Sex, Love, and Gender

Sex, Love, and Gender is the first volume to present a comprehensive philosophical theory that brings together all of Kant's practical philosophy—found across his works on ethics, justice, anthropology, history, and religion—and provide a critique of emotionally healthy and morally permissible sexual, loving, gendered being. By rethinking Kant's work on human nature and making space for sex, love, and gender within his moral accounts of freedom, the book shows how, despite his austere and even anti-sex, cisist, sexist, and heterosexist reputation, Kant's writings on happiness and virtue (Part I) and right (Part II) in fact yield fertile philosophical ground on which we can explore specific contemporary issues such as abortion, sexual orientation, sexual or gendered identity, marriage, trade in sexual services, and sex- or gender-based oppression. Indeed, Kant's philosophy provides us with resources to appreciate and value the diversity of human ways of loving and the existential importance of our embodied, social selves. Structured on a thematic basis, with introductions to assist those new to Kant's philosophy, this book will be a valuable resource for anyone who cares about these issues and wants to make sense of them.

Helga Varden is an associate professor at the University of Illinois at Urbana-Champaign. She has published on a range of classical philosophical issue—including Kant's answer to the murderer at the door, private property, political obligations, and political legitimacy—as well as on applied issues such as terrorism, poverty, and non-human animals. With a particular interest in Kant's contributions both to the philosophical canon and to contemporary issues, Varden is one of the few Kant scholars to have brought Kant's ideas to bear also on core issues in feminist philosophy as well as in the philosophy of sex and love, including abortion and same-sex marriage.

Praise for *Sex, Love, and Gender*

'sweeping, challenging, and imaginative'

Jennifer Ryan Lockhart, *SGIR Review*

'This groundbreaking book is quite simply a tour de force. Even Kant's defenders don't expect him to be a fruitful source of theorizing about gender, sexuality and sex, but Varden presents an impressively systematic and deep theory which synthesizes resources from his moral, political, legal and anthropological writings to give a rich account of our embodied, social human nature, the role in our lives of good sex, an analysis of sexual oppression and violence, and an important account on the role of the law and justice in relation to these. Clearly written, accessible, and avoiding jargon wherever possible, it will be a landmark in the literature for years to come.'

Lucy Allais, University of California

'*Sex, Love, and Gender* offers a unified philosophical theory of human nature, freedom, and political right that is at once ardently feminist and genuinely Kantian. Helga Varden brings out of Kant's philosophy a theory of human nature that explains our deepest needs and desires, and why sexual violence, gender oppression, and denial of full recognition of our sexual and gender identities are so deeply hurtful and wrong. Professor Varden applies these theories to controversial philosophical issues surrounding sex and gender, including pornography, sex work, and abortion, and derives powerful and novel arguments. This magnificent book will be widely read and influential in both Kant scholarship and feminist philosophy.'

Ann E. Cudd, University of Pittsburgh

'This book combines an impressively detailed and systematic exposition of Kant's practical philosophy, which forms the backbone of the argument, with analysis of a range of positions in law, anthropology, and social and political theory. Varden makes a powerful case for reading texts from the history of philosophy in light of present and urgent concerns. She combines originality, scholarship, and a quality not often found and rarely sought in philosophical arguments—passion. The book's compassionate advocacy of embodied social human nature makes this Kantian theory of sex, love, and gender nothing less than a theory of the human good.'

Katerina Deligiorgi, University of Sussex

Sex, Love, and Gender

A Kantian Theory

Helga Varden

OXFORD
UNIVERSITY PRESS

OXFORD
UNIVERSITY PRESS

Great Clarendon Street, Oxford, OX2 6DP,
United Kingdom

Oxford University Press is a department of the University of Oxford.
It furthers the University's objective of excellence in research, scholarship,
and education by publishing worldwide. Oxford is a registered trade mark of
Oxford University Press in the UK and in certain other countries

First published 2020
First published in paperback 2022

Published in the United States of America by Oxford University Press
198 Madison Avenue, New York, NY 10016, United States of America

British Library Cataloguing in Publication Data
Data available

Library of Congress Cataloging in Publication Data
Data available

ISBN 978-0-19-881283-8 (Hbk.)
ISBN 978-0-19-287231-9 (Pbk.)

To my loved ones

Contents

Preface

All human beings who spend any time on this planet face the challenges of sex and affectionate love. Indeed, even if one realizes that being sexually or affectionately intimate with others is something that one neither needs nor wants, one has not thereby avoided the issue; rather, one has found a way to engage these complexities that is good for oneself. Others do not want (intimate) sexual interactions with the same partners (only); one way they address their needs and wants is to pay others for sexual experiences. It is not an exaggeration to say, however, that many or even the majority of people (also) try to realize ongoing, longer-term, intimate affectionate and sexual relations with others, and that they experience this striving as a central concern in their lives. It seems fair to say that it is in these more intimate relations many people experience some of their most precious encounters as well as some of their most devastating failures and losses. We fall in love and we fall in lust; we sometimes live together as partners, and some of us marry, and some of us have children. At the same time, we break each other's hearts, we betray each other's trust, we need each other's forgiveness, or we must learn to deal with the fact that loved ones sometimes die far too early. A theory that could account for all these ever-so-common human experiences and challenges would be an improvement to existing theories, because most theories currently on offer aspire to explain only one or selected issues.

For the majority of people walking the globe—including all women and all members of sexual or gendered minorities—sex and love come with the added complexities of violence and/or oppression. These complexities, in turn, partly correspond to tendencies of cis men and sexual majorities to do bad things to women and sexual or gendered minorities, often in the name of the good or even God. Women are put in their "proper" subordinate place, and polyamorous and polysexual[1] persons as well as members of the LGBTQIA (Lesbian Gay Bisexual Trans Queer Intersex Asexual) community are stopped from "perverting nature" or "God's will" through their actions. The latter may find themselves or have their bodies subjected to physical or psychological violence to make them function in "normal" ways or as God "intended." And, often, cis men and sexual majorities not only get away with violent and/or oppressive behaviors against women and sexual or gendered minorities but may even perform them with legal approval, such as when legal systems deny the idea of marital rape; or through the state apparatuses, when they, for example, enforce sodomy laws or legally require the medical profession to undertake physical operations on intersex babies' genitalia to make them conform to prevalent gender norms in society. And only very recently and in very few

[1] Some use "polyamorous lives" to include polysexual lives. In this book, I use the term to distinguish those who have ongoing deeper, intimate, affectionately loving and romantic relations with more than one other person (polyamorous) from those who have only sexual interactions with more than one other person (polysexual).

places throughout the world has marriage become an institution that is open also to non-heterosexual couples, and though some countries permit cis men to marry more than one woman (but not vice versa), nowhere can polyamorous partners in symmetrical relationships marry.

A more complete and inclusive philosophical theory of sex, love, and gender must strive to cover all these issues. The current lack of such a theory is puzzling. After all, so much of history, and so much of our lives, concerns these aspects of human experience. Much more than half the global population constantly deals with the real threat or reality of related violence, and regardless of the extent of socioeconomic privilege held by particular women, polysexual or polyamorous people, and members of the LGBTQIA community, they must all deal with a world characterized by cisist, sexist, binary, heterosexist violence and oppression. Conversely, cis men and hetero-sexual people cannot avoid inheriting social identities that can tempt them to assume a point of view from which they are more equal than women and sexual or gendered minorities, and to wrong members of these less powerful social groups. In light of this, it is reasonable that both cis men and straight people would be deeply worried about these facts too, and that philosophers who are trying to develop comprehensive theories about human life would be rather preoccupied by these problems. However, neither the history nor the practice of philosophy has been particularly attentive to them. Indeed, still today, feminist philosophy and the philosophy of sex and love are not considered a challenge to theorize, or as theoretically important in most of mainstream, academic philosophy. To the best of my knowledge, since *On the Subjection of Women* (1869) by J. S. Mill, there has been only one book written by a cis, male philosopher—*Love and War: How Militarism Shapes Sexuality and Romance* by Tom Digby (2014)—that seeks to improve our understanding of and to criticize the problematic, inherited notions of cis masculinity.

Sex, Love, and Gender—A Kantian Theory aims to contribute to filling the void of theory in our philosophy practice (and thus also support the current efforts of changing related attitudes, behavior, and thinking) by developing a more compre-hensive theory of sex, love, and gender; that is, a rigorous and more complete analysis of these issues, and to accomplish it by utilizing the philosophical work left behind by Kant. As explained in more detail below, the ideas in this book have been developed over the last fifteen years and in close dialogue not only with Kant scholars but also with feminist philosophers, philosophers of sex and love, and philosophers working primarily within philosophical traditions that are not Kantian as well as with students and faculty from disciplines other than philosophy. This process of listening to talks and discussing my own work on sex, love, and gender with these colleagues and students has led me to conclude that we can bring feminist philosophy and the philosophy of sex and love a real step forward by taking on the challenge of developing more comprehensive theories.

Developing more comprehensive theories is currently possible and important because there is so much good work on sex, love, and gender that focuses on limited issues. For example, analyses that, say, take on one moral psychological or ethical or legal-political aspect of sex, love, or gender can be nuanced and improved if we can see how they fit together into more comprehensive theories, which, in turn, fit as parts of coherent philosophical systems. Classical philosophical theories—those of

Plato, Aristotle, Aquinas, Hobbes, Locke, Hume, Rousseau, and Kant, for example—do include discussions of sex, love, and gender, although all of these theories are cisist, sexist, and heterosexist in various ways.[2] Understanding why such incredible thinkers managed to get some of the basics about sex, love, and gender so very wrong is important to understand in itself (as it is important to understand our human temptation to evil). In addition, however, when we seek to figure out how our narrower theories fit into the philosophical systems we are thinking within, the classical texts can help us see which (kinds of) arguments are persuasive with regard to which questions and take care not to overstate how much work one (kind of) philosophical argument can do.

To illustrate the last point by means of a Kant-based example, we may point to Kant's view that there are significant limits to what you can do philosophically with the idea of the Categorical Imperative (CI). For example, the CI cannot explain the full structure of human phenomenology. The CI cannot explain all our desires and feelings and it cannot speak to human phenomena that are not moralizable in important ways. Thus, the CI cannot explain important moral psychological or anthropological aspects of phenomena such as falling in love, grieving, or presenting oneself socially in gendered ways. The CI also cannot be used to critique most of our legal-political system. The CI cannot explain things such as why forcibly removing my scarf from around my neck is battery whereas taking it when it lays on the table is mere theft—let alone explain what makes the scarf mine in the first place.

As I show in this book, a problem with the practice of philosophy, but not with Kant's own philosophical writings, is that for a long time, Kantians tried to critique moral psychology, moral anthropology, and legal-political philosophy by means of only his ethical and metaethical writings—philosophical ideas, such as the CI, that according to Kant himself could not have succeeded in providing such critiques. The effects of this interpretive assumption are particularly unfortunate when it comes both to understanding Kant's own theory, and to developing a revised Kantian theory of sex, love, and gender. More generally, although the classical texts of philosophy are insufficient in their analyses of sex, love, and gender, they are generative philosophical resources as we seek to develop more complete and robust theories. The classical systematic thinkers engage deeply with questions of how the many parts of a philosophical system do different philosophical work and still they all fit together into one philosophically coherent whole. As we take the next step with our theories of sex, love, and gender by developing them into more complex theories, we need also to take on the question of how they fit into more complex philosophical systems—and it behooves us to look to the classical theories for help.

In addition, the process of presenting my Kantian ideas to a variety of audiences over the years has led me to conclude that bridging the so-called "continental"/ "analytic" split in philosophy—and, for that matter, the emerging split between those philosophers who do not read the history of philosophy and those who do—requires that we strive to present the particular comprehensive, classical philosophical system we are drawn to in such a way that it is possible for everyone to see the strength and

---

[2] I return to Kant's sexism and heterosexism in the general introduction, where I also engage his racism.

importance of those ideas. Besides, this process of discussing these Kantian ideas with philosophically diverse interlocutors has taught me the value of conveying our ideas in a way that is sensitive to the strengths of philosophical traditions other than our own. We must fight the temptation to engage other philosophical systems and ideas through straw man interpretations and be willing to take the time to explain relevant background knowledge of our theories and their interpretive traditions. Throughout this book, I am doing my utmost to bridge disciplines by presenting Kant's ideas and my Kantian theory of sex, love, and gender in a way that it is accessible and useful to Kantian philosophers as well as to non-Kantian and non-philosophical audiences. I have also taken special care to write the introductions in such a way that they give uninitiated readers—whether to feminist philosophy, the philosophy of sex and love, or to Kant's practical philosophy—some help to see how the chapters fit into and build on the existing literature and Kant's philosophical system. Although it is plainly impossible within the scope of one book (and one human life) to engage all the relevant writings and arguments found in the other philosophical traditions, I hope that my close dialogue with many outside of the Kantian tradition, and outside of philosophy, has resulted in a book that is accessible and interesting across the disciplines. Insofar as I have succeeded, it is in large part thanks to the many audiences and wonderful colleagues and students who, over the years, have generously engaged my work through their questions and responses.

Sex, Love, and Gender—A Kantian Theory, then, provides a textually based, comprehensive Kantian theory of sex, love, and gender as embodied, social, ethical, and legal-political reality. The account seeks to overcome the philosophical mistakes and limitations of Kant's own work on these issues and to contribute a new kind of philosophical approach to the scholarly literature currently on offer. To do so, the book explores Kant's practical philosophy, understood as comprising his works on human nature generally and on freedom specifically, as I believe that Kant's philosophy, well read, can help us in our quests to develop our full human selves. I first show how Kant's claims about sex, love, and gender draw upon core ideas found in these works; then I reconstruct the relationships between some of these ideas. This allows me to draw different, better conclusions than those drawn by Kant and Kantians before and alongside me. Taking this approach therefore helps me to overcome Kant's own mistakes. It also helps me to surpass the limitations of current, narrower interpretations of Kant's thinking on sex, love, and gender and of related non-Kantian analyses, both of which tend to focus on particular, more restricted aspects. Kant's philosophy, I propose, has resources that can assist us not only in our searches for a moral theory (a theory of virtue/ethics and right/justice), but also in our pursuits for a theory of *all* aspects of the human good.

An advantage of my revised Kantian approach is that it can answer philosophical challenges presented by other theories, according to which sex, love, and gender are understood in terms of either choices (as existentialist theories of freedom do), violence (as postmodernist ideas of destructive forces do), or determinism (as the scientific conception of causality does). Kant's philosophy helps us see that these theories fail to do justice to our sexual, affectionately loving, and gendered lives because they fail, respectively, to appreciate how much of our condition is given (not open to choice), how much of ourselves is genuinely good (and not cynical, violent, or selfish), and how much we are free to change and transform ourselves. I argue that Kant's philosophy gives us the resources to transcend existentialist, postmodern, or scientific approaches without giving up on their many important insights. In this way, the book offers a way to bridge the insights of the continental and analytic philosophical traditions with regard to these issues, and also offers a way of seeing why the history of philosophy is important as we seek to improve our understanding of contemporary issues concerning sex, love, and gender. The result is a more complete theory that rests on and integrates core concerns of moral psychology, philosophical anthropology, ethics, law, and politics in a coherent whole that better positions us to see the complexity of the phenomena under investigation and to suggest ameliorative solutions that provide us with reasonable hope for a better future for each and for all.

The book has two parts. Part I, "Sex, Love, and Gender: Happiness and Virtue," lays out my Kant-based moral psychological theory of sex, love, and gender with a focus on the distinctive roles happiness and virtue play in good human lives. I engage and use Kant's writings throughout this analysis, explaining how his accounts of the faculty of desire, the predisposition to good, the propensity to evil, and aesthetic (the beautiful and the sublime) and teleological (parts and wholes) judgments shed light on some of the conclusions he draws about sex, love, and gender, such as those about sexual activity, marriage, and men and women. Recognition of the important roles these ideas play in Kant's practical philosophy enables us to understand why many readers of Kant are mistaken to think that he takes good sexual, affectionately loving, or gendered being, to be captured entirely by morality. For Kant, much of sex, love, and gender—such as becoming sexually excited, falling in love, and social presentation of gender—is experienced and can only be explained in terms of non-moralizable aspects of human being. Further, this attention to Kant's conception of human nature and his employment of aesthetic and teleological judgments allows us to identify and overcome Kant's own binary positions and, consequently, his cisism, sexism, and heterosexism. The result is a philosophical account that captures much of human phenomenology regarding sex, love, and gender as well as core related moral psychological issues, such as the evils of sexual violence and sexual oppression; along with central complexities concerning sexual or gender identities and sexual orientations. Finally, I integrate these insights with Kant's accounts of vital forces, perfect and imperfect duties, characters, and friendship to yield a richer account of our sexual, loving, gendered selves.

Part II, "Sex, Love, and Gender: Right," focuses on the legal-political aspects by engaging Kant's account of right (justice). Here, we see how my reconstructed Kantian theory can inform analyses of our innate and private rights and responsibilities to ourselves and others, as well as our public right claims on our shared public institutions. With these philosophical tools at hand, I explore core legal-political controversies regarding sex, love, and gender such as abortion, sodomy laws, marriage, trade in sexual services, and erotica. This part also outlines important legal-political means available to just states that strive to reform themselves so that they become better able to realize their inherent objective: a condition in which citizens can interact rightfully privately as well as govern themselves through active participation in public reason and public institutions. As a whole, the book provides a comprehensive theory that engages all of Kant's practical philosophical tools to offer a model and a way of thinking through emotionally healthy, morally justifiable sexual, loving, gendered actions and being.

Two final comments on method: First, in Günter Gaus's famous (1964) "Zur Person" interview Hannah Arendt responds to a criticism regarding the tone she sometimes uses when she writes about Eichmann. She explains that she cannot bring herself to apologize for her tone, because it expresses her very self as it responds to death and banal evil and, so, ultimately, is as it is. She believes she would laugh if someone as banal as Eichmann would take her to the gallows; laughing, she explains, is how she faces such devastating evil. As a Jew who had to flee Germany in the 1930s, Arendt knew herself in these regards. Being Jewish meant that she had first personal access—an emotional route internal to herself—to living with the threats of anti-Semitism and to facing death for who she is. Most Jews and most members of the LGBTQIA community living today have not personally faced the possibility of Hitler's death camps. Nevertheless, all Jews, women, and members of the LGBTQIA community do have first-personal access to living with existential threats facing their identities. Like Arendt, I find it right and necessary to write as I am—consistent with my temperament as a scholar and as a human being—around some of the hardest of these issues, such as betrayal, rejection, and the danger of being subjected to subjugating or lethal violence because of who I am. I know I would not laugh if taken to the gallows; I know I would withdraw, I would feel my sadness and seek to focus on the aspects of my life that have been precious, have filled me with awe and gratitude despite it all. Some will find my voice in those sections of the book too much (too sad, too angry, too non-worldly, etc.), while others will find it too little (insufficiently sad, insufficiently angry, insufficiently non-worldly, etc.). As other parts of my book explain, I believe Kant is correct in proposing that we are subjectively different in these temperamental regards. In any case, I have found that I could only write with integrity by using my own way of being around these matters, and, like Arendt, I do not want to apologize for that.

Second, this book is feminist and supportive of polyamorous, polysexual, and LGBTQIA lives in all their diversity. It is feminist in that it both seeks to understand sexist oppression and to envision a better future for women and for men. For some, feminism includes the philosophy of sex and love as pertaining to the LGBTQIA community and polyamorous and polysexual people. I do not presuppose such an understanding of feminism and the philosophy of sex and love in this book. One reason for not presupposing it is that I believe these two areas of philosophical inquiry are not co-extensive. Another is that I want clearly to distance myself and my theory from those who, in the name of feminism, write to undermine the reality of and/or to criticize people who are trans. As will become clear in the first part of the book, I hope a core contribution of my revised Kantian theory is its provision of a philosophical understanding of trans lives, as well as lesbian, gay, bisexual, queer, intersex, asexual, polyamorous, and polysexual lives. Additionally, it greatly saddens me to see what I consider to be the thoughtlessness with which many feminist (and other) philosophers relate to trans lives—a thoughtlessness that in my view is deeply connected with a lack of appreciation for the importance of genuinely listening to the persons whose lives we are critiquing with our philosophical theories.

Another way to get at this last problem is via the history of dehumanization of women, and gendered and sexual minorities by binary, heterosexist, cisist, sexist cultures, and its revealing of the dangers of a kind of cognitive stubbornness to refuse to see the lives of people as they are. Oscar Wilde (1990), in "The Case of Warder Martin: Some Cruelties of Prison Life," describes a fellow prisoner who has a mental illness and is losing his mind, but this goes unrecognized because it does not fit the doctor's theory. According to that theory, the prisoner is simply being difficult. As Wilde describes it, "At present it is a horrible duel between himself [the prisoner] and the doctor. The doctor is fighting for a theory. The man is fighting for his life. I am anxious that the man should win" (p. 903). My point is that in developing a theory, it is easy to end up in conflict with the people whose lives one seeks to critique: one stubbornly fights for one's theory while the people one theorizes are fighting for their lives *against the theory*. In fact, in due course, I argue that Kant's own discomfort with what he was saying about women and his anger when he writes on non-straight lives should have been red flags to him; something was wrong—and he, at the very least, had an unreflective awareness of it (as revealed in his discomfort and anger). You can, as Kant says, corrupt some of your own predispositions to good, but you cannot destroy ('eradicate') them—they remain a possible source of correction to your rationalization of bad behavior and destructive feelings, including bad philoso-phical theorizing. Kant should have recognized that his destructive feelings called for his attention and careful reflection. Similarly, good philosophical theories around sex, love, and gender, I believe, must be grounded in attentive listening to the people whose lives we are trying to make our theories speak to. Sometimes we have first personal access to these lives and sometimes not. Our general philosophical end, however, should not be to ignore, invent, or eliminate human lives through our theories. Rather, we must take seriously and take care around the fact that we are critiquing real, vulnerable lives—lives scholars have a moral duty to treat with respect and dignity, lives which can teach us wonderful things about being human if we dare to learn to be present in good ways.

Hannah Arendt's thoughts on fraught political times may also help us see why improving our understanding of the lives of people who are women, polysexual, polyamorous, and LGBTQIA might be particularly important at this moment in history. In *The Origins of Totalitarianism*, Arendt emphasizes time and again the serious mistake in failing to distinguish the old "Jew-hatred" from the anti-semitism that developed towards the late nineteenth century in Europe and that was consti-tutive of Hitler's totalitarian fascist movement. She furthermore emphasizes the importance of noticing that this change—from Jew-hatred to anti-semitism—came after the Jewish people were given equal rights alongside other social groupings. After legal-political processes result in securing rights not only for privileged social iden-tities, in other words, there is a danger of a totalitarian or fascist backlash partially aimed at destroying this progress. The final aim of Hitler's totalitarian movement, however, was not simply to destroy any particular groups as such, but to use the destruction of some groups (e.g., Jews, disabled people, the Roma people, gays) as a starting point for total, global destruction of spontaneous human life and dignity—all done in the name of the good. Arendt argues that Stalin's and Hitler's totalitarian undertakings were the first state-organized enterprises that aspired at nothing but the destruction of spontaneous human life and dignity as a whole. They were the first attempts at creating on the planet something humans before modernity had relegated to non-worldly life, namely to hell or Hades; all-consuming attempts to destroy being (to bring about non-being) under the guise of protecting and enabling being. Dehumanized social groups can be used in such political efforts of destruction because they are already seen as less human, as perverted, as sinful, etc. They also tend to be associated with their animality, while at the same time animality is denigrated. Accordingly, marginalized groups provide an opportunity for carrying out destructive, self-deceived political movements which deny the reality and complexity of the actual problems—for Arendt, dysfunctional legal-political structures that were not up to the challenges of refugees, new technology and science, and (post-)colonialization. Today, we seem to have the same problems in addition to serious concerns about the environment and the danger of rogue nations (and agents) with nuclear power. Rather than seeking solutions through changes in legal-political structures, those seeking destructive political power seek to establish a distorted sense of reality (a sham), according to which the real problem is these social groups. If we just restore "unperverted" humanity by restricting the freedom or cleansing humanity of these social groups and by putting women in their proper, subjugated place, this line of thinking goes, then all will be well again on the planet.

Like Jews, women and sexual or gendered minorities have faced violently oppressive conditions throughout most of history, and though women had gained some rights in many places by World War II, sexual and gendered minorities had not gained any. If Arendt is right, we saw above, there is a risk of backlash when marginalized and dehumanized groups make gains in legal-political equality, and in recent years, women and sexual or gendered minorities have gained rights in many countries. Certainly, we do not know if what we are seeing at the moment is "merely" the rise of dictators again or the beginning of processes that can lead to totalitarian dictators. Regardless, in recent years, we have seen formidable political forces in a large number of democracies seeking to take away women's rights, whether it be the right to abortion altogether or to its availability, denying women the right to decide what to wear in public, or by revoking laws criminalizing domestic violence. In addition, for the first time in history, people run for election on the basis of their commitment to stop and reverse legislation that secures equal rights for sexual or gendered minorities, such as by promising to revoke same-sex marriage laws or to institute laws that allow businesses to discriminate against people who are not cis or straight. It is possible to see these political movements as tools by means of which political forces of destruction currently seek a false description of reality, according to which our problems are not those of the environment, poverty, nuclear weapons, failing states, stateless peoples (refugees), migration crises, etc., but rather a problem of women and of sexual or gendered minorities or of certain dehumanized religious groups (especially Jews and Muslims). Although it will not solve all of these problems, we do seem to be at a point in our political history where understanding our sexual, loving, gendered natures better is particularly important, if not imperative. This includes a better comprehension of the temptation to disrespect and violate oneself and others because of sexuality, affectionate love, and/or gender. It also includes thinking deeply about how to build better emotional, social, ethical, and legal-political responses and safeguards against sex- and gender-based violence and oppression. I hope this book is a contribution to these practical efforts of working towards a better future for one and all.

The working out and writing up of the ideas in this book has, as mentioned above, taken about fifteen years. In the process, I have experienced some of the best there is in terms of genuine philosophical and collegial generosity, open-mindedness, and curiosity. My first ideas on sex, love, and gender were on same-sex marriage and they were developed as part of a side-project I had in graduate school (while writing my doctoral dissertation on the legal-political philosophy of Kant and Locke). From that time onwards, I have been extremely fortunate to have been able to trust and rely on the support and assistance of Arthur Ripstein, my Ph.D. supervisor, and Sergio Tenenbaum, dissertation committee member, when working on my understanding of, and texts regarding, sex, love, and gender. I am tremendously grateful for all their help and for showing me what ideals of responsible graduate student mentorship look like.

Second, I would like to thank Patricia Marino and everyone who presented their papers through the Society for the Philosophy of Sex and Love (SPSL) over the last decade or so. Marino and I ran the SPSL together from 2008 to 2018, and the conversations with her and with the scholars who participated in SPSL events have been incredibly useful to me. The philosophical courage and honest search for ways of understanding and dealing with complicated aspects of life and uncharted philosophical questions were characteristic of these conversations, and they have been constitutive for me finding my own way of doing this. An equally deepfelt thanks goes to New Voices in Legal Theory (NVLT) and my co-organizers there—Mary Anne Franks, Robin Kar, Eric Miller, Ekow N. Yankah, and Lorenzo Zucca—as well as the many presenters in NVLT workshops over the years. These SPSL and NVLT events and conversations over the last decade have been exceedingly valuable and productive. They have shown me, again and again, what wonderful philosophical conversation across the disciplines and philosophical traditions involve. The unwavering support these scholars have given me for my work has been precious.

During this time, I also have discussed and presented many of the ideas of this book at conferences and workshops organized by the American Philosophical Association, the American Section of the International Society for Law and Social Philosophy, the Association for Feminist Ethics and Social Theory, the International Association for Philosophy of Law and Social Philosophy, the North American Kant Society, the North American Society for Social Philosophy, and the Society for Analytical Feminism. In addition, I have presented some of the ideas at conferences and colloquia organized at universities and colleges around the world—too many to list them all here. Many, many colleagues, undergraduate and graduate students—at the University of Illinois at Urbana-Champaign (UIUC), at the University of Chicago, at Northwestern University, and at the University of St. Andrews—have listened to and engaged with most of the ideas now in this book as they were developing. I am tremendously grateful for all the constructive questions and other acts of scholarly generosity in these numerous and various settings.

I would also like to thank the UIUC for its research support through HASS funds, a fellowship at the Center for Advanced Study, a Humanities Teaching Release Time award, and for many Scholars' Travel awards. A big thank you also to Nancy Abelmann, Maria Gillombardo, Carol Symes, and the Office of the Vice Chancellor for Research, and to Sally Haslanger, Barbara Herman, Pauline Kleingeld, Martha Nussbaum, and Arthur Ripstein for having supported many a research funding application for the project over the years. Thanks too to the Centre for Ethics, Philosophy and Public Affairs at the Department of Philosophy, University of St. Andrews for having welcomed me as a visiting fellow in the spring of 2014, and to Northwestern University's Department of Philosophy and Brady Scholars Program for having welcomed me as their Brady Distinguished Visiting Associate Professor in the academic year of 2014/15. This research support—financial and scholarly hospitality—has been invaluable to this project. Thanks too to the following publications for permitting me to reprint text published as (parts of) articles in their journals and anthologies:

1) "Kant on Sex. Reconsidered: A Kantian Account of Sexuality: Sexual love, Sexual Identity, and Sexual Orientation" (2018), *Feminist Philosophy Quarterly* 4(1): 1-33.
2) "Kant and Women" (2015), *Pacific Philosophical Quarterly*, 98: 653-94. doi: 10.1111/papq.12103
3) "Kant's Moral Theory and Feminist Ethics: Women, Embodiment, Care Relations, and Systemic Injustice" (2018), in Pieranna Garavaso (ed.), *The Bloomsbury Companion to Analytic Feminism*, pp. 459-82. London: Bloomsbury Academic.
4) "Kant and Sexuality" (2017), in Matthew Altman (ed.), *The Palgrave Kant Handbook*, pp. 331-53. London: Palgrave Macmillan.
5) "Immanuel Kant: Justice as Freedom" (2015), in Guttorm Fløistad (ed.), *Philosophie de la justice / Philosophy of Justice*, Vol. 12, pp. 213-37. The "Contemporary Philosophy: A New Survey" series. New York: Springer.
6) "A Feminist, Kantian Conception of the Right to Bodily Integrity: The Cases of Abortion and Homosexuality" (2012), in Sharon L. Crasnow and Anita M. Superson (eds.), *Out from the Shadows*, pp. 33-57. Oxford: Oxford University Press.
7) "A Kantian Conception of Free Speech" (2010), in Deirdre Golash (ed.), *Free Speech in a Diverse World*, pp. 39-55. New York: Springer Publishing.
8) "A Kantian Conception of Rightful Sexual Relations: Sex, (Gay) Marriage and Prostitution" (2007), *Social Philosophy Today*, 22: 199-218.
9) "A Kantian Critique of the Care Tradition: Family Law and Systemic Justice" (2012), *Kantian Review*, 17(2): 327-56.
10) "Self-Governance and Reform in Kant's Liberal Republicanism: Ideal and Non-Ideal Theory in Kant's Doctrine of Right" (2016), *DoisPontos*, 13(2): 39-70.
11) "On a Supposed Right to Lie from Philanthropy" (2021), in Julian Wuerth (ed.), *The Cambridge Kant Lexicon*, pp. 691-95. Cambridge: Cambridge University Press.

Over the years, many friends and colleagues have helped me far beyond the call of duty. I would like to thank especially Lucy Allais, Sarah Broadie, Rachel Bryant, Ann

E. Cahill, Katerina Deligiorgi, Carol Hay, Barbara Herman, Eric Miller, Jordan Pascoe, Judy Rowan, Barbara Sattler, Richard Schacht, Jennifer K. Uleman, Shelley Weinberg, and Ekow N. Yankah. The number of important—and sometimes hard—conversations I have had with each of them on the ideas (and their presentation) in this book have been priceless to me. A special thanks also to Rachel Bryant and Shelley Weinberg for having read the whole manuscript—and some parts several times—with an eye to catch infelicitous formulations. Thanks too to Ingrid Albrecht, Joshua Dunigan, Maria Gillombardo, Krupa Patel, and James Warren who read parts of the manuscript for this purpose. I know the fact that I write in a second language involves work of this kind for those who care about me and I really appreciate those extra efforts. Thanks as well for many particularly important discussions of various ideas in, or whole chapters to, Ingrid Albrecht, Marcia Baron, Alyssa Bernstein, Jochen Bojanowski, Alix Cohen, Annette Dufner, Behrooz Ghamari, Sayed Kashua, Julia N. Kling, Alice MacLachlan, Benjamin Miller, Steve Naragon, Alexandra Newton, Elaine Olson, Ashley Say, and Sally Sedgwick. A special thanks is due Jen Cassandra Learn, who read the entire manuscript carefully at a very late stage, to the (anonymous) peer reviewers for Oxford University Press, to Peter Momtchiloff, whose editorial abilities have plainly been a gift to me, and to the wonderful team who produced the book in front of you, especially Jenny King (Assistant Commissioning Editor), Chandrasekaran Chandrakala (SPi Project Manager), Joy Mellor (copyeditor), and Rio Ruskin-Tompkins (cover designer). Finally, a heartfelt thanks to the participants at the two workshops on drafts of the manuscript—in Boston and in Chicago—in the summer of 2018: Anne Margaret Baxley, Elvira Basevich, Ann Cudd, Andrew Cutrofello, Kyla Ebels-Duggan, Lisa Fuller, Carol Hay, Eric Miller, Jordan Pascoe, Krupa Patel, Sandra Raponi, Susanne J. Sreedhar, Stephen White, and Rachel Zuckert—with a special thanks to Ann Cudd and Andrew Cutrofello for hosting these workshops.

It is a real possibility that if you as a reader particularly like some formulation or example in this book, it is thanks to one of the people mentioned above. It also goes without saying that there is no agreement among all these thinkers about the ideas in this book or about their presentation, but I hope it is evident to each of them that I have listened even though, in the end, I had to make the choices necessary to write this book in my own voice and way. Now, one might reasonably think that given my access to all this brilliant brain power, this book would be flawless. I am afraid, however, that this is not the case. The mistakes that have survived all these scholars' efforts to the contrary are obviously mine and mine alone.

Last but not least: thanks to my family and friends, whose patient generosity, wonderful ways, and sheer existence have made difficult times easier and fun times even better. A special thanks to Maja Andreasen, Barbara and Kim, Daniel Becht, Angelina Cotler, Julia Gasparro, Girls Night Out, Kari Kristensen, Kim Kramer, Nibal Lubbad, Brit Lunde, Cathrine Theodorsen, and Kat Yutzy—for hikes, talks, dinners, wine, tears, and laughter. The biggest, deepest thanks obviously go to my wife, Shelley Weinberg. Without her, many of my, and this book's, best bits would not be. It is that simple. And she is that amazingly wonderful.

Throughout this book, I refer to all of Kant's works by means of the standard Prussian Academy Pagination as well as the following abbreviations:

"A"	(*Anthropology*) for *Anthropology from a Pragmatic Point of View*
"BS"	for "Observations on the Feeling of the Beautiful and the Sublime"
"CB"	for "Conjectural Beginning of Human History"
"CPrR"	(or second *Critique*) for *Critique of Practical Reason*
"CPuR"	(or first *Critique*) for *Critique of Pure Reason*
"third *Critique*"	for *Critique of the Power of Judgment*
"GW"	(or *Groundwork*) for *Groundwork for the Metaphysics of Morals*
"LE"	for *Lectures on Ethics*
"LP"	for *Lectures on Pedagogy*
"LDPP"	for *Lectures and Drafts on Political Philosophy*
"MH"	for "Essay on the Maladies of the Head"
"MM"	for *The Metaphysics of Morals*
"PMB"	for "On the Philosophers' Medicine of the Body"
"PP"	for "Towards Perpetual Peace"
"R"	(*Religion*) for *Religion within the Boundaries of Mere Reason*
"SRL"	for "On the Supposed Right to Lie from Philanthropy"
"TP"	for "On the Common Saying: That May Be Correct in Theory, but It Is of No Use in Practice"
"IUH"	for "Idea for a Universal History with a Cosmopolitan Aim"
"UNHTH"	for *Universal Natural History and Theory of the Heavens*
"WE"	for "An Answer to the Question: What is Enlightenment?"
"WUPB"	for "On the Wrongfulness of Unauthorized Publication of Books"

Introduction

Many philosophers—Kantians or not—consider formulating an applied theory of sex, love, and gender to be an undertaking that is neither particularly difficult nor particularly important. In addition, that there has not yet been a comprehensive *Kantian* philosophical account of sex, love, and gender is perhaps not terribly surprising. After all, Kant views sexual activity as inherently morally problematic, and ethically permissible only as heterosexual procreative sexual activity within the legal confines of marriage. And in presenting these views, he makes many sexist and heterosexist assertions. For non-Kantian scholars working within feminist philosophy or the philosophy of sex and love, Kant's philosophy consequently has not stood out as a particularly interesting or useful resource for understanding human diversity when it comes to sex, love, and gender. Also, Kant's statements about sex, love, and gender are dispersed throughout his practical and aesthetic-teleological works. For a long time, no Kant (or any other) scholar found it philosophically worthwhile to engage these aspects of Kant's writings, let alone to take up the somewhat daunting task of gathering together and theorizing as a whole Kant's complex, yet not explicitly spelled-out, ideas on sex, love, and gender before reconstructing a philosophically more persuasive theory.

Change in the practice of philosophy began with the entrance of women into professional philosophy.[1] Some of the reason is that issues of sex, love, and gender, especially those regarding sexual and gender violence and oppression, were not pressing in professional philosophy when almost all the professional philosophers came from the privileged social group of cis men. It appears to be a rare phenomenon in human history that members of privileged social groups are so troubled by their disproportionate social power that they push for change. As women entered Kant scholarship, then, casting a light on sexual and gender difference and oppression became an important philosophical undertaking. The first two Ph.D. dissertations on Kant and gender[2] appeared in 1987 and 1988 and were written by two women, namely Else Wiestad and Ursula Pia Jauch, respectively. Shortly thereafter, Barbara Herman's seminal article on Kant on marriage and sexuality—"Could it be Worth Thinking about Kant on Marriage"—appeared (1993b), and gave clear attention to feminist concerns of objectification and vulnerabilities of women. The first major

---

[1] For an overview over the entrance of women into Kantian scholarship, see the introduction to Part I.

[2] Wiestad's dissertation was *Kjønn og ideologi. En studie av kvinnesynet hos Locke, Hume, Rousseau og Kant* and a shortened version was published under the same title with Solum Forlag (1989). Jauch's dissertation was *Immanuel Kant zur Geschlechterdifferenz. Aufklärerische Vorurteilskritik und bürgerliche Geschlechtsvormundschaft* and was published under the same title with Passagen Verlag (1988).

Sex, Love, and Gender: A Kantian Theory. Helga Varden, Oxford University Press (2020). © Helga Varden.
DOI: 10.1093/oso/9780198812838.001.0001

book on Kant and sexuality—*Sexual Solipsism*—was also written by a woman, Rae Langton (2009), and focused intently on feminist concerns of objectification. Similarly, many of the established women in Kant moral studies, such as Marcia Baron, Seyla Benhabib, B. Sharon Byrd, Robin S. Dillon, Jean Hampton, Pauline Kleingeld, Christine Korsgaard, Hjørdis Nerheim, Onora O'Neill, Herlinde Pauer-Studer, Sally Sedgwick, Susan Meld Shell, and Holly Wilson, like many of us who follow them, have all written about sex, love, and/or gender with a special attention to issues concerning women. As professional philosophy and society at large recently started to open up not only to cis women, but also to people whose gendered or sexual identities or sexual orientations fall into the categories of polyamory, poly-sexual,[3] and/or LGBTQIA—as mine does—and as it became politically safer, in the academy and elsewhere, to write on these topics, we saw an increased interest in philosophical investigations of issues concerning sex, love, and gender beyond the man-woman distinction.[4] This book continues on this path, and therefore is not aimed at understanding issues concerning women only, but also at understanding sex, love, and gender more broadly, and it seeks to do so in a way that improves our philosophical comprehension of polyamorous, polysexual, and LGBTQIA lives.

If we look at the existing secondary literature on Kant and sex, love, and gender as a whole, much of it engages Kant's first-personal ethics (virtue, or internal freedom) rather than also engaging his account of justice (right, or external freedom).[5] A main reason for this is that for a long time Kant's legal-political account as found in his Doctrine of Right was neglected in all Kant scholarship. In consequence, philo-sophers such as Rae Langton (2009), Sarah Clark Miller (2012), and Carol Hay (2013) wrote substantial, innovative monographs that explore questions of care, oppression, and objectification primarily through the lenses of Kant's ethical writ-ings. Articles written on these and other themes in feminist philosophy similarly tend to view Kant's ethics as providing the main philosophical resources with which to understand issues of sex, love, and gender, though some also attend to Kant's legal-political philosophy. For example, Kant's account of justice (right) with its special attention to issues of rightful coercion is central to Herman's analysis of marriage and O'Neill's (1990, 1996, 2000) shorter writings on women. By and large, however, Kant's legal-political philosophy has been underutilized in the scholarship on Kant and sex, love, and gender, a deficit that this work seeks to correct.[6]

---

[3] For my usage of the terms of polyamory and polysexual, see footnote 1 in the Preface.

[4] The first comprehensive philosophical engagement with ethical, social, and legal-political issues concerning gay and lesbian life is, I believe, that of my UIUC colleague Richard D. Mohr (1988, 1992, 2007). It pleases me to think that I am following in his footsteps: he received his Ph.D. from Toronto approximately thirty years (1977) before I did (2006) and he published his first book on these issues approximately thirty years (1988) before I finished mine (2019).

[5] For a more detailed overview of this literature, see the introductions to Parts I and II.

[6] My Ph.D. dissertation on the legal-political philosophy of Locke and Kant was undertaken at the University of Toronto in the period when Arthur Ripstein and Ernest Weinrib were doing groundbreaking work on Kant's Doctrine of Right. Their work made Kant's legal-political philosophy a real contender in the English-speaking philosophical world for the first time and, of course, my doctoral training under Ripstein gave me a base also as I sought to develop a Kantian understanding of right in relation to sex, love, and gender.

This book builds on and contributes to the existing literature by showing how a more complex (internal and external) freedom account of sex, love, and gender can bring together these analyses of virtue and of right while allowing each analysis to do its own philosophical work. More specifically, in Part I, I develop a Kant-based account of sex, love, and gender that engages Kant's account of first-personal ethics (or of virtue, which is a matter of internal freedom). In Part II, I engage Kant's account of justice (or of right, which is a matter of external freedom). In both analyses self-governance through law (autonomy) is a key orienting idea, but with regard to ethics the focus is on self-governance through virtuous internal freedom (The Categorical Imperative); and with regard to justice, it is self-governance through rightful external freedom (The Universal Principle of Right). As mentioned in the Preface, however, to arrive at a Kantian theory of sex, love, and gender, it is insufficient merely to appreciate how the perspectives of ethics (virtue) and justice (right) complement each other in a full Kantian account of freedom (internal and external, respectively). It also requires that we explore the relevance and importance of Kant's account of human nature as it goes beyond analyzing our human capacities for freedom. This emphasis on the importance of Kant's account of human nature as such—and related to this, Kant's take on philosophical anthropology—is not new in my approach to Kant studies. Here I join the efforts of, for example, Alix Cohen, Patrick Frierson, Robert B. Louden, Susan Shell, Allen Wood, and John Zammito. What I add to these discussions is a general emphasis on the phenomenological *structure* of Kant's account of human nature along with a particular emphasis on the importance of letting Kant's ideas of animality and humanity do their own, distinctive philosophical work in an overall account of our human nature. These two additions enable me to arrive at a Kantian account that can speak to key sexual, loving, gendered experiences and ways of being, including, crucially, their grounding or existential importance in human lives. Let me expand on some of these points.

Accounts that stay singularly focused on matters of moral freedom do not and cannot sufficiently answer central questions regarding human lives generally and human sexual or gender identity and sexual orientation more specifically. That is to say, Kant's theory of freedom does affirm that as a *person*, one has a moral right to set and pursue ends of one's own and to be treated with dignity and respect; and as a *citizen*, one has a set of basic innate, acquired (private), and systemic (public) rights. Nevertheless, neither of these inherently reflective analyses of moral (virtuous and rightful) freedom can engage questions regarding our sexual, affectionately loving, gendered being that require an appeal to importantly unreflective aspects of human phenomenology. It is because Kant's freedom accounts cannot answer many questions regarding *human* (rather than merely rational) being that Kant's (often offensive) teleological and aesthetic statements about sex, affectionate love, and gender are commonly set aside or explicitly rejected as irrelevant even by many Kantians. Yet focusing primarily on Kant's moral freedom writings, as so much of the secondary literature regarding Kant and sex, affectionate love, and gender does, makes it impossible to understand exactly *why and how* Kant consistently makes space for embodied, social concerns of human nature regarding sex, affectionate love, and gender within his moral accounts of freedom—indeed why he defends the philosophical importance of doing so. Being an emotionally healthy, morally good human being cannot be given a complete philosophical critique if we focus *solely* on our capacity to act in truly free ways, namely to set ends that are based on universalizable maxims from a moral motivation (The Categorical Imperative) or that are reconcilable with one another's innate right to freedom (The Universal Principle of Right).

Kantians who do pay special attention to our distinctly human (and not only rational) nature, furthermore, have a tendency to draw a distinction between morality (freedom) and happiness (non-moral concerns) without, unfortunately, much attention to the question of how Kant's account of happiness requires us to explore the phenomenological details of his account of animality and humanity. Therefore, neither the freedom accounts nor the human nature accounts on offer can capture why being able to realize one's sexual, affectionately loving, gendered being tends to be existentially central for human beings, as revealed in the lengths to which people go to live them out and the high suicide rates for people who are denied opportunities to do so. These existing accounts would also struggle to give a satisfying philosophical answer to the question of why sexual, intimate, and gendered violence is experienced as particularly heinous, as capable of damaging and ungrounding us in profound ways. More generally, existing interpretations seem to make invisible much of what is particularly valuable and particularly injurious in a human life with respect to sex, love, and gender. At the very least, these accounts place it outside of the scope of serious philosophical concern, by describing these aspects of us as something that merely makes it subjectively easier or more difficult to be moral and by reducing the various sources of our non-moral desires to a single, undifferentiated source (heteronomy).

It seems, then, that both as a matter of Kant interpretation and as a matter of philosophical theory, a more complex strategy is preferable, a strategy that shows how embodied, social aspects of our human nature in addition to our capacities for virtue and for right work together to yield a multifaceted theory of human sexual, loving, gendered actions and being. That is to say, while much excellent work has been done on Kant's moral psychology and philosophical anthropology in the past several decades, my focus is different. It is directed not so much at identifying the kinds of feelings and desires we need to cultivate in the service of our moral ends in order to qualify as virtuous by Kant's standards, but rather at how we can develop our full selves, including our animality and humanity, in order to become grounded, healthy, loving, affectionate, mindful, sexual, gendered beings and to live well as whole human beings. To do this, it is crucial to pay attention to the phenomenological structure of our various non-moralizable desires, understood as desires characterized by irreducibly unreflective aspects.

It is important to note that the fact that the available interpretations of Kant's moral psychology and anthropology tend to proceed in the ways sketched above is not an accident. For example, in the introduction to *The Metaphysics of Morals*, Kant explains that the counterpart to a metaphysics of morals "would be moral anthropology, which, however, would deal only with the subjective conditions in human nature that hinder people or help them in *fulfilling* the laws of a metaphysics of morals" (MM 6: 217). When reading this, it is tempting to conclude that everything that has to do with moral anthropology is not so important philosophically; what is really important is what a metaphysics of morals (principles of freedom) can give us.

On such a reading, *The Metaphysics of Morals*—with its Doctrine of Virtue and Doctrine of Right—then goes on to explicate self-governance through virtue (internal freedom) and self-governance through right (external freedom). Of course, I do not deny the importance or content of what Kant is saying here; quite the contrary. Rather, a basic interpretive assumption defended in this book is that when Kant says that moral anthropology deals with the subjective aspects of human nature that help or hinder morality, he is saying that *from the point of view of freedom*, non-moralizable aspects of our distinctively human being (animality and humanity) make it subjectively harder or easier to do what is right (to act truly freely). For example, it matters for how we praise or punish that something right was extremely hard to do or something wrong extraordinarily tempting. This does not mean, however, that non-moralizable aspects of our being in themselves are unimportant or not valuable in human lives. They are. Moreover, the embodied social aspects of our human being have their own work to do in good philosophical theories of human being, work that is additional to the work that explorations of our rational aspects can do. This is why Kant defines the highest good for human beings as a union between happiness and morality, and it is why he makes space for concerns grounded in our human (rather than merely rational) nature within his moral writings on virtue and right.

Correspondingly, because I am after a better philosophical understanding of the human phenomena of sex, love, and gender, Part I of my book is not merely written as an exploration of virtue, corresponding to Kant's Doctrine of Virtue. Instead, it is written as an exploration of the phenomena of sex, love, and gender, which explores *both* virtue and happiness with regard to these phenomena, and it pays special attention to the phenomenological structure of our embodied, social nature when exploring happiness. This is why Chapter 1, where I outline core philosophical ideas of Kant's that we need to understand sex, love, and gender, is proposed as a possible and fruitful interpretation of Kant with a target not only to capture virtue, but how virtue and happiness are achieved together in good human living as well as the difficulties humans typically encounter in trying to do so. What is more, because Kant made some serious mistakes in his analyses of women, sexual or gendered minorities, and of matters of sex, love, and gender more generally, I take my time (in Chapters 2 and 3, respectively) to show how he used his philosophical ideas to arrive at his cisist, sexist, and heterosexist conclusions. I then propose a different, and in my view better, way to use his philosophical ideas to critique these phenomena—one that is not cisist, sexist, or heterosexist. In Chapter 4, I use the ideas developed in the preceding chapters to explore the phenomena of sexual violence and oppression. Here I pay special attention to Kant's distinction between "material" and "formal" wrongdoing. I argue that because material and formal wrongdoing can come apart in human lives (since we are both rational *and* embodied social beings), we can find ourselves in situations where there are no morally good ways out.

In Part II of the book on right (justice), I start by expanding on Kant's account of innate right—as it is central to capture core legal issues concerning bodily integrity and speech—before using his principles of private and public right to address other central issues of right, such as marriage, trade in sexual services, and systemic injustice. In Part II, mostly because there is less that needs to be fixed and adjusted in Kant's own thinking and in the limited Kantian literature about these matters, I stay closer to Kant's general strategy. I first show what we can do with only the *a priori* principles of external freedom (right) when seeking a philosophical legal analysis of core issues regarding sex, love, and gender. Then I show possible ways in which we can accommodate embodied, social concerns of human beings into these freedom-based analyses such that we can reform the legal-political institutions we have inherited in ways that make them better means through which *human* (and not merely embodied rational) beings enable rightful relations among themselves and, so, flourishing, just societies. Finally, throughout these chapters, I use Kant's analysis of formal and material wrongdoing as well as his idea of "barbaric" regimes to explore the difficult questions of how to understand and what to do when (pockets of) the legal-political institutional reality either denies some group(s) of citizens access to rights or is wrongfully aimed at their oppression or demise.

If we turn from the Kant-based literature to non-Kantian feminist philosophy and philosophy of sex and love, four distinct types of theories analyzing sex, love, and gender are prominent. First, there are liberal—including libertarian—approaches, according to which one's sexual, loving, gendered self is a matter of choice. The most influential accounts here tend to take their lead from or argue in ways consistent with Simone de Beauvoir's brilliant, existentialist *The Second Sex* (2011/1949). On these approaches, one's sexual or gender identity and sexual orientation, for example, are ideally chosen ways of living. Consequently, although existing oppressive and prejudicial social norms make it more challenging to live out non-conventional sexualities or genders, what kind of sexual, loving, gendered life one wants to live is in principle a matter of free choice—there is no "givenness" to our sexual or gendered desires, identities, or orientations.

Second, postmodern accounts characteristically agree with Beauvoir that there is no innate givenness to our sexual, loving, gendered selves, but they depart from Beauvoir's optimistic, existentialist emphasis on free choices. These accounts instead tend to take their inspiration from groundbreaking work by Michel Foucault (as we find in *The History of Sexuality*) and/or Judith Butler (from *Gender Trouble* onwards)—sometimes in combination with work in the Freudian psychoanalytic tradition. These postmodern analyses tend to proceed on the (sometimes implicit) assumption that there is little (or no) hope of a better future—let alone that it is possible to say much about what a better future would look like and how we can get there—since there are no clearly better or right ways of dealing with sex, love, or gender. The sexual, loving, gendered relations that exist at any time are expressions of power, of how people struggle against each other to do what they want to do within (sometimes violently) oppressive social structures. Furthermore, people often undertake these struggles in deeply self-deceived ways; that is, they do bad things in the name of the good. Finally, the key to bringing about a better world tends to be *resistance* to harmful conceptions of sexuality and gender. Correspondingly, a philosophical weakness of these accounts is that they tend to offer little with which to clarify what "good" (non-harmful) conceptions of sexuality and gender, or even a better world, would look like. Sexuality tends to be presented as inherently a losing game with little real progress possible (beyond seeking to stop harm); after all, although there are gendered and sexed humans, and although there is violence, on these positions, there are no such things as sexual identities, sexual orientations, universal human rights, and freedom, ideally understood.

A third, more recently emerged approach, uses empirical science as its basis. It proposes that the most promising philosophical insights into sex, love, and gender will come from scientific explorations, such as comparisons of brain imagery and genetic studies (such as the search for a "gay gene"). On this approach, the ultimate answers to the puzzles of sex, love, and gender—why we act in this or that sexual, loving, or gendered way—will be found in a scientific laboratory or in scientific empirical studies of human bodies and deterministic behavior.

Fourth, virtue theory, including the "capability approach," has made many important contributions both in terms of emphasizing the importance of our social, embodied animality and the importance of seeking to develop ourselves as whole beings. In feminist philosophy and the philosophy of sex, love, and gender, the works of Martha Nussbaum are particularly prominent, comprehensive, and philosophically rich exemplars of this tradition. Indeed, it is in large part because of her work that many feminists and scholars working seriously on sex, love, and gender consider virtue theory or the capability framework as much more promising than Kant's philosophy when exploring these aspects of our embodied sociality.[7]

One particularly appealing aspect of Kant's philosophy, I argue in this book, results from the way in which it can engage the philosophical ideas and take on the philosophical challenges posed by these other theories, according to which sex, love, and gender can be understood in terms of choices (existentialist freedom), violence (postmodernist destructive forces), determinism (scientific causality), or virtuous embodied, social being (virtue/capability theory). As mentioned in the Preface, in this book I argue that we can use Kant's philosophy to transcend existentialist, postmodern, and scientific approaches without losing their many insights. Central to my view is that a philosophical theory of sex, love, and gender must be founded on both a more complex account of human nature and a more complex philosophical system than any of the first three types of theory have. In addition, a problem facing those working within a philosophical framework of available virtue/capabilities theories, in my view, is exactly their naturalized accounts of virtuous social embodiment as well as their relatively weaker (than Kant's) accounts of freedom. To give a brief example, it is very difficult to capture the experiences of being queer or trans or gay on such naturalized virtue/capability accounts, including Nussbaum's, because on these accounts, sexuality becomes either too much like a choice (as it is according to Nussbaum's capabilities approach) or too naturalized (naturally determined in a way that cannot explain human diversity, as it is on Aristotelian virtue approaches). As we will see, although Kant made mistakes about sexual and gendered minorities, his account of human nature gives us the philosophical resources we need to make

---

[7] In fact, it would not be hard to construct a theory of sex, love, and gender on the basis of Nussbaum's several works on feminist philosophy and on the philosophy of sex and love. I have not chosen this path, because I believe Kant's works on freedom in combination with his account of human nature yield a more compelling philosophical account. Discussing this question in any great detail is obviously (even if unfortunately) beyond the scope of this book, though it should be relatively easy to infer the kinds of reasons I would use to justify my choice from what is found here.

sense of polyamorous, polysexual, and LGBTQIA experiences and lives. In addition, the available virtue/capabilities theories tend to have fewer philosophical tools with which to understand the distinctions between ethics (virtue) and justice (right) as well as fewer ideas with which to explore justice (including the distinctions between innate, private, and public right) than does Kant's theory. In my view, therefore, Kant-based theories like the one I present in this book are more capable of capturing core aspects of sex, love, and gender than virtue/capabilities theories.

To put this latter point regarding complexity with reference to Kant studies only, this book maintains that sufficiently complex Kant-based account of sex, love, and gender will rest on his full account of human nature as we find it outlined in, for example, his *Religion within the Boundaries of Mere Reason* (hereafter *Religion*). Such an account provides us with the basis with which we can integrate the philosophical resources provided by Kant's analyses of freedom in the *Groundwork of the Metaphysics of Morals* (henceforward, *Groundwork*), *Critique of Practical Reason* (second *Critique*), and *The Metaphysics of Morals*, with his analysis of spontaneity and scientific causality found in the *Critique of Pure Reason* (first *Critique*), and with his ideas concerning aesthetic and teleological judgment that we find in the *Critique of the Power of Judgment* (third *Critique*). It is in part because the analyses of the first two kinds (first and second *Critiques*) yield objective principles and judgments, whereas those of the latter (third *Critique*) yield contingent judgments, I argue, that Kant's account of human nature is able to better capture our sexual, loving, gendered diversity than the other available accounts. Important too is the fact that many of Kant's own applied writings, such as those on anthropology, history, education, and politics, also combine philosophical insights found throughout his corpus to explore knotty (and sometimes thorny) human phenomena. By developing a fuller Kant-based theory of sex, love, and gender in a similar way, I seek to build and advance on both the existing Kant literature and non-Kantian writings on sex, love, and gender. I respond to both these literatures by showing how they capture important, but not all, aspects of the complex and complicated phenomena of sex, love, and gender, and how to unify core ideas in these writings into one, more comprehensive approach. In this way, the book also provides one way to bridge or merge the insights of the continental and of the analytic philosophical traditions with regard to core issues of sex, love, and gender, one that is based on Kant's account of human nature and his philosophical system as a whole.

These discussions of sex, love, and gender naturally connect with more general discussions in Kant studies and philosophy. An enduring source of skepticism towards Kant's practical philosophy is his deep conviction that morality must be understood in terms of universality. Whether we look to Kant's fundamental principle of virtue (The Categorical Imperative) or to his fundamental principle of right (The Universal Principle of Right), universality lies at the core of his analyses. We see this in Kant's ideas of universalizable maxims and acting from duty when it comes to virtue (ethics) and of interaction subject only to universal laws of freedom in his account of right (justice). A central worry of his critics is that by making universality the bedrock of morality, Kant fails to appreciate the importance of difference in societies, individual lives, and legal-political institutions when these are realized well. More specifically, Kant's approach seems unable to critique central aspects of normativity, namely the natures and roles of different social identities, including those tied to nations, cultures, and gender; those tied to different types of relationships, including differences between intimate and affectionate personal friendships, impersonal relationships involving strangers only, and purely professional relationships; and, finally, those tied to different historically situated legal-political systems. Insofar as contemporary Kantian theories maintain this deep commitment to universality, the critics continue, they will inherit the consequences of this serious philosophical mistake.

Indeed, one of the oldest, most persistent lines of criticism can be called the "universal formalism" objection, and it goes as follows: Kant considers the human self a purely rational subject that relates to everything as distinct from itself and that ought (morally) to relate to everything always in a thoroughly moralized, reflective way. Thus, as such subjects strive to lead lives that are as good and as moral as possible (as they should), they endeavor to act only on universalizable maxims (subjective rules of action) based in the motivation of duty (a self-reflective mode) with regard to everything and everyone at all times. And since the universalization test for maxims requires checking whether one's actions are consistent with respecting all persons as free and equal, it looks like all good or valuable actions and relations become moralized in a good person's life (since they always involve acting self-reflectively and are motivated by practical reason, or duty). In addition, living an emotionally healthy, morally good life appears to entail treating everyone—strangers and loved ones alike—as if they have an equal normative say and moral importance in our lives. Critics worry that an approach of this kind is unable to capture rich and meaningful human lives with profound, complex, and wonderful loves as well as brutal, devastating, and destabilizing losses. It also seems to be a morally and emotionally perverted kind of ideal: surely the purpose is not to live all aspects of our lives in such thoroughly reflective, moralized ways that requires treating everyone as equally important. Relatedly, such an approach appears incapable of capturing how non-moralized, unreflective emotions, as well as attachments to particular persons, are essential to many kinds of valuable human (inter)actions and evaluations. It also seems to ignore the central, constructive roles played by affectionate love, grief, and forgiveness, and the importance of particular histories, cultures, families, and loved ones, in lives lived well.

Variations of this worry about universal formalism—that it leaves no room for the importance of non-moralized, unreflective emotions and particularity in the lives of emotionally healthy human beings—have been raised against Kant's philosophy from the start by philosophers ranging from Fichte, Hegel, and Nietzsche to Beauvoir and Sartre to, more recently, many discussions motivating and surrounding important related work in both the analytic and continental philosophical traditions. For example, over the last few decades, feminist philosophers have fruitfully engaged these issues through concepts such as the "relational self" and "care."[8] Other particularly interesting treatments of these topics are found in contemporary work

---

[8] These discussions are sometimes framed in so-called "analytic" terms and sometimes in more "continental" terms.

inspired by P. F. Strawson's (1962) analysis of reactive attitudes;[9] by Bernard Williams' (1976) "one-thought-too-many" (hyper-reflection) objection to universal theories;[10] and, more recently, by Stephen Darwall's (2006) concept of the "second personal address." In addition, some discussions focus on the social nature of gender and sexuality, including its fundamental other-directedness—again, in ways often advancing arguments along the lines initiated by Beauvoir in *The Second Sex* and/or Butler in *Gender Trouble* onwards. Over the years, many Kantians have responded to this universal formalism objection by arguing that the Kantian agent is not as disembodied as the objection presupposes. In addition to responses from O'Neill, Herman, and Korsgaard, most Kantians who write on Kant's ethics and moral psychology address this objection, more or less explicitly.[11]

A second line of objection to Kantians, by Sally Sedgwick, gained prominence in the last couple of decades in a series of Hegelian criticisms of Barbara Herman's and Christine Korsgaard's work. This line of objection is as follows: even if the Kantian agent can be shown to be embodied and social—and the above universal formalist objections can be met—another, distinct "empty formalism" appears. Sedgwick argues that insofar as one makes Kant's or the Kantian agent more embodied and social in the ways Herman and Korsgaard do, the less well the position is able to respond to Hegel's classic objection to Kant that the source of morality for human beings cannot be Kant's noumenon (transcendental freedom). Indeed, the objection continues, insofar as these accounts succeed—and they no longer face, for example, Bernard Williams' problem of hyper-reflection ("one-thought-too-many")—there appears to be no difference anymore between the Kantian agent and the agent as defended in many other accounts. This point can be restated more generally: However we make this empty formalism objection—whether we do it with, say, Hegel or Mill—the claim is that it is impossible to use The Categorical Imperative to identify moral content. So understood, Kant's practical philosophy tries to derive content from form alone, but this is impossible; any morally horrible maxim, this kind of objection runs, can be universalized. Hence, Kant's moral philosophy is either a mere formalism or it cannot distinguish a moral maxim from a non-moral one. If Sedgwick is right, that is, Kantians appear to be stuck in a catch-22: if they can make the Kantian agent more embodied and social in order to avoid the universal formalism objection, then they encounter the empty formalism objection, namely the problem of losing the distinctive, noumenal (formal, transcendental freedom) aspects of Kant's practical philosophy. Relatedly, Katerina Deligiorgi (2012b) suggests that a drawback of embodied, social, and integrated accounts like those defended by Baron,

---

[9] For a Kantian example, see Allais (2008a, b, c).

[10] For Kantian examples, see Albrecht (2015/17) and Sussman (1996).

[11] For some other classical engagements, see related writings collected in Henry Allison (1990, 1996); Thomas E. Hill Jr. (1991, 1992); Paul Guyer (1993, 1996, 2000); Robert Louden (1986); Marcia Baron (1995, 2002); Engstrom and Whiting (1996); Nancy Sherman (1997); Allen Wood (1999); Karl Ameriks (2000); Engstrom (2002); and Andrews Reath (2006). Some newer engagements include David Sussman (2001); Patrick Frierson (2003, 2013, 2014); Jeanine M. Grenberg (2005, 2013); Jens Timmermann (2007); Alix Cohen (2009); Anne Margaret Baxley (2010); Jennifer K. Uleman (2010), Robert Johnson (2011); Katerina Deligiorgi (2012b); Kate Moran (2012); Julian Wuerth (2014); Lara Denis (2015); Oliver Sensen (2016); Melissa Merritt (2018); Pärttyli Rinne (2018); and Krista Thomason (2018).

Herman, Hill, and Korsgaard is that they fail to capture the distinct aspects of autonomy that speak to purely rational dimensions of our moral experience and which only a properly conceived formal account can reasonably aspire to comprehend or to provide an objective grounding. The general challenge, then, for embodied, social accounts such as mine, is to speak to this worry about form and content, which, as we will see, leads us to a discussion of truly free choices (so-called "free will") in Kant.

As mentioned above, I mean to contribute to these discussions by suggesting that a shortcoming of all the available accounts is that they pay insufficient attention to the *structure* of Kant's phenomenological account of the human being. More specifically, because they do not let what Kant calls our predispositions to "animality" and "humanity" do (enough of) their own important and distinctive philosophical work, they do not have a sufficient theoretical framework enabling us to speak philosophically to lives characterized by their social embodiment in general and to polyamorous, polysexual, and LGBTQIA lives in particular. On accounts currently and historically available in the Kant scholarship, "animality" and the social aspects of "humanity" are typically seen *only* as something that can help or hinder our ability to be morally good (virtuous). They too often group together all these non-moral desires of ours as if they were of one (heteronomous) kind. Or they identify heteronomy (with respect to morality) as the sole important characteristic of all of our non-moral desires, which entails that they cannot make good philosophical sense of how, for example, not being able to live out your sexuality or gender has a special existential significance for human beings. Somewhat simplified, if we apply these theories to the high rates of suicide among LGBTQIA persons living in oppressive contexts, at best it looks as if human beings who kill themselves because they cannot realize their sexuality or gender are doing something strange and irrational by inappropriately ascribing importance or value to their animality and/or social being. My account improves upon this unintended aspect of the available Kantian interpretations and theories by paying much closer attention to Kant's theory of the predisposition to good in human nature, which provides a philosophical account of the grounding role of animality and social aspects of humanity in general and thus of sexual or gendered identities and sexual orientations in particular. The specific way in which I do this locates my interpretive and philosophical position closest to the interpretations of Kant defended by Alix Cohen (given her account of Kant on feelings and desire) and Katerina Deligiorgi (given her account of the formal aspects of Kant on freedom and absolute moral prohibitions). But the main philosophical ideas should be interesting and acceptable (without too much revision) to all the other interpretations too. In the general conclusion to Part I, I first outline some of the features of my analysis of the human agent that enables it to avoid the first universalist formalism objection. I then use recent work by Lucy Allais and Katerina Deligiorgi on transcendental freedom and truly free choices ("free will") to expand upon this response by showing how my Kantian theory can respond to the empty formalism objection.

Independently of these worries about Kant's ideal of moral human agency, many philosophers object to what they consider Kant's and Kantians' singular focus on so-called "ideal" rather than "non-ideal" aspects of the human condition. These critics view Kantians as paying insufficient attention to the presence and impact of imperfect and destructive aspects of human nature and the actual human condition, such as bad behavior and violence, mean and twisted human characters, and systemic injustices. Moreover, although we find much work on systemic injustice in all the traditions of analytic philosophy,[12] it seems fair to say that the most interesting discussions to date of bodily and violent aspects of sex, love, and gender have occurred within the postmodern and phenomenological philosophical traditions as well as in the analytic feminist tradition.[13] A particularly influential strand of contemporary thinking concerned with sexuality and gender is found in the related aforementioned French philosophical tradition[14] and in the works of those inspired by it.[15] Importantly and somewhat ironically too, scholars working on sexuality and gender often argue that a major problem with Kant's philosophy is not, in a certain sense, its universalism, but its lack thereof. When it comes to women, and to people with non-straight, non-cis, non-binary sexual identities or orientations, it appears that Kant does not put such a high price on equality after all. The few times these differences come up in his works, he pays attention to them in the wrong ways. Instead of standing up to the oppression of social groups, for example, Kant appears to seek to justify it and thereby partakes in the project of rationalizing historically inherited prejudices and injustices in the name of universal moral theory.

In this book I argue that Kant's philosophy neither advocates moralized hyperreflective, alienating ways of being nor does it seek to justify his own and others' prejudices in the name of morality's universality. This is not to deny that Kant made serious philosophical mistakes in his writings on women and on LGBTQIA issues—just as he did in his writings on race—nor do I deny that we find some deep contradictions in Kant's thinking on these issues. Rather, I maintain four things. First, that exploring Kant's racist, sexist, and heterosexist remarks is philosophically important. As Lucy Allais (2016) also argues in "Kant's Racism," it is philosophically important to understand the structure of these destructive and damaging pathologies as we find them in Kant and in ourselves. More specifically, it is important seriously to engage the question of how these pathologies could and did find their way into the writings of one of, if not the most brilliant philosophers ever to have walked the planet—indeed, into the writings of the philosopher who, for the first time in the history of philosophy, was able to imagine a practical philosophical system founded on freedom. Second, as emphasized by Allais too, in Kant's writings we find valuable tools for understanding why and how these pathologies can and do take root in us.

[12] For some Kantian examples, see the works of Marcia Baron, Carol Hay, Barbara Herman, Thomas E. Hill Jr., Onora O'Neill, Arthur Ripstein, and me.
[13] In the analytical feminist tradition, I am thinking of philosophers such as Claudia Card, Ann Cudd, Carol Hay, Barbara Herman, Rebecca Kukla, Rae Langton, Jennifer Nedelsky, Martha Nussbaum, Onora O'Neill, Susanne Sreedhar, and Anita Superson.
[14] I am thinking especially of French thinkers like Hélène Cixous, Michel Foucault, Luce Irigiray, and Julia Kristeva, who in turn were often influenced not only by other French thinkers like Jacques Derrida and Jacques Lacan, but also by Sigmund Freud and the psychoanalytic tradition.
[15] In the English speaking tradition, many thinkers writing on these themes are profoundly inspired by philosophers in the French tradition, such as Linda Martín Alcoff, Susan Brison, Ann J. Cahill, Penelope Deutscher, Cressida Heyes, Jacob Hale, Laurie Shrage, and Chloë Taylor.

Kant's account of our ineradicable propensity to evil concerns, in part, our deep temptation to deceive ourselves and others, and, so, to do bad things in the name or under the guise of the good. Taking on the challenges these temptations and pathologies pose presumably go along with learning to identify, face, and relate well to these tendencies in ourselves and in our engagements with others, and thereby to take part in transforming inherited, damaging, and destructive patterns and systems of interaction into emotionally healthier, morally justifiable ones. A good future requires that our efforts at reform continue, making our societies better and freer for each and all—and constitutive of these reform efforts is engaging prejudicial temptations and pathologies as we find them in the classical philosophical texts. But, third, I argue that Kant put in place various safeguards against the influence of our prejudices: he was well aware of the dangerous temptation of mistaking our prejudices for insights, which is one reason why he maintained, as mentioned above, that arguments that are grounded on embodied, social considerations of moral psychology and moral anthropology—which his arguments about race, sex, affectionate love, and gender are—cannot take priority over or take the place of arguments grounded on considerations of freedom (persons and citizens). Fourth, as mentioned above, I propose that Kant's ideas of barbarism and formal and material wrongdoing are particularly useful as we seek to analyze conditions and situations involving profound wrongdoing. These, as we will see, are other reasons why engaging Kant's writings is a particularly fruitful philosophical enterprise.

Although the violences of racism, cisism, sexism, and heterosexism share important features—and I will draw attention to some of these shared characteristics in Chapter 4 on sexual violence and oppression—members of the LGBTQIA community, polyamorous, and polysexual people have often been denied the possibility of living out their sexuality and/or gender, which is existentially difficult in a different way than living subjected to racism. Polyamorous, polysexual, and LGBTQIA history is characterized by much suffering involving "living in the closet," damaging secrecy, and particularly high suicide rates. And as it has become possible to live these lives publicly in several countries in the world, those whose lives they are experience deep existential relief and joy. It is important for a theory of sex, love, and gender to be able to capture philosophically these particular kinds of joy and suffering, namely in such a way that those whose lives are being critiqued experience themselves as heard by the theory and find the theory useful for understanding and being around these aspects of their lives in good ways. A major aspiration in this book is therefore not only to investigate Kant's failures regarding sex, love, and gender, and to put forward a theory I believe Kant himself *should* have defended were he to stay consistent with his own, deep, philosophical commitments, but also one that captures the normative reality and human lives we are critiquing through philosophical theories of sex, love, and gender—a theory that listens to the lives it is seeking to explain.[16]

---

[16] Indeed, if one does, Kant's philosophical theory can explain why there are such things as sexual or gender identity and sexual orientation, and why, although there is racialization and racism, my analysis of sexual or gender identity and sexual orientation cannot be transferred to the complexities of racialization and the metaphysics of race. For example, the way I use "trans" in this analysis of sexual or gender identity

Kant's universalism is also often viewed as problematic from the perspective of legal-political philosophy. For example, many (Hobbesian) legal positivist theories, (Aristotelian) virtue theories, and (Hegelian) communitarian theories may be seen as unified in their judgment that Kant's universalism is impossible to defend since it does not capture the importance of historical context and the diversity of legal-political systems. There are many different legal-political systems, this line of criticism goes, which fail to satisfy Kant's Universal Principle of Right and his theory's liberal system of rights. Nonetheless, these systems do secure a legitimate rule of law for the peoples governed by and/or through them. Successful efforts at building good and just societies, including the rule of law, are not limited to projects grounded on (Kantian) principles of freedom. Rather, what determines the success of these efforts is the extent to which the laws, rules, or norms are recognized as valid by the people who are subjected to them.[17] In important ways, then, all the aforementioned non-Kantian legal-political philosophies share with their non-Kantian counterparts in ethics, moral psychology, and philosophical anthropology the belief that Kant's universalism is a major theory to refute and overcome. Part II of the book proposes a liberal republican reading of Kant's legal-political philosophy that does not fall subject to these objections. Instead, it shows how its universalism makes proper space for matters rooted in the history of particular legal-political communities. Further, it shows ways for oppressed groups to use the legal-political system to fight for their rights to be recognized, draws our attention to how legal-political cultures often are numb to the suffering of members of oppressed social groups, and points to ways we may start to reform these systems so as to make them better for realizing rightful interaction among us as distinctly *human* beings.

This book, in sum, suggests we need first to appreciate Kant's full account of human nature, which includes the predisposition to good and the propensity to evil, before exploring how Kant's theories of (virtuous internal and rightful external) freedom set the moral framework within which importantly unreflective or non-moralizable concerns of human nature are accommodated. We can then appreciate the ways in which Kant sees our faculty of desire as enabling both unreflective and reflective normative elements to be developed and work together as integrated wholes in emotionally healthy, morally good human beings, historical cultures, and legal-political systems. Kant's moral freedom theories (of virtue and of right) and the analyses that result from applying these freedom theories (with their universal principles) to actual interactions consequently do not demarcate the limits of his practical philosophy, and therefore they should not be the extent of our analyses of sex, love, and gender. Kant's full practical philosophy explains *both* how the non-reflective yet normative and the reflective parts of ourselves are realized in integrated

---

cannot simply be transferred and used for an analysis of racialization. A full engagement with the differences between sexuality and race is impossible within the scope of this book, however.

[17] This is a frequently used line of argument among legal positivists, whose historically informed accounts often draw on Hobbes. But Aristotle- and/or Hegel-inspired, communitarian political theorists like Alasdair MacIntyre, Charles Taylor, and Michael Sandel agree with legal positivists on the general point that Kant fails to appreciate the importance and role of historical difference in nation-building efforts. Addressing this issue here would take me too far afield.

ways in emotionally healthy, morally responsible human beings, cultures, and institutions *and* how we so easily fail at such realization. Importantly, each of the elements—the normative accounts of non-moralizable and moralizable aspects of ourselves and the account of evil—does its own independent philosophical work within Kant's overall practical philosophy, as it must do in theories of sex, love, and gender. As Kant appreciates the importance of non-moralizable emotions and particularity in human lives lived well, as well as the alluring dangers of rationalizing our emotional and moral shortcomings and failures and of mistaking our prejudices or particular practices for human ideals, so must we when we construct more comprehensive accounts of sex, love, and gender. Therefore, contrary to what some skeptics believe, these concerns are at the heart of Kant's practical philosophy, and they compose a main reason why the continuous engagement with and development of it should not simply be perceived as perpetuating a serious philosophical mistake, but as correcting mistakes while utilizing and continuing to develop some of the best, most exciting ideas of the Western philosophical tradition. My aim, then, is to bring out the productiveness of Kant's approach by addressing key areas of sex, love, and gender also in ways he did not do, something I could not have done without the help of related, philosophical work done by philosophers in the continental, postmodern, and feminist traditions, and by women, philosophers of sex and love, and feminist Kant scholars before me.

The book is divided into two parts. Part I—"Sex, Love, and Gender: Happiness and Virtue"—proposes a Kant-based moral psychological theory of sex, love, and gender in which happiness and virtue play their own, distinctive roles. The introduction to Part I offers an overview of the issues, of the emergence of women Kant scholars, and of the related secondary Kantian literature in feminist philosophy and the philosophy of sex and love. It seeks to situate the subsequent four chapters into the relevant history of Kant scholarship and show how those chapters contribute to the existing literature. Part I comprises Chapter 1 "Sexual and Affectionate Love: Happiness and Moral Responsibility"; Chapter 2 "Kant and Women"; Chapter 3 "Kant on Sex. Reconsidered"; and Chapter 4 "Kant on Sexual Violence and Oppression." In the general conclusion ("Concluding Part I: Reconciling Noumena and Embodied, Social Kantian Agents"), I re-engage the Hegelian empty formalism objection from Sedgwick to Herman with the help of work by Allais and Deligiorgi.

Part II—"Sex, Love, and Gender: Right"—moves to the legal-political aspects of sex, love, and gender by shifting the focus to matters of right, or justice. As discussed above, for a long time The Doctrine of Right was not given due attention in Kant scholarship. To help remedy this problem in the literature, and to set the stage for the analyses of justice in the second part of the book, the introduction to Part II explains the centrality of Kant's distinction between virtue (or ethics, which has to do with internal freedom) and right (or justice, which has to do with external freedom). Autonomy can thus be seen in two complementary, yet not co-extensive, ways: self-governance through virtue (internal freedom); and self-governance through right (external freedom). I also outline the emerging interpretive traditions as well as briefly explain why my approach can be located in what may be called the liberal republican interpretive tradition. I close this general introduction by explaining how Kant ensures that these freedom analyses make space for concerns of non-moralizable aspects of human nature and how the three chapters build upon and extend existing work on Kantian feminist philosophy and the philosophy of sex and love. With these ideas clarified, Part II of the book can make headway in a legal-political analysis of many of the core legal-political controversies regarding sex, love, and gender. More specifically, the three subsequent chapters are divided by means of Kant's distinction between innate, private, and public right. Throughout, I first use Kant's principles of right to analyze the general questions at stake before making space for considerations of our distinctively human nature. Part II comprises Chapter 5 "The Innate Right to Freedom: Abortion, Sodomy, and Obscenity Laws"; Chapter 6 "Private Right: Marriage and Trade in Sexual Services"; and Chapter 7 "Public Right: Systemic Justice." In the general conclusion ("Concluding Part II: Justice as Rightful, Human Freedom"), I return to some of the puzzles and objections that I have discussed above. I show how my right-based conception of sex, love, and gender combines both so-called ideal and non-ideal elements and shows one way to overcome the analytic/ continental split with regard to issues of justice. I also explain how my analysis reconciles core libertarian and other liberal ideas, just as it incorporates core insights of other legal-political traditions, such as legal positivist and communitarian traditions. I furthermore pay special attention to how the resulting account can engage, incorporate, and re-envision many of the insights developed in feminist thought, including the care tradition.

More detailed descriptions of each chapter are found at the end of the introductions to Parts I and II, since this makes it easier to see exactly how each chapter builds on and contributes to the existing literature. The reason why some of this literature is not directly integrated into the chapters themselves is because a major objective in this book is to outline my Kantian theory of sex, love, and gender. Consequently, I have integrated only what I believe is particularly useful for this purpose. To use my favorite analogy for understanding philosophical theories, one may think of our experience of "autostereograms." An autostereogram is a two-dimensional image with repeating patterns that hide a three-dimensional image—"a picture within a picture," so to speak. Understanding a philosophical theory is similar in that the many ideas and principles (the repeated patterns) suddenly show themselves as forming a coherent whole (the three-dimensional picture). Also, once the theory shows itself as clearly "three-dimensional," one can then "walk" around in it, think about it, and reconsider the various parts, combinations of parts, as well as the whole. I hope that the way in which the book is written helps the whole theory of sex, love, and gender emerge from the repeated patterns of the philosophical parts. I also hope that it lends to finding gaps or the need for any changes or nuancing.

Because of the subject matter of the book, and because I want the book to speak not only to (Kantian) philosophers, but to those the book is about, all of the chapters are written such that they can be read independently and in any order—although they build upon each other such that only together do they yield the complete, complex theory. Of course, this leads to some repetition in the chapters. Possibly reaching those who will personally relate to the difficulties of living with a marginalized sexual or gender identity or sexual orientation seemed to me to be of greater value than not attempting to do so. Notice too that the sophistication of the philosophical interpretation of Kant varies, with the greatest complexity coming in Chapters 1 (the first chapter in Part I) and 7 (the last chapter in Part II) as well as in the general conclusions to Parts I and II. These sections will probably be a more challenging read for those somewhat unfamiliar with the relevant literature and topics. In contrast, the introductions to Parts I and II aim to provide useful background information for people new to these philosophical discussions and the (related) Kantian tradition. My hope is that the construction of the book makes it accessible to people who are not already familiar with philosophy in general or with Kant's philosophy in particular, *and*, of great importance to me, to those who endeavor to improve their understanding of their own sexual, loving, or gendered lives through doing philosophy.

PART I
Sex, Love, and Gender
Happiness and Virtue

Introduction to Part I

When critiquing the conditions characteristic of everyday experiences of women and sexual or gendered minorities, capturing the nature of human embodiment and dependency relations is a principal interest. Analyses of embodiment and dependency relations are, for example, naturally at the center of critiques of abortion, domestic violence, systemic injustice, and oppression. Analyzing institutions such as marriage, prostitution, and pornography, and understanding phenomena involving sexual and affectionate love, sexual or gender identity, sexual orientation, sexual objectification, and sexual or gendered violence appear similarly impossible without involving concerns of embodiment and dependency. Explorations of embodiment and dependency also do important philosophical work in good analyses of relations involving caregivers and care receivers, especially in light of the asymmetry of these relations and of how the unpaid, physically and emotionally exhausting work of care has, historically, so often been deemed "women's work."

For scholars with serious interests in feminist philosophy, the philosophy of sex and love, and the history of philosophy, an unavoidable question arises: is it worthwhile to use the theories of classical thinkers to explore these issues? One problem is that most of the Western philosophical canon has been written by cis men, in ways that have done little to improve the conditions of women and sexual or gendered minorities—indeed, quite the opposite. In addition, for those who have research interests in the philosophy of Kant, the task of using his writings for feminist purposes has struck most thinkers as impossible. In contrast to J. S. Mill, for example, Kant is known neither for his rich, close, and interesting relationships with women, nor for being a champion of women's rights. Kant's closest friends appear to all have been men, and, as we will see in abundance in the subsequent chapters, when he speaks about women or about sexual or gendered minorities, he often expresses and affirms many sexist, cisist, heterosexist, and even homophobic beliefs and attitudes. Further, Kant's moral philosophy is commonly viewed as advocating a moral ideal of a rather disembodied kind. To many, Kant's ideal moral agent is the independent, hyper-reflective man who constantly strives to act only on universalizable maxims, and only from the motivation of duty. Kant's practical philosophy is therefore typically

Sex, Love, and Gender: A Kantian Theory. Helga Varden, Oxford University Press (2020). © Helga Varden.
DOI: 10.1093/oso/9780198812838.001.0001

deemed a particularly poor resource for understanding issues concerning human embodiment and dependency in general and for understanding the condition of woman[1] and sexual or gendered minorities in particular.

And yet, in recent years, a significant body of research—especially by women Kant scholars—has engaged Kant's writings anew. Some of these engagements challenge earlier readings of Kant, while others draw extensively on Kant's philosophy—commonly in dialogue with feminist philosophers writing in different philosophical traditions—as they seek to develop better philosophical theories of embodiment, dependency, and the condition of woman. A central idea informing many of these efforts is that although Kant's own judgment and analysis of the condition of woman presents serious problems that need overcoming, an undeniable strength of his practical philosophy is its abundance of philosophical resources for defenders of rights, understood in terms of freedom and equality, or in terms of autonomy. Indeed, as we will see below as well as in this book as a whole, some (including me) also argue that Kant's theory is particularly useful for defending women's rights and the rights of sexual or gendered minorities, for analyzing asymmetrical dependency (care) relations, and for appreciating the importance of our embodiment and sociality when seeking a better understanding of a range of related issues concerning virtue (ethics), right (justice), moral psychology, and philosophical anthropology. By setting the focus on issues of dependence and embodiment, work in feminist philosophy and in the philosophy of sex and love historically has and continues to radically improve our understanding of Kant's practical philosophy as one that is *not* (as it typically has been taken to be) about disembodied abstract rational agents. This book follows this path of interpretation and development of the Kantian philosophical enterprise.

To set the stage for the four chapters comprising this first part of the book, this introduction outlines this positive development in Kant scholarship in recent decades by taking us through major developments with regard first to the increased number of women Kant scholars; and, second, to the growth of philosophical resources in Kant scholarship dealing with issues concerning sex, love, and gender from the point of view of virtue (ethics), moral psychology, and moral (or philosophical) anthropology. Having this background knowledge should make it easier for philosophers generally and Kantians in particular to see how the account developed in the next four chapters builds upon, engages, and contributes to the existing literature. It will also be especially helpful in giving the philosophically trained reader a sense of where I believe the main, current interpretive and philosophical challenges lie. The corresponding overview of available Kant-interpretations on issues of right (justice) and sex, love, and gender, such as issues concerning abortion, marriage, and trade in sexual services, is provided in the introduction to Part II. That discussion sets the stage for seeing how the last three chapters of the book seek to advance the current literature on Kant's legal-political philosophy.

---

[1] I use "woman" rather than "women" here because I want to focus on what women share in virtue of being read as women rather than on questions focusing on the complexity of women's lives that track so-called intersectionality, that is, challenges related to, for example, class, racialization, sexual or gender identity, or sexual orientation.

Given the many problematic things Kant says about women, it may be surprising to learn that Kant scholarship is among the areas of philosophy that developed an impressive (and steadily increasing) number of outstanding women scholars early on. It is always difficult to name some and not others, but there is little risk of offending anyone by saying that Eva Schaper deserves special mention. Schaper received her Ph.D. from the University of Münster in 1950, and she made long-lasting contributions, especially to the study of Kant's third *Critique*. The pioneering Ingeborg Heidemann (Ph.D. Köln, 1955) is especially remembered for her work on and edition of Kant's first *Critique* and for having been an active force behind the historically most important Kant journal, namely *Kant-Studien*. Also among the earliest groundbreaking women, Mary J. Gregor (Ph.D. Toronto, 1958) is known both for her wonderful scholarship on Kant's practical philosophy and for her lasting contributions to the Kant and the wider philosophical communities through her excellent English translations of much of Kant's practical philosophy—indeed, many of the translations relied on in this book benefit from this work of hers.

A second, larger wave of trailblazing women Kant scholars includes Onora O'Neill (Ph.D. Harvard, 1969), Gertrud Scholz (Ph.D. Köln, 1972), Jill Buroker (Ph.D. Chicago, 1974), Karen Gloy (Ph.D. Heidelberg, 1974), Patricia Kitcher (Ph.D. Princeton, 1974), Barbara Herman (Ph.D. Harvard, 1975), and Seyla Benhabib (Ph.D. Yale, 1977). Although their Ph.D.'s were not in philosophy but in political science (Frankfurt am Main, 1971, and Harvard, 1975, respectively), Ingeborg Maus and Susan Meld Shell are also among those who paved the way for women Kantians. B. Sharon Byrd, who was originally educated in law (J.D. UCLA, 1972; LL.M. Columbia, 1987; J.S.D. Columbia, 1991), falls into these two categories as well. The 1980s saw another wave of influential women Kant scholars on both sides of the Atlantic, including Sharon Anderson-Gold (Ph.D. New School, 1980), Jean Hampton (Ph.D. Harvard, 1980), Béatrice Longuenesse (Ph.D. Paris-Sorbonne, 1980), Christine Korsgaard (Ph.D. Harvard, 1981), Adrian M. S. Piper (Ph.D. Harvard, 1981), Marcia W. Baron (Ph.D. North Carolina, 1982), Herlinde Pauer-Studer (Ph.D. Salzburg, 1983), Jane Kneller (Ph.D. Rochester, 1984), Claudia Langer (Ph.D. Heidelberg, 1984), Jean P. Rumsey (Ph.D. Wisconsin-Madison, 1985), Sally Sedgwick (Ph.D. Chicago, 1985), Robin S. Dillon (Ph.D. Pittsburgh, 1986), Ursula Pia Jauch (Ph.D. Zürich, 1988), Hannah Ginsborg (Ph.D. Harvard, 1989), and Holly L. Wilson (Ph.D. Penn. State, 1989). This decade also saw the first two women to take a Ph.D. in philosophy in the Nordic countries, namely the Kant scholars Hjørdis Nerheim and Else Wiestad (Oslo, 1986 and 1987, respectively). Nerheim is also the first woman to become a full professor in philosophy in these countries (in 1994, in Tromsø), whereas Wiestad is the first one to become a full professor in philosophy at the University of Oslo (in 2000).[2]

---

[2] I am grateful to Anne Margaret Baxley, Katrin Flikschuh, Howard Gold, André Grahle, Peter Niesen, Daniel Peres, Arthur Ripstein, Sally Sedgwick, Jens Timmermann, Rachel Zuckert, and Alice Pinheiro Walla for helping me construct this list. Any remaining imperfections are obviously entirely my responsibility. Also, please beware that this list is likely to be incomplete due to my insufficient knowledge of women Kant scholars and their publications on these issues in many countries and languages.

These scholars broke the philosophy equivalent of the glass ceiling for women to become Kant scholars and philosophers, and they have been tremendously important in innumerable ways for those of us coming after them. They have served, or still serve, as mentors, supervisors, teachers, role models, and transformers of the philosophical profession. Many of these scholars have focused their attention on topics other than practical philosophy, primarily on interpretive and philosophical issues concerning the first and the third *Critiques*, and most have not published on Kant in relation to feminist philosophy and the philosophy of sex and love. There is probably no simple or single reason why. For some, it may be a result of their research focus; for others, research interests may have been combined with (conscious or unconscious) strategic, career-building self-interest (given that feminist philosophy, let alone the philosophy of sex and love were for a long time not considered "serious scholarship" in the profession); and for yet others, it may have been influenced in part by how emotionally difficult it was to engage feminist philosophy and issues concerning the philosophy of sex and love when trying to succeed professionally as a woman in an academic discipline dominated by men.

The paths of women Kant scholars who wrote on practical philosophy developed quite differently. By the late 1980s to early 1990s, many of these women had begun publishing work on Kant and topics in feminist philosophy. As mentioned in the general Introduction, the first two Ph.D. dissertations on Kant and gender were defended in 1987, by Else Wiestad at the University of Oslo, and in 1988, by Ursual Pia Jauch at the University of Zürich. In the latter part of the 1980s, in the English-speaking world, Onora O'Neill, Barbara Herman, Christine Korsgaard, and Marcia Baron also wrote on Kant's practical philosophy—especially his ethics—by taking on the challenge from many quarters, including feminist philosophical quarters, to show how Kant's ethics could respond effectively to concerns regarding particularity, affective emotions, and our social natures (for example, see O'Neill 1990; Herman 1993a; Korsgaard 1996a,b; Baron 1995). An important, critical response to this literature's ability to face the more general and the explicitly feminist objections to Kant's ethics came from Sally Sedgwick in 1990.[3] Sedgwick argues in "Can Kant's Ethics Survive the Feminist Critique?" that although there are ways of overcoming many problems of sexism in Kant and despite efforts by Herman et al. to emphasize the role he awards feeling in his practical philosophy, pure reason nonetheless remains the basis of his supreme moral law. As a result, she claims, Kant's philosophy is unable to give a sufficient response to objections from feminist quarters—such as the worries expressed in Carol Gilligan's *In a Different Voice*—regarding the constitutive role of the emotions and particularity in morally good and emotionally healthy human relations, let alone care relations. As mentioned in the general Introduction, I return to this debate between Sedgwick and Herman in the conclusion to Part I, where I show its relevance both for the next generation women Kant scholars (represented by Lucy Allais, Alix Cohen, and Katerina Deligiorgi) and my project in this book.

---

[3] One of the very few (still classical) critical articles on Kant's take on women that existed at the time—"Kant: An Honest but Narrow-Minded Bourgeois?"—was written by another women, Susan Mendus (1987).

In 1992, Korsgaard published an important article that takes on explicitly feminist issues. In "Creating the Kingdom of Ends: Reciprocity and Responsibility in Personal Relations," Korsgaard focuses on how Kant's writings can capture dangers of sexuality and objectification as well as concerns regarding friendship in intimate relations. These issues are central to understanding Kant's account of the importance of marriage in general and for women in particular (even though the actual historical institution so often has been terrible for women). The year 1992 also saw the publication of a remarkable article by Rae Langton, "Duty and Desolation." Langton engages core ideas in Kant's moral philosophy by reflecting on a letter exchange between Kant and Maria von Herbert, a young woman who had been studying his philosophy together with friends and who came to him for moral advice. Langton argues that in addition to revealing Kant's inability to respond well to the challenge of von Herbert's difficult personal situation, the interchange between Kant and von Herbert reveals troublesome features of his moral philosophy, especially regarding his ideals of truth-telling and moral sainthood. Robin S. Dillon published her first two articles in 1992. In these as well as other articles published in the 1990s onwards, Dillon developed her Kant-inspired account of self-respect. A facet of her account explores connections with relations of care, and argues that a morally responsible, emotionally healthy life includes respecting ourselves and others not merely as rational beings but also as embodied, particular individuals.[4]

Another early groundbreaking contribution on Kant and women written in the English language was by Pauline Kleingeld, then a graduate student at the Dutch University of Leiden. In her 1993 "The Problematic Status of Gender-Neutral Language in the History of Philosophy: The Case of Kant," Kleingeld discusses the tension between Kant's sexism and the gender-neutral language of his moral and political theory. She criticizes the tradition of interpretation according to which this aspect of Kant's text is simply set aside as an unfortunate mistake. Also in 1993, the tremendously influential article "Could It Be Worth Thinking about Kant on Marriage?" by Barbara Herman was published. Herman not only presented an entirely new take on Kant and marriage—one that views Kant as aware of and concerned about the problematic, historical asymmetries between men and women—but also took up the important themes regarding sexual objectification addressed in Korsgaard's article. Herman's and O'Neill's discussions of particularity and the related importance of affect and direct emotional responses also received explicit attention in the work of Herlinde Pauer-Studer, who wrote a series of papers on feminist philosophy in the 1990s. In "Kant and Social Sentiments" (1994), she engages both O'Neill's and Herman's arguments by trying to show that neither successfully responds to the charge that Kant's philosophy is as disembodied and unsocial as feminists (and others) often argue. She proposes that the only way to overcome this limitation of Kant's ethics would be to complement it with an account of the good. These themes of embodiment, asymmetry, and particularity have become especially prominent in the so-called "care tradition" in philosophy. I return to them below.

---

[4] See, for example, (Dillon 1992a, b, c, d, 1997, 2001, 2003).

Robin M. Schott's *Feminist Interpretations of Kant* (1997) was the first anthology to focus exclusively on Kant and feminist issues. All of the articles and scholars included in this anthology deserve mention, but for our purposes here, I focus on the Kant scholars' contributions.[5] In "Kantian Ethics and Claims of Detachment," Marcia Baron begins by criticizing Kant's sexism before proceeding to explain why, in spite of that sexism, Kant's moral theory (with its basis in freedom and equality) is so empowering and useful for feminist causes. In "The Aesthetic Dimension of Kantian Autonomy," Jane Kneller discusses the role of aesthetic imagination in Kant's conception of autonomy.[6] In "Feminist Themes in Unlikely Places: Re-Reading Kant's *Critique of Judgment*," Marcia Moen too focuses on Kant's aesthetics to find support for feminist causes in Kant's philosophy, whereas Holly L. Wilson's contribution is, as its title suggests, an attempt at "Rethinking Kant from the Perspective of Ecofeminism." The year 1997 also saw a Kant-based response to claims of Kant's inability to meet the challenges regarding particularity and affect in Cynthia Stark's "Decision Procedures, Standards of Rightness, and Impartiality." The next year saw the publication of Jane Kneller and Sidney Axinn's anthology *Autonomy and Community: Readings in Contemporary Kantian Social Philosophy*, which includes exploratory papers on Kant in relation to feminist approaches to pregnancy and abortion (Feldman 1998) and marriage (Wilson 1998).

From the beginning, another important factor in the development of scholarship on Kant in relation to core feminist topics was the way in which some Kantian men directly engaged related topics in productive ways. Contributions especially deserving of mention include John Rawls's influential proposal of the family as a basic institution, which he put forth as early as 1971 in his original *A Theory of Justice*, and Thomas E. Hill, Jr.'s influential Kantian critique of the deferential wife in his "Servility and Self-Respect" (1973).[7] The first comprehensive—and still classic—engagement with Rawls' theory is Susan Moller Okin's *Justice, Gender, and the Family* (1989). A particularly significant engagement with Hill's paper is the 1985 interchange between Marilyn A. Friedman and Marcia Baron; their discussion of how to understand women's duties is continued in Carol Hay's (2013) work, where she proposes that women have an imperfect duty to fight their own oppression.

There is a series of general and more specific interpretive and philosophical questions facing anyone who approaches core questions in feminist philosophy and the philosophy of sex and love within a Kantian philosophical framework. Whether we look at the work referenced above or at the more recent work (discussed below), what we find is often determined by which of these questions the relevant scholars aspire to address. The interpretive questions are accompanied by efforts to establish exactly what Kant said and why he said what he said; this often leads these Kant scholars to explore structural interpretive issues, such as how to understand

---

[5] Sally Sedgwick's 1992 paper was also reprinted in a slightly edited form in this anthology.

[6] This article by Kneller was preceded by two 1993 articles on Kant's feminization of the faculty of imagination (Kneller 1993a, b).

[7] Mentioning Thomas E. Hill, Jr., and his supervisor, John Rawls, seems particularly appropriate because both are widely recognized as having helped empower women in the profession, including in their service as Ph.D. supervisors for several women.

Kant's accounts of ethics (virtue), justice (right), and human nature (including evil). Some then proceed with their general Kantian accounts—of virtue, and/or of right, and/or of human nature (including evil)—to explore what Kant wrote about specific issues concerning sex, love, and gender, such as women's sexuality, their "proper" roles in the home and in society, and so on. And some take on a next-level question as well, namely what Kant should have said about these various topics, once his accounts of virtue, right, and human nature are revised as they should be (whatever that is taken to involve). Others set these interpretive questions aside and instead proceed more directly, trying to determine what Kantians should say about sex, love, and gender when armed with the most defensible version of Kant's accounts of virtue, and/or of right, and/or of human nature.

All Kantians who want to contribute to contemporary discussions of sex, love, and gender employ some of Kant's philosophical tools to explore topics having to do with embodiment (e.g., sexual objectification, sexual activity, sexual violence, abortion); with care relations (e.g., marriage, dependents, servants); and with systemic injustice (e.g., poverty, prostitution, oppression). Furthermore, some of the Kant-based or Kant-inspired accounts also take part in bridging the Kantian and non-Kantian philosophical traditions by drawing attention to and making explicit the similarities and differences between their Kantian accounts and those offered by other kinds of philosophical approaches. Others go beyond the question of Kant and the condition of woman by using the Kantian framework in relation to other topics concerning diversity. Among these are some of the central issues in the philosophy of sex and love (e.g., non-conventional sexual activities, LGBTQIA identities and orientations, and polyamory), as well as issues brought to the fore by the philosophy of race and by the philosophy of disability. The following overview of many of these ongoing discussions regarding feminist philosophy and the philosophy of sex and love— and the related, burgeoning literature—is structured by a focus on themes rather than chronology, and most of the issues pertaining to Part II of this book (on justice) are not discussed.[8]

As noted in the general Introduction, part of the peculiarity of Kant's writings on women arises from the fact that they are predominantly found not in his moral writings on freedom but dispersed throughout other works: in the third *Critique*, the *Anthropology*, and shorter essays on history, politics, and aesthetics. In 2009, Susan Meld Shell published her *Kant and the Limits of Autonomy*, which extensively explores Kant's published and unpublished anthropological writings, including his (sexist) distinction between man and woman (Shell 2009; cf. Cohen 2009, Louden 2011, Wood 2008). This work does not take on the further task of exploring whether an improved account of human nature needs philosophical distinctions of the kinds Kant utilizes to make sense of gender or, relatedly, sexual or gender identity and sexual orientation. That it does not is symptomatic of how much of the scholarship on Kant's anthropology also does not explicitly address the question of whether the distinction between man and woman—or any other philosophical distinction(s)—is needed for a good philosophical theory of sex, love, and gender. Instead, these

---

[8] For a more general overview article, see Hampton (2004: ch. 7).

engagements tend to accept that Kant was sexist, explore ways in which he was or was not *as* sexist as many non-Kantians tend to think, and argue that his critical theory of freedom may be very useful for understanding the condition of woman and related concerns of feminist philosophy and the philosophy of sex and love. In Part I, I engage both the discussions of how to understand Kant's own conception of "woman" as well as the question of how he—and Kantians—should have used his philosophical resources to come up with a *better* conception of sexual love, sexual or gender identity, and sexual orientation.

Three fascinating, recent engagements with the question of how sexist Kant actually was are found in work by Mari Mikkola, Jordan Pascoe, and Jennifer K. Uleman. In "Kant on Moral Agency and Women's Nature," Mikkola (2011) argues that some of the earlier papers are too harsh in addressing Kant's actual views on women; Kant is not *as* sexist as many have read him to be. Pascoe and Uleman similarly aim to rectify earlier feminist readings of Kant. The discussion between Uleman (2000) and Pascoe (2011) centers on Kant's comments on the punishability of unwed mothers who committed infanticide—a common phenomenon in Prussia at Kant's time. Uleman (2000) presents an entirely new take on Kant's puzzling comments: she argues that contrary to what most thought at the time and what was prominently argued by Annette Baier (1993)—namely that Kant's comments revealed despicable callousness toward women and vulnerable newborns—his idea was sympathetic and important in that it questioned the punishability of women who, if they carried their babies to term, would doom themselves and their children to a life of shame and economic hardship. Uleman's paper is criticized by Pascoe (2011), who argues that Kant's sexism made him unable to hear the women's suffering. Despite being worried about the legal practice of severely punishing infanticide in Prussia at the time, Kant therefore ended up defending capital punishment for unwed mothers who committed infanticide. I engage the general question of Kant's sexism in Chapter 2, postponing the discussion of infanticide (and abortion) to Chapter 5.

Korsgaard's 1992 and Herman's 1993b papers on personal relations and marriage were groundbreaking in several ways, one of which is that they focus on sexuality and objectification. Herman's piece is also groundbreaking in how it explicitly draws attention to analogies between Kant's arguments on these issues and important related work in feminist philosophy, particularly that of Catharine MacKinnon and Andrea Dworkin. In *Sexual Solipsism* Rae Langton critically engages the arguments of both Herman and Korsgaard as she braids together threads of Kant, sexual objectification, intimate friendships, and adds to these the thread of pornography (Langton 2009). With respect to sexual activity and sexual objectification, in "Hunger for You: Kant and Kinky Sex," Pascoe (2012) takes up the themes laid out by Herman, Korsgaard, and Langton, arguing that Kant was aware of and is right in thinking that some sexual activities are morally dangerous. Nevertheless, it is not clear that all sexual activity is. Pascoe argues that Kant mistakes all sex for kinky sex. While kinky sex may be problematic, much other sex can be genuinely affirming, loving, and affectionately caring. Finally, in *Sexual Solipsism*, Langton (2009) also continues to bridge the gap between Kant and feminist philosophy as she undertakes to analyze Kant on feminist issues in relation to the philosophy of language. Many accounts of Kant in relation to sexuality and gender available today seek to bridge these gaps between Kant and feminist philosophy and/or between Kant and other areas of philosophy. I take on the questions of friendship, objectification, and dangers of sex in Chapters 3 and 4, postponing the discussion of erotic images (pornography) until Chapters 5 through 7.

As explained also in the general Introduction, this book is divided into two parts. Part I—"Sex, Love, and Gender: Happiness, and Virtue"—proposes a Kant-based moral psychological theory of sex, love, and gender in which happiness and ethics (virtue) play their own, distinctive roles. This part contains four chapters: Chapter 1 "Sexual and Affectionate Love: Happiness and Moral Responsibility," Chapter 2 "Kant and Women," Chapter 3 "Kant on Sex. Reconsidered," and Chapter 4 "Kant on Sexual Violence and Oppression." In the conclusion to Part I ("Concluding Part I: Reconciling Noumena and Embodied, Social Kantian Agents"), I re-engage the Hegelian empty formalism objection from Sedgwick to Herman with the help of work by Allais, Cohen, and Deligiorgi. Part II—"Sex, Love, and Gender: Right"— moves to the legal-political aspects of sex, love, and gender by shifting the focus to matters of right (justice). This part is composed of three chapters: Chapter 5 "The Innate Right to Freedom: Abortion, Sodomy, and Obscenity Laws," Chapter 6 "Private Right: Marriage and Trade in Sexual Services," and Chapter 7 "Public Right: Systemic Justice," as well as a conclusion ("Concluding Part II: Justice as Rightful, Human Freedom"). More detailed descriptions of the chapters in Part II are in the introduction to Part II. Below I give a short description of the arguments in the chapters of Part I.

Chapter 1 ("Sexual and Affectionate Love: Happiness and Moral Responsibility") presents a Kant-based account of the challenges involved in realizing affectionately loving, sexual, and gendered lives in ways that are emotionally healthy and morally responsible. To do this, I introduce and make use of Kant's accounts of the predisposition to good, the propensity to evil, the faculty of desire, truthfulness as our sacred moral duty, the highest good, vital forces, perfect and imperfect duties, characters (temperaments), and of friendship. The starting point is Kant's argument that our highest duty to ourselves and to each other is truthfulness, including and most importantly for our purposes, truthfulness regarding our own sexual, loving, gendered being—what we want and need when it comes to sexuality, affectionate love, and gender presentations. Because much of our sexual, affectionately loving, gendered being is experienced on an unreflective level, truthfulness regarding who we are and what we need and want—paying truthful attention to what feels richly and stably pleasant—is essential to emotionally healthy, morally good development of our sexual, loving, gendered selves. Ideally, our partially unreflective ways of being sexual, loving, and gendered are developed, transformed, and integrated through our faculty of desire such that they are in close union with what we morally approve of upon reflection. Through abstract conceptual, associative, and aesthetic-teleological means, our faculty of desire can enable us to develop our sexual, loving, gendered selves such that they are consistent with striving for the highest good understood as a union between happiness and morality and between our natural and moral vital forces. Although we have an ineradicable temptation to do bad things to ourselves and to one another, our faculty of desire enables us to assume responsibility for it such that we experience perfect duties not to do damaging things to ourselves or to one another as well as imperfect duties to further the development of ourselves and others as who we are in good ways. Although this chapter for the most part simply presents Kant's own philosophical ideas, I indicate that nothing of what is said requires that we draw Kant's cisist, heterosexist, or sexist conclusions. Although the account does maintain that a core challenge is to be able to realize the sexual, loving, gendered aspects of ourselves in ways that unite our non-moralizable emotional being with our moral being, it is a complex, complicated, and lifelong undertaking that cannot plausibly be seen to normatively prioritize—emotionally or morally—monogamous, binary, cis, and straight lives over polyamorous, polysexual, or LGBTQIA lives.

This is not to deny that Kant himself drew heterosexist and sexist conclusions, even if he did much better with regard to women than with regard to homosexuality. Chapter 2, "Kant and Women" gives an interpretation of Kant's own account of the traditional genders (man and woman) with particular attention to the historically oppressed gender (woman). I explain how Kant's full account of human nature, including his teleological arguments, in combination with how we use the imagination aesthetically when being sexual, inform his account of the traditional gender ideals of the man and the woman; the man is associated with the idea of the sublime, the woman with that of the beautiful. I explain how Kant, like Beauvoir after him, was deeply intrigued by Rousseau's account of the traditional genders. Moreover, though Beauvoir was able to see important problems with Rousseau's proposals for the gender ideals much more clearly than did Kant, I defend Kant's insistence that we should not reduce sexual or gender identity and sexual orientation to choice in the existentialist way Beauvoir does. I conclude the chapter by arguing that although Kant himself was not able to solve the puzzle of genders, sexual or gendered identities, and sexual orientations, including how they do not fit neatly into the two traditionally dominant categories of man and woman, his general suggestions that in addition to accounts of freedom and science, understanding sex, love, and gender requires appeals to embodied, social human nature, teleological judgments, and an aesthetic use of the imagination are worth exploring further. Thus, Chapter 2 sets the stage for Chapter 3, in which I offer a new Kantian theory of sex, love, sexual or gender identity, and sexual orientation by using Kant's philosophical ideas (as introduced in Chapter 1). I argue that Kant provided us with the resources needed for a complex, plausible philosophical account of sex, love, sexual or gender identity, and sexual orientation.

Chapter 3 ("Kant on Sex: Reconsidered"), then, outlines my reconsidered Kantian theory of sex, love, and gender, an account that seeks to overcome the problems plaguing Kant's own writings and that is philosophically interesting in its own right. The argument in this chapter is relatively straightforward, given the preceding chapter. I argue that in order to overcome the problems with Kant's own account, we simply need to do what he should have done. We need to correctly incorporate Kant's complex account of human nature into our theory of sex, love, and gender. Doing this requires us to heed the fact that insofar as our analyses of human sexual, affectionately loving, and gendered nature are enabled by philosophical ideas of the third *Critique* (as opposed to the necessary, objective analyses of the first and second

Critiques)—and so involve appealing to teleological or aesthetic judgments—they will include some inherent contingency and subjectivity. Our related claims about sex, love, and gender can therefore not be investigated or concluded with the same kind of objective, demonstrable certainty the two other engagements (of freedom and science) allow. By relying on recent research by Kantians working on non-conceptual content in the first *Critique*, in combination with recent insights by Kantians working on Kant's works on the third *Critique*, I argue that Kant's writings can show us a way to rethink sexual or gender identity and sexual orientation as capturing the various ways in which we subjectively (first-personally) experience our own embodied, sexual, and affectionate forcefulness—a basic way of feeling directed toward ourselves and others as embodied, social beings—that any good development of our sexual, affectionately loving, gendered selves must be attuned to. Additionally, once we unhook Kant's analysis of our teleological and aesthetic employment of the imagination regarding sexuality from his binary, cisist, heterosexual assumptions, we can engage the richness of human sex, love, and gender in the necessary nuanced, respectful ways. Having re-envisioned these two parts of Kant's actual view, we can develop a Kantian account of ourselves as sexual, loving, gendered beings that has the philosophical complexity we need in a persuasive account. We also have an account that responds to concerns of freedom, as Beauvoir's existentialist version and many other kinds of contemporary accounts do, but without courting problematic essentialist or deterministic conceptions of sex, love, or gender.

Chapter 4, "Kant on Sexual Violence and Oppression," links Kant's account of human nature to sexual activity and to the consequences of sexual or gendered violence and oppression. I use Kant's account of human nature, including evil, to explore the temptation of engaging in sexual violence and oppression, the damage sexual wrongdoing can do, why and how we can heal from sexual violence, why there are historical patterns to sexual violence and oppression, and why, despite the fact that our sexualities are unruly and have as possible corollaries the strongest of human emotions (passions), we are morally (ethically and legally) responsible for them. I argue that because of the threefold predisposition to good in human nature (animality, humanity, personality)—which underwrites the way in which we are in the world as animalistic, embodied, and social, yet morally responsible beings— sexual wrongdoing tends not only to be (physically) painful and damaging, but can also be existentially painful and damaging. Sexual wrongdoing can undermine our natural, implicit trust in the world as safe and good, a basic orientation we have in virtue of being constituted by the predisposition to good in human nature. Because we are embodied and because our bodies can be used in ways that subject us to others, we can be badly humiliated. Because we can be treated as if we have no worth, we can be made to feel ashamed and disgusting (by having been exposed, seen, physically mistreated, or subjected to another's bodily fluids, in ways that we do not want to be). Sexual wrongdoing can degrade us by robbing us of the otherwise always presumed ability to be able to act responsibly, according to our own choices. Those who commit sexual wrongdoing can do so due to the sexual pleasure they feel or they crave so strongly and/or because of the way in which they feel empowered by being able to force others to focus solely on affirming their own sense of self while they are doing terrible things to them—a pathology that reveals a deep lack of self-esteem.

In this chapter, I also argue that a strength of Kant's account of the propensity to evil is the way in which it is able to critique the heinousness and destructive force of sexual wrongdoing. Correspondingly, a strength of Kant's predisposition to good is the way in which it is able to provide an account of healing and of overcoming damage done to the self through sexual wrongdoing. The account is also able to explain why we tend not to want to assume moral responsibility for the effects of bad things done to us. It is very difficult to heal, as much of the emotional work involved is unreflective in nature. It concerns emotions enabled by our predisposition to animality and so go along with feeling the pain and fear from which we once fled in order to survive, to preserve ourselves. Whether perpetrator or victim, moreover, it is tempting to tell a story about ourselves and what we do that is not entirely truthful; it is hard to be truthful about our wrongdoing and it is hard to be truthful about the wrongs that have been inflicted upon us. But deception and self-deception for Kant is a path that can never lead to peace and wisdom. In addition to considering all of the challenges that accompany healing from the effects of sexual wrongdoing, the account can explain also why it is important and possible for us to assume responsibility for who we are, what we have done, and how we deal well with what has been done to us. Being able to account for all of these aspects of human being and what it takes to have healthy human lives is part of the strength of Kant's idea of the predisposition to good in human nature. Finally in this chapter, I argue that in addition to being able to capture the badness of sexual wrongdoing in general, Kant's account gives us tools with which to explain why the burdens of sexual wrongdoing are not evenly distributed, but are borne disproportionately by members of already dehumanized social groups, including women and sexual or gendered minorities. Together with Kant's account of what he calls "depraved hearts," this conception of dehumanization can explain how sexualized wrongdoing is used as part of violent oppression and atrocities. In addition, Kant's accounts of barbarism and formal and material wrongdoing enable us to describe how human beings can face conditions or situations in which there is no morally good way out (such as when we lie to people who wrongfully threaten us)—and we can do this without giving up on the idea of absolute moral prohibitions.

I conclude Part I by engaging the universal and empty formalism objections to Kant's philosophy. As mentioned in the general Introduction, the basic idea is that insofar as the account provided in the first four chapters (Part I) succeeds in overcoming the universal formalism objection, I may appear to take on the problem of empty formalism. After all, insofar as my Kantian agent no longer encounters the problems of being a disembodied, hyper-reflective purely rational self, my interpretation of Kant's theory may seem to leave no philosophical work for Kant's account of the noumenon. Indeed, it may seem as if my Kantian theory is indistinguishable from any other liberal or freedom-based theory. I argue that this inference is incorrect. To set the stage for this discussion, I first explain how my account of the structure of the human agent's phenomenology—in part due to the attention I pay to certain features of sex, love, and gender—has more clearly distinct, moving parts that do their own philosophical work than many other Kantian accounts (including that of Herman). I then show how my account has distinctive philosophical work done by absolute prohibitions and the noumenon. I illustrate this by drawing attention to how my account can be seen as complementary to Cohen's work on Kant on moral psychology and philosophical anthropology, and to Deligiorgi's work on Kant on absolute moral prohibitions, autonomy, metaphysics, and metaethics. Regardless of these internal Kant debates, I defend Herman's general claims against Sedgwick that Herman's account—and also my account—is not compatible with just any metaphysical account of freedom and that any account that is compatible with a distinctly Kantian account of freedom must have certain features. Here I lean on recent interpretations of transcendental freedom and "free will" by Allais and Deligiorgi. In addition, like Herman, I defend the importance of engaging human experiences from the "bottom up." Further, I argue that this is particularly important when we want to think with sufficient care about the complexities of human sexual, affectionately loving, gendered lives. As the history of the radical failures to adequately address sex, love, and gender shows, this is a site particularly vulnerable to erasure insofar as philosophical practices focus only on the reflective, moralized facets of human being. Sex, affectionately loving, and gendered aspects of human lives have too commonly been relegated to footnotes or considered philosophically unimportant; and all the while, brutal, indefensible violence—sometimes committed as part of atrocities—is or has been perpetrated against human beings because of their sexual, affectionately loving, gendered selves.

1

Sexual and Affectionate Love
Happiness and Moral Responsibility

Introduction

When we seek to use Kant's practical philosophy to increase our understanding of human sex, love, and gender, it is of central importance that we do not look only to Kant's account of virtue, but also to his richer account of human nature.[1] If we attend only to Kant's ideas about virtue, his comments about these topics are at best deeply puzzling, and we will not get far in our attempts to draw from Kant to capture why developing our human capacities for sex, love, and gender in emotionally healthy, morally good ways is a complex, challenging life-long project. A Kantian pure virtue account of sex, love, and gender struggles to capture many of our central experiences: It is unable to explain the existential importance sex, love, and gender tend to have in human lives and why human sexual love often is so unruly, indeed, why it is a site of so much personal and philosophical wrongdoing and failure. The purpose of this chapter, then, is to introduce core philosophical ideas from Kant's accounts of happiness and of virtue to show how they work together in full human lives. In Chapters 2–4, I explore Kant's own employment of these general philosophical ideas when considering central issues in feminist philosophy and the philosophy of sex and love before I re-envision how they can be better put to service in a full theory.

I start by outlining Kant's argument that truthfulness is our first and highest duty of virtue because truthfulness is a precondition for realizing ourselves well (section 1). To understand Kant's general take on what it means for human beings to develop well, we also need to understand his accounts of the predisposition to good in human nature (section 2) and of the faculty of desire (section 3). Important here is the fact that the three conscious structures constitutive of the predisposition to good in human nature (animality, humanity, and personality) differ in their inherent reflectiveness, which matters for the question of how we develop, transform, and integrate them through the faculty of desire. We will also begin to learn how the faculty of desire enables us to transform and integrate these conscious structures through reflection (abstract conceptual and associative thought) and imagination (aesthetic and teleological judgment involving the beautiful and the sublime, parts and wholes) when we are being sexual, affectionately loving, and gendered. (All of these

---

[1] As mentioned in the general Introduction, this chapter bears the heaviest weight of Kant interpretation and philosophy generally. Those new to either may want to skip to Chapters 2–4 or read this chapter last.

Sex, Love, and Gender: A Kantian Theory. Helga Varden, Oxford University Press (2020). © Helga Varden.
DOI: 10.1093/oso/9780198812838.001.0001

constituents of Kant's account will become clear as we move through the sections of the chapter.) This means that our sexual, loving, gendered self-development requires an ability to be emotionally grounded and also to engage in an aesthetic and/or teleological playfulness and presentation that is not based on an abstract conceptual or reason-based appreciation of oneself or an other.

Section 4 then shows how our propensity to evil complicates our efforts of self-development. We see how the propensity to evil comes in three degrees (frailty, impurity, depravity), and that with each degree it becomes subjectively more difficult to find one's way to emotional and moral health. With these arguments in place, we can see how Kant's account of virtue with its distinction between perfect and imperfect duties (section 5) complements this understanding of human flourishing. Because of the constitutive centrality of (uncontrollable) feelings in human lives, our perfect duties are negative in that they specify things we must not do, while our imperfect duties are positive and focus on fostering our emotional and moral growth as well as others'. In these ways, our moral duties are directed at our ability to act in morally responsible ways as *human* (embodied, social) beings by providing conditions protective of and conducive to emotional and moral growth. As we will see, our moral duties are correspondingly not aimed directly, but indirectly at our abilities to feel sexual, affectionate, and moral love.

All of this puts us in a position where we can appreciate Kant's account of our 'natural vital force' and 'moral vital force,' including his proposal that we should do our best to foster and to bring these two forces into close union (section 6). The account of the two vital forces is then connected with Kant's argument that the highest good is a close, harmonious union of happiness and moral responsibility (section 7). We see how we pursue our highest good by seeking to bring the inherently reflective and the importantly unreflective aspects of our being into harmonious union. With these accounts at hand, we can see how Kant's accounts of (sensible and moral) characters (section 8) and of (pragmatic and moral) friendships (section 9) add to his overall picture of the human challenge of developing ourselves in emotionally healthy, morally good ways. We notice too that difficulty is added by the fact that our projects of self-development start long before we are capable of moral responsibility and within familial and societal circumstances where we are subject to much bad behavior, including oppressive patterns of behavior, that result from others' immaturities, failures, and pathologies. Adding to this tangle of obstacles, those with whom we fall in love or lust or simply care for have their own unruly combination of these elements as well—and some of them die or get terribly ill much too young. For these reasons, developing ourselves as flourishing sexual, affectionately loving, morally responsible selves cannot be understood as an endeavor with a determinate end to be achieved; rather, it is an ongoing endeavor directed at emotional and moral improvement and growth that continues for life. I illustrate all of these ideas in section 10, emphasizing why Kant thinks that fuller accounts of sex, love, and gender require letting both unreflective and reflective aspects of our being do their own work. Here I also show how the basic approach developed in this chapter—which will be further developed in subsequent chapters—helps us understand both Kant's story of Henry VIII and Anne Boleyn and how he contrasts human beings with other, imaginable rational beings, such as angels.

1. Truthfulness

At the heart of getting through life in a good way, Kant argues, lies a fundamental commitment to truthfulness. "To be *truthful* (honest) in all declarations is," Kant says in the essay "On the Supposed Right to Lie from Philanthropy," "a sacred command of reason prescribing unconditionally, one not to be restricted by any conveniences" (SRL 8: 427). Being committed to truthfulness is not the same as being committed to telling the truth as such; after all, truth is objective and beyond what we can control by our will (SRL 8: 426). Kant's claim is also not that we have a duty always to answer all questions asked. For, surely, we do not; oftentimes the right thing to say is simply: "that is none of your business." Rather, truthfulness is a commitment to being honest in one's declarations of what is the case to the best of one's knowledge. Kant also suggests here that we should understand the command to be truthful as "sacred," by which he presumably means not only that we have a perfect duty not to lie, as we learn in *Groundwork* and second *Critique*, but also, as he argues in *The Metaphysics of Morals*, that lying ("the contrary of truthfulness") is "[t]he greatest violation of a human being's duty to himself regarded merely as a moral being (the humanity in his own person)" (MM 6: 429). Lying is contrary to a "*formal*" duty to oneself "as a moral being" and "to [one's] inner freedom, the innate dignity of a human being," and it is about making "one's basic principle to have no basic principle and hence no character" (MM 6: 420).

The reason why lying is so bad is that it conflicts with our *dignity* understood as an "inner worth," a pricelessness, or a value independent of human needs and inclinations; lying is a way of acting that is inconsistent with what gives us value as an "end in itself." What gives us dignity is our capacity to set ends of our own in morally responsible ways (autonomously): we are self-governing insofar as we act in ways consistent with respect for ourselves and each other as rational beings who obey "no law other than that which he himself at the same time gives" (GW 4: 434f.; cf. MM 6: 213-14, 226). Lying involves making it one's principle not to have a principle, because lying is to deceive someone—oneself or others—about what one is doing. Thus, lying entirely eschews the endeavor of living one's own life (setting ends of one's own) and owning the life one is living.[2] Indeed, as we will see below when exploring the propensity to evil, this is why Kant puts lying at the root of all evil and links self-deception (lying to oneself) to all of the ways in which we can lose our way in life, including always constitutive of the worst way, developing a "depraved heart." To appreciate the importance of truthfulness in Kant's account and to introduce more of the ideas needed to understand Kant's own and my Kantian theory of how to

---

[2] Relatedly, one important reason why lying is so bad is its link to the passions. In Chapter 4, we will see that trailing sexual desire is the temptation to develop passions (self- and other-destructive, obsessive desires). Developing a sexual or affectionate passion is a process whereby instead of developing the ability to enjoy sexual and affectionate love in an integrated, productive, and creative way, one becomes destructive by obsessing over sex or affection and one's related inability to have somebody else give one what one wants. Lying facilitates this process. As we will see there, because the main cause of passion is lack of truthfulness, the presence of truthfulness is passion's remedy and sometimes cure. Truthfulness is necessary for developing one's capacity for sexual and affectionate love in good (emotionally healthy, morally justifiable) ways.

develop, transform, and integrate our various feelings and desires in good ways, it is useful to understand Kant's account of the predisposition to good in human nature, which is the topic of the next section.

2. The Predisposition to Good in Human Nature

Like many before him in the history of philosophy, Kant has a threefold conception of human nature. Kant's approach distinguishes itself from his predecessors' by not including what, for example, Aristotle calls our "vegetative soul"—the one that is not conscious and that we share with plants. Kant also includes a part that concerns our capacity for freedom in what is for him the deepest sense of the word, namely an ability to act as motivated by our own practical reason and thereby to set ends of our own responsibly. So, whereas Aristotle divides the activities of the soul into vegetative, appetitive, and rational, Kant sees human nature as having these three predispositions: a predisposition to animality, which enables us to be "living beings," or animals; a predisposition to humanity, which enables us to be "rational beings," or to use reason to set ends of our own, and to have a social sense of self; and a predisposition to personality, which enables us to be "responsible beings" in that we can act as our practical reason deems necessary (R 6: 26). The structure of human phenomenology on a Kant-based account is centrally determined by the distinguishing features of each of these three conscious predispositions and by how they work together with our other capacities and faculties.

Animality, Kant proposes, should be seen as consisting of three conscious drives: the drive to "self-preservation"; the drive to "the propagation of the species, through the sexual drive," which is seen as including taking care of one's "offspring"; and the drive to "community with other human beings, i.e. the social drive" (R 6: 26). Although acting in these animalistic ways importantly involves teleological judgments (of parts and wholes, such as being in relation with others in a sexual and/or loving, affectionate "us"), it does not "require reason" (thinking through universal principles involving abstract concepts) (R 6: 26). And although the basic structure of the predisposition to animality is given to us by the relational categories of the understanding—self-preservation (substance), sex drive (causality), and basic sociality (community)—animality cannot be thought to "have reason at its root at all" (R 6: 28). Additionally, because these animalistic ways of being—preserving oneself, being sexual, being affectionately loving—do not require reason, they are something we share with non-human animals, and they are active in us even before we have developed the ability to use "I" or to reason (again, to think through universal principles involving abstract concepts). In an important sense, then, these ways of being do not require reflective self-consciousness and abstract conceptual reasoning powers—which in the practical sphere means the ability to act self-reflectively on maxims—and they have a basic directedness that is conscious and yet is not inherently self-reflective.

To illustrate the general ideas in the previous paragraph, consider newborns. Newborns reveal the animalistic aspect of our nature by expressing discomfort at hunger (self-preservation), by being responsive to sensuous touch (sex drive), and by being comforted by loving affection from caregivers (community). Hence, in uncomplicated cases, as soon as they are born, caring for them typically goes along with putting them on their caregivers' bodies, skin-to-skin, providing them with nourishment without delay, and speaking to and touching them in comforting ways. Kant proposes that to capture the animality of the human being, we need to understand these three natural, conscious drives as importantly unreflective, namely as not requiring self-reflective consciousness and abstract conceptual reasoning powers, but as self-reflexive conscious[3] ways in which we are oriented or striving animalistically.[4] This is not to deny that as we grow up, we continue to develop and transform these animalistic features also through self-reflective and abstract conceptual means (we do). Rather, the main point is that they are not rooted in a capacity for reflective self-consciousness and abstract conceptual reasoning powers. And to see that they are not so rooted is to appreciate the central importance to human lives of surviving, of being sexually excited, and of loving affectionately. As much of the literature on this explains, convincing accounts of human being must speak to how core aspects of these experiences are unreflective (and often associative). For example, self-reflective awareness and abstract, conceptual reasoning are not means through which I fall in love or become sexually excited or learn to handle heights—just as I cannot simply rationally choose to stop affectionately loving someone, choose not to be sexually affected by someone, or choose not to be scared of heights. Again, none of this means that I cannot be morally responsible for these aspects of myself or use self-reflection and abstract conceptual reasoning powers to deal with or develop, transform, and integrate them. Any complete account of human nature must speak to reason's role in such development, transformation, and integration, and I will do so below. However, to be morally responsible for these aspects of ourselves (our animality) is not to relate to them *as if* they were inherently reflective (rooted in our self-reflective capacity to reason through abstract concepts).

Another way to understand this predisposition is via Simone de Beauvoir's (1949/2011) account of our first (minimally) conscious experiences in the womb in the later stages of pregnancy and as newborns.[5] Drawing on psychoanalytic insights, Beauvoir suggests that central to understanding aspects of our basic emotional life is the fact that we at first experience the natural and the social as one unit: our initial conscious experiences take place inside another human being, where our needs are automatically satisfied and we comfortably float around in a liquid of perfect temperature without any notion of being distinct from our environment. Our first minimally conscious experiences are of being safe, at one, and deeply comfortable with the

---

[3] "Self-reflexive" consciousness means an awareness internal to any thought or action, whereas "self-reflective" consciousness means a first-personal *thinking about* what one is thinking or doing and that one is the one doing it. Self-reflective consciousness is a second-order awareness of what I am already self-reflexively conscious of.

[4] We share these basic ways of being with non-human animals, although non-human animals develop their animality differently from us as they think associatively and, so, do not have abstract conceptual reasoning powers nor an ability to set ends of their own responsibly. For more on this, see my (2020a).

[5] As mentioned in the general Introduction, drawing this link between Beauvoir and Kant is not accidental: both were deeply influenced by Rousseau's account of human nature in *Emile*. For more on the influence of Rousseau on Beauvoir, see Scholz (2010).

world—and all of this is enabled by another human being. Being born is therefore physically and existentially very painful, since for the first time we are not only cut off from the soothing body temperature liquid and the automatic food supply—and so we feel our physical needs in an intense, new way—but we are also physically separated from the being we have literally been existing inside of. It is in part because this whole separation process is so existentially traumatic that it is common in many cultures to put the baby immediately onto the caregiver's body and to tend to and comfort the baby throughout the first period of infanthood (no weaning). Such tending and comforting enable newborns to experience a safe, trustful way of being in the world. Correspondingly, for caregivers, making sure that the baby feels that the world as such is good becomes all-important. Moreover, when things go well (in good upbringings), young children learn to be comfortable with their own physical, including sensuous, embodiment. Thus, going back to Kant: realizing a healthy predisposition to good in animality requires developing a subjective (first-personal) sense of being safe and at home in the world as a living, embodied, social being, and it means becoming able to be with trust in the world as a good world (despite all the evidence to the contrary). Importantly, too, this kind of self-love is unreflective, yet good in that it enables us to be in the world as natural-social beings with non-moralized, yet normative, kinds of attitudes and emotions that express such implicit trust in the world as safe and good. To realize our animal nature well is to be fundamentally tuned in to the kinds of embodied social beings we are, such that we derive pleasure from that which is genuinely good for us.

In contrast to the predisposition to animality, the predisposition to humanity is inherently self-reflective and the rational part of it involves abstract conceptual thought and reasoning. As a whole, the predisposition to humanity enables us to be rational beings with a social sense of self. Rational beings can set and pursue ends of their own, and, so, it is because we are rational that we can each pursue our own, distinctive conception of happiness. Other animals, such as beavers and lions, indubitably also choose, but the kinds of ends they set are determined by their animalistic instincts. Beavers set beaver kinds of ends (they typically live in family groups, they build dams, they live in fresh water, they do not eat other animals, they locomote mostly by swimming, etc.); and, lions set lion kinds of ends (they are territorial, they live together in prides or coalitions, they hunt and eat other animals, they typically avoid having to swim, etc.). In contrast, there is no one set of ends for humans, and the kinds of ends we set are not originally predetermined by instincts. Rather, our reflective self-consciousness, abstract conceptual powers, and our powers of imagination enable us to set ends in a fundamentally open-ended way, including entirely new (kinds of) ends. Indeed, a core challenge for humans is to figure out exactly which (kinds of) ends make us happy as the particular beings we are; the activities that make me happy may be very different from those that make you happy—and what made me happy yesterday may not do so today. (More on this below.)

To elaborate on the social sense of self, Kant proposes that the predisposition to humanity "*involves comparison* (for which reason is required); that is, only in comparison with others does one judge oneself happy or unhappy" (R 6: 26). Kant also states that the predisposition to humanity is "rooted in a reason that is indeed practical, but only as subservient to other incentives" (R 6: 28) and that it should be seen as enabling an "inclination *to gain worth in the opinion of others*, originally, of course, merely *equal worth* ... but out of this arises gradually an unjust desire to acquire superiority for oneself over others" (R 6: 26). One way to appreciate some of what Kant is after here is to explore these statements by means of Jean-Jacques Rousseau's concept of *amour propre*. *Amour propre* is exactly this susceptibility we have to feel better or worse reactively and relatively to others. It captures how our feeling better or worse about ourselves (happy or unhappy) is so easily affected by how others are doing as compared to us. For example, a student may find themself happy about the A— they received on their paper *until* they come to class and hear that one of their friends received a straight A. Simply hearing that fact of the other's better grade can make them feel less happy even though nothing factually has changed about the accomplishment. Having a social sense of self means that how others affirm us, or how we see ourselves relative to others (being given an A— and not an A), can matter for how good we subjectively feel about ourselves.

Contrary to Rousseau, however, Kant thinks that this social sense of self is *originally* one of equal worth. That is to say, in its uncorrupted form, we affirm each other as having equal worth and we take joy in one another's happiness; indeed, another's happiness makes us more rather than less happy. To illustrate, having a social sense of self means that one is aware of and affected by how others perceive oneself. We see the nascent ability to have a social sense of self once babies start to interact with their caretakers through smiles and laughter. We also see the import- ance of this moment in the caretakers' behavior toward the babies' smiles and laughter. For example, when time and energy allow, it is common for caretakers when they change diapers to have a little lovefest where the caretaker and the baby smile and laugh together. Kant's point about how the uncorrupted version of this affective attitude is one of equal worth can be seen here: the caretakers and the babies take tremendous reciprocal delight and joy in each other's smiles and laughter—and experiencing each other's delight and joy only makes each of them happier. The temptation to bad behavior (*amour propre*), in contrast, can be seen once babies start to demand attention at all times or get upset if caretakers give affectionately loving attention also to others (like siblings); therein lies the temptation to develop unruly, destabilizing desires and bad inclinations—in this example, jealousy.

When the predisposition to humanity is developed well, then, in addition to mastering rational end-setting (acting on maxims that can hold as universal laws; more on this below), we experience a kind of love that is enabled by perceiving and being perceived by another as equally valuable. Correspondingly, insofar as we are realizing emotionally healthy intimate relationships, we regard each other as equally valuable in all our differences; we take joy in each other's successes, and we always assume that the other is directed towards us as we are towards them. When we fail, either intentionally or unintentionally, to affirm ourselves and others as having equal worth, we get hurt or hurt others. But then we can remedy the hurt. Insofar as we are emotionally healthy human beings in good relationships, we do all of this spontan- eously; it simply is the way we are predisposed emotionally to be oriented towards one another.

In addition to the predispositions to animality and humanity, there is the predis- position to personality, which makes it possible for us to be morally responsible for setting ends of our own, and so to act truly freely. About this predisposition, Kant says that it is

the susceptibility to respect for the moral law *as of itself a sufficient incentive to the power of choice*. This susceptibility to simple respect for the moral law within us would thus be the moral feeling... [as the] incentive of the power of choice. (R 6: 27)

Also, Kant emphasizes that this is the only predisposition that "is rooted in reason practical of itself, i.e. in reason legislating unconditionally," which is why it cannot be corrupted (R 6: 28). In short, Kant deems it impossible to account for the human ability to act as motivated by "the ought"—to act moved to do something *just because* it is the right thing to do—without invoking a human capacity for practical reason, understood as a self-reflective ability to think in principled, abstract, conceptual ways about action and to act as motivated by this process of reflection. It is this capacity for a distinctively moral valuing that gives us dignity (pricelessness).

As explanation, consider Kant's famous idea that human animals act in reflectively self-conscious ways on maxims ("subjective rules of action") (GW 4: 401n; cf. MM 6: 224). As we learn to drink from a glass, for example, we learn to hold an end in our mind and to move our entire body such that we can obtain that end; coordinating our action by an end is what it means to act on a maxim. Acting on a maxim is therefore a complex task, which is why it takes much longer for us than for other animals to learn to do some of the most natural things (or to perform actions at all). For example, it commonly takes roughly twelve months before human beings start the venture of learning how to walk, and it takes much longer before we can think about the fact that we are walking without losing our concentration and falling down. For instance, at first, when toddler Helga (who is learning how to walk) is interrupted in her efforts by someone saying "Look, Helga is walking!" she ceases to be able to orient her action toward that end and falls down. Much later, Helga is able not only to think about wanting to walk somewhere and make it clear that Helga wants to walk there, but she can also say, "*I* walk, mummy," or "Me walk, mummy!" That is to say, Helga reveals by being able to say this that she is starting not only to *think about* (reflect upon) what she wants but also that she is aware of herself as an "I," that she is acting from a first-personal, self-reflective perspective (expressed in statement that "*I*" or "*me*" "walk, mummy"). That is to say, in moving from just walking to thinking about ourselves as walking, we switch from acting on a maxim (acting in rationally directed or intentional ways) to thinking *about* both the maxim we are acting on and that *we* are acting on it (becoming reflectively conscious of ourselves and our maxim). With more practice, we get better at both and both come more easily. Indeed, we can even come to set for ourselves the task of intentionally perfecting our walking performance (perfecting our ability to act on the maxim of walking), including by figuring out how to walk in very many different, playful, and new ways, indeed to find our own, particular way of walking.

These are, then, core reasons why setting ends, for example, that of walking, are much more complex for humans than they are for non-humans. Because we have rational capacities that add complexity to our activities, we take more time than other animals to master even the simplest activities. Once we are able to do this, we also start the project of mastering the task of acting only on maxims that are consistent with the idea of a world of rational beings, that is, consistent with the idea of a world with beings who are able to set ends of their own just like we do. Continuing with the same example, we learn to walk in ways compatible with respect for other people's walking; we do not walk into or over them, for example. To boot, as noted above, because we have a social sense of self and use reason in comparative ways, we have emotions that reveal the existential importance for us of affirming others and of being affirmed by them, such as taking joy in each other's success and experiencing shame, jealousy, embarrassment, and envy. Back to the example of walking, we can take joy in walking, others' walking, and in walking with others, including in friendly competitions and challenges regarding walking, such as in creatively playing with funny ways of walking and with walking and running with each other in ways where the challenge is part of the fun. But we can also experience envy or shame in relation to walking, such as if others walk in cooler ways than I or if I fall down and feel ashamed of my clumsiness. Finally, we can use our ability to walk as a way to attract other's sexual attention or we can walk as a way to express our affection for each other, such as by walking close and synchronized so that we can lean against one another.

Today, most legal systems uphold laws according to which it takes eighteen years before we are deemed thoroughly and reliably capable not only of acting in these reflectively self-conscious rational ways, but also of owning or acting on a notion of "ought" or of what we should do. In Kantianese, it takes us eighteen years to be seen as capable of "deeds" or of viewing ourselves as the "authors" of our actions (MM 6: 223) in dependable ways with regard to all areas of our lives. As everyone who has read *Groundwork* knows, one of Kant's central proposals is that mastering the "ought" is something we can explain philosophically only if we can also give an account of human beings' ability to choose in truly free ways. To choose freely is both to act on maxims that are universalizable—on rules that can hold as laws for all rational beings—and to act as motivated by their universalizability. And being able to act on this motivation (to have moral feeling) is what makes personality (moral responsibility) possible for us, while simply having the capacity for it (in virtue of being born a human being) gives us dignity. I return shortly to give more details about the "ought" with a brief discussion of the moral law and perfect and imperfect duties. But before this, we need some more of Kant's ideas about human nature, starting with his account of our faculty of desire.

3. The Faculty of Desire

Kant denotes "living things" (so, as we saw above, all animals)[6] as beings that have a "faculty of desire," which enables them "to be by means of one's representations the cause of the objects of these representations" (MM 6: 211). In virtue of having the cognitive capacity to re-present something, living beings can relate to bits of reality as objects of representation, as somethings. In addition, Kant argues, living things can

---

[6] As we saw above, Kant's technical use of the term "living beings" does not include anything but animals. For example, it would not include plants.

feel in that they can take subjective pleasure or displeasure in such representations; as we have seen throughout the previous section, all animals have predispositions to good in their nature that enable them to be susceptive (to feel pleasure and pain) in certain ways. To illustrate, all living beings (all animals) have a capacity for choice, namely a faculty of desire that involves "a consciousness of the ability to bring about its object by one's action" (MM 6: 213). So, I can relate to something as something (say, relate to it as an object) that I feel drawn to (relate to it as something I would like to eat to preserve myself) and I can choose to obtain the object (pick and eat it). Now, both non-human and human animals can represent and choose in these ways; what distinguishes them concerns how complex their faculty of desire is and, so, what kinds of choices they can make. Consistent with the account of the predisposition to animality above, non-human animals' faculty of desire is accompanied only by associative thinking in response to strong (originally instinctual) inclinations: "animal choice…can be determined only by *inclination* (sensible impulse)" (MM 6: 213). (An animal can choose to eat the object as it identifies it instinctually or through habituation as a possible means to assuage hunger.) In contrast, human beings' faculty of desire also involves reflective self-consciousness and abstract conceptual cognitive powers that enable us to step back from what we want in the moment, to think about it, and then to choose to do something, including just because it is the right thing to do. For example, I relate to the object *as a* strawberry (abstract concept)—which I can think of as a small, red, seedy, watery, slightly hairy thing with a delicious scent (more abstract concepts)—and I can *think about* whether or not to eat it. On top of that, I can choose to give it to somebody else who needs it more because doing so is the right thing to do rather than, say, share it simply because I love that somebody or because I feel sympathy for them. Kant proposes that this human behavior is possible because our faculty of desire can function "in accordance with [abstract] concepts" (MM 6: 213); it is our ability to think about things by means of abstract concepts from a first-personal point of view—to act on maxims—that enables us to step back from what we want and to reflect upon whether or not setting a particular end is something we really want.

Let me illustrate this last point with an example that brings us back to the differences between the maturing of non-human and human animals. Although instinct can explain why both human babies and piglets drink milk from their mothers, because human babies have a more complex faculty of desire than pigs, as human babies mature, their appreciation for food and drink becomes more complex than that of pigs. Indeed, as newborns, babies and piglets are distinguished in that one of the first things human babies do after they have been born is to scream. One of the signs that things are good with newborn babies is exactly that they scream loudly and strongly—while piglets scream or squeak loudly only once they can smell their mother's milk. Kant argues that human babies' screams when born reveal our more complex faculty of desire; by screaming, the baby shows itself capable of a different kind of representation than non-human animals are capable of, namely one that expresses our frustration at not being able to act (exercise freedom) (A 7: 268). As we develop the human faculty of desire, moreover, our intended goal is no longer just to eat but to enjoy meals. For example, today when I am hungry not only do I notice that I am hungry and try to find something to eat, but I can think about being hungry, think about various types of food I can eat to assuage my hunger, and then choose to procure that kind of food. Not only can I think about what kind of taste and texture I want to enjoy, but also how to present the food in aesthetically pleasing ("agreeable") ways. Additionally, Kant argues, human beings can choose in ways such that the "determining ground" of their choice is their reason—they can do or not do something just because this choice is the right thing to do—which is to say that they have a "will" (MM 6: 213). Again, I can choose not to eat something (the strawberry) because it would be wrong to do so because somebody else needs it more than I do. In preparing a meal for some dear friends, I can also take into consideration all the foods my friends really like such that the meal shows them how I value them.[7] Alternatively, I may simply want to share with them a meal I have worked hard on because I want to share with exactly them some of the best I can do or have— some of my most precious and personal things—and they love that I really want to share exactly that with them.

As we have seen, the predisposition to animality is composed of three (reflexively self-) conscious orientations in us: the drives to self-preservation, to sex, and to basic community. Although these orientations are conscious, realizing them as such requires neither reflective self-consciousness nor abstract, conceptual reasoning abilities—or a distinctly *human* faculty of desire—as non-human animals (with self-reflexive consciousness and associative thought) can also realize them with their faculties of desire. Focusing on our ability to realize our capacity for sexual and affectionate love in good (emotionally healthy, morally sound) ways, it is important to note that we start this project as newborns not yet capable of acting as self-reflective subjects (apprehending the "I" reflectively) or in ways that involve abstract, conceptual thought (that involve reflectively acting on subjective maxims). As a result, much of our cognitive engagement at this point in life is self-reflexive and associative in nature (as it is for non-human animals). As we noted above, as newborns, we seek to survive, and we find it profoundly soothing to be cared for in affectionate, loving, sensuous ways; most of our behavior and responses at this stage are explainable through our animality (self-reflexively understood) in combination with associative thinking. For instance, as newborns, we associate certain smells, voices, touches, etc., with pleasure, and this alone explains our reactions to them. Thus, human and non-human animals can share the kind of being which fundamentally involves animality. And a human and a non-human animal can form affectionate, loving units ("us's")— even though the non-human's task of developing their animality is less complex than the human one due to a human's more complex faculty of desire.[8]

Finally, let me also link this brief exposition of the faculty of desire with the importance of aesthetic pleasures in human lives. Aesthetic pleasure, Kant suggests, is something "merely subjective" in that it is a response to "nothing at all in the object but simply a relation to the subject," namely it is a relation either to a desire (we find it agreeable) or to a non-desiring delight in it (it strikes us as beautiful) (MM 6: 212). The human faculty of desire therefore opens us up to aesthetic pleasures—pleasure taken in something's agreeableness and/or beauty. On the one hand, magnificent

---

[7] For one compatible, Kant-inspired account of this, see Albrecht (2015/17).

[8] See Varden (2020a) for more on non-human animals and our relations to them.

aesthetic experiences comprise an interplay between the imagination and the under-standing, something that reason (thinking through abstract concepts) cannot get hold of (subsume). Such experiences strike or move human minds with disinterested feelings (rather than feelings that are related to desires, or to something we want). It is part of human nature that we can experience both the natural world and various art forms—music, painting, dance—as aesthetically stunning or amazing in such disin-terested, yet deeply moving ways. Some of these natural experiences, such as the Victoria Falls or the Grand Canyon, are such that they can strike all human minds in these kinds of ways, while the purpose of much art is to give at least aesthetically mature minds such truly awe-inducing aesthetic experiences (provoking subjectively universal aesthetic judgments). On the other hand, we can experience things in aesthetic ways that do not aspire to anything that is universally recognized as aesthetically stunning, but simply as something that we, individually, find deeply agreeable, as something we—given how we are—really want or like (rather than something we think will or ought to strike everyone as aesthetically remarkable or incredible in a disinterested way).

Importantly, part of caring for oneself and others involves tending to and devel-oping these aspects of ourselves, that is, both our ability to be struck and moved by beautiful things and an understanding of what we like or find attractive (agreeable) with regard to embodiment (our own and that of others). Significantly too, aesthetic pleasure is not about abstract conceptual reasoning or a search for objective, dem-onstrable truths. That is to say, abstract conceptual reasoning strives to arrive at objectively justifiable or demonstrable truths. For Kant, whether we reason about spatio-temporal or moral reality, our aim is to establish which rules can hold as universal laws, meaning which rules can explain various events or actions as instances of a universal law. (More on this below.) Not so for aesthetic pleasures; they cannot be grasped in this way. Aesthetic pleasure is instead about being subjectively moved by an object in a way that feels deeply pleasant in an inherently playful, non-conceptual way. Also, because aesthetic appreciation is not reason-based, it is something humans can do at rather extraordinary levels relatively early on (as revealed, e.g., by musical aptitude or genius revealed in children). It is also something those whose cognitive reasoning abilities are damaged (temporarily or permanently) or are deteriorating (in dementia or Alzheimer's) can enjoy.

Our faculty of desire, in sum, is a core means through which we develop, transform, and integrate all aspects of our being—those that make us the emotionally healthy embodied, social, and aesthetically appreciative, morally responsible particu-lar beings we are—into good wholes. As we will see below, we also use the faculty of desire as we learn to deal with our various immaturities, failures, and pathologies in good ways. Before moving on to show how the propensity of evil adds to this account, however, let me note how the arguments in the above sections on the faculty of desire and on the predisposition to good in human nature naturally complement recent work by Alix Cohen.[9] Cohen (2018) argues that it is important to appreciate that, for

---

[9] This theme is central in much of Cohen's recent work and I am neither doing her nor the issues themselves full justice here. For more on these issues in Kant and for a more complete list of Cohen's recent, related work, see the Bibliography.

Kant, there is (only) one faculty of feeling and one faculty of desire. Consistent with my argument above, the faculty of feeling encompasses both non-moral and moral feelings (even though moral feeling cannot be explained philosophically without making a reference to our practical reason). We develop and transform both kinds of feelings through the faculty of desire. If we describe this point by means of my language above, we may say this: non-moralizable feelings are internally connected with the predisposition of animality as well as with the social aspects of the predisposition to humanity, whereas moral feeling is internally connected with the predisposition to personality. Additionally, both kinds of feelings are developed by means of the second aspect of the predisposition to humanity, namely the capacity to set ends of our own. This capacity to set ends is analytically linked with Kant's idea of the faculty of desire, since it is that faculty that enables us to represent something as desirable and to choose it. The faculty of desire enables us to use reflection (associative and abstract conceptual thinking as well as the reflective powers of the imagination) to relate to and develop, transform, and integrate into our lives something we find pleasant or desirable. Thus, the faculty of desire is also constitutive of developing feelings into inclinations (understood as "habitual desires," cf. MM 6: 212)—both good and bad—and of finding good ways of going about our lives (ideally, we will see in more detail below, inclinations and ways of living that can be grounded harmoniously on our vital and moral vital forces, which is about bringing happiness and morality into a close union). Hence, as we learn to set good ends, these ends can have their ground in aesthetic pleasures, in our animality, in the social aspects of our humanity, *or* in moral feeling, but we seek to bring all of them into a harmonious union that we can own as who we are (that genuinely makes us happy) and as morally responsible beings. What I add to Cohen's account so understood is a closer attention to the structure of our phenomenology. In the subsequent chapters, I return several times to the importance of appreciating how the reflectiveness of each of the predispositions to animality, humanity, and personality together with aesthetic pleasures as well as what comes in section 4, namely the propensity for evil, matters greatly for bringing out the nature of sex, love, and gender. Thus, paying attention to the un-/reflective nature of various parts of our being makes an important difference to our understanding of their existential importance, the nature of the feelings and emotions comprising them, the temptations to do various kinds of bad sexual or loving things, and the inherent unruliness of sexual and affectionate love in human lives.

4. The Propensity to Evil

Kant's account of the propensity to evil critiques human beings' deep temptation to do bad things. Kant thinks that given our embodied, social natures and our capacity for choice (to set ends of our own), doing bad things is empirically universal: we will all do them. Also, because we usually grow up in domestic settings (often families) and in cultures, for the first many years of our lives and before we are able to assume moral responsibility for ourselves, we live subject to others' pathologies and wrongdoing—so we inherit some bad patterns of associations and behavior that are difficult to become aware of and to assume responsibility for, let alone get rid of without significant residue. Although exactly how subjectively tempting bad behavior is is internally linked with how life or those around us have treated or do treat us, Kant's proposal is that we should think of our complex liability to do bad things—our propensity to evil—as something we bring upon ourselves through our choices and that this propensity comes in three degrees: "frailty," "impurity," and "depravity."[10]

The first two propensities—frailty and impurity—can be undertaken in both self-deceived and non-self-deceived ways. Frailty is to know what one ought to do and yet to do the opposite anyway. For example, I know that I should not have another chocolate, but then I have one anyway. If I do this in a self-deceived way, I might tell myself (wrongly) that "I deserve another one!", whereas if I do it without self-deception, I might tell myself that "I shouldn't have another one, but oh well!" Impurity goes along with a more patterned instability in my ways of feeling and associating such that I do not reliably respond to something in a good way. For example, if I have a pathology regarding orderliness (a generally good end), I might too easily respond with anger or upsetness to any instance of messiness (in the office, in the home, anywhere). If I am self-deceived about this pathological aspect of myself, I might tell myself a moralized story, according to which most others simply have not realized the importance of *always* having everything neat and tidy, whereas if I am not self-deceived, I realize that it is not others' habits but something about the way orderliness comforts me that is the reason why my reactions are as strong as they are and different from those of most other people.

Impurity is a higher degree of evil than frailty, on this approach, because where frailty concerns an instance of wrongdoing, impurity involves a pattern of bad behavior and is therefore much more difficult to get rid of. It is hard both to acknowledge it (say, that orderliness calms me, and so makes it subjectively easier for me to deal with the rest of life), let alone to do something about it (as it requires both trying to figure out why this is emotionally so important and trying to relearn aspects of how to feel the world as safe and comfortable without it). Finally, there is depravity, which is always self-deceived (doing bad in the name of the good), according to Kant. It consists in actions that are directed at damaging or destroying rational being. For example, serious domestic abuse can come in the form of impurity—a tendency to become too angry too easily—but it can also come as depravity, in which case the abusive man, for example, tells himself a story according to which his wife and children are intentionally unappreciative of his goodness, that they are constantly out to get him or to put him down. Although what he says and does is incompatible with respecting them—and actually harms, ruins, or even kills them—the story he tells himself is one where he is the only moral agent, even a heroic one. And, of course, in so doing, he is also destroying himself.

In sum, Kant's accounts of the predisposition to good and of the propensity to evil seek to get into view both how what we take pleasure in, value, and find meaningful (what makes us happy as the particular people we are) is subjective in that it is

---

[10] Kant's account of the propensity to evil is found in *Religion within the Boundaries of Mere Reason* (R 6: 29–45). How to understand Kant's conception of evil is controversial; I am merely presenting what I take to be Kant's own and the most convincing conception of evil. For more on this, see Varden (2021).

different from person to person, *and* how this subjectivity appears to be made up by shared structures and patterns. As we will see in more detail in the next few chapters, the above account of human nature, including evil gives us good philosophical tools to understand why it is so hard to flourish as sexual, affectionately loving, gendered people. The general challenge is that we want to exercise our capacity for setting ends of our own—freely chosen ends that affirm who we are—in morally responsible ways and thereby to develop, transform, and integrate ourselves as sexual and affectionately loving beings in a way that is also consistent with self-preservation (the third aspect of our animality) and with the social aspect of humanity (how we present ourselves to others and are affirmed as good by them). This enterprise is furthermore necessarily incomplete, since it is impossible to bring into complete, harmonious union our strivings towards happiness (through setting ends of our own) and morality (through limiting our ends to morally good ones). As we meet new people, as we develop, as we come up with new possible ends, as we mature, as our situations change, the imaginable whole changes and there will be aspects that no longer fit neatly and need to be developed and transformed to fit better (which may or may not be painful). And there is no end to this. Thinking that there is an obtainable end (that there is a point at which the union is complete or finished) reveals a form of confusion, immaturity, or pathology. To strive for the highest good, as we will see below, is to be oriented towards and to strive dynamically for a harmonious union, while realizing that it cannot be entirely obtained in a human life.

In addition, Kant's account of evil as presented above already enables us to see why it is tempting for us to take advantage of other people's sexual attraction to us, to yield to feelings of jealousy, to punish loved ones for presumed lack of attention, not to give our loved ones the credit they deserve for how they enable our flourishing (wanting to take all the credit for ourselves), or to passively-aggressively ignore people who love us in order to get more attention from them. I expand on this in Chapter 4, where I also explain how patterned bad behaviors related to sexual violence and oppression add to these efforts geared towards living well, including together with one another in intimate relationships. For now, notice that the above account of human nature also explains why, despite how tempting these actions may be, our predisposition to good as a whole enables us to avoid or stop these sorts of behaviors: our capacity for animality enables us to feel pain because such behaviors are incompatible with basic sociality; our capacity for humanity enables us to identify the maxim of our action and then feel the pain and irrationality of acting in ways that treat others as not equally valuable rational beings; and our capacity for personality enables us to avoid bad behavior *just because* the behavior is wrong and to engage in moral behavior *just because* it is the right thing to do. That is, our capacity for humanity enables us to stop and use our abstract conceptual reasoning powers to figure out what we are doing; and our capacity for personality enables us to do one thing rather than another *just because* it is right. A healthy animality makes all of this easier for us, but regardless it remains an emotional resource for us as we strive to do better.

Relatedly, in *Religion* Kant emphasizes that all three predispositions are both "original" (meaning that they "belong to the possibility of human nature") and "good" (meaning that "they do not resist the moral law," but rather "demand compliance with it," as this is exactly what moral feeling commands) (R 6: 28). That is to say, because the threefold predisposition to good in human nature is original and good, in spite of what we *de facto* feel like doing or want to do in the moment, we are equipped with unreflective and reflective emotional and rational resources that we can rely on as we seek to do better. When we act and live well, we use our reflective capacities to develop, transform, and integrate activities involving animality and humanity in such ways that they are consistent with moral feeling; our being is not, at its core, one where pleasures and pains and the rational capacities we have for developing them are at war with one another. We experience ourselves as at peace or harmonious when the various pleasures line up in a coherent whole. It makes sense, then, that, for Kant, our predisposition to personality can never be corrupted since it is only good—it is an ability that is enabled by our capacity for practical reason, which is beyond what we can choose to change—and, although the emotional structures that are enabled by the predispositions to animality and humanity can be profoundly off-kilter or corrupted (through accidents and the choices of others and ourselves), they cannot be destroyed ("eradicated") (R: 28). For that reason, although we are necessarily emotionally and morally imperfect, we can revisit old wounds to examine the patterns of our pathologies in order to heal: we can grow and become fuller, better human beings, with or without the guiding help of others. The most terrifying of human beings, therefore, are those who have lost their way so radically that their self-deception has made them numb or indifferent to any undertaking involving emotional or moral improvement, and they have replaced such efforts with false, moralized stories of their own greatness; such are people with depraved hearts. Let us now turn to how Kant's account of perfect and imperfect duties takes the account of the morally responsible human agent further.

5. Virtue: Perfect and Imperfect Duties

Kant suggests that when our choices are determined by practical reason—when I do something just because it is the right thing to do or do not do something just because it is wrong—then our choices are both negatively and positively free. They are negatively free in requiring that we step back from what our sensible impulses push us towards, and they are positively free in that they come along with a motivation stemming from our reasoning powers alone (MM 6: 213f.). When we act as motivated by reason alone (when we exercise positive freedom), Kant continues, we must be seen as motivated by the consideration of whether or not the maxim we want to act on can hold as a universal law for rational beings (MM 6: 214). After all, and as explained above, our maxims are subjective in that they concern what we—from our own subjective point of view—want. Accordingly, neither the content of our maxims nor our maxims as such can be what we as reasoners look to when we consider whether something we feel like doing is right or wrong to do. In other words, on the one hand, we can and should consider whether what we want right now is deeply consistent with the kinds of people we are (subjectively). Does choosing this fit with the kind of person I am, with what makes me happy, and with what kind of life I want to live? On the other hand, we can consider whether what we want is something that is morally good, something that is consistent with due respect for ourselves and for all other beings capable of rationality, namely of choosing ends of their own responsibly. Is my choice consistent with respect for rational being, so understood? As we become capable of moral responsibility, we learn to consider something from this inherently reflective, moral point of view. That is to say, when we consider whether or not what we want to do is morally good or at least morally permissible, Kant's proposal is that the only thing our reasoning powers look to is the form (not the subjective matter or content) of the maxim:

> pure reason applied to choice irrespective of its objects...does not have within it the matter of the law...as a faculty of principles (here practical principles, hence a lawgiving faculty), there is nothing it can make the supreme and determining ground of choice except the form, the fitness of maxims of choice to be universal law. And since the maxims of human beings, being based on subjective causes, do not of themselves conform with those objective principles, reason can prescribe this law only as an imperative that commands or prohibits absolutely.
>
> (MM 6: 214)

In other words, if our reason cannot look to the content of our maxims, but only to its form, what does it look to? Kant's proposal is that we consider whether or not the maxim we want to act on could function as an objective, universal law for all rational beings.

One quick way to illustrate this argument goes as follows. As mentioned above, Kant thinks that our reasoning capacities do something similar when we search for the scientific laws that govern events in spatio-temporal reality and when we act in morally responsible ways. In both cases, we search for objective principles that can be seen as laws that govern events or actions. More specifically, when we search for scientific laws, we start with some hypothesis (say, Newton's proposal for the law of gravity) and then we check to see whether it can explain all instances of objects falling to the surface of the earth (*ceteris paribus*). If it can, then we know that this hypothesis is a good candidate for a scientific law, indeed, one we may use when we try to do things like leave the planet and travel into other parts of the universe. If we find an exception to the rule, then we know that we did not find a scientific law after all; the exception shows that the hypothesis (rule) cannot hold as a scientific, causal law explaining all instances of objects falling to the ground. Kant thinks that when we think morally—and, so, when we look for the laws that should govern our ability to act spontaneously, to set ends of our own—we do something similar. We start with a rule (a maxim) that we (subjectively) want to act on and then we check whether or not this rule could hold as a law for all rational beings, for all beings that can set ends of their own. If the rule could hold as a universal law for rational beings, then the action is permissible, and if it could not, then the action is impermissible.[11]

---

[11] For example, in *Groundwork*, Kant writes: "A *maxim* is the subjective principle of acting, and must be distinguished from the *objective* principle, namely the practical law. The former contains the practical rule determined by reason conformably with the conditions of the subject (often his ignorance or also his inclinations), and is therefore the principle in accordance with which the subject *acts*; but the law is the objective principle valid for every rational being, and the principle in accordance with which he *ought to act*, i.e., an imperative" (G 4:421n).

To put this point in a way that resonates with the examples given earlier in this chapter, we can say that as a human being I can be reflectively conscious of what I am doing: I can think about what I am doing, or be aware of my maxim, understood as "the rule that the agent himself makes his principle on subjective grounds" (MM 6: 224; cf. GW 4: 401n) and I can become reflectively aware that *I* am the one doing it (I can think too about the fact that *I* am doing it). Therefore, as I set out to do something—which could be an action grounded in an animal concern for self-preservation, sex, or basic sociality—I orient myself and my causal powers to others by my maxim. My maxim (the subjective rule of my action) orients how I go about things in the world—what I do and do not do—in ways compatible with obtaining a particular end. In addition, Kant argues, when I do this well, I do it in such a way that my action is compatible with and furthers rational, human being (my own and that of others), including by affirming those with whom I interact as immeasurably valuable (as having dignity). This is what Kant means when—in *Groundwork* and elsewhere—he says that acting in morally permissible ways always requires acting on universalizable maxims, meaning maxims that can be both *thought* as universal laws for rational beings (they are consistent with our self- and other-regarding perfect duties to respect ourselves and others as ends in ourselves/themselves) and that can be *willed* as universal laws for rational beings (they are consistent with our self- and other-regarding imperfect duties to develop our capacities and talents and to assist others in their pursuit of happiness) (G 4:424). I can act as motivated by my practical reason—I can do something just because it is the right thing to do; I can be moved by moral feeling, including act "from duty." Moreover, when we do something *just because* it is the right thing to do (as determined by our practical reason), we act virtuously or act in a way that expresses a distinctively moral kind of valuing. That is to say, when I do this, I incorporate a moral motivation into my maxim and thereby add a distinctive, *moral* "worth" or value to my actions (G 4:401).

My predisposition to personality, in other words, shows itself in how I do and can feel and act. Because only human animals (as far as we know) are capable of acting from duty (acting as motivated by their practical reason), only human beings can be morally responsible for their actions. In addition, because we are embodied, social beings (we have predispositions to animality and humanity), the moral law—the principle constitutive of our reason—is experienced by us as a categorical imperative, as something we *must* or *ought* to do, namely "*act only in accordance with that maxim through which you can at the same time will that it become a universal law*" (G 4: 429). That is, as human beings it is possible for us to live well only if we develop an ability to figure out which ends we need and want to set given the kinds of persons we are and what we aspire to become in the circumstances we find ourselves—something each of us has to figure out, which amounts to a duty to try to figure out what makes us truly happy—and only if we make sure that the ends we want to set are compatible with (respectful of), and insofar as possible affirming and supportive of, others who are pursuing the ends that will make them happy in a similarly open-ended and reciprocally respectful way. Our basic moral orientation to ourselves and to others as beings capable of personhood (moral responsibility) therefore comes along with respecting and affirming our own and others' quests to set ends of our own, respecting and affirming the importance of how we are striving to realize our own lives.

Given the above understanding of virtue and respect, we can now also make sense of why Kant argues that we have perfect duties not to act viciously (i.e., not to infringe upon what another is owed in virtue of being a human being), whereas failure to act on imperfect duties is characterized by a lack of moral love and reveals not viciousness but merely a lack of virtue (a lack of commitment to humanity as such). In view of that, perfect duties are expressed negatively (they prohibit disrespectful or aggressive ways of acting), whereas imperfect duties are expressed positively (they require us to develop our abilities to set ends well and to assist others in their pursuit of happiness):

Failure to fulfill mere duties of [moral] love is *lack of virtue* (*peccatum*). But failure to fulfill the duty arising from the *respect* owed to every human being as such is a *vice* (*vitium*). For no one is wronged if duties of love are neglected; but a failure in the duty of respect infringes upon one's lawful claim.—The first violation is opposed to duty as its *contrary* (*contrarie oppositum virtuitis*). But what not only adds nothing moral but even abolishes the worth of what would otherwise be to the subject's good is *vice*.

For this reason, too, duties to one's fellow human beings arising from the respect due them are expressed only negatively, that is, the duty of virtue will be expressed *only indirectly* (through the prohibition of its opposite). (MM 6: 464f.)

To fail to act on one's imperfect duties, then, is to lack virtue whereas failing to act on one's perfect duties is to act viciously. The reason for this difference is that failing to act on perfect duties always is to act aggressively or in damaging ways; it is to act in ways inconsistent with showing respect for someone, to treat them (oneself or others) as having dignity (pricelessness). Such an action necessarily abolishes or destroys or damages moral valuing or rational being. In contrast, to fail to act on imperfect duties is not to destroy something, but simply not to further a more flourishing rational world. In either case, because moral valuing concerns being moved to do something *because* it is the right thing to do—moral feeling—we cannot control it (as we cannot control feelings). What we can control is our behavior, that we behave in ways consistent with respect for others as rational beings (ends in themselves), which is why duties of virtue that stem from moral feeling (respect) are negative and indirect by obliging us not to act in ways disrespectful of ourselves or others. Let us now move on to the question of how to relate the above ideas to Kant's accounts of vital forces, characters, and friendships.

6. Natural and Moral Vital Forces

As we saw above, Kant's account of the predisposition to good is an account of conscious, dispositional susceptibilities that we must assume to exist prior to any experience involving the feelings, emotions, and desires linked with animality, humanity, or personality. This is because these susceptibilities make such feelings, emotions, and desires possible for us. Kant's account of the predisposition to good thus helps us capture core elements of the structure of our phenomenology. The basic structure of the predisposition to animality, as we saw, is given to us by the relational categories of the understanding—self-preservation (substance), sex drive (causality), and community (basic sociality). In addition, however, Kant suggests that our sensible (phenomenal) nature as a whole is grounded in what he calls our natural "vital force." Our natural vital force, that is to say, is an embodied forcefulness constitutive of our predisposition to animality as a whole. Our non-sensible (noumenal) nature, in contrast, must be understood as grounded in our "moral vital force," meaning the forcefulness constitutive of our predisposition to personality. Corresponding to how, as we will see below, our highest end is to bring our happiness (internally linked with our natural vital force) into union with our morality (internally linked with our moral vital force), our objective with regard to both vital forces should be to realize them together in a harmonious whole.

Let us start exploring this by turning to two passages of Kant's, the first of which is among the most famous in the second *Critique*:

Two things fill the mind with ever new and increasing admiration and reverence, the more often and more steadily one reflects on them: *the starry heavens above me and the moral law within me.* I do not need to search for them and merely conjecture them as though they were veiled in obscurity or in the transcendent region beyond my horizon; I see them before me and connect them immediately with the consciousness of my existence. The first begins from the place I occupy in the external world of sense and extends the connection in which I stand into an unbounded magnitude with worlds upon worlds and systems upon systems, and moreover into the unbounded times of their periodic motion, their beginning and their duration. The second begins from my invisible self, my personality, and presents me in a world which has true infinity but which can be discovered only by the understanding, and I cognize that my connection with that world (and thereby with all those visible worlds as well) is not merely contingent, as in the first case, but universal and necessary. The first view of a countless multitude of worlds annihilates, as it were, my importance as an *animal creature*, which after it has been for a short time provided with vital force (one knows not how) must give back to the planet (a mere speck in the universe) the matter from which it came. The second, on the contrary, infinitely raises my worth as an *intelligence* by my personality, in which the moral law reveals to me a life independent of animality and even of the whole sensible world, at least so far as this may be inferred from the purposive determination of my existence by this law, a determination not restricted to the conditions and boundaries of this life but reaching into the infinite.   (CPrR 5: 162)

The second passage is from *The Metaphysics of Morals*:

It is inappropriate to call this [moral] feeling a moral *sense*, for by the word "sense" is usually understood a theoretical capacity for perception directed toward an object, whereas moral feeling (like pleasure and displeasure in general) is something merely subjective, which yields no cognition.—No human being is entirely without moral feeling, for were he completely lacking in receptivity to it he would be morally dead; and if (to speak in medical terms) the moral vital force could no longer excite this feeling, then humanity would dissolve (by chemical laws, as it were) into mere animality and be mixed irretrievably with the mass of other natural beings.—But we no more have a special *sense* for what is (morally) good and evil than for *truth*, although people often speak in this fashion. We have, rather, a *susceptivity* on the part of free choice to be moved by pure practical reason (and its law), and this is what we call moral feeling.   (MM 6: 400)

For reasons we cannot understand, Kant says here, we have two vital forces, one non-rational or natural vital force constitutive of our animality, and one rational or moral vital force constitutive of our personality. Besides, contemplating these forces (or aspects of my existence) is intimately connected with my reflective self-consciousness (the fact that I can be reflectively self-conscious about these aspects of my existence). Such contemplation fills me not only with admiration, but also awe (reverence), which is an aesthetic judgment of the sublime. Admiration for "the starry heavens above" comes from the realization that I am a tiny, contingent speck in the universe, and yet in virtue of having the animal vital force, I am an active speck. Awe (reverence) for "the moral law within" comes from the realization that I have a second kind of embodied forcefulness, namely one that is revealed in my capacity to choose ends of my own responsibly, namely as guided by my practical thinking. This capacity for moral responsibility is revealed in moral feeling, namely my susceptibility to be moved to act as a result of my thinking about whether what I am doing is consistent with respect for rational being. Indeed, without moral feeling I would be "morally dead," Kant argues in the second quote, meaning that without moral feeling I would not be capable of moral responsibility, as my only vital force would be that which all other animals living on the planet have. These reflections, Kant suggests, also push me towards the thought that human life has a kind of value that is of a distinctive, higher kind, one that it cannot have in virtue of its contingent existence on the planet, but that it has in virtue of somehow participating in all being in the universe. Moral feeling is a susceptibility that is enabled by my capacity for reflective self-consciousness, and that makes it possible for me both to know that the world as it appears cannot be all that there is. It also allows me and to choose in constructive, independent ways not determined by my vital animal force or by the causal forces in the world. The way in which I can act as motivated by my reason must be thought of as internally connected with the kind of being that is part of all that is (beyond what appears at any given time) and, hence, connected to me as a thing in itself or as noumenon.

The two vital forces, in turn, are constitutive of how we experience love, including self-love, in two ways: non-rationally and rationally. In addition, because we cannot have an obligation to have the vital forces—they are simply part of us for reasons we cannot understand and they reveal themselves in how we can take pleasure or displeasure in certain ways of loving—it is impossible to have duties or obligations to have the feelings of love (whether rational or non-rational) that the vital forces make possible. Kant therefore says that "*Love* is a matter of *feeling*, not of willing, and I cannot love because I *will* to, still less because I *ought* to (I cannot be constrained to love); so a *duty to love* is an absurdity" (MM 6: 401).[12] We cannot command love because we cannot command feelings. Rather, what we have a duty to do with regard to these feelings is to cultivate and strengthen our capacity for them (for feeling emotionally healthy and morally good (self-) love). We do this in part by contemplating how our animality (corresponding to the starry heavens above) is a source of admiration and our personality (corresponding to the moral law within) is a source

---

[12] For a more in-depth discussion of these passages—and earlier literature—that appears consistent with my discussion here, see Melissa Seymour Fahmy (2010; cf. 2009).

of awe. Our efforts to do this must be in line with how moral feeling (personality) enables us to be morally responsible, which is why Kant argues as follows:

Since any consciousness of obligation depends upon moral feeling to make us aware of the constraint present in the thought of duty, there can be no duty to have moral feeling or to acquire it; instead every human being (as a moral being) has it in [them][13] originally. Obligation with regard to moral feeling can be only to *cultivate* it and to strengthen it through wonder at its inscrutable source. This comes about by its being shown how it is set apart from any pathological stimulus and is induced most intensely in its purity by merely rational representation.   (MM 6: 300f.)

Now, it may be tempting to read this to mean that we have an obligation to cultivate and strengthen only our *moral* vital force, not our animal vital force. This seems incorrect textually because it goes against giving "the starry heavens" aspect of Kant's text its due. That is, Kant's basic proposal above is that our embodied nature requires us to understand ourselves as having two vital forces—one non-rational or animal-istic (phenomenal) and one rational or intellectual (noumenal)—and the contem-plation of them fills us with admiration or awe, respectively. Correspondingly, rather than seeing Kant as advocating that we should strive only to realize our moral vital force, it is more plausible to read Kant as making the following points. First, it is important to pay attention to how the two forces are different, and that it is the moral vital force that enables us to be morally responsible beings. Second, our capacity to set ends for ourselves—and so develop, transform, and integrate also our animalistic nature in abstract conceptual, associative, and aesthetic-teleological ways—must be developed in line with both basic vital forces where the moral force has normative priority since it enables me to be morally responsible for my end-setting.

Another way to get this into view starts with noting that Kant later in *The Metaphysics of Morals* claims that human beings can feel pleasure and displeasure in two kinds of ways, namely pathologically and morally:

Moral feeling... is to feel pleasure or displeasure merely from being aware that our actions are consistent with or contrary to the law of duty. Every determination of choice proceeds *from the representation of a possible action to* the deed through the feeling of pleasure or displeasure, taking an interest in the action or its effect. The state of *feeling* here (the way in which inner sense is affected) is either *pathological* or *moral*.—The former is that feeling which precedes the representation of the law; the latter, that which can only follow upon it.   (MM 6: 399)

So our end in life cannot be to squelch our (animalistic or non-rational) vital force and to foster only our moral vital force just as it cannot be an obligation to have either force (as having them is not something that is within reach of our possible choice or what we can control; they must be thought of as "original"). As we have seen, one's first-personal obligations regarding these forces as feelings are rather to strengthen them, including by being aware of their distinction, and then to develop, transform, and integrate one's animality so that it becomes *one's own* as the particular human being one is (again, through abstract conceptual, associative, and aesthetic-teleological

---

[13] The original German uses the male noun "Der Mensch" for "human being." Since English does not have gendered nouns and Kant does not write "Der Mann" (referring to man only here), I have replaced the "him" with "them" here.

means) and as a being capable of morally responsible end-setting. In Kant's words: "A human being has a duty to raise himself from the crude state of nature, from his animality, more and more toward humanity, by which he alone is capable of setting himself ends" (MM 6: 387).

This reading fits with how Kant argues in *Groundwork* that because a good will (which wills what is right *because* it is right) is the only thing that is unconditionally good and because moral feeling is made possible by our capacity for practical reason, what we can and ought to do is to cultivate our ability to use our capacity for practical reason to determine our actions as necessary (GW 4: 393-5). Kant argues likewise in the second *Critique* that "Pure practical reason merely *infringes upon* [animalistic] self-love, inasmuch as it only restricts it, as natural and active in us even prior to the moral law, to the condition of agreement with this law, and then it is called *rational self-love*" (CPrR 7: 73). Indeed, our moral objective is to perfect our ability to act out of rational self-love, to be able to act because it is the right thing to do (duty). In Kant's words,

A human being has a duty to carry the cultivation of his *will* up to the purest virtuous disposition, in which the *law* becomes also the incentive to his actions that conform with duty and he obeys the law from duty. This disposition is inner morally practical perfection . . . a feeling of the effect that the lawgiving will within the human being exercises on his capacity to act in accordance with his will . . . it is called *moral feeling*.   (MM 6: 387)[14]

Once more, this cannot plausibly be taken to mean that we should strive to act from duty at all times, but that we should strive to develop ourselves such that our rational and non-rational self-love are not in conflict with one another but in close union. We should therefore strive to perfect our ability to be aware of what we are doing and to act as motivated by moral feeling as appropriate; when we find ourselves in situations in which a particular kind of action is morally required, we should strive to perfect our ability to do that kind of action just because it is required. Playing soccer, for example, is neither in conformity nor in conflict with morality; there is simply no moral issue arising here. It is an activity through which I can experience much joy and playfulness, and, so is a way of experiencing non-rational self-love. However, when I play a game of soccer, I should not cheat, but follow the rules. So, not cheating is acting in conformity with morality. I should, however, strive to perfect my ability to play soccer without cheating because cheating is wrong. And insofar as I learnt to act in this way—have fun and play but never cheat—I bring into union non-rational and rational self-love in my life as a soccer player.

7. The Highest Good

In light of the above account of human nature, it is no longer surprising that Kant never argues that we should try to rid ourselves of our animality or that we should act

---

[14] Similarly, in "Theory and Practice," Kant says this: "Certainly, the will must have *motives*; but these are not certain objects proposed as ends related to *natural feeling*, but nothing other than the unconditional *law* itself; and the will's receptivity to finding itself subject to the law as unconditional necessitation is called *moral feeling*, which is therefore not the cause but the effect of the determination of the will, and we would not have the least perception of it within ourselves if that necessitation were not already present within us" (TP 8: 284).

from duty at all times; rather, he proposes that *the* human goal, "[the] highest good possible in the world...consists in the union and harmony of...human morality...and human happiness" (TP 8: 279). Another way of saying this is that for human beings, the highest good is a synthesis or union of the capacities for sensibility (phenomenon) and rationality (noumenon) (CPrR 5: 114f.). This is compatible with emphasizing that because we can be morally responsible for our actions, we have a distinctive interest in the "mere worthiness to be happy" (GW 4: 450) or with identifying a theory of morality or of virtue as "not properly the doctrine of how we are to *make* ourselves happy but of how we are to become *worthy* of happiness" (CPrR 5: 130). Rather it is to emphasize that for human beings, a full life—our highest good—is to strive to bring morality (virtue) and happiness into union. Kant says

inasmuch as virtue and happiness together constitute possession of the highest good in a person, and happiness distributed in exact proportion to morality (as the worth of a person and his worthiness to be happy) constitutes the *highest good* of a possible world, the latter means the whole, the complete good, in which, however, virtue as the condition is always the supreme good, since it has no further condition above it, whereas happiness is something that, though always pleasant to the possessor of it, is not of itself absolutely and in all respects good but always presupposes morally lawful conduct as its condition.   (CPrR 5: 110f.)

In a possible world, our happiness and our deservedness to be happy would align; in our actual world, however, our aim is to strive to bring the two into union.

Indeed, on my reading of Kant, there are three additional reasons why morality (virtue) cannot be a doctrine of how to make ourselves happy—how to love ourselves well in non-rational ways. First, there is not a single, universal answer to the question of how to be happy, either for human beings in general or for any particular human being. This is because many aspects of our being that determine our happiness are beyond our control, and because situations change and so are beyond what we can be morally responsible for in any direct way. As we have seen above, human beings begin to develop animalistic and social emotions prior to being capable of moral responsibility and life or others can and sometimes do terrible, devastating things to us before we can even understand what is going on. In addition, because these emotions are not inherently reflective and conceptual, these subjective aspects of us are not experienced in only one way. If we were to accept Kant's theory as presented in Chapter 2, for example, the subjective experience of sexual love is different for men and women; on my revised account in Chapter 3, the subjective experience of sexual love is not the same for those who are polyamorous, polysexual, binary, monogamous, cis, straight, or L, G, B, T, Q, I, or A. Second, because some aspects of our self-love or happiness concern our animality, our social sense of self, and our aesthetic-teleological powers, we can be morally responsible only *with regard to* them; our related moral duties are indirect just as our duty to assure our own and others' happiness is "indirect" (GW 4: 399).[15] Third, in an irreducible sense, what ends we set is open-ended in that we creatively find new ways of developing ourselves and our

---

[15] See my "Kant and Moral Responsibility for Animals" (Varden 2020a) for the argument that this is one reason why our moral duties regarding animals are indirect.

projects. This is also why Kant maintains that while human morality is an ideal of reason, human happiness is not; it is an ideal of the "imagination" (GW 4: 418).

In light of the above, we can see also quite clearly why truthfulness is our highest duty: in order to strengthen, transform, and develop my own embodied forcefulness (both vital forces) in creative, yet emotionally healthy, morally good ways, I need to learn to be able to be truthfully aware of what I actually feel and am doing; otherwise, I could neither act morally responsibly nor make improvements to how I go about my life. Without truthfulness, I would be acting in either self- or other destructive ways, rather than furthering myself as a rational, embodied, social being with my own life to live, and I would not be able to assist others in their pursuits to do the same for themselves. Notice how this helps us understand even better why Kant thinks that we cannot have a duty to feel respect even though our ineradicable feeling of respect for our own practical reason is what enables us to be responsible for acting in ways at least consistent with respecting our own and other human beings' capacity for personality. "Respect," Kant says in *The Metaphysics of Morals*, is

something merely subjective, a feeling of a special kind, not a judgment about an object that it would be a duty to bring about or promote. For, such a duty, regarded as a duty, could be represented to us only through the *respect* we have for it. A duty to have respect would thus amount to being put under obligation to duties.—Accordingly it is not correct to say that a human being has a *duty of self-esteem*; it must rather be said that the law within him unavoidably forces from him *respect* for his own being, and this feeling (which is of a special kind) is the basis of certain duties, that is, of certain actions that are consistent with his duty to himself. It cannot be said that he *has* a duty of respect toward himself, for he must have respect for the law within himself in order even to think of any duty whatsoever.   (MM 6: 402f.)[16]

That we can have feelings of respect or esteem for the kind of being we are, is possible to explain only if we understand these feelings as resulting from our shared capacity for practical reason. Respect and self-esteem are moral or inherently reflective feelings in that we can explain them philosophically only by an appeal to our capacity for practical reason—and so to our capacity for reflective self-consciousness and abstract, conceptual thought. Our capacity for practical reason must be understood as prior to moral feeling because it is something without which such a feeling would be impossible. Kant continues that it is only because we are capable of valuing ourselves as priceless—as having dignity in virtue of having this capacity for rational, responsible end-setting (autonomy)—that we are able to think of having distinctively moral duties. These are duties that are explainable in virtue either of being necessary to sustain the human world as one where rational being is not made impossible for anyone through our actions, or of being important to further everyone's ability to

---

[16] Similarly, it is no longer surprising that Kant says that 'so little is respect a feeling of *pleasure* that we give way to it only reluctantly with regard to a human being. We try to discover something that could lighten the burden of it for us, some fault in him to compensate us for the humiliation that comes upon us through such an example ... Even the moral law itself in its *solemn majesty* is exposed to this striving to resist respect for it ... But, in turn, *so little pleasure* is there in it that, once one had laid self-conceit aside and allowed practical influence to that respect, one can in turn never get enough of contemplating the majesty of this law, and the soul believes itself elevated in proportion as it sees the holy elevated above itself and its frail nature" (CPrR 5: 77).

unify this fundamental commitment with their pursuit of happy, flourishing lives. Accordingly, as we saw in section 5, we have two kinds of perfect duties and two kinds of imperfect duties. We have perfect duties to ourselves and to others, and they are similar in that they command us never to treat ourselves or others in ways inconsistent with respect for human dignity (for the capacities enabling autonomy). And we have imperfect duties to develop our own capacities and talents (to become capable of setting ends of our own rationally and responsibly) and to assist others in their pursuit of happiness insofar as circumstances allow.

8. Sensible and Moral Character

In the next two sections, I want to draw on two other aspects of Kant's writings on human nature, namely his accounts of the character of a person and of friendship. The goal is to bring out further complexities we need to understand the challenges involved in developing ourselves as sexual, affectionately loving, gendered beings, including as part of ongoing relationships. In this section, I outline Kant's account of the character of a person before moving on to his account of friendships in the next one.

Corresponding to how Kant views human beings as ideally seeking to realize, transform, and integrate two kinds of embodied forcefulness into a harmonious union, Kant thinks we can distinguish between two senses of having character. "The first," he argues, "is the distinguishing mark of the human being as a sensible or natural being," while "the second is the distinguishing mark of the human being as a rational being endowed with freedom" (A 7: 285). Also, given the way in which the predisposition to animality is different from the predisposition to humanity in that the latter necessarily goes along with end-setting and social, comparative reasoning but not morality (as it is not enabled by nor does it require a capacity to act as motivated by reason, or personality), we are unsurprised to learn that Kant suggests that we can distinguish two natural aspects of character, one tracking a "*natural aptitude* or natural predisposition" (animality) and one tracking a "*temperament* or sensibility*" (social sense of self and activity involving rational end-setting), and that these are areas where we see variety among humans (A 7: 285). Additionally, given how Kant sees the predisposition to personality as making it possible for us to do something just because we ought to (activity expressive of moral feeling)—because it is the right thing to do—and because this ought tracks the ability to act at least consistently with universalizable maxims, it is furthermore not surprising to learn that Kant thinks that the question of whether or not one has a moral character "purely and simply" concerns whether or not someone has "a way of thinking...or nothing at all" (A 7: 285). Kant equivalently summarizes the three predispositions to good in human nature by saying that "The first two predispositions indicate what can be made of the human being; the last (moral) predisposition indicates what [one] is prepared to make of [oneself]" (A 7: 285).

One's "natural aptitude," to repeat, is enabled by one's predisposition to animality, or one's basic way of striving to survive (self-preservation), to be sexual (sex drive), to feel affection for others (basic community). One's natural aptitude "more (subject-ively)" is about how one is susceptive "to the *feeling* of pleasure or displeasure" and how "one human being is affected by another"—"and in this [one's] natural aptitude can have something characteristic" (A 7: 286). "Objectively," one's natural aptitude has to do with "the *faculty of desire*," where "life manifests itself not merely in feeling, internally, but also in activity, externally, though merely in accordance with incentives of sensibility" (A 7: 286). Kant states that when we say that someone has a "good disposition," we point to how such a person is "not stubborn but compliant; that he may get angry, but is easily appeased and bears no grudge (is negatively good)" (A 7: 286). When we speak of "a good heart," Kant continues, then we add that such a person not only has a good disposition but also "an impulse toward the practical good" (A 7: 286). Indeed, because the person with *only* a good disposition or heart is not oriented by their capacity to act "according to principles" (as enabled by personality), both kinds of people are easily taken advantage of. Both kinds of people act on impulses or inclinations, and as a result, "both the person of good disposition and the person of good heart are people whom a shrewd guest can use as he pleases" (A 7: 286).

In contrast, Kant argues that when we make judgments about a human being's character in the sense of *temperament*, we speak neither about natural aptitudes (as understood above) nor about habits we may acquire through repetition, but rather about the excitability of a human being's feeling or activity level. Characters regarded as temperaments—or personalities in this vernacular sense of the term[17]—exist in the way in which people relate to their animalistic desires and are affected by others in their being so related. And Kant suggests that there are observable patterns among human beings here; we are not exactly the same regarding temperaments just as our differences are not simply individual. Indeed, Kant proceeds to argue, his account of human nature can be seen as engaging and transforming the old, presumably Medieval theories of temperaments, according to which there are four types. Let me explain.

Kant clarifies that he seeks neither to explore temperament from the "*physiological*" point of view—meaning one's "*physical constitution* (strong or weak build)"—nor is he interested in temperament understood in terms of "*complexion*"—meaning "fluid elements moving regularly through the body by means of the vital power, which also includes heat or cold in the treatment of these humors" (A 7: 287). Rather he is interested in temperament "considered *psychologically*...[as] temperament of the soul (faculties of feeling and desire)" (A 7: 287). If we borrow terms "from the constitution of the blood" as the old Medieval theories do, then these terms should be "introduced only in accordance with the analogy that the play of feelings and desires has with corporeal causes of movement (the most prominent of which is the blood)" (A 7: 287). In other words, it is perfectly fine to use non-Medieval terms to identify the philosophical distinctions we need in order to talk about temperaments. For example, we can explore these ideas in terms borrowed from contemporary psychological theories, such as the terms "extroverts" and "introverts." Kant also does not deny that there may be "corporeal factors in the

---

[17] Here "personality" here should therefore be understood only in the vernacular sense and not as equivalent to "personality" in the "predisposition to personality" above.

human being, as covertly contributing causes" of our temperaments (A 7: 287). Rather, he is chiefly interested in the ways in which our temperamental subjectivities appear patterned, and his idea of a natural vital force together with his account of human nature can make sense of these patterns; indeed, it can make sense of why the Medieval terms have been with us for such a long time.

More specifically, Kant argues, "since, *first*, they can be divided generally into temperaments of *feeling* and *activity*, and since, *second*, each of them can be connected with the excitability (*intensio*) or slackening (*remissio*) of the vital power, only **four** simple temperaments can be laid down...: the *sanguine*, the *melancholy*, the *choleric*, and the *phlegmatic*. By this means, the old forms can then be retained, and they only receive a more comfortable interpretation suited to the spirit of this doctrine of the temperaments" (A 7: 287). Kant emphasizes that the old theories were certainly wrong in thinking that it was something in the "*constitution of the blood*" that can

indicate the *cause* of the phenomena observed in a sensibly affected human being—whether according to the pathology of humors or of nerves: they serve only to classify these phenomena according to observed effects. For in order properly to give to a human being the title of a particular class, one does not need to know beforehand what chemical blood-mixture it is that authorizes the designation of a certain property of temperament; rather, one needs to know which feelings and inclinations one has observed combined in him.   (A 7: 287)

Before moving on to describe each temperament in more detail, notice that the point here is not that Kant's account of temperaments necessarily captures these aspects of us better than any other. Indeed, as Kant observes in his *Lectures on Pedagogy*, "Formerly, human beings did not even have a conception of the perfection which human beings can reach [since they did not understand freedom]. We ourselves are not even yet clear about this concept" (LP 9: 445). Rather, I suggest, the main point is that it is impossible to envision truly flourishing human lives—lives that flourish emotionally and morally, and so flourish when it comes to sexuality, affection, and love—without a philosophical account of people's sensible characters, in which an account of human temperaments has a central explanatory function.

Kant's proposal is that one can capture much about people's "sensible" character by categorizing temperaments according to the excitability, or lack thereof, of the animal vital power in regard to feelings or to activity. This yields a total of four temperaments: the "sanguine" and the "melancholy" as temperaments of feeling, and the "choleric" and the "phlegmatic" as temperaments of activity.[18] The distinction between the sanguine and the melancholy temperaments, Kant continues, is not so much a distinction between a tendency to "cheerfulness or sadness," but rather that the sanguine temperament "has the peculiarity that sensations are quickly and strongly affected," whereas the melancholy temperament experiences sensation as "less striking" but more "deeply penetrating ... [as getting] themselves rooted deeply" (A 7: 287). This is not to deny that a person with a melancholy temperament "broods over a sensation" and thereby "deprives gaiety of its easy variability," but to

---

[18] See Cohen (2017e, 2018) and Zammito (2002) for similar interpretations of Kant's account of the temperaments.

emphasize that doing so does not in itself produce sadness and to insist that "every change that one has under one's control generally stimulates and strengthens the mind" (A 7: 287). Thus, "he who makes light of whatever happens to him is certainly happier, if not wiser, than he who clings to sensations that benumb his vital power" (A 7: 287). Furthermore, what Kant is concerned with here are raw, sensible temperaments, that is, subjective tendencies that are not yet developed, transformed, and integrated through one's faculty of desire, namely through one's reflective (abstract conceptual and associative) and imaginative abilities and thereby also brought into closer union with one's moral powers.

It is helpful to expand a little on each temperament. The sanguine temperament is found in the *"light-blooded person"* and it is characterized by feeling strongly, quickly, and generally positively. Someone with the sanguine temperament is "carefree and of good cheer," he always "begins with hope of success," he "attributes a great importance to each thing for the moment, and the next moment may not give it another thought," and consequently he "thinks only superficially" (A 7: 288). A person with a sanguine temperament makes and breaks promises easily since they do not think through whether or not the promises they make in the moment are realistic. Therefore, such a person easily helps others, but they are a bad debtor; they are good, fun company but difficult to be in any kind of deeper relationships with because they do not

like to attribute great importance to anything (*Vive la bagatelle!*), and all human beings are his friends. He is not usually an evil human being, but he is a sinner hard to convert; indeed, he regrets something very much but quickly forgets this regret (which never becomes *grief*). Business tires him, and yet he busies himself indefatigably with things that are mere play; for play involves change, and perseverance is not his strength.   (A 7: 288)

The melancholy temperament of the *"heavy-blooded person"* is opposite in every way from the sanguine temperament. A person disposed to this temperament "attributes a great importance to all things that concern himself, finds cause for concern everywhere and directs his attention first to difficulties... [and] therefore... also thinks deeply" (A 7: 288). A person with such a temperament naturally also neither makes nor breaks promises easily, but this is not because it would be immoral to do so—"for we are speaking here of *sensible* incentives"—"but rather that the opposite inconveniences him, and just because of this makes him apprehensive, mistrustful, and suspicious, and thereby also insusceptible to cheerfulness... [and] he who must *himself* do without joy will find it hard not to begrudge it in others" (A 7: 288).

Turning to the temperaments of activity, the choleric temperament is found in the *"hot-blooded person"* (A 7: 289). This temperament is fiery. Persons who exhibit it are easily angered but "without hatred" and, so, if another person gives in to them, they also calm down quickly and indeed love "the other person all the more for quickly having given in" (A 7: 289). Choleric people are furthermore *"rash*, but not persistent... busy, but reluctant to undertake business" as this requires persistence, which is why the choleric person prefers to be "the mere commander in chief who presides over it" rather than having to carry things out themselves (A 7: 289). If passion accompanying the choleric temperament is allowed to develop, it will be "ambition"—and such a temperament is correspondingly conducive to taking "part in public affairs" and to activities that are "loudly praised" (A 7: 289). Anyone with a choleric temperament naturally loves "the *show* and pomp of *formalities*" and "gladly takes others under his wing and according to appearances is magnanimous, not from love, however, but from pride, for he loves himself more" (A 7: 289). Someone with such a temperament will also naturally have "a high opinion of *order* and therefore will appear to be cleverer than he is" (A 7: 289). A person with such a temperament, Kant continues,

is avaricious in order not to be stingy; polite, but with ceremony; stiff and affected in social intercourse, likes any flatterer who is the butt of his wit; suffers more wounds due to the opposition of others against his *avaricious* arrogance; for a little caustic wit directed at him completely blows away the aura of his importance... In short, the choleric temperament is the least happy of all, because it calls up the most opposition to itself.   (A 7: 289)

It is, in other words, because of the way in which the choleric temperament is naturally drawn to arrogance—which, we will see in Chapter 4, Kant understands as the perceived need to have others love oneself more than they love themselves—that those who have this temperament naturally attract a lot of opposition to themselves.

The final temperament is the phlegmatic one, which characterizes the "*cold-blooded person*" (A 7: 289). Such a person, Kant states, is not characterized by "indolence" or "lifelessness," but "*lack of emotion*" (A 7: 289). If we consider this natural temperament as a weakness, it shows itself as a "propensity to inactivity" (even if "strong incentives" are present), whereas as a strength, it shows itself in persistence and calm (A 7: 289). Moreover, Kant thinks that this kind of temperament reveals itself in persons who although only equipped with "a quite ordinary portion of reason" and "without being brilliant... still proceed from principles and not from instinct" (A 7: 290). Kant also suggests that because of the "fortunate" aspects of this kind of temperament, the phlegmatic temperament easily "takes the place of wisdom," which is why it is common to call people with this temperament philosophers and why many are happy to recognize them as "superior" without feeling this as an affront to their own vanity (A 7: 290). Such people are often also judged as "*sly*" since "all the bullets and projectiles fired at him bounce off him as from a sack of wool" (A 7: 290). Additionally, those who have this temperament quite easily establish dominion over those around them as they have the ability to seemingly "comply with everyone's wishes; for by his unbending but considerate will he knows how to bring their wills round to his" (A 7: 290).

Kant does not think that any of these temperaments can be combined harmoniously in the same person; if one finds two strands in one person, that person is simply characterized by "moodiness" rather than as having a temperament (A 7: 291). In addition, Kant argues that people who have some temperaments (and who thus exhibit particular patterns of being energized) do not easily (naturally) get along with or naturally seek out people who have others. In particular, he thinks the opposite temperaments (the sanguine and the melancholy, and the choleric and the phlegmatic) "*oppose*" each other, meaning that their temperaments balance each other out. In contrast, the sanguine and the choleric and the melancholy and the phlegmatic "*neutralize*" one another, meaning that their temperaments are naturally incompatible in that people with the sanguine temperament will naturally find it difficult to be around choleric people (and vice versa) and the melancholic and the phlegmatic will not naturally seek each other's company, either. The reason for this incompatibility (neutralization) is that a

> good-natured cheerfulness [sanguine] cannot be conceived of as being fused with forbidding anger [choleric] in one and the same act, any more than the pain of the self-tormentor [melancholic] can be conceived of as being fused with the contented repose of the self-sufficient mind [phlegmatic].   (A 7: 291)

As mentioned above, it is important to bear in mind that Kant is here concerned with raw temperaments, or patterns in our natural, sensible embodied forceful ways of feeling or being active. Kant suggests that if we simply let these subjective tendencies in us develop without restraint or transformation, we will exhibit one of four kinds of pathology. We will become pathologically self-loving in ways characterized by the sanguine, the melancholy, the choleric, or the phlegmatic temperament.

Notice too that each temperament, or character, is likely to have distinctive subjective strengths and challenges with regard to the projects of becoming emotionally healthy and morally good beings, and of flourishing while living together with others, such as in sexual and affectionately loving ways. The person with a sanguine temperament is naturally generously fun, joyous, affectionate, and sexually playful, for example, and yet they are also not naturally drawn to develop deep, intimate, and reliable relationships with others. The person with a melancholic temperament has the opposite set of strengths: such a person is a naturally reliable anchor with whom one can develop a deep relationship, and yet they are not naturally drawn to all the things that makes sexual and affectionate relationships fun, joyous, and playful. The person with a choleric temperament is naturally fiery, and so having the attention of such a person's sexual and loving energy is energizing and empowering, and they will like to be the center of attention and, so, will naturally want asymmetrical relations. Finally, the person with a phlegmatic temperament, like the melancholic one, is a reliable anchor once their sexual and affectionate loving attention is gained, and yet it takes a lot of outside energy to excite such an unresponsive person. In other words, if we simply let our temperaments develop "naturally," we become draining and damaging people; indeed, insofar as our temperaments are left untended, we become persons with whom it is increasingly difficult to flourish, both in general and with respect to our personal projects of sexual and affectionate loving emotional health in particular. Kant suggests that in order to develop and transform our temperaments such that they enable healthy relationships with ourselves and others, we must also develop moral character, namely our capacity to act in truthful ways in tune with moral feeling, and, correspondingly, insofar as necessary to act in ways demanded by our self- and other-regarding duties.

Kant starts his discussion of moral character by pointing out how it differs from the discussion of natural or sensible characters, each of which refers to a subjective "*way of sensing*" (linked, as we have seen, to the predisposition to animality and humanity, respectively). That is to say, when we move from sensible character to moral character, we move away from a discussion of character which says "a great deal about" someone, "what nature makes of the human being" (A 7: 292), or whether someone has "*this* or *that*" sensible character of temperament. Rather than talking about *which kind* of character a person has, when we are turning to the question of moral character, we are talking about whether or not someone "has a *character*" at all (A 7: 291). In consequence, if we say of someone that they have a character in this moral sense, we do not only describe that person, we also "*praise*" them, since moral character concerns "what the human being *makes of [themself]*," and it "is a rarity, which inspires profound respect and admiration" when someone makes of themself a person with moral character (A 7: 292). Having character in this moral sense, Kant continues, does not mean that one never makes mistakes; rather it concerns the general way in which one is oriented in the world:

to have... [moral] character signifies that property of the will by which the subject binds himself to definite practical principles that he has prescribed to himself irrevocably by his own reason. Although these principles may sometimes indeed be false and incorrect, nevertheless the formal element of the will in general, to act according to firm principles (not to fly off hither and yon, like a swarm of gnats)... has something precious and admirable; for it is also something rare. (A 7: 292)

To get these ideas better into view, Kant points out that some aspects of us, such as our talents and other contingent properties, have a "market price" in that they have exchange value, and thereby enable us to use them to pursue all kinds of purposes. Other aspects, namely our temperaments, are valuable affectively (they have an "Affektionspreis") since they enable us to enjoy spending time together. In contrast, moral character is priceless in that it cannot be exchanged for anything else or deemed instrumentally valuable; it simply has its own or "inner" worth (A 7: 292).

Corresponding to his argument that it is impossible to command oneself to feel, and that we must thus present perfect duties negatively—as things we must not do—Kant proposes that we should present "negatively the principles that relate to character" (A 7: 294). And given what Kant says in general about perfect duties and about the importance of being truthful, it is unsurprising that he also emphasizes that our duties with regard to developing moral character are negative and should be listed as prohibitions: do not lie ("say what is false"); do not "dissemble" ("appear... well disposed in public... [while] being hostile behind people's backs"); do not "break one's (legitimate) promises... including honoring... the *memory* of a friendship now broken off, and not abusing later on the former confidence and candor of the other person"; do not "enter into an association of taste with evil-minded human beings... limit the association only to business"; and do not "pay attention to gossip derived from the shallow and malicious judgment of others" (A 7: 294). Kant sums up his take on moral character as follows:

In a word, the only proof within a human being's consciousness that he has character is that he has made truthfulness his supreme maxim, in the heart of his confessions to himself as well as in his behavior toward everyone else; and since to have this is the minimum that one can demand of a reasonable human being, but at the same time also the maximum of inner worth (of human dignity), then to be a man of principles (to have a determinate character) must be possible for the most common reason and yet, according to its dignity, be superior to the greatest talent. (A 7: 295)

Interestingly, Kant also argues that there is a deep sense in which making truthfulness one's maxim, or the basic principle orienting how one goes about life, is something one must decide to do—in that having character is something that is not "innate" but must be "*acquired*" through exercising choice—and it is also commonly not experienced as something one gradually becomes capable of doing. Rather, pursuing a moral character is instead experienced as something that occurs at a moment in one's life when one makes a "vow to oneself," and doing so, Kant continues, is rarely attempted "before the age of thirty, and fewer still . . . have firmly established it before they are forty" (A 7: 294). Indeed, although it takes time to become good at this—very few are consistently successful at it before the age of 40, Kant judges—it is still the case that one does not envision the effort as something one wants to do gradually, step by step. Doing it step by step would be "a futile endeavor . . . since one impression dies out while one works on another; the grounding of character, however, is absolute unity of the inner principle of conduct as such" (A 7: 294). In other words, although everybody will fail morally in various ways, the decision to be oriented by truthfulness is a decision that must be thought of as grounding and as important for everything that one does, as it must be seen as involving a decision about what one strives to be all about.

Kant furthermore suggests that the fact that we do not commonly think about the task of owning and developing our lives as an ongoing commitment to truthfulness is not the fault of those whose special gift is story-telling, and whose stories enable to us feel others' subjectivity (e.g., the poets, novelists, and musicians). Nor is it the fault of religious leaders, whose authority is viewed as situated in between that of the Divine and that of earthly leaders. Both kinds of groups, Kant suggests, face situations in which it is rather impossible to do what they do best *and* live in such ways that truthfulness is their basic principle. Instead, Kant thinks that the failure of humankind clearly to appreciate the importance of truthfulness should be imputed to philosophers:

It is also said that *poets* have no character, for example, they would rather insult their best friends than give up a witty inspiration; or that character is not to be sought at all among courtiers, who must put up with all fashions; and that with clergymen, who court the Lord of Heaven as well as the lords of the earth in one and the same pitch, firmness of character is in a troublesome condition; and, accordingly, it probably is and will remain only a pious wish that they have inner (moral) character. But perhaps the *philosophers* are to blame for this, because they have never yet isolated this concept and placed it in a sufficiently bright light, and have sought to present virtue only in fragments but have never tried to present it *whole*, in its beautiful form, and to make it interesting for all human beings.   (A 7: 295)

As the serious joke goes, the better the poet, novelist, or musician, the more they enable us to get closer to truth, to the good, and to the beautiful by lying, such as, as we will see below, by telling a 10-year-old a moving, captivating, beautiful story of an honest man facing the most difficult of challenges—whether through words, verse, or music—a story that is not based on anything that actually happened (it is a lie and everybody knows that) but which enables the 10-year-old to become clear about what kind of person they aspire to become. The better religious leaders, in turn, enable the members of their religious community to hold onto themselves and their faith in the world as a good world through life's many meaningless disasters, and they help create ceremonies of joy to celebrate wonderful life experiences, such as the birth of children or marriages—often by using the powers of stories, verse, and music. Philosophy's job, in contrast, is to give philosophical accounts of how to go through life in practically wise ways—ways that are informed by the best philosophical accounts we have of what human nature and a human life is. For these reasons, Kant thinks, if humanity has not yet understood the importance of truthfulness to human lives lived well, because this commitment has not been presented to them in a clear, profoundly interesting, and meaningful way, then the blame for this belongs to us, the philosophers, rather than to the artists and clergy even though they too explore the three core questions in a human life, namely "What can I know? What should I do? What may I hope?" (CPuR: A805/B833).

9. Friendship

This section adds to the above account of the complexity of full human lives by exploring Kant's ideas of "pragmatic" and "moral" friendship. I draw from these ideas to argue that insofar as our sexual and/or affectionately loving relations are emotionally good and morally justifiable, they (i) reconcile both vital forces of each person in the relationship; (ii) give prominence to each person's moral vital force; and (iii) are pervaded by truthfulness.

Kant considers friendships among the most important things in our lives. Corresponding to how our being must be seen as striving to bring two vital forces into a harmonious, close union, friendships are viewed as unions between two persons characterized by reciprocal affectionate love and moral love (respect):

> *Friendship* (considered in its perfection) is the union of two persons through equal mutual love and respect.—It is easy to see that this is an ideal of each participating and sharing sympathetically in the other's well-being through the morally good will that unites them, the adoption of this ideal in their disposition toward each other makes them deserving of happiness; hence human beings have a duty of friendship.—But it is readily seen that friendship is only an idea (though a practically necessary one) and unattainable in practice, although striving for friendship (as a maximum of good disposition toward each other) is a duty set by reason, and no ordinary duty but an honorable one.   (MM 6: 469)

A perfect human friendship would be a relationship in which two people perfectly share in affectionate love and respect (moral love) towards one another. As a result, each person would happen to realize their predisposition to animality, humanity, and personality in such a way that they are perfectly satisfactory to the other person. It is plainly impossible for the lives of two distinct human beings to synchronize in this way—it is an unattainable idea and instead only an ideal to strive for—since human lives are too complex. This is both because each is seeking to set ends of their own, and because there are too many factors that are relevant to how each person feels, to what they need, and to what they want to do at any given time. Still, since friendship is characterized by shared lives—lives that involve affectionately and morally caring for one other—insofar as two people share their lives in this way, they deserve to be happy; indeed, the more they are able to live together in this way, the more they deserve to be happy.

Given his accounts of our predisposition to good and our propensity to evil, it is unsurprising that Kant deems friendships among the most difficult things to do well:

And how can he be sure that if the *love* of one is stronger, he may not, just because of this, forfeit something of the other's *respect*, so that it will be difficult for both to bring love and respect subjectively into that equal balance required for friendship?—For love can be regarded as attraction and respect as repulsion, and if the principle of love bids friends to draw closer, the principle of respect requires them to stay at a proper distance from each other. This limitation on intimacy, which is expressed in the rule that even the best of friends should not make themselves too familiar with each other, contains a maxim that holds not only for the superior in relation to the inferior but also the reverse. For the superior, before he realizes it, feels his pride wounded and may want the inferior's respect to be put aside for the moment, but not abolished. But once respect is violated, its presence within is irretrievably lost, even though the outward marks of it (manners) are brought back to their former course.   (MM 6: 470)

Affectionate and sexual love, on this account, are connected to our animality (our needs for sex, self-preservation, and affectionate love) and to our social sense of self (our humanity; our need to be affirmed as interesting, loveable, and sexually desirable), which are aspects of ourselves that make us seek to be closer to those with whom we have relationships. Moral love, in contrast, is enabled by our capacity for practical reason, and is intimately connected with our need to do our own things and to be in relationships in which the other(s) need and take delight in their own ventures (ventures independent of ours), and in which we enjoy and delight in them doing so. It follows from this that there is an important way in which this aspect of ourselves, as Kant argues in the passage above, pushes us away from one another. Or as Kant argues in his "Idea for a Universal History," we are not simply social beings; we are *unsocial* social beings. This "*unsociable sociability*" (IUH 8: 20) issues from the fact that we not only have a natural drive to "basic community" (as part of our animality) and a social sense of self (as part of our humanity), but we also have a need to set ends of our own (the other, rational part of our humanity). We are therefore beings who love to be with others *and* who naturally also like and need our own space (because we need to set ends of our own) and who enjoy, delight in, and respect others' need to do their own things too. Trailing the enjoyment we take in our own space (which in itself is good for us), there is a bad "propensity to *individualize* (isolate)" ourselves (IUH 8: 20)—just as trailing the predisposition to basic community, there is a bad propensity to set aside our need for a personal space. Besides, as we see in the passage above and in the account of sensible characters, each person has different needs for togetherness, and for distinct, personal spaces, and these differences give rise to bad temptations for both people in a friendship. It becomes inherently tempting to disrespect the other's needs by playing on one's strengths—whatever they are—rather than vulnerably and honestly working out ways that are productive for both parties. What is more, if there is no honesty and learning about these temptations, if they are simply yielded to time and time again and described in self-deceptive ways, then the party who is being treated badly will irretrievably lose respect for the other, even if they continue to treat the other with civility.

Another reason why true friendships are so difficult to realize is that friends have a duty to serve as one another's reality checks, including by pointing out each other's faults so that they can grow together:

From a moral point of view it is, of course, a duty for one of the friends to point out the other's faults to him; this is in the other's best interests and is therefore a duty of love. But the latter sees in this a lack of the respect he expected from his friend and thinks that he has either already lost or is in constant danger of losing something of his friend's respect, since he is observed and secretly criticized by him; and even the fact that his friend observes him and finds fault with him will seem in itself offensive.   (MM 6: 470)

Naturally, we do not like to hear that there are things we do not do well, and we especially do not like it from those who love us and who we want to adore us. In fact, when those who love us point out that there is something we are not doing well, we get agitated, partly because we are worried that since they clearly know that we are not perfect, they will lose respect for us and we fear that they (will soon) want to withdraw from us. And yet, the only way forward—for each and for the friendship itself—is by moving deeper together, including by getting rid of old fears, developing aspirations never given attention before, and being able to deliberate well about how to go about obtaining each person's goals together. As Barbara Herman puts it, "Human rational abilities are vulnerable to the effects of poverty, humiliation and sustained misdirection. Ignoring others' needs, demeaning their choices, making someone's life too hard or too easy can affect their ability to sustain or value rational activity" (Herman 2011: 53-4). The point, again, is being able to develop one's natural connection into a relationship, in which each can grow individually and both can grow together—ideally by neither making the task of growing together too easy or too hard on oneself or the other party.

The complexities of friendships make them something we deeply long for, and something we find it very difficult to do well. Appreciating these complexities also enables us to see both why we simply cannot understand how these relationships function if we try to understand them through the lenses of mutual advantages, and why it is impossible to develop truly good friendships if one seeks to ground them simply on feelings of attraction. Friendship requires that one genuinely engages in the endeavor of sharing a life, that one knows one is doing so, and that one is striving to learn how to do it better:

How one wishes for a friend in need (one who is, of course, an active friend, ready to help at his own expense)! But still it is also a heavy burden to feel chained to another's fate and encumbered with his needs.—Hence friendship cannot be a union aimed at mutual advantage but must rather be a purely moral one, and the help that each may count on from the other in case of need must not be regarded as the end and determining ground of friendship—for in that case one would lose the other's respect—but only as the outward manifestation of an inner heartfelt benevolence, which should not be put to the test since this is always dangerous; each is generously concerned with sparing the other his burden and bearing it all by himself, even concealing it altogether from his friend, while yet he can always flatter himself that in case of need he could confidently count on the other's help. But if one of them accepts a favor from the other, then he may well be able to count on equality in love, but not in respect; for he sees himself obviously a step lower in being under obligation without being able to impose obligation in turn.—Although it is sweet to feel in possession of each other that approaches fusion into one person, friendship is something so delicate (*teneritas amicitiae*) that it is never for a moment safe from interruptions if it is allowed to rest on feelings, and if this mutual sympathy and self-surrender are not subjected to principles or rules preventing excessive familiarity and limiting mutual love by requirements of respect. Such interruptions are common among uncultivated people, although they do not always result in a split (for the rabble fight and make up). Such people cannot part with each other, and yet they cannot be at one with each other since they need quarrels in order to savor the sweetness of being united in reconciliation.—But in any case the love in friendship cannot be an affect; for emotion is blind in its choice, and after a while it goes up in smoke.   (MM 6: 470f.)

Friendships are difficult, then, because they require us to value one another in ways that neither reduce to instrumental value (self-interest), nor to *Affectionpreis* (a relation based on affect), nor to a combination of them. Rather, friendships are ways of living together that include moments of deep unity, that involve being reliably there for one another (even though such support is not *why* friendships are sought), and they comprise shared ideas of what the friendship is all about since otherwise life's many interruptions will topple the friendship. Indeed, given the view Kant defends in the passage above, we can see how, as will be expanded upon in Chapter 3, his long-term relationship with Joseph Green in many ways was easier for him than it was for Green, since Green was not striving to write his own philosophy (nor had he any other similarly preoccupying creative projects); indeed, Green's deepest pleasure appears to have been to talk philosophy with Kant and to assist Kant's flourishing in this regard. Kant did not have the challenge of learning how to do anything similar in return—to learn how to cherish Green's happiness by helping him flourish creatively. Indeed, Green even took care of Kant's finances. Still, the way in which they lived together—the way in which they had clarified expectations and indeed maintained a close, intimate relationship for over twenty years—reveals that their friendship can plausibly be seen as a striving for the ideal. After all, Kant amended his way of life to make it compatible with living with Green, including by becoming reliably punctual and preferring to do activities that they could enjoy together, such as enjoying dinners together, rather than those that only one of them would enjoy, such as listening to music (Green was tone deaf). Indeed, their friendship seems to fit Kant's philosophical position that a real, stable relationship must be developed in part through abstract conceptual means; otherwise it stays based simply on feeling (as enabled by the two vital forces), which is too unstable a foundation for shared human lives.

The above interpretation, in addition, makes it possible to see why, for Kant, friendship is important insofar as the other makes oneself known, including to oneself, as Rae Langton emphasizes in her interpretation of Kant on this point.[19] Friends help us see what we do and what we do not do well, they help us discover who we are, and they help us clarify our thoughts. For example, Kant states that

The human being is a being meant for society (though he is also an unsociable one), and in cultivating the social state he feels strongly the need to *reveal* himself to others (even with no

---

[19] For more on this, see Chapter 3.

ulterior purpose). But on the other hand, hemmed in and cautioned by fear of the misuse others may make of his disclosing his thoughts, he finds himself constrained *to lock up* in himself a good part of his judgements (especially those about other people). He would like to discuss with someone what he thinks about his associates, the government, religion and so forth, but he cannot risk it: partly because the other person, while prudently keeping back his own judgments, might use this to harm him, and partly because, as regards disclosing his faults, the other person may conceal his own, so that he would lose something of the other's respect by presenting himself quite candidly to him. (MM 6: 471f.)

And yet, as we have seen, being known and knowing oneself is not *all* that Kant thinks friendships are about, contrary to what Langton claims. Rather, as Langton argues that Kant should have argued, Kant actually regards full friendships as ways of living together that bring into union affectionate and respectful ways of being together, of being an "us." As we saw above, the *idea* of these full friendships is unattainable, but like the highest good, they are still *ideals* worth striving for.

In contrast to the impossible, full idea of friendship, moral friendship is indeed possible, although it is rare. Moral friendship concerns those aspects of friendships that friends can bring under their control together.

Moral friendship (as distinguished from friendship based on feeling) is the complete confidence of two persons in revealing their secret judgments and feelings to each other, as far as such disclosures are consistent with mutual respect...If...[a person] finds someone intelligent—someone who, moreover, shares his general outlook on things—with whom he need not be anxious about this danger but can reveal himself with complete confidence, he can then air his views. He is not completely alone with his thoughts, as in a prison, but enjoys a freedom he cannot have with the masses, among whom he must shut himself up in himself. Every human being has his secrets and dare not confide blindly in others, partly because of a base cast of mind in most human beings to use them to one's disadvantage and partly because many people are indiscreet or incapable of judging and distinguishing what may or may not be repeated. The necessary combination of qualities is seldom found in one person (*rara avis in terries, niroque simillima cygno/a bird that is rare on earth, quite like a black swan*), especially since the closest friendship requires that a judicious and trusted friend be also bound not to share the secrets entrusted to him with anyone else, no matter how reliable he thinks him, without explicit permission to do so...This (merely moral friendship) is not just an ideal but (like black swans) actually exists here and there in its perfection. But that (pragmatic) friendship, which burdens itself with the ends of others, although out of love, can have neither the purity nor the completeness requisite for a precisely determinant maxim; it is an ideal of one's wishes, which knows no bounds in its rational concept but which must always be very limited in experience. (MM 6: 472)

As we see, part of what makes us want friends is that we can trust that we can share our views with them and not feel as if we are imprisoned with our thoughts. This, however, is not Kant's whole point here. He furthermore explains that moral friendship is characterized by truthfulness and by how each friend can trust going through life with the other at their side. We can discuss and think with our moral friends, knowing that important things that are said and that are private go no further without explicit consent—moral friendships provide spaces in which we ground ourselves in ways that are consistent with emotional and moral growth. Thus, too, moral friendships may or may not go hand-in-hand with or be integrated with affection or sexual relations, as trust and truthfulness can be features of any relationship—whether personal or professional—regardless of the extent to which the people in the relationship share other aspects of their lives.

Given what we have said above about personalities understood as characters of temperament, about our propensity to evil, and about the ways in which developing ourselves as who we are is a difficult, ongoing enterprise of integration and growth that includes animalistic, social, moral, and aesthetic-based elements of ourselves, and which is made more difficult by how we are subjected to others' combinations and challenges in these regards, it is not strange that most people fail to develop themselves as who they are together with another person for a longer period of time in a way that can plausibly be described as contributing to the flourishing of each. In addition, as we will see in Chapters 2 and 3, although Kant did not appreciate this but often ended up arguing in cisist, sexist, and heterosexist ways, it is not so strange that there simply is not one way to love affectionately or sexually that is both emotionally healthy and morally justifiable; not only are there LGBTQIA ways, but polyamorous and polysexual ways. In fact, it is no longer terribly perplexing that many who pursue highly creative lives—including philosophers—appear unable to live monogamous lives and seldom live together with another person who is equally creative (rather than with someone who enjoys less creative and more stabilizing aspects of life). After all, creative lives are importantly self- rather than other-centered and they easily stray into self-absorption and selfishness. Indeed, given the above, it is not terribly strange that insofar as one adds historical identities tracking oppression to such highly creative lives, shared lives between those whose identities are oppressed and those whose identities are not, seem particularly challenging: after all, those with oppressed identities are not "supposed" to live such ambitious lives according to these oppressive notions, and they are likely to be more sensitive to behavior that can be seen as holding them back than those who do not have such identities. All of this adds layers of complications to any attempts, including philosophers', to develop flourishing relationships. I return to many of these complexities in later chapters. For now, let me turn to one of Kant's illustrations of many of the main ideas concerning the complementarity of moralizable and non-moralizable aspects of human life outlined above, namely a story involving the tragic historical example of strong sexual, affectionate love having gone horribly wrong: Anne Boleyn and Henry VIII. This story also makes it easier to see how Kant distinguishes between rational, *human* beings and other imaginable rational beings such as angels.

10. Illustration: Anne Boleyn, Henry VIII, and Angels

Kant begins one of his illustrations of many of the above ideas by asking the question, "What, then, really is *pure* morality, by which as a touchstone one must test the moral content of every action?" Kant's first response is that it is "doubtful" that "only philosophers can make the decision of this question . . . for it is long since decided in common human reason, not indeed by abstract general formulae but by habitual use" (CPrR 5: 155; cf. GW 4: 411n). He then imagines how a 10-year-old would respond to a story about "an honest man whom someone wants to induce to join the calumni-ators of an innocent but otherwise powerless person (say, Anne Boleyn, accused by

Henry VIII of England)" (CPrR 5: 155). Kant then asks us to consider this honest person offered enormous advantages (gifts, rank, etc.) or subjected to the greatest losses (of friends and family betraying him, of material losses, etc.)—in the latter case a story so awful that it ends with the honest man wishing "that he had never lived to see the day that exposed him to such unutterable pain." If the honest man still "remains firm in his resolution to be truthful, without wavering or even doubting" (CPrR 5: 155), then the 10-year-old listener will respond by being

> raised step by step from mere approval to admiration, from that to amazement, and finally to the greatest veneration and a lively wish that he himself could be such a man (though certainly not in such circumstances); and yet virtue is here worth so much only because it costs so much, not because it brings any profit. All the admiration, and even the endeavor to resemble this character, here rests wholly on the purity of the moral principle, which can be clearly represented only if one removes from the incentive to action everything that people may reckon only to happiness. Thus morality must have more power over the human heart the more purely it is presented. From this it follows that if the law of morals and the image of holiness and virtue are to exercise any influence at all on our soul, they can do so only insofar as they are laid to heart in their purity as incentives, unmixed with any view to one's welfare, for it is in suffering that they show themselves most excellently. But that which, by being removed strengthens the effect of a moving force must also have been a hindrance. Consequently, every admixture of incentive taken from one's own happiness is a hindrance to providing the moral law with influence on the human heart. I maintain, further, that even in that admired action, if the motive from which it was done was esteem for one's duty, then it is just this respect for the law that straightaway has the greatest force on the mind of a spectator, and not, say, any pretension to inner magnanimity and most determinate influence on the mind but, when it is represented in the correct light of its inviolability, the most penetrating influence as well. (CPrR 5: 155f.)

For those familiar with *Groundwork*, the end of this example is reminiscent of how Kant there talks of good will. In particular, in *Groundwork*, Kant contends that even if disaster hits or if one is not by nature easily moved by sympathy, the good will "like a jewel would still shine by itself, as something that has its full worth in itself" (GW 4: 394); indeed, unfortunate circumstances and lack of natural dispositions would only make the good will "shine forth all the more brightly" (GW 4: 397). Similar to how it may be tempting to respond to these passages in *Groundwork* by thinking that Kant is advancing a position according to which the human moral ideal is not to be moved by any inclinations other than duty, it may be tempting to read the above passage from the second *Critique* as advocating that one should try to rid oneself of all non-moral incentives because removing them "strengthens the effect of a moving force that must also have been a hindrance" to practical reason's "influence on the human heart." I do not think this can plausibly be Kant's point in either place, however.

First, notice that Kant says nothing to suggest that it would be an emotionally healthy and morally good response to this story about "the honest man" to want to rid oneself of one's animality, including the social aspects of life enabled by this predisposition together with the predisposition to humanity. Kant is also not saying that the 10-year-old's response is to want to have to go through the honest man's pain, but rather that they want to become able to keep and to follow their own moral compass when faced with that sort of pain in the same way this honest man does. Second, Kant is arguing that being moved in this way shows us how morality gives us its own incentive, an incentive that inspires the highest regard possible in us. What impresses the child, then, is not that the honest man does not originally have a human life filled with friends, family, and material means, but that the honest man is able to face the challenges and hence is able to hold onto himself and what he (morally) stands for in a way that nothing and no one is able to take away from him even though everything he affectionately loves is taken away from him.

In *The Metaphysics of Morals*, Kant confirms the second point:

Virtue signifies a moral strength of the will. But this does not exhaust the concept; for such strength could also belong to a *holy* (superhuman) being, in whom no hindering impulses would impede the law of its will and who would thus gladly do everything in conformity with the law. Virtue is, therefore, the moral strength of a *human being's* will in fulfilling his duty, a moral *constraint* through his own lawgiving reason, insofar as this constitutes itself an authority *executing* the law.—Virtue itself, or possession of it, is not a duty (for then one would have to be put under obligation to duties); rather, it commands and accompanies its command with a moral constraint (a constraint possible in accordance with laws of inner freedom). But because this constraint is to be irresistible, strength is required, in a degree which we can assess only by the magnitude of the obstacles that the human being himself furnishes through his inclinations. The vices, the brood of dispositions opposing the law, are the monsters he has to fight. Accordingly this moral strength, as *courage* (*fortitude moralis*), also constitutes the greatest and the only true honor that a man can win in war and is, moreover, called *wisdom* in the strict sense, namely practical wisdom, since it makes the *final end* of his existence on earth its own end.—Only in its possession is he "free," "healthy," "rich," "a king," and so forth and can suffer no loss by chance or fate, since he is in possession of himself and the virtuous man cannot lose his virtue. (MM 6: 406)

I return to the idea of holy or superhuman beings below. For now, notice that if we read this in conjunction with the story of the honest man, Kant's suggestion is that what will impress the 10-year-old child is the moral strength (moral courage) displayed by the honest man in that he is able to hold onto himself and his commitment to truthfulness—and thereby his own dignity and human dignity in general—despite everyone around him failing to do so. The honest man is practically wise exactly in that he ultimately remains unmoved by anything other than what gives human beings dignity, which is to live in a way that is consistent with our being morally responsible animals. At the heart of this lies the honest man's commitment to truthfulness, which leads him to refuse to partake in an innocent person's unjust demise. Kant is saying that stories that seek to foster or strengthen our moral vital force—our moral strength to remain confident in doing the right thing because it is right—characteristically involve moments of (at least perceived) all-encompassing loss of human happiness for the hero(es), in the face of which they still do the right thing and thereby stay committed to what gives them and humans dignity. These features of the stories make apparent to us, Kant suggests, how "the law of morals and the image of holiness and virtue…influence our soul" as the protagonists "show themselves most excellently," and, so, move us from "approval" to "admiration" to "amazement" and "finally to the greatest veneration and a lively wish that" we ourselves could be such people. What we wish is that if push comes to shove, then like the honest man, we will feel it absolutely necessary to do what is right *just because* it is right. Naturally we wish that such awful situations never will occur in our lives, but if they do, given we are human begins with human lives, then we hope we feel as if there really is no other emotionally available choice to us and that this realization does not fill us with debilitating fear but that we will find ourselves able to work our way into a place where we can face our fears with calm resolution. As Kant explains elsewhere:

> Considered in its complete perfection, virtue is therefore represented not as if a human being possesses virtue but rather as if virtue possesses him; for in the former case it would look as if he still had a choice (for which he would need yet another virtue in order to choose virtue in preference to any other goods offered him).   (MM 6: 406)

Instead, "while virtue (in relation to human beings, not to the law) can be said here and there to be meritorious and to deserve to be rewarded, yet in itself, since it is its own end it must also be regarded as its own reward" (MM 6: 405f.).

Another way to make the same point is to return to Kant's mention of holy or superhuman beings (MM 6: 406, above). Notice that Kant does not say that the 10-year-old concludes from hearing this story that they wish that they were a holy being, such as an angel. Indeed, a plausible reading of Kant's take on angels (as we find them imagined in major religious texts) can help us see why Kant does not (and could not philosophically consistently) say such a thing. According to Kant, angels are possible beings only if we understand them in the following way: Angels (holy beings) do not have animality and though they have the social self-recognitional aspects of "humanity," they do not have the capacity to set ends of their own. Such beings, that is to say, cannot be viewed as having *personal* projects of animality, humanity, and personality, let alone the projects of integrating, transforming, and continuously seeking to become emotionally and morally better beings. Angels also act on maxims whose ends are set by the Divinity, namely to deliver various messages to humans from the Divinity. Such beings do not set their own ends grounded in their animality (since they do not have one) and thus cannot experience imperatives because they cannot experience moral feeling as internal calls for moral obligation or improvement; they do not have personality as revealed in a conscience.[20]

---

[20] For example, Kant says that "A will whose maxims necessarily harmonize with the laws of autonomy is a *holy*, absolutely good will. The dependence upon the principle of autonomy of a will that is not absolutely good (moral necessitation) is *obligation*. This, accordingly, cannot be attributed to a holy being. The objective necessity of an action from obligation is called *duty*" (GW 4: 439; cf. GW 4: 414, 439). Similarly, we find, "In the first case [of "human being" in contrast to "the infinite being as the supreme intelligence"]...the law has the form of an imperative, because in them, as rational beings, one can presuppose a *pure* will but, insofar as they are being affected by needs and sensible motives, not a *holy* will, that is, such a will as would not be capable of any maxim conflicting with the moral law" (CPrR 5: 32; cf. MM 6: 405). Along the same lines, we see that the concepts of "an *incentive*...an *interest*...and of a *maxim*...can be applied only to finite beings. For they all presuppose a limitation of the nature of a being, in that the subjective constitution of its choice does not of itself accord with the objective law of a practical reason; they presuppose a need to be impelled to activity by something because an obstacle is opposed to it. Thus they cannot be applied to the divine will" (CPrR 5: 79). Finally, regarding the saint, Kant says "human morality in its highest stage can still be nothing more than virtue, even if it be entirely pure (quite free from the influence of any incentive other than that of duty). In its highest stage it is an ideal...which is commonly personified by the *sage*" (MM 6: 383).

Interestingly, such a view of angels is consistent with the notion of fallen angels—similarly often invoked in religious imaginations—as beings who in virtue of their closeness to God develop a perverted desire to become God. But such a socially oriented desire, of say vanity or pride, arises not from animality, but from a social sense of self, which angels can have. After all, insofar as they do their jobs well, angels will be received by humans as voices of God that inspire feelings of awe and total subjection from humans. So, it is not conceptually impossible that they can obtain the desire to have this awe and subjection for themselves. Additionally, because angels do not have ends of their own, when fallen, their sole desire becomes to destroy God's will: They become "diabolic wills" in that the moral law becomes a perverted incentive to act; fallen angels seek to destroy the moral law (or, to destroy moral being). If this is the case, it furthermore makes sense that fallen angels are rather pathetic beings. Fallen angels do not create but only have destructive, derivative endeavors; they solely strive to destroy what God creates (being)—to turn being or things into non-being or nothing—and are solely driven by pride and vanity and so are lost in self-absorption and narcissism. Angels are therefore either fallen or not (rather than experiencing failure and continuously striving to do better).

In contrast, humans are not simply fallen or not—we can seek to improve our abilities to set ends, including by learning to handle social feelings such as vanity, admiration, and awe. As we will see in Chapter 3, Kant accordingly argues that "one can no more attribute passion to mere animals than to pure rational beings [including angels]" since neither one is capable of acting in the way that "presupposes a maxim on part of the subject, to act according to an end prescribed to him by his inclination" and yet that requires acting on "a *constant* principle with respect to its object" (A 7: 266). Non-human animals do not act on maxims in ways that require reflective self-consciousness, whereas angels have neither an animality nor personal ventures, and so do not experience morality as an imperative (an ought) in relation to how they go about realizing themselves. Only human beings have a nature that requires us to seek to realize our animality such that it is reconcilable with our capacities for rational end-setting (set ends of our own) and social sense of self as well as moral responsibility (personality). Hence, too, in contrast to an angel, a human being cannot be thought capable of being motivated to destroy the moral law, which is why Kant says, "one cannot rightly say that the malice of this human being is a quality of his character; for then it would be diabolic. The human being, however, never *sanctions* the evil in himself, and so there is actually no malice from principles; but only from the forsaking of them" (A 7: 293f.). This, then, is why human beings who lose their way the most radically—and develop "depraved hearts"—are always self-deceived when they act: they necessarily do bad under the guise of the good.

Notice that the above can explain too why humans need privacy and angels do not: again, angels are not *embodied* social beings with emotions tied to an animality, with lives of their own to live, and with needs for private spheres in which they live and can learn to do better, including together with their loved ones. It follows from this that one way in which we humans lose our way is by mistaking our nature with that of angels, in which case we may wrongly believe that, like angels, we do not need privacy. We, human beings, are embodied social persons who strive to live our lives—which is inseparable from striving to mature and to flourish as the particular beings we are—on our own and together with others, and privacy is constitutive of doing this. We see both the failure to realize that we are not angels and our need for privacy in some of the self-destructive and damaging behaviors on social media, behaviors that reveal an inability to distinguish between what is inherently personal and what is sharable in the social world.[21]

To illustrate further, a major challenge for humans who experience much fame and adoration (including, e.g., great musicians, religious leaders, novelists, athletes, singers, and surely also philosophers and other academics) is to avoid the temptation to try to live life as an angel, let alone a fallen angel. That is, we should endeavor to develop our creative abilities as an integrated part of a productive human life and not to use our ability to please a crowd as a rationalized means of seeking the experience captured by the concept of the Divine, namely the total subjection and awe of devoted admirers. This is similarly important for those whose jobs go along with assisting others in their efforts at becoming better, such as teachers and supervisors of students, therapists, religious leaders, etc. As the histories of all the related institutions show, it is inherently tempting for those who are in such mentoring positions to misuse their standing and, instead of assisting their students, patients, devotees, etc., in their efforts to become better at being who they are, to yield to the temptation to exert power over them by seeking to make them into adoring, dependent beings who function only to make the mentor feel important, powerful, smart, and/or wise.

The challenge for human beings, then, is to stay grounded in our own personal lives and to relate to our creative endeavors with the intensity they require in the moment without losing sight of our doings as *personal* projects—something angels cannot do. Indeed, humans have something that neither angels nor God have, and of which angels can be seen as envious, namely personal ventures grounded in animality.[22] It is in these efforts—of survival, of sexuality, and of affectionate love—that we get to experience some of our greatest joys, joys that angels and the Divine cannot have and that make sense of our human intuition that even if our "rational self" can be imagined to survive death, a purely rational existence after death would be irremediably boring or empty as compared to a full human life. In sum, then, human beings are embodied, social persons who strive to mature emotionally and morally and to flourish as the particular beings we are on our own (as Immanuel, as Joseph) and together with others (as Immanuel *and* Joseph). It is because all of this is so important to us—indeed, part of what makes a human life *human* rather than

---

[21] I return to issues of privacy in more depth in Chapter 5, but see also (Varden 2020c).

[22] This may be one reason the myths of some religions include gods that have human characteristics and personal enterprises that reach into lives of humans, and it may be one factor explaining the Jewish, Christian, and Muslim religious stories of Moses, Jesus, and Muhammad. These stories of gods embodying strong human emotions or of God reaching out to humans through prophets can help us engage our emotional and moral efforts at self- and world-improvement. Some of the ways they can do this are by comforting us through providing supernatural explanations for the difficulties we face (not even the gods are able to control their emotions), or by having us believe in a god who is called upon to intervene in our lives to help us preserve our faith in the world and in our own goodness despite all the evidence to the contrary, including our own failures. Also, the monotheistic religions' stories can be seen as powerful to many because they conceive of God as a being that understands and cares for each person's *personal* projects, struggles, and well-being even though God does not have such projects of its own and, so, lacks first-personal experience of them.

merely *rational*—that the 10-year-old child sincerely wishes that they would never have to experience anything like what the honest man has to experience even though they do wish that if they were to be so unlucky, they would be able to hold onto acting in a way that they can justify by means of capacities for moral responsibility in the way the honest man does.

11. Concluding Remarks

Let us now sum up some of what we have said above by drawing some implications only with regard to sexual and/or affectionately loving relations. Focusing on sexual and affectionate love, the above approach to human nature, self-development, morality, and friendship concludes a basic principle never to engage in non-consensual sex or non-consensual affectionate love with anyone. Non-consensual sex and affection are deeply disrespectful and destructive ways of relating to others. Correspondingly, they are inconsistent with self-respect and are self-destructive. Also, on this position, in flourishing lives, each person's challenge is to develop their ability to be an affectionately loving, sexual being in richer ways and as part of a complex life that they can also own morally. In subsequent chapters I argue that opportunities for personal development are inconsistent with socially and/or legally banning LGBTQIA or polyamorous or polysexual ways of life. Again, for some, self-development comes with growing as part of ongoing intimate relationships—whether monogamous or polyamorous—and for others, it requires more limited kinds of engagements and relationships with people (with different kinds of expectations). On this approach, there is also much space for accepting that often there is pain involved in growth. One reason is that growth sometimes requires facing and divesting ourselves of ingrained pathologies based on fear and on past bad behavior (one's own and that of others). Another reason is that growth and new sexual, affectionately loving connections and encounters sometimes strike us as things we do not immediately or unambiguously want (since if they did, we would already have those ways of being—of sexually and/or affectionately loving—as integrated parts of our lives). And indeed, some people pose a greater challenge to us than others: because loving them in an ongoing way that is true to (rather than a betrayal of) who we are, true to the grounding connection between us, *and* loving in a way that can be integrated in both persons' lives in good ways is possible only if one is able to learn something new, which can be difficult. And yet, walking away comes with an incalculable loss too. As a result, sometimes life can be lived well only if one is willing to give up one's former vision of what a good, whole integrated life looks like and if one trusts oneself, the other(s), and the experience itself to be transformable in a way that is true and constitutive of a (yet) better, even if more complex life.

As we grow emotionally (morally and non-morally), we develop our animality and our social, personal sense of self through exploring new associations, new abstract concepts, new uses of aesthetic and teleological imagination in ways that are consistent with who we are, with who we meet (who they are), with what each of us can own morally, and with the changing situations in which we find ourselves. And none of this is possible and none of it can be done better unless we are willing to be truthful about who we are—including about the fact that we are continuous works in progress. This might mean that some people find that they cannot have relationships with particular others as it is too hurtful or insufficiently satisfying in some important affectionate and/or sexual way (and so too limiting or even damaging) for reasons that cannot be overcome through personal work by either party or both. As Herman says, being and growing together should neither be too hard nor too easy—and we are likely sometimes to make it too hard and sometimes to make it too easy.

Finally, given the challenges stemming from both immaturities and self-deception, on this position it is also not surprising to learn that it is common for people not to start the undertaking of getting their sexual and affectionately loving selves into a truly integrated, flourishing, exciting gear until they are in their 30s, and most do not start to succeed more reliably until they are in their 40s. After all, as Kant tells us, the choice to live life truthfully is typically not made until one is in one's 30s (if at all), whereas truthfulness about who one is and what one does (having moral character) tends not to be more reliably realized until one is in one's 40s (again, if at all). To make matters worse, being truthful with people—even those we trust—gives them something they can use as a weapon against us. As Kant points out in his *Lectures on Ethics*, sharing truthfully can be dangerous as it can be taken advantage of by people who yield to the temptation to wrong us (LE 27: 448). Thus, although nothing is more meaningful than to dare to be who one is and to develop oneself in truthful, emotionally and morally maturing ways, both on one's own and together with others, doing so is among the most difficult things there is.

Now that I have laid out central ideas in Kant's theory of human nature, in Chapters 2-4, I first show how Kant employed these ideas in his treatment of sex, love, and gender. I then suggest how they can be employed somewhat differently to better capture our challenges, failures, and successes in striving to make sex, love, and gender constitutive parts of our human lives and being.

2

Kant and Women

Introduction

There is a glaring peculiarity in Kant's writings on women. On the one hand, he frequently appears to affirm the kind of view about women that has provoked much justified scorn from feminists, namely that the "nature" of woman prevents her (mysteriously) from being equal to man. Woman's nature is depicted as caring, nurturing, and attuned to the beautiful. In contrast, man's physicality and distinctively rational reasoning powers draw him towards the sublime. Consequently, Kant seems to be saying, woman is not capable of practical reasoning and moral responsibility (the moral ought) and should therefore restrict her activities to homemaking and the domestic sphere. In contrast, since man is capable of practical reasoning and moral responsibility, he should strive to engage in the public sphere as a scholar. This apparent position of Kant's also seems reflected in his assignation of men to the legal-political head of society and the family—active citizens who can participate fully in public life—and of women to the category of "passive" citizenship—citizens incapable of voting and holding public office, and so not of participating fully in public life.

On the other hand, Kant sometimes appears to say that woman ought to strive towards full autonomy ("majority"), that she is to be viewed as man's equal in the home, and that she should not be hindered in becoming equal to man, including by achieving active citizenship. And, indeed, this is the kind of position one would expect from Kant. Kant's *moral* philosophy is a theory of freedom in that it views the single-most important moral feature of human beings as their capacity to set and pursue ends of their own, subject only to and motivated by their own practical reason; having this capacity is what gives human beings dignity (unconditional value). The idea is that if all people regulate their actions by their practical reason, the constitutive principle of which is Kant's well-known "Categorical Imperative," human beings can respectfully coexist—in all their diversity—both together and as individuals. Furthermore, insofar as they are able to use their practical reason in this way, human beings have their actions morally imputed to them. Practical reason gives human beings this autonomy, which is also why they are regarded as both persons and citizens; they can and should be held morally (both ethically and legally) responsible for their actions. And anyone who is capable of such moral responsibility should strive to become self-governing in the all-inclusive sense: as a person responsible for their personal life and as a citizen responsible for the laws regulating their interactions with others. On such an account, if woman (like man) has the capacity to govern herself by her practical reason, she cannot, in principle, be regarded as

Sex, Love, and Gender: A Kantian Theory. Helga Varden, Oxford University Press (2020). © Helga Varden.
DOI: 10.1093/oso/9780198812838.001.0001

unequal to man. It does not even seem coherent to include within a moral theory of *freedom* an argument according to which one's "nature" determines any particular ends that one ought to pursue. A free person cannot be morally (virtuously or rightfully) forced to set and pursue any particular ends—"natural" or otherwise— which means that no one may justifiably impose any such boundaries on another person's choices. On such an account of morality as freedom, the only justifiable restrictions that we can coercively impose on one another's choices when interacting are those that come from freedom itself; the only justifiable, coercive restrictions are those that make reciprocal freedom under law possible in the first place (The Universal Principle of Right).

Historically, when interpreters have not simply disregarded Kant's views on woman as, at best, an embarrassing part of his scholarship, the most prominent response has been to argue that Kant held the former view, namely, that woman's nature prevents her from being man's moral equal.[1] And since that view is in tension with his theory of freedom, such interpretations contend that the texts reveal the depth of Kant's sexist and misogynist prejudices; Kant's work is seen as representing yet another example of the sexism prevalent in the Western philosophical canon. In contrast, interpreters more sympathetic to Kant's philosophical project as a whole typically argue that his sexist views should be set aside, because his overall moral philosophy is feminist friendly and, when it comes to the issue of woman and women's rights in particular, Kant's philosophy was ahead of Kant himself. Marcia Baron (in Schott 1997) captures this type of interpretation well when she says,

I do think that Kant's theory was *much* more progressive than he was. I deplore much of what he wrote regarding women but I do not think that it impugns his theory. I also think that feminists have reason to look favorably on his moral theory, principally because of its egalitarianism.   (147)[2]

---

[1]   Value-conservative thinkers like John Finnis (1994) hold that Kant's anthropological view of men and women is best understood as a moral ideal. Taking on and directly refuting Finnis's philosophical argument is not my concern here; this has already been done many times over. For a conclusive Kantian refutation, see Cheshire Calhoun (2000). Rather, my point below is that what Finnis is doing—viewing contingent ideals based on anthropological assumptions and observations as identifying the moral ideas of freedom (ethics or right)—is exactly the philosophical mistake that Kant warns us against.

[2]   Baron's paper is found in Schott's (1997) anthology *Feminist Interpretations of Kant*. As a whole, this collection of papers illustrates well the way in which most of the secondary literature concerning Kant on women breaks into two camps. All of the papers are more or less condemnatory of Kant's treatment of women, but those written by philosophers drawn to Kant's philosophy for other reasons, like Marcia Baron and Holly L. Wilson, still try to show that Kant's philosophical position (just not Kant himself) is feminist friendly. Commentaries written on Kant by non-Kantians in this anthology, such as those by Schott, Hannelore, and Schroeder, are more similar to the arguments presented by Genevieve Lloyd's (1993) *Man of Reason: "Male" and "Female" in Western Philosophy* or those of Irving Singer's (2000) "The Morality of Sex: Contra Kant." This type of interpretation typically does not take the second, constructive step of showing how Kant's philosophy (even if not Kant himself) can empower the feminist cause. Notice, too, that Pauline Kleingeld (1993) shares my interest in not simply setting aside Kant's view of man and woman. She differentiates the three common approaches to Kant on this issue, namely a conservative one (like Finnis) and the two feminist approaches mentioned above. A main difference between Kleingeld's and my interpretation is my proposal that Kant's conception captures quite well the traditional ideal of woman when understood as a powerful gender. For this reason, Kant's conception of woman is also not what Thomas E. Hill, Jr. (1991) in his paper on the deferential wife calls "a submissive person." Another

More recently, some Kant scholars have taken these more positive readings of Kant a step further by challenging core elements of the negative readings.[3]

This chapter supports these recent, more positive readings of Kant in maintaining that Kant never denies that woman is morally (ethically and legally) responsible for her actions. In addition, I argue that Kant's philosophy was not ahead of Kant here, and that it is not internally incoherent in the way even the most recent more positive interpretations worry it is. The chapter takes three steps beyond the current positive readings: first, in addition to arguing, as does Mari Mikkola, that what Kant was worried about was not woman's ability to be morally responsible for her actions (he never doubted that), I propose that what Kant was uncertain about was her ability to partake in public reason (understood as the legal-political reasoning constitutive of the public institutions as well as scholarly work); second, by showing how Kant uses the philosophical ideas presented in the previous chapter regarding human nature when he analyzes the traditional distinction between "man" and "woman," I provide a different, normative interpretation of woman's nature than do existing interpretations; and, third, I argue that Kant's legal-political account always only accommodates his normative, philosophical anthropological account of woman's nature and never denies woman the right to work herself into an active condition. Contrary to the available interpretations, therefore, I argue that Kant's conception of woman is more complex than they propose and that despite his mistakes and limitations, Kant makes some philosophically interesting moves in his account. Especially interesting is Kant's suggestion that the concept of woman should be understood in light of a normative, teleological-aesthetic theory of human nature and, consequently, his suggestion that our sexual, affectionately loving, and gendered being should be understood as profoundly informed also by our importantly unreflective embodied, social natures and not simply as spheres analyzable through morality (freedom) and empirical science (deterministically understood).

It is true that Kant believes the traditional man-woman distinction is unlikely to disappear; in his view, deep-seated reasons have made this distinction historically prevalent. As mentioned, what he is worried about is not whether or not women can be morally (ethically and legally) responsible for their actions—surely they can—but whether or not they can be scholars and active citizens. Indeed, it is because Kant deems it possible that the traditional ideal captures something accurate about woman's nature that he accommodates it in his legal-political philosophy by, for

---

difference is that I argue, in contrast to Kleingeld, that Kant does not only mean "men" when he discusses "humans" or "persons" in his moral writings.

[3] See, for example, Helga Varden (2007, 2012); Linda Papadaki (2010); Mari Mikkola (2011); and Carol Hay (2013). The main difference between this chapter and all of these accounts concerns the way in which it interprets Kant's theory of human nature as normative and hence as doing independent philosophical work with regard to capturing sex, love, and gender in his overall practical philosophy, that is, in addition to concerns that can be captured if one reads all Kant's work through the bifocal lenses of the rational (moral freedom) and the scientifically empirical. Another, related difference concerns the way in which I suggest that Kant's moral works accommodate these normative concerns; how, as we see below and also in later chapters, he envisions his moral writings to accommodate his moral (philosophical) anthropology. For a recent paper that also pays special attention to the teleological nature of Kant's account of gender, but comes to almost exactly opposite interpretive and philosophical conclusions, see Inder S. Marwah (2013).

example, assigning her to the category of "passive" citizenship. *But*, already in his earliest writings, Kant expresses discomfort and skepticism with the way he and the traditional gender ideals associate the capacity for active, public (scholarly and political) life (active citizenship) with the male gender only. And Kant never proposes the traditional normative ideals *as* the moral ideal; he rejects the idea that such a philosophical, or what he calls "moral" anthropological, account can establish the moral framework for free beings. This is why Kant's own writings on women are more consistent with his moral theory than is commonly thought; he never loses sight of the place his moral anthropological account of women should have within his freedom account of persons and citizens—indeed, this is why his moral texts on freedom are written in the gender-neutral language. It is also why Kant clarifies in The Doctrine of Right that although his legal-political philosophy can and should accommodate (also) his moral anthropological account of women, he still maintains that all citizens must have the right to work themselves into an active condition. And it is why Kant in his essay "What Is Enlightenment?" encourages *everyone*, including women, to use their reason autonomously and try not to capitulate under the pressure of those who discourage them from developing their reason to the fullest. Here he additionally emphasizes that attempts to prevent or discourage others from developing their reason are morally wrong.

To make my case, I begin by exploring (in section 1: "Kant on the Character of the Woman") the account Kant gives of the traditional genders in *Anthropology from a Pragmatic Point of View* (hereafter: *Anthropology*). I first explain how Kant's theory of traditional gender in *Anthropology* is informed by his broader theory of human nature as outlined in the previous chapter and as found in *Religion*. Next, I outline Kant's theory of gender in more detail before contrasting some important features of it with that of Simone de Beauvoir, whose writings on the traditional genders, like Kant's, was greatly influenced by Jean-Jacques Rousseau. I finish this section by considering some much quoted (and rather infamous) passages of Kant's that appear to undercut my proposed reading. In the subsequent section (section 2: "Kant on the Liberated Woman"), I explain how Kant's writings on legal-political freedom both make space for his conception of the traditional ideals of gender *and* defend the possibility of a somewhat different future regarding women's public participation, specifically once conditions of freedom have become better understood and established. I argue that although some things certainly went wrong in Kant's own account, we may want to explore further Kant's general, philosophical suggestion that morality must accommodate human nature (and not the other way around) by making space for related concerns of moral psychology and moral anthropology.

Finally, although my objective in this chapter is not to defend Kant's actual or a revised Kantian account of human sex, love, and gender, after pointing out obvious problems in Kant's own account, I conclude by suggesting that we might also want to engage more seriously Kant's general suggestion that human sex, love, and gender is difficult to capture without an appeal to embodied, social aspects of human nature. To capture sexual or gender identity or sexual orientation, for example, it seems we need to appreciate how aspects of our embodied, social natures requires appealing to normative, teleological, and aesthetic judgments, which in turn yields an account that can complement the empirical perspectives of science and the moral perspectives of freedom. It seems philosophically important to investigate the possibility that doing so increases our ability to understand human diverse ways of being sexual, affectionately loving, and gendered. We should not, in other words, dismiss too quickly Kant's suggestion that a better account of sex, love, and gender requires a normative perspective that does philosophical work different from, yet complementary to, what morality (freedom) and empirical science (scientific causality analyses) can give us. This sets the stage for Chapter 3—"Kant on Sex. Reconsidered"—where I argue that Kant does indeed provide us with the philosophical resources we need to critique more adequately than Kant did the human phenomena of sexual love, sexual or gendered identity, and sexual orientation.

1. Kant on the Character of the Woman

The interpretive consensus is that in order to establish Kant's actual view on any issue, we must attend carefully not only to which work Kant makes his statements in, but also to the overall point he is trying to make in the relevant sections of the texts. Employing this method to establish Kant's views on women is neither radical nor revolutionary, but it proves equally fruitful: an interesting pattern emerges when we discern whether Kant makes his claims about women within the context of his moral works on freedom or in his other normative works. Kant's sexist remarks predominantly occur *not* in his moral works on freedom, but rather in the other (less popular) works, and especially in his historical, anthropological, aesthetic, and religious writings. Below I first want to show how *Anthropology's* (1798) account of the traditional genders is more easily understood when seen in the context of Kant's 1793 account of human nature in *Religion*. I then explore Kant's distinction between the traditional ideals regarding woman and man in more detail before closing by attending to some interpretive puzzles. This sets the stage for section 2, which shows that Kant does no more than accommodate his normative account of gender in his moral works on freedom.

1.1 Kant on the Character of the Sexes

To appreciate the nature of Kant's discussion of women in *Anthropology*, it is important to establish Kant's overall aim in it. I take it as uncontroversial that any anthropology strives to elucidate the social meaning contained in people's ordinary interactions. Clearly, Kant has this objective too when he investigates the "character" of the sexes. But he is more ambitious than this; he wants to develop a "moral anthropology" (MM 6: 217). Kant provides his most general explanation of the concept of character he has in mind when he discusses the character of nations. Here he explains that the point is to present nations "as they are now, in some examples, and, as far as possible, systematically" (A 7: 312). Explaining something's character, then, is taken not only to require describing it in its current condition, but also to say as much as possible about the principles informing its permanence across time and space—and so resisting the temptation of too quickly appealing to social conditioning to do the explanatory work (A 7: 312). We furthermore get a clearer sense of his overall approach to the issue of the traditional genders, including which principles he views as central to their explanation, by appreciating how Kant's general account of human nature informs his analysis. As we will see shortly, the way in which Kant's full theory of human nature informs his account of the genders is important to capture why he does not take himself simply to be making empirical observations (possibly in combination with scientific explanations). Instead, his goal is to capture how gender inherently concerns the good development of our embodied, social natures, where the goodness involved is seen as something distinct from, yet enabling of, freedom and as involving a normative, teleological-aesthetic understanding of ourselves.

Kant's theory of human nature, and especially those aspects needed to understand his account of gender, is delineated in *Religion*: the distinction between three predispositions viewed as comprising one, overall original predisposition to good in human nature as well as the propensity to evil. Because I sketched these accounts of Kant's in the previous chapter, let me merely remind us of some of the key points here as well as add some supplementary ideas not mentioned there. The first predisposition—to "animality"—is taken to capture our natural drive to self-preservation, to have sex, and to seek affectionate community with others. The second predisposition—to "humanity"—is about both rational end-setting (acting on universalizable maxims) and a social sense of self enabled by comparative uses of reason. This predisposition enables both the setting of our own ends rationally and ideally a type of self-love that may be called "reciprocal" love as it is accompanied by the inclination *"to gain worth in the opinion of others*, originally, of course, merely *equal worth"* (R 6: 27) and an incentive to culture (R 6: 27). If we realize these two natural predispositions—animality and humanity—together and in a good way, then, not only will we be able to develop societies where healthy competition drives culture and progress, but we will find ourselves in a condition where reciprocal love among emotionally healthy, grounded people is realizable. There is therefore nothing inherently wrong with being in the world with these dispositions, even though they are importantly unreflective and operate on the affectionate, playful, and/or non-moral emotional level. Indeed, upon reflection, there is a moral push to have confidence in these partially unreflective ways of being as long as they operate well; after all, they ground us and are central to giving our personal lives meaning.

On the other hand, because these two natural predispositions are accompanied by desires and inclinations and since we have the capacity to choose, it is always tempting not to realize them in good ways—we have a propensity to evil—which is why we find ourselves in interactions characterized by certain kinds of vices. For example, the first predisposition ("animality") is associated with vices like gluttony, since we can choose to set the end of maximizing pleasure in the moment rather than properly tend to when, for example, we feel that pleasureable "full" feeling (and, so, stop eating). Similarly, trailing the second predisposition ("humanity"), we find vices like jealousy, rivalry, envy, and joy in the misfortune of others (Schadenfreude) because from the inclination to be valued as an equal "grows gradually an unjust desire to acquire superiority for oneself over others"—to dominate or have power over them (R 6: 27). We are, in other words, easily tempted to act in ways (and develop inclinations) that make us feel powerful in relation to others rather than ensuring that our emotions track equal worth. And good and not good ways of being are determined not only by whether or not these ways really are good for human beings (in the sense of comprising profound physical and emotional (unreflective)—embodied—contentment), but also by whether or not they are affirmable upon reflection by beings who have capacities of self-reflective consciousness and reasoning through abstract concepts and, so, freedom. Our susceptibility to act as motivated by considerations also from the point of view of reflection (freedom), we remember from Chapter 1, is enabled by what Kant calls the "third predisposition to good in nature," namely "personality."

The predisposition to personality concerns our susceptibility to morality's commands (the commands of freedom), or what Kant calls "moral feeling." Moral feeling is a susceptibility to want to act as motivated by thinking *about* whether or not what one is doing is right, that is, the ability to do what is right (follow The Categorical Imperative, obeying our practical reason) *just because* doing so is the right thing to do (act from duty). Thus, personality enables us to act upon or in response to the behavior connected with the first two (animality and humanity): when something we are doing is striking us as morally troubling, we can consider it from a reflective point of view (think about whether what we are doing is respectful to ourselves and each other as free beings capable of setting and pursuing ends of our own and/or furthering who we are in good ways), and we can act as motivated by this reflection (we can incorporate this motivation into our maxim). And, as we saw in the previous chapter, the kinds of self-love enabled by the first two predispositions are "natural and active in us even prior to the moral law," whereas the kind of self-love enabled by the third cannot exist without the moral law (practical reason), which is why it is this third kind that is internally related to moral responsibility (CPrR 5: 73). Furthermore, when we restrict our natural or social inclinations in the ways commanded by our practical reason—we do something just because it is the right thing to do—then we act out of *rational self-love* (rather than simply in conformity with rational self-love) (CPrR 5: 73). Finally, even though the first two predispositions, which concern our basic natural affective and social natures, cannot be "eradicated," they can, as mentioned above, be used and habituated in bad ways. In contrast, the third predisposition, which enables rational self-love, cannot be corrupted, since it provides an incentive to act simply as practical reason commands (R 6: 28).

That Kant has this view of human nature explains why he emphasizes, in *Anthropology*, that to realize our sexual, loving, gendered natures as men and women is not to realize morality as such; sexuality, affectionate love, and gender primarily concern (in the sense of being enabled by) the first two predispositions (animality and humanity) and not the third (personality). This is why Kant instead argues that our sexual, affectionate loving, gendered (social) natures are normative (valuable), rather than strictly empirical or moral. And in a certain developmental sense they are prior to morality in that developing our embodied social natures prepares us for morality—individually and as societies. The way the traditional genders treat each other when they realize their sexual, loving, gendered natures well together does not serve to teach each other morality, he argues, but instead to teach each other "moral decency, which is the preparation for morality and its recommendation" (A 7: 306). Kant also claims that women play an especially important role in preparing both genders for morality: the woman is the *primus motor* by virtue of her superior social skills, such as her speech, charm, gentleness, and courtesy (A 7: 306). In some ways, therefore, Kant affirms the old feminist joke about why God created man first, since it is always important to make a sketch before you set out to make the real thing: Woman has a more complex social character because of her more complex natural function, and consequently it is not surprising that "the provision of nature put more art into the organization of the female part than of the male" (A 7: 303). And because woman's nature is the more complex one, Kant explains, his focus in *Anthropology* is on her (A 7: 303).

Further evidence for reading Kant's theory of the traditional genders in *Anthropology* together with his threefold analysis of the predisposition to good in human nature in *Religion* is found in the final section on the "Character of the Species" in *Anthropology*. Here Kant says,

Among the living *inhabitants of the earth* the human being is markedly distinguished from all other living beings by his *technical* predisposition for manipulating things (mechanically joined with consciousness), by his *pragmatic* predisposition (to use other human beings skillfully for his purposes), and by the *moral* predisposition in his being (to treat himself and others according to the principle of freedom under laws). And any one of these three levels can by itself alone already distinguish the human being characteristically as opposed to the other inhabitants of the earth.   (A 7: 322; cf. 328)

It makes good sense to view Kant's three distinctions here in *Anthropology* as corresponding to the threefold predisposition to good in human nature outlined in *Religion*, that is, to view them as connected, respectively, to the predispositions to animality and humanity (the two, which, if realized well together, enables "moral decency"), and personality (which, if realized, enables "morality"). The interpretive plausibility of doing this is bolstered by Kant's elaboration on the pragmatic disposition:

The pragmatic predisposition to become civilized through culture, particularly through the cultivation of social qualities, and the natural tendency of his species in social relations to come out of the crudity of mere personal force and to become well-mannered (if not yet moral) being destined for concord, is now a higher step.   (R 7: 323)

This view parallels Kant's description of the predisposition to humanity in *Religion*, the realization of which presupposes also realizing the predisposition to animality. In addition, just as developing the natural, social predispositions (animality and humanity) is insufficient for morality (since developing morality requires us to develop the predisposition to personality too), developing the technical and pragmatic predispositions is insufficient for morality, but they are sufficient for moving us out of a crude state of nature characterized by "personal force" and become social (well-mannered), or for establishing moral decency. Realizing animality and humanity is therefore not to realize morality as such, but realizing them is a normative achievement (moral decency), and when realized well, they are directed and pushing towards morality (as freedom).[4]

---

[4] Observe also how Kant explains that developing the pragmatic disposition requires learning how to use other persons skillfully; it necessarily involves social skills (including understanding how one is seen by others). Notice too that Kant emphasizes that progress with regard to the pragmatic disposition occurs in the species as a whole over the course of generations—it is not something that one individual can realize

Notice, too, in this section (of *Anthropology*) Kant stresses that the highest disposition is the moral disposition, which is constitutive of the human being and that insofar as we are capable of "personality" (moral responsibility for our actions) we are always aware of it, regardless of historical circumstances. A human being is, Kant explains,

a being endowed with the power of practical reason and consciousness of freedom of his power of choice (a person) [who] sees themself[5] in this consciousness, even in the midst of the darkest representations, subject to a law of duty and to the feeling (which is then called moral feeling) that justice or injustice is done to them or, by them, to others. Now this in itself is already the *intelligible* character of humanity as such, and in this respect the human being is *good* according to their dispositions (good by nature).   (A 7: 324)

To realize the first two historical stages (the technical and the pragmatic conditions) in a society, then, is not to realize the human *moral* ideal. Realizing them well is a process by which individuals and societies develop from barbaric conditions to more cultured or civilized ways of life, to conditions of moral decency. Yet even in these less free conditions (the technical and pragmatic conditions), people know and feel when they are being wronged (when their freedom is disrespected) and when they are wronging others (disrespecting others' freedom). And Kant wants to show that as individuals and societies become more flourishing, their social interactions become increasingly geared towards freedom—what is good and what is right line up.

Correspondingly, Kant views the traditional gender ideals as constitutive parts of the process towards civilization because he views civilized societies as precursors to free societies. This implies, though, that to realize the traditional gender ideals is not thereby to realize a free society. In traditional (or "pragmatic") societies there is moral feeling (recognition of the moral ought), but freedom has not become a pervasive and prominent part of managing and living human life well. People have not come to reflect upon or become used to reason in terms of freedom as they organize their lives and build their legal-political institutions.[6] According to Kant, and as we will see more clearly below, this freedom-stage of human development did not really begin until the Enlightenment. Before that, societies were predominantly either barbaric (characterized by brute force) *or* pragmatic (morally decent), even though human beings have always been fundamentally oriented toward, or susceptible to the moral ought (freedom's commands). Insofar as these societies were in the pragmatic condition, the prominent norms for interaction came from culture and

---

alone (A 7: 322). Understanding our pragmatic disposition requires us to investigate our species from the point of view of nature, considered teleologically. From this point of view, it is reasonable to think that we develop and progress in culture and civilization *as a species*, not as particular individuals. This means that appreciation of and respect for women cannot be realized by one individual acting alone; this is something that people must develop together. And to do so, they must first develop culture and civilized interaction (moral decency), as those are precursors to establishing conditions of freedom. Moreover, if people use their pragmatic skills only to control and destroy each other, then there obviously is no progress of culture or civilization occurring in that society as it thereby degenerated into a barbaric condition where people have yielded to inclinations accompanying the predisposition to humanity, specifically, the inclination to take pleasure in dominating others.

[5] I have changed Gregor's translation here into a gender neutral one.
[6] For more on how this point is related to Kant's idea of public reason, see Chapter 7.

moral decency (freedom's precursor). This does not mean that realizing oneself in a free way requires eschewing tradition, but it does require understanding that the source of the moral *justification* for traditions is, ultimately, respect for everyone's freedom; after all, traditions concern one's natural, embodied sociality (realizing the predispositions to animality and humanity) the healthy realization of which points *towards* freedom (realizing the predisposition to personality). Having sketched Kant's general approach in *Anthropology*, let me turn to his account of the two traditional genders in some more detail.

1.2 Kant on the Complementarity of the Man's and the Woman's Gender Ideals

Kant begins his argument in *Anthropology* by discussing the first and second preconditions to good in human nature (animality and humanity) as it relates to sexual unions. As expected in light of the discussion of the *Religion* account of human nature above, Kant first emphasizes that humans are not only rational beings who set and pursue ends of their own responsibly, but are also affective, embodied social beings with a sexual drive. Additionally, in order to reconcile their sexual end of preserving their species with their rational and social, affectionate being, humans create a domestic union, a home (A 7: 303). Sharing a home—a personal life—in this intimate, including sexual, way feels profoundly good to beings like us. It does so not only because it is accompanied by regular satisfaction of our sexual desires with someone we find sexually attractive, but it is done together with another who is likewise oriented towards us, including affectionately and emotionally. Accordingly, on this approach, the home is a context that, at its best, enables the satisfaction of these desires in the challenging, open, and vulnerable way humans can experience them at their fullest—and feel profoundly affirmed, good, and safe (rather than unappreciated, uneasy, and at risk) as who we are when being so emotionally oriented towards another. In these ways, the shared home is taken to enable the realization of the predispositions to animality and humanity in good ways.

Kant proceeds by discussing a particular challenge that trails the second precondition to good (to humanity), namely, the problem of possible, endless competition between the two persons who create a home—one personal space—together. Kant argues that the home of two rational persons must be organized so that each adult is "superior in a different way." Nothing productive results when two adults both try to take charge of every sphere of their shared domestic life, since then "self-love produces nothing but squabbling" (A 7: 303). This introduces the question: in which ways is each of the genders superior with regard to the other? Here, too, Kant's response arises from his view that our sexual natures must be understood in light of our species' two natural, social predispositions: animality and humanity. Regarding animality, Kant argues that because woman carries the offspring in her womb, she is rendered more vulnerable, and so naturally fears physical danger more than man does. Moreover, since the work of maintaining a safe home must be divided between the two adults, and only the woman gets pregnant, the man bears the main responsibility for physically providing for and protecting the home. Woman's superiority, in contrast, arises from being the one charged with the daily running of the home; she is responsible for cultivating in the home a social environment that grounds the family, or enables it to live well and thrive. This is why the woman is in charge of ensuring that the children healthily develop their natural affective, social natures in the home and the supporting social world surrounding it (A 7: 303, 306).

What about the second predisposition, to humanity? Again, once we read the more specific argument concerning women in *Anthropology* together with the broader argument concerning our competitive inclinations in *Religion*, then it is no longer surprising to find Kant asserting in *Anthropology* that what really needs explanation is *not* that everyone has an inclination to dominate (since that is the tempting, bad inclination trailing the predisposition to humanity).[7] Rather, he argues, what is puzzling is a specific element in the interaction between the genders, namely, that "[w]oman wants to dominate, man to be dominated" (A 7: 306).[8] To put the challenge back into the language of the second predisposition to the good of *Religion*, the problem is to see how the cohabitation between man and woman can be realized such that it leads not to endless competition between them, but to reciprocal love and "equal worth." And to explain this in relation to the genders, Kant argues in *Anthropology*, one must explain how man can want to be dominated by woman in their shared home.

To explain this Kant suggests not only that the couple cannot endlessly compete in the home as that is self-destructive (for reasons given above), but also that this possibility of peaceful co-habituation is partially enabled by the inherent connections between the female and the beautiful and the male and the sublime. More specifically, Kant argues that the man gets a personal, embodied experience of the beautiful primarily through the woman and, likewise, the woman gets an experience of the

---

[7] As we will see in Chapter 4 on "Kant on Sexual Violence and Oppression," this does not mean that Kant thinks history can be described as both sexes oppressing each other. Rather, Kant argues that the historical pattern is that men have oppressed and are oppressing women—a pattern that tracks the fact that men tend to be physically stronger than women.

[8] It is important to note Kant's careful rejection of a certain view, which he attributes to Pope, namely that "the female sex (the cultivated part of it, of course)... [can be characterized] by two points: the inclination to *dominate* and the inclination to *enjoyment*... [*please*]" (A 7: 305). (Because Gregor's translation here (of "Vergnügen" as "please") is both possible and has advantages that Louden's (of "Vergnügen" as "enjoyment") does not, I include both.) On Kant's view, this description fails to capture the character of women. For one thing, this characterization fails to "*characterize*" women as a group distinct from men. After all, *everyone*—man or woman—has a natural inclination to dominate ("to acquire superiority for oneself over others"). As we saw also in Kant's account of human nature in *Religion*, this dangerous inclination (to dominate) accompanies the comparative social predisposition to humanity (to be valued as an equal with others). This point can also be stated in the related language of *Religion*: everyone has a natural inclination to dominate because the inclination of gaining worth in the eyes of others is the natural inclination that accompanies the natural predisposition to humanity. From this natural inclination "arises gradually an unjust desire to acquire superiority for oneself over others" (R 6: 27). Furthermore, viewing women as characterized by both the inclinations to domination and enjoyment misses, Kant thinks, the way in which woman's superior social skills—her artful abilities to please and charm others—are simply means to dominate. Kant writes in *Anthropology*, "inclination to *dominate* is woman's real aim, while *enjoyment* [or *pleasing*] in *public*, by which the scope of her charm is widened, is only the means for providing the effect of that inclination" (A 7: 305). According to Kant, Pope is wrong to think that women have two fundamental social inclinations: just like men, they have only one, namely to dominate.

sublime primarily through the man. The woman's aesthetic power is that of easily mastering the beautiful, which includes the power to allure and attract, while man's aesthetic power is that of mastering the sublime, which includes the power to be forceful or strong and overtake or overflow. Thus, to experience the beautiful, the man has to subject himself to the power of the woman; he must be invited in, to be embraced by, and give himself over to it. Indeed, this is Kant's explanation for why the man "courts" the woman, whereas the woman "refuses" the man (A 7: 306). To experience oneself as affirmed as beautiful (the woman) or affirmed as sublime (the man) in good ways is also something the other person holds the key to; it is the other that opens up this possibility since each reveals themself to the other, and is affirmed by the other as irresistible in these ways.

Kant continues that since the home is predominantly a sphere of intimacy and the beautiful, the woman has to be in control of it. The woman's power makes the man want to give himself over to (and be dominated by) the woman in their personal relations. The woman's primary means of domination is her ability to "master his desire for her," though she supports her efforts with her superior ability to deal with issues concerning intimacy; she is more willing and able to support her stance with her "tongue" in domestic fights (A 7: 304). Certainly, it may be tempting to read these and similar statements of Kant's as *simply* confirmations of his sexist prejudices against women. But I do not think they are. Rather, I think that with such statements he is pointing out how social knowledge is power, and how one can use this knowledge for good or for bad. Earlier, we saw how he thinks that man and woman can bring out the best in each other. Here, we see how he thinks they can use their abilities as purely self-interested tools for getting another to do what they want them to do. As Louden (2011) frequently emphasizes in his commentaries on Kant's *Anthropology*, social knowledge is a means of power—it is something one can use to steer others towards what one wants, including using the other simply to gain a sense of being powerful (to make another orient themselves such that all they can do, at all times, is to try to please one or make one feel important). And if Kant is right that according to the "character" or traditional ideal of woman and man, the woman has superior social knowledge (knowledge of intimate relationships such that she can win a domestic quarrel), then it follows that she has a kind of social-aesthetic power that the man lacks—a power she can use for good or for bad. Equivalently, of course, the man can use his social-aesthetic power for good or bad too.

Both the man and the woman, then, have a natural inclination to dominate (accompanying the predisposition to humanity), but they have different ways of dominating. So, if the man and the woman are to live well together, they must have different roles in relation to both the world and their shared home. Related to this is Kant's view that the characteristic male virtues—those suited to the man's natural protective function—are those connected with the power of the sublime: physical power, industriousness, and reason (A 7: 306). Comparably, the characteristic female virtues are those connected with the powers of the beautiful and a well-functioning home: sensitivity, patience, and financial prudence. When this division is realized, Kant maintains, their natural inclination to dominate does not turn them against each other and so to internal squabbling and unhealthy competition. When the two persons are able to dominate and be dominated in these complementary ways, instead, true reciprocal love is fostered—the kind constitutive of emotionally healthy, happy human beings.

Again, in these ways, reading *Anthropology* together with his account of human nature from *Religion* suggests that Kant envisions the home as the personal sphere in which two people of opposite sexes realize together their natural, embodied sociality (through both mechanical and reciprocal self-love) in a way that is consistent with their respect for each other as persons (as affirmable from the point of view of "rational" self-love). It is also from this personal, shared sphere that they, as a team, engage the outside world. As we will also see in more detail below, Kant's proposal seems to be that the traditional genders complement each other both in the home and in the larger social world; the traditional gender ideals enable the two people sharing a home to be emotionally healthy, grounded beings by enabling a good realization of intimate, personal aspects of the predispositions to animality and humanity for each other. In contrast, the arena for healthy competition (of the kind that drives cultural progress) is seen as the social sphere beyond the home (and so not in the home). Before detailing this account, remember that, for Kant, an emotionally healthy human being who only realizes the first two natural predispositions to good (to animality and humanity) does not thereby realize morality. These predispositions concern only our natural, embodied sociality, and although the second predisposition (to humanity) requires comparative reason, it does not require practical reason in the sense of moral reasoning. Rather, to realize these predispositions in a good way is to become an emotionally healthy and grounded embodied, social being—a way of being that affirms and supports morality.

To illustrate the complementarity between the man and the woman Kant draws an (infamous) analogy between the man's power in the home and the minister's power in a monarchy:

> the woman should *dominate* and the man *govern*; for inclination dominates and understanding governs.—The husband's behavior must show that to him the welfare of his wife is closest to his heart. But since the man must know best how he stands and how far he can go, he will be like a minister to his monarch who is mindful only of enjoyment . . . so . . . the most high and mighty master can do all that he wills, but under the condition that his minister suggests to him what his will is.   (A 7:309f.)

Read unsympathetically, Kant can be understood to think that women, like monarchs, concern themselves only with amusement and therefore are fundamentally irrational and irresponsible. But such a reading really would be unfair. To start with, it would be extraordinary if Kant thought that all monarchs *necessarily* think only of amusements; after all, Kant was extremely well read, so it would be hard to support such an interpretation. Also, this passage comes just after a point in which Kant emphasizes that "woman's [economic activity] is saving" (A 7:308). And finally, before making this statement, Kant describes his analogy as a "gallant" expression of the man-woman relation, though "not without truth" (A 7: 309); that is, the expression is taken to be an exaggeration of something he believes is true.

A more sympathetic interpretation of the analogy is available. The minister to a monarch who thinks only of amusements has a duty to correct the monarch's views. Similarly, the husband of a financially imprudent wife must ensure that her spending decisions are not in excess of what they can afford. Not to correct his wife's decisions in these situations would reveal that he is not firmly committed to her welfare in the way that his knowledge of their finances and the world and his special responsibilities to her and their shared home require him to be. Just as the minister is the one who must ensure that what the monarch wants is financially prudent if need be, the man is the one who must ensure that what his wife wants for their home is financially wise; after all, he is responsible for the relationship between their home and the world. Flipping the example on its head, as we can imagine a wise monarch with a minister who is incapable of doing what is right, we can imagine a wise wife with an unwise husband. In such a case, the wife's best chance (in such a traditional relationship) is to ensure that she controls her husband's desires, so that his strongest desire is the desire not to disappoint her—and this is why, at the end of the day, he sets responsible financial ends. And insofar as a woman is like a monarch and a man like a minister, Kant maintains, only fools believe the "feminine ways" are weaknesses: "reasonable men know very well that they are precisely the rudders women use to steer men and use them for their own purposes" (R 7: 303f.).

So the man, like the woman, has an inclination to dominate. Although the man wants to be dominated (and the woman wants to dominate) in the home and the family's social spheres, the man wants to dominate in the relation between the home and the world. Yet, Kant argues, because the woman is naturally dependent on the man to protect her physically and provide for the home, the woman is fundamentally attuned to pleasing even strangers and is sensitive to how every man perceives her. Not only does having such interpersonal skills make her powerful in general, but being perceived as pleasing is prudent, in case she becomes widowed and needs a new husband.[9] As a result, the woman has more personal and social power than the man does; the woman is more capable of being around the other gender and of controlling their social interactions; the woman has, so to speak, a higher "social IQ" than the man. In Kant's words: "Early in life she becomes confident of pleasing; the young man is always afraid of displeasing, so that he is self-conscious (embarrassed) in the company of ladies" (A 7: 306). In fact, Kant thinks that the woman is so tuned in to pleasing the public that "the scholarly woman uses her *books* in the same way as her *watch* . . . which she carries so that people will see that she has one, though it is usually not running or not set by the sun" (A 7: 307). The woman is very aware of how the world perceives her, and everything she does is sensitive to its judging eye. And, undeniably, focusing on independent ventures and being less concerned with the "public" eye breaks with the traditional ideal, and does not generally go unpunished—a point that Simone de Beauvoir emphasizes too in *The Second Sex*.

---

[9] This is why, Kant explains, "The man is jealous *when he loves*; the woman is jealous even when she does not love, because every lover gained by other women is one lost to her circle of admirers.—The man has his *own* taste: the woman makes herself the object of *everyone's* taste" (A 7: 308; cf. 304f.). Since the woman by nature is much more vulnerable than the man, she is much more dependent upon public opinion than he is.

1.3 Kant vs. Beauvoir on the Traditional Ideals of the Genders

In fact, reading Kant and Beauvoir on the traditional genders against each other is particularly useful to bring out some features of Kant's account. As explained earlier, this is hardly a coincidence. Neither Kant nor Beauvoir took their accounts of the traditional genders out of thin air; they were both profoundly inspired by Rousseau's writings on the issue, especially his *Emile*. But there are some important differences between them, mainly resulting from how although Beauvoir incorporated Rousseau's emphasis on the social (though she developed this point by utilizing psychoanalytic insights), she did not work with the teleological, aesthetic elements of Rousseau's account of human nature. Kant, in contrast, kept all elements of Rousseau's social account of human nature, and so ended up with a more complex threefold approach to sexuality: scientific (empirical) facts, teleological-aesthetic and social human nature, and human freedom, rather than Beauvoir's scientific (empirical) facts, sociality (being seen by the other), and human freedom. Let me sketch a few key differences between them regarding the points mentioned so far since this enables us to see why choosing the more complex route may be more promising as we seek to revise their theories of sex, love, and gender, including by ridding Kant's account of his mistakes.[10]

First, in contrast to Beauvoir, who views the traditional female ideal as submissive (as involving living as a mere means), Kant sees any such actual, historical submissive ideal of womanhood as a perverted version of the normative, traditional ideal (the traditional female ideal realizable by the first two predispositions to good in human nature, to animality and humanity). Kant contends that both the male and the female traditional gender ideals are strong figures.[11] He argues that because the genders have an interpersonal component, their natures are only discernible in civilized societies— societies where a relatively flourishing culture has developed. In "uncivilized societies," Kant contends, "superiority is simply on the side of the man" (A 7: 303); "in the crude state of nature...the woman is a domestic animal" (A 7:304), and "a barbaric civil constitution makes polygamy legal...[where the woman lives in the man's] kennel [or prison[12]]" (A 7: 304).[13] In these barbaric societies, woman is man's

---

[10] Kant explicitly discusses Rousseau in *Anthropology* at 7: 326f. See Robert B. Louden (2011) and Susan Meld Shell (2009) for further discussions of Rousseau's influence on Kant here. For a discussion of Rousseau's deep influence on Beauvoir, see Sally Scholz (2010).

[11] This kind of approach is perhaps most well known in contemporary writings by care theorists who follow Carol Gilligan's lead in her influential *In a Different Voice: Psychological Theory and Women's Development*. Gilligan also argues not only that women's reasoning powers are different than those of men, but that rather than viewing them as weaknesses, we should see them as strengths in their own rights. It follows from my criticism of Kant below that even this kind of care approach is insufficiently complex in its critique of sex, love, and gender.

[12] Gregor here translates the original German "Zwinger" as "prison." Presumably, Louden chose "kennel"—another possible translation of "Zwinger"—due to Kant's reference to domestic animals earlier in this paragraph. Gregor's translation has the strength of capturing Kant's reference (where "Zwinger" is mentioned) to the concept of a "barbaric civil constitution," which makes a term like "prison" a good choice. This is why I have kept both translations here.

[13] According to Kant, barbaric societies are characterized by "force without freedom and law" (A 7: 331). By "polygamy," Kant here means asymmetrical marriages in which one man is married to several

tool for reproduction and/or sexual pleasure (or both) (A 7: 304). Unlike Beauvoir, who thinks that on the traditional ideal the woman amounts to such a tool—"an object" and not "a subject," Kant believes that this historical, actual "ideal" is, rather, a perverted or barbaric version of the traditional one. Furthermore, the traditional ideal or "character" of the sexes only becomes discernible as culture advances and the "morally decent" society establishes itself. Only under those conditions do we realize our natures in the right, complete ways: as two genders that complement each other in a way compatible with the preservation and development of the species. In this more civilized society, the two persons form a lifelong, domestic, sexual union in which reciprocity of superiority and subjection occurs (as monogamous, heterosexual marriage). The man and the woman thereby ensure that the natural inclinations that accompany the predispositions to animality and humanity are realized such that reciprocal love is enabled; the two persons ground each other as the embodied, sexual, social beings they are. In other words, the kinds of desires and emotions comprising sexual love are not just like most of our desires. They can be realized in ways that enable us to exist as the embodied, affective, social beings we are, exactly by each affirming the other at the intimate, personal level. This also means, however, that sexually loving desires and emotions are of the kinds that can unground or unmoor us, if misfortune hits or if we wrongly open ourselves up to particular others who, rather than affirm us, merely use us in bad ways, such as simply to satisfy their own sexual itches or to make sure another constantly affirms their own sense of self (power).

Another, related point of difference between Kant and Beauvoir revolves around Kant's idea that both men and women (traditionally) consider creating a home together an essential part of life. For Kant, in contrast to Beauvoir, on the traditional ideal, the home is not merely a site where reproduction occurs and services are provided to the man as he goes about his "real" business in the outside world. Rather, as we saw above, Kant believes the traditional ideal maintains that "The husband's behavior must, at all times, show that the welfare of his wife is closest to his heart" (A 7: 309f.). Why? Because, I take it, being so oriented (including emotionally) is necessary to be grounding for the other (or, for the wife, or for the woman) in the way that grounding—empowering reciprocal love—involves. Being so directed towards her is important not only to ensure that one's home is safe and taken care of, but because it is necessary in order to be emotionally open in the constructive and healthy (rather than self-destructive, damaging, and draining) ways sexual love is. So, Kant does not agree with Beauvoir that according to the traditional ideal, women necessarily consider themselves mere objects for men (or that traditional men consider women as mere objects for themselves). Instead, Kant thinks that by empowering each other in the gendered ways he describes, both members of the

---

women. This is not consistent with equal freedom since the man gets more than what each of the women gets: the women each get a legal right to $1/n$th of the man (where n=the number of women the man is married to), whereas the man gets a legal right to 100 percent of each woman (MM 6: 278). As a result, polygamies of this kind are "barbaric" or inconsistent with each person's right to freedom. (The question of whether there could be symmetrical polygamies consistent with respecting each as equals I deal with in Chapter 6.)

couple ground and complement each other (they enable each other to realize their embodied, social natures together in good ways). This enables them to form a good social unit—an us—with which they engage the rest of the world. Where woman is considered a mere object whose only purpose is to please others, there are no healthy interpersonal relations, whether at the personal or cultural level. Treating women as mere objects is a way of interacting at odds not only with healthy realizations of the predispositions to animality and humanity, but also with the predisposition to personality, since this predisposition depends upon developing ways of interacting and being that respect all persons as ends in themselves. Societies in which women are mere (reproductive, sexual, domestic, etc.) tools for men who have their own enterprises in the outside world are therefore, for Kant, in a perverted or barbaric condition. Such a condition is inherently inconsistent with the three predispositions to good in human nature, and so, deeply disrespectful of women.

It may be tempting to think that these two differences between Kant and Beauvoir are not very interesting philosophically or practically (when we read societies through the lenses of these theories), but I believe this is mistaken. First, part of the difference here is that Kant has available, through his social, teleological-aesthetic account of human nature, a perspective that does normative work independent from, although supportive of the perspectives of empirical science and freedom, whereas a theory like Beauvoir's ultimately moralizes her analysis of everything (including sociality and empirical desires), such that truly free sexuality becomes a rather disembodied sexuality of free choice. To put the point differently, on the one hand, Beauvoir reads human reality through a less complex, threefold perspective (scientific empirical facts; sociality; and freedom), whereas Kant reads it through a more complex threefold perspective (scientific empirical facts; human nature that has distinctive animalistic, social, and teleological-aesthetic components; and freedom). On the other hand, because of the way in which Kant includes not only an account of sociality, but a richer account of human nature, his resulting account of the trad-itional ideals becomes more complex—his approach gives more substance to the way in which sexuality (whatever the true account is) is not simply a matter of free, disembodied choices even if any justification of what we do in the name of morality has to be undertaken in terms of respect for freedom. The advantage of Kant's view is therefore that it opens up human reality in a more complex way without comprom-ising his commitment to the claim that the ultimate justification for moral interaction is human freedom. As I will return to later, the combination of a philosophical account that lets teleological-aesthetic aspects of human nature do their own nor-mative work has an advantage over a social, freedom-based account such as that of Beauvoir in that the former allows us to capture more of sexuality. Some of these advantages are that it can capture how we—whether straight, gay, bi, trans, queer, asexual—find our sexuality or gender to have a basic givenness in its direction (rather than it being simply a matter of choice); how we typically find the issue of teleological-aesthetic social embodiment central; and how we experience not being able to live out our sexual or gendered being as existentially traumatic. Beauvoir's account struggles to capture all of these phenomena, since on her normative analysis of sex, love, and gender, good realizations of these phenomena (properly understood) is simply a matter of free choice and respectful reciprocal, affirmation.

Let me illustrate this last point of the advantage of the more complex analysis in a different way with regard to the issue at stake: a difference and advantage of Kant's view relative to that of Beauvoir concerns the way in which Kant identifies a normative critical standard internal to traditional societies that is different in kind, though supportive of, the critical (reflective) standard of freedom. It seems to me that Kant's conceptions of "womanhood" and the importance of the home to both man and woman are exactly the ideals affirmed by various traditional, conservative interpretations of religions—a fact that strengthens the claim that Kant's anthropological account of gender and his basic claim that teleological-aesthetic aspects of human nature (and not just empirical science and freedom) may be part of the fuller, better account. As we shall see later, this is also why correcting Kant's account of sex, love, and gender is particularly useful: he makes the same mistake that religions traditionally have made in their lack of appropriate responses to sex, love, and gender's diversity and failure to realize women's equal abilities for scholarly work and public, legal-political participation. That is to say, conservative interpretations of religions such as Christianity, Islam, and Judaism consider the man's and the woman's characters as given, though they are not given by nature alone (understood scientifically), but rather by God's teleological-aesthetic structuring of embodied, social human nature. Correspondingly, conservative interpretations of these religions typically conceive of the "home" as the "proper" primary focus of both the man and the woman. And they consider the "proper" relationship between man and woman as involving a home in which the (Muslim, Jewish, or Christian) mother is ultimately the more powerful domestic figure, although the father deals with "the world" and thus has the right and duty to "put his foot down" in the home to prevent family members from pursuing irrational or unwise ends in the world. On these interpretations, happily married husbands adore their wives, and being a "real man" inherently involves (only) adoring his woman. Only bad men relate to their women as mere means, including as mere sexual tools or as someone who should tiptoe around men in constant efforts to please them. Similarly, Kant's interpretation of the traditional ideal of woman can make sense of why certain conservative religious people in more stable, flourishing cultures, in contrast to what Beauvoir seems to say, identify the proper sexual aim not merely as the man's satisfaction, but as both the husband's and the wife's sexual satisfaction.[14]

The important point here is that Kant's account appears to capture better these traditional religious positions, including how they criticize those who, in their opinion, show insufficient respect for and appreciation of women. In my view, the fact that Kant is able to capture these traditional, normative accounts of men and

---

[14] According to Beauvoir, sex among couples who live in accordance with traditional gender ideals within the context of marriage is a rather sad affair (since women view themselves and are viewed by men as mere objects for men), whereas sex under conditions of freedom (without the historical institution of marriage) can be quite satisfying. For Kant, I have argued here, the opposite seems to be the case, since only under barbaric conditions do women view themselves, and do men view women as mere objects for men, whereas sex consistent with personality (morality) poses a problem only marriage can overcome. To me Kant's account of traditional sex is superior to that of Beauvoir, but Kant's accounts of sexual love and gender, including good sex still contain serious philosophical mistakes. I address these issues further in subsequent chapters.

women is a strength, rather than a weakness, of his anthropological account. Since Beauvoir lets her conception of freedom set the complete, normative framework for her anthropological and psychological investigations, she appears incapable of drawing a distinction between better ("decent") and worse ("barbaric") instantiations of the traditional ideals. Moreover, as we will see below Kant's philosophy as a whole can and does protect everyone's rights to work themselves into active citizenship, and it can explain where and why not only he himself failed, but also why and where these traditional religious institutions typically have failed similarly and so why many of them have been or are currently transforming their associated ideals of sexual or gender identity, sexual orientation, and gender. Kant was fully aware that he (and the traditional institutions) may be mistaking what he thought he was seeing for what is possible and good (especially under conditions of freedom), and he made sure that his philosophical system safeguarded against perpetuating such prejudicial, rationalized mistakes through his conception of morally justifiable construction of legal-political institutions. In addition, I maintain below, his theory of human nature shows why he was responsible for his mistakes; it shows what he should have tended to better in himself in order to correct these mistakes (namely his own discomfort), and why he was obligated to do so (because he was capable of freedom). In the next chapter, I then show how a revised Kantian theory of sex, love, and gender can utilize Kant's philosophy to overcome the mistakes inherent in many of the traditional views, and, so, provides philosophical resources also to conservative (religious-philosophical) thinkers who are trying to identify and overcome the interpretive and philosophical mistakes of those who preceded them.

1.4 Revisiting Some Textual Puzzles

At this point, it is worth taking a break to emphasize that my reading is certainly not the only possible reading of Kant's *Anthropology* or the other relevant works. In fact, the following statement of Kant's seems to resist my reading:

> When refined luxury has reached a high level, the woman appears demure only by compulsion and makes no secret of wishing she might rather be a man, so that she could give her inclinations larger and freer latitude; no man, however, would want to be a woman.
>
> (A 7: 307)

In this passage, Kant appears to argue that when conditions are plentiful, women will wish to be men so that they can give their inclinations "larger and freer latitude" and their modest or reserved (demure) behavior is maintained only by some kind of compulsion. Men, in contrast, never want to be women, regardless of circumstance. Kant seems to be saying that the expectation that women behave "demurely" is a demand of virtue[15]—that is, a requirement of freedom. If Kant indeed advocates here that women are ethically obliged to live in accordance with a set of specific "natural" ends and pursue the traditional female ideals that correspond to these ends (e.g., by being demure) rather than to seek to realize their freedom, then the reading of Kant I presented above is incorrect.

---

[15] This is how Gregor understands this statement, since she translates the relevant part of it as "a woman shows herself virtuous only under constraint."

And, certainly, the textual case against my proposed reading can be strengthened by pointing to the fact that *Anthropology* is not the only place wherein Kant makes statements that seemingly undermine it. In "On the Common Saying: That May Be Correct in Theory, but It Is of No Use in Practice" (hereafter: "Theory and Practice") for example, Kant explains that women cannot be voting citizens because woman, like children, lack a "*natural*" prerequisite (TP 8: 295). In other words, women cannot be persons who fully participate in public reason because something crucial is missing from their nature. Additionally, one might argue that Kant held this position already in his very earliest writings, for in the "Observations on the Feeling of the Beautiful and the Sublime" essay he remarks that "The fair sex has just as much understanding as the male, only it is a **beautiful understanding**, while ours [men's] should be a **deeper understanding**, which is an expression that means the same thing as the sublime" (BS 2: 229). To make matters worse for my reading, perhaps, earlier in the same work Kant says that although both sexes have elements of both the beautiful and the sublime, they are unequally distributed and that

All education and instruction must keep this before it, and likewise all effort to promote the ethical perfection of the one or the other, unless the one would make unrecognizable the charming difference that nature sought to establish between the two human genders...one must also not forget that these human beings are not all of the same sort.   (BS 2: 228)

In addition, when commenting on some extraordinary women scholars in his time (Dacier and Châtelet), he says that they "might as well also wear a beard; for that might perhaps better express the mien of depth for which they strive" (BS 2: 230). And later, in the same text, he even adds, "It is difficult for me to believe that the fair sex [woman] is capable of principles" (BS 2: 232). One might reasonably contend that it is these kinds of sexist views that led Kant to draw the conclusion in *The Metaphysics of Morals* that women are incapable of full, active participation in public life (which would mean being politicians, public officials, or scholars, for instance), because they simply do not possess the practical (self-reflective) reason such participation requires.[16]

If Kant really means that women and men have a moral (ethical and legal) obligation to pursue the traditional gendered personal and interpersonal ideals as well as interrelated "natural" ends, then there is no doubt that his practical philosophy as a whole ends up in a rather formidable contradiction, since it is a moral theory of freedom. On Kant's moral theory of freedom, persons are free in virtue of setting and pursuing their own ends in a manner respectful of others doing the same and subjected only to their own practical reason. Kant famously rejects the idea that there is a "natural end" that is our moral end; he even rejects the idea that happiness can be understood as our moral end.[17] In my view, though, we ought not rush to the

---

[16] Susan Meld Shell's *Kant and the Limits of Autonomy* is a particularly useful resource for further textual evidence as to how common such statements from Kant were in his unpublished lecture notes on anthropology, as well as in some other earlier texts.

[17] For example, in *Groundwork*, Kant says: "In the natural constitution of an organized being, that is, one constituted purposively for life, we assume as a principle that there will be found in it no instrument for some end other than what is also most appropriate to that end and best adapted to it. Now in a being that has reason and a will, if the proper end of nature were its *preservation*, its *welfare*, in a word its *happiness*, then

conclusion that Kant's philosophy collapses in contradiction. While it is true that Kant believes there is wisdom in the traditional gendered (teleological-aesthetic, social) interpretation of our human nature—after all, his goal *is* to identify a correct account of human nature, here investigated in relation to our gendered being more specifically—he never holds up this traditional ideal *as* the moral ideal. Rather, Kant's overall point, as I elaborate below, is that if the normative ideals he has identified really do capture something important about our human nature, then our ideals of ethical and legal perfection should recognize and accommodate those ideals. Realizing our personhood in a way that we find meaningful requires dealing with aspects of ourselves that concern our (partly unreflective) embodied, social sexuality. Correspondingly, Kant also thinks that our natures present us with various "natural" or subjective (unreflective) challenges to realizing (self-reflective) reason and freedom. Yet Kant neither advocates that it would be unethical or should be illegal to act contrary to the anthropological (traditional) ideals of gender, nor does he claim that this moral (philosophical) anthropological ideal is the moral ideal.[18] And he seems open to being wrong or not being able to see this complexity clearly enough.

In my view, Kant's main point is to draw attention to the difference—and the importance thereof—between human moral anthropological ideals and human moral rational ideas of freedom. Kant draws our attention to this difference in the introduction to *The Metaphysics of Morals*, when he explains how he perceives the relationship between his accounts of morality and moral anthropology. Here, he first states that "a metaphysics of morals cannot be based upon anthropology but can still be applied to it" (MM 6: 217). Then he contends that the "counterpart of a metaphysics of morals" in a complete practical philosophy

> would be moral anthropology, which, however, would deal only with the subjective conditions in human nature that hinder people or help them in *fulfilling* the laws of a metaphysics of morals.... It cannot be dispensed with, but it must not precede a metaphysics of morals or be mixed with it; for one would then run the risk of bringing forth false or at least indulgent moral laws, which would misrepresent as unattainable what has only not been attained just because the law has not been seen and presented in its purity... or because spurious or impure incentives were used for what is itself in conformity with duty and good.   (MM 6: 217)

As emphasized in Chapter 1, Kant's complete practical philosophy contains his strictly moral works (the works of freedom: of ethics and of legal-political

---

nature would have hit upon a very bad arrangement in selecting the reason of the creature to carry out this purpose... the whole rule of its conduct, would be marked out for it far more accurately by instinct... nature would have taken care that reason should not break forth into *practical use*" (GW 4: 395).

[18] Kant's moral philosophy (his ethics and his legal-political philosophy) resists the notion that people ought (or can be forced) to live their lives in this traditional way. Not only that, but Kant himself—in his own life—certainly did not realize important aspects of the traditional ideal of manhood, as he neither married nor had children. We might even say that Kant is after an explanation for why people, insofar as they uphold the traditional ideals of manhood and womanhood, would consider Kant less of a "man" than any man who is sexually virile, married, and has a family. Kant never (to use his own wording) let himself experience the great pleasure of being dominated by a woman. The traditionalists who confuse morality and anthropology are even likely to say that Kant might have been one of the greatest philosophers of all time, but since he was not sexually active, married, or a father, he was a somewhat pitiful man—not a "Real Man."

philosophy) *as well as* the accounts that deal with those normative aspects of us that do not belong within moral philosophy proper (within freedom as such), but with our distinctly *human* nature—namely our embodied, social being as explored in his normative works of history, religion, education, and anthropology.[19] (Empirical anthropology, in contrast, would simply be describing various societies and their particular ideals; such accounts would not be what Kant calls "moral" anthropology.) Kant also emphasizes here that a moral anthropological account concerning various elements of our human nature must not be mixed into an account of the metaphysics of morals. And, insofar as moral anthropology is relevant to morality, it concerns various subjective conditions that may make it easier or more difficult for human beings to realize the moral commands of freedom.[20] But, these subjective challenges, which stem from our natures, do not reveal or establish the moral ideals of freedom. They identify neither a set of objective natural boundaries within which people must exercise their freedom nor any natural ends everyone must pursue. If Kant were to claim, instead, that people can be ethically bound to realize or legally required to act in conformity with certain natural ends, then he would be letting his prejudices speak rather than his reason and he would be contradicting himself; he would be doing bad philosophy. But this does not seem to be what he holds. Rather, he clearly states that an approach according to which one permits moral anthropology to set the framework for morality (freedom) is dangerous and fundamentally misguided, since it runs the danger of "misrepresent[ing] as unattainable what has only not been attained." Finally, notice that none of this means that a critique of a full human life does not require both elements—it does—but that when we are after the objective ideals, the contingent embodied, social aspects of our nature must be abstracted away and we must search only for the principles of freedom.

Although I recognize the possibility that Kant was an incorrigible sexist who was neither worried about his own views on women nor never even partially cured, let me give some further reasons to resist that conclusion for just a little while longer. To start with, let us look more closely at the statement Kant makes in *Anthropology*, about wives who wish they were men (although husbands never wish they were women). Kant makes this statement while emphasizing the way in which women, including married women, are sensitive to the public eye. So, the complete relevant passage reads as follows:

In marriage the man woos only his *own* wife, but the woman has an inclination for *all* men; out of jealousy, she *dresses up* only for the eyes of her own sex, in order to outdo other women in charm and fashionableness. The man, on the other hand, dresses up only for the feminine sex; if one can call this dressing up, when it goes only so far as not to disgrace his wife by his clothes .... When refined luxury has reached a high level, the woman appears demure only by

---

[19] In addition, there are practically relevant facts that are in themselves not normative, namely empirical (including scientific) facts.

[20] See Louden (2011), especially ch. 6, "Applying Kant's Ethics: The Role of Anthropology," and ch. 7, "Anthropology from a Kantian Point of View: Toward a Cosmopolitan Conception of Human Nature," for a good exposition of how *Anthropology* is "pragmatic" (how it merely aims at capturing human nature) and not "moral" (it does not aim to show how morality should be applied to anthropology).

compulsion and makes no secret of wishing that she might rather be a man, so that she could give her inclinations larger and freer latitude; no man, however, would want to be a woman.
(A 7: 307)

A sympathetic reading of Kant will pay attention to the context in which this statement is found. Attending to the context, we see that the badness of the wife who wants to be a man lies in her using her increased means (her power) to unleash her inclinations accompanying her social skills and thereby obtain control over many men, rather than limiting her use of her ability to please men to her husband. In other words, more powerful women (i.e., women with more material resources) will be tempted to use their skills at seduction to obtain the kind of social power (i.e., political power) that only men have in traditional society. Yet doing this is wrong, Kant argues, and only self-constraint keeps women from pursuing political power (or traditionally male power) in this way. Additionally, men do not wish to be "women" as the sum of their material means increases, since (traditional) women do not have political power. Men, in contrast, do not have a temptation to obtain social power by controlling the desires of everyone else; they are tempted, instead, wrongly to obtain social power through strategic reason and violence. Therefore, on Kant's account, (traditional) men only dress up for the other sex and their own wives, not for the world. Kant's argument here is therefore also not meant to show that a woman can never prove herself capable of good political power; this is left an open question.

What about the other passage, the one from "Theory and Practice" which states that the nature of women, just like the nature of children, makes it impossible for them to vote? Why are women "passive" rather than "active" citizens, according to Kant? I believe that a sympathetic reading of Kant on this point starts from the assumption that Kant presumably does not mean that there is something in women's physical chemistry or genes (scientifically understood) that precludes them from active citizenship (including voting). After all, if that were the case, then we could understand gender through an empirical, scientific lens, a possibility that Kant clearly rejects by advocating that gender should be understood through the moral anthropological perspective informed by his normative, teleological-aesthetic account of human nature. So, "nature" here presumably refers to Kant's normative, anthropological account of women, as outlined above; this is the one he accommodates in his theory of freedom. Moreover, since his claims about women are exactly normative, anthropological claims informed by the relevant teleological-aesthetic aspects of his account of human nature, however, are only *accommodated* within the theory of freedom, they are not (because they must not be) setting the framework for freedom.

I believe that we can cut Kant a little slack with regard to his sexist comments in "Beautiful and Sublime" too. By paying attention to the surrounding text, Kant's statement again becomes more nuanced than first impressions suggest. In "Beautiful and Sublime," Kant first asserts that he does not want to "give offense," and then he continues by saying that "It is difficult for me to believe that the fair sex is capable of principles ... for these are also extremely rare among the male sex" (BS 2: 232). In other words, Kant emphasizes that his view may come across as offensive, yet he believes that "the fair sex is [in]capable of principles," presumably because he did not believe he had witnessed brilliant scholarly women. Indeed, he claims that the same holds for most men, as principled reasoning is "extremely rare" among them too; in fact, we could argue that his "beard comment" actually reflects that he judged the mien (character) with which the extraordinary women scholars of his time, such as Dacier and Châtelet, were pursuing scholarly questions as just as impressive as that of the scholarly men.[21] Thus, with this statement, Kant does not seem to have in mind the principled thinking characteristic of practical reasoning—he is not, as he never is, maintaining that women cannot be morally (including legally) responsible for their actions—but rather that he has not yet seen genius women producing brilliant scholarship (abstract academic reasoning) although he does think that the serious-ness with which the women scholars he knew about are going about their work matches that of men.[22] It is noteworthy too that two of his examples of exceptional men in this part of the text are Newton and Descartes—philosophers who

[21] Now, immediately before saying this Kant emphasizes that he thinks women are motivated by love and the beautiful when they act. They do what is right not because it is right (or, dutiful) but because "they love to," and because they consider evil "ugly" and "insufferable... virtuous actions... are [strike women as] ethically beautiful. Nothing of ought, nothing of must, nothing of obligation" (BS 2: 232). Obviously, Kant could be saying here that human beings who are women are not persons, that their practical reason is not constituted by categorical moral principles, and so they do not recognize the ought and cannot be morally obligated in general. But this does not strike me as a particularly plausible reading, since, among other things, it makes it unclear why Kant says that women appear incapable of "principles"—and not "*the* principle" (The Categorical Imperative). In my view, these comments of Kant's concern why he thinks that the "natural" motivation of women (i.e., if we consider women merely in terms of their social natures and not their personhood) draws them towards love and the beautiful, whereas men's natural motivation draws them towards the sublime, making them "naturally" closer to reason and duty. Kant does not therefore deny that women recognize what is morally correct to do—the moral ought, as such. Rather, what he writes here is in line with his overall point in these sections, namely, that he deeply suspects that women are not capable of abstract academic work (such as philosophy), or (presumably) any profession that requires understanding abstract science or the moral principles constitutive of legal-political institutions, and that a healthy realization of the female ideal within the context of traditional society will be conducive to and supportive of morality, though it will be expressed predominantly in social-aesthetic, affectionate concepts and emotions. In other words, to interpret this passage, it seems more relevant to examine how Kant had been, in the previous pages, talking about how woman's "philosophical wisdom is not reasoning but sentiment" (BS 2: 230).

[22] For more on why it simply seems unreasonable to claim that Kant ever thought that women are incapable of moral responsibility for their actions, see Mikkola (2011). The passage that is commonly cited to give evidence for the textual claim that Kant thought women incapable of moral reasoning, is in *Anthropology*: "[women] cannot personally defend their rights and pursue civil affairs for themselves, but only by means of a representative" (A 7: 209). Notice, first, though, that Kant is not talking about being incapable of *moral* (ethical or legal) responsibility, but of an inability to represent oneself in court. The negative, feminist interpretations of Kant struggle to make sense of this claim, as Mikkola shows so well. I do believe, however, that Mikkola is mistaken when she then moves on to claim that although Kant deems women capable of representing themselves, they "*should not* do so" (Mikkola 2011: 101). In my view, Kant's view in *Anthropology* and in his Doctrine of Right is that women at the time were incapable of the abstract, principled public reasoning constitutive of legal reasoning, which is why they must be seen as having a right to have a legal representative (trained in the laws) if charged with a legal wrong, such as a crime. This is also why, for example, Kant continues, in the very next sentence in *Anthropology*, to describe this (current, in his time) inability of women as an "immaturity." If the inability of women to represent themselves is an immaturity, it is something that presumably can be overcome (by education) and if so, women defending themselves is not a moral wrong in itself (which it would be on Mikkola's interpreta-tion). Also, if this inability is an immaturity, then it is not revealing an *a priori* impossibility for women (which it is on the very negative, feminist interpretations of Kant). Viewing the inability as an immaturity (and not *a priori* impossibility) also has the advantage of being consistent with Kant's view that ideals of moral anthropology—which woman is—cannot be understood as objectively demonstrable since they do not rest on objective science or on *a priori* principles of freedom.

revolutionized philosophy and science—so his standard for proof of scholarly genius is obviously very high here.

The "Beautiful and Sublime" essay was Kant's earliest piece on the topic of gender, and clearly, he was uncomfortable with his take on women and with sharing it. Kant emphasizes that he means no offense with his statements and that, like the other views he presents in this essay, it should be understood as resulting from mere "glances" on various "peculiarities of human nature" from "the eye of an observer [rather than] of the philosopher" (BS 2: 207). He does not present his view—that only men engage in principled public reasoning or become scholarly geniuses—as an *a priori* truth or as a claim backed up by irrefutable empirical proof. Rather, his claim is based on his observations and experiences. Read even more sympathetically, Kant's idea is that until we have established conditions of freedom, we cannot know whether members of both genders will prove themselves capable of truly principled public reasoning or brilliant scholarly reasoning. (Indeed, as we will see below, such a reading appears supported by his "What Is Enlightenment?" essay.)

Finally, in partial defense of Kant on this point, it is worth pointing out that Beauvoir, writing in the twentieth century, likewise thought that the traditional male gender ideal (of transcendence) was closer to the scholarly ideal commanded by freedom. And neither did she believe that history had yet witnessed female scholarly genius; she did not think that the societal conditions necessary for the development of such genius had existed yet for women. For example, Beauvoir writes, "If truth be told, one is not born, but becomes, a genius: and the feminine condition has, until now, rendered this becoming impossible" (Beauvoir 1949/2011: 152). Therefore, in my view, the major problem with Kant's account in this early essay was his failure to uncover the source of his own discomfort with his claims about women and brilliant principled reasoning. He managed only to note that there was something distressing about his own take on this issue, something not quite right, and to emphasize that he was largely sharing his observations at the time rather than sharing what he took to be a philosophically justifiable position. Throughout his life, as indicated above in relation to his published writings on anthropology and as we will see even more clearly below, Kant remained skeptical about the wisdom of his own judgment here.

2. Kant on the Liberated Woman

Turning to his moral writings, it is useful to remind ourselves of the distinction Kant draws between justice (right) and ethics (virtue).[23] Put briefly, ethics concerns how one ought to live one's life, whereas justice concerns what one can rightfully be coerced to do. In addition, it is important to keep in mind that Kantians generally recognize what I have stated above, namely that most of Kant's ethical and legal-political argumentation is carried out in gender-neutral terms—in terms of persons and citizens (not men and women). To the best of my knowledge, Kant never has the distinction between the genders do any philosophical work in his ethical freedom works, but only in one of his major moral works (The Doctrine of Right in

---

[23] For more on this, see the earlier introductions as well as the introduction to Part II.

The Metaphysics of Morals) and in one short essay ("What is Enlightenment?").[24] In the latter piece, I argue below, Kant draws the distinction to criticize both women's and men's roles in keeping women "in minority." In The Doctrine of Right, he writes of both "men" and "women" in his accounts of marriage and of "active" and "passive" citizens. In neither work does Kant defend the view that women are incapable of moral (ethical and legal) responsibility, that they are morally inferior or unequal to men, or that reason commands us to treat women as subjected to men. In fact, as we shall see, in The Doctrine of Right Kant argues that women cannot be prevented from working their way into active citizenship, and in the "Enlightenment" essay, he contends that everyone (also women) ought to use their reason to the fullest (and see where this takes them) and that anyone would be wrong to hold them back.

2.1 The Woman in The Doctrine of Right[25]

As noted above, Kant draws the man/woman distinction in The Doctrine of Right only in his accounts of marriage and of "active" vs. "passive" citizens. Critics of Kant (on this point) typically read these accounts as affirming that (a) men should be in charge of the family, and (b) women should always be "passive citizens," whose actions should be restricted to the domestic sphere. In contrast, below I argue that Kant maintains that one cannot rightfully deny women the possibility of working themselves into active citizenship and that men do not have an unconditional, *a priori* or perpetual right to be in charge of the home.

Let me start by briefly engaging the relevant parts concerning Kant's view of marriage. This argument is found in the private right section of The Doctrine of Right. It focuses primarily on establishing the principles of marriage that are constitutive of private right, meaning the principles Kant believes any sound liberal legal system will uphold in private (family) law.[26] More specifically, most of Kant's argument regarding marriage concerns why, as a matter of private right, marriage must establish the two spouses as equals who share a legally recognized home. As equals, they have a right not to be abandoned by each other, a right that the other does not engage in sexual activities with anyone else, and a right to share all their private property and honorary titles (MM 6: 277-9). After sketching this argument, which (among other things) leads him to reject the enforceability of contracts involving concubines, sex work, and morganatic[27] marriages, Kant makes an infamous statement that has attracted much scorn from many feminists:

If the question is therefore posed, whether it is also in conflict with the equality of the partners for the law to say of the husband's relation to the wife, he is to be your master (he is the party to direct, she is to obey): this cannot be regarded as conflicting with the natural equality of a

---

[24] I believe that regarding an issue as controversial as sexuality and gender, it is only fair to stick to Kant's published works when interpreting his views, rather than unpublished lecture notes taken by his male students. After all, the risk of inaccurate notetaking is particularly high here.

[25] In order to give a more complete interpretation of Kant on women, I chose to include this discussion of Kant's from The Doctrine of Right although the general rule structuring this book is that discussions concerning right come in Part II.

[26] I return to Kant's account of private right, including marriage, in Chapter 6.

[27] Morganatic marriages are ones in which the two spouses are not recognized by law as equals in all regards. For more discussion, see Chapter 6.

couple if this dominance is based only on the natural superiority of the husband to the wife in his capacity to promote the common interest of the household, and the right to direct that is based on this can be derived from the very duty of unity and equality with respect to the *end*. (MM 6: 279)

Many feminists conclude from this passage—and not without reason—that Kant argues that the natural superiority of the husband over the wife entails that the law can legitimately specify that the man is the one who commands, whereas the woman is the one who obeys.[28] Yet in light of the account I have presented above, it seems more reasonable to interpret Kant differently. I suggest that Kant's claim is that such laws are permissible *if and only if* (a) the account of the "subjective challenges" that inhibit women in their ability to deal with the relation between the home and the world is correct, and (b) the decision in question concerns those subjective challenges. This entails too, however, that such laws are permissible only insofar as women are in fact incapable of assuming equal responsibility for relations between the home and the rest of the world, and, consequently, such a law will be legitimate only insofar as we are in a historical condition in which traditional ideals of women and men prevail (a condition of moral decency). That is to say, such a law will be permissible under traditional conditions and it will be permissible under conditions of freedom *if and only if* experience shows that the traditional ideal is not backward-looking in a problematic sense. Furthermore, as we have seen, Kant considers it a real possibility (from his first publication, "Beautiful and Sublime," onwards) that he and the traditional ideal may be wrong in regarding only men as capable of an active public life, as public leaders and scholars. Below we will see that in the "Enlightenment" essay Kant encourages women to prove him wrong, whereas here, in The Doctrine of Right, we will see that he protects everyone's right to prove not only him, but the legal-political systems in which they find themselves, wrong.[29]

In The Doctrine of Right Kant draws the distinction between men and women also in his account of passive and active citizens. At first glance, it certainly does seem as though Kant affirms the view that women can (and should) only ever be passive citizens. Kant first explains that women, like children and servants, are "passive citizens" because they lack independence, in the sense that they depend "upon the will of others" (MM 6: 314). Women, children, and servants lack sufficient ability to engage in public self-government (partaking in the public government of civil society through public reason): children lack both material and mental powers; servants lack material and possibly intellectual ability (as they lack education); and, women (presumably) lack either intellectual ability (the ability to participate actively in the public sphere through the

---

[28] It may be worth pointing out that Kant is not saying here that regardless of how bad a man is, he is still necessarily better than any woman. Presumably, this passage concerns only the moral permissibility of the way the law of Kant's time gave the man the ultimate say on certain family matters (where there were no complicating factors, such as incapacitating alcohol abuse). And Kant argues that such laws are legally permissible.

[29] This reading, which emphasizes that Kant keeps his language in the moral writings gender-neutral for deep-seated reasons, is consistent with how Mika LaVaque-Manty (2006, 2012) in his writings on Kant on education regards Kant's use of gender-neutral language. Again, in my view, this aspect of Kant was truly important to him, as it reflects his concern that he (like traditional ideals) might have been wrong about aspects of the gender ideals.

use of reason) or material ability (private property or material powers), or both. As a result, children, women, and servants are judged to be passive citizens.

Why, then, is it reasonable to argue that Kant *does not* believe women must necessarily remain passive citizens? First, were he to mean that women are perpetual passive citizens, then, again, he would explicitly introduce a philosophical contradiction into this philosophical system by subjecting morality (freedom) to moral anthropology. Second, Kant would then also contradict himself within the space of two paragraphs, because in the very next paragraph he argues that any laws posited in a just state must "not be contrary to the natural laws of freedom and of the equality of everyone in the people corresponding to this freedom, namely that anyone can work... [their][30] way up from this passive condition to an active one" (MM 6: 315). In other words, in a just state all members, including women, have a right to work themselves into active citizenship. One might worry here that while servants and children can change their condition (they can grow up, obtain an education, or make enough money to become materially independent), surely women cannot stop being women?!

Assuming, sympathetically, that Kant does not contradict himself within the scope of two paragraphs, I do not think that ceasing to be women is the kind of change he has in mind. Instead, I believe Kant means that women have a right to work their way into active citizenship by showing themselves capable of scholarly work and legal-political (or public) participation (of the kind that the traditional ideal—and Kant himself too—was skeptical they could do). Women must dare to take on the challenges of the public sphere, and men do not have a right to prevent women from doing so; men cannot pass laws according to which women—a moral anthropological category—cannot work themselves into an active condition. Moral anthropology concerns, among other things, the subjective conditions in human nature that hinder people from or help them to fulfill the laws of a metaphysics of morals. As such, our moral theories of freedom should accommodate moral anthropology (including the traditional ideals), but moral anthropology cannot set the parameters within which freedom must operate; the conditional cannot limit the unconditional. As we saw above, letting moral anthropology (the conditional) set those parameters risks the danger of

bringing forth false or at least indulgent moral laws, which would misrepresent as unattainable what has only not been attained just because the law has not been seen and presented in its purity... or because spurious or impure incentives were used for what is itself in conformity with duty and good.   (MM 6: 217)

And in fact, not only was this an important theme for Kant in *The Metaphysics of Morals*, he makes the same point in *Groundwork*. There too he emphasizes that although the laws of freedom are *a priori*, correct application to actual circumstances requires "a judgment sharpened by experience" (GW 4: 389). As we have seen, already from the first publication ("Beautiful and Sublime") Kant was unsure about

---

[30] I have changed the gendered "his way" in Gregor's translation to "their" since in the original German text, Kant makes this point using the gender-neutral "Volk," that is, he argues that respecting the equality of every member of the people entails that each and every one of them should be able to work themselves into an active condition.

KANT ON THE LIBERATED WOMAN

his own experience with human life under conditions of freedom (in Prussian *Königsberg*), in particular that his judgment of women, including under conditions of freedom was good enough. To judge this issue wisely was very difficult for him, and he knew that. And in fact, he did not manage to get it right; his prejudices were very strong and his experience with women and human life as it flourishes under conditions of freedom too limited. It is also some of Simone de Beauvoir's brilliance that she focused much of her argument exactly on how women were denied access to public spheres as equals—as legal-political leaders and as scholars. Indeed, she not only proved her own philosophical and scholarly genius in authoring *The Second Sex*, but also paved the way for other women to do the same—to enter and be successful in the academy. The possibility of exactly my sitting here writing this book is as much thanks to her as it is to Kant.

Although Kant was sexist—he has many sexist beliefs, attitudes, emotional responses, and associations—and although he accommodates, to some extent, the two traditional ideals of gender in The Doctrine of Right, his practical philosophy as a whole is still not inherently anti-feminist. His account explicitly blocks the possibility that just states can pass laws that make it illegal for women to work themselves into active citizenship. This interpretation has the benefit of being consistent with how Kant conceives of the relationship between moral theories (ethics and law) of freedom and moral (philosophical) anthropology. Additionally, it avoids having to charge Kant with explicitly contradicting himself both within the space of two paragraphs and within his philosophy generally. Finally, as I elaborate below, this interpretation is consistent with what Kant says about the distinction between men and women in "An Answer to the Question: What is Enlightenment?"

2.2 Women in "What is Enlightenment?"

Let me now move on to Kant's brief note on men and women in the essay "What is Enlightenment?" Given how controversial this is as a matter of interpretation, it is worth quoting the passage in full:

> *Enlightenment is the human being's emergence from his self-incurred minority. Minority* is inability to make use of one's own understanding without direction from another. This minority is *self-incurred* when its cause lies not in lack of understanding but in lack of resolution and courage to use it without direction from another. *Sapere aude!* Have courage to make use of your *own* understanding! [dare to know/dare to be wise] is thus the motto of enlightenment.

> It is because of laziness and cowardice that so great a part of humankind, after nature has long since emancipated them from other people's direction ... nevertheless gladly remains minors for life, and that it becomes so easy for others to set themselves up as their guardians. It is so comfortable to be a minor! ... That by far the greatest part of humankind (including the entire fair sex) should hold the step towards majority to be not only troublesome but also highly dangerous will soon be seen to by those guardians who have kindly taken it upon themselves to supervise them; after they have made their domesticated animals dumb and carefully prevented these placid creatures from daring to take a single step without the walking cart in which they have confined them, they then show them the danger that threatens them if they try to walk alone. Now this danger is not in fact so great, for by a few falls they would eventually learn to walk; but an example of this kind makes them timid and usually frightens them away from any further attempt.

Thus it is difficult for any single individual to extricate himself from the minority that has become almost nature to him. He has even grown fond of it and is really unable for the time being to make use of his own understanding, because he was never allowed to make the attempt. Precepts and formulas, those mechanical instruments of a rational use, or rather misuse, of his natural endowments, are the ball and chain of an everlasting minority. And anyone who did throw them off would still make only an uncertain leap over even the narrowest ditch, since he would not be accustomed to free movement of this kind. Hence there are only a few who have succeeded, by their own cultivation of their spirit, in extricating themselves from minority and yet walking confidently.

But that a public should enlighten itself is more possible; indeed this is almost inevitable, if only it is left its freedom. For there will always be a few independent thinkers, even among the established guardians of the great masses, after having themselves cast off the yoke of minority. (WE 8: 35f.)[31]

What are we to make of this? To start, I believe that we must pay attention to the fact that this account is not written from the perspective of moral (philosophical) anthropology, but from that of freedom (morality).[32] In addition, in this essay, Kant is not restricting his analysis to the perspective of rightful freedom (right) or ethical freedom (virtue), but vacillates between these two perspectives. As such, he writes more generally in order to encourage us all to promote freedom, to dare be free. And I suggest that once he assumes these moral freedom-perspectives, he reasons in a way that will strike feminists as quite similar to the work of Beauvoir in *The Second Sex*. First, like Beauvoir, he criticizes women (and anyone) for not stepping up to the task of leaving their minority behind, insofar as it is self-inflicted. He criticizes them for choosing to live as minors who need guardians (namely, men) to assume responsibility for their lives, for choosing the comfort of life as a dependent (or, minor) rather than facing the fears that accompany freedom—the fears of failing and of having to seek answers on one's own rather than having them provided by others. To put the point in Beauvoir's language: when it is a possible choice, woman must step up to the challenges of freedom and govern her actions by her own reason (live in "transcendence" and not in "immanence"). She must stop living as if the manuscript for her life is already written for her (live as an "object")—regardless of how comfortable this is—she must dare to write it for herself (live as a "subject").

Second, again like Beauvoir, Kant condemns men for being ever so willing to make women their "dumb domesticated animals," for "carefully prevent[ing] ... these placid creatures from daring to take a single step without the walking cart in which they have confined them," and for presenting the world as a dangerous place that women should be deeply afraid of.[33] Finally, like Beauvoir, Kant emphasizes the

---

[31] The original German uses the male noun "Der Mensch" or "human being" (this translation: "the individual"), which is why the remainder of the paragraph uses the pronouns "he" and "himself." Also note that Kant here clearly uses the concept of humankind ("die Menschen" in the original German, or "human beings") to cover both sexes, since he explicitly points out what he thinks is special for women.

[32] Much of "What is Enlightenment?" deals with political philosophy, but the opening pages focus on individuals and what they ought to leave behind—namely, "minority."

[33] Kant argues similarly in *Anthropology*. After having argued that women's inability to represent themselves in court should be understood as an immaturity, he states: "But to *make* oneself immature, degrading as it may be, is nevertheless very comfortable, and naturally it has not escaped leaders who know

difficulty for any single person, including a woman, to leave minority behind on their own under such conditions. Yet, again like Beauvoir, Kant maintains that even under conditions where minority is encouraged, so long as freedom is not made impossible, there will be a few extraordinary individuals who will choose freedom and majority anyway. And despite the odds, these independent thinkers will push towards conditions of majority for all (which are also the conditions under which scholarly genius can develop). Sometimes these independent thinkers will be members of the privileged class, like J. S. Mill in *The Subjection of Women*, and sometimes they will be members of the oppressed classes, though they will more often be somewhat privileged members of the oppressed classes (here, socially fairly privileged women) as they experience more freedom. Examples of the latter case range from George Elliot (Mary Anne Evans) to Madam Curie to Simone de Beauvoir to Vigdís Finnbogadóttir.[34] But Kant calls on everyone, generally: women must dare to leave oppression and minority behind insofar as this is a possible choice. In the language of *Anthropology*, everyone must dare to realize their human nature—animality, humanity, personality—to the fullest, "Sapere Aude!" ("dare to know"/"dare to be wise"), including dare to see what this means in terms of possibly reforming the anthropological ideals we have been handed over through traditions.[35]

And indeed, it is actually not random, according to Kant's philosophical system, that brilliant legal-political public reasoning—like the reasoning found in great judges—and academic brilliance from women was slow to appear: brilliant legal-political reasoning and academic brilliance both require training in reasoning in a way that creative arts—such as music—do not. So there is Mozart-the-genius-musical-child, but no Kant-the-genius-philosophical-child. As explained in Chapter 1, the reason for this difference, according to Kant's philosophical system, is that central to brilliance in the creative arts is use of the imagination unbound by reason (the third *Critique*)—and so can be found already in children—whereas brilliant legal-political reasoning and academic brilliance requires training of abstract conceptual reasoning skills to a much larger extent (the first and second *Critique*)—and, so, cannot be found in children. This is not to deny that excellent education enhances art or that the history of tremendously talented, oppressed women scholars is only currently being written. Rather, it is to point out the obvious fact that although some of George Eliot's brilliance in *Middlemarch* clearly reveals Mary Ann Evan's education, she could come before Simone de Beauvoir in history because Beauvoir

---

how to use this docility of the masses (because they hardly unite on their own); and to represent the danger of making use of one's *own* understanding without the guidance of another as very great, even lethal" (A 7: 209).

[34] Vigdís Finnbogadóttir was the first female President in Europe, and in 1980 became the first democratically elected female head of state (in Iceland).

[35] See also Jauch (1988, 2014) for particularly interesting engagements with the question of whether Kant knew about, whether his philosophy was the inspiration for, or maybe even that he was the (co-)author of (together with his friend Theodor Gottlieb von Hippel) an anonymous publication advocating for women's rights. As we can see from her discussion, consistent with the above interpretation, although Kant explicitly denied being the author of the publication, he never says that the idea of equal rights defended in the publication—that men and women should have equal rights—is inconsistent with his philosophy. Indeed, as Jauch points out, in one of Kant's newspaper articles, if we read in between the lines, Kant says the exact opposite: he affirms that Hippel had applied his philosophy correctly to this issue (Jauch 2018: 286–8).

needed her academic, university training and setting to write her brilliant *The Second Sex*—something not available to women living in Evan's time and that held back the philosophical efforts of scholarly women before they could enter academia as men's equals. Given the above analysis, it is additionally no longer so strange that although history has seen many great queens—women entrusted with and capable of mastering national political emotions—it took much longer before we got the first women ministers, let alone democratically elected prime ministers and presidents. Indeed, it is not implausible to argue that the impossibility of combining serious philosophical interests with being a queen in (hetero)sexist societies is revealed in the life of Queen Kristina of Sweden, who abdicated. And it is also no longer so surprising that the two first women US Supreme Court Justices—Sandra Day O'Connor (b. 1930) and Ruth Bader Ginsburg (b. 1933)—appeared on the Supreme Court as late as in 1981 and 1993 (respectively). In addition to how the US legal-political world had to become less sexist for their appointments to be possible, O'Connor and Ginsburg first had to be trained academically and then practice as lawyers and judges before they were ready for the Supreme Court.

And, as we have seen, Kant was well aware that his views of women might simply have been expressions of his own prejudices and sought to ensure that his philosophy as a whole was wiser than he was. Kant's philosophical writings on freedom leave room for concerns of moral anthropology and moral psychology *and* they leave room to revise claims made in those domains. That is, what we find in the moral anthropological and relevant psychological writings (unlike the freedom writings and yet consistent with them) are not objective, universal claims, but inherently contingent ones. This is why the freedom writings set the framework within which these contingent claims are accommodated (rather than the other way around), which explains the few appearances of "men" and "women" in Kant's moral writings on freedom. Regardless of whether we accept this interpretive claim, Kant would certainly have held that it is not a given that the positive development regarding women in philosophy generally and in the Kant community in particular over the last few decades will continue. Shortly after the comments quoted above, Kant says,

a public can achieve enlightenment only slowly. A revolution may well bring about a falling off of personal despotism and of avaricious or tyrannical oppression, but never a true reform in one's way of thinking; instead new prejudices will serve just as well as old ones to harness the great unthinking masses.   (WE 8: 36)

Indeed, the strong political women's rights movement—with everything it involved and led to—proved not only how challenging it is to bring about sustained change, but also that the traditional ideal of woman as incapable of abstract scholarly reasoning and full public participation is proven wrong once and for all. Under conditions of increasing freedom, there were at first a few remarkable individual women who successfully broke loose (some of whom are mentioned above) and a few men and other women who defended and supported them, including by recognizing, affirming, and delighting in their abilities. And soon more women and men joined the movement. Obviously, there is still a long way to go and set-backs keep occurring, but the changes we have witnessed since Kant's time have been enormous. Recently, several of the greatest legal-political leaders have been or are women, and many of the best of minds coming out of various education systems are women. In fact, many of the leading Kant scholars in all areas of his philosophy, are women.[36] Kant himself admitted from the start that this could happen, even if he had not himself observed it and even if he was as skeptical about this as he was of his own judgment of women. When I am feeling most fond of Kant, such as after I have read him as he nails European colonizers to the wall, I tend to think that if he could come back from the dead and see what has happened—see how many women philosophers first proved him wrong precisely by further developing his philosophy; indeed, that so many women befriended his critical philosophy as they sought to realize themselves as free and as philosophers—he would smile. At all other times, I would at least expect him to want to learn to love it and support him in his efforts to learn to live it.

3. Concluding Remarks

Kant never presents or defends his account of the traditional woman as a moral ideal. Kant never thinks that women cannot be morally (legally or ethically) responsible for their actions; and he explicitly encourages everyone (including women) to dare to be free—to dare to guide their actions by their own reason (be autonomous). What Kant was uncertain about was not whether or not women could be morally responsible for their actions, but whether they were capable of active citizenship and the special kind of abstract reasoning constitutive of public, or legal-political and scholarly reasoning. He deemed it possible that their philosophical wisdom lays elsewhere, in the kind of caring, affectionate reasoning constitutive of well-functioning social and personal spheres for embodied, social beings like us. His account of the traditional woman aspires to capture this moral anthropological ideal, including by fundamentally informing it with his normative account of human nature—and it is this anthropo-logical ideal he makes space for in his moral, and especially his legal-political writings on freedom. He thought that the traditional ideals of men and women capture different, equally valuable, and complementary ways for human beings to be wise. Both are crucial to a society fit for emotionally healthy human beings; such a society requires both types of philosophical wisdom: the one more closely tied to human nature understood in terms of personal affection, sociality, and the beautiful as well as the one more closely tied to human nature understood in terms of force, compe-tition, and the sublime. A world in which there is only the one is a bad world to live in for human beings. The kind of beings we are requires the realization of both types of being and reasoning, or philosophical wisdom. If he is right, then realizing oneself is inseparable from realizing one's nature—male or female—as this is what will make one most profoundly happy and what will be affirmed upon reflection (morally). Thus, Kant's views on this matter are not inconsistent in that one can be morally (ethically and legally) responsible without being capable of the kind of argument constitutive of public (legal-political and scholarly) reasoning.

Still, undeniably, Kant did not get all of this right. And indeed, Kant was clearly aware of the possibility that he did not see these things quite in the right way, that he

---

[36] For an overview over the emergence of women Kant scholars, see "Introduction to Part I."

was mistaking what he believed he was seeing (the traditional ideals) for what was possible (gender ideals possible under conditions of freedom). This worry was something he was generally concerned about from the start and something he explicitly emphasized in the introduction to *The Metaphysics of Morals* by arguing that though moral works (of freedom) make space for normative claims based on a fuller (moral anthropological) account of human nature, this is all it can and should do; a good practical philosophy cannot present moral anthropology as yielding principles that can take the place of moral principles of freedom. And, so, this is what he does, including when he analyzes women's rights: it cannot be illegal for anyone to work themselves into active citizenship. Only in this way does ideal theory (concerned with moral freedom) make space for non-ideal theory (concerned with other aspects of human nature, including our propensity to act in bad ways) in a way that is compatible with humankind correcting its errors over time, exactly by show-ing how some of what has been deemed impossible was only impossible until conditions of freedom were established.

In my view, therefore, it is not a coincidence that most of Kant's comments on women are found in his non-moral, yet normative works, such as his works on history and on anthropology. His account of morality, in turn, is found in his works on freedom, including *Groundwork*, second *Critique*, and *The Metaphysics of Morals*. Kant intends these moral works to capture our freedom, which is why they almost never discuss the distinction between men and women, but instead refer to "persons" and "citizens"—gender-neutral terms. One might be tempted to think that by "persons" and "citizens" Kant merely means only "men" and not also "women," as appears to be the case in the quoted passage above. But the male pronoun appears above not because Kant writes "men" in the German text, but because the German term for human being is "Der Mensch," which is a male noun. Still, one might object that this makes no difference, because, for Kant, "der Mensch" really refers only to men. It seems somewhat unfair, though, to accuse Kant of being this rather nasty version of Humpty Dumpty (of saying one thing while meaning something else entirely) since he almost always draws a distinction between men and women when it strikes him as important to do so, including as we have seen, when he (correctly) believes his views will come across as offensive. Instead, in these works, he accom-modates the traditional ideals where and in the ways he thinks they should be, and then insists on how the just state must not mistake these normative (philosophical anthropological) ideals for moral ideas by never making it illegal for anyone to work oneself into active citizenship.

Assume for a moment that the interpretation I present in this chapter is fair, including that Kant's view captures well the traditional ideals of the man and the woman. For the sake of argument, accept too my claim that Kant made space for and even encouraged women to dare to be free. If all this is correct, then it seems fair to say that the first mistake Kant made was to pay insufficient attention to, or to not be open, both to women who did not fit the traditional mold and to the sexual and gendered diversity surrounding him. By exploring his own discomfort here further—a discomfort so clear to him that he drew attention to it already in his earliest writings on the topic; indeed, a discomfort so present and vivid to him that his own theory of moral psychology and anthropology should have made him tend to it much more carefully.

After all such discomfort is often, according to this theory, an indication that one is rationalizing about something one is unable to deal with well—he could have taken his project the next logical step. This step, I believe, would require him to realize that although his account of moral anthropology—with its supporting, full account of human nature—clearly captures important normative principles central to the exploration and development of our own embodied, social, and teleologically-aesthetically informed sexualities *and* explains how these principles can produce the two traditional gender ideals in civilized (as contrasted with barbaric) ways, it fails to account for sex, love, and gender's diversity even in fairly traditional societies like his own. Take one obvious example: as Kant's account stands, it cannot make good sense of homosexuality or any kind of gender-bending—and that is obviously a big problem for an adequate philosophical account of sex, love, and gender. After all, these are not historically new phenomena and people have often been willing to risk everything to live them out, to hold on to and live as who they are. In fact, even today, in one of the more liberal societies the planet has seen, the suicide-attempt rate among people who identify as trans is 41 percent, 10-20 percent among gay and lesbians, and only 4.6 percent among people who identify as straight.[37] A philosophical engagement that ends up being blind to people's lives and suffering in the way Kant's is—one that deems LGBTQIA lives as perverted—reveals a philosopher doing bad work. In addition, this brings home the importance of appreciating how good philosophy combines both kinds of philosophical wisdom: those Kant labels the female and the male.

Still, although something obviously went wrong in Kant's account of human nature (and complementary accounts of moral anthropology and moral psychology) such that it leads him to these mistakes, there seem to be good reasons to think that the better Kantian theory does not reject what I take to be a major philosophical contribution—that to understand sex, love, and gender, we cannot have a theory driven only by perspectives of freedom and deterministic empirical science (or, with Beauvoir, with the addition of sociality as such). We have not found sexual orientation genes or any other necessarily physical causal factors. Therefore, any theories that remain philosophically committed to such facts to explain sex, love, and gender remain incapable of explaining (which good philosophical theories will do) the experience of people who, for example, have always found themselves sexually attracted to and sexually most at home in the world with people identifying as of the same sex, and that this makes profound, existential sense to them. Similarly, without finding genes or any necessary physical laws that can explain sexual or gender identity, the resulting theories remain equally toothless philosophically. And in this case, it appears even more unlikely that such genes will be found: after all, part of the challenge involved in explaining trans lives is to explain how those who have transitioned feel at home in the world for the first time as the embodied, sexual, or gendered beings they always have felt themselves to be. And better accounts will have to explain why, even though these same people have not yet had those embodied experiences (including those physical experiences that transitioning opens up). Kant's theory of women is therefore not only historically interesting, but

---

[37] See the recent National Transgender Discrimination Survey for more information: http://williamsinstitute.law.ucla.edu/wp-content/uploads/AFSP-Williams-Suicide-Report-Final.pdf

philosophically interesting in that it recommends that we employ a trifold perspective when we try to get human sex, love, and gender into view: empirical science (necessary causal laws), embodied, social human nature where teleology and aesthetic judgments are also given their due, and freedom (moral laws). What we will see in Chapter 3 is that we need not reject out of hand Kant's philosophical account of human nature in order to accommodate or even celebrate the remarkable diversity that characterize human sexual, loving, and gendered ways as well as overcome Kant's own prejudices, failures, and limitations in these regards.

Finally, insofar as we are able to create conditions of freedom, it is becoming increasingly obvious (and, so, increasingly difficult to deny by any minimally reasonable mind) that people find it profoundly meaningful to combine the ideas of the sublime and the beautiful with the predispositions to animality, humanity, and personality in many different ways. Increasingly, therefore, in free societies, *many* distinct normative ideals are becoming socially visible; different new ways of working out profoundly meaningful lives—and not only the two captured by the two traditional, dominant gender ideals. We learn not only that some of the best politicians, judges, scientists, philosophers, etc., are women, but that patterns regarding sexual or gender identity and sexual orientation cannot be understood by appeal to some selection of and contrasts between biological features (in various ways); sometimes one's sexual or gender identity does not track basic components of the biological embodiment one is born with; many people are able to and profoundly enjoy "changing gears" being drawn to the sublime with regard to some areas of their life or sometimes, and the beautiful in others or at other times; some feel most at home in the world if they can be sexual, affectionately loved, or sexually loved by more than one; others find some, much, or all of sexuality and intimacy rather boring or uncomfortable in the first place. We are learning too, it seems, that healthy politics and a healthy public (including academic) life requires social skills of the kind traditionally associated with women, for example, the ability to know and further healthy (rather than unhealthy) love of country and of knowledge. Without these, states and learning institutions easily go awry in their justice- or knowledge-seeking efforts.

All of this, however, seems consistent with Kant's basic insight: knowing one's subjective self requires one to know one's own nature—it is not something understandable simply from the reflective, objective points of view of empirical science or of freedom, but must additionally be informed by an unreflective point of view that invokes irreducible subjective, teleological, aesthetic, embodied, social elements. One can explore this in good ways by tending to what makes one feel truly at home in the world, as a good place, as the sexually or gendered embodied, social person one is. Trustable others, including good theory, only make this process of exploration easier. These developments are also consistent with Kant's other, fundamental claim, namely that when done well, various realizations of human nature affirm human freedom, including upon reflection: they are experienced as profoundly meaningful, good ways of living one's life as who one is and that one can do well, including together with others. Indeed, in Chapter 3, I argue that this is the kind of position Kant *should* have defended given both the human experiences and lives he was engaging philosophically and his own, relevant philosophical commitments.

3

Kant on Sex. Reconsidered

Introduction

Mentioning Kant and sex in the same sentence evokes in most philosophers associations of the following kinds: a lifelong celibate philosopher; a peculiar defense of a natural teleological view of sexuality; a peculiar incorporation of this natural teleological view within his liberal, freedom-based moral theory; and a stark ethical condemnation of uninhibited sexual desire and activity in general and of non-procreative sexual desire and activity in particular. Certainly, Kant says many things to induce these associations throughout his works. For example, natural teleological assumptions are typically present when sexuality is being discussed, such as in his description of "sexual love" as "destined by it [nature] to preserve the species...a *natural* end" (MM 6: 424). Among his moralized and teleologically informed condemnations of most kinds of sexual desire and activity, Kant says that ethically permissible sex occurs only within marriage and comprises only procreative sexual activities since "one may not, at least, act contrary to that [natural] end" (MM 6: 426). Indeed, after having clarified that marriage is between men and women in *The Metaphysics of Morals*, Kant emphasizes that unnatural sexual use takes place

either with a person of the same sex or with an animal of the nonhuman species...such transgressions of laws, called unnatural...[carnal crimes against nature] or also unmentionable vices, do wrong to humanity in our own person, [and] there are no limitations or exceptions whatsoever that can save them from being repudiated completely. (MM 6: 277)

Along similar lines, Kant claims that any non-procreative sexual activity (even masturbating with fantasies) involves a "*defiling* (not merely a debasing) of the humanity in his [one's] own person" and "debases him [one] beneath the beasts" and is "contrary to morality in its highest degree"; in fact, even thinking about sex *within* marriage is a rather shameful activity, which is why sex can only be talked about in "delicate" ways in "polite society" (MM 6: 424ff.). And as if this were not bad enough, Kant maintains that all non-procreative sex is to be considered worse than suicide, even though both kinds of activities are inconsistent with "mere animal nature" (MM 6: 277). After all, a person who commits suicide must at least have courage, whereas the person engaging in unnatural sex thereby "abandons...his personality (throwing it away)" and instead simply "surrenders" to "animal inclination" in a way that deprives them of all self-respect (MM 6: 425). From reading these and similar passages, it seems that the best we can do, according to Kant, is to engage in ethically permissible sex understood as strictly procreative sexual activities within

Sex, Love, and Gender: A Kantian Theory. Helga Varden, Oxford University Press (2020). © Helga Varden.
DOI: 10.1093/oso/9780198812838.001.0001

a marital context, and we should avoid experimenting or enjoying even that too much—a rather grim vision indeed.

When first encountering these statements, most people—and maybe especially those who find Kant's general ways of doing philosophy fruitful and compelling—find them philosophically puzzling. One puzzle is why Kant—a stout defender of freedom and natural science—employs the perspective of natural teleology in the middle of his discussion of morally permissible sex. Another general puzzle concerns why Kant seems to think that marriage can transform an allegedly inherently unethical activity—sexual activity as such ("sexual love")—into an ethically permissible one. Sexual love in a narrow sense of the word is—as we will explore in more detail in Chapter 4—a type of pleasure that can become the strongest form of pleasure (a "passion"), and it combines sensuous pleasure with pleasures "from the *enjoyment* of another person" (MM 6: 426). In addition, the special kind of pleasure sexual love enables is distinct from both moral love and delight in another person since sexual love includes the desire for carnal enjoyment of the other (objectification), whereas both moral love and delight "instead, deter one from carnal enjoyment" (MM 6: 426). Kant furthermore says that sexual love can enter into "a close union with ... [moral love] under the limiting conditions of practical reason" (MM 6: 426), which presumably occurs when sexual activity is undertaken in procreative ways within a marital context (MM 6: 277). This leads us back to the question: why is marriage deemed capable of performing such moral magic on otherwise immoral activities?

Sometimes, exploring these seemingly enigmatic statements concerning sexuality in Kant's writings leads not to simple puzzlement but also to sadness. Most of us who are accustomed to encountering heterosexism and homophobia register Kant as advancing both; indeed, the kind of language Kant uses can be the same language used when we are subjected to emotional and/or physical sexual violence. Kant is aggressive and condemning: sometimes, such as when reading the texts where we find the language of "defiling" and "debasing" quoted above, it feels as if Kant is having angry panic attacks in the middle of his texts. Why did he not do better? What is it about sex, love, and gender that makes it so easy and tempting to join damaging social forces, to turn as aggressive, cognitively stubborn, dehumanizing, and narrow-minded, as Kant did? Why did Kant not dare to be wiser about sex, love, and gender? And, of course, reading what Kant says—what are for many statements about oneself, about one's loved ones, or about others whose sexual or gendered identities or orientations are not cis, binary, or straight—is emotionally hard work, as is trying to fix the account for Kant. This chapter is therefore not setting aside, defending, or offering an apology for Kant's many awful statements about sex, love, and gender. Quite the opposite: I am proceeding on the assumption that it is important to explore these troublesome aspects of Kant's writings if we are to understand them in all their complexity and the complicated phenomena we then encounter, including his cisism, binary heterosexism, and homophobia. Understanding Kant's mistakes is important not only to understand Kant's vulnerabilities in these regards, but also our own, and it is necessary to finding a better, reconsidered Kantian theory of sex, love, and gender. In addition, I argue that by making Kant's basic philosophical framework and insights more consistent, we can derive from them a compelling approach to sexual love, sexual or gendered identity, and sexual orientation.

A good account of sexual love, sexual or gender identity, and sexual orientation requires at least four elements. It must explain how activities and relations involving these aspects of ourselves are deeply personal and can have a grounding function for us; they can make us feel safe and at home in the world as who we are. Second, sexual love, sexual or gender identity, and sexual orientations are often accompanied by a certain creative playfulness of which the experiences of the beautiful and the sublime in oneself and in another often are constitutive parts. Third, although sexual love is unruly in nature, we can assume moral responsibility for how we go about developing our capacity for it. Fourth, a minimally plausible account of sexual love, sexual or gender identity, and sexual orientation cannot end up with a cisist, binary, heterosexual analyses since that makes it incapable of speaking to polyamorous, polysexual, and LGBTQIA being and experiences in meaningful ways. Importantly—and this makes Kant's thinking difficult here—the first two elements concern ways in which sex, love, and gender, for the most part, is experienced in unreflective, non-moralizable ways. In fact, in order for reflections on our sexually loving or gendered selves to track reality, they must be informed by how we are oriented in unreflective, embodied, intimately social ways in life. Contrary to standard interpretations and common caricatures, I argue that Kant would agree with this.

More specifically, section 1 ("Kant on Sexual Love") reminds us of core relevant features of Kant's account of human nature (section 1.1)[1] and of the union between unreflective and reflective elements of the emotionally healthy, morally good human self as explored in Chapter 1. I expand on how Kant envisions the imagination—especially principles involving teleology (parts and wholes) and aesthetics (the beautiful and the sublime)—as informing and enabling human sexual, loving, gendered activity and being before revisiting some textual puzzles. Section 2 ("Reconsidering Kant on Sexual Love, Sexual or Gender Identity, and Sexual Orientation") develops important elements of Kant's own account, arguing that a more plausible account of morally justifiable, emotionally healthy human sex, love, and gender that encompasses the diversity of human sexual or gender identities and orientations can be found without abandoning Kant's basic philosophical framework. In this section, I also revisit the special relationship that existed between Kant and Joseph Green, arguing that it may be internally linked with Kant's anger around gay sexuality. I finish the chapter by indicating how we can use Kant's philosophical ideas to move beyond his own writings and search for more plausible engagements with human sex, love, and gender diversity. This re-envisioning of Kant's philosophy with regard to sex, love, and gender is achieved by reconceiving how we develop and transform our embodied animalistic forcefulness (our natural vital force) through our faculty of desire—through associative, abstract conceptual, teleological, and aesthetic means—in such a way that it is also brought into union with what morality requires (our moral vital force).

[1] For more on Kant's account of human nature and more explanation of the technical Kant language used below, see Chapter 1.

1. Kant on Sexual Love

As mentioned above, a sufficiently complex theory of sex, love, and gender needs an account of how an aesthetic-teleological employment of the imagination constitutes important aspects of it for many human beings (for Kant, as enabled by our employment of the beautiful and the sublime and of parts and wholes), and it needs a way to conceive of sex, love, and gender that avoids binary, cisist, and heterosexist binaries. Since I provided an interpretation of Kant's take on affectionate love in friendships in Chapter 1 and on the traditional genders ("man" and "woman") in the Chapter 2, here I only sketch his account with an eye to issues relevant to reconsidering his account of sex, love, and gender. More specifically in this section, I outline Kant's suggestion for how aesthetic and teleological use of the imagination is constitutive of sexual love, which enables us, in the next section, to overcome Kant's binary, cisist heterosexism.

To start, as we saw in Chapter 2, Kant's general suggestion is that emotionally healthy sexuality occurs when we use aesthetic and teleological imagination to experience complementary female and male sexual embodiment. More specifically, the beautiful (female) embodied power irresistibly allures and hence makes the sublime (male) embodied power want to subject itself to and become one with it, whereas the beautiful wants to be empowered by the sublime and hence wants to become one with it. In this way, the animalistic sexual union becomes a (teleological) union—an us—between two kinds of equally powerful, embodied principles; the female experiences sublime, forceful embodiment through her union with the male— through having it wanting her and yet being in control of it—and the male experiences beautiful, forceful embodiment through his union with the female. In addition, Kant argues, it is a union that is compatible with procreation and, so, with a teleological species-maintaining use of the imagination.[2] When things go well, Kant furthermore argues, this sexual union matures into a social, self-sustaining union in that the two people respect and affirm each other's worth as equals, and in which they split between themselves the emotional, physical, and social work, so that they complement each other in their shared life in addition to pursuing ends of their own. In this way, aesthetic-teleological employment of the imagination and moral judgment (respect) is constitutive of sexual love between men and women, which makes this union between human animals more complex than it is between other kinds of animals.

An illustration of this line of argument is found in his "Conjectural Beginning of Human History" essay, where Kant interprets the Judeo-Christian story of Adam and Eve in just this way. Part of Kant's purpose here, I believe, is to explain features of this story that help us to see how human beings' reasoning and imaginative powers set them apart from other animals both cognitively and emotionally (CB 7: 322, 328). To do this and consistent with the interpretation of the account of human nature provided in Chapter 1, Kant first emphasizes that though human beings share with other animals the natural drive for nourishment, our capacity for self-reflective

---

[2] Thomas Nagel (1969) comes close to philosophically defending something like Kant's own conception of "natural sexuality." For an interpretation much closer to the one I am defending here, see Wood (2008).

consciousness and reason (abstract, conceptual powers)—and, so, our more complex faculty of desire—enables us not only to be at a reflective distance from our natural, instinctual desires, but also to imagine new ways of satisfying them. Accordingly, humans can set new kinds of ends regarding our instinctual desire for nourishment rather than merely satisfying natural instincts. Contrarily, since other animals do not have self-reflective consciousness and abstract conceptual reasoning powers, their end-setting is fundamentally determined by instincts and natural desires. What is more, we (humans) can develop, transform, and enhance the sensuous experience itself also by utilizing our aesthetic appreciation of the beautiful and the sublime. For example, we enhance the experience of eating by combining tastes of various kinds of foods as well as through the aesthetic presentation of food as delicate (beautiful) or elegant (sublime), such as by manipulating colors and shapes. Again, as noted in Chapter 1, mature human beings do not only eat; we enjoy meals.

Second, and relatedly, humans can develop a more complex version of the natural sexual instinct. This instinct, Kant suggests, is that by means of which all animals, including humans, "care for the preservation of the[ir] kind" (CB 8: 113). Yet, our more complex faculty of desire enables us to develop and transform our natural sexual instinct too:

The human being soon found that the stimulus to sex, which with animals rests merely on a transient, for the most part periodic impulse, was capable for [them][3] of being prolonged and even increased through the power of the imagination, whose concern, to be sure, is more with moderation, yet at the same time works more enduringly and uniformly the more its object is *withdrawn from the senses*, and [they] found that it prevents the boredom that comes along with the satisfaction of a merely animal desire. The figleaf...was thus the product of a far greater manifestation of reason than that which it had demonstrated in the first stage of its development. For to make an inclination more inward and enduring by its withdrawing its object from the senses, shows already the consciousness of some dominion of reason over impulse and not merely, as in the first step, a faculty for doing service to those impulses within a lesser or greater extension. *Refusal* was the first artifice for leading from the merely sensed stimulus over to ideal ones, from merely animal desire gradually over to love, and with the latter from the feeling of the merely agreeable over to the taste for beauty, in the beginning only in human beings but then, however, also in nature. Moreover, *propriety*, an inclination by good conduct to influence others to show respect for us (through the concealment of that which could incite low esteem), as the genuine foundation of all true sociability, gave the first hint toward the formation of the human being as a moral creature.—A small beginning, which, however, is epoch-making, in that it gives an entirely new direction to the mode of thought— and is more important than the entire immeasurable extensions of culture that followed upon it.   (CB 8: 112-13)

Again, our reflective self-consciousness and abstract conceptual reasoning powers enable us to have a certain distance from our sexual desires such that we can develop, transform, and enhance them, including through a playful, aesthetic game of concealing and revealing our bodies to each other. I take it that although straightforward procreative sex in response to sexual impulse is obviously very satisfying (for people

---

[3] As usual, I have changed the translation of this quote insofar as necessary to make it more true to the original, gender-neutral German.

who enjoy straight sex), in the long run doing only this gets rather boring for human beings. We make it more exciting—and enrich the sexual pleasures experienced—by engaging in various sexual games of concealment, allurement, refusal, and acceptance.

Notice too that part of Kant's point here seems to be that we develop and transform our basic, animalistic affectionate sociality so that it is integrated into the self-recognitional kind of sociality enabled by our predisposition to humanity. That is, engaging in these kinds of sexual activities expresses our ability to affirm one another as equally valuable. The way in which our faculty of desire enables us to engage the world in new and playful ways is therefore seen as promoting more complex ways of desiring one another and as developing, transforming, and integrating sexual desire into mutual and affirmational sexual love. As the sexual, loving relation matures emotionally, each person develops an ability to be profoundly affectionate, emotionally open to, and affirmative of one another in the course of the sexual activity itself. Our being emotionally open to and affirming of another in terms of our sexuality is one way in which we are open to being struck by another as beautiful and/or sublime. It opens up our ability to experience the world as beautiful and/or sublime in an embodied way—to be, as Kant says, awe-struck or filled with awe.

The analysis above also helps bring out Kant's claims that being sexually attracted to someone is to want their *person*—and not just their body—as we want the other to show us their aesthetic, creative playfulness and invite us to be part of their endeavor to develop themselves as who they are, an endeavor that requires us to learn to show respect for one another in this process and, so, pushes us towards morality. This aspect of the analysis even helps to understand Kant's condemnation of masturbation. That is to say, being fully directed towards another in an emotionally open, sexually loving way is being directed towards the person, and not just the body of the person. One wants the other to see how one reveals oneself—as who one truly is, in all one's spontaneous, creative expressions—and one wants the other to want exactly this, to find exactly this irresistible, and to affirm one as revealed (and vice versa). And with time, we want to be part of each other's developing, transforming, and integrating this ability into something more than it was. If this is right, then Kant's worry about masturbation is that it is not other-directed in the right kinds of ways; it is narcissistically self-oriented rather than other-oriented. Additionally, for human beings, the point of sexuality cannot simply be orgasms; if it were, then sexuality would reveal us as "lower than the beasts" and involve "throwing away one's personality" since it would require focusing simply on one's animalistic capacity for intensely pleasant physical feelings rather than using our faculty of desire to develop and transform these capacities in an integrated life where our capacity for aesthetic appreciation as well as predisposition for humanity and personality are also realized as fully as possible and in a close union. We live in ways that bring our natural and our moral vital forces into union or we pursue the highest good understood as a union between morality and happiness.

Even though I believe this is too simplified a view of masturbation for emotionally healthy human beings (I provide a revised analysis below), it seems fair to say that a danger internal to sexual self-gratification is that sexuality simply becomes an occasion to feel sexual pleasures strongly and that a danger internal to sexual interaction is that there may not be reciprocity in emotional openness. Sexual love becomes either reduced to sexual pleasure or merely a more complex way of masturbating, where one is treating the other simply as a masturbation tool with the gratifying capacity to affirm one's sense of self.[4] Now, none of this is to say that this account is necessary or sufficient: after all, it is simply not the case that the binary, cisist, heterosexual way is how very many experience fulfilling sexual love—indeed, not even many who do identify as cis and heterosexual experience their own sexuality in such a binary way. In order to address these complexities, we need to use Kant's own philosophical tools to go beyond his texts, which is the purpose of section 2 below. Before doing so, however, let us revisit some of the textual puzzles noted at the beginning of this chapter and how my interpretation above can add to prominent existing Kantian engagements with them.

1.1 Some Textual Puzzles Revisited

As we saw in the introduction, Kant affirms a binary, cisist, heterosexist view of sexuality, according to which morally justifiable and emotionally healthy sex tracks procreation and ought to be undertaken only within the confines of lifelong marriage. Many, such as Barbara Herman (1993b), have noted that it is truly puzzling why Kant thinks that marriage can do such moral magic on inherently unethical activities (having sex). Although Kant certainly seems mistaken to think that sex is morally permissible only within the setting of cis heterosexual marriage (for reasons that will become clearer below), notice that it does seem plausible that encouraging an other to be as emotionally open as they can be in intimate, sexually loving affectionate relationships is justifiable only if one is equally open oneself. In my view, this is why Kant argues that when we realize our sexuality in ways that involve good realizations not only of our animality and humanity, but also of our personality, we do so in the context of marriages. Obviously, like several Kantians before me, I do not agree with Kant in this. I do not think emotionally healthy and morally good sexual encounters and relationships require marriage or that real relationships are this simple to make good; surely they are not. And yet, that Kant viewed marriage—a public, lifelong commitment of two people to each other—as fulfilling the criterion of reciprocal openness is not so strange: it may help explain why marriage is such an important human institution to so many (regardless of their sexual orientations or identities). Thus, this account can say something as to why Kant thinks that marriage is emotionally and morally important to many.

Notice too that this interpretation fits with Kant's argument that the only way in which sexual love itself can develop into a damaging, obsessive passion is if it is not reciprocated (A 7: 266). Like all passionate longings, unrequited love "gnaw[s] and consume[s] the heart or, so to speak, bind[s] the vital force with shackles" (PMB 15: 940) and "the capacity of the understanding is of little help against it; for the end of enchanted human being sees very well indeed the reasons against [their] favorite

---

[4] I cannot develop this argument here, but I believe the implied conception of moral development is broadly consistent with, for example, those we find in Herman (2008) and Abramson and Leite (2011).

inclination, but... [they feel] powerless to give them active emphasis" (MH 2: 261).[5] Sexual passion driven by unrequited love is emotionally and morally damaging because it can make it increasingly difficult for one to live one's own life; instead one's life becomes too focused on or obsessed with one unsatisfied aspect of life that one cannot develop, transform, and integrate into it. Marriage, then, for Kant, is one way to secure oneself against this morally dangerous aspect of sexuality; it captures how one reasonably expects anyone who wants profound, intimate emotional openness towards one to be(come) similarly oriented themselves, and to aim for a lifelong relationship since any other orientation involves exposing both oneself and an other to self-damaging passions.

To bring out other aspects of the above account, notice too how it allows us to improve upon existing interpretations of Kant by adding phenomenological structure to Kant's account, namely one informed by his account of human nature. For example, Barbara Herman (1993b) interprets,

although on Kant's view sexuality creates a morally impermissible relation between the sexual partners, it is neither desirable nor possible to forbid sexual activity. Sexual intercourse is the now standard (then necessary) means for procreation, and love relations with sexual components are essential to happiness (for many). So we have a kind of relationship that we cannot forego (as the kind of beings we are) but that is not morally acceptable. Marriage is supposed to solve the problem—resetting the moral stage so that there is a morally permissible way for sexual life to take place without inevitable moral loss or danger. (64-5)

She continues later,

The idea seems to be that through the mediation by law, the natural tendencies to objectification, and so dominance and exploitation, in sexual relations are blocked. The institution of marriage in this way resolves the moral difficulty arising from sexual activity. (67)

Herman proceeds,

The purpose of the institution of marriage is to block the transformation of regard that comes with sexual appetite.... What... [the rights and responsibilities] are to do is to secure regard for one's partner as a person with a life, which is what the sexual appetite by itself causes one to disregard. (68)

Consistent with Herman that sexual desire for Kant is inherently objectifying, Christine Korsgaard (1992) identifies the main problem somewhat differently, as being one of desiring to possess the other: "Viewed through the eyes of sexual desire another person is seen as something wantable, desirable, and, therefore, inevitably, possessable" (310). Marriage solves this problem of objectification, Korsgaard continues, because of how it enables reciprocal possession: "perfect reciprocity is the only condition under which the sexual relation is morally legitimate; and Kant thinks this condition is only possible in marriage, where the reciprocity of surrender has been pledged" (311). For sure, neither Herman nor Korsgaard thinks that the historical institution of marriage—or "marriage-as-we-know-it" (Herman) or "marriage as it

---

[5] As usual, I have changed the translation into the gender-neutral noun (they) here to make it more true to the original German.

has usually existed" (Korsgaard)—has been the solution; as Herman points out, *that* institution is a "nasty thing" (Herman 2002: 65) and "has hardly been a solution to *this* problem [of objectification]" (Korsgaard 1992: 311).[6] In *Sexual Solipsism*, Rae Langton (2009) engages these readings of Herman's and Korsgaard's and argues that even if Herman's reading of Kant's worries about sex (sexual love being "a desire for a person *qua* body, a *reductive* desire") or Korsgaard's reading (which understands sexual love as "a desire for a person *qua* person, but ... an *invasive* desire") is a correct interpretation, both take sexual desires to be "certain pathologies." This basic assumption appears affirmed by Jordan Pascoe (2012) as well in "Kant and Kinky Sex," where her main argument is that Kant mistakes all sex for kinky sex—before proceeding to explain how one can also engage in kinky (highly objectifying and consequently highly morally dangerous) sex in morally responsible ways. Finally, Langton (2009) concludes her engagement with Herman and Korsgaard by arguing that even if Kant held such a view, we should not see *all* sexual desire that way—and Pascoe agrees.

My interpretation adds to these discussions by showing how Kant's account of human nature informs his comments about sexuality. We have seen that according to Kant, simple animalistic sexual love is objectifying and bad because it does not involve a realization of our threefold predisposition to good in human nature; it is to live as if our beings are composed of only one aspect. Thus Kant sees only a dichotomy: "natural sexual union takes place either in accordance with mere animal nature ... or in accordance with *law* [which is *marriage*]" (MM 6: 277). Now, given Kant's account of sexual teleology, this is also why he thinks that the only thing worse than simple objectifying animalistic sex is *unnatural* objectifying sex; in this case, we not only live as if we are beings with sheer animality, but we use our capacities to choose to pervert this animality. This is why Kant says things like, "unnatural sex" involves

transgressions of laws, called unnatural [carnal crimes against nature] or even unmentionable vices, [which] do wrong to humanity in our own person, [and] there are no limitations or exceptions whatsoever that can save them from being repudiated completely;   (MM 6: 277)

unnatural sex goes along with a "*defiling* (not merely a debasing) of the humanity in his [one's] own person" and "debases him [one] beneath the beasts" and is "contrary to morality in its highest degree" (MM 6: 424-5); and unnatural sex is worse than suicide since a person who commits suicide must at least have courage, whereas the person engaging in unnatural sex thereby "abandons ... his personality (throwing it

---

[6] In Varden (2007, 2012a) as well as in Chapter 6 below, I argue that although the ideal legal institution of marriage does have such remedial virtues according to Kant, his argument succeeds without making objectifying features of sexual desire do such philosophical work. However, since the aim here is merely to see how Kant's account of human nature informs his comments on sexuality and how marriage can be emotionally healthy and a safeguard against our tendencies to do bad things, I am setting aside this issue here. Also, notice that if this argument is persuasive, it gives us interpretive resources with which both to show that Kant does not lack an account of the good, as Herlinde Pauer-Studer (1994) objects to Kant and Kantian defenders such as Barbara Herman and Christine Korsgaard. Also added is more structure to the Kantian phenomenology than we find to date in the work of Herman, Korsgaard, and other prominent Kantian ethicists.

away)" and instead simply "surrenders" to "animal inclination" in such a way that deprives them of all self-respect (MM 6: 425). "Mere" objectifying sex, in contrast, is to use one's own ability to choose (to exercise one's humanity) in such a way that one reduces oneself and the other to mere things—to animality—and so it is bad too, but not as bad.

In contrast, acting well for Kant involves developing one's sexual animality through one's faculty of desire in such a way that it is developed, transformed, and integrated into a unified whole that tends to have as a corollary aesthetic appreciation of one another and affirms both one's humanity and one's personality, and the only way to do this, we have seen Kant say, is to engage only in procreative sex activities within the confines of marriage. Only then is sexuality realized in non-pathological and morally justifiable ways. Below I argue, in a spirit similar to Langton and Pascoe, that although Kant is right to argue that human sexuality is morally dangerous, Kant is wrong to argue that the only way to realize emotionally healthy and morally good sexuality is through binary, cis, and heterosexual procreative sexual activities within the confines of marriage. Indeed, I argue, my reconsidered account of human sexuality is what Kant himself *should* have argued, given his core, basic philosophical commitments.

2. Reconsidering Kant on Sexual Love, Sexual or Gender Identity, and Sexual Orientation

The previous section outlined Kant's take on sexuality, which brings us back to the question asked at the beginning of this chapter: what went wrong philosophically such that Kant ended up defending the binary, cisist, heterosexist un/natural distinction, and how can we overcome this problem in his theory? In my view, the answers to these questions are also found in Kant's discussion of human nature, especially how his account of the three original predispositions to good is integrated with discussions of teleology and the beautiful and the sublime so as to show how we develop our natural animalistic vital force in emotionally healthy, morally good ways.[7] My proposal is that Kant should have conceived of this process somewhat differently, since only then would it be possible to capture how emotionally and morally healthy human sexual, loving being is not invariably experienced as binary, cis heterosexuality. I proceed without giving up on Kant's insight that there is more to human sexuality than what can be captured through scientific, deterministic analyses of strict causality (as would be the perspective of the first *Critique*) or through the moral perspective of freedom (as would be the perspective of the second *Critique*). I maintain that sex, love, and gender requires an analysis of the development of our animalistic vital force through the faculty of desire, where aesthetic-teleological imagination (the perspective of the third *Critique*) in addition to our humanity (rational end-setting and social sense of self) and personality (our moral vital force) are given due importance. The resulting account, I conclude, is what Kant *should* have defended, since it can capture the predispositional aspect of human

---

[7] See Chapter 1 for more detail.

sexuality and our experience of our own directedness towards others without ending up in unsustainable, binary, cisist heterosexism. I first outline what I take to be Kant's important insight that human sexuality should not be understood in terms of deterministic science or moralized accounts of free choices. I then show how we can overcome the binary, cisist, heterosexist shortcomings of Kant's own approach by means of his own philosophical ideas.

2.1 On the Givenness of Sexual or Gender Identity and Sexual Orientation

What Kant clearly seems correct in saying is that there is a certain givenness to the experience of one's own sexual, loving being, and that this is interconnected with feeling at home in the world as an embodied, animalistically forceful being; an animalism that is based on a natural vital force. Kant furthermore seems right that this embodied animalistic forcefulness concerns how we can feel safe in the world (self-preservation), how we can feel sexually excited (sex drive), and how we can feel ourselves as an affectionately loving us with others (basic sociality). In other words, Kant's suggestion that we develop our natural vital force as animalistic forcefulness through the relational categories of the understanding employed teleologically— understood as a part-whole reasoning—seems to track much human sexual, loving, and gendered experience and life. How one orients sexually, for example, such as whether one identifies oneself as straight, lesbian, gay, bisexual, polyamorous, and so forth, is experienced as tracking something true about oneself with regard to how one feels others can complete one safely in sexual and/or affectionately loving activities as an us. Similarly, sexual or gender identity and sexual orientation concerns, among other things, how one can experience oneself as a good part of a good world. Moreover, Kant seems right to argue that if we try to explore this givenness through the perspectives of deterministic science or unbounded/free choices, we simply cannot get it properly into view; such approaches fail to capture the importantly unreflective, subjective sense of givenness to one's sexual or gender identity and sexual orientation. There is something to get right about one's sexual or gender identity and sexual orientation and in an irreducible sense, only each individual can explore this. Yet what Kant, like so many others, seems clearly *wrong* about is the idea that this is simply a question of realizing oneself in line with a particular selection of the biological attributes one is born with. Therefore, even if we grant that there are cultural and biological tendencies that can be generalized into binary, cis heterosexuality, it is simply not the case that much flourishing human sexuality can be meaningfully understood in this way.

To illustrate the philosophical problem and how my revised Kantian account solves it, let me start with an example of sexual or gender identity, namely an experience common to some people who identify as trans. In my view, a good philosophical theory of sex, love, and gender must be able to make good sense of being trans, including the transitioning experience. It must, for example, address how some people who identify as trans are deeply uncomfortable with their current embodiment, a discomfort that can be alleviated only through transitioning. That is to say, the account must be able to explain how some people have a deep desire or need to go through the physical surgeries involved in transitioning, to change their physiology, and how, after undergoing these changes, they describe finally feeling peacefully at home in the world as the embodied beings they have always felt themselves to be. In my view, it is very hard to make good philosophical sense of this if we understand sex, love, and gender simply as a matter of choices (including in response to existing desires) or science (strict, deterministic spatio-temporal causality relations—in this case genetics and physiology). Both types of account struggle to get into focus the existential importance of the surgeries as well as the existential relief experienced when the process has been completed successfully. A sufficiently complex account needs to be able to capture how these people have not until after transitioning had the positive, life-affirming embodied experiences (including physical ones) that the medical interventions enable, and for which they have longed for so long. The choice (freedom) and science (determinism) accounts are not able to capture this. After all, before the surgeries, these people have not yet had the physical embodiment that they are longing for, meaning that their existing physicality pre-surgery cannot explain their desires pre-surgery, and so cannot explain why their discomfort is alleviated through transitioning and finally having those physical experiences. It seems more plausible to argue that such transitioning is better understood as fulfilling a deeply felt need to adjust one's physical embodiment so that it fits better with one's subjective experience of oneself as a forceful embodied part of the natural-social world (one's natural vital force), and as having the sexual functions and physical attributes important for one's sense of being beautiful, at home in the world, and for participating in profoundly fulfilling intimate relations. Virtue theories and capability approaches appear to do better here, since they, like Kant, let our embodied, social natures do important work in addition to freedom and natural science. However, to me it seems that naturalist virtue accounts that follow Aristotle's route struggle to get into view the way in which biology cannot do the necessary philosophical work, whereas capabilities approaches similar to Nussbaum's encounter a problem similar to those of the choice accounts. After all, also on the capabilities approaches it seems difficult to capture the subjective, existential necessity of transitioning for some (and not others) who identify as trans.

Let me try to illustrate these points with regard to sexual orientation, as well. Although most of us are significantly more flexible about sexuality than conventional theories seem to allow, it still seems true that many experience a basic sexual orientation with a certain givenness to it. They experience their sexual orientation as neither sheer choice nor as determined by strict causality (by their genetic and physiological structure)—and, again, it appears tricky to explain the existential importance of sexual orientation by the paths available through (naturalized) virtue accounts or capabilities theories. For example, straight people experience themselves as most comfortable sexually, including most sexually aroused and most easily sexually aroused, when they are sexually connecting with and physically complemented by people who identify as belonging to the opposite sex; gay people are most comfortable sexually with people who identify as belonging to the same sex, bisexuals with both, and queer people with people who present in non-binary ways. Again, this is to deny neither that there is much playfulness that crosses these boundaries for all sexual orientations nor that there is a deep openness characteristic of all mature human sexuality. Rather, the point is that these distinctions regarding sexual orientations do track something experienced as existentially important—an importance revealed both in how empowered one can feel oneself sexually (our strong natural vital force) and in how deeply and increasingly difficult it is for someone to be denied the possibility of living out their sexuality by developing and integrating it into their way of living life (the shackling or numbing of the natural vital force). And the more plausible philosophical accounts must be able capture this existential importance of one's sexual orientation for many lesbian, gay, bisexual, and queer people.[8]

I believe we can add to our understanding of the nature of our sex, love, and gender by reconsidering both the way in which Kant links the ideas of the sublime to the male and the beautiful to the female, and how we might understand ourselves teleologically as embodied beings. It seems to me that we do not, nor should we, have to link these ideas rigidly to the binary male and female, or to how the male and female perspectives can complement each other, such as in various ways of taking (power) and being taken (subjection), of being inviting and alluring as well as feeling oneself drawn towards and completed by another. Nevertheless, these principles of the beautiful and the sublime do seem important for how many go about realizing their sexuality one way or another, including when femme is attracted to femme or for those who playfully engage different principles at different times, in different situations. The philosophical mistake, therefore, does not lie in Kant's argument that many of us experience sexuality partially through the embodied employment of the aesthetic principles of the sublime and the beautiful or that teleological principles concerning unions (in Kant's words, the coming together of various kinds of parts and wholes) seem central to the experience for many. Both kinds of principles seem important to how many of us see ourselves as part of the natural world and as acknowledged and affirmed as attractive and as who we are by others; they are important to our feelings of being valued and of belonging or being grounded in the (natural-social) world. Teleological judgments also appear important in accounting for why it is common (albeit certainly not universally the case), regardless of one's sexual orientation and identity, to experience a deep desire to have children with one's deep sexual loves. For example, from the start, the rights to adopt and access to artificial insemination have been central to many members of the LGBTQIA community. Again, Kant's mistake is, rather, the way in which he lets the binary, cisist, heterosexist male-female distinction run through the entire analysis.

Although Kant himself was stuck in a binary, cisist, heterosexist perspective, I believe that it was philosophical considerations along these lines that informed his insistence that the phenomenon of sex, love, and gender cannot be understood through the *a priori*, non-contingent perspectives of either pure reason (first *Critique*) or pure practical reason (second *Critique*); sexuality is contingent and subjective in a way that neither perspective captures or allows. In the end, the distinction between men and women does not track spatio-temporal causal necessities, and it is simply not the case that most people find their basic sex, love, or

---

[8] As we saw also in Chapter 2, according to the recent National Transgender Discrimination Survey (Haas, Rogers, and Herman 2014), the suicide-attempt rate among people identifying as trans is 41 percent, 10–20 percent among gay and lesbians, and only 4.6 percent among people who identify as heterosexual.

gender to be something they can simply choose in unbounded ways, let alone find meaningful when undertaken out of a sense of (moral) duty. My approach is consistent too with Kant's basic suggestion that sexuality as such requires an analysis of our natural vital force through the perspective of human nature (the predisposition to good in human nature) in combination with an analysis of the beautiful and the sublime (third *Critique*). What we are exploring is not, in other words, our bodies qua spatio-temporal objects to be studied scientifically or qua objects we can choose to do sexual things with. Rather, we are exploring partially unreflective aspects of ourselves as having an embodied, animalistic, aesthetically responsive forcefulness. We are tending not only to the fact that there is a certain direction to our sexual forcefulness, but also to the nature of it—how it feels when we imaginatively develop our embodied forcefulness (our vital force) in enhancing our productive sexual and affectionately loving ways, when engaging it feels comfortable, safe, good, and aesthetically deeply pleasing as who we are, from a first-personal, subjective, and unreflective point of view. We are paying attention also to ways in which we respond and others complement and affirm us through their own sexual and affectionately loving forcefulness. And when we do this well, as who we are, we seek and are invited to affirm one another in playful, aesthetic, sexual, erotic, affectionately loving, and respectful—and so personally empowering—ways.[9] Thus, again, in Kantianese, what our faculty of desire picks out in intuition (as explored in the first *Critique*)—our natural vital force—is engaged, developed, and transformed in an inherently subjective way enabled both by the power of judgment (as explored in the third *Critique*) and through our associative and abstract conceptual powers in ways that brings it into union with what we can morally own (our moral vital force).[10] Thus, neither the perspective of deterministic science, nor that of choice[11] nor that of language[12] (construction) goes all the way when it comes to sex, love, and gender. There is something in us—a direction or structure to our embodied forcefulness—that we are in tune with, first-personally, when we are getting all of this basically right about ourselves.

In addition, when we do this well, rather than acting in ways that are destructive and damaging for our basic, embodied forcefulness (what we might, with Kant, call ways of "bind[ing] . . . the [natural] vital force with shackles" (PMB 15: 940)) we enable it, and so we enable ourselves, to develop, transform, and integrate our

---

[9] Because the three aspects of the predisposition to animality are enabled by Kant's relational categories of the understanding, one might say that this forcefulness in ourselves that we can pick up by intuition is what we engage at the animalistic level by means of the relational categories of the understanding though employed in teleological ways. And, in turn, this way of relating to ourselves is complemented in an integrated way by the emotional orientations enabled by our capacities for aesthetic appreciation, a social self-recognitional sense of self, and rational (open) and morally responsible end-setting.

[10] Here I am especially indebted to the work of Lucy Allais (2015) on the first *Critique* and Rachel Zuckert (2007) on the third *Critique*, but I do not think that the ideas I present presuppose their interpretations in particular.

[11] Thus, existentialist philosophy, including Beauvoir, as was noted earlier, is wrong on this point.

[12] If so, then much continental philosophy and related (hermeneutic) language-style interpretations of Kant get this wrong, which is a main reason why they fail to get all of sex, love, and gender into view, and tend to focus only on socially oppressive and violent aspects of it.

animalistic desires in aesthetically pleasing and morally good, emotionally healthy ways (constitutive of our humanity and personality). Again, if this is more or less right, we also see that my revised Kantian account can capture much of what makes people lean toward capabilities accounts or virtue theory—namely their ability to capture our embodied, social natures—but without having to pay the price such accounts share with choice and deterministic accounts, which is an inability to give satisfactory philosophical explanations of non-binary, non-straight, non-cis sexual, loving ways as both existentially important and good.

Notice too that if my revised Kantian account is correct, then it can provide some explanation why sexual love tends to be so unruly and difficult to handle well. I return to these issues in more detail in Chapter 4 on sexual violence, but for now notice that sexuality concerns deeply unreflective aspects of us, namely basic ways in which we feel at one with ourselves, at home in the world as who we are, including when together with others. It follows that one cannot alleviate one's discomfort with one's way of being sexually loving simply by thinking about it (reflecting). Reflection can make one aware of problems, and although it is a central means of dealing with some problems, much of the work is unreflective. It requires relearning (or learning for the first time) how to be vulnerable and true to oneself without feeling powerless. Or, to put the point differently: how we experience ourselves in sexually loving ways cannot be simply chosen (away). Relatedly, the above account can explain why it is difficult to understand a different way of being sexually loving than one's own: one's sexual loving self is inherently contingent and first-personal, and so another's different sexually loving self is something one can gain access to only by living closely and in an emotionally open reciprocity with that person. It would also explain why many seek to understand different subjectivities in these regards through art (paintings, songs, novels, plays, movies, books, etc.): art can offer a sense of what it is like to experience life through the eyes—or different sexuality—of another.

Various types of sexual oppression and aggression—the anger often referred to with the term "homophobia"— furthermore makes sense on the above account. If one is uncomfortable around sexuality or if one seeks to understand it only through the bifocal lenses of male and female or maybe even as simply being a matter of choice or of lived lives in language-structured realities, one may never quite under-stand and tend to the source of one's discomfort in the right way. To give this also a Beauvoirian spin consistent with what I have said above, it seems plausible to argue that facing the fact of flexibility in sexual love can be very confusing and scary. Some fears expressed as aggression ("homophobia") may be internally connected *not* to repressing one's deep sexually loving tendencies—such as those tracking one's sexual or gender identity or sexual orientation—but to fear of being seduced into realizing the possibility of one's more fluid, potential, and playful appreciation of sexual love. Additionally, appreciating the givenness of our sexually loving or gendered self—the way we basically *are*—can be one reason why people can get so terribly aggressive and violent against non-binary, non-cis, and/or non-straight people. It is as if the aggressors want to beat this given nature out of them—an end that is, obviously, impossible to achieve. And yet, a person's wanting to do so is, I think, best explained by how they are not feeling at home in the world—as a sexually loving or gendered self—and by how they find it disempowering that others actually are, even though those others are not even conforming to the dominant social norms regarding sex, love, or gender.[13]

None of this is to deny that if one finds oneself living in a cisist, sexist, and heterosexist society or as a member of a sub-culture in which physical, social, and emotional abuse against people who do not conform to binary, cisist, heterosexist norms are commonplace, then it takes much moral courage to stand up to it. It is, as Lucy Allais (2016) argues in relation to racism, much more tempting to rationalize one's (and much of society's) bad behavior by dehumanizing those who are wronged and hurt by the behavior, and by repressing (rather than exploring) the cognitive dissonance involved. Much aggression and violence against sexual or gendered minorities, for example, is rationalized through thinking that these people have sexually loving or gendered selves that depend upon corruption or perversion of human nature. For people like Kant, who are deeply committed to ideas such as respect for the dignity of human beings, the felt need to rationalize oppressive aggressive behavior such that it is seemingly consistent with respect for human dignity is great. For persons deeply committed to doing what is right—whether for moral, philosophical, or religious reasons—admitting that they have got something this important so very wrong, that they did not register human suffering *as suffering*, and even wanted to or have already inflicted more suffering on vulnerable others, maybe even loved ones, is a truly difficult thing to do, in Kant's time as it is now. I do not deny this—quite the contrary. In addition, although with respect to his racist and sexist statements, Kant appears to have improved with regard to the former and to have never been fully convinced of the latter, he never improved when it came to his binary, cisist heterosexism or his homophobia.[14] As well, even if we accept that Kant's account of natural teleology and his social context help explain his binary, cisist heterosexism, it does not suffice to explain his homophobia; his anger remains puzzling.

2.2 *The Curious Case of Immanuel Kant and Joseph Green*

So, how do we explain Kant's homophobia? As argued above, explaining homophobia—the turn from simple heterosexism (inability to perceive diversity) to homophobia (anger at human sexual diversity)—is difficult unless we somehow relate it to the angry persons' discomfort with their own sexuality. And indeed, if the tales of Kant and Joseph Green are correct, one source of Kant's homophobia may have been his inability to fully accept his own way of loving. According to the story, as noted earlier, Kant and Mr. Green developed a most special and intimate relationship, one that lasted from around 1765 until Mr. Green died in 1786.[15] We all

---

[13] I return to some of these complexities in Chapter 4, "Kant on Sexual Violence and Oppression."

[14] For discussion on this point, including whether or not I have been insufficiently harsh on Kant in my "Kant and Women" (2015c/2017) and in Chapter 2, see Huseyinzadegan (2018).

[15] For more on the special friendship between Kant and Mr. Green, see Hoffman (1902) and Gensichen (2004). I am most grateful to Terry Pinkard for drawing my attention to the relationship between Kant and Mr. Green, including these references to Gensichen and Hoffman. Many years ago, Pinkard also alerted Manfred Kuehn to these aspects of and related literature regarding Kant's life. For Kuehn's interpretation, according to which Kant and Mr. Green were simply best friends, see Kuehn (2001), and for further details see (Kuehn 2001: 154–8, 219, 222, 228, 240ff., 322ff.). For an interpretation of the relationship between

know the story of how everyone in Köningsberg could align their clocks with Kant's meticulously regular daily walk. However, what the story typically does not reveal is that Kant's regularity was due to his daily visits with Mr. Green. For many years, every afternoon Kant would walk to Mr. Green's house, where mostly he would find his dear friend sleeping in a chair. Kant would walk in, pull his chair up to Mr. Green's, and fall asleep there, until, at a specific time, they were both awakened. They then spent time together—talking about philosophy, life, politics, and literature—until Kant would leave at exactly 7 p.m. (9 p.m. on Sundays) to return home to work again. Reliably structured, this daily ritual was a central, precious part of how they lived their everyday lives together.

Kant's relationship with Mr. Green was special in other ways too. For example, the two would go for buggy rides and holidays together in the countryside outside of Köningsberg. And, indeed, the expectations regarding reliability and punctuality (set by Mr. Green) were very high also here. For example, once when Kant (who did not have a punctual nature) forgot the time and arrived a few minutes late, Mr. Green left without him—with Kant running down the street after the buggy. Mr. Green (a banker) was also entrusted with Kant's financial investments—something Mr. Green did so well that Kant was relatively well off in his later years. Mr. Green furthermore read and discussed all of Kant's philosophical writings with him in this period—including the entire first *Critique* as it was developing—and together, they were invited every Sunday for dinner at two friends' (the Motherbys') house. These ways of living together and caring for one another do not characterize ordinary friendships. The relationship is much more intimate, has more structure and daily involvement, and is accompanied by much higher expectations than do ordinary friendships. The relationship includes features that simply cannot be explained without a notion of intimate, affectionate, reciprocal love. It is therefore also not surprising to learn that when Mr. Green passed away, Kant had a crisis and in important ways withdrew from the world. (Kant later re-entered the world in a new way, which included his famous dinner parties.)[16] Now, Kant and Mr. Green never seem to have taken their relationship to physical, sexual levels, and judging from Kant's anger when he writes on sexuality, one reason could very well be a discomfort with this aspect of himself. Of course, for those of us who live out non-heterosexual sexualities, we intimately understand the challenges of doing so. Indeed, the more sexually oppressive the society we have grown up in, the better we grasp the difficulty. We are correspondingly not surprised by such a story about Kant, by how it can be the reason for his homophobic anger. We know that sexual discomfort and/or self-hatred sometimes manifests itself in this way; tragically sometimes those who hate us the most are the same as we are.

Kant and Mr. Green that I consider closer to my own, see Jauch (2014); see also this work of hers for an interpretation of Kant's other significant male relationships. For other philosophical engagements (and other references to bibliographical texts) with the relationship between Kant and Mr. Green, see Steve Naragon (2017), who includes a rather extensive overview of early sources on the issue, and Zammito (2002).

[16] For two particularly interesting explorations of Kant's dinner parties, see Cohen (2008) and Jauch (2014).

2.3 *Eroticism and Sexual Diversity—Moving Further Beyond Kant*

Another problem with Kant's reflections upon sexuality, which can also be explained through his own discomfort around it and which the above revision of his account can make better sense of, is his writings' inability to capture the erotic as opposed to the sexual. In particular, eroticism may be seen as distinct from sexuality in that erotic experiences are characterized by delighting in another or in oneself as an embodied sensuously and aesthetically appealing being. Accordingly, the erotic aspect of our sexuality is not about wanting another person or wanting another person to want oneself. Rather, this part of sexuality is more about delighting in oneself or in another person as the sensuously embodied yet particular being that one, or that the other, is. This is not to say that eroticism does not involve arousal, but that the arousal involved is not of an alluring, dominating, or possessive kind. And I take it that erotic arousal can be one way in which another can give rise to awe in us; we can find ourselves profoundly struck by the beauty of another, whether in person or in an artistic depiction. And a lot of intimate, sexual interaction switches between these ways of engaging one another—the sexual (wanting and wanting to be wanted by the other) and the erotic (delighting in oneself and in an other).

Kant's own account of sexuality is also unable to account for how good sexual interaction does not always come with deep emotional connections, how it sometimes is not limited to only one other person, and how some do not experience themselves as particularly sexual at all. I believe my revised account can. It seems undeniable that many people genuinely enjoy casual sexual encounters, including with strangers, and that these can be experienced as emotionally and morally uncomplicated for all parties involved. On my revised Kantian account, this fact should not be seen as all that surprising. Under uncomplicated conditions, developing sexual desires in meaningful, playful ways, including together with others, needs neither always to require deep emotional connections nor morally corrupting objectification. For example, one may compare a morally good, emotionally healthy casual sexual encounter with a game of squash (though this example runs the risk of not communicating this point to those who do not find sports—or other physical games—deeply enjoyable). So, finding a great squash partner is truly wonderful: that particular partner knows exactly how to challenge you, it is always a good game with that partner, and good games are just fantastic fun; they challenge you and enable you to grow in all kinds of playful, deeply satisfying ways. They give you a good game even on a pretty bad day. Still, sometimes it is fun to play with someone you have not played with before, and not only because playing squash is a fun way to get to know someone. Sometimes playing squash with someone new is fun because it is just a different game, sometimes because newness is fun in its sheer unpredictability, and sometimes because, for some reason, that particular player is able to challenge you in a different way, a way you find very satisfying; they intuitively get your way of playing in such a way that they can challenge you in ways no one has before. And for some, playing squash is a way of being in the world that is so important and so enjoyable that they seek to establish or join clubs where they are likely to be able to live this out with similarly minded people in good ways, etc.

I do not think that having emotionally healthy, morally justified sex, as such, is all that different from a good game of squash, which is not to belittle either. And it is not universalizable, meaning that it is not the same for all. For some, the best games are with one's one-and-only or one's few fellow players—the one or those who know you so very well and with whom you have had or aspire to have long-lasting, committed connections and relationships. For others, all that emotion and history is a little burdensome, and it is lovely and light to have new partners. And some seek to take squash to a different level together with others who have similar strong desires. I believe these are simply subjective, individual, personal differences. It is just the way it is (and we are). Which does not mean that those who mostly prefer to play one way cannot ever enjoy doing it another way. Or that some people find it OK once in a while, but not all that often. And it is not to deny that some folks do not like to play squash at all. They really, really do not like it: they find it physically exhausting and sweaty (rather than thrilling and exuberating), smelly and messy (rather than luscious), and drainingly dramatic and emotional (rather than, simply, amazingly wonderfully fun and challenging). And that is all right too. Obviously. We really just are that different. Or to put these points back into the sexual framework: we might think of the various ways in which we are sexually and erotically oriented as coming with a range of volume switches—some of them may be generally turned up quite high, whereas others are turned down very low or off. We have therefore many combinations of types of sexual or gender identity and orientation as well as differing subjective enjoyments of various types of sexual and erotic activity, depending on how we are—first-personally. Rather, paying attention in an attempt to understand ourselves sexually and erotically, gives us clues as to what (and who) can help us flourish in this aspect of our being.[17]

Judging only by divorce rates, it is likely that very many of us do not subjectively fit the traditional monogamous, cis, heterosexual ideals of sex, loving, gendered relations. My account of sex, love, and gender gives us reason to think that for some exploring open (polysexual or polyamorous) arrangements or marriages is likely to be better, whereas for others, it is giving up the expectation of cis or straightness that is necessary to start exploring more meaningful sexual, loving ways. Doing any of it in truthful, authentic ways—ways that feel deeply good and are morally justifiable for oneself and one's partners—is not easy. It is difficult to develop, transform, and integrate one's sexually loving self together with others in ways that are productive to each and all. Yet as the various, relevant statistics of divorce rates for monogamous, cis, heterosexual marriages, and the suicide rates for sexual or gendered minorities show, trying to uphold the traditional, heterosexual, binary social norms is undesirable and unwise for all as they are impossible and damaging norms to many people. After all, the fact that there is much room for playfulness and variety (including much space for casual sexual encounters in human lives lived well) does not undermine the fact that sexual love comprises very strong forces; they can make us

---

[17] Chapter 4—on sexual violence and oppression—can also help us speak to how being able to enjoy sexual interactions of the kinds one wants is harder for those whose social identities are oppressed. For example, it is harder in today's world to be able to find enjoyable, safe, casual interactions for straight cis women than it is for straight cis men. Additionally, regardless of which non-traditional sexual interactions one needs and wants to flourish, one cannot simply rely on tradition as guidelines and, so, it requires more carefulness about figuring out how to go about realizing them.

risk it all, and not being able live, transform, develop, and integrate our sexual, loving, gendered selves in good ways can make us lose our way in life and find self- and other-destructive ways irresistibly tempting.

To sum up, I believe that Kant is right that there is something about sexual love and gender that is first-personally experienced as given and that there is something about this self that we can only get into view if we invoke the aesthetic ideas of the beautiful and the sublime as well as teleological concepts of complementary parts and wholes. Kant's mistake concerns how he thinks this entails that good (emotionally healthy, morally justifiable) sexual, affectionately loving, gendered ways comes in only two good forms (male and female), that those who are biologically more male always identify with the sublime and those biologically more female always identify with the beautiful, and that good sexual, affectionately loving, gendered activity can only contain binary, cis, procreative heterosexual activities within the confines of marriage. Once we give these up and add the other elements in the ways indicated above, I believe the result is a powerful account of human sex, love, and gender. The revised position can account for the non-moralized features of human sexuality and it is also no longer binary, cisist, or heterosexist. My revised account can explain how our sexually loving, gendered selves are experienced as given, grounding, embodied, social, deeply personal, and aesthetically playful. Engaging our sexually loving, gendered selves, I have furthermore argued, fundamentally concerns how we experience ourselves as embodied forces that others can complement, strengthen, and value in embodied, affectionate, aesthetic, and respectful ways. The revised account can therefore explain how sex, love, and gender encompasses extraordinary interpersonal power and empowerment; it centrally engages and affirms our sense of being valuable, even beautiful and precious, in the interactions with, and eyes of others. That is, the way in which many of us engage and develop our sexuality very much incorporates a playful use of teleological as well as aesthetic principles, of power and subjection, parts and wholes, and of the beautiful and the sublime. Insofar as we do this in good ways, we sympathetically and correlatively track one another's particular ways of being and enable ourselves to become even more playful in sexual, loving, and aesthetic ways—and so we also experience a feeling of seeing others and of being seen as who we are and desired as such. Being sexually loving in mature ways is therefore not about "throwing away one's personality," even though it does consist of, in important ways, letting go of the self-reflective, moralized perspective; it is importantly about learning to let go and trust—albeit supported by good reasons—both oneself and another or others through directly and affirmatively engaging each other in caring ways through revealed sexual, affective, and aesthetic playfulness. In the words of Rae Langton, the point of letting oneself love and be loved is not primarily to know oneself, but because living together in affectionately affirming, loving ways (including sexual ones) is one of the most meaningful things we can experience, it is like daring to go through an open gate "to a garden, an orchard of fruits where things are growing (calamus and cinnamon, myrrh and aloe), where there are cool breezes, the sound of water—and [from where] someone seems to be calling" (Langton 2009, 381).

The above is not to deny that sometimes morality (ethics and the law) comes in to limit sexually loving behavior—indeed, our tendency to do bad things is empirically universal. I expand on these two complexities in other chapters, but for now, let us simply note that for morally responsible persons, the law primarily only engages with other-destructive, coercive (non-consensual) behavior, creates conditions under which one can form legal obligations, including a legally recognized "us" (marriage), and it deals with systemic injustices that track sex, love, and gender, such as poverty and oppression. Ethics, in contrast, comes in as a limiting force also in consensual interaction and any destructive sexual behavior. As we know, for Kant there are two types of ethical duties—perfect and imperfect[18]—and I take it that there are two main ethical alerts that something is off. Aligning with our perfect duties is behavior that is either self- or other-destructive, in which case the behavior violates one's perfect duties to self and others. For example, if one is gay, ethics manifests as bad conscience if one pushes oneself to engage in straight sex that one really does not want and which makes one feel that one is acting in numbing, damaging, or self-destructive ways towards oneself. Aligning with our imperfect duties is to develop oneself and assist others in their pursuit of happiness, which in this context means striving to feel at home with oneself and in the world in terms of one's sexually loving, gendered self. It is also to help one's partner(s) and loved one(s) develop theirs. Finally, affirming what Kant says elsewhere, until all are living under conditions of freedom, we do not really know which of a culture's dominant beliefs about the inherently contingent issues of moral anthropology—here sexually loving, gendered selves—are prejudices and which are insights (MM 6: 217). Consequently, we must let the objective principles of freedom set the framework within which we make space for considerations of moral anthropology, and then some people will break free from the prejudices and others will follow thereafter. As we saw in Chapter 2, the previous century brought a good deal of liberation from historically common prejudices for women; in this century, we are, with hope, seeing the beginning of a similar development for the flourishing of non-binary and LGBTQIA identities and orientations.

3. Concluding Remarks

In this chapter, I have suggested that we can explore sexuality's or gender's givenness by means of an idea of embodied, animalistic forcefulness (natural vital force) that is engaged and developed, transformed, and integrated through our faculty of desire— through abstract conceptual, associative, and aesthetic-teleological means—in such a way that it is also brought into union with our moral vital force. If so, notice that we then have a suggestion for how Kant's metaphysics can be seen as working to explain aspects of our sexually loving, gendered selves and we can furthermore solve certain puzzles in contemporary philosophical discussions of sexual or gender identity and sexual orientation. On the one hand, we have seen that we can make sense of the experience of givenness of sexual or gender identity and sexual orientation without invoking a notion of an "essence"—whether understood in rationalist ways (e.g., the idea of "femaleness") or in scientific ways (e.g., the idea expressed in search for the

---

[18] For more on how I read Kant's distinction between perfect and imperfect duties, see Chapter 1.

"gay gene" deterministically understood).[19] On the other hand, we have an analysis that avoids understanding our sexual loving, gendered selves simply as a matter of choice—whether an existentialist type of analysis of free choice à la Simone de Beauvoir in *The Second Sex* or a postmodern analysis of more or less coerced performances à la Judith Butler in *Gender Trouble*—something that for long has been a central objection to both types of theories, especially from members of the LGBTQIA community.[20] Instead, the account draws on these philosophers'—and inspired works'—important insights and moves beyond them by being able to speak better to how members of the LGBTQIA community, again and again, call on philosophers to listen to them when they say that their sexual, loving, gendered selves are experienced neither as essences nor simply as free choices. In so doing, the account also presents itself as a strong alternative to virtue theory, including capabilities accounts.

Finally, notice that one interesting feature of the account is the way in which the third *Critique* provides the clue for understanding the nature of sex, love, and gender. Our sexual, loving, gendered selves concern our embodied forcefulness, but constitutive of developing it well is our capacity for reflective judgment (the imagination), namely our capacity to relate to our own embodied forcefulness (natural vital force) aesthetically and teleologically as "purposive without a purpose," that is, without a claim to objective, universal (scientific or moral) validity—which is why any attempt at reducing our sexually loving, gendered selves to the perspective of deterministic science and/or to free choices will fail. If Kant is right about this, then, as we have seen, our sexually loving, gendered selves involves engaging with an embodied forcefulness (our natural vital force) that we can pick out by intuition (in ourselves or in others) that we then develop through our faculty of desire. Doing so consists of developing, transforming, and integrating it in ways consistent with our animality, humanity, and personality functioning as a unified whole—both our natural and our moral vital forces—that is also aesthetically pleasing as such (beautiful/sublime) or to us in particular (what we like; agreeable).[21] On the latter point, regardless of how we sexually identify or orient, for example, we can all agree that someone can present in a "hot" way, such that those who do not see it as "hot" are failing to perceive something just as would be the case when someone does not see that an incredible painting is beautiful. One is not seeing or getting something there to be got. Gender

---

[19] It may be worth pointing out that because of the way in which human sexuality involves our embodied forcefulness, it is entirely consistent with my theory that there is a science (i.e., a strict spatio-temporal causal analysis) of some aspects of our sexuality, as there is of any other aspects of our physical bodies. My theory is also consistent with some animalistic aspects of our sexuality being explorable through biological sciences and the contingency they allow. For example, current research on the so-called "gay gene," although still in its infancy, has not revealed strict causal relations but rather certain tendencies with respect to some sexual desires. Rather than denying any roles for science and biology, I have argued that human sexuality cannot be fully understood by either approach.

[20] We see Butler acknowledge in an interview by Molly Fischer for the *New York Magazine* (2016), that she is "thrilled to see the work that has gone beyond hers." Of *Gender Trouble* in particular, she says, "I didn't take on trans very well. The book doesn't account for the experience of gender that someone like Caitlyn Jenner describes when she says her brain feels 'much more female than it is male,' for example. So, in many ways, it's a very dated book."

[21] For more on Kant's distinction between the beautiful and the agreeable, see Chapter 1.

presentations work—we can all pick up on gender presentations that are, say, "butch," "tomboy," "queer," and they work on this conception because gender is something that opens up to us by means of our shared capacity for aesthetic judgment. Sometimes, however, we present more intimately to those who really like us, including in response to what they really like; we use aesthetic judgment in its capacity to appreciate something as "agreeable," as something we simply like (rather than something we necessarily think should strike everyone as cool or beautiful).

If all these appeals to Kant's arguments in the third *Critique* are along the correct lines, then they can also explain why so many of the philosophical writings on the phenomenology of sex, love, and gender are written within the continental or postmodern tradition. As we know, the philosophers in this tradition are not only closely connected with those thinkers particularly inspired by Kant's third *Critique*, but they also follow their basic philosophical judgment that core features of sex, love, and gender are impossible to get good hold of if we limit our analyses to the objective lenses enabled by deterministic science (first *Critique*) and free choices (second *Critique*). Contrary to what they and many think, however, Kant would agree: exploring subjectivity so understood is at the heart of the matter. And so do I.

4

Kant on Sexual Violence and Oppression

Introduction

"I am the love that dare not speak its name," Lord Alfred Douglas ends his beautiful poem "Two Loves." Oscar Wilde surely was right that the love Douglas had in mind was the sexual, erotic, and/or affectionate love that can exist between older and younger men, the kind Socrates seems to have experienced in some of his relationships with younger men. Equally surely, however, the reason why Douglas touches so many of us with his poem is because its reach is not limited in this way. Douglas's poem speaks to those of us who know first-personally the sadness that comes with loving in a way that often does not dare to be spoken. It expresses the sadness of living a life that is not commonly recognized and affirmed as a loving life, as a life that tracks some of the best of who we are. Indeed, some of the sadness tracks how the one who does not dare to speak its name, to own it, sometimes is oneself. Knowing that Douglas himself later in life not only failed to embrace the way he loved, but publicly denounced his relationship with Oscar Wilde and actively promoted homophobia only makes the poem more powerful.

Douglas's poem also gives voice to how sometimes the reason we—polyamorous, polysexual, or members of the LGBTQIA community—choose to be silent is fear that voicing our love may attract all-consuming (emotional and/or physical) violence from people belonging to the majority, from people who love themselves and others in socially powerful ways. We know that those who love in socially powerful ways are tempted to maintain that we should know our place—in the shadows, quiet, sad, grateful for their permission to exist at all—or we will be made to feel their power, their wrath. Anyone who loves in polyamorous, polysexual, and/or LGBTQIA ways knows this dangerous, phobic anger intimately: it is a dehumanizing violence that can turn into a deadly rage that seeks not only to subordinate but to destroy one's being. And we know that this anger can come from strangers, from people who love us, and from people who love like we do. It can be done in the name of knowing and loving us better than we do ourselves, and it can even be done in God's name. Presenting one's polyamorous, polysexual, or LGBTQIA identity or orientation with confidence, joy, and without shame is internally connected with an increased likelihood that the anger and violence becomes directed at you. At the moment, the most

Sex, Love, and Gender: A Kantian Theory. Helga Varden, Oxford University Press (2020). © Helga Varden.
DOI: 10.1093/oso/9780198812838.001.0001

difficult LGBTQIA lives are trans lives,[1] but all polyamorous and polysexual people and members of the LGBTQIA community—including those whose social situation permits them to live relatively safely out in the world—know more intimately than others the importance of being able to love quietly and to trust themselves and their loved ones in their way of loving. Belonging to any of these sexual or gendered minorities requires, as Douglas says, one to deal better with loneliness and violent threats than being monogamous, cis, and straight does. To keep the threats at bay often requires that one chooses the loneliness of silence. Besides, being able to live such a life well requires that one must try to find ways that do not lead one down paths of self- and other-destruction. It requires one to learn both to own the complexity of one's life without running away from it in (or due to others') anger and violence (as Douglas did in the end). It furthermore requires one to distinguish when it is possible to work with privileged others to peacefully improve conditions from when it is not, and to be able to handle both situations.

Living a life that continuously requires dealing with harassment and oppression, with the real threat of becoming subjected to sexual violence, and with the expectation that one should be silent is not only part of the history of and reality for polyamorous and polysexual people as well as members of the LGBTQIA community, however. It is similarly characteristic of the conditions of sex workers and of women. Sex workers live with a high risk of being subjected to sexual violence.[2] Without exception, sex workers are poorly protected in the existing legal-political systems. And in many places, offering sexual services for sale as such is criminalized in addition to carrying severe social stigma. Criminalization and social stigma, in turn, radically affect sex workers' abilities to use the legal system, the health care systems, the economy, the financial system, etc., as systemic means through which they can freely set and pursue ends safely and as others' equals. In fact, participating in these systems if one is a sex worker often comes with a real risk of further wrongdoing being done to oneself by people who take advantage of one's social and legal-political vulnerability.

As the #MeToo movement has shown so clearly, women in every country also live with a real threat of being sexually harassed or assaulted, including being raped; there is no country on the planet where women, across the board, are paid the same as men for the same jobs or can climb as easily as men can career-wise; most women live under conditions where social indications of sexual confidence are positively correlated with increased danger of social condemnation and violence; many women live in societies where there is little to no legal protection against domestic violence; almost no states have a system that enables women safely to flee from abusive husbands; a large number of women are traded as sex slaves internationally; women comprise by far the largest number of servants in the world, doing work that commonly goes along with a real danger of being subject to sexual violence without any (real) legal recourse; many women find themselves in situations where obtaining a home of their own or access to other forms of financial security requires them to marry men or to engage in

---

[1] As a reminder, the suicide-attempt rate among people who are trans in the US is 41 percent, 10–20 percent among gay and lesbians, and only 4.6 percent among people who identify as straight.

[2] See Deering et al. (2014) for a relatively recent overview of violence against sex workers.

dangerous, frequently illegal practices of selling sexual services; and, finally, some heterosexual men equate sexuality with a kind of unilateral subjugating violence, which makes sexual violence a part of what some heterosexual men and women think of as normal sex. Indeed, we need an account of sexual and gendered wrongdoing that can make sense of what Margaret Atwood puts her finger on when she says, "Men are afraid that women will laugh at them. Women are afraid that men will kill them."

Some of the complexities mentioned above, such as most of those contained in the buying and selling of sexual services and the legal institution of marriage will be dealt with in later chapters. The primary objective here is to use Kant's philosophical resources to provide a critique of (emotional and physical) sexual violence and wrongdoing in a broad sense of the term, meaning that it refers to violence that is aimed at or motivated in part by perceived sexual or gendered differences. This will include providing answers to questions such as why sexuality is morally dangerous; why sexuality is a site of abuse that is emotionally and morally bad on so many dimensions; what distinguishes sexual violence from other kinds of violence such as racial and ethnic violence, even though these aggressions sometimes come in the form of sexual violence; and, finally, how we may deal more wisely with various forms of sexualized violence. I start by using Kant's account of human nature in combination with his account of "affect" and "passions" to give a general critique of sexual violence, of why it is tempting for human beings generally and can be not only harmful, but damaging. Affects and passions, we will see below, make it subjectively more difficult to control our lives by means of our practical reason, and when we face experiences of sexual love, we face the challenges of integrating, transforming, and developing ourselves such that we are not ruled by affects and passions. More specifically, affects temporarily disable our ability to act from practical reason, whereas passions depend upon thinking processes that makes us not want to act in emotionally healthy, morally justifiable ways. As we will also see, Kant distinguishes between direct and indirect dangers of passions, where (in the context of sexuality) the *direct* dangers concern how trailing sexual love is the temptation to develop what he calls the "inflamed" or hot (affect-involving) passions of "sex" and "freedom," whereas the *indirect* dangers concern how men are tempted to use their relative physical strength as part of developing the "cold" (reason-involving) passion of domination over women.

With these philosophical tools at hand, we can then see that the temptations of the hot passions of sex and freedom can explain the "inflamed" types of violence against women, sex workers, polysexual and polyamorous people, and members of the LBGTQIA community, such as some very violent rapes and enraged, sexualized phobic beatings. Another strength of Kant's account, I propose, is its ability to capture the moral psychology of the dehumanization of social groups—to capture why human beings can bring themselves into a state where they do not register other human beings' suffering *as* suffering—which is necessary to account for both the patterned frequency of sexual violence against women, sex workers, and sexual minorities, and the heinousness of some of these attacks. In addition, the cold passion of domination can help us understand cold, binary, sexist, cisist, and heterosexist violence, such as the denial of educational opportunities for women, exclusion of polyamorous people or sex workers from normal community life, or refusing to hire members of the LGBTQIA community. The two other cold passions—for honor and for possession—can explain both how sex workers, polyamorous and polysexual people, and members of the LGBTQIA community often are required to be silent, and some ways in which sexual violence can be used as a tool of war and oppression. This account also enables us to see how the sexual violence that is part of the oppression of sex workers and women is different in kind from the sexualized violence that is part of the oppression of polyamorous and polysexual people as well as the LGBTQIA community: the former typically seeks to put sex workers and women "in their place" of subordination, whereas the latter typically seeks to ostracize or to annihilate. In addition, sexual violence against sex workers and women in radically bad situations, including those enabling sex slavery, characteristically consist of treating these persons as mere means or as possessions.

Once we have clarified these arguments of Kant's, we are in a position to use the account to explain how someone with a "depraved" heart can manipulate and channel people's liabilities to act in affective and passionate ways so as to draw people into participating in ethnic and racial atrocities in which sexual violence serves as a tool. I finish by arguing that sexuality is one area of life where we can face situations or conditions in which some other(s) makes it impossible to interact in respectful ways and, so, where there may not be any emotionally and morally good ways out for the targeted individuals or groups of individuals, as we see revealed in the phenomenon of choosing to be silent. To explore this set of issues, I make use of Kant's distinction between "material" and "formal" wrongdoing and his related idea of "doing wrong in the highest degree." Doing so helps us see the challenges of learning to live with such experiences or in such oppressive conditions without succumbing to self- and other-destructive desires, including those involving damaging passions such as revenge.

1. The Temptation and Damaging Nature of Sexual Violence: Affects and Passions

Kant's account of human nature—of the predisposition to good and the propensity to evil especially—together with his accounts of "affect" and "passions" enable us to explain why (emotional and physical) sexual violence can be both very tempting and very damaging for human beings. Although we are not fragile and can handle quite a lot of bad behavior from people around us—including those we love—sexual violence can be very damaging because sexual violence attacks us at both the level of animality and the level of humanity. That is to say, even though sexual violence always disrespects us (our personality), the effect can be profound also because of the way in which our embodied sociality is being used against us and because of the importantly unreflective, existential nature of the emotions enabled by animality and humanity. The emotions lodged at both levels concern our embodied, social make up; they concern our emotional openness to others and our sense of being safe in the world; they concern our sense of ourselves as loveable and loved, interesting and precious, which is why sexual attacks can undo us or make it hard for us to hold onto ourselves. Likewise, sexual violence can be tempting both because it can make us feel seen, powerful, loved, sexually affirmed, and alive, and because it can be a means of escaping one's own challenge of emotional and moral improvement. Furthermore, the way in which these emotions are inherently unreflective can make it difficult for us—especially in the heat of the moment—to know exactly what we are doing: whether what we *think* we are doing is actually what we *are* doing. These embodied, social aspects of ourselves, therefore, can involve emotions that are very strong and unruly, and they are such that it is very easy and tempting to lose our way with regard to them. Once we have drawn from Kant's philosophy to clarify how to approach all of these questions—why the combination of the predisposition to good and the propensity to evil (section 1.1) and affects (section 1.2) and passions (section 1.3) create such an emotionally powerful, disobedient mix with regard to human sexuality—we turn to the questions of the patterned and particularly heinous aspects of sexualized violence.

1.1 The Predisposition to Good and the Propensity to Evil—A Quick Reminder

As explained in previous chapters, according to Kant, the predisposition to good in human nature enables us to use our faculty of desire to develop, transform, and integrate three aspects of ourselves into one harmonious whole: our animality (our conscious striving for self-preservation, sex, and basic community), our humanity (our social sense of self and rational end-setting), and our personality (moral feeling). Animality enables conscious, emotional orientations in the world that are importantly unreflective in nature—they are internally linked with our animalistic, natural vital power—and thus that are not under the direct control of our reflective, cognitive powers. In addition, our predisposition to animality is constitutive of some of our biggest thrills, joys, and griefs, such as those involved in falling in love, feeling sexual lust, losing loved ones, facing dangers, etc. Humanity concerns challenges contained in developing our basic, social sense of self as well as our capacity to set ends of our own rationally. These aspects of ourselves require reflective powers and reason in that they consist of both comparative emotions and acting on (universalizable) maxims. As a result, developing this aspect of ourselves involves tremendously powerful social emotions, such as taking joy in others' ventures as well as experiencing shame, jealousy, envy, and Schadenfreude. What is more, humanity enables us to develop ourselves through pursuing personal projects freely (set ends of our own open-endedly) and rationally (through setting ends of our own in justifiable ways). Personality, in turn, is what enables us to do one thing rather than another *just because* it is right—to act as motivated by practical reason—and it is internally linked with our moral vital power. Now, as we seek to do all of this well—as we seek the highest good understood as a harmonious union between human happiness (internally linked with our animalistic, natural vital power) and human morality (internally linked with our moral vital power)—we additionally use our imagination in both the teleological ways central to striving towards becoming good and whole as well as in the aesthetic ways that enable us to develop and appreciate ourselves, each other, and the lives we live as involving the principles of the beautiful and/or the sublime.

As we have also seen in previous chapters, trailing our predisposition to good is the propensity to evil, which comes in three degrees. At each level, there is a particular way in which it is tempting for us to do bad things and to develop inclinations that make it subjectively more difficult for us to live lives that are truly good and morally justifiable: *frailty* is the temptation not to do what we know we ought to do; *impurity* is the temptation to act on bad motivations; and *depravity* is the temptation to reverse the order of motivations so that rather than seeking to act in ways that are morally justifiable upon reflection, we use our reflective, cognitive abilities self-deceptively to do bad (destroy what is good and right) in the name of or under the guise of the good. When we are wronged, switching now from the perspective of wrongdoers to the perspective of being wronged, our trust in others is challenged in three degrees: by someone committing a wrong against us (frailty); by someone being more generally unreliable or untrustworthy in that they are not able to act consistently from the right kind of motivations in various situations (impurity); and, finally, by someone striving to do terrible things to us, and feeling morally justified and emotionally content in the moment of doing them (depravity). That there are three degrees reflects how seriously we can lose our way in life (as we move from frailty to impurity to depravity), and although the first two degrees can come in both self-deceived and non-self-deceived forms, the last one—acting in ways that reveal a depraved heart—is always self-deceived.

1.2 Affects

Kant argues that our conscious orientations enabled by our predispositions to animality and humanity can give rise to affects and passions, both of which subjectively challenge our ability to be in practical (moral) control of how we act. Affects are, in *The Metaphysics of Morals*, internally connected with feeling in that they "preced [e] reflection" and make reflection "impossible or more difficult" (MM 6: 408). In the *Anthropology*, Kant compatibly describes affect as

surprise through sensation, by means of which the mind's composure ... is suspended. Affect is therefore rash, that is, it quickly grows to a degree of feeling that makes reflection impossible (it is thoughtless).... What the affect of anger does not accomplish quickly, it does not do at all; and it forgets easily.... Affect works like water that breaks through a dam.... Affect works on our health like an apoplectic fit. Affect is like drunkenness that one sleeps off, although a headache follows afterward.... Where a great deal of affect is present, there is generally little passion.... Affects are honest and open. (A 7: 252)

Affects, then, are honest, open, and thoughtless, and they include strong feelings such as anger, joy, astonishment, fear, hope, and indignation. Being taken over by affect is similar to being a little drunk, something which is not always bad for us even though it does make it more difficult to control how we are acting; in fact, generally speaking, it seems healthy to be a little tipsy now and then. Moreover, it is because of the way in which it precedes reason and is internally connected only with feeling that affect "does not enter into kinship with vice so readily as does a passion" (MM 6: 408). Hence, although affects involve a (partial) suspension of reason, they can be good for us.[3]

---

[3] This reading contrasts with other readings in that it views affects as not only bad. For an alternative, more negative reading of affect and for an overview over much of the existing Kantian literature, see Frierson (2014).

In "On the Philosophers' Medicine of the Body," Kant correlatively describes the affects by saying that although they

agitate the body by a certain assault on it, they can be healthful, provided they do not reach the point of enervating it. The affects of joy and indignation, which sometimes pour out in heated words, are healthful. So too is astonishment.... [Similarly, games involving] fear and hope... produce a good deal of stimulation that can help the ailing body, primarily because the mind is not fixed on any object but wanders, moving quickly over a great many things which, indeed, are to be reckoned of no account.   (PMB 15: 940)

Although affects can be healthy, they can be very bad for us too. This is why we should relate to affect by what Kant calls "the duty of *apathy*," meaning that we have a duty to learn how to feel and be around affects without necessarily acting on them (MM 6: 408).[4] That is, we must learn to govern or be in charge of our feelings rather than giving ourselves over to affect as a way of life (MM 6: 408). Affects involve a suspension of reason, and, therefore, they open up the possibility and temptation of blocking reason. Affect can make it tempting for us to act on anger or on sexual desire and, so, can make it tempting for us to do bad things. Indeed, I take it that some rapes and other kinds of sexualized violence are best explained by appeal to affect and as involving frailty, meaning that committing such acts consists of knowing that one ought not to commit them, but then one does so anyway. For example, people can find themselves very sexually excited and can choose to yield to that excitement and to block the call of apathy as a duty. Alternatively, some parents react to learning their children not being cis or straight by getting angry and lashing out. In these cases, once the action (the rape, the hitting) is done and the sexual excitement or anger is gone, the wrongdoers can be morally horrified by what they have done. They cannot quite bring themselves to understand how it was possible that they did what they did: after all, they "do not do" such terrible things. And yet they did—that once. This is what they have to learn to own and live with truthfully, that for a moment they failed to register the suffering of another human being— someone they are sexually attracted to or whom they love (their child)—and instead chose to yield to their craving for sexual satisfaction or to their anger.

1.3 Passions

Passions differ from affect in that they are internally connected not with (thought-less) feelings, but with lasting inclinations and desire—and so with choices, reflection, and reason.[5] In addition, Kant maintains, although we speak loosely and fondly of

---

[4] See Langton (1992) for a relevant, yet quite different, take on Kant's duty of apathy (and conception of the human self).

[5] In the *Anthropology*, Kant describes desire as "the self-determination of a subject's power through the representation of something in the future as an effect of this representation. Habitual sensible desire is called *inclination*... Inclination that can be conquered only with difficulty or not at all by the subject's reason is *passion*. On the other hand, the feeling of a pleasure or displeasure in the subject's present state that does not let him rise to *reflection* (the representation by means of reason as to whether he should give himself up to it or refuse it) is *affect*.... [Being] subject to affects and passions is probably always an *illness of the mind*, because both affect and passion shut out the sovereignty of reason. Both are also equally vehement [*heftig*] in degree; but as concerns their quality they are essentially different from each other, both with regard to the method of prevention and to that of the cure that the physician would have to

passions in non-philosophical contexts, such as when we write poems—Kant's example being: "If reason is a magnet, then the passions are the wind"—it is still the case that on a strict and precise philosophical analysis passions are always only bad (A 7: 267). More specifically, in contrast to the spontaneous, stormy yet fleeting, and honest nature of affect, passion not only

> takes its time, in order to root itself deeply and think about its opponent . . . [but is] like a river that digs itself deeper and deeper into its bed . . . passion . . . [works on our health] like consumption or emaciation . . . passions . . . are deceitful and hidden.   (A 7: 252)

In contrast to affects, passions signify true evil, because whereas affects, such as anger are intimately linked to feelings, passions, such as hatred, are intimately linked with inclinations (habitual sensible desires) and reflection and thinking.

Similarly, in *The Metaphysics of Morals*, Kant says,

> [t]he calm with which one gives oneself up to it [passion] permits reflection and allows the mind to form principles upon it and so, if inclination lights upon something contrary to the law, to brood upon it, to get it rooted deeply, and so take up what is evil (as something premeditated) into its maxim. And the evil is then *properly* evil, that is, a true *vice*.   (MM 6: 408)

Likewise, in the *Anthropology* Kant notes,

> Since passions can be paired with the calmest reflection, it is easy to see that they are not thoughtless, like affects, nor stormy and transitory; rather, they take root and can even co-exist with rationalizing.—It is also easy to see that they do greatest damage to freedom, and if affect is *drunkenness*, then passion is an *illness* that abhors all medicine, and it is therefore far worse than all those transitory emotions that at least stir up the resolutions to be better; instead, passion is an enchantment that also refuses recuperation.   (A 7: 265-6)[6]

---

apply . . . passion (as a state of mind belonging to the faculty of desire) takes its time and reflects, no matter how fierce it may be, in order to reach its end . . . passion is regarded as a sickness that comes from swallowing poison. . . . The person who *loves* to be sure can still remain quite clear-sighted; but the person who *falls in love* is inevitably blind to the faults of the beloved object . . . no human being wishes to have passion. For who wants to have himself put in chains when he can be free" (A 7: 251ff.).

[6] Similarly, in the *Anthropology* we find, "The subjective possibility of the emergence of a certain desire, which precedes the representation of its object, is propensity (*propensio*);—the inner *necessitation* of the faculty of desire to take possession of this object before one even knows it, is *instinct*. . . . A sensible desire that serves the subject as a rule (habit) is called inclination (*inclinatio*). Inclination that prevents reason from comparing it with the sum of all inclinations in respect to a certain choice is *passion* (*passio animi*). . . . Passions are cancerous sores for pure practical reason, and for the most part they are incurable because the sick person does not want to be cured and flees from the domination of principles, by which alone a cure could occur. . . . In the sensibly practical too, reason goes from the general to the particular according to the principle: not to please one inclination by placing all the rest in the shade or in a dark corner, but rather see to it that it can exist together with the totality of *all* inclinations. . . . It is folly (making *part* of one's end the *whole*), which directly contradicts the formal principle of reason itself. . . . That is why passions are not, like affects, merely *unfortunate* states of mind full of many ills, but are without exception *evil* as well. And the most good-natured desire, even when it aims at what (according to matter) belongs to virtue, for example, beneficence, is still (according to form) not merely *pragmatically* ruinous but also *morally* reprehensible, as soon as it turns into passion.

Affect does a momentary damage to freedom and domination over oneself. Passion abandons them and finds its pleasure and satisfaction in a slavish mind. But because reason still does not ease off with its summons to inner freedom, the unhappy man groans in his chains, which he nevertheless cannot break away from because they have already grown together with his limbs, so to speak" (A 7: 265-7).

Correspondingly, Kant argues that although passions are only possible for human beings in virtue of our faculty of desire and reason, it is characteristic of the passions that we feel unable to control them; they make us feel as if our practical reason is powerless. Passions characteristically make it impossible for us to transform, integrate, and develop all our desires into a harmonious whole, since they make us want to focus on only one inclination, one that we are not able to develop holistically. For example, in the "Essay on the Maladies of the Head," Kant says,

> The drives of human nature, which are called passions when they are of a high degree, are the moving forces of the will; the understanding only comes in to assess both the entire result of the satisfaction of all inclinations taken together from the end represented and to find the means to this end. If, e.g., a passion is especially powerful, the capacity of the understanding is of little help against it; for the end of the enchanted human being sees very well indeed the reasons against his favorite inclination, but he feels powerless to give them active emphasis.
>
> (MH 2: 261)

Accordingly, although passions can be extremely violent or forceful, Kant says elsewhere, they are in a fundamental sense, "still sheer *weaknesses* in view of what reason prescribes to the human being" (A 7: 271f.). In addition, because passions are always "inclinations directed by human beings to human beings," a person's passions can only "be satisfied" by another human being (A 7: 270).[7]

Kant furthermore proposes that there are two kinds of passions, namely passions "of *natural* (innate) inclination and passions of inclination that result from human *culture* (acquired)" (A 7: 267). Natural passions comprise the passions of freedom and sex, and because they are "connected with affect," they are "inflamed" or fiery. The passion of freedom is the passion not to be restricted by others. To see the affective root of freedom as a passion, we may return one more time to Kant's example of newborn babies. As seen in Chapter 1, Kant argues that a newborn who

> has just wrenched itself from the mother's womb ... enters the world with loud cries, unlike all other animals, simply because it regards the inability to make use of its limbs as *constraint*, and thus immediately announces its claims to freedom (a representation no other animal has).
>
> (A 7: 268)

In other words, the baby's cry reveals an affective striving for freedom, explained by reference both to the baby's representation of itself as free (as wanting to set its own ends) and to the frustration of not being able to do so. If unrestrained or untransformed, children will seek to turn the affect into a passion, by having parents (and everyone else around them) satisfy their every desire, and so they become little monsters. (The animalistic desires for self-preservation, or for food, drink, and basic community or affectionate love can also develop into passions—strong desires that the child demands be met constantly, in which case the child becomes a three-headed monster.) We see two other examples of the passion of freedom in nomadic and hunting peoples—and we

---

[7] Consistent with the analysis, non-human animals cannot experience passions: "With mere animals, even the most violent inclination (for example, the inclination to sexual union) is not called passion: because they have no reason, which alone establishes the concept of freedom and with which passion comes into collision.... Passions ... are directed only to human beings and can also only be satisfied by them" (A 7: 269).

could presumably add other traveling groups, such as many sailors—insofar as they feel "ennobled" by the way they are untied to a particular place but can (and subjectively feel that they absolutely must) move about freely (A 7: 269).

On the topic of sex as a passion, Kant states that

> Sexual love, in turn, can become a passion when it is not reciprocated, . . . when it is not a case of *being in* love. The reason is that once the latter desire [sexual love] has been satisfied (by enjoyment), the desire, at least with regard to the very person involved, also stops. So one can list being passionately in love [among the passions] (as long as the other party persists in refusal), but one cannot list any physical love as passion, because it does not contain a *constant* principle with respect to its object. Passion always presupposes a maxim on the part of the subject, to act according to an end prescribed to him by his inclination. Passion is therefore always connected with his reason, and one can no more attribute passion to mere animals than to pure rational beings.   (A 7: 266)

So, physical love—simply having sex—is not a passion, since the power sexual attraction (understood purely "animalistically") holds over persons ends as soon as they are (physically) sexually satisfied. Sexual love as passion, in contrast, involves a "*constant* principle with respect to its object," namely the other person and that person's refusal. That is to say, sexual love as a passion is about a person being drawn to another both with respect to their animality (in particular, their need for affectionate love and/or their sex drive) and their humanity (their capacity for rational end-setting and/or their sense of self), and either the other does not experience the same draw or is unable to figure out how to respond to it, or, which is obviously much worse, manipulatively refuses to develop the connection into a relationship (whereby the attraction becomes transformed, developed, and integrated into both or all parties' lives, and, so, becomes controllable by practical reason). In such circumstances, if the one whose sexual love is not reciprocated does not withdraw, passion develops. Unable to form a harmonious whole with the other person, that lack becomes a consuming focus, it becomes sexual passion that "gnaw[s] and consume[s] the heart or, so to speak, bind[s] the [natural] vital force with shackles" (PMB 15: 940).

Along with the natural passions of freedom and sex there is the second, "acquired" or "cultured" kind, which fundamentally concerns inclinations to have power or influence over other human beings. These cultured or acquired passions are, in other words, intimately connected with the predisposition to humanity, and especially with how others can be means to realizing ends of one's own and how others' affirmation of oneself is so important to one's own sense of self. Thus, this inclination that seeks dominance or influence

> comes closest to technically practical reason, that is, to the maxim of prudence.—For getting other human beings' inclinations into one's power, so that one can direct and determine them according to one's intentions, is almost the same as *possessing* others as mere tools of one's will. No wonder that the striving after such a *capacity* becomes a passion.   (A 7: 271)

Kant continues that we may think of this capacity to have influence over others as threefold. More specifically, if one can acquire

> *honor*, *authority*, and *money*, [then] one can get to every human being and use him according to his purpose, if not by means of another.—The inclinations for this, if they become passions,

are the *manias for honor, for domination,* and *for possession.* It is true that here the human being becomes the dupe (the deceived) of his own inclinations, and in his use of such means he misses his final end; but here we are not speaking of *wisdom,* which admits of no passions at all, but only of *prudence,* by which one can manage fools.   (A 7: 271)

When one develops one's ability to control others through honor, authority, or money into a passion, one develops a "mania" for honor, domination, or possession. Such living is unwise, since it consists of emotionally unhealthy ways of being as well as actions that are morally unjustifiable. One ends up enslaved by one's own inclinations, and hence, insofar as one yields to them, one becomes incapable of pursuing the highest good—a harmonious, close union between morality and happiness. This is why Kant says,

Mania for honor is the weakness of human beings which enables a person to have influence on them through their *opinion; mania for domination* through their *fear;* and *mania for possession,* through their own *interest.*—Each is a slavish disposition by means of which another person, when he has taken possession of it, has the capacity to use a person's own inclinations for his purposes.   (A 7: 272)

As well, developing such powers is incompatible with loving, affectionate friendships and respect from others: "the first makes one *hated,* the second makes one *feared,* and the third makes one *despised*" (A 7: 274).

   To explain the historical pattern of men dominating women, Kant focuses on the "mania for domination":

This passion is intrinsically unjust, and its manifestation summons everything against it. It starts, however, from the fear of being dominated by others, and is then soon intent on placing the advantage of force over them; which is nevertheless a precarious and unjust means of using other human beings for one's own purposes: in part it is *imprudent* because it arouses opposition, and in part it is *unjust* because it is contrary to freedom under law, to which everyone can lay claim.—As concerns the *indirect* art of domination, for example, that of the female sex by means of love which she inspires in the male sex, in order to use him for her purposes, it is not included under this title; for it does not employ force, but knows how to dominate and bind its subject through his own inclination.—Not that the female part of our species is free from the inclination to dominate the male part (exactly the opposite is true), but it does not use the same *means* for this purpose as the male part, that is, it does not use the advantage of *strength* (which is here what is meant by the word *dominate);* but rather the advantage of *charm,* which comprehends an inclination of the other part to be comprehended.
(A 7: 273)

We are all naturally afraid to be dominated by others, and this fear expresses itself in how we are naturally tempted to seek to dominate. In addition, as we saw in Chapter 2, Kant thinks that women are tempted to seek to dominate through their social skills—their abilities to charm and to read social situations—and, so, to dominate through emotional control. This emotional forcefulness is not physically coercive, however. In contrast, men have a tendency to seek to dominate through physical force, since men tend to be physically stronger than women. This, then, is Kant's explanation of why—to return to the Margaret Atwood quote at the beginning of this chapter—men fear that women will (use their relative social strength to) laugh at (humiliate) them, whereas women fear that men will (use their relative physical strength to) kill them. There is an internal temptation for men to develop passions involving their relative physical strength (even a passion for killing) when women do not give them what they want, while women's main tool for dominance is emotional manipulation, including the humiliation of men.[8] The power to kill trumps the power to manipulate. So, when both men and women have been willing to use their respective powers to the hilt, men have dominated women, not the other way around. Notice too that it is entirely consistent with this view to argue that one reason why there is so much sexist harassment in the history of institutions in which some people bear authority over others (from educational to medical to political institutions) in sexist societies, is that men are tempted to use the threat of their physical power to implicitly or explicitly threaten women into consenting to "offers they cannot refuse." Finally, although our propensity to want to dominate in combination with strength is what Kant proposes as the ultimate reason why there has been so much oppression of women in history, it is compatible with expanding the argument to include the other two cultured passions/manias (for honor and possession) as well as the two natural passions/manias (for freedom and sex) in a more complete account of oppression.

In order to explain how sexual violence can be used as part of sexual, racial, or ethnic oppression, the other two passions (the manias for honor and possession) are more useful starting points. Let me begin with an explanation of a kind of forced silence about their way of loving on the part of polyamorous, polysexual, and members of the LGBTQIA community as the result of sexual majorities developing a mania for honor. As Kant explains,

[It] is not *love of honor*, an esteem that the human being is permitted to expect from others because of his inner (moral) worth; rather it is striving after the *reputation of honor*, where semblance suffices. Here arrogance is permitted (an unjustified demand that others think little of themselves in comparison with us, a foolishness that acts contrary to its own end)—this arrogance, I say, needs only to be *flattered*, and one already has control over the fool by means of this passion. Flatterers, the yes-men who gladly concede high-sounding talk to an important man, nourish this passion that makes him weak, and are the ruin of the great and powerful who abandon themselves to this spell.

Arrogance is an inappropriate desire for honor that acts contrary to its own end, and cannot be regarded as an intentional means of using other human beings (whom it repels) for one's ends; rather the arrogant man is an instrument of rogues, and is called a fool.... Since arrogance is the unjustified demand on another person that he *despise* himself in comparison to others, such a thought cannot enter the head of anyone except one who feels ready to debase himself, and that arrogance itself already supplies a never-deceiving, foreboding sign of the baseness of such human beings. (A 7: 272–3; cf. MM 6: 465f.)

---

[8] Simone de Beauvoir, I believe, makes a consistent point in *The Second Sex* that it is significant in the context of sexual violence that only men have penises. This is not to deny that women rape men and women rape women—women do rape men and women do rape women—but raping without a penis is simply more technically difficult than raping with one, especially if the one raping wants it to be physically pleasant in addition to giving one a social sense of empowerment. The point here is not to account for every instance of sexual violence or all patterns of oppression—some of the other sexual instances and patterns are dealt with elsewhere in this chapter—but to explain the pattern of men sexually oppressing women.

Because a central aspect of sexual identity and orientation concerns gender presentation, which is a form of social presentation in the world and because polyamorous and polysexual people as well as members of the LGBTQIA community will always be outnumbered by the cis, straight, monogamous majority, the latter face a temptation to use its social power by denying equal recognition (honor) to LGBTQIA- and poly-presentations. This mania for honor can also explain how cis, straight, and monogamous people can be tempted to use the threat of condemnation or even wrath to require sex workers, polyamorous and polysexual people as well as members of the LGBTQIA community to despise themselves—to view themselves as socially lower than monogamous, cis, straight people—and to be subservient, to not ask to be affirmed by cis, monogamous, and straight people, or to be silent about who they are. On the flip side, for Kant the only reason why one would develop the passion of wrath—violent anger towards others—is because one despises oneself; otherwise one simply cannot form the desire to act so violently against others. This seems consistent with how cis, monogamous, and straight people who are deeply secure about who they are sexually tend to be binary, cisist, and/or heterosexist at their worst, and at their best they do what they can to protect members of sexual minorities from sexualized violence. Even if they tend to deny sexual minorities an approving social confirmation—one that affirms them as their equals—they are not drawn to violent, dehumanizing behavior. (The more insecure they are with their own sexuality, the more despicable they are to themselves, and the more likely they are to engage in sexualized violence.)

As argued in Chapter 3, one can plausibly read Kant's wrath against non-straight behavior as coming from such a place of self-hatred, and one can view the behavior of those around Kant and Mr. Green—friends who normalized their relationship by inviting them for Sunday dinners and simply relating to the two of them as if the relationship were the most natural thing in the world—as having enabled them to live this relationship without social resistance for so long. Historically powerful social institutions, such as royal families, the Vatican, and universities like Oxford and Cambridge, have similarly protected their own, at the very least by not drawing public attention to those among them who lived non-cis, non-straight, non-monogamous lives. And sex workers too tend to have been relatively protected parts of such socially powerful scenes.[9] Indeed, the many old stories about the "two spinsters" or "the two bachelors" who lived together so that "at least they do not have to be lonely" have similar implications. In spite of having the space to live together, the price to be paid by those who lived these lives in such sexually phobic societies is that, typically, at the very least, they have been pushed into silence even by those protecting them. True friends, however, would not have such expectations, as they are inconsistent with due deep affectionate love and genuine respect for others.[10]

---

[9] It is important not to sugar coat this, however, since many of these institutions protected their own only because doing so was in their interest. They therefore have histories not only of protecting sex workers and members of the LGBTQIA community who deserved to be protected, but also of protecting sexual predators such as Roman Catholic clergy who raped their parishioners (including children) and professors who have sexually harassed or sexually assaulted their students.

[10] See Chapter 1 for more on Kant's account of friendship.

A similar analysis plausibly explains ethnic and racial oppression and violence as these patterned behaviors are also about someone wanting others to think of themselves as less human than that person. And it seems plausible to argue that wars and ethnic and racial oppression can use sexual violence because of its ability to make victims feel unsafe, humiliated, or ashamed to be who they are in their own bodies; sexual violence can be devastatingly effective in this regard. In addition, it seems plausible to appeal to the mania for possession to explain sexual violence that involves money in dehumanizing ways: one's ability to control others and their bodies through one's monetary control over them can give one a sense of power with respect to things that in themselves have nothing to do with money. Kant puts it,

> Money is the solution, and all doors that are closed to the man of lesser wealth open to him whom Plutus favors. The invention of this means, which does not have (or at least should not have) any use other than that of serving merely as a means for the exchange of human beings' industry, and with it however everything that is also physically good among them, has, especially after it was represented by metal, brought forth a mania for possession which finally, even without enjoyment in the mere possession, and even with the renunciation (of the miser) to make any use of it, contains a power that people believe satisfactorily replaces the lack of every other power. This passion is, if not always morally reprehensible, completely banal [*ganz geistlos*], is cultivated merely mechanically, and is attached especially to old people (as a substitute for their natural incapacity). (A 7: 274)

Applying this argument about money to sex, some people use money as a substitute for powers they do not have. Hence, *some* people, especially men, use their money to buy sexual services so as to obtain a sense of sexual superiority by controlling other beings' (sex workers') sexuality as a compensation for the fact that they are unable to realize a sexual sense of self through physical violence (let alone in emotionally healthy, morally justifiable ways).[11] That they can buy sex and feel in possession of vulnerable people—most commonly women—and that they feel a subjective sense of satisfaction in possessing another can only be explained by a passion. For their satisfaction is felt by doing something morally reprehensible (rather than in a kind of sexual security that would enable them to seek ways of being that are emotionally healthy, sexually empowering, and suitably vulnerable). Some patterns of trade in sexual services (including sex slavery) therefore track human beings who have a liability to seek a sense of sexual security and empowerment through using their money to feel in possession of other people, and they do so to compensate for lacking an empowering sexual sense of self. None of this is to deny that explaining the complexity of the vicious behaviors contained in some kinds of sexual (emotional and/or physical) abuse requires us to posit the presence of the other passions—of sex, freedom, domination, and honor—as well.

The above discussion of destructive patterns tracking women, sex workers, sexual or gender identities, and sexual orientations—in individuals and societies—does not entail denying that there are temptations to act badly with regard to both our

---

[11] This argument does not apply to all buying and selling of sexual services, but only to the emotionally unhealthy, violently oppressive kinds. I return to the issue of buying and selling of sexual services in more detail in Chapters 6 and 7.

animality and humanity in *all* human relationships. Quite the contrary: even when we do not participate in sexual violence and oppression, we can find ourselves doing things we ought not to (exhibiting frailty) and acting towards others as the result of bad motivations (exhibiting impurity). Furthermore, sexual love is fertile ground for passions, and for that reason we can be tempted to cease striving to live emotionally good, morally justifiable lives, and to let our lives instead be organized around chasing the intense experiences of sexual drama. After all, our nature is such that we tend to have deep desires to feel cared for and caring, attracted and attractive, excited and exciting, challenged and challenging, stimulated and stimulating, in sexual, physical, and creative, etc., ways. As well, our personal challenges to feel safe and attractive make it tempting to be both jealous and envious of each other and/ or to commit adultery; our desires to set ends of our own in creative ways make us liable to be selfish or possessive with regard to our resources (material, money, time, etc.); our desires to please and love others make it tempting for us *not* to be a source of correction for them when they do not handle things well; and so on. Moreover, as discussed earlier, what is subjectively important to us depends in part on the kinds of persons we are—the different personalities or temperaments we have—and, so, on our spontaneous affective responses, on what we tend to value (more or less) and how we value it, and on which aspects of life we are good at and which not. And no one is good at everything. Also, because we have all grown up in families or in institutional settings where we have been subject to other persons' pathologies and bad behaviors, we all bear scars and wounds. Growing emotionally and morally sometimes means facing old fears and re-opening old wounds so that they can heal in better ways. As we all know, this is not something we "naturally" want to do.

In addition, as we grow, we change—and we typically do not grow and experience success all the time, at the same rate, or at the same time. Importantly too, regardless of whether we are right or wrong in our judgments about one another's behavior being bad or hurtful, the way in which we are emotionally open to the other means that, subjectively, we feel hurt or wronged, which is to feel pain. Naturally, we react by wanting to fight or flee (whether physically or psychologically). And because these emotions are not directly under control by our reflective cognitive powers—they are not inherently reflective—it is especially difficult to relate to them truthfully, such as being able to evaluate whether or not what one is feeling right now is appropriate. It is, in other words, inherently tempting to rationalize the interaction and what we feel, to describe it such that one puts oneself or the other in a more favorable light than is actually warranted. Besides, some of the challenge as one grows is to be neither too dependent on one another for how one feels and what one chooses to do nor careless about the effects of one's choices and words on the others, and vice versa. In fortunate lives, personal growth comes with generous space for the other person(s) to seek experiences, friendships, and personal growth on their own as well as with other people, trusting that the other(s) will be able to handle the challenges involved. And we do want ourselves and others, whether alone or together, to live in ways deeply consistent with who we are. But each needs to be responsible for these choices. To make matters worse, we inherit societies and ways of thinking and being that contain sexist, homophobic, racist, and ethnic prejudices, which add their own challenges to any attempt at realizing good relationships as these prejudices consist of patterns of feelings and associations at at least the impure level of evil for both those who inherit the oppressed and the oppressive identities or orientations. (More on this in section 1.4.) It is, in other words, not very surprising that long-term sexual, loving intimate relationships—even those that start from the best of places and aim for the best of things—are very difficult, why they all go along with behavior that can feel violently hurtful, why more of them end in a break-up than not, and why most do not lead to flourishing lives for each individually and for both (or more) involved as an us.

1.4 Perfect and Imperfect Duties Regarding Sexual Oppression and Harassment

Let me end this part with a note on how the above account of the temptation of sexual wrongdoing may help move forward our understanding of perfect and imperfect duties with regard to sexual oppression and harassment. Sexual oppression is systemic; sexual harassment is not but becomes a patterned problem under sexually oppressive conditions. Sexual oppression is not simply a case of individual wrongdoing, but of societal prejudices and the legal-political system working together to create conditions in which some can get away with treating others badly, including by harassing them, and where the totality of laws and public policies fails to establish conditions that enable and protect everyone's ability to interact as free and equal. Sexual harassment under these same conditions is typically individual wrongdoing by means of which one privileged person treats another less privileged person badly, and where the presence or absence of privilege is determined by the sexually oppressive conditions in which the interacting persons find themselves. So far in human history, there has yet to be a legal-political system that has not been or is not sexually oppressive. Therefore, conditions have been that sexually privileged people (straight people, cis men) have been able to harass sexually unprivileged people (sex workers, polyamorous, polysexual, members of the LGBTQIA community, women) without consequence. Notice too that if Kant and the Kantian theory presented above are correct, then sexual violence and oppression will always remain a temptation and challenge for us as individuals, as groups of individuals, and as societies. Therefore, it is an important issue for us to address. Below the focus is on how one should understand one's individual, first-personal ethical duties to resist and fight sexual oppression and harassment, and on how to handle one's own sexual oppression and harassment. In Chapter 7, I consider how the state should handle challenges regarding sexual harassment and oppression.

The challenge of analyzing our ethical duties regarding sexual oppression is amplified by the fact that Kant himself does not explicitly address it, and by the fact that it is difficult to figure out exactly how to understand our related ethical duties in terms of Kant's simple distinction between perfect and imperfect duties.[12] It is uncontroversial that Kant thinks that we have perfect duties not to treat ourselves and each other in aggressive (destructive and damaging) ways, while we have imperfect duties to develop our own capacities and talents, and to assist others in their pursuit of happiness. In light of this, it is not difficult to see that we have a

---

[12] For more on my general take on the distinction between perfect and imperfect duties, see Chapter 1.

perfect duty not to oppress others, but what about our duty to fight our own oppression? Is this duty perfect or imperfect, and is it a duty to self or to others? Ann Cudd, in *Analyzing Oppression* (2006), argues that the duty to fight oppression is an imperfect duty to others. It comes from the duty not to harm others, which we do, she argues, if we do not resist oppression or oppressors' social group. Cudd furthermore argues that we have an imperfect duty to others to resist the oppression of our own social group in cases where we can do so without risking something worse happening to us. She also argues that we have leeway with regard to our choice of how to resist, and that fighting oppression, when doing so comes with the risk of worse things happening to us, is supererogatory. Were it otherwise, then having a duty to fight our own oppression, given how pervasive the system of sexual oppression is, would result in not only others wronging us but also that their bad behavior makes it the case that we must spend much of our life fighting their wrongdoing. In addition, it is impossible successfully to defeat problems of systemic injustice on one's own. In part in response to these worries of Cudd's, Carol Hay, in *Kantianism, Liberalism, and Feminism: Resisting Oppression* (2013) argues in agreement that women's duty to fight their own oppression and harassment is an imperfect duty, but that it is a duty women have to themselves. Their imperfect duty is to work towards a better world for themselves.

Although I agree with much in both groundbreaking analyses of oppression,[13] if my above account works, then the duty to resist and fight one's own oppression and harassment is perfect, and it is a duty we have to ourselves and to others (not to wrong them). Similarly, Thomas E. Hill, Jr.'s (1973) "deferential wife" and women who face what Onora O'Neill (2000) calls "offers one cannot resist" are facing a call of morality that has the form of a perfect duty, which is yet another reason why life under sexually oppressive conditions is so emotionally draining. None of this is to deny that we also have imperfect duties to improve our abilities to deal with these kinds of wrongdoing and to assist others in their efforts to do so too; quite the opposite—if we cannot even *think* or conceive of the maxims involving not resisting or fighting oppression as universal laws of freedom, we certainly cannot *will* them as such. Finally, under conditions of pervasive sexual oppression and harassment, sometimes all one can do to resist is to be truthful to oneself about what is going on, or engage in what Hay (2013: 141) calls "internal resistance." As we will see below and drawing on the analysis in Chapter 3, my proposal is that many of the considerations that lead Hay (2013: 137) to revise Kant's account of perfect and imperfect duties—and to propose that on her revised account, the duty to fight oppression is imperfect rather than perfect—can be dealt with by exploring Kant's argument that sometimes it is impossible to match one's "formal" duties (to fight oppression) with "material" ones. That is to say, we (embodied, social human beings) may face conditions in which "wrongdoing in the highest degree" is impossible to avoid (even if other kinds of imaginable rational, embodied social beings would not face such problems). I return to this issue in more detail below.

---

[13] I have engaged both works in my commentary (Varden 2009) on Ann Cudd's *Analyzing Oppression* and in my review (Varden 2013) of Carol Hay's *Kantianism, Liberalism, Feminism: Resisting Oppression.*

Let me emphasize that it follows from the above account that a single explanation cannot capture all of the kinds of sexualized violence that occur against sex workers, women, and sexual or gendered minorities. Sexual violence is not simple, it is multifaceted and can consist of emotional violence or extremely violent killings, beatings, and rape that are best explained through either affect or the inflamed passions of sex and freedom *and/or* the cool passions of domination, honor, and possession.[14] Notice too that even if we accept all of the above as correct, then we have not yet explained how sexual violence happens as part of atrocities. That is, the above account of sexual violence and oppression draws only from Kant's ideas about affects and passions and frailty and impurity. To explain how atrocities can take place and how they often involve sexualized violence, I suggest that Kant's account of depraved hearts must play a distinct role. In other words, it is not the case that atrocities take place only because of temptations of frailty or impurity in combinations with affects and passions; rather, people's liabilities to yield to these forces are steered into destruction by someone who stands at a distance from being ruled by them and who is able to manipulate and channel these forces in others into a unified, all-consuming destructive force or movement. Or so I will argue in section 2.

2. Sexual Violence under Barbaric Conditions: Wars, Atrocities, and Violent Oppression

In her important work *The Atrocity Problem—A Theory of Evil*, Claudia Card (2002) argues that Kant's moral philosophy is unable to capture atrocities in all their morally horrible destructiveness. More specifically, Card argues that the reason Kant's account of evil cannot make sense of atrocities is that it does "not distinguish evils from less serious wrongdoing" (2002: 83), where "evils have two basic components: (intolerable) harm and (culpable) wrongdoing" (2002: 4).[15] Below I argue that the above philosophical resources together with Kant's account of depraved hearts can explain how sexual violence can be used as a tool in atrocities and when extreme violence takes place. In addition, if this as well as the above analysis is correct, then it follows that we—as individuals or as members of various social groups whose identities are oppressed and dehumanized—may face situations or conditions in which respect for our humanity is denied and where any assertion of our humanity is likely to be met with (more, even lethal) violence. So, what do we do? As Kant would put it, what do we do when we find ourselves facing "barbaric" violence or barbaric conditions? To answer, I draw on Kant's account of formal and material wrongdoing as well as on the idea of doing wrong in the highest degree to capture the difficulty of living with one's choices when facing the threat of barbaric violence. In the end, in these situations, there simply is no good way out, and whatever one does will require either suffering severe wrongdoing or perpetrating extreme violence in

[14] See also Ann J. Cahill (2001) and Linda Martín Alcoff (2018) for arguments that sexual violence, including rape, is not one thing but something that comes in many forms.
[15] Although it would take me too far afield to do so here, I believe that my account of evil presented here can also respond to Card's (2010) "Kant's Excluded Middle."

protective measures—towards oneself (self-sacrifice) or towards others—that one cannot feel morally authorized to do.

As we have seen, Kant suggests that part of what makes affects morally dangerous is that they contain a suspension of reason, whereas passions are even more dangerous because they consist of using reason in ways that give others destructive control over us. Furthermore, it is because affects and passions make it so arduous for us to guide our lives by our practical reason (morally) that they are weaknesses. We have additionally seen that insofar as we have grown up in societies that are corrupted by sexist, heterosexist, racist, and ethnic prejudices, those whose lives are not characterized by oppressed identities are liable to develop passions of honor, domination, and possession. One symptom of these passions is an inability truthfully to tell the history of the oppressed (and instead to rationalize this history, by, for example, claiming that it was "their fault" or "it wasn't that bad"). Another is an inability to relate to their own or others' gender or sexuality as parts of good, flourishing lives. It follows from this that when someone is able to stimulate profoundly hateful, destructive political movements—movements the purpose of which is to violently oppress or destroy some groups of human beings or humanity as such—that person may best be described by means of Kant's account of depraved hearts. Because they are using their reflective, thinking capacities to maximize human destruction, when successful, it is not because they themselves are driven by these passions (for sex, freedom, honor, domination, and possession), but that they know how to manipulate others into acting in affective and passionate ways—into doing the morally horrible things for them. This is why these manipulators are so terrifyingly dangerous. In other words, sexual violence can become part of an atrocity when someone is able to stimulate other people's various liabilities to affect and passions and to unify them into a destructive force. Without people with depraved hearts, others' affects and passions are not organized for mass destruction. For example, individual soldiers at war may develop passions for freedom (which, as we saw above, consist of a heightened subjective sense of empowerment to subject others to evil without consequence), and, so, can (and do) sometimes commit war crimes (they rape, torture, or kill innocent civilians, for example) on their own initiative. But contrast this with soldiers committing the same kinds of crimes as part of a coordinated, political movement directed at destruction. Such a political movement—or atrocity— can only be generated by someone who is themself not driven by these affects and passions, but who can manipulate other people's affects and passions in such a way that they work as constitutive parts of a unified destructive force. Such are those with depraved hearts.

If this is correct and the most vicious human beings are not themselves driven by affects and passions when they act, then what drives them, what are the incentives underlying their actions? The answer is, I believe, profoundly perverted forms of self-love, which is why these manipulators tend to have elaborate self-deceptive stories, according to which they are better than the other human beings, and what they are doing is enabling a grand moral, emotional movement for "the whole" people. If so, this is also why they are able to direct those who are driven by affects and passions, as they are themselves not driven by them; to be driven by affects and the passions, you must still be actively engaged in your own life as a human being in a way that those with depraved hearts are not; one must still be striving to develop one's animality, humanity, and personality into a unified (emotionally healthy, morally good) whole. For some reason, being (let alone honestly and vulnerably) engaged in their own lives is too scary for them; it is an endeavor they have given up a long time ago.[16] Notice too that if the above account is correct, then sexualized violence as part of atrocities will tend to make women and religious, ethnic, sexual, and racial minorities their victims, since in oppressive societies, these groups are already dehumanized, and they are either on the whole somewhat physically weaker (women) or they are weaker as social groups (in relation to the majority), which is why they tend to be targeted, again and again, when wars and atrocities take place.

Before concluding, let me briefly address the question of what to do if one is a woman, sex worker, or a member of the LGBTQIA community when facing the threat of individual, dehumanizing violence, or when facing conditions of serious, barbaric injustice. As mentioned in the discussion of perfect and imperfect duties, a Kant-based answer to this question would benefit from Kant's idea of "doing wrong in the highest degree," and from his distinction between "formal" and "material" wrongdoing. Starting with the former, at the very end of his discussion of private right in The Doctrine of Right, Kant says,

Given the intention to be and to remain in this state of externally lawless freedom, men do one another no wrong at all when they feud among themselves; for what holds for one holds also in turn for the other, as if by mutual consent (*uti partes de iure suo disponunt, ita ius est.*) [*the party who displaces another's right has the same right himself.*] But in general they do wrong in the highest degree* by willing to be and to remain in a condition that is not rightful, that is, in which no one is assured of what is his against violence.   (MM 6: 307f.)

Kant clarifies the * in a footnote:

This distinction between what is merely formally wrong and what is also materially wrong has many applications in the doctrine of right. An enemy who, instead of honorably carrying out his surrender agreement with the garrison of a besieged fortress, mistreats them as they march out or otherwise breaks the agreement, cannot complain of being wronged if his opponent plays the same trick on him when he can. But in general they do wrong in the highest degree, because they take away any validity from the concept of right itself and hand everything over to savage violence, as if by law, and so subvert the right of human beings as such.   (MM 6: 307f.)

---

[16] I believe this is consistent with my argument that Anders Behring-Breivik, like Adolph Eichmann before him, was not terribly successful in his attempt to be in charge of a political movement aimed at destroying humanity, but he also seems to share with Eichmann a similar kind of fairly advanced emotional numbness in combination with deep narcissistic self-deception (Varden 2014a). It seems plausible to argue that those who are successful at initiating or leading political movements that aim at the destruction of humanity as such are much further along the process of self-deception in that they no longer have a sense of themselves as distinct from the destructive political movement—and this is why they are much better at manipulating others' affects and passions (which do track their own personal efforts). So, Eichmann wanted to have a successful career and Behring-Breivik wanted to become famous—and, consequently, neither viewed themselves as existing only through an inherently destructive political movement in the way totalitarian political leaders do, which is a precondition for barbarism turning into totalitarian barbarism. Regarding these latter kind of individuals—such as Stalin or Hitler—I believe my Kantian analysis philosophically joins up with Hannah Arendt's in *The Origins of Totalitarianism*, but this argument will have to wait for another time.

So, doing wrong in the highest degree is to displace right with might (violence); it does not necessarily involve a material wrongdoing (wronging another particular human being, as in these examples of Kant's), but it always involves a formal wrongdoing (using force in ways that cannot be justified, namely subjecting another person to one's unilateral violence rather than to force authorized by the general will[17]). Thus, insofar as you are a woman, a sex worker, polyamorous, polysexual, or a member of the LGBTQIA community, you may, in other words, face situations where another is trying to wrong you (materially and formally), in which case you might choose to defend yourself with lies or with lethal force (if you can). Self-defense by means of lies or lethal force is a right of justice each person has, but exercising it is something you will experience as difficult to live with as you cannot justify it: you do not, after all, find that you have the moral authority to lie or to take another's life (you commit a formal wrong by lying or killing).[18] Moral repair or healing, in other words, requires learning to live with what you did to survive or protect yourself, which can consist in going back to humanize the wrongdoer when it is safe to do so.

In addition, however, women and sexual or gendered minorities can face general conditions in which this sort of violence as self-protection will be done secretly. The reason why this has to be done secretly is not only because the violence one is subjected to—such as sexual violence, including marital rape or rape during what was set up as a sexual transaction for money—is not recognized by the law as wrong, but it can also be that living consistently as one is—as LGBTQIA, for example—is deemed a criminal offense (in some places, a criminal offense that carries the death penalty). In these cases, the actual legal-political system itself can be a lethal threat. One may therefore find oneself in a situation where public officials, such as the police, will not protect one against sexualized violence, but will treat one as a criminal in virtue of who one is or for having tried to protect oneself, and hence meet and treat one with a dehumanized conception of oneself. Indeed, the worse (more barbaric) the oppression, the higher the risk that the public officials themselves will pose a threat as they know they will not be held accountable for any wrongdoing. Accordingly, although sex workers, women, polyamorous, polysexual, and members of the

---

[17] For more on how I understand this point, see Part II.

[18] We see Kant make this distinction, for example, in The Doctrine of Virtue, where he says, for example, that "In the doctrine of right an intentional untruth is called a lie only if it violates another's right; but in ethics, where no authorization is derived from harmlessness, it is clear of itself that no intentional untruth in the expression of one's thoughts can refuse this harsh name" (MM 6: 429). See also Kant's Lectures and Drafts on Political Philosophy, where he says, "A case of necessity is when I take the law into my own hands and am my own judge.... Nature rules in lieu of right when there is no valid administration of right, e.g. saving one's life.... There is never any case of necessity which justifies lying, yet speaking an untruth is in accord with right" (LDPP 19: 242; cf. LE 27: 448). Speaking an untruth as such is not a legal wrong, but lying in self-defense can never be *justified*: lying in self-defense always involves replacing right (rightful interactions) with might (nature)—or, in accordance with the above, such lying always is a formal wrong (doing something that cannot be morally justified) even if it does not constitute a material wrong (wronging anyone in particular). I discuss lying and wrongdoing in the highest degree also in Varden (2010a, 2021); for legal-political discussions of wrongdoing in the highest degree and lying that I consider largely compatible with mine, Weinrib (2008); Wood (2008); Ripstein (2009); and Sussman (2009). As mentioned in the general Introduction and as will be expanded upon in the conclusion to Part I, this is where I believe my analysis of doing wrong in the highest degree matches up with Deligiorgi's analysis of Kant's idea of absolute moral prohibitions.

LGBTQIA community may find themselves living within the confines of civil society in many regards—they may have basic formal rights to private property, to contract, and so on—it may still be the case that they find themselves facing what Kant calls a "barbaric" condition in regard to their sex work, gender or sexual identity, or sexual orientation.[19] Let me explain.

The state of nature (the pre-state condition), Kant argues, is a condition where in the best of worlds we have peaceful anarchy, understood as "Law and freedom without force"; barbarism, in contrast, is characterized by "Force without freedom and law" (A 7:330f.).[20] In conditions of serious sexual oppression, not only may sex workers, women, and members of the LGBTQIA community find themselves in a situation where they must secretly exercise lethal violence against other private persons to survive—say against a husband who repeatedly rapes his wife, against people who demean or use violence against sex workers, or against someone who acts out his sexual phobic violence on a member of the LGBTQIA community—but they may even have to do so against someone who understands themself as acting as a public person when they subject them to unjustifiable, dehumanizing violence. In either scenario, life can put us in situations in which there is no emotionally or morally good way out, in which we must choose between *either* being wronged in the highest degree (materially and formally) *or* protecting ourselves by doing wrong in the highest degree (formally).[21] Regardless, the ultimate aspiration is always to replace violence with rightful solutions, when possible. In part, this is because doing so is the only way to avoid the deep temptation to develop the tremendously strong and damaging passion for revenge rather than deal in emotionally and morally healthier ways with the dehumanizing, morally horrible acts that cannot be undone.[22]

In later chapters, I explore why this kind of position still precludes violent revolution—"burning it all down"—as a solution to serious problems of injustice.[23] For now, let me only emphasize that on this position, part of the challenge of responding well to having been treated unjustly—including having to live in conditions of oppression—is not to develop passions. For, Kant argues, experiences

---

[19] See also Varden (2012c). I return to this issue in Chapters 5 and 7.

[20] Chapter 7 treats Kant's account of the state of nature and the four juridical conditions (anarchy, barbarism, despotism, republic) in more detail.

[21] This is not to say that lethal responses are the only possible ones. Insofar as the responses involve wrongdoing in the highest degree, they use aggression that is inconsistent with perfect duties to oneself or to others, but they can also involve various responses that break with imperfect duties. For a classic, literary portrayal of how sexism places women in situations from which there are no morally good ways forward, see Henrik Ibsen's character "Nora" in *A Doll's House*; for a classic feminist analysis of the impossible scenarios women face, see Marilyn Frye's (1983) account of "double binds"; for a Kantian analysis of these complexities, see Hay's (2013).

[22] In my (2014a) on the terrorist attacks, I argue that a major problem with Breivik's sentence is that the punishment is not in principle matching the wrong done (as the punishment by law was only twenty-one years for all the killings). Thus, it was not able to provide the rightful means to settle the case in the conclusive way it should have done—and, so, it did not help calm the passions for revenge as it should have done.

[23] As we will see, proposing a right to violent revolution wrongfully presupposes the possibility of justice in the state of nature. This is not to deny that there can be injustice in the state of nature—to rape someone, for example, always has been and always will be unjust: it involves formal and material wrongdoing—but it is to deny that unilateral uses of force (violence) can be correctly described as conclusively rightful.

involving what he calls "outer freedom," and, so physical interactions in the world—
have a very strong effect on us as embodied beings:

> hatred arising from an injustice we have suffered, that is, the *desire for vengeance*, is a passion
> that follows irresistibly from the nature of the human being, and, malicious as it may be,
> maxims of reason are nevertheless interwoven with the inclination by virtue of the permissible
> *desire for justice*, whose analogue it is. This is why the desire for vengeance is one of the most
> violent and deeply rooted passions; even when it seems to have disappeared, a secret hatred,
> called *rancor*, is always left over, like a fire smoldering under the ashes.

> The *desire* to be in a state and relation with one's fellow human beings such that each can have
> the share that justice allots him is certainly no passion, but only a determining ground of free
> choice through pure practical reason. But the *excitability* of this desire through mere self-love,
> that is, just for one's own advantage, not for the purpose of legislation for everyone, is the
> sensible impulse of hatred, hatred not of injustice, but rather against *he who is unjust* to us.
> Since this inclination (to pursue and destroy) is based on an idea, although admittedly the idea
> is applied selfishly, it transforms the desire for justice against the offender into the passion for
> retaliation, which is often violent to the point of madness, leading a man to expose himself to
> ruin if only his enemy does not escape it, and (in blood vengeance) making this hatred
> hereditary even between tribes, because, it is said, the blood of someone offended but not yet
> avenged *cries out* until the innocently spilled blood has once again been washed away with
> blood—even if this blood should be one of the offending man's innocent descendants.

(A 7: 270-1)

Insofar as we are inheriting societies whose histories and current functioning contains patters of sexualized violence and oppression, those who bear oppressed and
violated identities face a special emotional and moral challenge. In particular, this is
because when one has or is being denied the opportunity to live justly with others,
one can become tempted not to develop the complex and complicated emotionally
and morally wiser ways of engaging reality that are consistent with the possibility of
justice and instead develop the passion for revenge. If one develops the passion for
revenge, one not only desires something that is impossible—passions cannot be
satisfied—but one might rationalize one's desires with self-deceptive stories according to which one is simply putting things right. However, in such cases, one in fact
endeavors to destroy oneself as well as the hope for a better future for anyone
affected. And, if one does give in to these temptations, one becomes more easily
manipulated by those with "depraved hearts"—those who are no longer driven by
affects and passions in confused pursuits of their personal enterprises, but who stand
at a distance from passions and in accordance with profoundly self-deceptive,
moralized stories will seek to exploit others' weaknesses in order to orchestrate
political movements geared only towards destruction (atrocities).

3. Concluding Remarks

In her extraordinary essay "Duty and Desolation," Rae Langton (1992) argues that
Kant's interactions with Maria von Herbert reveal not only his personal limitations
with regard to interactions with women, but also the limits of his moral philosophy.
In short, von Herbert wrote to Kant to seek moral advice. She writes that as a result of
having entrusted a secret regarding her intimate past to a man with whom she was

developing an intimate relationship and who asked about her intimate past, the man withdrew and ended the courtship, and instead offered to be just a friend instead. The complications surrounding this failed relationship leads von Herbert to consider suicide, and she seeks to engage Kant on the question of whether or not it is a perfect duty not to commit suicide. Kant's response to von Herbert does not engage the topic of suicide. Instead, Kant says that if this was a true *moral* friendship, then she has nothing to fear (as her friend will return), whereas if all the man was after in the first place was a physical friendship, then she might as well face this fact right away; in that case, the relationship did not have the moral fiber that she needs in a true friendship after all and life simply goes along with many such disappointments. As it turns out, Kant was correct in his judgment and the man did come back to von Herbert and offered intimate friendship, but then von Herbert did not want it any longer; she found it and life boring. Von Herbert then writes to Kant one more time, a letter that reveals that she is again clearly struggling with suicidal thoughts, and in which she explains that she would like to visit Kant, partly to see how he manages life in accordance with his own philosophy. Kant at this point has sought knowledge from a common acquaintance regarding what von Herbert's secret was all about, and he learns that she had had a sexually intimate relationship with another man before, and that this man had taken advantage of her. Kant decides not to respond to von Herbert, and instead bundles the letters up with a note on how there is a lesson in von Herbert's letters on how dangerous *enthusiasm* (an affective mental state) is and gave both to Elizabeth Motherby—the daughter of Kant and Mr. Green's friends, the Motherbys. We also learn from Langton that von Herbert finally gives in to her suicidal longings and kills herself.

Langton argues that this story clearly reveals how Kant fails to appreciate the dangers of truth-telling. Indeed, it seems plausible, she argues, that von Herbert *should* have lied to her friend; after all, this would have been a rational, prudent way of dealing with a terribly sexist society in which not only had she been taken advantage of, but in which revealing this fact could be met with more sexist behavior (as in fact it was). In addition, she finds it rather callous that Kant does not respond to von Herbert's suicidal frustration and that he simply hands over the letters to Mrs. Motherby.

In light of the above and previous chapters, let me suggest a different way to read this story. To start, Kant does not think that we can have a moral *duty* to lie. We can therefore not argue that von Herbert *should* have lied to her new friend. This does not mean that we must answer every question we are asked; we are not even obligated always to answer our intimate friends' questions. But we might plausibly imagine von Herbert facing a situation in which not answering the question would be understood either as a "yes, I have had intimate relations before" or "no, I don't want this kind of deep intimacy with you (even though that is exactly what we are doing right now, and, so, I don't make sense and you should walk away from me)." We can imagine that the only way to get out of trouble would be to lie. Now, Langton seems right to emphasize that facing these kinds of challenges is much more strenuous for women than Kant seems to have appreciated, and one could argue that he should have given a version of his argument of lying to the murderer at the door. The new intimate partner should have known not to seek such power over his new girlfriend (by asking her such a dangerous question about her intimate past). And von Herbert could have lied, thus committing a formal, but not a material wrong, although this would have been difficult for her to live with, and it would have held back their friendship.

Alternatively, we could argue that Kant did the right thing. He did not want to engage with a stranger's difficult suicidal thoughts, as doing so well would only have been appropriate within a much closer relationship, which is why he did not invite von Herbert to visit. It seems fair to say it would have better if he had been able to acknowledge her depression, express his feeling sorry for her situation, and maybe even say that he does not feel he knows her well enough to talk to the suicidal longings or to have her visit. But it seems to me that not being able to react so is more likely to reveal a kind of immaturity than cruelty or callousness. In any case, Kant does share a caring kind of advice: he points out that if the new partner is a true friend—one with whom the fullest kind of friendship is possible, a moral friendship that involves a development, transformation, and integration of a way of living lives together—then she should not put too much emphasis on the immediate spontaneous, affective, or even passionate responses in the situation. If the new partner is the real thing—and not yet another person who would just like to experience intense physical or social pleasures (relating to animality and humanity) with her—then he will overcome these irrational emotional challenges and come back to her. Indeed, in light of Kant's relationship with Mr. Green, it was not just on the basis of his philosophy that he said this, but also on the basis of his lived life. True friends—including Kant—mess up in all kinds of ways, but their way of being oriented towards you is such that they do not just walk away (even if they do so temporarily, in the heat of the moment). They will take on the challenge of growth that you offer, and will offer the same to you. Or to put this point from a different angle, if the friendship is the real thing—if neither one of them is simply seeking a relationship based on feeling (enthusiastic affect)—then it is not over. If it is not the real thing, then it may be better to deal with it right away rather than to postpone it; dealing with life requires us to be able to handle such complex and complicated facts.

To suggest that Kant responded well to von Herbert is not to deny that perhaps Kant should not have shared this story with Elizabeth Motherby.[24] Then again, maybe not. After all, she was the daughter of two of his best friends; he was at the Motherbys' house for dinner together with Mr. Green every Sunday for many, many years. It is not inconceivable that they had had discussions about the dangers of "enthusiasm," and that he thought that this interchange revealed some of the seriousness of this affective temptation; indeed, that his note to Elizabeth Motherby indicates that they have had discussions regarding the danger of basing friendships on affect only (enthusiasm) could refer to conversations they have had many times about the nature of relationships.[25] If you base your relationships on enthusiasm, then they remain vulnerable and unstable in this way. Indeed, we could add, having heterosexual relationships in sexist societies has this kind of challenge: some of the reactions of either party are going to track pathologies and oppressive/defensive

---

[24] Arnulf Zweig's introduction to Kant's (1999: 28–9) *Correspondence* discusses Kant's response to von Herbert. On the difference between lying and reticence, see Walla (2013).

[25] More detail on Kant's account of friendships is found in Chapter 1.

behaviors that need careful handling if things are going to go well. Additionally, in light of the analysis in this chapter, perhaps we can see in this story of von Herbert some of the difficulties of living and loving in a world of oppressed identities, including the difficulty of being tempted not to face the challenges of oppression, but to run away (temporarily or permanently) in affective ways instead. In other words, Kant's sharing of the letter may very well have been inappropriate—perhaps the relationships we have as important adult figures in our friends' children's lives are incompatible with sharing in this way even if sharing such a difficult experience with our closest friends is part of how we handle them well. Still, even if it is inappropriate to share such experiences with people for whom we perform a guiding function, it would be a very human mistake.

Concluding Part I

Reconciling Noumena and Embodied, Social Kantian Agents

To conclude this first part of the book, let me revisit a core challenge mentioned in the general Introduction.[1] Insofar as Kantians humanize their agents by showing them to be more embodied and social (and not only rational), as I have done, they appear to encounter a new problem: their accounts of human agency appear not to be distinctively Kantian. This Hegelian "empty formalism" line maintains that the more embodied and social the Kantian conception of the human agent, the less that conception can capture Kant's emphasis on the noumenon, how human beings are distinct from all other animals in that they can act in truly free ways—they have "free will"—which lies at the heart of Kant's conception of morality. Kantian ethicists therefore face a dilemma: either they must choose formalism, in which case they cannot capture the (importance of the) embodied, social nature of human beings, or they lose the formalism distinctive of Kant's position. Kantians cannot have it both ways. Having chosen the path of humanizing the Kantian moral agent and having argued that it is the path that Kant himself chose (even if Kant and I disagree on how best to understand issues of sex, love, and gender), it is important to explain why my theory has not lost Kant's formalism, and its distinctive value, along the way. I owe an explanation as to why my theory can capture the philosophical insights in, and even requires, Kant's distinction between noumenon and phenomenon, of transcendental freedom, and a "free will."[2] It is true, as I emphasized at the end of the general Introduction, that many of the philosophical ideas and moves offered in my theory are acceptable to many non-Kantian theories. Nevertheless, I believe that Kant's

---

[1] As mentioned in the general Introduction to this book, this conclusion is quite advanced in relation to philosophy generally and Kant's philosophy particularly. Those newer to these discussions may therefore find it best to skip this conclusion on the first go-around and continue directly to Part II.

[2] Although much of this debate is carried out in terms of "free will," in my view, this is not Kant's favored way to describe human beings' ability to choose truly freely. In the introduction to *The Metaphysics of Morals*, Kant says, "Laws proceed from the will, *maxims* from choice. In [the hu]man [being] the latter is free choice; the will, which is directed at nothing beyond the law itself, cannot be called either free or unfree since it is not directed to actions but immediately to giving laws for the maxims of actions (and is, therefore, practical reason itself). Only *choice* can therefore be called *free*" (MM 6: 226; cf. 6: 213f.). (Here is another place where I have amended Gregor's translation as she translates the German "in dem Menschen" as "in man," which is an unfortunate choice. Although "Mensch" in German is a male noun, it refers to any human being (not only a man, which would be "der Mann") and since Kant also writes "im" which is an abbreviation for "in dem," I believe a better here translation here is "the human being.")

Sex, Love, and Gender: A Kantian Theory. Helga Varden, Oxford University Press (2020). © Helga Varden.
DOI: 10.1093/oso/9780198812838.001.0001

ability to capture human freedom sets it apart and makes it a better theory than the others; otherwise I would not have chosen this path. Thus, it is important that I engage this topic before moving on to sex, love, and gender in relation to justice in Part II.

To set the stage for a discussion of what is distinctive about Kant's ability to capture true freedom ("free will") such that I regard it the most philosophically attractive account, I first engage the most recent discussion on the topic between Sally Sedgwick and Barbara Herman. Second, I lean on recent work by Katerina Deligiorgi and Alix Cohen to bring out how my account of sex, love, and gender can be seen as responding to the Hegelian objection. I finish by using recent work by Lucy Allais and Katerina Deligiorgi to indicate what kind of metaphysical conceptions of transcendental freedom and free will my own account is compatible with and needs—a kind of account that is not subject to Sedgwick's empty formalism objection.[3]

Echoing Hegel's objections to Kant, one of Sedgwick's persistent objections to Herman's Kantianism over the last two decades is that it falls prey to a specific problem of "empty formalism." In her critical engagement[4] with Herman's *Moral Literacy*, Sedgwick (2011: 33f.) first notes that Herman's account does not fall prey to the classical (universal formalist) objection that Kant's idea of the agent "in her [Herman's] words ... [is] ... 'denatured, abstract, simplified' (Herman 2008: vii)." Rather, Sedgwick worries that Herman does not and cannot address a different classical, Hegelian charge, namely of empty formalism; and that, in fact, Herman's "form of Kantianism provides fuel for its fire" (Sedgwick 2011: 34). The more embodied the agent becomes in an interpretation of Kant's practical philosophy— and so the better the interpretation responds to criticisms that focus on philosophical problems with "disembodied accounts" of the Kantian agent—Sedgwick argues, the less the formal, noumenal aspects of Kant's practical philosophy perform any important, distinctive philosophical work in the interpretation. Furthermore, if this is the case, then the interpretation and resulting philosophical position no longer appears to be one of or based distinctly on *Kant's* practical philosophy because nothing distinguishes it from other moral theories, such as Rawls's, in which ideas like freedom, respect, and rights are also foundational.

Sedgwick (2011: 43) additionally clarifies that her main worry about Herman's Kantianism is "not about the law's special status as universally and necessarily valid" as such, but about her ability to capture the law's *"meaning."* More specifically, Sedgwick is concerned that Herman does not engage the formal, noumenal aspects of Kant's account to explore this question of meaning to the satisfaction of those who share those concerns. Sedgwick finds it unsatisfactory to say that The Categorical Imperative commands us to respect human freedom—many kinds of positions can say that—since what the Kantian must explain is how "the [moral] law is necessarily

---

[3] This is not to say that I could not have done the same by utilizing the work of other Kantians. I have chosen these three as they fit particularly well with how I have argued in this book and to celebrate the fact that, as mentioned at the end of Chapter 2, at this point in time, it is actually a natural choice to use the work of three women Kantians, as some of the best Kant scholars today are women.

[4] For a much earlier formulation of this set of worries regarding contemporary Kantian practical accounts, see Sedgwick (1997).

valid for all rational natures... [how] the categorical imperative is the one and only supreme practical principle for all cultures, all traditions, at all times" (Sedgwick 2011: 43), and this is a difficult claim to defend. And yet, doing so is the task of the Kantian: The Categorical Imperative yields absolute commands for all rational, yet embodied beings—beings with capacity for truly free choices, or a "free will."

On the topic of transcendental freedom, Sedgwick notes that Herman appears uneasy about Henry Allison's (1983) classical "two-standpoint" interpretation of Kant's distinction between noumenon and phenomenon (according to which the "world-as-it-appears" and the "world-as-it-is" is simply an epistemological distinction) and unsure "whether there can be a metaphysically acceptable account of the kind of cause Kant thinks the will is" (Herman 2008: 174/Sedgwick 2011: 46). Indeed, Sedgwick argues, Herman appears disposed to think

that the doctrine of the noumenal will is dispensable, and that we can get at the idea of a mental cause without it. This indicates a significant departure from Kant. Although it may be that Herman is right to assert that the idea of a mental cause, 'does not by itself require noumenal causality', *Kant's* conception of practical agency requires noumenal causality. The freedom Kant attributes to the moral agent is *not* that of a mere mental form of causation. A mere mental or 'internal' freedom, as he calls it, is nothing more in his view than the 'freedom of a turnspit'; it is the compatibilist version of freedom he so passionately rejects (Kant 1996b: [97]). On Kant's account, only one kind of freedom is capable of grounding a metaphysics of morals, and that is the freedom he refers to as 'transcendental'. The agent who is free in the transcendental sense acts not just from a mental cause; she is capable of initiating a causal series from a standpoint outside time [A551/B579].

Applying this objection to Herman (et al.) to my account of the Kantian agent as presented in Part I, the question becomes: does my account require Kant's distinction between phenomena and noumena, that is, does it require an idea of rational agency which can explain why something is *always* wrong (independent of culture, traditions, etc.)? Additionally, if Herman's and my accounts do presuppose a distinction between phenomena and noumena, do the accounts thereby appeal to some suspect, magical, or otherwise unjustifiable metaphysical notion of a rational agent who can initiate a causal series in time by acting from outside of time? Along with Herman, I answer "yes" to the first question. I will then show why my theory needs a distinction between the noumenal and the phenomenal. Indeed, I need it even more than Herman's because of the way in which I use the distinction between formal and material wrongdoing throughout this book. By leaning on recent work by Deligiorgi, I will argue that this distinction may be an advantage rather than a disadvantage of my account. In due course, along with Herman, I will answer "no" to the second question before employing recent work by Allais and Deligiorgi to show what kind of metaphysical and metaethical conceptions of freedom and free will my position can take onboard and even requires.

Herman responds to Sedgwick by arguing first that we can tell the applied story—for Herman: moral literacy; for me: human sex, love, and gender—from the top down where the consistent focus is on the formal. However, starting with the formal features of the account and then carrying these formal features down to the complex human experiences we are engaging philosophically, Herman and I agree, is not an effective way to develop a philosophical understanding of moral literacy and human sex, love, and gender that is "interesting for all human beings" (A 7: 295), to use Kant's formulation of this point. This is one reason why I have tried to tell the formal Kantianese story only as required in the previous chapters. In this way, I hope that anyone who picks up this book—including non-Kantians and readers who are not necessarily experienced with doing philosophy—can read it and appreciate the usefulness of formal aspects of theory to understand complex human experiences (here by Kantian lights) without being bombarded by more complexity than is necessary along the way.

Another reason not to choose such a top-down approach, Herman explains and I agree, is that it is important not to shy away from the complexities of actual human lives when we do practical philosophy. An important goal is to make clear how our philosophical theories capture this complexity. In fact, a major reason why I have chosen to tell much of the story from the "bottom-up" is that I believe that the failure of Kantians (and others) to appreciate the actual circumstances of lived human lives is one reason why philosophy has been for so long practically indifferent to, and not a force for stopping wrongdoing against, including the harming and dehumanization of women, sex workers, polysexual, polyamorous, and members of the LGBTQIA community. When we keep our focus only on Kant's moral freedom writings and utilize only the arguments we thereby have available, the issues of sex, love, and gender barely surface in Kant's texts or philosophically. And as the related secondary literature on Kant reveals, the statements we find in Kant's texts remain rather inscrutable and seem more like strange, uncomfortable, prejudicial afterthoughts resulting in philosophical accounts that are insufficiently complex to yield satisfying analyses of much human experience. To arrive at a more complex philosophical understanding of sex, love, and gender, Kant's full account of human nature is necessary and we must pay attention to how animality and the social aspects of our humanity do their own, distinctive philosophical work here.

In addition, one of the great services done by Herman and so many other Kantian ethicists and moral psychologists since the 1970s is to emphasize that if we attend only to Kant's moral freedom writings and the formal arguments we find in them, we will misrepresent Kant's practical philosophy. Kant's practical philosophy is not exhausted by his moral freedom writings. To understand his practical philosophy well, we must ask the question of how the moral freedom writings are a constituent part of it, such that the sum is a consistent whole that captures the complexities of human lives. Indeed, as I have argued in Part I, if the reason why one sets aside Kant's other (anthropological, historical, religious) works as well as his related comments within his moral freedom works is that one finds them too disturbing in their cisism, sexism, and heterosexism (and racism), then one deprives philosophy as a whole of a useful resource with which to understand our human capacity for evil. After all, we find these awful statements in the writings of perhaps the best philosopher in the Western philosophical tradition; indeed, in the one who revolutionized practical philosophy by proposing that the basic principle of moral philosophy is freedom and whose only long-term, intimate companion in life was another man. Understanding how Kant could get some of these sexual, affectionate, gendered aspects of our lives so wrong is important to understand in itself and because it helps us to understand our propensity to evil.

Important to the writing of this book has been the judgment that by simply setting these problems aside, we set aside the challenge of figuring out how to overcome these limitations of Kant's own philosophical writings. To make matters worse, if we primarily focus on the formal aspects of Kant's position, we facilitate and maintain philosophy as a discourse and practice that appears cruelly insensitive to much of human life, and one that appears to put the sexual, loving, gendered aspects of our lives in the same category as much of our other phenomenal ("heteronomous") existence: in the category of things we like, such as playing soccer, eating chocolate, or having a good glass of wine. But, surely, finding these sorts of things as existentially important as sex, love, and gender in a human life lived well is to make a category mistake. The consequences are that the theory ends up being unable to pay attention to or to explain foundational, critical facts such as how being denied conditions in which one can realize one's sexual, affectionately loving, gendered self is internally connected with radically high numbers of suicides for human beings: the suffering for many is simply too much to bear. As seen in earlier chapters, if formalism is our only primary focus when doing practical philosophy, not only is our theory unable to register human suffering, but we (as theorists) run closer to the danger of becoming tempted by vanity, that is, the danger of developing the brutalizing cognitive stubbornness characteristic of Oscar Wilde's physician who cannot bring himself to see his patients' suffering *as* suffering because doing so falsifies his theory.

Even in the more recent work by Kantians who do explore Kant's writings on history, on anthropology, moral psychology, and on biology, there is a tendency to stay focused on the general rather than also the applied aspects of the theory, including by never really making it to issues of sex, love, and gender (beyond sometimes noting that Kant was sexist and, sometimes, heterosexist and homophobic). And again, this is deeply unfortunate since the stakes are so high here; after all, this is an area where there has been and is so much suffering and wrongdoing and where happens much of what makes human life meaningful, full, and precious for many. Further, in my view, sex, love, and gender is one of the areas where Kant's own work needs improvement through philosophical argument—where he makes mistakes that are intimately connected with terrible practices in human history, including philosophical practice. Thus, correcting these mistakes appears important in itself. In addition, understanding the nature and cause of those errors helps us to understand the rest of his philosophy. We can come to appreciate the importance of, for example, the connection between reflective (teleological and aesthetic) judgment and contingency. Therefore, viewing these "applied" questions as always coming further downstream—only after we have satisfactorily explored the formal or general philosophical framework—when we do interpretive and philosophical work in much practical philosophy seems, at best, ill-advised.

To set the stage for addressing how my theory uses Kant's distinction between the noumenal and phenomenal, let me first note that, like Herman, I can express much of the analysis in the previous chapters in Kantianese and in such a way that the formal features of the account are front and center. To start, I could emphasize throughout that the predisposition to animality explains how we use the three relational categories of the understanding (substance/self-preservation, causality/sex drive, community/basic sociality) teleologically in relation to a given, animalistic embodied forcefulness (natural vital force) that we can pick out through intuition understood non-conceptually. In turn, this natural vital force must be thought of as internally linked to our being as part of the universe as it appears, even though we can only make sense of how it appears to us through our rational capacities if we allow for there being things beyond what appears, or things-in-themselves. When we engage and develop these aspects of ourselves well through our faculty of desire (through setting ends of our own in complex ways that involve abstract, associative, teleo-logical and aesthetic cognitive means), we transform, develop, and integrate them in ways that feel deeply pleasant or that we reasonably expect ourselves to learn to genuinely enjoy with time. In addition, we find ourselves with a moral forcefulness that we can make sense of philosophically only if we consider it to be made possible by our practical reason, meaning our capacities for reflective self-conscious being and for acting as motivated by our faculty of practical reason. Hence, we obtain know-ledge of the world by engaging it through abstract concepts and searching for universal laws—how it is constituted insofar as we can engage and know it theoret-ically (and through empirical science)—and we additionally figure out how to govern ourselves as beings who set ends of our own by truthfully thinking through abstract concepts (specifically, maxims) and by living in accordance with universal laws (universalizable maxims) that we give ourselves. In addition, in contrast to how the thing-in-itself functions as a place-holder for what there must be beyond being as we can know it (the thing-as-it-appears), the way in which human beings can govern themselves through giving laws to themselves must be understood not as internally connected with our being as it appears, but as it is in itself. Finally, insofar as we develop, transform, and integrate our animalistic desires as they are internally linked to our natural vital force such that they are consistent with our moral vital force, we live our particular lives—we exercise our freedom—in a(n also socially affirming) way consistent with striving for the highest good for human beings: namely, a close, harmonious union between happiness and morality. Although my account maintains that it is impossible to give philosophical accounts of our vital forces and the basic kinds of feelings we have, it does maintain that there are aspects of our reflective self-consciousness (including associative, abstract conceptual, and imaginative cognitive powers) which must be presupposed to enable these feelings, and which consequently are preconditions of their possibility.[5]

On this account, then, we—human beings—must think of ourselves as having two kinds of embodied forcefulness, one that is at the heart of what makes us *embodied, social* rational animals and the other that makes us embodied, social *rational* animals. Moreover, in exploring both aspects of ourselves insofar as we can obtain objective knowledge about them and morally own them, we use our rational capacities, our capacities to engage the world by means of universalizable maxims and the

---

[5] This claim does not, however, appear any more metaphysically suspect than, for example, the claim that all there is (being as such) is what there is in space and time—as the truth of this claim cannot be verified by anything in space and time.

principles of understanding. Furthermore, it is having a capacity for giving laws to ourselves—as constitutive of our being—that gives human beings dignity (priceless-ness). In particular, insofar as we realize this capacity, we seek to live lives in which all our maxims can at least be *thought* as universal laws for rational beings (perfect duties), and insofar as possible, can also be *willed* as universal laws for rational beings (imperfect duties). Human beings, that is to say, are capable of moral responsibility because we can act on practical reasons (maxims that can be thought and/or willed as universal laws); and when we do this well, we affirm ourselves (also socially) and others as having dignity. Also, we are unsocial social beings: since we set ends of our own (personal ends) and yet are social too, there is an irreducible sense in which we are both drawn towards one another (through affectionate love, creative playfulness, desire to help, etc.), and yet there is an irreducible sense in which we need our own space to set our personal, individual ends, to become Immanuel, Helga, and so on. In addition, we have seen that the highest good for human beings is a close, harmonious union between happiness and morality, and that one of our challenges is not to treat this ideal as something we can fully realize; the most we can accomplish is to strive to realize it, and so to deserve to be happy.

As I described in Part I, even though we must appeal to the rational (noumenal) side of us in order to explain our capacity for moral responsibility, it does not follow that the objective in a *human* life should be to live as if we were only *rational* beings, as if we were angels (holy beings) or gods. Although Kant does think that some people will be subjectively most attracted to such a life, and will lead one in impressive ways—in ways that we describe as saintly, because they realize a morally estimable ideal—it is not a moral duty to lead such a life, nor should it be understood as *the* human ideal. After all, there is a significant human cost to living a saintly life since it is to live as a human being without enjoying this kind of life to its fullest. If one truly is a saint, one lives one's life in such a way that it is primarily devoted to the well-being of others; a saint makes it easier for others to handle life's many challenges well. In addition, part of the challenge for a human rational being who loves another human being is to live life in such a way that this other human becomes constitutive of one's own life—that this human being *matters* for how one goes about life—and yet that this way of living together is consistent with each being a *rational* being too, a being whose ends are open-ended and who has a distinctive individual life of their own to live and who can do so in morally responsible ways because of their practical reason. As I have emphasized, some of the challenge of human beings sexually and affectionately loving one another concerns how there is a certain givenness to our sexual animality and sociality about which we need to be truthful and attentive to get all of this right. There are things we need to be sexually aroused (sex drive), feel affectionately loved (basic community), and to be safe (self-preservation) and ways in which we need to be affirmed socially (as important and valuable to oneself) that are not universal but contingent and yet central to having a good sexual, affectionately loving, gendered life. And there is besides a deep sense in which in our meetings with other human beings, there is a fundamental openness to the experience(s) as we are, exactly, beings who creatively set ends of our own and accordingly, beings whose ongoing open-ended activity can never be fully captured by concepts. To love someone in a grounding and caring, yet open way that allows for change of the kind constitutive of genuine growth is one of the most meaningful, yet hardest, accomplishments for human beings.

In the previous chapters, I have also explained that Kant's account of human beings is not one according to which we always strive to do the good and the right things. We have, we have seen, an ineradicable temptation to do bad things—a propensity to evil that trails our basic desire to do the good, right things. This temptation comes in three degrees—frailty, impurity, and depravity—which track increasingly serious ways in which we can lose our emotional and moral way in life. No human being is able entirely to avoid doing bad things; it is an empirically universal fact that humans will do bad things, and that they will often do them in ways that contain self-deception. Indeed, our deep desire to be good comes with its own dangers, one of which is to describe what we are doing in such a way that it makes us feel good (we do bad in the name of the good). It is in part because of this danger of self-deception that Kant proposes that truthfulness is our first or a sacred duty of virtue, though it is our first duty also because only if we are truthful about what we are doing can we possibly succeed at governing ourselves through our practical reason. This account of human nature therefore gives us a model for the basic phenomenal structure of a human (social, embodied) being who can be trapped in situations in which the only morally good way out is internally connected with unhappiness, or in situations from which there actually is no morally good way out. That is to say, we can find ourselves in situations in which choosing to do the morally right thing (choosing not to partake in formal and material wrongdoing against an innocent person), entails choosing an unhappy life. Further, we can find ourselves in bad, oppressive conditions, where we do not materially wrong anyone when using even lethal violence against others (since we are protecting ourselves against their attempt to unjustifiably coerce or violate us) and yet we do commit a formal wrong ("wrong in the highest degree") as we do not have the moral authority to use lethal force against other human beings (we do not have the moral authority to be the ultimate decider over life and death). Perpetrating such violence against others, even though it is to protect oneself against evil, is to act in ways that are inconsistent with treating human beings as having dignity.

Given the nature of human evil, each individual will find themselves drawn to the temptation of destructive inclinations. We will often deceive ourselves about this, and we may even develop patterns of giving in to destructive inclinations (e.g., we may develop passions, or we may allow our affect to guide our behavior when we should not). And so will societies. Although revolution ("burning it all down") cannot in principle solve these problems when they emerge at the societal level, the best response may be to forcefully refuse to go on (resistance), and to face the (threat of) barbarism in particular interactions or conditions as individuals. On this view, individual histories will not *necessarily* go well, but if a person stays committed to truthfulness as a way of life, despite the undignified, brutal ways in which others may treat them, no one can diminish the dignity with which they go through life or even face their own wrongful demise. There is reasonable hope on this position. Human nature is "crooked timber," but each of us (and, so, each culture) has what it takes internally to assume moral responsibility for our own failures, to deal with the bad things done by others, and to move on in better, healing ways, towards a better future, although it will be subjectively easier for us to do so if others assist us in our efforts to do so.

There are virtues to telling the story of my Kantian theory of sex, love, and gender as I just did, placing emphasis on its formal and general features. For the philosophically trained mind, it is in some ways easier to read the text above than the previous chapters. But! This book seeks to provide and present a theory of sex, love, and gender that can be useful not only to (Kantian) philosophers, but to anyone who is genuinely interested in using (or learning to use) philosophy to understand these human phenomena. Thus, in my view, it is important that I can reasonably hope that the above paragraphs and this conclusion to Part I can be understood, at least more or less, by anyone who has read the previous chapters, and thus that the text can enable readers to see why it may be helpful to engage philosophy as they try to live well and understand their lives better. In my view, insofar as I have succeeded at doing this, it is a virtue of my text just as it is a virtue of Herman's *Moral Literacy*.

There are, in other words, good reasons to choose a bottom-up approach when using philosophy to engage complex human experiences, such as moral literacy or sex, love, and gender. And this way of engaging and developing Kant's philosophy does not entail—on my or Herman's approach—that the formal aspects of his position play no role. Before moving on to the question of whether or not Kantian positions like Herman's or mine must appeal to some suspect metaphysical magic to explain rational agency, I would like to show that this worry is perhaps even more worrisome on my account since the formal does even more work in it but that this is a strength rather than a weakness vis-à-vis Herman's account. To show this, I want to draw on recent work by Deligiorgi as well as Cohen.

In *The Scope of Autonomy: Kant and the Morality of Freedom* (2012b), Deligiorgi raises an important objection—one that is related to Sedgwick's above worries regarding Herman—to many "psychological" contemporary Kantian approaches, such as those defended by Marcia Baron, Paul Guyer, Barbara Herman, Thomas E. Hill, Jr., and Christine Korsgaard.[6] Deligiorgi argues that these accounts put too much pressure on psychology to do all the philosophical work, since this inevitably leads to one-sided accounts of self-organization. Once these Kantians had done the corrective and much needed work with respect to Kant interpretation of the Kantian agent, Deligiorgi continues, they leave us with no reason to follow Kant as someone who has something very different to offer than basically a hierarchical account of autonomy which asks us to take others into account, that is, to organize our internal affairs properly, not to claim independence or to find happiness, but in order not to hurt, harm, or wrong others. Such approaches, she argues, obviously have much to offer, which Sedgwick would agree with, but what is not captured by them, Deligiorgi emphasizes, is Kant's idea that *absolute prohibitions* and so *categorical imperatives* are essential to morality like no other area of human activity; and such imperatives are possible only if they can be unconditional, where unconditional is the most demanding sense of objective there is (unlike the theoretical objective). Nothing of this kind is found in nature (which is

---

[6] Deligiorgi's (2012b) critique focuses on these works: Korsgaard (1986, 1992, 1996a, 1996b, 1996c, 1997, 1998, 2002, 2003, 2009); Hill (1991, 1992, 2002); Guyer (1993, 1995, 1996, 2000, 2007), Herman (1993a); and and Baron (1997b).

not to say it is some supernatural thing); rather, it is a formal notion which gives us the formula of autonomy. But she then asks, why call it autonomy? Her answer is that it is autonomy because it is the uptake by beings capable of rational thought of this very idea that morality has this sort of objectivity. Once we cut off this autonomy dimension of Kant's thought, we still have a rich ethics, but a heteronomous ethics: that is to say, we have accounts of self-governance where our capacity to act truly freely—paradigmatically as revealed in our ability to recognize and act on absolute prohibitions—is not doing its own, distinctive philosophical work.

Obviously Herman et al. do not need me to answer for them, so let me instead point to certain features of my position, as well as how it can be seen as consistent with and complemented by important, recent work by Alix Cohen, to show how I believe this objection does not apply to my theory as presented in Part I. First, notice the emphasis I have placed on viewing the highest good as a union of happiness and morality; on the fact that our attempts at unifying these two aspects of ourselves can never fully succeed; on how the philosophical account of either part must do its own philosophical work in the overall account of sex, love, and gender; on how we must let the reflective and unreflective aspects of our being do their own, distinctive normative work in our accounts; and on how the absolute claims morality makes on us (human beings) entails that we can find ourselves in situations in which there is no good way out (even though we can imagine other rational beings, for whom that would not be the case). Second, rather than viewing all sources of human value as moral value and viewing all other aspects of human life as valuable only insofar as they make it easier or more difficult to do what morality demands, I have argued that a rich human life requires us to seek to realize both morality and happiness. The challenge for us is to strive to realize ourselves such that we develop our vital force and our moral vital force into a close union. This point, in my view, connects at a fundamental level with Alix Cohen's (2018) argument that there is one faculty of feeling for Kant—non-moral and moral feelings—and one faculty of desire, whereby we develop our ways of living in ways that transform and integrate these two kinds of feelings into full human lives. My account, like those of Deligiorgi and Cohen, contrasts many of the psychological accounts that emphasize showing what an integrated human life looks like. Our accounts have an ineliminable differentiation at the center of the analysis in that non-moralizable and moralizable feelings and ways of being cannot take each other's place or be meshed together in the philosophical analysis. One is not reducible to or replaceable by the other; and, on my account, morality does issue absolute prohibitions. A distinctive argument throughout the book is the distinction I draw between formal and material wrongdoing, which helps me speak both to how our practical reason commands us absolutely and yet how, in human lives, we can find ourselves trapped in situations where there are no morally good ways out; we can end up in situations where formal wrongdoing is unavoidable in that the only other choice is to let someone else do material and formal wrongdoing to us.[7] Where my account in Part I of this book moves beyond

---

[7] This feature of the account corresponds to how I argue elsewhere that lying, for Kant, *always* involves (formal) wrongdoing (doing wrong in the highest degree). In contrast, most of the "psychological theories"

Cohen's and Deligiorgi's accounts (though I believe in ways compatible with their accounts)—and so beyond the other existing Kantian accounts—concerns the way in which I add an emphasis on the structure of human phenomenology. This enables me to speak to why, although it is true that non-moralizable aspects of human life help or hinder moral being, it is mistaken to think that they are not sources (and not only one kind of source) of genuine value in human lives lived well also on a Kant-based account, including when we critique issues of sex, love, and gender.

Regardless of this internal dispute among Kantians on the question of how to capture Kant's formalism with regard to absolute commands, if the formal aspects do play a role, what about Sedgwick's criticism that Herman's argument assumes that plural, non-Kantian metaphysical theories or principles could ground Herman's moral philosophical theory? Let me first explain why I agree with Herman in her response to this challenge, and then try to solve the problem Herman does not try to solve by drawing on recent work by Allais and Deligiorgi on transcendental freedom and free will.

Herman (2011: 57) starts her response to Sedgwick on this point by emphasizing that nothing she says in *Moral Literacy* affirms that there is "Kantian pluralism about moral first principles," and I take it that nothing I have said in the previous chapters entails such pluralism either. Herman then argues that leaving open the question of whether a metaphysical account other than Kant's own can do the philosophical work needed on her account of moral literacy is not to say that it is compatible with just *any* kind of account. In particular, Herman emphasizes that any plausible candidate must be able to capture

some idea of rational causality. One question is: how much further must we go? Kant holds that we cannot regard rational causality, the causality of the rational will, as part of the temporal sequence of things in experience; that the idea of an autonomous will requires transcendental freedom, independent of but also connected to the material causality of nature. I see no reason to be shy about discomfort here. Kant is rather bold in his own discomfort, arguing that, in the end, it is enough to show that an idea we have to have for practical purposes is not impossible, and even helps make sense of other ideas we have to have about the understanding. The commitment we cannot forego is Kant's core insight in the practical domain: that the will is a rational, norm-constituted causal power. The practical investigations that I have made explore what follows from the idea that the moral law, an a priori principle of practical reason, is the constitutive principle of such a will's causality. Does Kant have the best or the only account of the possibility conditions of such a principle or capacity? I don't see that his core insight is compromised if the answer is 'no'. To sustain the core insight we need a way to maintain the idea of reason as a distinctive ability that has a normative and effective role with respect to what we think and do. But there are many reasons to want to have that.

The core insight does require a particular understanding of the motives of a rational being, and so of us. Rather than an element of a system's hydraulics, a motive is a determination of the will—that is, a piece of practical reasoning. Here is the picture that is not right: I recognize a morally salient fact; I figure out what I ought to do, given that fact; but what happens depends on the presence (or absence) of a sufficiently strong motivational source to get me from

mentioned by Deligiorgi as well as other Kantian answers to this puzzle by revising Kant's own account by arguing that he should have argued that lying is wrong *most* of the time.

recognition to action. Rather, on Kant's view, the practical cognition is itself sufficient for action. Of course means and opportunity need to be secured, and there can be impedances to and failures of reasoning. But there is no extra motivational element beyond the agent's reasoning.   (Herman 2011: 59-60)

Like Herman, I believe that an advantage of Kant's philosophy is that it provides a philosophical account of our capacity to be rational causal agents in virtue of being capable of practical reasoning. Any account that is not able to explain this cannot yield the philosophical ideas and distinctions required for the account of sex, love, and gender presented in the previous chapters, or in Herman's *Moral Literacy*.

At the same time, until one has mastered all the relevant metaphysical accounts available in the history of philosophy and at least the relevant features of Kant's metaphysics, and one feels satisfied that one has a good explanation not only of how Kant's own argument works but also why it is better than at least many of the alternatives, and one's account does not invoke any appeal to metaphysical magic, one should not—and I believe Herman is right to say this—take a more conclusive stand on this metaphysical issue regarding causality, and being uncomfortable around this complexity seems appropriate. After all, metaphysics is an area of philosophy where mistakes are easily made and the consequences of these mistakes are real and can be drastic. In the context in which I am writing, one should not underestimate this fact. For much of Western history, for example, most philo-sophers sided with Aristotle, according to whose metaphysical mistake, women and natural slaves do not have the full rational soul that men capable of being citizens have, as they lack part of the rational soul that makes it possible for them to reason abstractly or theoretically for themselves, although women can deliberate practically (and, so, are capable of phronesis, at least to some extent). Subsequent philosophers could instead have sided with Plato's *Meno* or *Republic*, according to which also children who are girls and/or whose parents are slaves can become philosopher kings in a just world. In such a world, all children need to be educated—and then demonstrated skill determines who is best suited to which kinds of lives. It is not clear, however, that Plato's rationalism is the best way to account for the human capacity for practical reason, let alone the only one needed to avoid Aristotle's mistake or to give a good account of human sexuality, love, and gender. Metaphysics matters, in other words.

None of this undermines the fact that my account of human agency—like the account presented in *Moral Literacy*—appeals and draws attention to the need for metaphysics as part of developing practical philosophies. In particular, my account presupposes an idea of a so-called "free will"—or truly free choices—to make sense of how we can be morally responsible for our actions. My account is similarly incom-patible with many kinds of metaphysical accounts, indeed with any metaphysical account that is rational (including conceptual or constructive) or empirical all the way down. But we may reformulate this question in the following way: Herman is worried about any appeal to a notion of rational causality outside of time that applies inside of space-time, and Sedgwick appears to argue that this *is* the Kantian account. If we want Kant, we therefore have to want this. Is this true? Alternatively, what kind of work is it that Kant's account of transcendental freedom and free will have to do in my Kantian theory? To answer these questions, in this last section, I will lean on the work by Allais and Deligiorgi to show what kind of metaphysical conceptions of transcendental freedom and of free will an account like mine requires.

This brings us back to the second question noted at the outset of this conclusion: if my account does presuppose a distinction between phenomena and noumena, does it thereby appeal to some suspect, magical, or otherwise unjustifiable metaphysical notion of an agent who can initiate a causal series in time by acting from outside of time? Sedgwick (2011: 46) thinks that when Herman or other Kantians say things like "Kant holds that we cannot regard rational causality, the causality of the rational will, as part of the temporal sequence of things in experience; that the idea of an autonomous will requires transcendental freedom, independent of but also con-nected to the material causality of nature" (Herman 2011: 60), then such a Kantian must appeal to a notion of an agent acting effectively in space-time from a standpoint "outside of time"—indeed, she argues, Kant himself asserts this (CPuR A551/B579). And as we see above, this is a worry that in important ways Herman has too; she is concerned about any conception of the rational agent who is taken to be able act in space-time from outside of time. Notice also that if there is such a conception, in my case, it must be a conception that can handle three ideas concerning causality: first, causality as we encounter it in science understood deterministically (necessary laws); second, causality as we understand it in relation to teleological-aesthetic judgments (parts and wholes and aesthetic appreciation); and, third, causality as we understand it in relation to moral responsibility (acting on practical reasons). I appeal to all three conceptions of causality throughout my analysis of sex, love, and gender in the previous chapters. And if this an unresolvable worry, then I should be no less worried than I am with regard to Aristotle: after all, it appears that Kant and the Kantians (must) argue that the human agent in part is able to assume a perspective it may be humanly impossible to imagine; a perspective from outside of time. Fortunately, I do not think that Kantians have to read Kant or the Kantian position as appealing to such metaphysical magic. Both Allais and Deligiorgi put forward readings of Kant and the better Kantian philosophical position that avoid these interpretive and philosophical problems and, consequently, also yield a truly compelling understand-ing of transcendental freedom and free will that can complement my theory while avoiding Sedgwick's objection. I start with Allais and with a focus on transcendental freedom before moving on to Deligiorgi where the focus is primarily on free will.

In current work[8] Allais argues that transcendental freedom in the first *Critique* is importantly negative in that it makes space for moral freedom but cannot prove it through metaphysical arguments. To show this, Allais begins by proposing that the philosophical position in question (a metaphysical freedom that makes room for moral freedom) can be clarified by using the contemporary terms "compatibilitism" and "incompatibiliasm" as Allen Wood does in his description of Kant's position as

---

[8] Allais (unpublished manuscript). There is much in Allais's discussion, including textual engagement with the first *Critique* and the existing secondary literature that goes beyond my concerns here. My aim is simply to sketch the way in which this kind of interpretation is a good starting point for further explorations of these metaphysical questions of freedom in a way that is compatible with the interpretation and philosophical account presented in this book. I thank Allais for permission to cite this work.

an "incompatibilist compatibilism." Such a description can help us see why Kant's first *Critique* argument regarding transcendental freedom allows for three kinds of causality I employ in Part I: scientific necessity, whole-part causation, and human freedom. And I see no reason to think that aesthetic playfulness is not compatible as well, since whole-part causation falls under the same umbrella (third *Critique*). My intent here is not to make a conclusive argument in favor of Allais's position—doing that is beyond my current philosophical abilities—for my purposes, it suffices to sketch some of the main interpretive and philosophical moves and show how they are of the kind my Kantian theory needs.

That Kant makes space for human freedom in the first *Critique* only negatively, argues Allais, rests on his ambition to show that despite that "everything that happens in space and time has a cause that falls under a deterministic law," this "does not make human free actions impossible." Allais's aim is to forge a kind of compatibilism in Kant—a reconciliation of human freedom and determinism. Yet, she continues, Kant's conception of freedom is "incompatibilist" in that it appeals to

a causal capacity to initiate actions that are not a determined function of previous states of the universe, and he wants to show that our having this kind of causal capacity is not made impossible by the fact that everything that happens in space and time has a cause that falls under a deterministic law that shows how it has to follow from a previous state of the universe.

Allais (unpublished manuscript: n.p.)

Allais then makes three arguments from which emerge two central ideas in such an incompatibilist compatibilist interpretation of Kant's philosophical position.

First, Allais argues that Kant does not think that we can prove or understand human freedom metaphysically. According to Kant,

we cannot prove [by metaphysical argumentation] that we actually have the causality of freedom; all we can show is that its possibility is not ruled out. Further, we cannot even really understand it [freedom] metaphysically, as a form of causality. Our only metaphysical understanding of freedom is negative: the idea of a capacity to initiate something that is *not* a determined function of previous states of the universe. Kant does not think that this negative claim is yet a conception of freedom: it is compatible with things occurring randomly, or by chance. We need a positive conception of freedom in addition, to rule out mere randomness or chance, and he holds that the only way we can give a positive characterisation of the causality of freedom comes not from metaphysics but from practical reason, and involves a capacity to act for reasons, where this is understood as governed by recognition of higher-order rational constraints on what counts as a reason for action.   Allais (unpublished manuscript: n.p.)

According to Allais, Kant neither tries nor thinks it is possible to prove or understand human freedom by means of metaphysical arguments; metaphysics will only take us as far as a *negative* conception—a space opened up for freedom in human action. The proof that humans have a capacity for truly free (*positively* free) choices ("free will") is revealed in the human ability to recognize the authority of moral reasons (practical rationality), in a sense to be in the space where we recognize that we *ought* not to do something just because doing so would be wrong or we *ought* to do something because doing so would be right. As Kant argues time and time again in *Groundwork*, we cannot appeal to anything but the form of reasoning itself in order to grasp the moral authority encapsulated by the ought; if the rule (maxim) I am considering acting on cannot be thought as holding as a universal law for rational beings, I ought not to act on it. Thus, the moral law is experienced as a categorical imperative. To be able to act on a categorical imperative just is positive freedom: it is an ability to choose as motivated by practical reason, which is all my account in the previous chapters requires. This understanding of freedom complements my applied, normative, and moral interpretations and arguments in the first part of this book. I expand on this idea of free will below with the help of Deligiorgi's recent work.

Second, Allais argues that the most interpretively and philosophically plausible engagement with Kant's account of transcendental freedom involves appreciating how a commitment to determinist science does not commit us to the metaphysical position she calls "Total Metaphysical Determinism," according to which "at any time t there is a total set of facts and a total set of laws which together entail all the facts about the future." Instead, scientific determinism can be complemented by the (more plausible) conception of scientific necessity, namely "Law Determinism," which holds that "the laws of nature are deterministic ... [and] every thing that happens in space and time has a cause that falls under a law of nature" Allais (unpublished manuscript: n.p.). She furthermore argues that although contemporary compatibilists tend to side with Total Metaphysical Determinism and consequently steer away from an incompatibilist account of human freedom, Kant and the Kantians can and should defend Law Determinism, which *is* compatible with human freedom as we experience it also commonsensically (as the feeling of the *ought*'s pull). Indeed, Allais argues,

Law Determinism is a transcendental condition of empirical cognition and as such can be known to be true of the world in space and time, while Total Metaphysical Determinism is a transcendent metaphysical claim which goes beyond human cognition, and features for us as a mesmerising metaphysical illusion that arises from the empiricist side of human thought.

Allais (unpublished manuscript: n.p.)

In other words, thinking that we can in principle know all there is through scientific investigations of what happens in space and time is exactly what Kant takes his transcendental idealism to refute; he takes it to refute the empiricist temptation to consider things-as-they-appear-to-us as though they were things-as-they-are-in-themselves.

Third, Allais argues that a Law Determinism account of scientific causality views the future as possibly "open," meaning that although "everything that happens in space and time has a cause that falls under a deterministic law," this does not mean that what could happen in the future must be thought of as determined at the beginning of space and time. At any given point in time there could be more than one possible future. My position in the previous chapters requires an open-ended understanding of causation like this one, as it involves human agents setting ends of their own, and it appeals to imagination, which includes teleological and aesthetic judgments. Allais does not attend specifically to aesthetic judgments, but she does engage the teleological part-whole complexity, arguing that transcendental idealism does not rule it out:

This account allows for the reality of top-down or whole-part causation ... we have neither empirical nor a priori reasons to rule out its possibility. For whole-part causation to be logically ruled out we would need an a priori reason to think that there is a most fundamental level of explanation and that there are complete causal explanations at this level of explanation. This is not a claim made within science (including the science of matter) and it is not consistent with transcendental idealism.   Allais (unpublished manuscript: n.p.)

To make this argument, Allais also draws on important work in the philosophy of science by Nancy Cartwright and Helen Steward. According to the latter (2012: 231), "There is absolutely no *scientific reason* to endorse the claim that purely physical laws are sufficient to dictate the movements of any physical thing... there is only the grip of a mesmerising world view." Allais illustrates this point by using the example of how to explain all movements of an animal. She argues that if we suppose that there is

whole-part causation, we are supposing that the explanation as to why the animal moved its body in certain ways will require reference to its purposes and behaviours which can be understood only at the level of the whole animal and its environment. This is compatible with the idea that, whichever thing the animal did, there will be causal processes in its brain chemistry that explain how it moved.   Allais (unpublished manuscript: n.p.)

In the same manner that such whole-part causal explanations (holistic causal explanations) of aspects of animal behavior are not in principle inconsistent with scientific causal explanations, neither of these causal explanations are in principle inconsistent with the transcendental freedom that is necessary to account for human beings' capacity for moral responsibility, or for the aesthetic playfulness to which I appeal. Rather, just as "top-down" or "whole-part" physical causation does not appeal to acting for reasons in order to explain human movements, aesthetic playfulness need not appeal to scientific causal laws to explain human actions. Both acting for reasons and aesthetic playfulness must be seen as having a different kind of causality than strict, scientific causal necessity.

Allais's account is additionally fully compatible with what is required for my account of how we, as human beings, seek to develop ourselves as the particular beings we are and as part of a complex enterprise of realizing the embodied, social, and aesthetically playful aspects of ourselves in such a way that it can be seen as seeking a harmonious union with responsiveness to act on practical reasons. These philosophical moves in my position are consistent with Allais's basic claim that such interpretations of Kant's philosophy attribute to him a denial of the claim "that there are complete explanations at the fundamental level"; indeed, they claim that such a denial "is just what transcendental idealism asserts" by maintaining that

appearances are not things in themselves... since... if they were "then nature is the completely determining cause, sufficient in itself, of every occurrence, and the condition for an occurrence is always only in the series of appearances that, along with their effect, are necessary under the law of nature" (A563/B564).   Allais (unpublished manuscript: n.p.)

This account of transcendental freedom is therefore one according to which "both whole-part and physical causation could be genuinely operative [and different in nature]. Whole-part causation is not the same as explanation involving freedom" (Allais unpublished manuscript: n.p.). Furthermore, such an interpretation is consistent with the arguments I have put forward in this first part of the book: it is a plausible candidate for my (and other embodied, social Kantian) accounts of the human agent, and it should help alleviate the worry that my account necessarily suffers from Sedgwick's Hegelian empty formalism charge.

This, then, is a good time to take a moment to engage directly the question of how this understanding of Kantian transcendental freedom can respond to Sedgwick's objection to Herman that such an agent can act effectively in space-time from a point of view or place "outside of time." Allais argues,

> We have seen that thinking that particular events have particular determining causes does not entail that the whole state of the universe entails the particular event. But when (Kant thinks) we cognize the objective temporal order this involves seeing how the way things are has flowed from the way they were in the past. When we do this, we are following the events as they fell under determining causes, and seeing them as something that had to happen. Because we cannot cognize free acts in the way (Kant thinks) we cognize the world in science, we cannot explain them as flowing from or being determined by previous states of the universe. This gives a sense in which they are outside of the way we cognize the temporal order. But we need not read this as an assertion of a different kind of, non-temporal, causation. Our ways of thinking of things without time tend to be misleading—they tend to involve pictures of time, and then ways of trying to see events outside of it in relation to all of it. In my view, Kant is more consistent when he sticks with the negative way of making his point: rather than saying that things are *not* temporal as they are in themselves, we can merely say that our spatio-temporal forms of intuition do not present us with things as they are in themselves. This is not a positive claim about reality in itself. The point need not be that free acts are outside of time, but rather that to the extent that we cannot cognize the choices as having to follow from previous states, we cannot cognize them as determining parts of the temporal order. The way we cognize the relevant events as part of the temporal order is in terms of the physical events and their particular determining causes, which are always in operation.
>
> Allais (unpublished manuscript: n.p.)

In other words, Kant's claim that human freedom requires the idea of an absolute beginning is most productively understood in light of his overall transcendental metaphysics. In that light, the claim appeals to a kind of beginning that we cannot conceive of as analyzable through spatio-temporal intuition, just as the idea of "things-as-they-are-in-themselves" cannot be engaged through such intuition. To make the full philosophical and interpretive case for this is the job of metaphysics, which starts where the analysis in this book ends. In noting the limits of her metaphysical account of freedom, Allais appears to advocate a similar philosophical division of labor:

> To give a complete Kantian account of human freedom requires far more than showing that the universality of the causality of nature does not rule out the possibility of the causality of freedom. It requires, at a minimum, giving a Kantian account of what it is to act for reasons, why acting for reasons commits us to recognising [one's own and] the humanity of others as a constraint on what counts as a reason, why understanding acting for reasons in this way is a conception of freedom, why a reasons-responsive causal capacity requires [the possibility of] an open future, how our [human] reasons-responsive causal capacity is embodied and relates to the causality of nature. A full account would also include an account of self-governance through virtue, would ideally also relate to Kant's account of what grounds political freedom, as well as of how [human agency] goes wrong and is corrupted, and of how to understand Kant's notion of intelligible character ... [Here m]y concern ... is simply with one part of what

is required for the total picture: showing that the metaphysics that we need to make sense of science doesn't undermine the possibility of the causality of freedom. It is important to keep in mind that this metaphysical picture does not give a positive conception of freedom.

Allais (unpublished manuscript: n.p.)

So, what kind of positive conception of freedom—of "free will"—does my position require and how can it avoid the objections advanced by Sedgwick and also avoids Herman's own worries? In my view, Deligiorgi's work on metaphysics and metaethics is tremendously helpful to see what such a path looks like; her and Allais's work on metaphysics (as outlined above) are in deep agreement and there are also deep agreements between her related concerns in metaethics and mine as explored in this book. Deligiorgi's work also helps us see why Kant's account of acting for reasons is a conception of freedom.

As previously explained, I agree with Deligiorgi in her claim that part of what stands out in Kant is his account of categorical imperatives—that some actions are absolutely prohibited. Throughout this book, I use this idea to capture some of the complexity of human life: we can find ourselves in situations where our practical reason issues absolute commands such as that we should not lie or kill and yet sometimes if we follow this command, wrongdoing will happen either to us or to somebody else. In the language of this book, formal and material wrongdoing can come apart in human lives since we are both rational *and* embodied, social beings living together on a planet; we can end up in situations where although we do not wrong anyone by engaging in material wrongdoing, we do "wrong in the highest degree" by engaging in formal wrongdoing.

Now, a philosophical challenge contained in these absolute commands, Deligiorgi argues in "Interest and Agency," is to explain their ground or source, which "lead[s] us straight into metaphysical territory" (2017: 20). And just as Allais can be seen to be responding to Sedgwick's objection that Kantian agents appear to act in space-time from outside of time, Deligiorgi argues that although

Kant claims that the matter of grounds is beyond our comprehension . . . [he] insists that we can *think* this more fundamental sense of freedom, which 'contains nothing borrowed from experience' (KrV A 522/B 561). When we consider an action that realizes some end empirically, we ascribe it to some agent as its proximate source, spatially and temporally. If the thought of freedom as first ground is to contain nothing borrowed from experience, 'beginning' cannot be understood temporally nor 'origination' spatially. In addition, excluding from our thought temporal properties means that we cannot think of the performance of an action in terms of efficient causality. This leaves us with nothing much, except for the term 'spontaneity'.

(2017: 20-1)

As I have argued throughout this book, our predisposition to humanity enables us to set ends of our own, to be the source of originally set ends, and our possible choices are limited to what is within our control. It is tempting, but mistaken, Deligiorgi proposes here, to understand this way in which we are original sources of our actions in terms of efficient causality as we do in scientific investigations. If we do, then we (in vain) look for a notion of acting from outside of time and space that is also effective in space-time, which is non-sensical. However, because, Kant's metaphysical argument in the first *Critique* does not foreclose the possible compatibility of science and freedom, it is also not necessary to look for such (incoherent) notions. Instead, Deligiorgi (2017: 21) proposes, Kant urges us to

understand spontaneity, in the practical context, as a relation agents have to ends ... it states simply that ends are *set* by agents.... [Moreover, the advantage of this is that i]nterpreting spontaneity teleologically ... allows us to side-step the topic of efficient causality by focusing narrowly on ends (rather than effects). Importantly, this conception of spontaneity counteracts the worry that we are programmed to pursue pre-given ends.

So, by switching from investigations into things that can be understood scientifically (in terms of efficient causality) to investigations into human spontaneity as it concerns our capacity to act, the door is open to an account of freedom.

Deligiorgi (2017: 22) continues by suggesting that this kind of argument forces us to think about whether or not "we have good reason to believe that we have a power of spontaneity ... which [not only] underwrites the freedom of choice, [but] which [also] enables specific instances of control." That is to say, if we can be original sources of action (be spontaneous or free), do we have any reason to think that we are able to control these actions or be responsible for them? After all, because we cannot give a metaphysical argument that proves that we can "know" or "prove" our spontaneity; "our claim to this concept [of spontaneity] is not theoretically secure" Deligiorgi (2017: 22). This is where, Deligiorgi suggests, the importance of categorical imperatives and absolute prohibitions shows itself. How? Because they reveal human beings' ability to control their spontaneity, "it is both cognizable *and* enforceable [by the agents themselves] 'as soon as it comes to doing our duty' (*Dohna* 28: 677)" (2017: 22). Why? Because doing our duty shows us as "addressees of the moral law and so as standing 'independent of the whole of nature' ... [we show that] we commit ourselves to the idea that we *can* deliberate about ends" (2017: 22). In being such addressees—in recognizing the moral ought or categorical imperatives—we (human beings) show ourselves as having an active deliberative interest "in the notion of morally guided evaluative control (*Wille*)" or a "rational interest in freedom" (2017: 22). And central to such a rational interest is the notion of an "unconditional ... type of norm [absolute prohibitions] ... that is external to all series of conditional goods, a location given as 'transcendental freedom'" (2017: 22). By recognizing absolute or unconditional prohibitions, we show, in other words, that our thinking about ends is not merely of the "means-end" (teleological) kind; rather we recognize normative commands external to any such conditional means-end thinking process.

On Deligiorgi's account, then, choice is free "because it consists in deliberation about ends in light of reasons and the formation of the intention to act in the pursuit of some end in light of said reasons ... [and choice is free in virtue of] spontaneity, given here as the power human beings have to set ends ... [which is] the farthest limit of our epistemic powers" (2017: 23). Hence, Deligiorgi continues, these epistemic limits, in turn, are reached by a

regressive argument, which is not designed to offer the binding conclusions that deductive arguments, for example, are supposed to offer. To clinch the argument Kant shifts the discussion to the idea of morally guided evaluative control. And because morally guided evaluative control is guidance by authoritative normative standards, the discussion about [free or spontaneous] agency ... connects with ... [our] rational interest in freedom (2017: 23)

To put these points in the language used in the first part of this book: in virtue of having the predisposition to humanity, we, human beings can set ends of our own (we are free or spontaneous in this sense of the term). In addition, when we act, we act on maxims, which is possible for us because we are self-reflectively conscious beings who can use abstract concepts. In addition, however, when we think well about which ends to pursue, we deliberate, or use practical reason, and when we do, our recognition of the fact that there are some things we must absolutely not do reveals that we have an interest in our end-setting that must be understood as purely rational and formal in nature. When we do this, we do not, as we saw in the earlier sections on perfect and imperfect duties (Chapter 1), look only to the content of our maxims (whether what we want to do is something that will make us happy) but to their form; we ask whether we can *think* or *will* the maxims we want to act on as universal laws. Moral feeling—recognizing the ought—reveals to us that we have such a purely rational interest in our own end-setting. Our susceptivity to the moral ought and paradigmatically absolute prohibitions reveal that we have what it takes (our practical reason) to be able to participate actively by setting ends of our own (spontaneously) in morally responsible (and not destructive) ways in the universe.

Central to Deligiorgi's interpretation is therefore the way in which the ideas of free (spontaneous) and rational (practically reasoning) agency complement each other: "The end-setting claim about human agency is a non-normative fact about the sort of being we are talking about, more precisely the sort of powers such a being possesses. The claim about strong authoritative normative standards, which is unconditioned, i.e. has no deniable antecedent, is a normative fact, a fact of reason no less" (2017: 23). To put this point in the language of Part I of this book, it is important to distinguish between the predisposition to personality and the predisposition to humanity: the latter concerns our capacity to set ends of our own, whereas the former makes it possible to act morally responsibly or as our practical reason requires. Moreover, the predisposition to personality is revealed in moral feeling—paradigmatically in the feeling that although we want to do something, we must not do it—and, Kant argues, this feeling can only be explained philosophically by our capacity for practical reason.

Finally, Deligiorgi agrees with both Allais and with the argument I have put forward in this book that

the distinctively Kantian way of thinking about freedom ... [refers] not just ... [to] the content [but also to] the procedure. Kant invites us to think about freedom in a way that manages to respect distinct areas of enquiry while also showing the way they interconnect. Although, of course, morality is central to his concerns, moral theory is not the sole load-bearing component of his theory of freedom. And it is part of his negative argument that metaphysics cannot do the job alone either.   (2017: 23)

Indeed, Deligiorgi concludes,

Taking forward this [Kantian project] is not just a matter of adding detail and definition to the parts presented here [proper boundaries of component enquiries and method] ... it is also a matter of identifying and calibrating the component parts proper to the topic.   (2017: 23-4)

One can correspondingly see my book as requiring the kinds of accounts of transcendental freedom and free will defended by Allais and Deligiorgi but as seeking to provide one way of taking up the argument where Allais and Deligiorgi leave it off, by identifying and calibrating the component parts proper to the topics of human sex, love, and gender—areas where our capacities for rational being and morality cannot do all the philosophical work on their own. Rather, the embodied social aspects of our human being have their own additional work to do.

In this first part of the book, the focus has been on our embodied, social, rational being as it pertains to realizing happiness and self-governance through virtuous internal freedom. In Part II, the focus will be on our embodied, social, rational being insofar as it pertains to realizing flourishing human societies and self-governance through rightful external freedom.

PART II

Sex, Love, and Gender
Right

Introduction to Part II

It is our capacity to act truly freely that makes it possible for us to be morally responsible for our actions. It is what sets us apart from all other living creatures we have encountered so far in the universe and enables us to be autonomous, self-governing through practical reason. In turn, understanding Kant's conception of freedom requires us to pay close attention to his distinction between internal freedom (virtue or first-personal ethics) and external freedom (right or justice). It is this complex idea of human freedom that informs all Kant's practical works, regardless of whether the work in question focuses on ethics (virtue), religion, politics, right (justice), history, education, or anthropology—just as it centrally informs the structure of and theory presented in this book. Part I also emphasizes the importance of looking to his fuller account of human nature and letting the various parts of that account do their own philosophical work in the integrated whole that is Kant's practical philosophy. This idea is central to the analyses presented in the subsequent three chapters as well. The book as a whole proceeds on the interpretive and philosophical assumption that in order to be able to describe, evaluate, or improve our actions, interactions, cultures, societies, histories, religions, and legal-political institutions, we need to understand our distinctly rational ability to be free as well as our distinctly human embodied, social being.

There is no doubt that the aspect of Kant's practical philosophy that has received the most attention in (the history of) philosophy are his works on internal freedom (virtue), particularly (meta)ethics. Kant's first major work in practical philosophy—*Groundwork*—was published in 1785, four years after the first *Critique* (1781). *Groundwork* is a short book of about eighty pages, concerning practical philosophy in general and first-personal (meta)ethics in particular—with an ongoing critique of the human, moral "ought." Kant thought that this would be his most popular work, explaining that he wrote it with an eye to its content being accessible to any enlightened, interested person—not only to philosophers. Given how inaccessible *Groundwork* actually is, it is somewhat surprising that Kant correctly predicted that it would be his most popular work. In addition, for a long time, and somewhat regrettably, (Kantian) philosophers took *Groundwork* not as an attempt to reach a

Sex, Love, and Gender: A Kantian Theory. Helga Varden, Oxford University Press (2020). © Helga Varden.
DOI: 10.1093/oso/9780198812838.001.0001

wider public or as a primer for what was to come, but as capturing the essence of Kant's practical philosophy—and viewed the second *Critique* and the other practical works as supplements to it. An unfortunate consequence is that the importance and interest of other aspects of Kant's practical philosophy often have been downplayed. Hence, much scholarly work has focused on the categorical imperative, duty, and im/perfect duties, leading many to try to solve all normative problems in practical philosophy with these philosophical tools alone. A large majority of students have been—and some places they still are—taught that these arguments about the categorical imperative, duty, and im/perfect duties are what Kant's practical philosophy is all about. Not until the 1970s did this problem in Kant interpretation—at least in the English-speaking world—begin to be properly remedied with regard to Kant's ethics (virtue), and not until the late 1980s/90s did philosophers properly attend to Kant's main work on justice (right), The Doctrine of Right.

The Doctrine of Right and The Doctrine of Virtue compose the first and second halves of *The Metaphysics of Morals*, one of Kant's latest published works (1797). The Doctrine of Right is the only place where Kant systematically outlines the basic structure of his theory of right (justice). All his other published works on right and politics are essays discussing more limited questions. Among the most important of those essays are: "An Answer to the Question: What is Enlightenment?" (1784); "On the Wrongfulness of Unauthorized Publication of Books" (1785); "On the Common Saying: That May Be Correct in Theory, but It Is of No Use in Practice" (1793); "Toward Perpetual Peace" (1795); and "On a Supposed Right to Lie from Philanthropy" (1797). Although scholars historically have given greater attention to these shorter essays than to The Doctrine of Right, it is reasonable to assume that Kant wrote the essays as complements to The Doctrine of Right. Part II of this book is written under that interpretive assumption.

To set the stage for the three chapters to come, below I first delineate Kant's distinction between right (justice) and virtue (ethics). I then sketch his answer to the classical question of why we establish public legal-political systems (states) at all. I briefly present his distinction between innate, private, and public right before providing an overview of Kant's core ideas concerning how we should incorporate concerns of our distinctly *human* nature in our lawmaking in general and as we seek to reform the very imperfect legal-political frameworks we inherit. Finally, I indicate how these analyses in Part II complement the general literature on Kant's legal-political philosophy, other Kantian analyses of sex, love, and gender, and related non-Kantian work in feminist philosophy and the philosophy of sex and love. In these ways, this introduction sets the stage for the following three chapters on Kant's legal-political philosophy in relation to issues concerning sex, love, and gender. The overall aim of this introduction is to make it easier to see how the three chapters in Part II together build on and add to the existing literature as well as yield a more complete legal-political theory of sex, love, and gender. Like the chapters composing Part I, these are written so that they can be read relatively independently of one another.

The opening lines of Jean-Jacques Rousseau's *Of the Social Contract* (1762) are among the most famous in the history of philosophy: "Man is born free, and everywhere he is in chains. One believes himself the others' master, and yet is more a slave than they. How did this change come about? I do not know. What can make it legitimate? I believe I can solve this question" (Rousseau 1997: 351).[1] Rousseau's deep influence on Kant's legal-political philosophy is hardly disputed. Like Rousseau, Kant's analysis of right focuses on the question of which coercive limitations can be placed on our actions in the name of freedom. Indeed, which coercive limitations our actions can be subjected to without our freedom being thereby disrespected is a core, organizing question in both Kant's shorter legal-political writings and in The Doctrine of Right. Kant repeatedly emphasizes that right fundamentally concerns the question of the authority to use coercion, or rightful uses of coercion. For example, Kant writes in The Doctrine of Right that

Resistance that counteracts the hindering of an effect promotes this effect and is consistent with it. Now whatever is wrong is a hindrance to freedom in accordance with universal laws. But coercion is a hindrance or resistance to freedom. Therefore, if a certain use of freedom is itself a hindrance to freedom in accordance with universal laws (i.e., wrong), coercion that is opposed to this (as a *hindering of a hindrance to freedom*) is consistent with freedom in accordance with universal laws, that is, it is right. Hence there is connected with right by principle of contradiction an authorization to coerce someone who infringes upon it.

(MM 6: 231)

For Kant, rightful uses of coercion—the "chains" or enforceable laws we can justify— are those that restrict us only in ways that are necessary to enable our reciprocally respectful exercises of freedom under universal laws. The only rightful limitations (laws) are those that are necessary because they make interaction under universal laws of freedom possible. Kant thereby sets a high threshold for rightful uses of coercion.

To understand Kant's approach to justice, it is important to appreciate the emphasis he places on distinguishing clearly between right (justice) and virtue (ethics). The Doctrine of Virtue (first-personal ethics) is an analysis of what we *ought* to do as individuals, or of the ways of acting through which we are truly free— in both the negative sense of abstaining from doing something because it is wrong to do it and the positive sense of doing something just because it is the right thing to do. The analysis of virtue does *not* issue the restrictions upon our actions that can be *rightfully enforced*; investigating uses of force or coercion is the main topic in The Doctrine of Right. The centrality of this point to Kant's philosophy of right cannot be exaggerated, in part because it entails that his analysis of virtuous actions in, for example, *Groundwork* and the second *Critique* cannot be directly applied to or used to explore the sphere of right (justice).

Some key arguments from Kant's (meta)ethical theory help to illustrate this distinction between right and virtue. Recall from Part I that in *Groundwork*, Kant maintains that acting virtuously involves *both* acting on the basis of maxims (first-personal or subjective rules of action) that can be "universalized" (can hold as universal laws), *and* acting as we do *because* it is the right thing to do (actions have "moral worth" only when the moral motivation is incorporated into the maxim upon which we act). We also saw that our perfect duties concern our obligations never to act aggressively or destructively against ourselves or others (never to act on a maxim

---

[1] The textual reference uses the standard pagination, but the translation is Rousseau (1997).

that cannot be *thought* as a universal law), while imperfect duties concern our obligations to develop our own capacities and talents and to assist others in their pursuit of happiness (our duty to act on maxims that can be *willed* as universal laws). Hence, we have perfect duties not to kill or lie, for example, while we have imperfect duties to improve our knowledge of the world in which we live and to provide aid to those who are struggling. Furthermore, if we abstain from killing others only because we are afraid of ending up in jail, then we do not act virtuously, but strategically. In this case, our choice (not to kill) is in agreement with what our reason (morality) demands of us, but it does not have "moral worth" because the moral motivation is absent (we are not refraining from killing *because* killing is wrong). Similarly, Kant argues, if we give money to the poor *because* we want others to think that we are such wonderful, virtuous people, we are not practicing beneficence (rather, we are feeding our narcissistic propensities or acting in our self-interest).

In the introductions to *The Metaphysics of Morals* and The Doctrine of Right, Kant highlights some important consequences of the fact that virtue essentially concerns maxims, which include the incentive or motivation on which one acts. First, he argues, because virtue involves a distinctly internal motivation, right cannot "reach" virtue; being forced to act in a way consistent with virtue is not to be forced to act virtuously. Virtue, Kant argues, concerns "internal" (subjective or first-personal) lawgiving, while right concerns "external" (coercively enforceable) lawgiving (MM 6: 224-6; cf. 213-14). To act virtuously is to act on universalizable maxims from a moral motivation; without both of these elements present, what we are doing may be emotionally healthy, morally permissible, and morally responsible, but it does not involve moral valuing (on the part of the actor) or acting virtuously. Furthermore, the maxim (including the motivation) upon which we are acting is accessible only from an internal, first-personal perspective: only I can know what I am doing (which maxim I am acting on, or which end I am pursuing), including the motivation of my action (whether I am doing it simply because it is the right thing to do). Coercion (the use of external force) can make me act consistently with certain ends, but it cannot make me set those ends (act on particular maxims), let alone do so *because* they are the correct ones (act from a moral motivation). Since no one can be forced to set a particular end from a moral motivation, no one can be forced to perform beneficent actions, for example, which is to say that "duties of benevolence, even though they are external duties ... are still assigned to ethics" (MM 6: 220). This is true, according to Kant, despite the fact that rich people can, of course, be forced to give up some of their money, which can then be given to poor people, and rich people can be threatened or shamed into acting in a way consistent with virtuous ends, such as by giving money to the poor. At most, then, coercion can function as a threat, and thereby give people a prudential incentive to act in ways that lead to a certain end being achieved. In Kant's own words: "No external lawgiving can bring about some-one's setting an end for [themselves] (because this is an internal act of the mind), although it may prescribe external actions that lead to an end without the subject making it [their] end" (MM 6: 239).

It follows from this that everything having to do with virtue or first-personal ethics necessarily lies beyond the scope of right or justice, whereas everything that lies within the domain of right can be also within the domain of virtue or ethics. That is,

I can feel and act on the obligation to obey just laws *just because* following them is the right thing to do. Hence, the sphere of virtue is wider than and encompasses the sphere of right, and while duty (the moral "ought") is the motivation of or incentive for virtue, any motivation (including the threat of coercion and self-interest) can be the motivation or incentive operative in the legal sphere (MM 6: 218-19). Although right and virtue are not diametrically opposed, from the point of view of right, all that is required is that our actions fall within the boundaries of the law, while from the point of view of virtue, an action must be done *because* it is the right thing to do in order not only to be permissible, but to have "moral worth" (MM 6: 220). Or to put the point from a different angle:

> The mere conformity or nonconformity of an action with law, irrespective of the incentive to it, is called its *legality* (lawfulness); but that conformity in which the idea of duty arising from the law is also the incentive to the action is called its *morality*... [Hence, e]thical lawgiving... is that which *cannot* be external; juridical lawgiving is that which can also be external.
> (MM 6: 219; cf. 230)

In the introduction to The Doctrine of Right, Kant expands upon the implications of the distinction between right and virtue by elaborating upon what is characteristic of principles of a legal-political theory that conceives of right in terms of external freedom. To start, he emphasizes that although right is inherently normative and concerned with questions about how to act morally, it is of crucial importance to note three limits to the scope of these concerns. First, right does not concern all action; it only concerns *interaction*. Therefore, as long as one does not interact with others, such as if one is alone on a deserted island, issues of right (justice) do not arise; in such a scenario only ethical questions concerning how to take care of and develop oneself will arise. Not until another person comes on the scene and interaction starts does right become an issue. One must then take up the challenge of figuring out how to interact in such a way that reciprocal freedom under universal laws of freedom is possible. Second, right concerns only whether a person's actions are reconcilable with others' right to freedom, including their rights to set and pursue their own ends using their own means (separately or together with others) under laws of freedom. Right is not concerned with whether a person's ends are ethical or virtuous; it does not ask whether or not we set ends or use our means in ways virtue demands. Not only does this entail that imperfect duties, such as beneficence or generosity, cannot be enforceable duties of right; but also, importantly, that the duties of right are not identical to or co-extensive with the perfect duties of virtue. For example, even if I live in conflict with my perfect duty of virtue not to act in self-destructive ways—if I waste all my money on parties or gambling—I have not thereby done anything wrong from the point of view of right. Third, a theory of right that takes freedom seriously cannot predetermine specific ends anyone must pursue. This is not merely a reiteration of the observation that no one can be forced to act on a specific maxim (i.e., to set any particular ends) since we can at most be forced to act in conformity with particular ends. Rather, Kant's point is that everyone has a right to pursue ends of their own with their means insofar as doing so is consistent with respecting everybody else's right to do the same. Rightful laws are laws of freedom; they cannot presuppose any specific ends on the part of those who live subject to those laws. Right secures reciprocal or equal freedom for persons interacting under universal laws of freedom, which means that no particular private ends can be presupposed by the principles enforced (MM 6: 230).

Combining the above arguments, it might appear that Kant rejects both the notion that the rich can be forced to assist the poor and the notion that states can establish welfare institutions to protect their poor. For a long time, many Kant scholars drew exactly this conclusion about Kant's theory of right (and many non-Kantian scholars still have this belief about Kant's philosophy). Consequently, early in the exploration of Kant's legal-political writings, some Kant scholars tried to develop Kantian theories of justice that overcame this apparent consequence, such as John Rawls in *A Theory of Justice* and Onora O'Neill in *Constructions of Reason, Towards Justice and Virtue* and *Bounds of Justice*. Others used arguments they found in Kant to criticize these Kantian developments. The most famous debate of this kind is the one surrounding Robert Nozick's libertarian criticism of the redistributive "difference principle" in John Rawls's *A Theory of Justice*. In *Anarchy, State, and Utopia*, Nozick argues at length that the difference principle makes Rawls's theory irreconcilable with the normative fact that respecting freedom demands that no one can ever be forced to help others *simply* because they are in need of help. Of course, Nozick argues, it is ethically wrong not to assist if one can, but failure to do so ought not be seen as unjust, legal (let alone criminal) wrong. The failure to help is an ethical, not a legal wrong in a just (liberal) state. Along Kant-inspired lines, Nozick argues that failing to respect others' rights to set their own ends (including selfish ones) with their means is to treat them as mere means and not as ends in themselves. Nozick also argues that it follows from this that a just state cannot tax its citizens in order to provide need-based assistance to the poor (which would be coercive redistribution). Consequently, on his account, the existence of even extreme poverty *as such* is not a sign of injustice in a state.[2] The just state is "minimal" in that it does not tax its population to redistribute resources in response to the needs of the poor.

As we will see below in the overview of the literature on states' rights (public right), some contemporary libertarian Kantians still maintain this line of interpretation regarding Kant's idea of the state. Other contemporary Kantians (in the liberal republican interpretive tradition) maintain that even if Nozick correctly interprets Kant as rejecting the idea that the state can tax some citizens *merely* in response to other citizens' needs, Nozick incorrectly concludes that Kant rejects all forms of poverty relief by the state. These interpretations hold that The Doctrine of Right convincingly refutes an assumption that Nozick's argument requires, namely the assumption that (excluding the administrative laws needed for the establishment of a legal-political institutional order) the rights of the state (public right) are, in principle, identical with the rights that private citizens have in relation to each other

---

[2] For Nozick, whether or not an instantiation of extreme poverty is a sign of injustice depends on how it came about; more specifically, it depends on whether or not the history yielding current private property holdings is consistent with his version of Locke's so-called "enough-and-as-good" proviso. See Varden (2012b, 2015a, 2016b) for more on this issue, including how securing the rights of the poor remains a live issue in the Lockean tradition, one that separates "right-wing" from "left-wing" Lockeans.

(innate and private right). As I argue in Chapter 7 on systemic justice, once we reject this assumption (because holding onto it is irreconcilable with building a legal-political system grounded on upon each person's innate right to freedom), the conclusion that the state must be "minimal" no longer follows; the state is not only permitted to provide unconditional poverty relief but is required to do so (as it must secure unconditional legal access to means for each citizen). This argument is important when we seek to analyze issues such as trade in sexual services, because the related historical institutions ("prostitution" and "pornography") track the effects of various forms of oppression in seriously problematic ways. As also indicated below and expanded upon in Chapter 7, the above arguments regarding both the unenforceability of virtue and systemic justice (public right) inform some of my resistance to Kant interpretations and to Kantian proposals that expect imperfect duties to do the bulk of the philosophical work to solve problems of systemic justice, including oppression of women and sexual or gendered minorities.

As we saw in Part I, the fact that Kant views his complete practical philosophy as irreducible to his moral analyses of freedom is textually clear; all his moral analyses (those of virtue and those of right) leave room for and integrate our distinctively *human* phenomenology. As we also saw in Part I, in *The Metaphysics of Morals*, Kant states that the necessary counterpart to his account of freedom in internal and external uses of choice (virtue and right, respectively) in a complete practical philosophy is a

> moral anthropology, which, however, would deal only with the subjective conditions in human nature that hinder people or help them in *fulfilling* the laws of a metaphysics of morals.... It cannot be dispensed with, but it must not precede a metaphysics of morals or be mixed with it; for one would then run the risk of bringing forth false or at least indulgent moral laws, which would misrepresent as unattainable what has only not been attained just because the law has not been seen and presented in its purity...or because spurious or impure incentives were used for what is itself in conformity with duty and good.   (MM 6: 217)

Kant's practical philosophy is, again, not a philosophy that consists only of his freedom writings (on virtue and on right). Instead, it is a practical philosophy that views *morality* as captured by his *Groundwork* and second *Critique* and the related writings on freedom (virtue and right), but which also includes writings on human nature; and so, his complete practical philosophy includes his writings on philosophical anthropology, moral psychology, politics, history, religion, and so on. For Kant, each part—freedom (virtue and right) and embodied, social, and aesthetic aspects of human nature, etc.—does its own philosophical work in the interconnected whole that is his complete practical philosophy. Moreover, as we envision how each part does its own, appropriate work, it is central to appreciate that the objective certainty we can have about the principles of freedom cannot be had about non-moralizeable ideas necessary to understand our human nature more fully. As the above passage makes clear, Kant is adamant that his writings on freedom must set the framework within which embodied, social, teleological-aesthetic aspects of human nature are given their due. A complete understanding of various human phenomena must therefore make space for the inherently contingent considerations of moral psychology and moral anthropology. This matters centrally when we seek to understand how Kant integrates his account of human nature (including evil) into his writings on virtue, as we saw in Part I, but also on right or legal-political freedom, including when we seek to understand legal matters concerning sex, love, and gender. Hence, as we develop full accounts of various complex legal-political human phenomena, such as marriage, rape, or abortion, each part will do complementary, yet different philosophical work and freedom will set the framework within which we give non-moralizable aspects of our human nature their due concern. Not only is the whole of Kant's legal-political philosophy complex; the parts comprising them are themselves complex.

That Kant often develops many ideas at once adds another layer of complexity in his legal-political writings. For example, sometimes his suggested ideas are proposed as improvements on notions handed down to him by the tradition of legal-political philosophy. Thus Kant's theory of right responds to central features and concerns of earlier theories, including the theories of justice that were prominent in his time, such as the "natural right" theories defended by, for example, Hobbes, Rousseau, and Locke. That Kant incorporates the different juridical categories of innate, private, and public right (law) adds even more complexity to the theory. So does Kant's practice of periodically situating his theory of right within the whole of his philosophical system. In my view, part of what makes Kant's theory of right so attractive to those who want to use philosophy to understand legal-political questions regarding sex, love, and gender is that it is these complexities that open up the argumentative spaces we need in a theory thereof. The way in which Kant brings together and develops different principles and ideas of right to form a coherent whole founded on each person's right to freedom and the way in which this whole fits into his greater philosophical system is tremendously helpful as we try to think through the complex and complicated phenomena of sex, love, and gender.

The natural right theories that dominated in Kant's day are so named in part because they typically begin their accounts of justice by analyzing which "natural" rights and duties individuals have in relation to each other. To do this, these theories often appeal to a thought experiment that involves imagining "the state of nature" or the "natural condition"—how humans (would) live (together) before (in the absence of) legal-political institutions (states).[3] They typically include arguments concerning why and how legal-political systems ought to be or are likely to be established, which in turn inform their analyses of what characterizes just legal-political frameworks (just states). Kant's theory is no exception to this model. He proposes a set of principles that should regulate individuals' interaction in the state of nature— principles analytically (the rights to rightful honor, to our own bodies, and to free speech) or synthetically (the principles of private right: private property rights, contract rights, and status right) linked with our innate right to freedom—in order to enable "provisional" justice, *and* he offers arguments for why people establish domestic legal-political systems and for how those systems (public right) should

---

[3] Sometimes these accounts involve analyses of how people actually did live together before states/legal systems were established.

function to enable and secure "conclusive" justice for each person subjected to its monopoly on coercion.[4]

Kant scholars still disagree extensively about many parts of Kant's analysis of the state of nature, and of how and which kind of just legal-political system should be established and structured—as they do with regard to virtually any other aspect of Kant's philosophy. But let me start with the aspects that are not, at least any longer, very controversial. To get a good grasp of Kant's analysis of innate and private right, it is useful to make two important observations. First, for embodied, social, rational beings, the innate right to freedom corresponds to a duty to "*Be an honourable human being...*," or to maintain "*Rightful honour...* [which] consists in asserting one's worth as a human being in relation to others" (MM 6: 236). To defend one's rightful honor is to defend one's right to be recognized publicly by others solely by the deeds one has performed. One's reputation, Kant explains, "is an innate external belonging" (MM 6: 295); it can originally belong only to the person whose deeds are in question. Second, for embodied, social, rational beings like us (even if not for all imaginable rational beings, such as angels), the right to freedom relates analytically to two other rights, namely the right to our own bodies and the right to free speech.

Starting with the latter, Kant explains in The Doctrine of Right that we cannot do wrong with words as such, not even with lies: "such things as merely communicating his thoughts to them [others], telling or promising them something, whether what he says is true and sincere or untrue and insincere" do not constitute legal wrongdoing because "it is entirely up to them [the listeners] whether they want to believe him or not" (MM 6: 238). Hence, even though being truthful in one's declarations of fact (not to lie) is a perfect duty of virtue—indeed, as we saw in Part I, truthfulness is the *first* or a sacred duty of virtue—lying is not a legal wrong as such.[5]

To see why our legal personhood and our right to our bodies are in an analytic relation, we need to familiarize ourselves with two important ideas that structure Kant's arguments in The Doctrine of Right, namely his account of possession and his distinction between "phenomenal" and "noumenal" possession. More specifically— and I return with more detail on this shortly—Kant suggests that there are three kinds of things external to or distinct from us that we can describe as "our own" in that we think we can possess them in some way: objects, other persons' actions (industry), and other persons. For example, we might say things like "this is my coffee mug," "you owe me three hours of work," and "this is my daughter." Moreover, Kant emphasizes the importance of noticing that the possessive relation expressed in these statements is thoroughly normative and not empirical. In other words, if the mug really is mine, it is not only my mug while I hold it in my hand and have empirical, or—to use one of Kant's favorite terms, phenomenal—possession of it. Rather, it is also mine once I put it on the table and leave it there for a while; I have normative, or—to use another of Kant's favorite terms, noumenal—possession of it. To describe something as *mine* is therefore not to make an inherently empirical

---

[4] Kant also discusses international and cosmopolitan public right in The Doctrine of Right, but exploring these arguments and issues would take me beyond this book's aims.
[5] The literature on lying in Kant is vast. For my take on the classic issue of Kant and lying to the murderer at the door, see Varden (2010a, 2021).

statement. It is to make an inherently normative one. Furthermore, noumenal possession describes not a relation between a person and an empirical thing (since empirical things cannot act normatively and so cannot be "in relation"), but a normative relation among persons with regard to an empirical object.

Empirical and normative possession only coincide, Kant then holds, in our possession of our own bodies: from a juridical (external freedom or spatio-temporal) point of view, my person and my body are one; they are in an *analytic* relation (MM 6: 249-50). Hence, we each necessarily have both empirical and normative possession of our own body, and we are each born with a right to our body. Besides, to infringe someone's bodily integrity is to commit a particularly grave legal wrong; from the legal point of view, to violate another's body is to violate their person (their legal personhood). This argument regarding the analyticity of the relationship between my legal personhood and my body is central to the analysis of bodily rights in Chapter 5.

In contrast, all other possessive relations are *synthetic*: they inherently involve seeing persons as normatively related to objects distinct from themselves, such as the mug being mine also after I put it down on the table. Moreover, the normative fact that we can make objects distinct from us our own (what Kant calls "external objects of our choice" or "our own") is constitutive of our external use of freedom. For embodied beings, external freedom involves setting and pursuing ends in the world, which in turn involves making things distinct from us—like a coffee mug—our own. Therefore, being able to make external objects our own is constitutive of exercising external freedom. The kinds of things we can control (without thereby damaging or destroying them) and make into our means set the limits for the kinds of ends we can choose to set for ourselves. For example, though I wish I could fly like Peter Pan, I cannot choose to do so since my body does not have the function of flight. In order to fly, I have to make an airplane by transforming materials appropriately in the world. And to do this, I need to be able to make these materials (these means) my own. Kant's theory of private right provides an account of the *a priori* principles we use when we make objects external to us our own, namely principles that delineate the boundaries of private property, contractual relations, and personal relations (familial or household relations, which Kant calls "status" relations). Moreover, the fact that there are three principles of private right (private property, contract, and status right) is a result of how we use the three relational categories of the understanding (substance, causality, and community) in this normative way (respectively) that is constitutive of making external freedom possible (MM 6: 247). Although the details of Kant's account of acquired, private right are beyond our interests here, a brief exposition is helpful.

According to Kant, the three principles of private right are structurally distinct from each other: we apply the principle of private property right unilaterally; we apply the principle of contract right bilaterally (together as two); and we apply the principle of status right omnilaterally (together as many). Regarding the principle of private property, Kant argues that our first step in making something unowned into our private property is to apply our own power or force to it so that we can control it. Then we signal to others that we have taken such control of it (MM 6: 258). For example, I may take possession of a piece of land on which I plan to grow vegetables and fruit, and I signal this to others by putting up a fence. By taking possession of the land in this way, I make it into a means for myself. This account differs from those historical accounts (such as Locke's), according to which my *labor* on the land (or natural resources) makes it mine. Kant instead follows the lead of those historical accounts (such as Hobbes's), according to which the first step toward possessing something is taking *control* over it through physical power. These different types of accounts of possession imply different answers to classical questions in the philosophy of right concerning private property, including land ownership. For example, who owns the hare that gets shot if two different hunters, unbeknownst to each other, have chased it? Or, if my bees fly away and settle on land that is not mine, do I still own them? And why can we not own the oceans? As Nozick puts it in his famous objection to Locke's labor theory of acquisition: why do I not get to own the ocean when I pour tomato juice into it (and in doing so mix my labor with it), but I do obtain possession of a field when I plough it and plant vegetables in it? Kant's answer is: it is not the mixing of labor that is the clue here, but control; you cannot control the ocean, whereas you can control the field. All we can control with regard to the oceans is the water close to the shore, that part of the water can be controlled from land, or so "as far as our canons can reach." Hence the oceans cannot be owned, but coastal waters can. In addition to proposing a way to deal with these classical legal puzzles, Kant also focuses on another central philosophical question in the discussion of private property right, namely, how the fact that I have taken something under my control can obligate others to abstain from using it? That is to say, does my unilateral choice to subject something, such as a piece of land, to my physical power (force) give rise to an obligation—a moral command—for others to stay away from it? And if it does not, am I permitted to use physical force to keep them away? We return to this issue shortly. Kant's understanding of private property as centrally matters of control and exclusion informs the arguments concerning private property in Chapter 7.

The second type of private right is contract right. Kant maintains that a binding contract is a normative agreement between two parties (MM 6: 271f.). Specifically, it is a bilateral agreement that each party will do something (they will exercise their causal powers, their industry) for the other and as the other wants. For example, you and I may enter a binding agreement, according to which I will paint your garage in exchange for a certain amount of money from you. Or, we might agree that you will give me your horse and I will give you my Cadillac. Kant's proposed principle for this type of agreement is that ownership is transferred only once something material changes hands. Only once I have put the paint on your wall is it yours and only once the horse has been delivered to me, is it mine; up until the point of its delivery it is not yours or mine even though we do have legal claim on one another to deliver. I will use this argument together with Kant's emphasis on how legal personhood and bodies must be understood as analytically related in my account of rightful trade in sexual services in Chapter 6.

Finally, status relations—or "rights to persons akin to rights to things [Von dem dinglichen Art persönlichen Recht]" (MM 6: 276)—concern how two or more people can share a legally recognized home or have standing within one another's private or domestic lives (MM 6: 276). These relations pertain to a certain kind of legal claim we can have on other people, including that they are "ours" in an important sense and how they become "ours" in a way that carries legal obligations. Kant presents three categories of status relations: relations between parents and children; relations between spouses; and relations among families and their servants (MM 6: 277). Although these types of relation are all omnilateral (all involve the establishment of a shared private life), they are importantly distinct from each other. Children are neither equals with their parents nor free: children do not and cannot give authorizing consent to be a part of the family; they are born without having given such consent; they are not yet capable of being responsible for their choices; and they are born into their parents' family (MM 6: 280). Unlike children, two spouses are both free and equal, which is why each must choose the other (say "yes" as part of the legal marriage ceremony). And finally, unlike children, servants are free (they are morally responsible) and so must give their authorizing consent to become servants, but unlike spouses they are not equal. That is, within the home, they are not the equals of the heads of the family (employers) and they lack the material means required for setting up their own independent households.

Kant emphasizes that status relations are especially vulnerable by virtue of involving claims on one another's *person* and a related fusion of several people's private lives in a legally recognized home, which is why Kant views them as requiring their own analysis (rather than subsuming them under an analysis of private property or contract right)[6] (MM 6: 276). The unique danger within status relations is that there is a real possibility for the shared home to become a place where might replaces right, and the weaker become enslaved to the stronger. That is to say, the lives and choices of the more vulnerable members of the household can easily be subjected to the decisions of the stronger; the home becomes the "man's castle," the "parents' castle," the "heads of family's castle." Recognizing these problems of asymmetry and dependency, Kant proposes a separate set of private right principles for relations in private homes (relations between parents and children, between spouses, and among families and their servants). His private right principles for relations of status propose a way of realizing right in the home, so that homes do not become inherently unjust spaces ("castles") where the force of the stronger rules.[7] I draw upon this account of status relations in the next three chapters, especially in my analysis of the legal institution of marriage in Chapter 6.

So far, I have been describing straightforward and relatively uncontroversial aspects of Kant's account of private right. The rest of his account is either too labyrinthine or too disputed to be treated at length in an introduction such as this. Yet it is worth briefly mapping some of the main lines of interpretation in the secondary literature on Kant's account of private right. I do so in order to help those readers trying to orient themselves in this literature, to locate the chapters in Part II of this book within it, and to show how these chapters aim to contribute to it. As we will see, some of the main lines of interpretation emerge when we focus on the

---

[6] Indeed, Kant views his account of status right as a separate category of private right—separate from the categories of private property and contract right—as an addition to the history of philosophy (MM 6: 282).

[7] These topics are very important in much feminist theory. The care tradition has been particularly active in bringing them to the forefront. For my engagement with the care tradition, see Varden (2012a, 2020b).

relationship between Kant's theory of justice and other theories that were prominent in his time. More specifically, some of the disagreements in the secondary literature can be traced back to whether the authors assume that the structure of Kant's theory is fundamentally similar to Hobbes's absolutist legal positivism, to Locke's libertarian theory, or is a liberal republican development of Rousseau (that aims to transcend the kinds of natural right theories that Hobbes and Locke defend). For reasons of space, I start by sketching the approaches of different interpretive traditions to Kant's account of why we must establish states (public legal-political institutional systems backed by a monopoly on coercion) at all. Then I match the interpretive approaches with outlines of their conceptions of the legal-political institutions constitutive of a (minimally) just state.

According to Hobbesian interpretations of Kant's legal-political theory, Kant agrees with Hobbes's claim in the *Leviathan* that it is impossible to realize rightful interactions in the state of nature because in such a condition peaceful interaction is impossible. As Hobbes famously argues, life in the state of nature is characterized by "continuall feare, and danger of violent death;' indeed the "life of man" in this condition is "solitary, poore, nasty, brutish, and short" (Hobbes 1996: 89). Hence, given human nature and the context of the state of nature (where everyone must fend for themselves and trust their own judgment at all times), the trust required for peaceful, rightful interaction cannot exist there. Moreover, since he views our practical reason as fundamentally prudential or strategic, Hobbes argues that we do not have a right to remain in the state of nature. That is, we do not have a right to make choices that are as stupid, irrational, or imprudent as the choice to stay in the state of nature is. Consequently, we can be forced to leave the state of nature and enter the civil condition by becoming subjects of a Leviathan (a public authority or a state)—and when we so yield to the Leviathan by becoming its subjects, we thereby consent to the state's legitimacy.

Hobbes's conception of the civil condition, in turn, is characterized by law-regulated stability, which is grounded on each subject's right to self-preservation, and backed up by overwhelming force. This force provides assurance to everyone that law will be upheld and in virtue of the stability such a legal-political system offers, it is strategically wiser to live within its boundaries even when the actual laws are unfair and oppressive; choosing to live under bad laws is more rational—prudentially speaking—than choosing to stay in the brutal condition of the state of nature, where human lives characteristically are miserable and end in premature, violent deaths. Hobbesian interpreters of Kant's theory of right do not, of course, attribute to Kant Hobbes's view that human beings' practical reason is inherently and solely prudential. Rather, they emphasize Kant's descriptions of human beings as both good and bad—such as his claim that we are made out of so very crooked timber ("aus so krummem Holze") (IUH 8: 23)—and maintain that this view explains Kant's position that we cannot realize right (justice) in the state of nature. They read Kant to argue that because of our unreliable characters (our liability to vice), we are incapable of interacting rightfully on our own (in the state of nature), and therefore we can be rightfully forced into the civil condition. In the civil condition, our propensity to act in evil ways is tamed by the real threat of punishment from the state; the risk of getting in trouble if we interact inconsistently with others' rights produces its own, strong incentive or motivation for us not to do so. This Hobbesian approach to Kant's theory entails that we can be obliged to obey a public authority even if we have not freely consented (without threats or yielding to violence) to its establishment or existence. Indeed, on these readings, Kant maintains that we can be politically obliged to obey public authorities that are not grounded on a firm legal commitment to each citizen's right to freedom.[8]

A second prominent line of interpretation of Kant's theory of right views it as structurally similar to Lockean/libertarian theories of justice. According to this interpretive tradition, we can realize justice in the state of nature, namely by each individual respecting everyone else's right to freedom. (This basic claim is sometimes matched with interpretive arguments concerning how rightful interaction in the state of nature involves respecting one's right to bodily integrity, to speech, and to having relations involving external objects of choice regulated by the three principles of private right.) Those who read Kant in this way typically agree with the Hobbesian interpreters that it is our crooked or violent natures—for the libertarian interpretations, it is our frequently stupid, ignorant, imprudent, biased, and evil actions or challenges similar to those Locke famously calls "inconveniences" of the state of nature (Locke 1988: 352/II: § 127)—that are the main impediments to realizing justice in the state of nature. Hence, they agree that the establishment of the state more effectively realizes justice; living under laws that are posited by legislators, applied by impartial judges, and enforced by the police is a much more prudent way of realizing justice in our interactions than is allowing individuals to make, apply, and execute laws all on their own. In addition, they continue, because we are obliged to assume responsibility for our inherent badness (our ineliminable propensity to act in wrongful ways), we can be forced to enter the state since the state provides each person with security against everyone else's badness. At this point, Lockean/libertarian interpretations of Kant clearly diverge from Hobbesian ones. The former argue against Hobbesians' absolutist legal positivism, according to which any law-governed monopoly on coercion can issue political obligations. Lockean/libertarian interpreters typically argue that since we have knowledge of the laws of nature, including knowledge of how to apply them in the state of nature, and since the laws of nature are laws of freedom, the only rightful state we can establish is the liberal state, the legal foundation of which is the same laws of freedom that individuals in the state of nature ought to use to regulate their interactions. Hence, only such liberal states can issue political obligations, according to Lockean/libertarian interpretations of Kant.[9]

The third line of interpretation of Kant's theory of right is the (liberal) republican tradition, whose proponents often sees themselves as incorporating and developing important Rousseauian ideas.[10] These republican interpreters maintain that Kant

---

[8] See, for example, Howard L. Williams (1986) and Onora O'Neill (2000).

[9] Most recently, Sharon B. Byrd and Joachim Hruschka (2010) defend an interpretation along such libertarian lines.

[10] Of course, the nature of these republican interpretations of Kant's private right argument vary greatly. For example, compare and contrast the republican interpretations by Julius Ebbinghaus (1953); Wolfgang Kersting (1984/1993); Thomas Pogge (1988); Ernest Weinrib (1995); Jeremy Waldron (2006); Katrin Flikschuh (2008); Helga Varden (2008), and Arthur Ripstein (2009).

challenges a presupposition shared by both the legal positivist and the libertarian strands of interpretations, namely the proposition that it is fundamentally *only* our troublesome nature that prevents the realization of justice in the state of nature. In contrast, republican interpretations typically contend that Kant also provides *ideal* reasons—that is, reasons that are neither simply prudential or appeal to our propensity to evil—for why justice requires the civil condition (or the establishment of a public authority). Hence, on these readings, even on the (unrealistic) assumption that we never act imprudently or violently and always happen to agree about how to interact peaceably, justice (rightful interactions) remains impossible in the state of nature; the state is *ideally* constitutive of the realization of justice by being the only means through which rightful interactions are possible. These interpretations argue that it is impossible in the state of nature to use coercion rightfully or to establish a private coercive power that can politically obligate everyone to obey it. In the state of nature, any use of coercion in the state of nature is irreducibly private (unilateral), which means it expresses some (set of) private individual's arbitrary (contingent) choices. But no one can be obliged to subject themselves to or obey another private person's arbitrary choices because everyone has an innate right to freedom, which is a right to be subject only to universal law, and not to another's arbitrary choices. Correspondingly, rightful coercion occurs when interaction is subjected only to universal law of freedom that restricts interacting persons reciprocally—and this can be accomplished by the establishment of a distinctly *public* (inherently shared) authority. Hence justice requires a public authority: a rightful, institutional public "us" with a monopoly on coercion. To realize justice, we need to establish a forceful, representative public "us," meaning a legal-political "us" that can be understood as a public representation of what Rousseau usefully calls a "general will." Only if we establish such a public "us" through which laws of freedom are specified, applied, and enforced is it possible to transform the threat and/or use of force from wrongful violence to rightful coercion. We establish public legal-political institutions or authorities (states), therefore, not only because we so often act in imprudent and non-virtuous ways, but also because we cannot enable and secure rightful interaction without establishing a rightful, authoritative *public* use of coercion. According to republican interpretations of Kant's theory of justice, we establish public authorities because doing so is the only means through which we can enable rightful relations when we interact; namely, interaction consistent with each person's innate right to freedom.

Since the republican interpretations are slightly more difficult than the Hobbesian and Lockean ones, let me illustrate them with an example. As mentioned, the republican approach to Kant typically involves arguing that our propensity for imprudent or evil actions is not the only reason why we cannot specify, apply, and enforce the principles of private right rightfully in the state of nature. Because in any given situation there are many ways to specify and apply the principles of private right, one cannot rightfully use coercion to enforce one's own (unilateral) choice of specification without thereby forcing others to subject themselves to one's arbitrary choice (as opposed to subjecting their interactions to universal laws). Consider Locke's theory of private property appropriation, according to which individuals have a right to a fair share of the world's natural resources (his so-called and-as-good proviso"), and they have a right to use coercion to take and defend their fair share. According to Kant, even if we accept this as the correct principle of private property appropriation (which, as we saw above, Kant does *not* do), it is impossible to figure out exactly which particular parts of the world's natural or material resources are, objectively speaking, mine, or yours, or any other particular person's.[11] After all, it is impossible to decide how much any specific part or piece is objectively worth since there is no objective value—"quantity" ("enough") or "quality" ("as good") (MM 6: 266/ Locke 1988: 288/II: §27)—that attaches to empirical objects in the world, like an objective value of specific coconuts, trees, pieces of land, lakes, etc. Therefore, my decision to make something mine remains morally problematic, since if I use force to exclude you from it, it subjects our interactions regarding what is yours and mine to my arbitrary choice about the matter (rather than simply to objective, universal laws). Of course, interacting persons may all happen to agree on the value of each specific thing and who gets to possess it, so that no one ever needs to use coercion to settle any disagreement. But this would be an accident: because disagreements about ownership do not necessarily result from unreasonableness, there is no objectively valid reason why all must reach agreement. Besides, even if we do happen never to disagree on anything in the state of nature, what we have is neither a condition of justice nor of injustice, but rather a condition "devoid of justice" (MM 6: 312). In such a scenario, it is mere chance—an accident—that no one disagrees, and because the resulting peace depends on contingent facts (our chance agreement), we do not have an enforceable right to remain in that condition, a condition where justice (enforceable rights) is impossible. Indeed, we have an enforceable *duty* to enter civil society, since rightful coercion is only possible through the public, legal-political institutions that make up the state. Because the establishment of civil society is therefore constitutive of justice, we do not have a right to stay in the state of nature. This is why, republican interpretations tend to maintain, Kant concludes his discussion of private right and the state of nature by claiming that choosing to stay in the state of nature is to do "wrong in the highest degree" (MM 6: 307).

These disagreements concerning Kant's explanation for why we have states at all are reflected in the different traditions' interpretations of Kant's conception of the rightful or (minimally) just state. Simply put, the (absolutist legal positivist) Hobbesian interpretations maintain that according to Kant, any stable system of law that is enforced by a sufficiently powerful state is legitimate. If one considers the

---

[11] Sometimes this is referred to as the "indeterminacy" arguments regarding general and particular specification of the laws of freedom in relation to actual interactions. A separate kind of argument is sometimes referred to as the "assurance" argument, which can be seen as a sophisticated, ideal development of Hobbes's assurance argument as we found it above. To what extent republican Kant interpreters defend both arguments or only one of them varies. I defend the position that Kant provides the assurance argument—in part because I believe this is how Kant shows that rightful relations require a motivation (external force) different from moral motivation (internal obligation or duty)—*as well as* two kinds of indeterminacy arguments (first, specification of general law and second, application of these laws to particular cases). These three arguments yield a critique of the tripartite public authority: the indeterminacy problems are solved by the legislative authority (general specification) and the judiciary (particular specification in particular cases) and the assurance problem is solved by the executive authority (impartial, overwhelming force).

civil condition as the solution to an extremely dangerous state of nature, this view follows, because almost any state will be more capable of preserving life than will individuals on their own in the state of nature. It is easy to find support for such lines of interpretation in Kant's texts. For example, they fit quite well with Kant's claim that we do not have a right to revolution, not even under very unjust conditions (MM 6: 318ff.). They also accord with some of Kant's remarks about the French Revolution, especially those in which he seems to say that no one had a right to participate in it, even though it took humankind in the right direction (towards freedom).[12] The Kantians who defend such readings of Kant are also typically frustrated with his theory of right and its apparent implication that one is politically obliged to obey even the most oppressive and unjust states, paradigmatically Hitler's Nazi Germany. Consequently, these interpreters often attempt to develop (what they see as) revisionist Kantian theories of justice that can explain why one is not politically obliged to obey *any* rule-governed gruesome regime with a monopoly on coercion.

Libertarian/Lockean types of interpretations, in contrast, typically hold that a just and legitimate state is one that establishes a legal-political system to specify, apply, and enforce the innate and private right principles, by means of which individuals ideally regulate their interactions in the state of nature. The major difference between the rights of the state (public right) and the rights of individuals (innate and private right) is that the state has certain additional rights in consequence of it having to establish a legal-political institutional system. For example, the state has to establish laws of public administration, something individuals obviously have no need of in the state of nature. Still, on such libertarian readings, Kant's idea of a rightful state is a "minimal" one. It is minimal because, beyond the public laws it needs to fulfill its administrative tasks (public right), a just state does not have any rights and laws that do not exist in a state of nature; the state simply posits the laws that are needed to secure the basic rights individuals already possess in the state of nature. Moreover, once established, if a state does not respect the rights of individuals in its use of power, then, on these interpretations, there ceases to be a civil condition. Since in such circumstances individuals find themselves thrown back into the state of nature, they have to defend their rights against violations as best they can. Hence, on this interpretive line, when individuals in these circumstances resist or use force against (*de facto*) "state officials," they are actually not engaging in revolution (strictly speaking), but instead they are, yet again, enforcing their rights by their own means (individually) in the state of nature.[13]

---

[12] Generally, those who read Kant's Doctrine of Right in this absolutist way are likely to emphasize these aspects: the so-called assurance or security arguments one finds in the first chapter of the private right part (MM 6: 245–57); Kant's arguments in support of the claim that citizens do not have a right to use coercion against the public authority (MM 6: 339–40, 370–2); and Kant's conclusion of the private right discussion (MM 6: 305–8) as well as his opening paragraphs of the public right discussion (MM 6: 311–13).

[13] Naturally, these interpretations pay careful attention to Kant's arguments about assurance or security, but they also emphasize that individual rights are what must be secured. Especially important parts of Kant's text, for these scholars, tend to be Chapter 2 in The Doctrine of Right, which concerns the private right principles (especially the principles concerning private property and contract right, MM 6: 258–80, 284–6), and the concluding arguments and claims in the private right section (MM 6: 256–7, 305–8).

The republican interpretation considers Kant's state a (Rousseauian) republican alternative to (Hobbesian) absolutist legal positivism and (Lockean) libertarianism.[14] Republican interpretations object to the absolutist claim that any stable, law-regulated uses of power (ones that ultimately track prudential reasoning) qualify as civil conditions and can generate political obligations. A Kantian republic, they argue, must establish "freedom as independence," which involves creating a representative public authority with a certain institutional structure. What this institutional structure must be is a matter of great controversy, however. Some liberal republican interpretations hold that Kant's distinction between "barbarian" and "civil" conditions hinges on whether or not the laws of the state *represent* the people, which means that they simply seek to secure certain basic (*a priori*) principles of right for all citizens, thereby guaranteeing their status as free, equal, and independent.[15] Other republican interpreters contend that with the term "representation," Kant firmly commits himself to democracy as the only just form of government.[16] Finally, yet other republican interpretations downplay aspects of Kant's text that seem to imply a distinctively liberal notion of rights, and argue instead for normative, yet non-absolutist, legal positivist interpretations of Kant. According to these interpretations, a state is legitimate as long as the stability it provides is recognized by its citizens' normative (and not merely *de facto*) recognition of the state's authority over them.[17]

Despite these internal disagreements about the importance of liberal rights and democracy, all republican interpreters agree with the libertarian interpreters that not just *any* form of rule-governed use of power constitutes a legitimate state on Kant's position. They agree and argue against the libertarian claim that the Kantian position can recognize an individual's *right* to realize justice on their own if they find themselves subjected to an illegitimate state. Hence, such individual uses of coercion cannot be an exercise of a *right* to revolution as we cannot call such uses of coercion *rightful*. Since justice is in principle impossible in the state of nature, we cannot have a *right* to return to this condition, and we cannot describe what we are doing when using violence in these ways as re-establishing rightful relations (since rightful relations are only possible in civil society). My interpretation of Kant's political theory falls within the liberal republican tradition. We saw this in Part I, in my discussion of what to do when we face conditions of extreme oppression, where I drew on republican ideas to describe the morally impossible choices that face human beings that find themselves in barbarous situations or conditions. In the chapters in Part II, I use these republican ideas to analyze issues such as abortion, rightful sexual interaction, and sexual oppression. The preceding outline of three

---

[14] To defend their position, republican interpreters often point to what Kant says in the beginning of the "public right" section (MM 6: 311–13), in addition to challenging the readings of the text absolutist and libertarian interpretations highlight.

[15] In my view, Waldron (2006), Ripstein (2009), and Varden (2010b) fall within this camp of interpreters.

[16] Both Ingeborg Maus (1992) and Pauline Kleingeld (2010) defend such democratic interpretations of Kant.

[17] In my view, Hans Kelsen (1992) is a good representative of this interpretive tradition.

approaches to interpreting Kant's legal-political theory also helps us see the many kinds of ways in which Kantians and non-Kantians alike can challenge my philosophical position. One might wield (absolutist) legal positivist or libertarian arguments to object to any part of it. In addition, of course, objections can be raised from within the republican interpretive framework. The chapters to come are written such that those with a philosophically trained eye can anticipate how I would respond to such objections, but for reasons of space and to make the chapters readable for non-Kantians, I do not engage these disagreements to any great extent.

Let me finish this general sketch of Kant's theory of justice by returning to the question that frames the above discussion of "What responsibilities, if any, does the state have to alleviate poverty among its citizens?" Answers to this question illustrate some of the key differences among what I have called Hobbesian absolutist legal positivist, Lockean libertarian, and liberal republican interpretations, and are particularly useful to appreciate the analysis that follows in the next three chapters, and especially Chapter 7. According to Hobbesian absolutist legal positivist interpretations, the answer is (or at least should be) quite simple. Presupposing, as these interpretations do, that on Kant's view, all stable, law-governed states are legitimate, such states may or may not redistribute resources without this affecting their political legitimacy one way or the other. On these readings, the will of the sovereign authority properly determines how the state responds to problems concerning poverty among citizens. Problematically, however, these interpretations require us (insofar as they stay consistent with their own basic philosophical commitments) to disregard most of what Kant says directly about the issue of poverty, including in The Doctrine of Right, and to treat it as irrelevant to understanding the public institutional structure defended by Kant's legal-political theory. This is a puzzling move, though, because poverty and the distribution of material resources are among the central issues for Kant (also) in this work. In The Doctrine of Right, Kant says,

To the supreme commander there belongs indirectly, that is, insofar as he has taken over the duty of the people, the right to impose taxes on the people for its own preservation, such as taxes to support organizations for the poor, foundling homes, and church organizations, usually called charitable or pious institutions.... The wealthy have acquired an obligation to the commonwealth, since they owe their existence to an act of submitting to its protection and care, which they need in order to live; on this obligation the state now bases its right to contribute what is theirs to maintaining their fellow citizens.... [The state] will do this by way of coercion (since we are speaking here only of the *right* of the state against the people), by public taxation, not merely by *voluntary* contributions.   (MM 6: 325f.)

So, Kant certainly does think that the state has a right to tax its citizens and cannot justifiably try to deal with poverty by relying on voluntary contributions. But why? Also, here Kant appears to appeal to the distinctly *human* needs of protection and material means, which raises the question of how such an appeal is possible within an account that understands right in terms of freedom.[18]

---

[18] The literature on Kant and poverty at this point is significant. For an overview of much of it prior to 2006, see Varden (2006); for an overview of later literature up to 2012, see Ebels-Duggan (2012).

An interpretive challenge for the Lockeans/libertarians is that they also struggle to attribute a philosophically coherent account of poverty relief to Kant, one that is also able to incorporate what he says about poverty. Recall that on the Lockean/libertarian interpretations the rights of the state (public right) are co-extensive with the rights of individuals (innate and private right) when we exclude public administrative rights. As a result, in order for the state to have a right to redistribute resources to the poor, individuals (in the state of nature) must have the same right in relation to each other. But Kant clearly seems to reject this, for reasons similar to those for which Nozick rejects it in his famous response to Rawls. Both Kant and Nozick argue that a private individual cannot have an enforceable obligation to redistribute goods in response to the needs of the poor, because that would be irreconcilable with each person's right to set their own ends with their own means. Consequently, it seems that on libertarian approaches, Kant would agree that the state cannot have such a right either. Notice, too, that even if one can refute Nozick's objection to Rawls, and make a Kantian case for the state's right to enforce redistribution of resources in response to problems of poverty, one must show that this forced redistribution does not amount to forced beneficence; otherwise, it will contradict Kant's observation that forced beneficence is in principle impossible.

Broadly speaking, the liberal republican interpreters reject (or should reject for consistency's sake) all of the above approaches to the state's responsibility to relieve its citizens of poverty. On the one hand, they can and should reject any absolutist or legal positivist claim that a legitimate state would be justified both in relieving poverty and in not relieving it; and, on the other hand, they can and should reject the libertarians' claim that the right of the state to relieve poverty are co-extensive with those of the individuals. In my view, the most promising republican line of argument proceeds as follows: A state can rightfully establish a monopoly on coercion only if it also ensures that the legal system as a whole is reconcilable with each citizen's innate right to freedom. The only way to do this is by securing everyone's right to freedom (understood as a right to independence from subjection to others' choices, and to be subject only to laws of freedom) by legally guaranteeing or securing each citizen's rightful (legal) access to means. In other words, if some citizen does not own anything at all and everything already belongs to someone else, then this destitute citizen can obtain access to means only by committing a crime (stealing from those with means) *or* by benefiting from the choice of those with means to give them charity or employment. In the latter situation, the poor citizen's possibility of freedom depends on the arbitrary, private choices of those with means—to provide them (or not) with charity or employment—and this is irreconcilable with the poor citizen's right to freedom as independence from having the possibility of one's freedom subjected to another person's private choice. Rather, freedom as independence requires that our choices are subject only to universal laws of freedom. For this reason, the minimally just or legitimate state must guarantee each and all of its citizens legal access to means as part of public right, namely as a claim citizens have on their own public authority (and not directly on each other as private citizens). The right to poverty relief should therefore be understood as a public right and not a private right.

On this liberal republican approach, poverty is a systemic problem of justice arising from the state's necessary establishment of a monopoly on coercion, and it is a problem the state must assume responsibility for by legally guaranteeing (securing) every citizen's legal access to means through public law. In order to transform provisionally rightful property claims into conclusively rightful property claims, the state must reconcile its monopoly on coercion with each citizen's rights to freedom by providing unconditional poverty relief; that is, by securing legal access to means for all its citizens at any given time. It should be noted that the state can address this systemic problem of poverty *minimally* either by regulating private charitable organizations entrusted with fulfilling this function (by committing to give all people equal access to them without having to declare allegiance to a particular religion, for example) *or* by establishing public shelters. The main point is that the state assumes responsibility for ensuring that all citizens have legal access to means that is not subject to other citizens' private, arbitrary choices (to exercise charity or employ them); all citizens are to have their exercise of freedom (including its possibility) dependent on law only (and not other citizens' private, arbitrary choices). In my view, a strength of this liberal republican line of interpretation is that it accords with Kant's claim that public welfare institutions should not be considered forced charity or beneficence; the reason why the state has to guarantee unconditional poverty relief is that doing so is the minimal, necessary institutional solution to the systemic problem of poverty. Unconditional poverty relief is necessary in order to reconcile the state's monopoly on coercion with each citizen's innate right to freedom; it is constitutive of trans-forming provisionally rightful private property claims (in the state of nature) into conclusively rightful property claims (in civil society).

Another strength of this republican line of interpretation is that it is not vulnerable to Nozick's criticism of Rawls. That criticism presupposes that the rights of the state (public right) are co-extensive with the rights of individuals (innate and private right). In contrast, the liberal republican argument shows that citizens have certain claims as citizens on their common public authority (public right) that they do not have against each other as private persons (innate and private right). Consequently, liberal states have a right and a duty to provide welfare institutions that address problems of poverty, which involves coercive redistribution, despite the fact that private individuals do not have a corresponding legal right and duty against each other. In addition, as we will see in Chapter 7, this minimal condition of uncondi-tional poverty relief is not the end of the Kantian story of how to establish a republic in which citizens govern themselves through public law. More specifically, extending the argument from the rights of free beings to the rights of embodied, social *human* beings, means that the state must guarantee a right to the safe shelter, material sustenance, and privacy that such beings require to survive and that an early developmental project for new states is to fight the problem of homelessness.[19] These arguments regarding how to make the legal-political system more suitable to

---

[19] Among the earliest papers that may be described as fitting within the liberal republican tradition's treatment of poverty are, I believe, those of Weinrib (2003), Varden (2006), and Ripstein (2009), but many Kantians since have published articles that share at least deep agreements with these interpretive and philosophical lines of argument. For a critical engagement with this interpretive approach directed at the work of Ripstein and myself, see Kleingeld (2010); for my response to Kleingeld, see Varden (2014b) and for Kleingeld's response to this response, see Kleingeld (2014). I return to a recent, critical engagement with this type of approach and develop my account a little further in Chapter 7, where I also discuss Christopher Essert's (2016) criticism of Kantians on this point through a discussion of homelessness.

human beings will also be used to discuss some aspects of the systemic problems of poverty and oppression as they relate to the institutions of trade in sexual services and goods ("prostitution" and "pornography").

Let us now turn our attention from issues concerning the overall structure of Kant's legal-political philosophy to the existing deployment of Kant's philosophical framework to discuss issues of sex, love, and gender from a legal-political point of view. As mentioned above, on most topics, the secondary Kantian literature is rather scarce. Notice too that as with the chapters in the first part of the book, the chapters in this second part aim to develop a Kantian theory of sex, love, and gender by building upon Kant's own works, upon the secondary literature, and upon feminist philosophy and writings in the philosophy of sex and love. To do so, I have divided this account of rightful sexual relations into three chapters, each of which engages the philosophical resources of Kant's analyses of innate, private, and public right respectively. More specifically, Chapter 5 ("The Innate Right to Freedom: Abortion, Sodomy, and Obscenity Laws") primarily makes use of Kant's arguments that our innate right to freedom is analytically related to our rights to rightful honor, bodily integrity, and free speech; Chapter 6 ("Private Right: Marriage and Trade in Sexual Services") employs Kant's arguments regarding acquired private rights to status relations and contract right; and, finally, Chapter 7 ("Public Right: Systemic Justice") takes up Kant's arguments regarding systemic, public right. In addition to using Kant's legal-political theory to develop the related analyses of rightful sexual, loving, and gendered relations, the chapters draw upon much of the related (Kantian and non-Kantian) literature. To indicate the arguments of Part II, below are short descriptions of how each chapter engages contemporary discussions of sex, love, and gender.

Pregnant women and persons engaging in non-procreative, and especially non-straight, non-cis, non-binary sexual activities compose groups that have been and still are among those most severely subjected to coercive, legally enforced restrictions regarding their own bodies. From a historical point of view, it is a recent and rare phenomenon that legal systems recognize women's right to abortion and legally responsible adults' right to engage in non-procreative sexual interactions, including those involving erotica.[20] Today most liberal states do recognize these rights, at least to some extent, and yet they are frequently under attack—sometimes by violent protest—from various political movements. Important too when seeking a legal-political understanding of our sexual, loving, gendered lives is that there is a tendency among those living with repressed sexualities, including members of the LGBTQIA community, the BDSM community, and polyamorous and polysexual communities, to use erotica as sources of empowerment. At the same time, there is a tendency among dominant social groups to use erotica in ways that sustain and even support oppressive patterns regarding sexuality. For example, historical patterns characteristic of the

---

[20] I am using "erotica" as the umbrella term to refer both to (potentially) liberating sexual images and pornography and to morally problematic sexual images for two reasons: (1) insofar as one makes, uses, or sells/buys erotica, one is legally responsible for doing so; and (2) it is impossible to establish any *a priori* principles that can identify morally problematic sexual images as such, since what is damaging depends on the historical or particular context of the image.

so-called "mainstream" pornography industry include a labor force where the majority of the sex workers are women and/or predominantly from lower socioeconomic conditions. It also includes a kind of erotica that reinforces oppressive, dehumanizing racial and ethnic depictions, and much of the erotic material is anything but an empowerment of women's sexuality. On the latter point, in much mainstream erotica, women are presented as not having a choice to say no when men want to have sex with them, as beings who men want to sexually engage in demeaning, subjugating ways, as beings who want and enjoy being subjected to violence while having sex, as beings whose sexual pleasure is irrelevant to the activity itself, and, relatedly, as beings who, for some inscrutable reason, appear to take enormous and only joy in giving men sexual pleasure. These deeply disturbing patterns in the pornography industry involving women are explored in much feminist philosophy. For example, it is central to Rae Langton's (2009) Kantian philosophy of language-based analysis of the damaging effects of pornography on women, and it has led many feminist philosophers to follow Andrea Dworkin's (1981) and Catharine A. MacKinnon's (1979, 1987, 1989, 1994, 2003; Dworkin and MacKinnon 1988) lead in arguing for (at least) severe legal restrictions on the production of pornography for sale. Indeed, in her research, Lori Watson (2007, 2014; Watson and Flannigan 2019) continues the line of argument from Dworkin and MacKinnon by arguing that what some call "sex work" should not be called "work" at all. More generally, liberal, including much liberal feminist theory tend to be at least somewhat wary as to how the law should deal with these emotionally and morally problematic patterns in erotica, while defending people's right to enjoy erotica as such and being positive to patterns showing that erotica can empower oppressed sexualities.[21] In the next three chapters, I engage all these discussions.

Chapter 5 begins with a Kantian account of innate right in relation to the issues of abortion, sodomy, and obscenity laws. Although contemporary liberal theories of justice typically defend women's rights to abortion and legally responsible citizens' right to engage in non-procreative sexual activities and to use erotica as part of their sexual activities, these theories often struggle to capture the fundamental nature and ground of these rights. For example, it appears hard for many liberal theories to say exactly why and when only the woman and not the embryo/fetus has rights, and why the right to certain sexual practices is not on par with rights to satisfy other preferences. Contemporary liberal theories of justice therefore also tend to struggle to identify what distinguishes questions of abortion and sexual activities from other

---

[21] For excellent overviews over much of the existing literature and debates on both pornography and prostitution, see Watson (2010, 2013), and for an especially interesting interpretation of the patterns of anti-porn feminism in recent decades, see Anne W. Eaton (2007). Engaging all of this literature is beyond the scope of this book, but note that the account in the next three chapters is consistent with core ideas of the different, existing traditions. I defend people's right to have, sell, buy sex; and to make, have, and use erotica as such (including what Watson et al. would call "pornography," which is limited to sexualized images that have women in subjugating positions and, so, is plausibly seen as internally related to the ongoing harm done to women through the industry of pornography). On my account, the making, having, and selling/buying of erotica (including pornography) is not a legal wrong, let alone a crime as such. This, however, is consistent with legal regulations on erotica and its production, with permitting legal arguments in the courtroom that appeal to various kinds of harm, and with the state's right and duty to fight the systemic conditions of oppression characterizing the sex work industries.

questions of right and thereby to capture the gravity of the wrongdoing involved in denying women's right to have abortions and denying people the right to engage in sexual interactions authorized by consent. These theories also tend to be wary around questions of whether or not, from a legal point of view, the only thing that matters is the presence of continuous consent as well as the question of whether or not one can consent to no longer have the right to say no: are there, in other words, limits on what authorizing work consent can do with regard to making sexual interactions legally permissible? Finally, insofar as liberal theories do not follow the feminist routes of the anti-porn kind, they tend to either be rather silent on questions regarding the truly morally and emotionally disturbing patterns of the pornography industry or argue that as long as the exchanges involved are consensual, they are beyond the proper reach of the law.

At first blush, Kant does not appear to have much to offer as we seek plausible philosophical accounts of the legal permissibility of abortion, authorizing consent for sexual activities, and the use of erotica. To be sure, as we have seen in previous chapters, Kant's own related writings at their worst are filled with anger, discomfort, and prejudices, and at their best are rather confusing and perplexing. To give some relevant examples, in The Doctrine of Right—where Kant proposes his theory of justice as freedom—we are faced with his brief description of human beings as persons upon conception[22] and with his teleologically based and notoriously phobic statements about homosexuality.[23] In The Doctrine of Virtue, we also find fierce condemnations of sexual lust that involve sexual imaginations as sources of sexual pleasure, which may reasonably lead us to think that he regards any use of erotica can be only bad.[24] Despite these texts, in Chapter 5, I argue that Kant's legal-political writings give us the philosophical resources required for a legal conception of authorizing consent with regard to sexual activities and the legal permissibility of abortion, non-procreative or non-binary sexual activities, and erotica as such; indeed,

[22] For example, about whether a fetus is a person, Kant says: "For the offspring is a *person*, and it is impossible to form a concept of the production of a being endowed with freedom through a physical operation. So from a *practical point of view* it is a quite correct and even necessary idea to regard the act of procreation as one by which we have brought a person into the world without his consent and on our own initiative, for which deed the parents incur an obligation to make the child content with his condition so far as they can" (MM 6: 280f.). In the note on the same page, Kant continues, "If the philosophic jurist reflects on the difficulty of the problem to be resolved and the necessity of solving it to satisfy the principles of right in this matter, he will not hold this investigation, all the way back to the first elements of transcendental philosophy in a metaphysics of morals, to be unnecessary pondering that gets lost in pointless obscurity" (MM 6: 280n). As will become clear in Chapter 5, these passages are compatible with arguing that from the point of view of ethics, personhood may be attributed upon conception, but from the point of view of law, evidence of rationally unified spontaneous activity is the normatively significant moment.

[23] About non-procreative sexuality, Kant says, among other things, that homosexual interaction involves an "*unnatural*" use" of one another's "sexual organs and capacities" (MM 6: 277), and that because "such transgressions of laws...do wrong to humanity in our own person, there are no limitations or exceptions whatsoever that can save them from being repudiated completely" (MM 6: 277).

[24] On sexual lust aroused by the imagination, Kant maintains, "Lust is called *unnatural* if one is aroused to it not by a real object but by his imagining it, so that he himself creates one, contrary to [natural] purposes; for in this way imagination brings forth a desire contrary to nature's end...such an unnatural use...of one's sexual attribute is a violation of duty *to oneself*...indeed one contrary to morality in its highest degree" (MM 6: 425). For more of Kant's statements about sexuality, see especially Chapter 2.

his philosophical ideas can help us capture the seriousness of the wrongdoing involved in outlawing these things as such, not just for embodied, social rational beings—which is serious enough—but for embodied, social *human* beings. I argue that Kant's account of human nature and evil (from Part I) can explain why we consider sexual violence particularly serious (because sexual violence is partially aimed at our persons) and heinous (because of our embodied, social emotional make-up, it can do existential, psychological damage).

Chapter 6 provides a Kantian account of private right in relation to marriage and trade in sexual services. Perhaps the topic that has received the most attention in the first decade of the twenty-first century in Kantian, feminist debates is the topic of marriage—and in large part because of the influence of Barbara Herman's (1993b) groundbreaking article on this issue. As mentioned earlier, a particularly impressive aspect of Herman's paper is the way in which it draws explicit attention to Kant's distinction between virtue and right. What followed in subsequent work by others was an emphasis on one or the other (on virtue or on right), or both. Regardless of this difference, all of this work explores the more general question of whether, in spite of the horrible history of the legal institution of marriage for women, Kant may still be correct in thinking that it is an institution worth maintaining and reforming, and by extension of Kant's theoretical framework, regarding same-sex couples as well. I engage this discussion by developing a core idea I pursued in an early (2007) paper and which Herman does not explore in her article—that in addition to various non-ideal reasons and reasons based on equality that make same-sex couples want to have a right to marry, there are ideal reasons why they want such a right. I also extend this argument to defend the right to marry for non-binary, symmetrical polyamorous partners.

Hence, against the trend in feminist philosophy and the philosophy of sex and love, such as the influential, related writings by Martha Nussbaum (2010) and Elizabeth Brake (2012), I argue with Kant that marriage should not be understood in terms of ordinary contract right, which is also one reason why it should not be conceived of as possible to break down into smaller, less extensive contracts. Instead we should follow Kant's lead by viewing marriage in terms of the category of status right, and if we do, we can make better sense also of the legal concerns of the diversity of loving unions who want the legal right to marry. I explain why marriage contracts are not like other contracts because they involve our persons and shared homes. That Kant recognizes this difference forms the ground for my argument that Kant's account of marriage is particularly apt to capture why many same-sex couples have fought so hard for the right to marry. On this account, creating a shared, legally recognized home is constitutive of creating such rightful relations with another person. There are many well-known prudential reasons for and against the institution of marriage, but it is Kant's ideal argument that shows us why it is a legal institution we should want to keep reforming. I argue that the importance of how the law must protect the creation of a shared home—a legally recognized *us*—becomes particularly obvious when couples or non-binary partnerships spilt up: the legal system provides a way of dividing up what we have owned and acquired in our time together that protects the freedom of each party, as opposed to any one party finding themselves subject to the unilateral choices of the other. These are reasons why not having the right to marry has been so devastating for same-sex couples and non-binary partnerships: without a right to marry, their relations stay in the state of nature, without the legal protections needed for a legally recognized and protected *us* as well as legal provisions for rightful dissolution of a shared home. I then make space for concerns of moral anthropology, as discussed in Part I, by explaining why having such a legal right is also emotionally important for many human beings. In this way, I show that a Kantian position like mine can accommodate our distinctly *human* nature without abandoning Kant's own framework; and that doing so has some advantages over following Brake's or Nussbaum's lead on this question.

The second topic in Chapter 6—trade in sexual services—has also received considerable attention in recent years, and Rae Langton's analysis of pornography has been the most influential one in the Kant literature. First, I focus on the question of how to understand trade in sexual services, maintaining that Kant's account of bodily rights can explain why one never gets an enforceable right to have sex with another person even if one has a right to get some of the money back if a contract is broken. On the one hand, as explained in Chapter 5, no one can have enforceable rights to my body since this would give them enforceable rights to my legal person (which would amount to a right to enslave me). Therefore, continuous authorizing consent is always necessary for rightful sexual interaction with others, which also means that contracts involving sexual services never give anyone an enforceable right to engage another person in sexual activities. On the other hand, we have the challenge of explaining whether or not this means that no one can ever rightfully decide voluntarily to exchange sexual services for money. Importantly, regardless of what someone may think from the point of view of virtue or religion—that is, regardless of whether one thinks it is ethically wrong or a sin to sell sexual services—from the point of view of right, the question is only whether or not one has a *right* to engage in a reciprocal and voluntary buying and selling of sexual services with another person or persons. In Part I, I explained why sex is emotionally and morally dangerous, why having sex one really does not want can be emotionally damaging, and why we have perfect and imperfect duties with regard to sexual activity. Here, I argue that concerns regarding the risk of emotional damage can explain the practice of paying for sexual services *before* they are rendered and always stopping sexual activity if the person providing it changes their mind. After all, a sex worker can give back a portion of their fee, but they cannot get back what is taken from them if the sex turns non-consensual.

None of these arguments concerning private right deal with the added problems that the institution of sex work typically brings with it, namely that most of those selling sex are women and/or come from poorer socioeconomic conditions. Moreover, given human phenomenology and the fact that much sex work involves physical interactions, including various kinds of bodily penetrations, problems concerning a lack of choice are particularly urgent in just states. These activities are emotionally and morally dangerous for human beings, which matters for our legal analyses in that a primary aim of law must be to make it safe for those who sell sexual services. Other questions of concerning how erotic images can be damaging for women living in an oppressively sexist world as well as what the institutions of trade in sexual services do to (also racialized) women and members of the LBGTQIA community in oppressive societies are addressed in Chapter 7.

In Chapter 7, the focus is on systemic justice. Issues of poverty have been at the center of much discussion in liberal theories of justice generally and have been at the core of much feminist philosophy of systemic justice in recent decades. This is not surprising. For most of history, women have not been able to own private property, to access higher education, and they have not been permitted to vote or take part in the legal-political processes that determined the coercive legal-political framework within which they lived their lives. It has been, and still often is, the case that for many women the only access to private homes and means independent of their parents runs through marriage to men. It is also the case that women are not paid equally to men for the same jobs, and it is the case that many women are forced, or that the least bad of the choices available is, to engage in sex work they really do not want to do. An important aspect of O'Neill's work is her focus on these issues of poverty and the systemic aspects of women's oppression. Poverty has been a core concern in her research from the start, with her engagement with Rawls's Kantian proposal for how the state should respond to human material needs. In addition, an emerging feature of all the feminist work on this topic—such as the work of Ann Cudd (2006), Sarah Clark Miller (2012), and Carol Hay (2013)—is the acknowledgement that issues like poverty cannot be understood simply as analyses of individuals' interactions. These issues must also be seen as involving identities that track historical oppression and systemic injustice.

This final chapter engages these complexities concerning systemic justice. It aims to illustrate how the philosophical ideas in Kant's account of public right (citizens' claims on their public institutions), in combination with his full account of human nature, yields a position that can take on systemic issues of dependency and oppression from within his theory of right. My approach, I argue, has interpretive as well as philosophical advantages. On the one hand, it does not appeal to virtue or imperfect duties to account for the state's duty to secure systemic justice for all (including problems tracking historical oppression), though it understands the corresponding duties of virtue as perfect in nature. On the other hand, it can explain why minimally just states can and should reform themselves so that those who work in sexual service industries, including to produce erotica, do not consent to do so because they are given offers they cannot refuse.

Keeping in mind the special problems arising with trade in sexual services—that socioeconomic factors play a huge role and that there are special dangers, moral, emotional, and physical—there is still the question of whether, and if so how, these services should be publicly regulated. I propose in the final part of Chapter 7 that Kant's legal-political theory, well read, supports the following set of claims: First, the state cannot authorize the criminalization of the sale of sexual services and goods. Second, whether or not buying such services should be illegal is a question to which there is no *a priori* answer. Rather the general political principle should be that as the state builds institutions that protect everyone's systemic rights in better ways, it must strive to make sure that the systemic, legal measures undertaken do not make a safe, rightful existence even harder for those who are already vulnerable. The aim is to seek the best possible ways right now to protect those who are providing these services, which may or may not involve legalizing the buying of sex. Then the task is, over time, to build better systemic institutions that secure all citizens' choices by securing a condition wherein each citizen has real paths available, according to which their hard work, within a reasonable amount of time, secures them the means required for a good life as they perceive of it—something they may or may not decide to involve selling sexual services. As we will also see, it is not an accident that states that understand their own authority through their citizens' basic right to freedom often do not posit or enforce certain kinds of laws—such as abortion laws or laws prohibiting sex trade on the street—unless they can also properly protect their citizens by having in place appropriate public institutional systems. I also argue that Kant's account of different kinds of uses of external force people may find themselves subjected to—"barbaric," "anarchic," "despotic," and "republican"—capture the moral complexity facing oppressed and vulnerable populations in different legal-political circumstances. Finally, I argue that the ultimate aim for states is to create a legal-political whole characterized by the citizens governing themselves wisely through active participation in public debate and public institutions.

5

The Innate Right to Freedom
Abortion, Sodomy, and Obscenity Laws

Introduction

It is uncontroversial to say that pregnancies and sexual activities are tremendously important aspects of our lives and that, consequently, it is not accidental that they are major concerns for both ethical and theological theories. In this chapter, however, I am concerned neither with ethical nor theological evaluations of pregnancies and sexual relations nor with the justifiability of various ethical and theological theories as they have been utilized to explore these issues. Instead, I simply give an account of why, from the point of view of *justice*—or what Kant calls "right" (German: "Recht")—it is a grave wrong coercively to prevent, let alone to outlaw or to criminalize, abortion as such or non-procreative sexual activity, including the making, possessing, exchanging, or using of erotic images.[1] This account therefore goes against several trends in contemporary writings on these issues. For example, it is often assumed that an analysis of what is right and wrong from the point of view of ethics or theology must yield the same or at least similar results as an analysis from the point of view of justice. Alternatively, it is thought that conclusions drawn about what rights we have are dependent on conclusions drawn about what is ethically or religiously required. These kinds of assumptions are prominent in a large proportion of the papers and books written on abortion and sexual activity over the last few decades. My argument below challenges them.[2] In addition, I contest the view that the ways in which liberal states recognize rights to abortion and non-procreative sexual activity should simply be seen as the result of considerations of prudence or tolerance. According to this line of argument, only by granting such rights can we peacefully coexist in a pluralist world given our different ethical and religious convictions.[3]

---

[1] For more on Kant's distinction between virtue and right—as well as all the technical Kant concepts used in this chapter—see the introduction to Part II.

[2] For some historically influential articles, see note 14 below.

[3] This is not to say that distinguishing between analyzing an issue from the point of view of justice and from the point of view of ethics or theology is novel. In her seminal article "A Defense of Abortion," Judith Jarvis Thomson argues along similar lines, though it is not entirely clear exactly on the basis of what she draws the distinction (beyond an appeal to some of our common intuitions about the matter). See (Thomson 1971: 60–1). Similarly, the stronger readings of John Rawls's later philosophy, as found, for example, in *Justice as Fairness: A Restatement* (2001b) and in *Political Liberalism* (1996), proceed on a similar assumption. Note, however, that it is tempting to read Thomson and Rawls as defending "tolerance" arguments, meaning arguments according to which the great differences in overall moral or religious

Sex, Love, and Gender: A Kantian Theory. Helga Varden, Oxford University Press (2020). © Helga Varden.
DOI: 10.1093/oso/9780198812838.001.0001

Contrary to these dominant views, I defend the claim that we cannot deny one another the right to have abortions as such or to engage in non-procreative sexual activity without thereby refusing to interact rightfully, that is, in a way reconcilable with each person's innate right to freedom. One's innate right to freedom is the right to have one's interactions with others restricted reciprocally by universal laws of freedom. Justice concerns rightful interaction in the world, or moral relations that are in principle enforceable as they hinder hindrances to external freedom (in space and time) under universal laws. All we can and should do through legal means is to ensure that people interact in ways consistent with respect for each other's innate right to freedom. The point is not only that even if we try, it is impossible to force people to be religiously good or to be ethically virtuous, but that if we use force in this way, we wrong those we so subject to coercion. It is therefore entirely possible that what is rightfully enforceable is not co-extensive with what we deem ethically justifiable, religiously defensible, or prudent; in fact, it is of central importance not to confuse legal ideals with ethical, religious, or prudential ideals. If we do confuse these ideals, then we necessarily fail to achieve what we are trying to do and the legal principles we end up enforcing deprive those subjected to them of their innate right to freedom. Therefore, even if the Kantian position defended below is consistent with prudential, ethical, or religious ideals (it is), prudence, ethics, or religion is not what justifies the uses of coercion involved.

To best employ Kant's legal-political theory to discuss the legal questions of abortion and authorizing consent in sexual interaction, we must take seriously the fact that human beings are embodied persons, which means that the material limits of our legal personhood are co-extensive with our embodiment. Because we are embodied beings, and because the restrictions on abortion and sexual activity under consideration are coercive restrictions on what we can do with our own bodies, to force people to act in accordance with the pursuit of a natural end or to punish them for not acting consistent with the pursuit of a natural end is to deny them their right to freedom; it is to deprive them of their legal personhood. And because the state, in establishing itself as a public authority, must provide conditions in which its citizens can interact rightfully—consistent with respecting each other's right to freedom and legal personhood—it cannot justifiably enforce such restrictions. Also, the fact that Kant (or anyone) considers abortion or some sexual ends to be more or less natural or virtuous than other sexual ends cannot be a relevant consideration when determining these questions only from the point of view of right. A legal system that

---

conceptions entail that justice must stay neutral amongst them. Such an interpretation is advanced by Robert P. George (1997) in "Public Reason and Political Conflict: Abortion and Homosexuality." I believe that this interpretation of both Rawls and Thomson is mistaken and fails to capture the strength of their positions. In contrast, with respect to Rawls, I believe that the better interpretation is the one provided by Arthur Ripstein in "Private Order and Public Justice: Kant and Rawls" (2006), and I believe the stronger reading of Thomson follows similar interpretive lines. Consequently, I am not defending a "neutrality tolerance" argument of the kind criticized by George. My view is that it is *wrong* from the point of view of justice to deny persons a right to obtain an abortion or to engage in non-procreative, including homosexual, activity independently of conclusions drawn from the points of view of tolerance, ethics, and religion. (This is not to say that I think George's argument is persuasive from the point of view of ethics or religion—I do not—but addressing this question is beyond my interests in this chapter.)

that forces everyone to act consistent with a particular natural end enforces an inherently contingent restriction and not a law of freedom; such a coercive rule will necessarily conflict with each person's right to freedom and it is therefore unjustifiable as a law.

Nevertheless, my analysis does not entail that there are no rightful restrictions on abortions or that there are no limits on the kinds of sexual interaction that can be authorized by consent: states that provide real opportunities for pregnant persons to have abortions can require those persons to make their decisions before a certain time; and some sexual interactions are not legally permissible because consent can neither legally authorize slave-contracts (they are necessarily void) nor killing (partial or full). Although good laws permit risky behavior as we have a right to take risks, they do not permit just anything and they do hold people responsible for the bad consequences of negligent risk taking. Furthermore, once we have analyzed abortion and sexual interaction authorized by consent through the lens of rightful freedom, we can and should consider our moral psychology/anthropology in order to ensure that our laws are sensitive not only to the fact that we are embodied, social beings capable of freedom, but also to the fact that we are embodied, social *human* beings. Such consideration makes clear the inherent heinousness of enforcing laws that outlaw or criminalize abortion and non-procreative sexual interactions. Finally, once we consider our specific human phenomenology, we can speak to some of the dangers of mistaking legal ideals for emotional and ethical ideals, such as thinking that all there is to appreciate about abortion, erotica, and/or sexual activity and interaction—in general or in particular cases—can be captured by the legal ideal of rightful freedom and the central emphasis it places on continuous, authorizing consent. With these ideas in hand, we can turn to how trade in sexual services and goods, including erotica, call for their own, distinctive analyses of right, which is a main topic in Chapters 6 and 7.

1. The Right to Bodily Integrity

At the foundation of Kant's conception of justice lies what he calls our "Only One Innate Right," namely each person's innate right to freedom (MM 6: 237). Each person's innate right to freedom is defined as their right to "independence from being constrained by another's choice . . . insofar as it [their exercise of freedom] can coexist with the freedom of every other in accordance with a universal law" (MM 6: 237). The same idea informs Kant's basic principle of justice, namely The Universal Principle of Right: "Any action is *right* if it can coexist with everyone's freedom in accordance with a universal law, or if on its maxim the freedom of choice of each can coexist with everyone's freedom in accordance with a universal law" (MM 6: 230–1). Right, then, for Kant, is solely concerned with people's actions in space and time, or what he calls their "external use of choice" (MM 6: 213f., 224ff.). When we deem each other and ourselves capable of deeds, meaning that we see each other and ourselves as the authors of our actions, we "impute" these actions to each other and to ourselves. Such imputation, Kant argues, shows that we judge ourselves and each other to be capable of freedom under laws we give to ourselves, or capable of moral responsibility for our actions (MM 6: 227). Besides, when we interact, we need to enable reciprocal external freedom, meaning that we must find a way of interacting that is consistent with respecting everybody's external freedom. And this is where justice, or right, comes in. Right is the relation between interacting persons' external freedom such that reciprocal external freedom under laws of freedom is realized (MM 6: 230). This is what Kant means when he says that rightful interactions are interactions reconcilable with each person's innate right to freedom such that universal laws of freedom (rather than anyone's arbitrary choices) reciprocally regulate interacting individuals' external use of choice (external freedom).

As noted above and explained in the general introduction to Part II, a first upshot of this conception of right is that first-personal ethics (virtue) is beyond right's (legality's) proper grasp. Right concerns only external freedom, which is limited to what can be rightfully hindered in space and time (coerced), whereas virtue concerns internal freedom ("internal use of choice"), which requires acting on universalizable maxims with a moral motivation (which cannot be coercively enforced). This is why Kant maintains that only freedom with regard to interacting persons' external use of choice (right) can be coercively enforced; freedom with regard to *both* internal (virtue) and external use of choice (right)—morality as a whole—cannot be coercively enforced (MM 6: 220f.). And it is in virtue of being persons—beings capable of assuming moral responsibility for our actions—that notions of rights and duties are possible at all. And it is because human beings are embodied (spatio-temporal) persons that we must determine how we should interact in the empirical world. Right, then, concerns how we—embodied persons—interact and can be forced to interact in space and time in the name of freedom.[4]

From the point of view of right, the fact that we are embodied beings entails, as we saw in the introduction to Part II, that the relation between my person and my body must be considered "analytic," meaning that it must be seen as one of necessary unity. Therefore, when conceptualizing a person's legal rights, we must think of a person and their body as one.[5] We see this clearly in Kant's discussion of the relation comprising empirical possession:

All propositions about right are *a priori* propositions, since they are laws of reason... An *a priori* proposition about right with regard to *empirical possession* is *analytic*, for it says nothing more than what follows from empirical possession in accordance with the principle of contradiction, namely, that if I am holding a thing (and so physically connected with it), someone who affects it without my consent (e.g., snatches an apple from my hand) affects and diminishes what is internally mine (my freedom), so that [this person's] maxim is in direct

---

[4] For example, Kant explains, "In contrast to laws of nature, the... laws of freedom are called *moral* laws. As directed merely to external actions and their conformity to law they are called *juridical* laws; but if they also require that they (the laws) themselves be the determining grounds of actions, they are *ethical* laws, and then one says that conformity with juridical laws is the *legality* of an action and conformity with ethical laws is its *morality*" (MM 6: 220; cf. 225). For more on this, see again the general introduction to Part II.

[5] Angels are therefore not legal persons since they are not embodied (spatio-temporal), but we can imagine other existing embodied, non-human persons (morally responsible beings), as we do in science fiction and fantasy novels, for example. The account of rightful relations—including the analytic relation between legal personhood and embodiment—would apply to relations between such non-human, embodied persons and between such beings and human beings.

contradiction with the axiom of right. So the proposition about empirical possession in conformity with right does not go beyond the right of a person with regard to [themself].

(MM 6: 249–50)

Since right is a moral[6] perspective tracking external interaction in space and time—a third-personal point of view—it is impossible from the point of view of right to distinguish between a person and their body. The distinction between the person and the body is available only from the internal first-personal perspective, but this perspective is tied to "inner sense," which is our ability to relate to objects in time only, and which enables the moral, inherently reflective perspective of inner freedom (virtue) (MM 6: 214). The distinction between my person and my body is also one I can draw by means of metaphysical arguments of various kinds. However, from the point of view of right—from the point of view of space-time—such a distinction is not available or discernable. Since my body and my person are always in the same spatio-temporal location—and relating to my body necessarily involves "outer sense," or the capacity to relate to an object in time *and space* (MM 6: 214)—the empirical boundaries of my person are identical with those of my body from a legal point of view; the extent of my body is the spatial extent of my legal personhood.

We can illustrate the analytic relation between—the necessary unity of—a person and their body by contrasting it to the synthetic relation between a person and their private property. A person's private property is not necessarily united with their person; I may obtain private property through certain actions, and, indeed, if something is mine, then it is mine even if I am not physically holding it. Thus, if someone takes my property, they wrong me, but they do not wrong my person. For example, if I forget my scarf at your house one evening, then the scarf is still mine even though I no longer have it with me. If you steal my scarf, you do not wrong my person since you do not touch my body, but you still wrong me by depriving me of my rightful property.[7] In contrast, were you to forcibly grab the scarf from around my neck as I am leaving your house, not only would you wrong me by depriving me of my property (you would steal), but also you would wrong my person by touching my body in unauthorized ways (you would commit battery). Or to use an example that tracks the long history of oppression against women: no one has a right to force anyone to dress in a particular way or to use state power to punish them if they do not dress in that way. For example, no one has a right to force women to wear certain kinds of (religious) headwear, such as niqabs or hijabs, just as no one has a right to force women not to wear them. Only the women themselves have a right to decide which religious clothing they will wear. From the point of view of justice, then, my embodiment entails that when you violate my bodily integrity, such as by coercively dressing or undressing it, you wrong my person (commit battery). Because violations against my body are violations against my person, they are more serious than wrongs involving only my private property. Consequently, forcing someone to wear or not to wear religious clothing is to wrong their person; it is to commit battery. Finally, once

---

[6] Here I am using "moral" in the broad sense to include both virtue (ethics) and right (justice/legality).

[7] For other discussions of Kant's idea of innate right and questions of embodiment, see Ripstein (2009); Flikschuh (2017); and Palliakkathayil (2017).

we make space for human phenomenology in this freedom-argument, we may capture why such uses of violence are particularly heinous: because of the way in which clothing and religious clothing in particular relates to human beings' sense of being safe in their own bodies and part of a good and even awe-inspiring world, using force or threat to make women wear or not wear certain pieces of clothing is both particularly wrongful (as it is to refuse to interact with women as legal persons) *and* particularly heinous.

Liberal theories of justice affirm some version of the view that everyone has an innate right to freedom, meaning that everyone has a right to set and pursue ends of their own, as long as in doing so they respect the rights of others to do the same, subject to laws of freedom restricting reciprocally. Besides, according to the account of justice presented in the previous paragraphs, the fact of our embodiment entails that our innate right to freedom contains a right to our own bodies—as contrasted with acquired rights to material possessions (private property). To be free in this "external" sense—to have what Kant calls "external freedom"—is to be recognized both as an embodied person that can never be treated as a mere means (as a being that has dignity) and as a being who can acquire rightful possessions with which to set and pursue ends of our own under universal laws of freedom. Thus, when we *interact*, we are free insofar as we are setting and pursuing ends of our own in ways that are consistent with each and all of us being embodied persons and subject only to universal laws of freedom that restrict us reciprocally. This, for Kant, is rightful freedom.

One way to clarify this conception of rightful freedom is to contrast it with being enslaved and with being deprived of rights by the legal-political system(s) to which one is subjected. I return to this topic in Chapter 7, but for now notice that enslaved people are subjected to a set of coercive rules, according to which they are not seen as having the right to set and pursue ends of their own. According to such rules, the enslavers are seen as literally owning the people they enslave. These enslaved people are regarded as the possessions of the owners, that is, they are treated as mere means with which the owners can set and pursue their own ends. Enslaved people are therefore not only deprived of all rights, that is, of rights to set and pursue ends of their own (they are denied the right to have rights at all), but everything they do, all their bodily activity, is in principle subject to the approval of their alleged owners. According to Kant's conception of right, the reason why such rules regarding slavery are necessarily void is that they could not oblige persons; indeed, they rest on an incoherent notion of rights. Such rules lack the form of a law for all free beings and, so, they cannot hold as laws for any being capable of external freedom. Rules permitting slavery are incoherent in that they assume that some groups of human beings are mere means (things) for others, and so incapable of obligations, and yet at the same time they are deemed capable of obligations (such as to their enslavers), and, so, are not mere means (things) after all. Therefore, if enslaved people were mere means (things), then they could not be obligated by the rules imposed on them, or be held legally responsible for following them, whereas if these laws were to be obligating, then these human beings cannot be thought of as mere means (things).[8]

---

[8] Obviously, one can point to how at various points in our lives—when we are children or incapacitated in various ways—we are not capable of full responsibility, and then one can try to argue that "naturally enslaved peoples" are of a similar kind. Slavery does not follow from granting this premise, however. What

Consequently, enslavement rules (whether understood in terms of "possessions" or "contracts") can never be rightfully enforced as laws by states. In contrast, being denied access to rights in a state is not thereby to be regarded as ownable by someone else as a mere means (as a thing), but it is to be forced to stay in the state of nature in one's relations with others. Both kinds of cases involve the denial of a right to freedom, understood as the right to set and pursue ends of one's own independently of the arbitrary choices of others and as subjected only to universal laws of freedom that restrict persons' interactions reciprocally.

As we will see shortly, the most common problem with coercive restrictions that outlaw or criminalize abortions and non-procreative sexual interactions (so-called "sodomy" and/or "obscenity" laws) is not that they enslave pregnant persons[9] or people who engage in non-procreative sexual activities. Rather, the main problem with such rules is that they deny pregnant persons and people who engage in non-procreative sexual activity a right to have or to enjoy rights by denying them the right to their own bodies.[10] And since human bodies and persons must be seen as necessarily (analytically) united from the (spatio-temporal) point of view of right, laws that forbid abortion or non-procreative sex are irreconcilable with respect for one another's legal personhood, which is the foundation of any system of law based on persons' innate right to freedom. Consequently, a state that enforces such rules fails to establish a civil condition in these regards (since the civil condition just is a public legal-political institution by means of which everyone can interact in ways consistent with respecting everyone else's basic right to freedom).[11] Such a state therefore fails to provide conditions under which each and all citizens can interact as legal persons or on terms consistent with each other's innate right to freedom. Instead, in this regard, such a state forces its subjects to interact as they would in a barbaric[12] version of the state of nature, in which the many or the powerful refuse to interact in ways consistent with respect for everyone's right to freedom. The legal-political system is corrupted by people who have made it a means through which they pursue their private, wrongful end of depriving others of their innate right to freedom (rather than enabling and securing rightful interactions among everyone). And if

---

follows is a right to a legal guardian, or to be cared for in accordance with laws of freedom. For more on rightful care relations, see Varden (2012a, 2020a).

[9] I am using the phrase "pregnant persons" rather than "pregnant women" because not only people who identify as women get pregnant (also people who identify as trans men, as ungendered, as queer, and some people who identify as intersex get pregnant). In addition, it is possible that in the future technology will make it possible for other kinds of human beings to get pregnant or that we meet non-human, embodied species in the universe (besides animal species) that also get pregnant.

[10] This has sometimes, but not always, been a legal fact of slavery too.

[11] I expand upon this point below, but it may be useful to note that this does not entail that the state thereby fails to establish rightful relations across the board, since it may, for example, have succeeded in establishing rightful private property relations.

[12] In the *Anthropology*, Kant defines barbarism as the condition of a society in which there is "Power without freedom and law" (A 7: 331), and so refers to a condition that is fundamentally in conflict with the demands of practical reason. As shown below, since criminalizing abortion and homosexuality is inconsistent with respect for a person's legal personhood, it is inconsistent with basic requirements of rightful freedom (and so is inconsistent with what practical reason demands). Notice too that it matters not to the barbarity of the restrictions whether they are enforced by a *de facto* state or an individual, since in enforcing a rule that contradicts the fundamental ground for justice (the innate right to freedom) the state ceases to yield political obligations in this regard. I return to these issues below and in Chapter 7.

anything is wrong, this is wrong because it violates the very foundation of a just state, namely each person's innate right to freedom. As will be argued below, under such conditions, pregnant persons who are denied the right to have abortions, polyamorous or polysexual people as well as members of the LGBTIQA community who are denied the right to engage in sexual love consistent with who they are (sodomy laws), or people who are denied the right to enjoy erotica as such (obscenity laws) are forced into a position where they must do what they can to protect themselves from the violence threatened or perpetrated against them by others—including the state's representatives who are trying to subject them to such unjustifiable violence—to the best of their ability even though doing so is to do wrong in the highest degree. Additionally, once we acknowledge that those who are subjected to this serious wrongdoing are human beings—with humans' specific phenomenological make-up—we realize that the histories of oppression of women, of members of various sexual or gendered communities through abortion, sodomy, and obscenity laws is something about which we, humankind, would appropriately feel shame, remorse, and sadness. Indeed, as will be expanded upon in Chapter 7, this is one reason why some state leaders have started the important process of publicly recognizing and apologizing for having failed LGBTQIA communities. Let me now turn to the legality of abortion and non-procreative sexual, loving, and gendered activities in some more detail, starting with abortion.

1.1 Abortion

If we look at the many discussions surrounding abortion, both in popular media and philosophical literature, we may distinguish cases in which legal rights to abortion are commonly considered easier to justify from those in which they are more difficult to justify. Below I first use and develop the analysis of justice developed in the previous section to engage the easier cases, which raise the questions of who can legally decide whether a pregnant person can terminate their pregnancy, and whether a person has the right to terminate a pregnancy that results from rape or that endangers their life. I then engage what many consider the more difficult cases, namely those in which no such considerations apply. Here I develop this Kantian approach further by showing how it can yield a way to move beyond the current deadlock between those who argue for and those who argue against a right to abortion. I then argue that under conditions where the state cannot secure access to abortion for all its pregnant citizens, neither can it enforce any abortion laws. I furthermore argue that in some medical cases abortions must be legal beyond the normal time limit. I finish by arguing that the interpretive and philosophical plausibility of this argument is strengthened by the fact that it can explain why Kant maintained that the many unmarried women who committed infanticide in his time should not be subjected to the death penalty for murder and why he was onto something important in so maintaining.

Let us start with the easier issues concerning abortion. If a state is just, it will reject any proposed law that would subject a pregnant person's decision regarding abortion to another private person's choice. For example, a just state will reject proposed laws that would give the pregnant person's parents, or the person whose sperm fertilized their egg, the authority to veto the pregnant person's choice to have an abortion.

According to my Kantian account of rightful relations, the reason why just states reject such restrictions is that they enslave pregnant persons. Such rules are fundamentally inconsistent with pregnant persons' right to be subject only to universal laws of freedom because such rules subject the pregnant persons' legal persons (by subjecting their body) to the arbitrary choices of other private persons (the parents, or the person whose sperm fertilized their egg). Such rules are fundamentally inconsistent with each person's innate right to freedom because they deprive legally responsible persons (pregnant persons) of the right to make such decisions regarding their own persons.

In addition, laws of freedom are inconsistent with any notion that pregnant persons have a legal duty to carry forward pregnancies that are the result of a crime, such as sexual assault (rape) or gaining access to another's body through deception (e.g. intentionally using dysfunctional condoms). After all, if a state were to force pregnant persons to carry to term pregnancies that are the result of crimes, it would permit some to use a crime as a means to an end. Laws that would make abortion illegal in such circumstances would permit the wrongdoers to take advantage of a person's particular kind of embodiment—human beings can get pregnant as a result of battery and deception—as a way of forcing that person to become a mere means to a particular end (to carry forward a pregnancy). For a state to permit this would be for it to deprive some of its citizens—the pregnant ones—of a right to freedom and to permit the replacement of right (rightful coercion) with might (violence). In both cases, the proposed rules could not hold as laws of freedom since they are inconsistent with all persons'—here pregnant persons'—basic right to bodily integrity, and, so, they cannot be seen as authoritative (constitutive of a rightful authority) but only as sheer, unjustifiable violence.

Additionally, if a state is just, it does not ascribe equal rights to pregnant persons and their fetuses; in a just state, fetuses acquire full rights only once they are born. Up until the point of birth, the life and health of the pregnant person has priority, which means that if carrying the fetus to term presents a health risk to the pregnant person, the pregnant person has a right to abort beyond the usual legal time limit. With Kant, we can suggest that the just state functions in these ways because the full enjoyment of the right to freedom is something persons can only be seen as born with (which is one literal meaning of *innate*). The full enjoyment of the right to freedom is not something that persons can have prior to birth. The reason is simply that a just state requires its laws to be consistent with each citizen's right to freedom, namely each citizen's right to independence from subjection to another's choices and instead a right to be subjected to universal laws of freedom only. Thus, for the sake of this argument we can assume that fetuses are persons. But even if we do, the argument is that if one person is inside another and dependent on this other person to survive, and even if the fetus and the pregnant person are an analytic unity, then the dependent person cannot have equal rights until they are no longer inside the other person; otherwise the law would make the independent person into a mere means for the dependent person, which is inconsistent with the idea of a right to freedom. What is more, in the human case, this means that since human beings are embodied beings who start their lives inside other human beings and since (at least at this point in history) only human beings with a uterus can gestate and give birth to babies, the only way to protect pregnant persons' legal personhood—to protect their basic rights as citizens—is by giving them priority over their fetuses. To treat fetuses otherwise—to treat fetuses as if they were independently existing persons prior to birth—is necessarily to deprive the pregnant persons of their bodily integrity and therefore of their legal personhood. To give the fetus and the pregnant person equal rights would be to treat the pregnant person merely as a means for the fetus and not as an independently existing legal person—and this no state based on each citizen's right to freedom can permit or do.

At this point, it is important to pay attention to the importance of the fact that the persons getting pregnant (on this planet, at least) are human beings. That is to say, because of human beings' phenomenological make-up,[13] many experience rapes and sexual deception as ungrounding, as something that makes them feel unsafe in their bodies and in the world—and for many, it takes a tremendous amount of emotional work to get through such experiences in good ways. In addition, a pregnancy brought to term radically affects the pregnant person's body for over nine months. So, forcing people to bring pregnancies to term means forcing them to endure (for nine months!) serious, increasing physical manifestations *in their own bodies* of the violence and deception done to them. Some of these effects might permanently change, or even damage, their bodies. What is more, if the laws also deemed pregnant persons legally responsible for the babies that result from their forced pregnancies, these persons would be forced into being legally responsible for a major consequence of the original crime done to them; they would be forced to assume responsibility for a vulnerable human being who needs human care and loving affection to be able to develop into an emotionally healthy, morally good human being. It seems that only the pregnant persons themselves can possibly evaluate whether or not this is something they can and want to do, and no law can force them to do this in the name of protecting and enabling rightful (human) freedom.

The above examples illustrate easy cases for most theories of justice, including the Kantian theory, and they do not, in my view, get to the heart of the current controversies surrounding abortion. After all, legal-political theories of many different kinds (not only freedom-based ones) as well as many ethical/theological positions which argue against a general right of abortion have ways of justifying the unequal legal status of mother and fetus until birth, and the legal termination of pregnancies that are the result of crimes of sexual assault and deception. These kinds of cases do not bring out the core of the controversy surrounding abortion, since most participants in current discussions agree that the above cases are at least exceptions to the general rule. Rather, the real controversy concerns what the general rule should be: should pregnant persons have a general right to abortion? Much of this debate focuses not only on the assumption granted in the arguments above, namely that the fetus is a person, but also on the question of whether the embryo is a person. The reason for this focus seems to be that both camps in the debate tend to agree that if we accept that an embryo/fetus is a person—for metaethical or theological reasons— then we must also accept the general rule that abortion in all stages of embryonic/

---

[13] See Part I for more on this.

fetal development should be coercively prevented, outlawed, or even criminalized (with exceptions for enslavement, protecting the life or health of the mother, deception, and sexual assault). Consequently, much effort on the part of those in favor of abortion focuses on challenging this assumption with regard to earlier stages of embryonic/fetal development, whereas anti-abortion defenders often focus on justifying it. Thus, the current debate tends to get mired in trying, to this point unsuccessfully, to give some sort of conclusive metaethical, metaphysical, or theological argument for the stage—if any—at which we should consider the embryo/fetus a person.[14]

The most important challenge to the assumption that there is some metaethical, metaphysical, or theological argument that will solve the problem of whether or not abortion should be prohibited comes from Judith Jarvis Thomson in her momentous 1971 "A Defense of Abortion." Thomson grants the assumption that the fetus is a person in all stages of development, and then argues that it does not follow that abortion can be coercively prevented, outlawed, or criminalized. (Famously, she makes her argument through the example of a violinist who is physiologically hooked up to another, kidnapped person, and whose life depends on being hooked up in this way for nine months). As is evident by now, I agree with Thomson's conclusion. Nevertheless, I believe that Thomson's argument succeeds only in justifying the exceptions to the general rule outlined above. That is, it demonstrates, with reasoning similar to the Kantian analysis above, only that laws must not give anyone an

---

[14] For some historically influential engagements here, see, for example, Michael Tooley (1972; cf. 1983); H. Tristram Engelhardt, Jr. (1974); and L. W. Sumner (1974; cf. 1983). Moreover, whether the fetus is or is not granted the status of a person, arguments are typically provided for or against the conclusion that it is always wrong to kill it. For example, for Michael Tooley (1983: 37–8), "One reason the question of the morality of infanticide is worth examining is that it seems very difficult to formulate a completely satisfactory liberal position on abortion without coming to grips with the infanticide issue. The problem the liberal encounters is essentially that of specifying a cutoff-point which is not arbitrary: at what stage in the development of a human being does it cease to be morally permissible to destroy it?" Tooley argues that in order to justify the criminalization of abortion as such, we must establish the moral impermissibility of it. Therefore, the two analyses (from right and from virtue) are seen as yielding the same results, which means that the analysis of justice is dependent upon the (meta)ethical analysis of abortion. See also Norman C. Gillespie (1977), Don Marquis (1989), and Robert P. George (1997) for arguments that proceed on the same assumption. For a brief overview of both kinds of arguments (for and against), see Marquis (1989: 183–9). Marquis grants that a fetus is not a person, but a potential person. However, he sees this difference as irrelevant to the issue of abortion, since what makes killing immoral is that one deprives another being of a valuable future. Hence, whether one kills a potential or an actual person, the immorality of the action is deemed the same (1989: 189–92). Tooley (1983) also famously argues that if it is correct that fetuses are not persons because they lack self-consciousness in some minimal sense, then one must not only defend the right to abortion until birth, but also the right to infanticide. Given how important Thomson's (1971) paper—to which I turn in the next paragraph—has been, including to motivate these papers, and how ingenious it is in making more accessible how dramatic a pregnancy is for many in so many ways, it is interesting to note that almost without exception these papers and books are all written by cis men who cannot get pregnant. Even more noteworthy is the lack of puzzle, let alone expression of worry, that they attempt to write authoritatively about rights involving a kind of embodiment that none of them have experienced or can experience. The prominent exception among cis men scholars on this topic is Sumner (1974, 1983), who takes the experiences of pregnant persons (and his own subjective limitations in these regards) seriously. For a recent engagement with the abortion issue that presupposes the significance of the personhood of fetuses and embryos and an overview of much of the more recent literature, see Kate Greasley (2017).

arbitrary veto power over the pregnant person, that they must give the pregnant person priority over the fetus, as well as the right to abort pregnancies that result from sexual assault. What we are looking for, however, is a stronger argument, one that demonstrates the unjustifiability of outlawing ordinary abortions, not just exceptional ones.[15] That argument, I suggest, must tackle the trickier question of whether or not it matters from the point of view of justice that the pregnant person has freely chosen to let embryonic/fetal development reach a certain stage, an argument that can also, fortunately, grant Thomson's point that to have sex involving procreative activities is not thereby to tacitly consent to getting pregnant, even though it often comes with the risk of getting pregnant. The stronger justification of a right to abortion shows that even if we grant personhood upon conception for metaethical, metaphysical, or theological reasons, this does not entail that as a matter of justice, normal cases of abortion can be coercively prevented, outlawed, or criminalized. Additionally, if we can show why requiring pregnant persons to choose whether or not to abort before a certain stage of fetal development is not, as such, unreasonable, we might have an argument convincing to both camps in this debate. This argument can therefore provide a way out of the current deadlock between pro-choice and anti-abortion activists and advocates, by driving home the point that their disagreement is about metaethical, metaphysical, or theological positions on person-hood and not about considerations of justice, because *legal* personhood is the only kind of personhood that is relevant to the rightfulness or legality of abortion.

This third approach to abortion that I am providing requires us to accept the view that an analysis from the point of view of right is in an important sense not the same as or co-extensive with an analysis from the points of view of virtue (ethics and/or theology). This is not a terribly upsetting assumption for most people. No major religions, for example, argue that one can be forced to become religious. Although in history there is the phenomenon of forced conversions, over time and in peaceful times, religions tend to maintain that one is only a truly religious person if one has freely accepted the religion, taken it "to heart," and so on. In addition, most people's use of common sense agrees with the claim that much of what might be considered ethically praiseworthy or blameworthy should not be made a matter of law. For example, people do not commonly think that it should be a matter of justice that we should act in generous, kind, friendly, or considerate ways—or that we should outlaw or criminalize all stingy, unkind, unfriendly, or inconsiderate actions. Assuming responsibility for these aspects of our lives lie with each individual, not the law. Because rightful interaction tracks only what is coercively enforceable, ethics and religiosity are fundamentally beyond the proper grasp of coercive legislation. Being religious, just as being virtuous, fundamentally requires a first-personal involvement and motivation that coercion cannot in principle reach and therefore we cannot legislate virtue or religiosity. It follows that having laws that prescribe virtuous or

---

[15] The argument I am providing is a dependency argument of the kind Thomson (1971: 58) mentions. If successful, it shows that pregnant persons living under conditions in which abortion is legally secured (including economically) and who choose not to abort before the deadline as legally defined has, as Thomson says, a "special kind of responsibility for it [the fetus]," since in this case they have freely chosen to let another person (as legally defined) become dependent upon their bodies.

religiously inspired actions (or virtuousness or religiosity) are nonsensical and rely on confused metaphysical assumptions. In addition, laws demanding religiosity or virtue are fundamentally inconsistent with each person's fundamental right to set and pursue ends of their own, which is to say that such laws are inconsistent with each person's innate right to freedom. The innate right to freedom therefore includes the right to choose one's own religious beliefs and lifestyles; it even includes the right to set and pursue non-violent, unethical ends, such as by undertaking stingy or unfriendly actions.

What will strike many as controversial, rather, and accordingly what is important to show, is that the legal issue of abortion also requires us to distinguish between what the law and what first-personal ethics or religion can demand in the name of protecting and enabling our freedom. Abortion, I am proposing, is an issue whose complexity we cannot grasp unless we pay attention to how the analyses of right (justice) and virtue/religion (ethics/theology) are not identical: to determine what the law should be on these questions, ethical and theological arguments are not, and therefore should not be considered to be, determining or directly relevant. Consequently, when we as citizens, as politicians, as legislators, or as judges think about whether or not abortion should be outlawed or criminalized, ethical or theological arguments must not be what settles the issue for us. Rather, what is important from the point of view of justice is how to make our interactions in the world rightful or consistent with respect for one another's right to freedom, and the challenge then is to show how legal personhood and embodiment relate. In addition, as we search for our conceptions, it is important to remember that rightful inter-action concerns external freedom. External freedom requires the ability consciously to set and pursue ends of one's own in the world, and rightfulness is a relation between persons' responsible exercise of external freedom, namely one that enables *interaction* under laws of freedom that restrict reciprocally. It is because external freedom is exercised in space and time that it can be coerced, since to coerce is to hinder the exercise of external freedom (the setting and pursuing of ends in the world in space and time).

How, then, does this conception of rightful interaction help us see why abortion as such cannot be rightfully and coercively prevented, outlawed, or criminalized? To see this, it may help first to remember that justice, and consequently legal argumentation, is limited to the kinds of beings who are capable of external freedom, even if this ability is not fully developed and even if it is temporarily incapacitated.[16] In light of this consideration, it is important that at very early stages of pregnancy the embry-onic cells do nothing but divide and multiply as an organic whole. To explain how they divide as an organic whole—as not just as an unstructured mass—one needs to explain how cells of an organic whole signal to one another, but any appeal to a capacity for unified, rational action is not needed or even helpful to explain this. At this stage, that is to say, there is as yet no spatio-temporal being that has developed this subjective, rational capacity for choice (as such) in a minimal sense, the one that

---

[16] The unconscious or comatose patient, for example, is only temporarily unable to exercise external freedom, not permanently unable to do so. In contrast, the minimally acting fetus, I argue below, has started to develop this capacity or exercise the ability in minimal ways.

for human beings becomes the ability to act as morally responsible beings.[17] At this stage, what the embryo "does" neither requires nor is reasonably explained by rationally unified, conscious spontaneous activity (even in its most rudimentary forms). Therefore, we cannot justifiably attribute legal rights or legal personhood upon conception even if we, for metaethical, metaphysical, or theological reasons, attribute ethical/religious personhood upon conception. Consequently, legal personhood is necessarily limited to beings with a spatio-temporally detectable subjective capacity for spontaneous, rationally unified action, whereas ethical/religious personhood may not be so limited.

To clarify this point, let me draw an analogy to some discussions surrounding legal death. Although there is significant disagreement exactly when legal death occurs, most states consider persons legally dead when they are, for example, "brain dead" meaning that there is no longer functional brain activity. So, from the point of view of justice, the crucial consideration is whether or not the persons in question are presumed (by medical experts) permanently to have lost their spatio-temporal, subjective capacity (let alone their ability) for external freedom, that is, to act in spontaneously, rationally unified ways. When this happens, legal guardians have the right (they are legally authorized) to end life-sustaining medical treatment. The main reason why legal guardians are not *required* to end treatment at this point, I believe, is to ensure that the legal system is compatible with some brain-dead human beings' previous and some legal guardians' deep metaethical or religious beliefs, namely that the brain-dead human being is still a person.[18] Analogously, at early stages of pregnancy, when the unit of cells (the embryo) merely divides and multiplies as an organic whole, there is no spatio-temporal human capacity, let alone minimal ability spontaneously to act in a rationally unified way, and, so, no legal personhood.[19] Until it does have such a capacity, the embryo/fetus cannot be viewed as having acquired any legal rights, and the decision whether or not to abort lies entirely with the person who is pregnant. In other words, we may grant that from a metaethical or religious point of view, the person already exists, say, as a being only in time, as a potential or an immaterial being, but justice and the law must restrict themselves to regulating interaction in space and time between beings with a capacity for external freedom (as evidenced by action that requires an appeal to rationally unified, spontaneous action). They thus can only regulate interactions between beings each who have

[17] Kant would say that there is neither "outer" and "inner" sense nor "outer" and "inner" use of choice, which is why it is absurd to say that at this stage there exists a capacity for choice even in its minimal sense. Certainly, at these early stages it is impossible to detect anything that would distinguish the human being from many other animals at embryonic stages of development, but since we are paying attention to the early stages of human capacities (constitutive of a *human* being inside another *human* being), this fact is irrelevant here. For more on this point, see my "Kant and Moral Responsibility for Animals" (2020a).

[18] The two US exceptions to the rule are New Jersey and New York, where in addition to brain death, the heart and the lungs must also have stopped functioning before death is pronounced. For our purposes, this difference seems irrelevant—and not only because in the absence of technological intervention, the loss of heart and lung function quickly follows brain death—since the important point is that even though death cannot be pronounced until also the heart and lungs have stopped functioning, the legal guardians have the right to stop treatment at the point of brain death.

[19] In Kantian language, the capacity for spontaneous, unified external action, is the capacity enabling "outer sense" and "outer use of choice."

the capacity to act consciously and spontaneously in rationally unified ways. Such a capacity cannot plausibly be ascribed to the cells dividing and multiplying as an organic whole at early stages of embryonic development (just as they cannot plausibly be attributed to a brain-dead human being). Hence, legal rights as such (legal personhood) can be conferred only at the point at which the fetus has developed into a rationally unified spatio-temporal being, one with minimal capacities for rationally unified spontaneous action. This developmental point, therefore, is the normatively important moment from the point of view of justice and the law. Since justice and the law are limited to regulating external freedom—interaction in space and time— justice and the law must always grant the right to abort until the human capacity for minimal, rationally unified spontaneous external action can plausibly be said to exist in the embryo/fetus.

It follows from this that from the point of conception until the point at which the embryo/fetus is able spontaneously to act in this minimally rational, unified sense, the embryo/fetus cannot be given legal personhood (legal rights) and the law cannot coercively restrict abortion. Up until this point, the pregnant person's own metaethical and/or religious considerations are what should regulate their thoughts and actions about the matter. To *legislate* otherwise is to deprive pregnant persons (even if they would choose not to abort out of metaethical or religious reasons) of their innate right to freedom in a most radical sense. Having coercive restrictions that require pregnant persons to carry forward pregnancies before the embryo/fetus for good reasons can be ascribed legal personhood is to treat pregnant persons as being subject to the law in a different way or for different reasons than anyone else, namely not in ways that are grounded on rightful interaction between legal persons. Pregnant persons are therefore denied equal protection under the law.[20] And, to emphasize again, even if we concede either that metaethical or metaphysical considerations require us to attribute ethical personhood upon conception, as does Kant, we have not thereby established that we can rightfully outlaw, let alone criminalize abortion. Kant's distinction between virtue and right therefore shows us that we need a distinction between (meta)ethical or theological conceptions of personhood and legal personhood, and the law cannot attribute legal personhood before minimal capacity for external freedom is evidenced and reasonably explained. Finally, it is understanding what is required for legal personhood that allows me to extend the embodiment argument (as we find in Thomson) to a right to abortion generally.

As there is reasonable disagreement about the point at which one should be proclaimed legally dead, so there is also reasonable disagreement about exactly when legal rights should be conferred on a fetus.[21] Indeed, there is significant, informed disagreement about this within and among states that protect pregnant persons' right to abortion. For example, some advocate the time of viability, others

---

[20] This would be a philosophical argument for why the 14th amendment to the US Constitution cannot permit restricting abortion in early stages of pregnancies.

[21] The distinction between embryo and fetus is often drawn at twelve weeks—a time that corresponds with much, but not all, countries' legislation on this issue. For the argument pursued here, this roughly agreed but somewhat arbitrary timing is not particularly significant or determining.

230 ABORTION, SODOMY, AND OBSCENITY LAWS

the moment of "quickening," still others the emergence of certain neurological processes, and so on. The effect of this reasonable disagreement is that states that (correctly) protect pregnant persons' right to abortion have different laws determining the time after which abortion is no longer legally permissible (under normal circumstances). Some states permit pregnant persons to abort only up until the twelfth week, others later. Still, what is common to all these reasonable suggestions is that they focus on evidence of the development of human cells into what may be deemed a rationally unified, spontaneously acting human being. Therefore, each suggestion identifies a reasonable empirical operationalization or application of the same normative principle. As a result, the disagreement seems not only to be reasonable, but also inevitable, because answering the question "when can we ascribe rationally unified actions (as opposed to mere movements) to a fetus?" requires making a normative judgment. Specifically, it requires making a judgment about when it is *reasonable* to explain the movements of the fetus as having been spontaneously initiated by the fetus in a rationally unified way rather than as having been determined by teleological principles of biological organisms or by scientific laws of necessary causality. Because we are looking for a normative principle to determine the issue, there will be more than one reasonable suggestion. Some suggestions will be unreasonable; again, there are no good reasons to argue that cells dividing and multiplying as an organic whole at early stages of embryonic developments involve spontaneous, rationally unified action (action that must be seen as originating in the consciousness of the growing being). Yet although some empirical suggestions are more reasonable than others, it will not be possible to determine one single, objectively correct empirical answer to the question of exactly when the growing being begins to evince spontaneous, rationally unified action originating in the consciousness of the growing being—and hence there are many reasonable legal determinations in different legal systems.

Because there can be *reasonable* disagreement regarding the correct application of the normative principle determining legal personhood, only the *public* authority—and not private individuals—can apply the principle: only a public authority can have the right to specify, apply, and enforce any specific restrictions on abortion. That is to say, since many of the choices are equally reasonable, for any particular private person to make the legal determination is merely for that party arbitrarily to impose their private choice on others. This would result in one person being seen as having the right to subject another person's body and legal person to their arbitrary choices, which is inconsistent with due respect for that person's right to freedom. Only a public authority can be seen as representing everyone and yet no one in particular and so can be thought of as a means through which we determine rules for interaction where there is no one reasonable choice with regard to how to specify and apply the normative principle. This, then, is why only a public authority can issue a restriction on abortions that can be deemed impartial in principle. Therefore, only a state can impose abortion restrictions on pregnant persons, namely, legal requirements that pregnant persons terminate their pregnancies before a particular stage of gestation.

Moreover, only once the baby is born and is no longer physically dependent on the pregnant person's body, does it have full legal rights, including the right that both (or

THE RIGHT TO BODILY INTEGRITY 231

all) parents take care of it (MM 6: 28of.).[22] On the latter point, the baby has not consented to being born, but is the result of the parents' actions and hence it is reasonable to claim that they are responsible for the baby. The parents must act on behalf of the child and, insofar as possible, provide the child with what it needs to become capable of emotional health and moral responsibility.[23]

I have defended the position that states should not restrict abortions before a certain legally significant stage of embryonic or fetal development—the stage at which the embryo or fetus acquires some legal rights due to having developed a capability to act in spontaneous, rationally unified ways in space and time (minimally understood). And only the state can legitimately determine what this developmental stage is.[24] Therefore, up until the point at which an embryo/fetus acquires legal personhood, the choice whether or not to abort a pregnancy can only lie with the pregnant person. In addition, if the pregnant person chooses to let the embryo/fetus develop beyond this point, they must also accept that the fetus has acquired some legal rights, while full rights are only ascribable after birth. At this point, the question arises: Can a state *always* enforce laws that restrict abortion? In my view, the answer to this question must be "no." The state can enforce such abortion laws only if it ensures that every pregnant person, whether adolescent or adult, actually has access to the resources required for safe abortions before the legal deadline. Thus, in a just state, adolescents must be guaranteed information and financial help in order to make sure that they are not subjected to their parents' lack of ability or unwillingness to pay for or otherwise to facilitate both access to pregnancy tests and the abortion itself, since this would be to allow the parents to enslave their children (in the sense described above). Poor persons' rights to abortion must also be guaranteed by any state that enforces abortion laws. Such guarantees are necessary to ensure that poor persons have real choices regarding abortions, that is, that they live in conditions under which their choices to abort are not subject to other private persons' arbitrary choices to provide them with the required means (such as through charitable donations). After all, a pregnant person cannot make a choice to abort or to remain pregnant if they do not have the material means necessary to carry out their choice, such as by there not being a sufficient number of affordable abortion clinics within

[22] This is also why a non-pregnant parent may have duties to the *pregnant person* before the child is born, since they are partially responsible for the pregnancy, but they do not have rights or duties to the *fetus or child* until it is born. This position also maintains that if the person whose sperm is used to fertilize the egg wants the pregnant person to abort but the pregnant person chooses not to, then the person whose sperm is used by the pregnant person must be able to reject legal responsibility for the fetus. Similarly, those who contribute to sperm-banks neither incur legal responsibility for the child born nor do they have legal standing with regard to the child.

[23] Once the child is born, the nature of the dependency changes since it is not physically united with the pregnant person. Still, the previously pregnant person continues to act on behalf of the child, since the infant is not yet capable of exercising choice or external freedom responsibly—children are not capable of "deeds" or "rightful interaction." The scope and justification of children's rights is naturally beyond the parameters of this chapter. For more on these issues, see Varden (2006, 2012a).

[24] For example, my position appears to support the general principle that if there is good evidence that the fetus has such serious impairments that (a) if born, it will commit the parent(s) to the dependency relation for the rest of their life, and (b) this evidence is available only after the general deadline, then there might be an extension of the time by which the decision must be made.

reach. Accordingly, if a state imposes and enforces a deadline on abortions, then it must also institutionally guarantee all pregnant subjects actual access to the required means, say, through distributive welfare measures, that make either choice (to abort or not to abort) possible. If a state upholds a monopoly on coercion and a legal system in which pregnant persons neither have the appropriate knowledge nor the requisite actual access to services to exercise their freedom, it fails to provide rightful conditions for them. Instead, it forces some of its subjects to be subject to the arbitrary private choices of others on the matter, namely, to others' private choices to provide charity. The state must set up its monopoly on coercion such that it is reconcilable with each person's innate right to freedom, which requires systemic institutional guarantees against anyone being trapped in such unjustifiable private dependency relations. If it does not provide such institutional guarantees, it cannot justly or rightfully enforce abortion laws.[25]

It is also important to note that there is space within this position to capture how states should make and enforce abortion laws that accommodate concerns of natural teleology—moral psychology/moral anthropology. For example, the position can speak to why just legal systems do not allow others to interfere if pregnant persons want to risk their lives in carrying their pregnancies to term, or in carrying them until the child can survive outside of the uterus. I believe my position takes seriously the fact that we make laws not merely for embodied, social rational beings, but for embodied, social *human* beings. As argued in Chapter 1, because of the structure of our phenomenological make-up, human beings are partially emotionally grounded in their unreflective, affectionate loving relations: this is part of how we realize our animality ("basic community") and social aspects of "humanity" (social sense of self), and it is constitutive of how we go about our lives in meaningful ways. When someone becomes pregnant, their self-understanding sometimes has or will be transformed. Some shift to seeing themselves and their fetus as in the process of becoming an affectionate loving, grounding "us." They then see more at stake than their own life or they now feel their own life as including that of the fetus in an ineliminable sense. For these reasons, good laws ensure that no one but the pregnant person has the right to decide whether or not to take on the risk of carrying forward a dangerous pregnancy. Others, including healthcare professionals, can guide and advise, but only the pregnant persons can decide whether or not to accept the risk of continuing their pregnancy. Healthcare professionals will be legally required to intervene (to act as legal guardians and as specified by the relevant laws) only if things suddenly go severely wrong and the patient is no longer able to choose what should be done. Then the healthcare professionals will first save the pregnant person. Good laws see the priority of decision-making in this way for two reasons. On the one hand, although one is permitted to act in risky ways, healthcare professionals are not

---

[25] This is does not, however, entail that those who live in a state with sodomy or anti-abortion laws cannot have *any* political obligations. The issue of political obligations is not exclusively disjunctive: persons may have political obligations to obey a state's laws governing many relations, such as private property and contract laws, but nevertheless cannot be politically obligated to obey laws governing all relations, in this case laws governing abortion. I return to these complexities in Chapter 7.

required to stand by in cases where the risk of death is irrational or no longer can be rationally chosen and death can be prevented. On the other hand, because the pregnant persons have to live with the decisions made, they are the only ones who can have the right to make them. I return to similar analyses of risk and sexual behavior below.

Relatedly, this position also defends the legal permissibility of later abortions when continued pregnancy would threaten the pregnant person's mental health. On this position, if carrying out the pregnancy beyond the legal limit becomes very difficult for the pregnant person for mental health reasons—it is simply too overwhelming— then this position defends their right to abort. Nevertheless, as would also be the case in early births, if the fetus is viable, the medical personnel involved will be legally required to try to deliver the fetus such that it maximizes the fetus' chances of survival once it is outside the pregnant person's body (unless, as always, doing so involves increased risks for the pregnant person). Hence, it is impossible, on this position, to defend the state (or anyone else's, such as a husband's) right to act as a legal guardian for the pregnant person on the grounds that that pregnant person is not competent to make medical decisions *and then* in the name of acting as a legal guardian to force the pregnant person to carry the pregnancy that they cannot handle mentally through to term.

Notice too that if we use the argument above as well as the argument, which informs the whole book, that the principles of freedom must set the framework within which morality accommodates human nature, then we may also have a solution to the classic interpretive puzzle raised by Kant's cryptic remarks on infanticide, which was not uncommonly committed by unwed mothers in his time. In a passage addressing capital punishment for these mothers (as well as for duelers who kill their opponent) Kant says,

Here penal justice finds itself very much in a quandary. Either it must declare by law that the concept of honor (which is here no illusion) counts for nothing and so must punish with death, or else it must remove from the crime the capital punishment appropriate to it, and so be either cruel or indulgent. The knot can be undone in the following way: the categorical imperative of penal justice remains (unlawful killing of another must be punished by death); but the legislation itself (and consequently also the civil constitution), so long as it remains barbarous and undeveloped, is responsible for the discrepancy between the incentives of honor in the people (subjectively) and the measures that are (objectively) suitable for its purposes. So the public justice arising from the state becomes an *injustice* from the perspective arising from the people.   (MM 6: 337)

Jennifer K. Uleman (2000) and Jordan Pascoe (2012) differ in their judgment of whether or not Kant's analysis of unwed mothers' infanticides is sensitive to the women's suffering, but they both agree that Kant decides that the death penalty is appropriate not only for killing during dueling but also for these mothers. David Sussman (2008) is less conclusive in his discussion of these cases, maintaining that it is not clear that Kant affirms the state's right to punish with the death penalty here. All three find these passages somewhat inscrutable. The above account suggests a new way to think about the problem: if the state simply upholds the objectively correct law—and, for the sake of argument, we can accept Kant's view that this law demands the death penalty for infanticide—in situations that are themselves not rightful, but undeveloped and barbaric, then it will do something that is correctly experienced as an act of injustice from the subjective point of view of the people (the unwed mothers), and the state is responsible for this injustice. Therefore, this penal law cannot rightfully be enforced in full effect (these women must not be sentenced to death) until the state is able to provide minimally rightful conditions for its people, which includes a right for both mother and child not to be doomed to a life in poverty and shame because the baby has been born out of wedlock. This, I believe, implies the following: if the state upholds the death penalty in these cases, it does wrong; and if people (the unwed mothers) protect themselves against such unjust uses of force by surreptitiously killing their newborn, they will wrong their babies *and* they thereby do wrong in the highest degree. But there is not yet established a public, legal-political authority that can hold them accountable for this by punishing them—the authority that is supposed to enable their rightful co-existence with others is radically failing in its ability to do so by permitting some spheres of interaction to remain "barbarous." Consequently, the pregnant persons who find themselves in this impossible position will have to live with whatever they do in response to it, but there is no rightful authority that can judge or punish what they do. If the unwed mothers do commit infanticide and their actions are discovered, then, according to this interpretation of Kant, the state must assume responsibility for its own failures by not fully punishing them (by sparing them the death penalty). I return to the complexities raised by barbaric laws in Chapter 7.

Let me finish this section by addressing the question of whether there corresponds to the right to abortion a duty on behalf of healthcare professionals to facilitate it. The general answer to this question is, I take it, yes: to become publicly authorized to be a healthcare professional on this view is not only to demonstrate that one has a certain level of medical knowledge through relevant academic exams, but one must become publicly "licensed" meaning that one must become authorized by the state to act as a specific kind of legal guardian with regard to citizens in need of medical assistance (one's patients). To act as legal guardians, healthcare providers must act so as to secure their patients' basic rights to freedom as specified by law, and in just states, these laws will affirm pregnant persons' right to abortion. Part of the expectation of anyone seeking a public license to practice as a healthcare provider, in other words, is that they are able to engage with patients in the ways the relevant public laws and policies specify. On this position, that is to say, the relationship between healthcare providers and their patients is fiduciary. After all, if contracts between healthcare providers and patients were considered normal contracts, they would enslave patients, for they would legally authorize (consensually, or non-consensually in emergency situations) healthcare providers to subject to their arbitrary choices one aspect of their patients' lives (one aspect of their patients' embodied freedom). Such subjection amounts to enslavement, which Kant's freedom ideal explicitly opposes. States must ground their laws on each person's right to freedom, namely the right to independence from having one's freedom subject to another's private, arbitrary choices and the right instead to have all one's interactions subject only to universal laws of freedom. Hence, contracts between patients and healthcare providers must instead be understood as involving a kind of fiduciary (status) relationship that is made rightful by the healthcare providers acting within the laws and policies constitutive of their rightful, public authority and thereby enable patients to deal with aspects of their own embodiment with their expert medical assistance.

By becoming legally authorized as a healthcare provider (through professional, public licenses), then, one chooses to act within such a legal framework and, accordingly, one is legally bound to secure one's patients' rights to freedom; failure to do so would result in losing one's professional health practitioner license.[26] As usual, however, on this position, there is space for accommodating human nature with regard to how these laws operate in order to protect both parties. Surely, it is undesirable for vulnerable patients to be treated by healthcare providers who for religious reasons, say, are uncomfortable enabling all the rights of pregnant persons with respect to their bodies. And surely it is desirable for us to create societies where people are able to live not only their private lives, but also their professional lives in accordance with their religious beliefs. Exactly where the state should draw the line between reasonable and unreasonable discomfort here is a question to which there is no single answer. Thus, this is a question that the state—through public deliberation—should settle. It is likely, however, that a just state will put laws and policies in place that, for example, legally require individual healthcare providers to make public any limitations they may have when it comes to ensuring the rights of pregnant persons and to require that medical clinics hire a sufficient number of medical professionals who are able to interact professionally and secure *all* patients' rights. The related responsibility of the state, in turn, is to ensure that pregnant persons have access to qualified healthcare providers to meet their medical needs. In Chapter 7, I return to these issues by attending to the state's responsibility to secure systemic justice.

1.2 Sexual Interaction Authorized by Consent

As we have seen, Kant defends a relational conception of justice grounded on what he takes to be the only justifiable basis for a theory of justice, namely each person's innate right to freedom. On this conception, justice arises only among interacting persons, and the rightfulness of their interactions consists in the relation established between them when they interact. Kant argues that a person's innate right to freedom is respected only if their choices—their setting and pursuit of ends—are never subjected to another person's arbitrary choice, but only to universal laws of freedom. A person's freedom is subjected to another's arbitrary choice when this other person decides how they can set ends, for example by treating their bodies with violence or by accessing their means without their consent. These wrongful uses of coercion reveal the coercer's refusal to interact according to laws of freedom. In contrast, rightful restrictions are non-contingent and symmetrical restrictions upon the

---

[26] On this position, being publicly licensed as a healthcare professional is to be authorized to act on behalf of one's patients in the ways specified by the law. Because healthcare professionals must act within the boundaries set by the law, when we find ourselves so subject to licensed healthcare professionals, we are still subject to choices that are not the healthcare professional's private choices, but to inherently public choices that represent one's own choices in virtue of being a part of the general will represented by the public authority (which is why being so subjected is not irrational nor inconsistent with one's right to freedom). For more on this, see Varden (2012a).

interacting persons' actions that are consistent with each of their innate rights to freedom. Kant's conception of justice is inherently relational in that it characterizes political freedom as the absence of arbitrary (contingent and asymmetrical) imposition of might amongst interacting persons by demanding that interacting persons are constrained only by universal laws of freedom that restrict reciprocally.

Given that Kant grounds his theory of justice in each person's innate right to freedom, it is, as mentioned several times in this book, most surprising to discover that his analysis of sexual practices is fundamentally informed by a distinction between natural and unnatural acts. To repeat one of the examples, in his discussion of marriage in The Doctrine of Right, Kant states,

Sexual union is... the reciprocal use that one human being makes of the sexual organs and capacities of another.... This is either a natural use (by which procreation of a being of the same kind is possible) or an unnatural use... with a person of the same sex.... Since such transgression of laws, called unnatural... do wrong to humanity in our own person, there are no limitations or exceptions whatsoever that can save them from being repudiated completely.
(MM 6: 277)

"Natural" sexual union refers to sexual deeds involving two persons of opposite sexes who make reciprocal use of each other's sexual organs and capacities in a way that is consistent with procreation. To engage in any other sexual practices, Kant appears to argue, conflicts with our innate right to freedom, because it is an unnatural use of our sexual organs and capacities. Procreative, heterosexual interactions are the only natural ones, whereas all other interactions are unnatural—including, of course, homosexual interactions.[27] Now it is not clear what Kant means by such actions being "repudiated" here, whether he thinks that they should be ethically condemned, outlawed, or even criminalized, or whether he thinks the people who engage in them should be denied legal recognition by not having the right to marry, or something else. In Part I of this book, I argued that Kant himself and Kantians should recognize polyamorous, polysexual, as well as non-straight, non-cis, and non-procreative sexual activity as emotionally healthy and morally good, which means that justifiable legal and ethical analyses of marriage should do so too. I return to some of these legal issues in Chapter 6. For our purposes here, the more important question to evaluate is whether or not Kant by his condemnation of "unnatural" sexual interaction can justifiably mean—that is, without contradicting his own basic legal principles—that non-procreative sexual activities (including the making, possession, and use of erotica) should be outlawed or criminalized through so-called sodomy and obscenity laws.

If Kant did mean that non-procreative sexual activities, including making, having, or using erotica should be outlawed or criminalized through sodomy and obscenity laws, he surely was mistaken about his own theory. The reason is simply that sexual interactions that do not aim at procreation are not in conflict with our innate right to freedom. The innate right to freedom gives each person a right to independence from having their freedom subjected to another person's arbitrary choice and there simply is no such wrongful subjection involved in consensual, non-procreative sexual interactions among legally responsible persons. That is, according to Kant's

---

[27] For more on Kant's discussion of "unnatural" sexual practices, see Chapter 3.

legal-political theory, sexual relations are rightful as long as they are authorized by continuous consent. So even if we could give an explanation of why consensual non-procreative practices of various sorts involve ethically or religiously more objection-able subjection to animalistic or social or aesthetic desires than do heterosexual practices consistent with reproduction[28]—which, as we know from Part I, I do not think is possible to do convincingly—the explanation would be irrelevant to deter-mining the legality of these interactions. Hence, Kant's considered opinion, at least, should be that a legally responsible person has the right to choose which sexual ends they want to set, on their own or consensually together with other legally responsible persons. A person can, of course, change their mind at any point, and if their sexual partners do not respect this, then they are legally wronged: they are victims of sexual assault.[29] But the general principle is that insofar as the sexual interaction is author-ized by the interacting persons' consent, their sexual interaction is legally permissible.

For these reasons, given Kant's core commitments, he cannot claim that certain sexual activities, such as same-sex practices, anal sex, oral sex, three- or moresomes, or filming or taking pictures of sexual activities should be legally impermissible as such.[30] If we remain faithful to Kant's systematic commitment to the individual's right to freedom, the number, the kind of sexual pleasure, the sexual or gender identity, and the sexual orientation of the sexual partners are irrelevant to the legality of their interactions and practices. According to this philosophical position, only a lack of authorizing consent can make a sexual deed wrong in the legal sense, or, conversely, authorizing consent is constitutive of any rightful sexual interaction. Persons who are not capable of legal responsibility for their actions (and so are not capable of *deeds* rather than merely actions), which includes children and all of us when we are relevantly incapacitated, cannot give such consent. That is to say, if the consenting persons cannot be seen as capable of deeds, either due to immaturity (children), mental impairment (disability or illness) or intoxication (alcohol, or drugs), or if their consent is empty because it was given in response to deception, threats, or threatening behavior, then their utterance of consensual words is insuf-ficient to authorize sexual interaction with them. Moreover, if persons fail to take sufficient precaution in their sexual behavior, such as if they fail to ensure that the persons with whom they have sexual interaction are old enough to be capable of consent, then, as a general rule, they are culpable of some form of legal negligence. But for persons who are capable of legal responsibility for their interactions, con-tinuous authorizing consent is the main factor that determines the legality of sexual interactions under laws of freedom.

---

[28] This is the interpretation Kant seems to encourage here, namely that reproduction is morally permissible because it furthers human kind or rational agency as such. For more on this, see Herman (1993b).

[29] Of course, if one deceives another person in order to obtain consent, such as by lying when asked if one has a sexually transmitted disease, the consent is vitiated by the deceit, and such unauthorized access to another person's body is considered battery. The deceiving party therefore commits a criminal wrong and is legally responsible for the full consequences thereof.

[30] I return to the complexities surrounding economic exchanges involving sexual services and goods in Chapters 6 and 7.

Another way to reach this conclusion is to argue that attempts to justify coercive restrictions on non-procreative or non-binary sexual interactions, including criminalization, encounter problems similar to those faced by attempts to justify coercive restrictions on abortion as such. Because a human being is an embodied person, their innate right to freedom gives them a right to bodily integrity. Restrictions on sexual activity, like restrictions on abortion as such, fail to respect an individual's right to bodily integrity. The main difference between the two cases is that the argument against coercively restricting sexual activity in ways that track sexual orientation or identities is simpler and more straightforward, since these sexual interactions involve consensual interactions between two or more legally responsible embodied persons. In short, coercively preventing, including criminalizing, non-procreative, non-binary sexual interaction involves arbitrarily denying some persons sole control over their own bodies and thus over their own legal persons. Instead, it permits some people to use the threat of violence to make others use their own bodies only consistent with specific ends, and in doing so it permits some people to refuse to interact consistently with each person's innate right to freedom. Therefore, such legal restrictions on sexual activity function to annihilate bodily rights—and thus respect for legal personhood—as such. Moreover, a state that enforces such restrictions fails to institute civil society. By positing and enforcing laws that fail to treat each citizen as having an innate right to freedom, such a "de facto" state fails to set itself up as a *public* authority, for it fails to represent each of its citizens and yet no one in particular. The state thereby forces non-straight, non-cis, polyamorous, and polysexual persons to stay in the pre-state condition, or the so-called "state of nature" in this regard and, indeed, in a particularly barbaric or brutal version thereof, namely, one in which there is no respect for their legal personhood with regard to their own bodies. Hence, no one can be obliged to obey such coercive restrictions, and they must defend themselves, even against the state and its representatives, as best they can even though doing so involves doing wrong in the highest degree. As mentioned previously, I return to this issue of what to do when faced with (the threat of) such barbaric violence in Chapter 7.

As far as I can see, then, it is impossible to justify any restriction on sexual activity that legitimizes only cis, heterosexual, binary, monogamous activity, because such a restriction would result in contingent, asymmetrical legal restrictions that are inconsistent with each person's innate right to freedom. This is not to say that there cannot and should not be any legal restrictions on sexual interactions, but that their rightfulness will not depend on whether or not they are binary and procreative. So what legal restrictions are important to have in place for all sexual activity, whether heterosexual, homosexual, involving group-sex, or otherwise? To find the considered Kantian answer to this question, I believe we must start by yet again looking to Kant's account of enslavement as well as his account of murder, including "partial" murder (MM 6: 421): we do not have a right to enslave one another and we do not have a right to kill each other regardless of whether or not we actually consent to being enslaved or being killed. We do not, in other words, have a right to give up our right to interact as persons. As we noted in relation to the slave contract, any such agreement cannot be understood as authorizing consent; such a contract is necessarily void. If someone, for whatever reason, wants to give up their right to interact as a person, then this cannot authorize anyone else to start treating them as if they were a mere thing. If the person who has this desire is capable of moral responsibility, then others must refuse to accept the offer of treating them as a mere thing *or* if the expression of this desire reveals that this person no longer is capable of relating to their own actions in the way required by moral responsibility (relating to their actions as deeds, as exercises of causality for which they are morally responsible), then those around them have a legal right and ethical duty to care for them as legal guardians (temporarily, while they call the public healthcare authorities; or permanently, depending on their status relation to that person).

Similarly, no one can authorize anyone else to destroy or permanently damage their physical or cognitive capacities, namely those in virtue of which they are capable of external freedom. We cannot, in other words, give *authorizing* consent to destroying our bodies, or parts of them. We—human beings—cannot legally consent to someone destroying our limbs, our eyes, our (sexual) organs, our ears, etc., because from the legal point of view, the spatial extension of our bodies is the extension of our legal personhood. Exactly where we draw the line between destroying and merely changing or transforming cannot be determined *a priori*, of course, but would be one that needs to be arrived at through public deliberation. We are permitted to authorize and engage in risky behavior with others, but we cannot authorize or engage in behavior that aims or inevitably entails permanently doing damage to anyone's legal person, including our own. Consequently, when a wife neither leaves nor presses charges against her physically abusive husband, she does not thereby authorize his abuse. He commits a legal wrong every time he abuses her. The only ideal reasons the state could have for refraining from coercively stopping the possibility of one person abusing another who will not press charges are reasons having to do with procedural justice, privacy, and the fact that one has a right to *risk* becoming subjected to wrongful behavior. (These ideal reasons differ from the merely pragmatic reason that many states are unable to secure homes for women who flee physically abusive husbands—an issue I take up in more detail in Chapter 7.)

Just as basing rights to abortion on the right to external freedom does not prevent abortion law from taking human phenomenology seriously, the fact that a person cannot legally consent to an interaction that will destroy (partially or fully) their capacity for external freedom does not prevent laws that regulate physically risky behavior from taking our phenomenology seriously. To illustrate, the legal impossibility of consent to self-destruction is consistent with a person's right to risk shortening their life by undergoing invasive surgery (e.g., nephrectomy, partial hepatectomy) in order to donate an organ to someone who needs it, and it is consistent with their basic right to have gender-affirming surgery. In recognizing both of these rights, a system of laws based in the principle of freedom accommodates human beings' embodied, social self-love—our deep loving care for others (basic community) and for ourselves (self-preservation). It can do this because these rights are required by and consistent with demands of freedom, and because our system of laws is one not only for embodied, free beings, but for embodied, free, social *human* beings. What laws based in the principle of freedom cannot legally permit is for people to undergo organ removal for profit. Otherwise, the state would authorize contracts according to which some persons are paid to be partially, physically damaged or destroyed simply to benefit others (which is not to say that the victims can be punished), and this is inconsistent with the state functioning as a *public* authority that acts on behalf of each and no one in particular. Furthermore, such behavior could not be justified by appeal to emotionally healthy self-love like donating to save life and gender-affirming surgeries can.

Notice too that as with abortion, a main reason why the state is essential to ensuring rightful sexual interaction is that there appear to be problems of indeterminacy, albeit of a different sort. Indeterminacy with respect to abortion arises because there is reasonable disagreement about how to apply the normative principle that identifies the stage of fetal development up until which abortion should be legal. In contrast, indeterminacy with respect to the legality of sexual activities seems to arise when there is reasonable disagreement about whether or not a person has given or can give their authorizing consent to a sexual interaction. So, although continuous, mutual, authorizing consent among legally responsible persons is the main normative principle we all must accept as governing the rightfulness of any particular sexual interaction, situations may arise in which there is reasonable disagreement in the application of this principle (whether or not consent has been given in a particular situation). For example, there are questions of required maturity, the use of alcohol and drugs, relations involving asymmetrical power (such as relations between physicians and their patients), and so on. Hence, unless the public authority, which represents both interacting parties and yet neither of them (or anyone else) in particular, determines restrictions on consent and applies these restrictions when controversies arise, we appear to have another situation in which one person's choice runs roughshod over another's. Similarly, some sexual activities—including some BDSM (bondage, discipline, domination, submission, sadism, masochism) activities—essentially involve pain and higher than usual risk of bodily harm. Again, we do have a right to engage in consensual risky behavior—sexual or otherwise—but this does not mean that all risky behavior can be authorized by consent and it does mean that one can be held legally responsible for the bad consequences of taking such risks. Again, any reasonable evaluation of such risk must take into account that we are not only embodied, social beings capable of external freedom, but *human* beings. The upshot of this last point is twofold: (1) private individuals cannot be seen as having the right to determine, apply, and enforce restrictions in cases involving the question of whether or not there is authorizing consent; and (2) states that outlaw non-straight, non-cis, non-monogamous sexual activity fail to provide rightful solutions to wrongdoing among those who engage in such activities. Instead, such a state forces mere might (violence) to reign between the disputants: the question of whether or not a person has been wronged cannot be settled or brought before a court of law without the plaintiff thereby being charged with a legal wrong or a crime. Again, I delve deeper into these and related issues in Chapter 7.

Finally, as with the argument against legal restrictions on abortion, this argument against legal restrictions on non-cis, non-straight, or non-binary sexual activity is irrelevant to, and therefore reconcilable with, very different ethical and theological views, including deeply confused ones. Because the demands of justice are not co-extensive with the demands of ethics or religion, the argument against restrictions on sexual activity can be affirmed by people who deem non-cis, non-straight, or non-binary sexual activities as immoral and/or sinful from an ethical or religious point of view. It is important to note that this argument also does not require an appeal to tolerance (though it can be complemented by it). The reason why non-cis, non-straight, or non-monogamous activity cannot be coercively restricted is not primarily that we must tolerate our differences in order to achieve a minimum of stability and peace (although this is of course true). It is also not a fairness argument of the kind: "if heterosexuals have the right, then in all fairness homosexuals must have it too (etc.)." The argument is not and does not require such an appeal to fairness (though it can be complemented by it). Rather, the argument is that from the point of view of right, a coercive public authority must be reconcilable with each person's innate right to freedom, and so its laws must afford everyone the right to engage in any sexual interaction that can be authorized by consent. To arrive at this conclusion, ethical and religious discussions and disagreements are irrelevant, and considerations of tolerance and fairness as such do not do the main justificatory work. From the point of view of right, no state can outlaw or criminalize sexual interactions authorized by consent without thereby failing to act as a public authority. The problem with binary, cisist, heterosexist restrictions on people's sexual activity authorized by consent is correspondingly that they involve state-organized wrongdoing because they deny those persons a right to bodily integrity, which is to deny them their legal personhood.

2. Free Speech: The Case of Erotica

Kant is a staunch defender of free speech. In fact, some see his defense of free speech as his sole objection to Hobbes's absolutism. Even so, these same interpreters tend to find it genuinely puzzling why and problematic that Kant chooses free speech as the sole condition on political legitimacy rather than, say, Hobbes's unconditional right to self-preservation.[31] Given Kant's strong defense of free speech, it is natural to think that he rejects any rightful limits on what private individuals can say to one another in public spaces. Any such limitation, it seems, would be an unjust limitation on free speech. At the same time, if Kant's view really is that people can communicate whatever they want, then he does not have much to contribute to contemporary legal debates surrounding free speech in general and erotica in particular. I will argue the contrary: a closer analysis of Kant's texts in light of his philosophical commitments regarding the importance of privacy and the wrongfulness of unauthorized publications of others' writings and art provide us with some of the philosophical ideas we need to understand important legal complexities surrounding erotica.[32] More specifically, I first explain how Kant's distinction between internal and external uses of choice illuminates why most ways in which persons use words and images in their interactions with one another do not involve wrongdoing from the point of view of right. I then use this argument to justify legally responsible persons' general right to use erotic images before explaining why no one has a right to publish private

---

[31] For overviews over the secondary literature on this point, see Varden (2010c, 2015b).

[32] Whether or not there can be limits on speech in public spaces beyond criminalization of unauthorized publications and discussion of related issues is found in Chapter 7.

sexual or erotic images of others without authorizing consent. I finish this section by showing how our distinctive human phenomenology makes sexual privacy so important to human beings, and how it can explain why the use of erotica comes with its own dangers. In Chapters 6 and 7, I return to problems concerning the production and sale of erotica.

The general reason why speech cannot be outlawed, Kant argues, is simply that words as such do not have coercive power.[33] In The Doctrine of Right, Kant explains that "such things as merely communicating his thoughts to them [others], telling or promising them something, whether what he says is true and sincere or untrue and insincere" do not constitute wrongdoing because "it is entirely up to them [the listeners] whether they want to believe him or not" (MM 6: 238). Words do not have the physical power to hinder others' external freedom, either by affecting their bodies or by depriving them of their means. Since words as such cannot exert physical power over people, it is impossible to use them as a means of coercion against another. For example, if you block my way, you coerce me by physically hindering me from choosing to move in certain ways: you hinder my external freedom. If, however, you simply tell me not to move, you have done nothing coercive, nothing that *thereby* hinders my external freedom, as I can simply ignore what you are saying and walk past you. So, even though by means of your words, you attempt to influence my internal use of choice by providing me with possible reasons for acting one way rather than another, you accomplish nothing coercive. You may *wish* that I take on your proposal for action, but you do nothing to force me to do so. Whether or not I *choose to act* on your suggestion is still entirely up to me; you cannot, in other words, choose for me and your words as such cannot control my end-setting. Indeed, even if what you suggest is the virtuous thing to do, your words cannot make me do it. Virtuous action requires not only that I pursue the right end, but that I pursue it because it is the right thing to do. Because the choice of maxims is beyond the grasp of coercion, Kant holds that most uses of words, including immoral ones such as lying, cannot be seen as involving wrongdoing from the point of view of right.

Three further clarifications are in order before we can see how this conception of right delineates the boundaries of free speech, including how it pertains to the issue of speech involving erotic images. First, even though lying is not a wrong from the point of view of right, it is important to emphasize that if one lies, one is legally responsible for the bad consequences of the lie. The reason is that by lying one voluntarily sets the framework within which another person acts. If the other person accepts my invitation to trust my false description of reality, then I am responsible for the bad consequences of the other person having believed me. For example, say you ask me for directions to the library and I, due to my extraordinarily bad sense of humor, lie. It happens that my lie directs you away from the library and through the most dangerous part of town, where you become the victim of wrongdoing. Because my lie sets the framework within which you choose your route—it constructs the set of presumed descriptive facts by reference to which you make your choice—I become

---

[33] I deal with the right to participate in public debate in Chapter 7.

partly responsible for what happens to you. My words have set the framework within which you exercise your external freedom and consequently, even if unbeknownst to me, I send you into a dangerous neighborhood, I am still partly responsible for what happens to you there. Since the wrongdoing befell you as a result of my words, I am responsible for the bad consequences resulting from it.

Second, it is important to distinguish threats of coercion from merely immoral speech. When you threaten me, you tell me that you do not intend to interact rightfully with me in the future unless my behavior is of a certain kind. Simply uttering a threat does not deprive me of anything that is mine, of course, but if you are serious and have the ability to harm me—if you really are threatening me—then you intend to back up your words with physical force. Hence, when you threaten me, you are neither uttering "empty words" nor are you taking yourself to be doing so. For example, assume that instead of yielding to your threat, I begin to walk away. You then move forward to block my retreat. This signals your intention to follow through with the threat. In fact, you might engage in other acts to signal that the threat is not empty. Perhaps you crush my hat under your foot or take a baseball bat to my car. In cases like these the words contained in the threat no longer function merely as speech but take on the role of communicating the intention to wrong me unless my behavior is of a certain kind. Hence, threats are not considered mere speech on this view.

Third, speech must be distinguished from uses of words that debilitate others in virtue of their causal effect on their human bodies. After all, some words are communicated by means of sound waves, which exist in space and time and hence can have coercive power in relation to human bodies. For example, I believe that this account affirms the view that if your words debilitate another's physical functioning, whether intentionally or unintentionally, there is legal wrongdoing. If you are standing on the edge of a cliff, and I sneak up behind you and say "Boo!", I am responsible for the consequences. In this case, it is the effect of the noise on your body, the effect on your body of the noise having surprised or startled you, rather than the word ('boo') that hinders your external freedom, namely by hindering your choice to stay on the edge of the cliff. In the same vein, playing Herbjørg Kråkevik's latest album extremely loudly out the windows of my house night and day—say, to enlighten my frustratingly ignorant neighbors about contemporary Norwegian folk music—has the debilitating effect that those close by cannot concentrate on work, relax, or sleep. Ultimately, the extremely loud music will result in their inability to function physically. In this case my speech clearly deprives others of what is theirs, namely the functioning of their bodies, due to the stress created by being subject to constant, high levels of noise. Nevertheless, it is not the words or their content as such that constitutes my wrongdoing, but the noise. The point is that when an act that involves speech significantly affects another human being's physical ability to set and pursue ends with their own means, that act is coercive; it hinders another human beings' external freedom.[34] And note that this is fully consistent with Kant's general

---

[34] The analysis changes if the music is not extremely loud, but merely annoying or causing inconvenience. In these cases, the sound waves do not have the debilitating effect I describe above. The judgment of particular cases—whether they are merely annoying, debilitating, intentional or non-intentional—falls to the public authority, as we will see shortly.

claim that speech as such cannot be a legal wrong, since the three acts above are each wrong in virtue of features other than, or in addition to, the fact that they are forms of speech.

It is because people typically cannot deprive others of what is theirs by means of speech alone that most immoral uses of words, including lies, do not involve legal wrongdoing. Instead of attaching to immorality in general and lies in particular, legal wrongdoing merely tracks the few instances in which speech alone has coercive power. It should therefore not come as a surprise that the general rule does not protect the liar in instances when lying speech has coercive power: first, lying as part of a contractual negotiation; and, second, defamation and libel. The reason contractual lies have coercive power is that if I lie when I make a contract with you and you believe me, then my intention is to deprive you non-consensually of something that is yours. For example, assuming that were I honest about what you will receive for your hard-earned money, I strongly suspect you would not contract with me, say, to buy swampland in Florida. Thus, by lying I non-consensually deprive you of something that is yours, which as a part of contractual negotiations is a private wrong (MM 6: 238, 238n, 429).[35] I return to this complexity in Chapter 6 when discussing trade in sexual services.

What about defamation and libel; how does it involve coercion? Attempts at defamation and libel also constitute attempts non-consensually to deprive others of what is theirs, namely their good reputations as determined by their actions. As mentioned in the introduction to Part II, according to Kant, one's duty to "*Be an honourable human being.... Rightful honour*... [which] consists in asserting one's worth as a human being in relation to others" (MM 6: 236) corresponds to one's innate right to freedom. To defend one's rightful honor is to defend one's right to be publicly recognized by others solely by the deeds one has performed. One's reputation, Kant explains, "is an innate external belonging" (MM 6: 295); it can originally belong only to the person whose deeds are in question. If others publish falsehoods about the life you have lived, then you have the right and duty to challenge their lies publicly, for your reputation belongs only to you and to no one else. Your reputation is not a means subject to other people's choice; it is not a means that others have a right to manipulate in order to pursue their own ends. To permit this, Kant argues, would be to permit others to use your person as their own means, or to "make yourself a mere means for others" rather than also being "at the same time an end for them" (MM 6: 236). The absence of defamation and libel is necessary for public opinion to be reconcilable with each person's right to freedom and the corresponding duty to be an honorable being.[36]

---

[35] For more on Kant and lying, see Varden (2010a).

[36] In The Doctrine of Right Kant says that defamation is not punishable by "the criminal court," but only by "public opinion, which in accordance with the right of retribution, inflicts on him the same loss of the honor he diminishes in another" (MM 6: 296n). One might be tempted to conclude that Kant rejects the idea that defamation is a legal issue at all. But this would be mistaken, for in MM 6: 295, Kant explicitly confirms that defamation after death can "take effect only in a public rightful condition, but... [it is] not *based* only on its constitution and the chosen statutes in it... [it is] also conceivable *a priori* in the state of nature and must be conceived as prior to such status, in order that laws in the civil constitution may afterwards be adapted to them." Reading defamation to be a legal issue also gains support from this passage

Given the above account of rightful freedom, it is not hard to see that legally responsible persons have a right to make, have, exchange, and use erotica (erotic images) on their own and together with other legally responsible persons. Erotica consists in images and speech and as such does not have coercive (physical) power, and so neither making, nor having, nor sharing erotica among legally responsible adults can, as such, be legally wrong. Although we have set aside for Chapters 6 and 7 the main discussion of the selling and buying of such images, and of the industry that produces many of them, a question we do need to address now is this: if words and images cannot coerce and the general rule is that we can legally say what we want and even lie, why is the *unauthorized* publication of others' words and images—here erotic words and images—a serious legal wrong? Indeed, I will propose that unauthorized publication of private erotic images and speech (such as so-called "revenge porn") should be deemed a particularly serious and heinous act of legal wrongdoing. To justify the claim that it should be a legal wrong to publish another's words and images in unauthorized ways, I appeal to Kant's account of the wrongfulness of unauthorized publishing as well as to a Kant-based account of privacy. To get at a fuller explanation of why unauthorized publication of erotic words and images is particularly heinous, I once again appeal to the importance of incorporating the fact that we make laws not only for any embodied, social, rational beings, but for embodied, social *human* beings with lives of their own to live. For human beings, unauthorized publishing of sexual and erotic speech and images that were intended only for private, intimate use can be emotionally devastating and ungrounding.

There are good reasons why we cannot publish erotic speech, including images, without authorization of the person whose speech or image it is. Kant's essay, "On the Wrongfulness of Unauthorized Publication of Books," provides some of these reasons. In this essay, Kant argues that if we publish another's writings without their authorization (against their will), we wrong the author by undertaking the author's "affairs in . . . [their] name" (WUPB 8: 79f.). More specifically, a publisher of written work is merely the *"mute instrument for delivering the author's speech to the public . . . by printing it,"* which means that it is something that one necessarily does in another's (the author's) name. This is why one can rightfully publish an author's work only insofar as one is authorized by the author to do so. Moreover, Kant emphasizes that simply to have a copy of someone's speech is not thereby to have the right to publish it since a right to publish in another's name is not part of or conferred by a right to the copy of the speech (WUPB 8: 83). Hence, merely to have a copy of someone's writings is not to have a right to publish these writings, including to reprint them. An author's public writings are necessarily "actions" by means of which they address the public in their own name, and if the author has not approved one as

in The Doctrine of Virtue: *"false* defamation . . . [is] to be taken before a court" (MM 6: 466). Consequently, when Kant argues in The Doctrine of Right that defamation cases should not be taken before a criminal court, he should be seen as identifying the proper venue for defamation cases, namely civil (rather than criminal) court. And when Kant says that the punishment should be loss of honor, he means that the main punishment meted out by the civil court is loss of honor by a guilty verdict, though one can presumably also sue for damages as a result of the wrongful defamation.

the publisher of their work, one cannot say that the author speaks through one as their publisher.

In contrast, for Kant, "*works of art*, as things, can be copied or cast from a copy that has been rightfully acquired, and the copies of it can be traded publicly without the consent of the artist who made the original" (WUPB 8: 85). Since works of art are *works* and not actions (by means of which one addresses the public), works of art "can exist on their own" whereas publications "have their existence only in a person" (WUPB 8: 86). Erotica can be viewed as encompassing both categories: it can be speech by means of which one addresses the public, or it can be a work of art that exists on its own. Regardless of which category a piece of erotic writing or an erotic image falls into, in order rightfully to publish or to reproduce it for public consumption, either one must be authorized to publish it (to be someone through which the author addresses the public), or one must have rightfully acquired possession of it as a work of art (e.g., by having bought it or by having been given it as a work of art). Thus, no one ever has the right to originally publish or reproduce a piece of erotic writing or an erotic image without the author's or artist's authorizing consent; that someone else has been entrusted with access to the writing or the images in a private or intimate context is not such authorization.

To boot, once we acknowledge the human temptation to publicize privately shared erotica (e.g., the temptation to publish "revenge-porn"), and the typically devastating effects of this on the person whose private writing or image has been made public, we can capture why laws in free societies not only should criminalize the unauthorized publication of private erotica but should treat it as a particularly heinous crime. That is to say, all embodied, social rational beings can be seen as having a right to privacy, and having such a right is commonly emotionally very important to human beings since we need personal spaces in which we can flourish safely as the sexual, loving persons we are and where we can strive to improve and live in better ways. Alternatively, on the Kantian interpretation of angels we met in Chapter 1, such imaginary beings cannot be thought of as having a right to privacy—nor would they need it. Kant's interpretation of various religious writings on angels sees them as possible beings that are neither embodied nor have animality nor set ends of their own. Angels must be thought of as only having the social aspects of "humanity," which is why such beings do not have a right to and would not need privacy. Such imaginable beings cannot be viewed as embodied or having *personal* projects of animality, humanity, and personality, let alone the projects of integrating, transforming, and continuously seeking to become emotionally and morally better beings. Angels must be thought of as acting on maxims where their ends are set by the Divinity, namely to deliver various messages to humans from the Divinity. Correspondingly, such beings do not have external use of choice (external freedom) nor could they experience imperatives (because they do not have animality), including internal calls for moral improvement (personality as revealed in a conscience). In contrast, embodied, social rational beings that can be responsible for their actions do have a right to privacy—to a space that is only one's own—and beings that also have an animality need it very much. Indeed, even ideal kinds of human beings such as saints—imperfect beings who have lives of their own to live but dispositions only for good—have a right to and need privacy no matter how good and "rechtliebend" (right-loving) they may be (MM 6: 312). The rest of us—who also have real struggles with the propensity to evil—need it a lot.

To expand on these latter points, it is important to emphasize that the feelings and emotions that are intimately connected with our animality and the self-recognitional aspects of our sociality are not simply under the direct control of our reason; they are also parts of us that we can and do stimulate by means of erotica, which is why protecting them is particularly important.[37] We can be ungrounded or undone—not know how to move on or what to do—by things that affect our animality, such as deaths of loved ones, or by things that affect the social aspects of our humanity, such as the shame (an inherently social emotion that disempowers us) we can feel if someone publishes an image of us that was intended for intimate, private, sexual or erotic use only. It is because of the important existential role of these animalistic and social emotions and their partially unreflective nature (and related sheer psychological strength) in human lives lived well, that we need to take care around them. In addition, because of our liability to do bad things, and because these animalistic and social aspects of us are emotionally strong, unruly, and have inherently unreflective elements, they are morally dangerous. We can be tempted to develop these animalistic and social aspects of ourselves in bad ways, with resulting bad actions. The existence of "revenge porn" shows how someone who is unable to handle a breakup can be tempted to make intimate, erotic images of their ex-partner publicly available online. Violating another's privacy in this way can hurt them immensely and can radically disempower and damage them because it takes away their control of who sees how they reveal themselves in intimate spheres, including to loved ones. Besides, because assuming moral responsibility—including by repairing and developing our embodied, emotional selves in good ways—is such a challenging, slow, never-ending, and personal project, we never outgrow the need for privacy; indeed, the more we mature, the more we appreciate its importance. Finally, it is because these animalistic and social aspects of ourselves are both very emotionally powerful and unruly that it is particularly mean-spirited to disrespect the boundaries set by privacy and why, as we will see below, the law should treat such behavior as particularly heinous. Again, this is not to deny that imaginary, morally responsible, embodied beings that have neither animality, personal projects, nor a liability to act in bad ways would have a right to privacy; it is rather to emphasize the importance of it for *human* beings.

To sum up, given the Kantian account of human nature in Part I, including our propensity for evil, it is not surprising that people use erotica in good and bad ways. On the one hand, given human beings' animalistic and social sense of self, erotic images are, for many, a playful and even empowering source of sexual stimulation. On the other hand, human beings also have a propensity to evil, which makes sexual relations, including the use of erotica, emotionally and morally challenging and even dangerous. Erotica can be also addictive since, like most forms of addictive stimuli, using it can become an easy way to experience intense, yet simple and immature

---

[37] I take it that one way in which erotica can be self-damaging would be to develop what Kant calls "passions" in relation to it, meaning that being stimulated by erotica is the only way in which one can engage in sexual or erotic activities, in which case it hinders one's project of integrating, transforming, and developing one's enjoyment of sexual activity. For more on angels, passions, and saints, see Chapter 3.

pleasures, and to escape one's project of emotional, sexual, and moral improvement. Similarly, the fear of sexuality and intimacy can express itself as extreme anger against the use of sexual images, and hence other people's enjoyment of erotica as such can make one feel powerless, which in turn can make one angry with those who use it. Therefore, emotionally healthy and morally good uses of erotica do not come easily. In addition, human history is characterized by many kinds of oppression (sexism, racism, heterosexism, etc.) that find expression in erotic images and speech, and so when used uncritically, erotica can reinforce and perpetuate oppressive patterns of behavior. I do not think, however, that beyond enforcing age limits that shield people from exposure to erotica until they can assume moral (ethical and legal) responsibility for their own sexuality, the law can outlaw having, making, or using of it. From the point of view of law, responsibility for the emotional and moral challenges of using erotica in empowering and playful ways must lie with each individual and us as a society. This does not mean, however, that just states will not have laws in place to regulate the production and public display of erotica—as it does for sex work generally. The nature of such laws is addressed in Chapters 6 and 7.

3. Concluding Remarks

The most important task for a theory of justice is to delineate legitimate from illegitimate types of coercion—whether by individuals or by states. To do this we need a criterion of distinguishing between the two (legitimate and illegitimate uses of coercion); an account of to whom these principles apply, how to accommodate the fact of human phenomenology in the law; and examples of actions/behaviors that fall on either side of the line, all of which is what I have tried to provide above. As we have seen, all uses of coercion must be reconcilable with each person's right to freedom, and ultimately no private person has a right to use coercion against another without thereby doing (at least formal) wrong. It also follows from the arguments made in this chapter that no one can ever obtain a right to have sex with another person, just as no one has the right coercively to prevent abortion and non-procreative sexual interaction (including as it involves erotica) authorized by consent; any such restrictions, aside from regulating timing (abortion) or age or ability to consent (sexual interactions), are irreconcilable with each person's innate right to freedom.

We have also seen that there are two reasons why laws that disrespect our bodily integrity in the ways that much abortion, sodomy, and obscenity legislation does involve a graver form of injustice than many other unjust laws. Because our bodies and legal personhood are analytically related, using sexual force against others' bodies, using force so that they remain pregnant against their will, or denying them the possibility to have consensual, non-procreative sex with one another, or to subject another to punishment for having done so, is to deprive them of inter-action consistent with their legal personhood. Furthermore, by upholding such laws, states thereby fail to establish themselves as public authorities with regard to abortion and sexual activity. That is, they fail to represent all and yet no one in particular by positing, applying, and enforcing only laws that enable their citizens to interact in ways that are reconcilable with each citizen's innate right to freedom. Instead such states allow its legal-political machinery to be a means through which some private persons subject other persons' freedom to their arbitrary, private choices about what lives to live and thereby force those subjected to such violence to fend for themselves against inherently unjust, barbaric uses of force. Finally, because the persons subjected to such barbaric violence are *human* beings, it dehumanizes and can unground them by making life feel impossible to live as who one is. Denying people their basic rights to bodily integrity, speech, and privacy in the ways that abortion, sodomy, and obscenity laws traditionally have done in most legal-political frameworks and still is done in many countries are therefore particularly serious (barbaric) cases of state failures to provide basic conditions of rightful freedom for all its citizen.

6

Private Right
Marriage and Trade in Sexual Services

Introduction

Why do same-sex couples want to marry? Indeed, why does anybody want to marry; why do we not just love each other instead? Given the bad history of marriage, especially for women, should we not simply want to avoid or dismantle this institution altogether? And if we do marry, must marriage and sexual love be only between two persons, and do marriage contracts have to be so all-encompassing and combine both legal and personal, including religious ceremonies? Also, should the sale of sexual services and goods be legally permitted, and should it be permitted as well, or even especially, when the ones providing the services and images are predominantly poor (or otherwise seriously struggling) and/or oppressed women and/or sexually oppressed minorities? These are some of the increasingly prominent questions in both public discourse and academic discussions in feminist philosophy and the philosophy of sex and love over the last few decades. This chapter utilizes Kant's account of private right—more specifically status right and contract right—to provide accounts of marriage and trade in sexual services grounded on Kant's innate right to freedom. Moreover, while Chapter 5 focused on rights analytically (internally) connected with our innate right to freedom, in focusing on private right, this chapter analyzes rights synthetically (externally) connected with our innate right to freedom; it focuses on principles by means of which we can obtain legal claims on persons and things *distinct from* or *external to* us. The general claim defended is that the just state acts as a public enabler and guarantor for both domestic and contract relations (private right), meaning that the just state makes possible legally rightful claims regarding marriage and trade in sexual services.

After exploring Kant's position on domestic right ("status relations"), I argue that denying people in same-sex or symmetrical polyamorous relationships the right to marry is to deprive them of their right to establish a rightful, shared, personal domestic sphere—a legally recognized home—together with others as their equal(s). This account additionally gives us good reasons to question the recent suggestion—from Kantians and others—that it would be better to replace the all-encompassing marriage rights with more limited, "à la carte" contracts regarding aspects of our domestic or personal lives. I also argue that although Kant's arguments address only issues of freedom in providing a general framework for understanding the legal aspects of marriage, for human beings it is wise, but not necessary, for the legal marriage ceremony to integrate religious or personal practices. In section 2, I argue

Sex, Love, and Gender: A Kantian Theory. Helga Varden, Oxford University Press (2020). © Helga Varden.
DOI: 10.1093/oso/9780198812838.001.0001

that Kant's account of rightful contract relations shows that there is nothing legally impermissible about consensual trade in sexual services as such; yet such contracts cannot be viewed as giving an enforceable right to have sex with another person.

Throughout, the aim is to demonstrate that Kant's relational conception of justice entails that legally enforceable claims regarding sexual deeds are fully justifiable only insofar as they are determined and enforced by a public authority whose uses of coercion are justified and delimited by principles of freedom consistent with each citizen's right to freedom. In addition, I show how to accommodate distinctly *human* concerns within this framework set by legal principles of rightful external freedom so as to enable societies characterized by rightful, human freedom. This chapter also sets the stage for Chapter 7, which attends to the morally problematic asymmetries that characterize marriages and trade in sexual services and goods insofar as they involve oppressed sexual or gendered identities and orientations.

1. Reconsidering Kant's Account of Marriage

Kant's explicit discussion of enforceable legal claims with respect to domestic sexual relations is found in his account of "Personal Right Akin to Right concerning Corporeal Things" (MM 6: 276), or what he also calls "status relations." Kant enumerates three types of status relations: those arising when parents obtain children, when husbands obtain wives, and when families obtain servants (MM 6: 277; cf. LE 27: 642).[1] At first glance it is puzzling why Kant puts these three relations in the same category: what, if anything, makes him think that there is a similarity or link between these apparently very different relations? In my view, Kant considers these relationships similar to one another and distinct from all other legal relationships in that they are about legally enforceable claims concerning the private life of another person. This is why Kant explains that a status relation is a relation between persons in which one person has the right to "make arrangements" affecting another person's private life (MM 6: 259), why he argues that status relations concern "what is mine or yours *domestically*" (MM 6: 259), and why claims that the right to make arrangements for another is the "most personal" of all rights (MM 6: 277). In fact, one of Kant's more remarkable claims is that this *personal* kind of right, or this type of "possession" can be analyzed neither as a right "to a thing [property right] . . . [n]or a right against a person [contract-right]" (MM 6: 277). This is because property right cannot capture that it is *a person* who is the "external object" of possession, and contract right cannot capture how "personal" rights result in one person obtaining legal standing or status in relation to how *another* person conducts their own private life. Therefore, neither property nor contract right (neither rights to things nor rights to services) can provide the framework with which to analyze this type of right.

It is not hard to understand why property right cannot be the mode through which to analyze the marital relation between husbands and their wives. After all, if it were, then we would possess persons as things, which, as we saw in Chapter 5, would be to deprive them of rights all together. But why can we not analyze marriage simply as

---

[1] For a fuller discussion of Kant's category of status relations, see Varden (2012a, 2020b).

any other contractual relation? The reason, Kant suggests, is that a contractual analysis of marriage would make the marriage contract into a slave contract, which is also why Kant argues that in status relations consent cannot do the legitimating work it does in contracts.[2] The problem is that status relations give rights *to* persons rather than rights *against* persons, which in Kant's times meant "a *man* acquires a *wife*" and thereby obtains legal standing with regard to how his wife lives her private life. As we saw in Chapter 5, a person cannot give authorizing consent to enter into a relation in which their own legal person is no longer subject to their own choice but rather to another person's arbitrary choice. Such asymmetrical subjection is slavery. Therefore, even if a woman consented to subject herself (her private life) to her husband's arbitrary choices in this way, their agreement cannot be legally recognized as an enforceable contract as it would necessarily be void. To restate, wives are legally responsible persons, and their consent is necessary for rightful relations. Yet their consent to give their husband standing with regard to their private lives is insufficient to give rise to legally enforceable claims. The problem is not only that wives perform a rather open-ended set of (morally permissible) tasks that can be loosely understood as supporting their husbands. And the problem is not only that wives are legally bound to assist their husbands *themselves*, in the sense that wives cannot sub-contract their tasks of loving and caring for their husbands to others in the same way that, for example, a carpenter can hire another carpenter to fulfill their contractual obligations for them. Rather, the reason why the kinds of agreements constitutive of domestic relations are classified by Kant as belonging to the category of *status* is that husbands obtain legally enforceable claims to the private lives of their wives; they acquire the right to partially dictate the framework within which another sets her own ends. Through marriage the husband obtains a certain legal status within his wife's private life: that she shares a home, including her sexual life, with him only and that he has a say about how that home is to function. Such a (status) right analyzed under contract right is tantamount to a slave contract. Therefore, status relations regulated by contract right are not legally enforceable; they are necessarily void and enforcing them is necessarily wrong.

The first step, then, to make such "status" relations rightful, Kant's suggestion is, is to make the legal claims between the persons *reciprocal*. Husbands and wives therefore must have legal claims to *each other's* person. It cannot, in other words, be the case that only the husband obtains standing with regard to his wife's private life. The wife must obtain the same standing with respect to her husband; she also obtains a right to share a home (not be abandoned), to fidelity, and to have a say in which ends will be set in the home and pursued using the family's shared means. Giving husbands and wives reciprocal claims to each other's person is the only way in which provisionally to secure both parties' rights to freedom. Only through marriage can the husband obtain legal standing to the *person* of his wife, because marriage gives the wife the same rights to the person of the husband. Only through marriage can two legally responsible persons give each other legal standing

---

[2] My interpretation here is consistent with the writings of Herman (1993b) and Ripstein (2004) in that they also emphasize that the problem Kant addresses in status relations cannot be solved by appealing to consent.

within each of their private spheres or become a legally recognized personal "us." The open-ended subjection of one's private life to the choices of another that occurs in unifying one's private life and home with another require reciprocal subjection to each other's choices. The marriage contract achieves this reciprocity between spouses by giving each the same standing with respect to how they now set ends with their rightful means, which comprises important decisions regarding their bodies, their causal powers, and their shared private property.

More specifically, in marriage two private spheres are unified into one rightful domestic sphere by providing the following three conditions: First, the spouses' previous personal property and titles become common private property and titles. This is why Kant argues that the "morganatic marriage," meaning a marriage in which one party does not get all the titles, privileges, and estates of the other party, is not a rightful marriage. Kant argues a marriage of this kind is unjustifiable because it "takes advantage of the inequality of estate of the two parties to give one of them domination over the other" (MM 6: 279; cf. LE 27: 641).[3] A rightful marriage requires that the two parties share each other's means fully—with no such restriction. Their common private property is subject to their choices as a couple. This is also why Kant rejects the rightfulness (in the sense of enforceability) of concubine contracts. Such a contract, Kant states,

> would be a contract to *let* and *hire*… a member for another's use, in which, because of the inseparable unity of members in a person, she would be surrendering herself as a thing to the other's choice. Accordingly, either party can cancel the contract with the other as soon as it pleases without the other having grounds for complaining about any infringements of its rights. (MM 6: 279)

Second, marriage achieves a rightful domestic sphere by each spouse giving the other legal standing with regard to how they use their causality, namely with respect to decisions concerning how to organize their individual work and leisure time. By marrying, persons give one another a right to know about and often have a say in choices that affect their shared life so that each is able to have a private life with the other in a way agreeable to both. For example, the two persons also authorize each other to know about and participate in what otherwise are strictly personal decisions, say, decisions concerning one's own health.

Third, the spouses in a rightful marriage are under a legal obligation to restrict all their sexual activities to each other (MM 6: 278f.). Prior to marriage, there is no legal wrongdoing when one partner engages in sexual relations with a person other than their partner, but after marriage decisions concerning either partner's sexuality become shared decisions. So, Kant argues that adultery legally wrongs one's spouse—and, so, presumably, provides a legal ground for divorce, the settlement of which favors the non-adulterer. For example, one may reasonably argue that the person who has not committed adultery has the first claim to the shared home (since it is the adulterer who violated the marriage contract), and that the violated party also

---

[3] For example, the British Royal House considered whether or not Prince Charles should form a morganatic marriage with Camilla Parker-Bowles. Like the argument presented here, they decided against it, since it would not be a marriage of equals.

has a right to damages. It also seems that this position is consistent with sexual practices such as "open" (non-exclusive) marriages, as long as the decision whether or not to engage with other sexual partners is agreed upon by the spouses. It is one of the many things about which married persons—in virtue of marrying—have made a legally significant commitment to each other, namely to work these things out together.

It is also important to note that Kant's account recognizes marital rape as a criminal act. Remember from Chapter 5 that a lack of authorizing consent always makes sexual interactions wrongful; nothing Kant says about marriage changes this fundamental claim. Rather, Kant's conception of marriage is driven by the concern that consent alone cannot give rise to legally enforceable claims to one's consensual sexual partner. It is implausible, therefore, to think that Kant considers consent *after* marriage superfluous. What Kant wants to establish are the ways in which we can consensually "make use" of one another's bodies and have legal claims that involve them—such as not to be abandoned or to have legal claims rooted in adultery— without thereby disrespecting one another's innate right to freedom. Thus, spouses are never entitled to use coercion to obtain access to each other's sexual organs; the only thing that suffices to gain rightful access within the marital setting, as within any other setting, is continuous, authorizing consent. That this is the philosophically most convincing position, and the most plausible reading of Kant, is supported by Kant's argument that being married does not mean that one has a right to have sexual intercourse. He says that if two persons marry with the "awareness that one or both [partners] are incapable of it [sexual intercourse]," then the contract is not legally binding. However, he continues, "if incapacity appears only afterwards, that right cannot be forfeited through this accident for which no one is at fault" (MM 6: 279; cf. 426). Here it is reasonable to interpret Kant as arguing that marriage does not give rise to a right to sexual services from one's partner. Rather, Kant argues that one remains legally obliged to stay sexually faithful towards one's partner *even if* they discover after being married that one party is incapable of enjoying sexual activities and therefore does not want to engage in them.[4]

In the three ways briefly outlined above (joint decision-making regarding bodies, causality, and private property), two persons when marrying unite their previous, separate domestic spheres into a single domestic unit under their mutual control.[5] Decisions regarding where to live, sexual enjoyment, health, career, and private property become decisions subject to their joint deliberations. In my view, the better interpretation of the Kantian position will defend a person's right to divorce, but this does not change the fundamental claim that, *as* married, persons have unified their domestic lives in such a way that important decisions which impact them both are not for one spouse to make unilaterally.

---

[4] This is not to deny that marrying comes with expectations of reciprocal caring for the other, of wanting and working to make the other happy, which in this imagined case could result in the person who does not enjoy sexual activity allowing the person who does enjoy sexual activity to enjoy it with others.

[5] This is consistent with the home being split between two or more residences; it just means that insofar as these residences are residences, all spouses should be on all the titles as no home can be sold without all spouses' consent.

Though the reciprocal claims engendered through marriage make up rightful relations between husband and wife, rightful relations are not thereby realized. The problem is that marriage contracts are not rightfully *enforceable* in the state of nature. The reason is that within the conceptual framework of the state of nature (a pre-state condition), there is no person outside of a particular status relation with rightful authority to intervene in it. When there is disagreement about whether the parties are acting in accordance with the marriage contract, more than likely the stronger person in the relationship becomes the judge. Without a public authority to act as a "civil guardian" of the parties in status relations, it is impossible to ensure that their domestic relationship is rightful rather than one where might rules. The basic problem is not just that the terms of such contracts are indeterminate, namely, that it is impossible to determine exactly the rightful boundaries concerning choices that affect the common domestic sphere. Rather, the trickier problem with ensuring the rightfulness of domestic relations is that the contracts are open-ended and personal. And because they are open-ended and personal, it is impossible, in the state of nature, to characterize the distinction between rightful and wrongful end-setting in status relations (beyond what is determined by respect for bodily integrity) since there is no position outside of these private relations from which one can have standing to evaluate their end-setting. In this condition, there exist only self-contained private domestic spheres, and no one outside of such a private sphere has rightful standing to evaluate whether or not the ends they set for each other within this private sphere are reasonable. The problem, therefore, is not one of determining what the contract involves, although that might also be problematic; the problem is one of rightful uses of coercion within the contract, namely within the domestic relation. Again, as we know from Chapter 5, such coercion is never rightfully used on the persons themselves—doing so is always only wrong. Coercion is acceptable only with respect to which ends to set with their shared means, and since there is no one objective answer about which ends to set, there is no possibility in the state of nature of a rightful solution to such domestic conflicts: the person who decides to enforce their decision will subject their partner to their arbitrary choice, whereas the one who lets the other have it their way will subject themself to their partner's arbitrary choice. There is therefore no rightful solution to marital, domestic conflicts in the state of nature. Because there is no rightful coercion, there can be no rightful domestic relation in the state of nature; at best there can be provisionally rightful relations or relations devoid of injustice, which will occur when there happens—accidentally— never to be any disagreements between the partners.

To establish domestic right there must be a public person with the appropriate standing to determine boundaries on unilateral choices and to adjudicate disputes among adults sharing a domestic sphere. Only a public authority can have this standing, since only a public person can represent the will of each spouse and yet the will of no one (including no one else) in particular, and hence make rightfully enforceable decisions when conflicts arise between the two parties. A private third person cannot be designated to adjudicate and enforce domestic right since no private individual can enjoy the requisite standing to coercively enforce rights. And consent cannot do the work of establishing such appropriate standing of the third party, since, as we have seen, the contractual subjection of one's private sphere to the decisions of another private person is, essentially, a slave-contract. The appeal to an impartial private individual to settle domestic disputes merely replicates and complicates rather than solves the original problem of legally enforceable claims involving the private lives of persons.

The only way to solve these problems, then, is by giving marriage a public institutional setting. That is, a public authority is a necessary condition for enforceable domestic (marriage) rights, because only by constituting a *public* authority with standing in domestic relations can there be legally enforceable claims between spouses. The solution is the establishment of a public authority because only it is non-contingent in that it represents the united will of interacting, private persons (and no one else), and only it enables the symmetrical subjection of individuals to a law that can resolve their conflicts. Because the public institution of marriage can yield lawful restrictions upon the married couple consistent with treating each of them as free and equal, it can generate those enforceable claims with regard to the spouses' domestic sphere that are necessary for rightful domestic relations (MM 6: 277f.). Civil society is therefore an enforceable precondition for domestic right because it is the means through which we enable the possibility of rightful domestic relations involving a legally shared, personal home with others as free and as our equals. Only through a marriage that is authorized and enforced by a public authority in its role as a civil guardian with regard to domestic relations are both domestic partners subject to coercively enforceable restrictions regarding their shared personal life. The public authority specifies the content of marriage laws and as the civil guardian of domestic right it establishes those institutions necessary to ensure that all domestic relations are rightful. For example, the public authority can determine which contracts (such as those regarding loans and the selling or buying of property) require each spouse's authorization, what kind of information (such as medical information) spouses have a right to know about each other, and so on. That is to say, it is impossible, to specify a priori exactly how the state fulfills its role as civil guardian in all historical circumstances; the only thing we can say a priori is that it must set up legal-political institutions by which it endeavors to fulfill its role of enabling legal homes between free and equal partners and which kinds of laws are among likely candidates.

Kant's position on the rightfulness of domestic relations, correctly understood, then, sheds some much needed light on what most take to be three very puzzling arguments in Kant's discussion of private right with regard to husbands and wives. First, most interpreters think that Kant's position entails that in order to justify rightful sexual relations between two persons, they must marry.[6] The reason is that sexual relations are considered immoral, and the only remedy is marriage, which amounts to reciprocal sexual exploitation. The puzzle is, as Herman notes so succinctly, that it is unclear why Kant would think *reciprocal* sexual exploitation makes an otherwise immoral act okay. Second, as Howard Williams (1983: 117) points out,

---

[6] This is a common objection to Kant's conception of marriage. For example, see Nussbaum (1999); Singer (2000); Soble (2002).

an important premise of Kant's argument is that sexual relations necessarily involve treating oneself and one's partner as things. But there is no reason at all, why this premise should be accepted. And, indeed, to demonstrate convincingly that marriage is the only ethically desirable context for sex, Kant ought to start from better premises than these.

The problem with Kant's argument, according to Williams, is that it seems to rest on a rather grim view of sexual relations, and there is no good reason to accept this premise. And as we have seen earlier, Jordan Pascoe, Rae Langton, and many Kantians agree with Williams here; after all, there is caring, loving, generous, playful, etc., sex. Consequently, Kant's argument that only marriage can make sexual relations moral rests on rather shaky ground if this is the ground.[7] Third, because Kant argues that a husband is fully entitled to bring his wife back "under his control" (MM 6: 278) if she runs away, it seems that upon marrying, a husband obtains something close to private ownership of his wife. If marriage is supposed to solve the problem of treating others as things, then, clearly, arguing that the marriage relation is a private property relation cannot be the solution.

My interpretation of Kant's understanding of rightful domestic relations can solve these three interpretive puzzles by bringing together the following points. First, we have seen that Kant's entire position is motivated by the thought that it is incorrect to try to analyze marriage in terms of private property. Therefore, we must understand the relation between two persons in marriage to be different from the relation a person has to a thing they own. Second, we have also seen that any rightful access to another person's body *always* requires authorizing consent. Kant's account of marriage neither contradicts nor alters this fundamental claim, which underscores the important point that marriage is not needed to make sexual deeds rightful as such. Hence, none of this entails that consensual sexual relations outside of marriage in civil society should be illegal.[8] It merely means that they cannot give rise to any legally enforceable claims, since such claims require marriage—and so concubine contracts, for example, do not contain enforceable claims to the other person (they lack the required reciprocity with respect to one another's person that characterize rightful status relations). Rather, the public institution of marriage is needed in order for an agreement between two persons to share a personal life to give rise to a rightful domestic sphere understood as a legally recognized, shared home and legal standing within each other's personal lives. Legal, public marriage is required to make sure that the shared domestic sphere is free of unjustifiable power relations and is one in which there are reciprocal enforceable claims to mutually control their shared private life. Rightful marital relations therefore require two things: reciprocal rights to one another's person (private right) and the establishment of a public authority with standing in the relationship (public right).

What exactly does Kant mean, then, when he asserts that a husband is entitled to bring his wife back "under his control"? In part, the point of Kant's argument is that within the conceptual framework of private right, there is a deep sense in which the

---

[7] See also earlier chapters on this point on what (good) sex is both as a matter of interpretation of Kant and of the Kantian position.

[8] Kant does seem to think that sexual relations outside of marriage are unethical, but, as we have seen in previous chapters, that is a separate issue.

husband who forcibly brings his wife back under his control is simply upholding their marriage agreement. By marrying, they agreed to share a domestic sphere, and consequently the wife cannot simply abandon her spouse when what she perceives as a better opportunity comes along. The better reading of Kant, however, never loses sight of the fact that he makes this comment about the husband fetching back the wife within his discussion of private right *in the state of nature* where there is no public institution of marital law. Thus, it is crucial also to notice that Kant ends this discussion of private right by saying that if both parties choose to stay and fight it out in the state of nature, they do not wrong one another, but they do wrong in the highest degree (MM 6: 307). Consequently, if the husband chooses to enforce his domestic rights against his wife (not to be abandoned) in the state of nature rather than to enter civil society where their disagreements can be adjudicated in a court of (family) law, he not only does wrong in the highest degree, but he additionally wrongs his wife by subjecting her to unilateral and unjustifiable violence. That is to say, *conclusively* (rather than merely provisionally) rightful marital relations are possible only in civil society, and since in the state of nature the husband has not entered into truly rightful relations with his wife, this means that he does not have the right to *enforce* his rights against her. The problem, then, is that there is no rightful resolution to conflicts in marriages in the state of nature. Because there is no public authority, there is no one with the standing to judge whether a right has been infringed. And one person unilaterally enforcing their own judgment as to whether or not their rights have been infringed amounts to wrongdoing, since the potential wrongdoer has become the judge in their own case. Therefore, once we understand that marriage can make domestic relations between husbands and wives rightful only in civil society, we see that the three puzzles are solved: rightful sexual relations require reciprocity because obligations corresponding to rights *to* other persons must be reciprocal; the immorality of sexual deeds is irrelevant to the marriage argument; and the full argument concerning "fetching back one's wife" also highlights the wrongfulness (in the highest degree) of such violence rather than simply explaining the general, private provisional wrongfulness of abandoning one's spouse.

If we discount Kant's personal discomfort with non-cis, non-heterosexual, and non-monogamous practices, this interpretation of his philosophical position on marriage gives us the resources to explain why it is so important that same-sex couples obtain the right to marry. Essentially, if same-sex couples are not given the right to marry, then they are also not given access to laws constitutive of a rightful legal personal, domestic "us," and they are also not given legal protection against many types of domestic wrongdoing in their shared, personal homes. By denying same-sex couples the right to marry, the state forces their relationship to stay in the state of nature and thereby denies them access to (legal) ways of sharing personal lives in the domestic setting that are reconcilable with their innate right to freedom. Since without a right to marry, same-sex couples have no legal claims to one another as spouses, continuous authorizing consent with regard to each action institute the end of their legal rights with respect to each other. This means that it is impossible for same-sex couples to unify their private lives into homes without thereby subjecting each member of the couple to the other's unilateral decisions regarding the most intimate and important aspects of their personal lives. It means that when one party no longer consents to let their private life be under their reciprocal control, or no longer wants to disclose important information concerning how they conduct their private life, or simply wants to quit the agreement, the other party has no legal claims to them beyond what everyone else has too. When same-sex couples are denied the right to legal marriage, they are forced to stay in a state of nature where it is impossible for them to avoid subjecting one another to a kind of unilateral use of force that only a public institution of marriage can overcome.[9] Or to put the point positively, by being denied a right to marry, same-sex couples are precluded from the possibility of respecting their co-habiting partner's right to independence with regard to their shared private home, since it is impossible for them together to create a rightful common private sphere (a personal legal us of which a shared home is a constituent part) or to enjoy rightful domestic relations.

I have defended Kant's claim that marriage contracts are different in kind from other contracts and that to treat them simply as standard contracts is to fail to capture the *open-ended* and *personal* nature of the marriage contract. An alternative is to argue that there is nothing essentially different about the marriage contract and that to deny same-sex couples the right to marry is simply to deny them equal contract rights. As we have seen, a problem with this alternative argument is that if marriage contracts are treated just like any other contract, then the open-endedness and personal character of their terms makes traditional marriage contracts like slave contracts, which undercut the very possibility of rightful relations. One might agree with my analysis and argue that rather than maintaining the position that same-sex couples should have the same right to marry as do heterosexual couples, no one should have the right to marry in the traditional sense; the all-encompassing marriage institution should be decomposed into smaller, less inclusive contracts. But this strategy does not escape unscathed, as we will see below.

1.1 Polyamorous Marriage

The above account of marriage focuses on the right to marry one other person, but what about polyamorous marriages? On my Kantian account the main problem with the historically dominant forms of polyamorous marriages is their gendered asymmetries: they have tended to be marriage contracts according to which the husband gets a full (100 percent) claim to each of his several wives, whereas each wife gets 1/Nth of a claim to the husband, where N is the number of wives and is a number that changes with the husband's related decisions. Kant maintains, accordingly, that the problem with traditional polygamies, in which one man marries several women, is that the woman "who surrenders herself gains only a part of the man who gets her completely, and therefore makes herself into a mere thing" (MM 6: 278). This

---

[9] This point is tragically clear in situations where longstanding same-sex partners who cannot marry are denied the right to make decisions (set ends) for each other in cases of incapacitation due to sickness or impairment. As we know, such gay and lesbian couples have no legally enforceable claims against the families of their partners when sickness or the need for caretaking decisions occurs. Instead, the original family of the sick partner is given legally enforceable rights with regard to the partner, including the right to deny visitation to the healthy partner and the right to decide any other matter deemed in the best interest of the sick partner.

arrangement is therefore problematic because of its asymmetry, because of how this asymmetry correlates with the oppression of women, and finally because of how the wives' legal claims are fundamentally subjected to the arbitrary choices of the husband in that each time the husband unilaterally chooses to marry another wife, the other wives' claims on the husband are reduced (from, say, 1/3rd to 1/4th). I do not know and cannot think of any good, freedom-based arguments by means of which to question this argument.[10] But does accepting it entail that as we reform our states and make them more consistent with their grounding principles of freedom, nothing but monogamous marriages can be legally recognized? I do not think so, but I also do not think that the currently prominent proposal that we rethink marriage as decomposable into various sub-contracts, of which we may choose one or more, paves a way forward either.

To start, insofar as we appeal only to concerns of reciprocal freedom—as we should on an account of justice as rightful freedom—it seems that we have no good reason to limit marriages to unions between two persons only. Surely, caring for and wanting to share a life with just one person at a time does not seem to be the only way human beings love; various forms of polyamorous relationships are not uncommon in human history. It also seems that reasons of freedom do not demand limiting marriage to monogamy. To be sure, loving relations that consist of odd numbers of people, such as full threesomes, do yield the principled problem of two persons against one, but this problem of asymmetry can be solved by the law requiring important decisions to be explicitly authorized by all three persons, not only two. In addition, relationships involving more than two persons certainly have their own sources of instability, but they also have their own sources of stability, so this concern about potential instability of polyamorous marriages does not appear to be a significant, let alone decisive, point either. I therefore do not see that there are any reasons why partners in symmetrical, non-binary relationships should not have a right to marry just as partners in binary relationships do.

In addition, it seems to me that we also do not have good reasons to think of marriage right as decomposable to a bundle of contract rights, of which we may (in a freer future) choose a smaller or larger bundle. Accordingly, I do not find this trend in contemporary writings on marriage—exemplified by Elizabeth Brake's (2012) conception of "minimizing marriage" or Martha C. Nussbaum's (2010) "disaggregating civil unions"—persuasive, although I agree with much of what Brake and Nussbaum say otherwise about sex, love, and gender, such as problems with the historical institution of marriages. The main problem with such minimizing or disaggregated approaches, in my view, is that they allow one person's freedom to be subjected to another's arbitrary, unilateral choice rather than to universal laws of freedom. For the sake of space, let me briefly illustrate this with regard to Nussbaum's account. In the next section, I then turn to another important issue in both her and

---

[10] The best one I know of—I cannot remember if anyone else has already made it, though it is likely that they have—goes like this: we can imagine terrible historical periods in which wars left many widows behind, and in which the prevailing sexism made it impossible for these women to secure their own income. In such conditions, perhaps one way to secure these women's safety would have been to permit asymmetrical polygamies.

many other recent writings on marriage, namely how to make space for the fact that the *human* institution of marriage contains important emotional concerns beyond those captured by laws that only appeals to concerns of freedom.

In *From Disgust to Humanity: Sexual Orientation & Constitutional Law* (2010), Nussbaum argues that if things go well, a "disaggregated," "non-expressive" conception of civil union law will take the place of current marriage law.[11] Her suggestion is that instead of the current system of state issued marriage certificates, in the future the state will simply issue civil union certificates. The main difference between the two is that civil unions do not include a so-called "expressive" element, which is the committed couples' public expression of their "love and commitment in front of witnesses" (2010: 129). This expressive component, Nussbaum suggests, properly belongs only to the private aspect of marriage, which may or may not be a religious ceremony (2010: 162-4). So, in the future the civil union is envisioned as a legally binding contract between two (or more) persons regarding a reciprocal, personal commitment with respect to some aspect of their private lives. In contrast, in the future, "marriage" will refer to the comprehensive institution, which includes the legally binding, civil union as well as the private, non-enforceable promise of personal love and commitment (the expressive element) (2010: 163). Nussbaum furthermore suggests that states will probably want to offer different types of civil union contracts, which will vary with respect to how comprehensive they are or how many aspects of a couple's private lives they include. This is what Nussbaum calls the "disaggregated" element of the suggested civil union law. That is, in the future, liberal governments will want to offer different kinds of legally binding civil union packages, where the "benefits" of any particular package depend on the nature of the personal commitments and relations it includes.[12]

If we use Kant's analysis of marriage right to evaluate the "disaggregated" aspect of this proposal, a first problem is that any one of the contracting parties unilaterally can choose to change the application of the contract. For example, assume that I have a financial contract with one person (my financial partner) and a contract regarding my sexual fidelity with another (my sexual partner). Now, I can unilaterally choose to affect the means available to my financial partner simply by choosing to act contrary to my sexual contract, since my sexual partner presumably gets a claim on my

[11] Nussbaum's analysis in *From Disgust to Humanity* also does not seem to explain why the state should be involved in the business of marrying or creating civil unions at all. As far as I can see, the philosophical position Nussbaum defends entails that the state could and perhaps even should hand the whole business of commitments to join private lives over to the private persons themselves, or to their chosen private organizations, religious or otherwise. In fact, Nussbaum's analysis seems compatible with the state simply not enforcing personal commitments to share private lives. It also seems compatible with state's proper role in a break-up being limited to solving problems of the division of private property in accordance with who owes and owns what.

[12] For example, as Nussbaum (2010: 163) says, "People who share a household may not be sexual partners, and committed sexual partners may have separate finances... Our analysis suggests that constitutional law does not require the state to offer any particular package of benefits. The disaggregated approach would pass constitutional muster if both equal access and due process liberty were sufficiently protected. I believe there are many reasons to favor such disaggregated rethinking, both about the interests that need protection and about the different groups that might receive entitlements."

material means (as compensation for breach of contract). Alternatively, assume I have contracted with one person regarding my sexual fidelity, and then I sign another contract with a second person regarding my personal support and encouragement, and yet another one with a third person regarding my home. Again, I appear to have the right to change the application (or effective terms) of my first contract by signing additional contracts that concern my person (my personal support and encouragement and my shared domicile). By choosing to give two additional people claims to my person, I necessarily become less available to (have sex with) the first person. Another problem is that the unilateral choices of my partners seem to affect my contractual relations with my other partners. For example, assume that the partner with whom I have a contract regarding personal support and encouragement decides to pursue a really difficult path for a while—say a really challenging career—with the implication that I must provide more support and encouragement. As a result, more of my time and energy will be put towards supporting them and less time and energy will be available to increase my wealth, have sex, and take care of my home. The unilateral choice of one of my partners changes the external freedom of my other partners—people with whom no one but I have contracted.

In sum, I do not quite see how more than one person at a time can have legal claims to my person (to my body, including to my sexual or non-sexual company) and shared ownership of my personal belongings in this binary way. But the disaggregated picture seems to require (or at least allow for) exactly this possibility. In addition, even if we can solve this problem, we also need an account of which relation or relations, in principle, should be privileged when actual, including reasonable, disagreements occur between the involved persons. I suspect that it is impossible to solve these problems in a way compatible with freedom defined as everyone having a right to themself (including their body) and their own means and any access or change to their personal freedom (defined as their person and their private means) goes only through their authorizing consent.[13] The underlying reason why it seems impossible is that, as exemplified above, each person's private life or personal freedom can become subjected not only to the unilateral choices of their partner(s) but also to the arbitrary choices of their partners' partners, that is, persons with whom they have not signed any contract. The only way to avoid these problems, I believe, would be to argue that one can enter into only one of these types of partial civil unions at a time. So, if I make a personal, sexual contract with one person, I cannot also make contracts with anyone else to share my encouragement and support, my home, or my finances. The problem with this solution is that it entails that if I make any one of these more limited contracts, in effect I become legally restricted in all my other personal relations too. In sum, the disaggregated picture appears to leave us with a dilemma: either my person (including body) or my material means become subject both to the unilateral choices of those with whom I have contracted and of some with whom I have not (any others with whom any of

---

[13] Merely appealing to the partners' consent will not do here, since we are after restrictions on freedom that are enforceable in principle.

my partners have contracted); or as soon as I choose one of these personal contracts, I thereby also choose never to make any legally binding personal contracts with a third party. So, the disaggregated account of civil unions has the result that the idea of justice as rightful freedom is not preserved.

What about equality? I do not think disaggregated civil unions fare any better here. In the disaggregated scenarios above, the idea is that we become equals in some personal regard, say with respect to sexual fidelity or home-sharing, but not in all regards, say not with respect to personal encouragement and support, or to finances. Now, if we assume that we can make many of these personal contracts, then a person who actually does make several such contracts thereby is in a position where they can choose to be less committed to any one of their partners who makes fewer contracts than they do. After all, the number of personal contracts any one person makes determines how available they and their means are for another. It determines the degree to which they can be legally obligated to another person. If one person has five personal contracts and each of their partners only has one contract, then the person with five contracts gets their partners' full attention in the relevant regard, since there are no in principle competing, legally enforceable contracts. At any given time, each of the partners can (in principle) fulfill 100 percent of their personal contracts. For the person with multiple partners, in contrast, there are competing enforceable contracts that make demands on their private life, which means that at any one time they may only be able to fulfill 1/5th of their personal contractual obligations. And so, the possibility of many disaggregated unions does not secure equality between persons with regard to their private lives. If we choose the other option, according to which we can enter into only one such personal contract, the state would be enforcing contracts between persons who choose to share only one aspect of their private lives. This is, as we know, one of the options that many of the powerful groups of people in history have wanted. Rich men have often not wanted to share their wealth with their wives, and often they have also not wanted to sign sexual fidelity contracts. Instead they have wanted to make only parental and home-sharing agreements. A major problem with such agreements is that the weaker party always gets the short straw: in effect, she does not obtain an equal say in the shared home (after all, she has little or no money of her own); her exit options are limited (as she has little or no money); she has no claim on any wealth creation enabled by their private union (since their private money is separate from the contract); and so on.

These problems of securing the possibility of enforceable contracts regarding shared private lives between free and equal persons are why, I believe, marriage or comprehensive civil union is necessary for private legal unions of two or more persons. Marriage contracts are the means through which two or more persons can unify their private lives into *one* shared private life *as equals*. This is not to deny the usefulness of prenuptial agreements and the like, but it is to argue that their main purpose is to ensure that people do not take advantage of each other by means of marriage, say, by marrying, getting the money, and running, but are seriously committed to sharing a private life together as equals. This is why such prenuptial agreements should have legal expiration dates as, when one marries, the intention is to marry as equals for life.

1.2 Accommodating Human Nature in Marriage Ceremonies and Legal Reasoning Surrounding Sexual Love

In the vast literature on marriage in relation to Kant's philosophy that has been written since Herman's (1993b) groundbreaking article on the issues, there has been a mix of papers on Kant from the point of view of right and those that (also) seek to capture how marriage for human beings are accompanied by deep, practically potent emotions.[14] What should be the proper space for these concerns in a legal-political theory—and, so, in a legal-political system—that seeks to understand and justify rightful coercion in terms of each person's right to freedom? In this section, I illustrate my approach to these questions partly through an engagement with Nussbaum's claim that the "expressive aspect" of the marriage ceremony should be private only (not public), and with her argument that (Supreme Court) judges who evaluate these laws should use their imagination to make sure that the laws they uphold speak to our humanity in the right way. I suggest *pace* Nussbaum that it is neither surprising nor unfortunate that human beings want to integrate an expressive element into the legal ceremony. In addition, although I agree with Nussbaum that Supreme Court justices should humanize laws and their judgments, the arguments that ground their basic decisions regarding whether or not a law must be repealed or changed neither needs to nor should appeal to facts concerning our specifically human phenomenology (humanization). These decisions should appeal only to considerations of reciprocal freedom. Concerns of human phenomenology come in, I suggest, in relation to engaging the heinousness of the wrongdoing involved in a legal system that has upheld laws that dehumanize sexual or gendered minorities. It seems plausible, on the position formulated here, that wise Supreme Court justices (and public leaders in general) recognize the importance of expressing sincere sadness and regret for past wrongdoing against and suffering by those who have been subjected to dehumanizing laws as part of the legal-political process of repealing such laws.

Let me start with Nussbaum's criticism of the legal practice of including an "expressive" element in the marriage ceremony. The expressive aspect of the marriage ceremony is the public expression of mutual love and commitment, which on Nussbaum's view is not necessary to initiate comprehensive civil unions, let alone to initiate disaggregated ones. I think she is right in holding that people may choose not to include this element, but in my view, they should always have a right to insist on doing so. This is because, it seems to me, when *human* (and not merely rational, embodied, social) beings commit to marry each other, they can reasonably be expected to do so out of or with a firm commitment to love one another, as any other reason is unlikely to hold for such an endeavor. As indicated in the previous arguments, I believe there are moral arguments (based in reasons of justice) why marriage is the only way in which the unification of private lives can carry legal obligations. But in my view, our legal traditions are right to make space for people

---

[14] For example, see Holly Wilson (1998); Allegra De Laurentiis (2000); Lara Denis (2001); Kory Schaff (2001); Allan Beever (2003); Donald Wilson (2004); Elizabeth Brake (2005); Jane Kneller (2006); Varden (2007), on which the analysis in this chapter is based; Allen W. Wood (2007); Matthew C. Altman (2010, 2011); Linda Papadaki (2010); Jordan Pascoe (2013, 2015, 2018); and Elizabeth Robinson (2017).

who find that reasons of justice are insufficient to motivate a commitment to marriage. They are insufficient because living together as a married couple without the intention of loving each other affectionately and morally is both very risky and likely self-destructive for human beings, and the law therefore generally allows for a distinctively human emotional element to be part of the ceremony. That is to say, to love someone is to be respectfully, yet affectionately and caringly oriented towards them. To be in a respectful yet affectionately loving relationship involves enabling and furthering an other's (strong) personal sense of self—something, which, if the theory presented in Part I of this book is correct, is impossible for a human being to do unless their basic non-moral and moral feelings about the other are of the right kinds. Indeed, trying to force oneself or others to love another (non-morally or morally) is, as we saw in Chapter 1, impossible; it inevitably leads to self-destructive hatred or, worse, resentment of oneself and the other.

So, marriages that are not based on the firm commitment to both moral and affectionate love are highly susceptible to becoming self- (and other-) destructive. In states that are grounded on a right to freedom, the law can never recognize obligations that require self-destruction or too great a risk of self-destruction. For this reason, it is not puzzling that the legal marriage ceremony includes an element in which the marrying couple expressly affirms their commitment to strive to live in respectful ways with one another (their commitment to morally love), their current affection for one another, and their desire and commitment to strive to keep affectionately and respectfully loving one another. The marriage ceremony provides an opportunity to integrate affectionate and moral love, to express and affirm one's commitment to love and care for one another in the full sense. The promise the partners make is to strive to love and care in such a way that affectionate and moral love keep forming the basis for an integrated practical orientation towards one another as the particular human beings they are.[15] The point is that it is less ideal for the state to authorize a non-loving private union that bears coercively enforceable obligations between human beings because such a union is likely to be self-destructive, and no one can be under a coercively enforceable obligation to destroy oneself.[16] If one cannot honestly commit to both the moral and the non-moral, yet normative, aspects of marriage, then in normal circumstances, it is unwise to marry, as doing so is too risky an undertaking for oneself and the other person. This is why the state's legal marriage ceremony is not antithetical, but typically welcoming of an expressive moment. Again, this does not mean that we cannot envision conditions in which we would marry for reasons other than affectionate love—for instance, we might marry a person to save them from destruction in their country (as marriage to us would give them citizenship in our country). But such marriages are ways of trying to deal with a barbaric world, in which, in fact, the lying involved (in this case by

---

[15] Notice that the account, as it is presented, is compatible with marriages in traditional societies where the parties can first affirm only the *intention* to love—believing that with more time and familiarity, they can and will grow to love one another—even though they have insufficient knowledge of each other to be certain that their belief is correct.

[16] This does not mean that we do not have a right to divorce; indeed, it yields a reason why a right to divorce is important.

proclaiming affectionate love for someone we do not so love) would be formal, but not a material (let alone punishable) wrong.[17]

As mentioned above, in addition to worrying about the expressive element of current marriage ceremonies, Nussbaum has worries about "purely legalistic" conceptions of marriage. She notes, "when cases reach the U. S. Supreme Court, they are usually legally difficult cases, to which formal legal analysis has suggested no unequivocal solution" (2010: xxi). Hence, when difficult constitutional cases are heard by the Supreme Court, Nussbaum continues, the court must employ not only a formal analysis of respect for citizens' freedom and equality, but also "sympathetic imagination and responsiveness to the complexities of another's situation...namely to understand the issues in their historical and cultural setting and with an eye to the human beings they embody" (2010: xxi). This complex combination of respect and responsive, sympathetic imagination is essential to what Nussbaum calls "the politics of humanity." So her argument goes as follows: to deal with the difficult cases in question, Supreme Court justices must first move *from* an unreflective mode of perception—their experience of something as disgusting—*to* the perspective of humanity—a reflective mode that zooms in on a general description of people's actual actions, such as their sexual activity, combined with a general sympathy for human beings in their pursuit of happiness. The justices must then use their imagination to see that the activity that might have unreflectively struck them as disgusting is actually one possible way in which respectful (non-harmful) sexual activity can be engaged in and, in fact, is for some the only meaningful way. Thus, Nussbaum advocates judges' active use of respectful, responsive, sympathetic imagination when considering how legally to relate to the ways in which various minority groups, such as gays and lesbians, pursue happiness.

It is important to emphasize that although Nussbaum worries about purely formal legalistic arguments, she does not reject the importance and persuasiveness of legalistic arguments in their own right. On the contrary, she provides convincing formal legal arguments regarding both private and systemic issues related to our sexuality. For example, along with Mill she argues that consensual voluntary sexual interaction and personal commitments that are important to people's pursuit of happiness and cause no harm cannot be outlawed as such. She also convincingly argues that there is simply no plausible justification for states to limit the kind of sex that is legally permitted to "straight" sex (whatever that is) between two people in their private home. Nor is there any plausible justification for legally permitting only opposite sex persons to marry. All the currently proposed reasons in favor of not extending these legal protections to all legally responsible citizens[18] are plainly irreconcilable with a basic commitment to the idea of citizens as free and equal. Nussbaum's argument regarding systemic issues, and in particular issues of discrimination in the various sectors of the economy, for instance the housing or the job

---

[17] For more on this, see both Part I and Chapter 6.

[18] Because I only engage Kant's account of domestic right here, I am avoiding dealing with issues concerning illegal and legal residents. On this account, everyone residing on the territory has basic rights to freedom and the question of whether or not one is illegally residing has no bearing on these basic issues. For reasons of space, however, I am setting aside these questions and just writing "citizens" here.

markets, is similar in structure. Nussbaum argues that there are no good reasons to exclude gays and lesbians and others who have "non-traditional" sexual identities, orientations, and preferences from being treated as equals in these markets. One can justify certain restrictions, such as the requirement to provide safe and hygienic conditions in private sex clubs, but this is an argument that in principle applies to any private economic institution where people's bodily fluids are shared, such as in public baths and swimming pools. In addition, she argues, one can make an exception for religious institutions: they are and should be permitted to hire only people of their own religious convictions to fulfill inherently religious, institutional functions. Consequently, people who disagree with some basic tenet of the shared religious beliefs, such as those pertaining to the moral rightness or wrongness of gays and lesbians and their sexual activities, can be excluded. None of these considerations, however, are sufficient to deny people a right to be treated as equals in the economy as such, just as considerations of race, religion, and gender do not undermine this right. Yet insofar as religious institutions extend themselves into the economy beyond their strictly religious purposes, say by purchasing and renting property, they are subject to the same restrictions as any other private business.

Why, then, does Nussbaum see these arguments grounded in respect for citizens' freedom and equality as insufficient grounds for judicial decisions? She holds them to be insufficient, if I read her correctly, because many judges have to deal with the fact that they often find the sexual activities of gays and lesbians, for example, to be disgusting and the arguments presented in favor of limiting their legal protection typically employ the language of disgust: non-traditional or minority sexual practices are viewed as disgusting by the majorities—as are the people who take part in them. To end up on the right side of these issues and to be convincing, the judges need to supplement the formal arguments by engaging in what Nussbaum calls "the practice of imagination." In this way, the judges force everyone, including themselves, to move from an unreflective mode of disgust to a reflective mode of respect and responsive sympathy for humanity in general and for non-traditional minorities in particular. Thus judges can help to bring the whole process of legal reflection in line with the politics of humanity.

Now, as hinted above, I do not believe Nussbaum is correct in arguing that we need to appeal to judges' reflective, responsive sympathy and imagination in order to justify the claim that our fundamental rights include a right to marry, to human sodomy, to join private sex clubs, to participation in the economic and financial systems as equals, and so on. I think (private and public right) arguments that appeal simply to the public authority representing each of its citizens as free and equal should and can carry the day.[19] That is, the possibility of justice should not be

---

[19] If one were to outline the defense of the above points regarding private and systemic issues in Kantian rather than Nussbaum's Millian terms, the argument would be this: The constitution of any liberal state must secure each citizen certain basic, private rights to freedom of conscience, thought, and speech, to their own bodies, and to the basic categories of private right (private property, contract and family/fiduciary relations—or what Kant calls "status relations,") which include the right to marry. To be a citizen is to have a right to these things. Additionally, because the state establishes a monopoly on coercion, it must make sure that the freedom-determining systems upon which citizens are made dependent are reconcilable with the citizens being free and equal. For example, this is why it regulates the economy and the financial system by certain public right measures, namely to ensure that they function as systems within which people can

dependent on judges' ability to humanize the persons whose lives are subjected to their authority. Rather, arguments for marriage and other sexual interactions authorized by consent should be made solely in terms of respect for each person's right to freedom. As far as I can see, judges can and should employ only these formal, innate, private, and public (systemic) rightful freedom arguments, since they are sufficient to solve the difficult legal cases that they adjudicate. Judges can and should proceed purely "legalistically," which is to say from the reflective mode of arguing in terms of citizens' basic innate, private, and public rights to freedom. Arguments that appeal to anyone's unreflective disgust or reflective, imagined sympathy are irrelevant in that they do nothing to determine the correct interpretation of the constitution in these cases, or in any other cases; such humanized arguments provide no legal justification when it comes to constitutional rights.

This is not to say that imaginations involving active humanization of dehumanized people and processes are not important in the legal-political institutional framework as such: I think Nussbaum is right that many judges need to and will find it useful or necessary to go through such exercises to make it subjectively easier for them to use their reason correctly and wisely, and they may be important as one writes up parts of the rulings such that they express awareness of how difficult it is for human beings to have been forced to live with a denial of rights and how painful it is for human beings to be met with disgust and shaming behavior for who one is or how ones loves. But the point is that by employing only legal justification, what is protected is what must be protected in a just society—everyone's equal right to freedom—and the justification for its protection can be apparent to everyone regardless of their basic, unreflective, emotional responses to various sexual activities or even their "comprehensive doctrines" to use Rawls's famous phrase. Any legal argument to the contrary will necessarily be a bad legal argument, which is why liberal democracies—one by one—currently are in the process of abandoning legislation that outlaws human sodomy and private sex clubs (as such) and are permitting marriages for all of its legally responsible citizens, whether straight or gay. In other words, these legal cases should not be and are not that difficult as long as one keeps the argument within a framework grounded on citizens' freedom and equality. Again, once these purely legal, freedom-based arguments have been made, there is space for incorporating the fact that we are making laws not only for spatio-temporal rational beings, but for *human* beings: doing so helps us appreciate the gravity of wrongdoing involved in denying human beings these rights, the heinousness of subjecting people to such wrongdoing, and—as I believe Nussbaum is quite right to say—to fight our evil temptation to dehumanize others and the lives they live.

From this Kantian account of marriage, notice, finally, there follow some principles for divorce. When we divorce, we disunite our shared, legal homes and doing so requires establishing distinctions that are compatible with each person moving on, on

exercise their freedom as equals. Consequently, all private businesses in the private economy must, as a general rule, treat all of their customers as equals and they must provide accessible, safe, and hygienic conditions for all. Consequently too, citizens do not only have public right claims—or claims against the public institutions—to be secured basic private rights, but they also have public right claims in relation to the common land, and to the economic and financial systems upon which any exercise of freedom depends. I return to these arguments regarding public right (systemic justice) in Chapter 7.

their own. Consequently, although the law will permit divorcing couples to make their own contractual arrangements for their separation, it will not recognize terms of these contracts—if they are brought to court—that serve not to end the marriage after all. Although there is space for alimonies and for arrangements for children, these arrangements cannot be such that they make it impossible for anyone to marry another person as an equal. When one divorces, the marriage is over; it does not continue with enforceable contractual claims that make new marriages impossible (as then one's new spouse becomes subjected to the ex-spouses' arbitrary choices). Otherwise, the problems characteristic of Nussbaum's and others' proposals for disaggregated civil unions would be replicated.

2. Rightful Trade in Sexual Services

Kant's take on rightful sexual relations falling within marriage are interesting, in my view, because of the distinction he draws between domestic ("status") relations and either regular contract or property relations. However, Kant also makes interesting comments on rightful sexual relations falling *outside* of marriage, comments we can clarify by seeing them together with his general account of embodied rights and contract right. Again, part of what is fascinating about Kant's argument regarding private right is that it shows how legal claims with regard to trade in sexual services actually can be enforceable claims only on public institutions; we never have the right to use force against one another directly. Additionally, the combination of his general argument that one does not own something by contract until it has been physically given to one and his explanation of why it is impossible to have a right to have sex with another person together yield a promising approach to understand contractual exchanges involving sexual services. To many people it is not particularly problematic to let go of Kant's assumption that sexual activities outside of marriage are inherently unethical. But even if we do give up this view, it still seems difficult to explain why persons cannot legally contract to perform (unethical) sexual services for one another. In addition, contrary to what many fear, what arises from Kant's analysis is not the rather scary libertarian one, according to which anything goes as long as the contractors are adults and they have voluntarily consented to a particular contract. Indeed, that some libertarians argue that these contracts are even enforceable, especially in light of human phenomenology and the damage sexual interactions can do, is a profoundly disturbing thought. Rather, the legality of sexual contracts on the Kantian position defended here gives rise to something much more appealing to minds that understand justice in terms of (human) freedom. In this section, I focus on the nature of the exchange itself. In Chapter 7, I use Kant's understanding of the functioning of minimally and more robustly just states to show why contracts involving exchanges of sexual services need not threaten the freedom of either party.

Kant calls contract right "personal right," which is a kind of right one person has against another to perform a certain deed.[20] These acquisitions are consequently

---

[20] Kant delineates three main types of contracts corresponding to the three categories of property acquisition (MM 6: 259f.): unilateral; bilateral (of which there are two types: permanent alienation and letting and hiring); and omnilateral contracts. Each of these contracts has three sub-categories,

undertaken only by persons capable of deeds, that is, morally (ethically and legally) responsible persons. Furthermore, since each person has an innate right to freedom, they cannot rightfully be coerced into performing a deed themselves (by using their bodies in particular ways). So, we can neither have a right to acquire somebody else's deeds (external choices) *originally* (since this would be a right to coercively subject that person's external use of choice to our arbitrary choices) nor can we have a right to use embodied force or threat of force against someone to make them do something. Therefore, "personal right" can arise only through a voluntary bilateral or "united" choice, namely a contract. A contract, for Kant, is "[a]n act of the united choice of two persons by which anything at all that belongs to one passes to the other" (MM 6: 271). Contracts do not give us a right directly to a thing as it is a right of one person against another to perform a particular deed, namely to perform some service or transfer some thing. Contracts, therefore, enable the rightful transfer of rightful possessions (goods and services) between people. In addition, just as with original appropriation of private property, contracts are relations between persons rather than relations between persons and things. Thus, through a contract, the promisee acquires a legal claim against a person to deliver an object or perform a service—not a claim to the object or service itself. And since contracts are relations between persons, the *final* title to actual objects is not transferred before the thing or service has actually been delivered. If the promisor fails to deliver, the promisee is entitled to compensation, but not necessarily to the thing or service contracted (MM 6: 271-6).[21]

Consistent with Kant's general analysis of rights, including contract right in the state of nature,[22] we can expect that contractual arrangements between persons in the state of nature do not generate conclusive, but only provisional contract rights. But Kant offers little explicit explanation for why this would be. Nevertheless, a reasonable account can be suggested. First, there is an ideal problem of indeterminacy regarding how to enact an agreed upon exchange. Contracts invoke a normative idea of a united choice among (two or more) persons. This idea consists in what the persons see themselves as having agreed to in their commitments to exchange goods or services. The problem arises because there are many equally reasonable ways in which this normative idea can be realized in our actual exchanges. Well-intentioned, reasonable persons may very well find that they have differing conceptions about how to carry out what they have agreed to—leading to disputes about whether or not

---

corresponding to the three ways in which persons can engage in relations with each other with respect to goods and services (unilaterally, bilaterally, and omnilaterally). Thus, in total, there are twelve *a priori* types of contracts (MM 6: 284-6).

[21] "By a contract I acquire something external" says Kant, "[b]ut what is it that I acquire? Since it is only the causality of another's choice with respect to a performance he has promised me, what I acquire directly by a contract is not an external thing but rather his deed, by which that thing is brought under my control so that I make it mine.—By a contract I therefore acquire another's promise (not what he promised), and yet something is added to my external belongings; I have become *enriched*... by acquiring an active obligation on the freedom and means of the other.—This *right* of mine is, however, only a right *against a person*, namely a right against a *specific* physical person, and indeed a right to act upon his causality (his choice) to *perform* something for me" (MM 6: 273f.).

[22] For more on this, see the introduction to Part II.

the contract has been fulfilled. For example, assume that I have hired you to paint my garage. Given your conception of garage painting, you believe that you are required to give the garage one coat of primer followed by one coat of paint, while I believe that fulfilling the contract requires that the garage be given one coat of primer followed by two coats of paint. Alternatively, we may have differing conceptions of the way in which the contract deals with unforeseeable empirical circumstances, such as whether the deadline should be met independently of the weather, illness, etc. Because of such indeterminacies, situations can occur where it is impossible for any one of the parties objectively or correctly to determine whether the contract has been fulfilled, and therefore, the contract is not rightfully enforceable. Thus, Kant concludes that without a public authority there is "no judge competent to render a verdict having rightful force" (MM 6: 312).

Contractual interactions, like private property relations, must be subject only to non-contingent and symmetrical restrictions. Therefore, contract right also calls for a public authority because private solutions prove insufficient. That is to say, private persons certainly may consent to let a third party settle their disagreements, but such a private solution does not suffice to generate enforceable contract right. The problem with an external private arbiter is twofold. On the one hand, since the establishment of an external private arbiter is subject to the consent of the disputing parties, there is no reason why the parties should ever come to agreement about who in particular should arbitrate the dispute. After all, the arbiter is no better equipped to solve the dispute than the parties themselves when the disagreements are reasonable.[23] What is more, consenting to an arbiter seems irrational in that the parties merely subject themselves to the arbiter's contingent judgment rather than to their own—say to the arbiter's view about whether the garage should be painted with one or two coats of paint. Solution by way of a private arbiter does not allow the contracting parties independence from the arbitrary (private) choices of others, but subjects them to the arbiter's (private) arbitrary choice. On the other hand, there may arise conflicts over whether an agreed upon arbiter performs their duty. In this case, the parties need another arbiter to solve the dispute about whether or not the first arbiter appropriately has exercised their entrusted task—potentially resulting in an infinite regress of arbitration. The third party private solution therefore is not sufficient for *enforceable* contract right: as a contractual solution to the problem of contracts, it merely generates the indeterminacy problem once again. The reason why a contractual solution is insufficient to solve the contractual problem is that it leads to an infinite regress of contracts.

Solving the contractual problem requires a judge who is impartial in their *form*—a *public* judge—who has standing in contractual relations. The public judge's rightful standing in contractual relations derives from the fact that their rulings are consistent with the requirements of justice: the public judge enables us to settle our disagreements such that they can be seen as the reciprocal application of laws of freedom. Since such public judges *qua* judges have no private interests and are trained and

---

[23] Obviously if the dispute is a result of bias on the part of one or both parties, the arbiter's impartiality is an asset. Nevertheless, remember that in our scenario the dispute does not result from bias or unreasonableness, but simply because of the indeterminacy of actual contract fulfilment.

authorized only to apply laws consistent with each person's basic rights to freedom to particular cases (and to make sure that the laws are so consistent), their judgments have an impartial form.[24] Only by ensuring that contracts are undertaken within such public legal framework, can we make sure that in contracting we do not hinder one another's external use of choice arbitrarily, but only in accordance with universal law. That is to say, only when the arbiter is a public authority, namely impartial in its form—by representing each and no one in particular and subjecting the interactions to laws of freedom—can it enjoy the proper standing from which to adjudicate disputes and enforce contract right independent of the contracting parties' actual consent. It is this standing that enables the public judge to determine the rightful use of coercion to resolve a conflict conclusively *even if* one of the parties would prefer to use private might to settle it. For these reasons, rightful contractual relations require civil society.

The state enables enforceable contracts—it acts as the public enabler of contract right—by setting up a public court with public judges who adjudicate particular disputes in accordance with posited contract law. In a just state, then, all contracts, including trade in sexual services, are regulated and enforced by public institutions in the sense that the public authority decides whether or not a contract was valid, was broken, and if any compensation is to be paid. And again, it is central to appreciate that contracts are relations between people with regard to things and services, which is why Kant argues that one obtains title to a thing or service only once it has been delivered (MM 6: 273ff.). This entails that if, for example, a sex worker fails to or no longer wants to deliver the sexual service they have been paid to deliver, then the customer does not have a claim to have the service delivered, but a right to reimbursement and, possibly, compensation. Moreover, insofar as the sex work involves one's body, then if the buyer fails to respect the seller's change of mind— if the buyer does not heed the seller's "no"—and resorts to force to complete the sexual interaction, then this is battery, which is a more serious kind of wrongdoing than, for example, theft or breach of contract. This is why Kant argues that

hiring [somone] for [sexual] enjoyment on one occasion (*pactrum focnicationis*) is a contract that cannot hold in right...everyone will admit that a person who has concluded such a contract could not rightfully be held to the fulfillment of her promise if she regrets it.

(MM 6: 279)

As we have seen above, no contracts involving deeds—claims against morally responsible persons—are enforceable in that one cannot be forced to perform a deed. In the case of sex, this becomes an even more urgent point because of human beings' particular phenomenological make-up. A system of laws based in human freedom will deem sexual violence particularly heinous since it can devastate and unground human beings. Indeed, it is plausible to think that the seriousness of the wrong of sexual violence explains the common practice of paying for sexual services before receiving them: after all, if a sex worker changes their mind or

---

[24] Because the court enforces only the terms of the contracts, it can never be a court of equity. To allow for equity the judge would be seen as dealing with their own private interests rather than representing the general, united will of the contractual parties. Thus Kant rejects courts of equity at (MM 6: 234f.).

disagrees with a client about what they contracted to do, they can give some of the money back—the exact amount can be settled by a court—while there is no way to take back the wrong the client does if they disrespect the autonomy of the sex worker by not regarding continuous, authorizing consent as what makes the sexual interaction legally permissible.

3. Concluding Remarks

In this chapter, I have continued the argument started in Chapter 5, according to which it is impossible to have an enforceable right to have sex with another person, and lack of authorizing consent always makes sexual interactions legally wrong. In addition, I have defended Kant's view that any legal, enforceable claims regarding sexual practices are possible only in a civil society, where the state acts as the civil guardian over domestic relations and as the public enabler of contract right. I have argued that Kant's considered position must conclude that refusing legally responsible persons a right to marry is to deny them the possibility of rightful domestic relations involving a shared home as equals, and that it is unjustifiable to deny same-sex couples and people in symmetrical polyamorous relations access to the legal institution of marriage. Finally, I have argued that a legal framework based on each person's right to freedom can and should accommodate specifically human concerns, but, as usual, these concerns should not take the place of freedom arguments when we deliberate about the laws regarding marriage and trade in sexual services.

Notice that this chapter combined with Chapter 5 could be seen as yielding a classical, libertarian natural rights analysis of sexual love. That is to say, there is nothing in the analyses presented in this chapter and Chapter 5 that libertarians who understand justice in terms of each individual's right to freedom cannot accept as such. In addition, libertarian analyses that follow in Locke's footsteps would typically insist that this chapter and Chapter 5 make up the complete analysis of a just state's coercive authority: on such a position, the rights of the just state are coextensive with the rights of individuals (if we set aside public administrative right). In Chapter 7, I follow Kant's lead in challenging this assumption. I argue that the state's monopoly on coercion must be reconciled with each person's right to freedom, which necessarily means that the state must secure the operations of the legal-political institutional system as a whole through a series of systemic, public right principles (public law). And, I argue, none of these arguments can be rejected on the grounds that they are irreconcilable with each person's right to freedom; indeed, establishing a legal-political system founded on each person's right to freedom demands these systemic institutional protections of public right. In addition, we see that in its focus on reforming historical conditions of severe oppression of sub-sections of the citizenry, my liberal republican position has much to offer legal positivist, communitarian, and virtue ethical legal-political approaches, as it does to much feminist and postmodern theory.

7

Public Right

Systemic Justice

Introduction

Human history is characterized by a pervasive failure of legal-political institutions to treat women and sexual or gendered minorities in rightful ways; indeed, none of the states that have existed or currently do exist have secured conditions of rightful freedom for these groups. And if Kant's account of our propensity to evil is correct, it is at best naïve to think that these problems will ever be permanently overcome by humankind.[1] In fact, on the theory of sex, love, and gender presented in this book, one of the signs that a society or state is deteriorating is exactly that women and sexual or gendered minorities are once again becoming objects of hatred, harassment, violence, and oppression, and that legal consequences for such treatment are disappearing. Considering these facts of human history, we may ask the following questions: What kinds of political obligations do women and members of sexual or gendered minorities have under the different kinds of conditions in which they may find themselves, and how can we reform our inherited legal-political institutions to improve and safeguard the rights of women and sexual or gendered minorities? In this chapter, I propose that Kant's account of public right together with his ideas about how theories of justice as freedom must make space both for human nature and for recognition of the faulty features of the legal-political situation in which we currently find ourselves are particularly useful as we grapple with these questions in general and in relation to the realities of women and oppressed sexualities or genders in particular. Kant's ideas enable us to identify when a state is minimally just and can issue political obligations, to suggest paths of reform that can bring our inherited, imperfect legal-political institutions closer to their own, more robust ideals of justice as rightful human freedom, and to speak to the question of what our options are when reform is not yet possible. On this account, what our obligations are at present is often difficult to answer: with regard to some parts of our lives, we may have political obligations and be obliged to reform the related legal-political institutions, while with regard to others, we may find ourselves left to our own devices with no available emotionally good, morally justifiable choices.

This chapter is divided into two main sections. The first main section ("Kant's Conception of a Minimally Just State ('Rechtsstaat')") focuses on Kant's account of a minimally just state, which he calls a "republic" and which I will also call, using

[1] For more on this, see Chapter 4.

Sex, Love, and Gender: A Kantian Theory. Helga Varden, Oxford University Press (2020). © Helga Varden.
DOI: 10.1093/oso/9780198812838.001.0001

German, a "Rechtsstaat." Section 1 is divided into two main sub-sections: the first ("1.1 The Form of Public Authority I: Republican Principles of Innate and Private Right") focuses on questions concerning the *a priori* principles of innate and private right that are constitutive of a minimally just state. The second section ("1.2 The Form of the Public Authority II: Republican Systemic Principles of Public Right") focuses on questions concerning the *a priori*, systemic principles of public right that are constitutive of a minimally just state. The second main section—"Reforming Our Imperfect, Inherited Legal-Political Frameworks into Well-Functioning, Robustly Just States"—explores questions of institutional reform of imperfect public institutions in different political circumstances. This section is also divided into two sub-sections. The first sub-section ("2.1 From Right to Politics") focuses on the general issue of how to reform our states in light of the particular histories and political circumstances in which we find ourselves. The second sub-section ("2.2 Active Self-Governance through Public Institutions") concentrates on questions concerning the reform of inherited legal-political institutions and the transformation of these institutions in ways that are conducive to citizens' active self-governance through participation in public reason (engaging in public discussions and holding public offices). Throughout these discussions, the focus is, as always, on core issues regarding sex, love, and gender. I conclude this chapter by arguing that constitutive of good reform efforts is a state's public recognition of its own failures to secure the rights of various vulnerable groups, including women and sexual or gendered minorities. These failures have placed these citizens in situations in which they have either been excluded from access to legal institutions or been forced to protect themselves against barbaric, heinous violence to the best of their abilities. Public recognition of these failures is important because people have a right not to be treated in these ways and because our laws are made for and by human beings whose historical progress (rather than regress) as a moral species requires telling truthful histories. The process of legal-political institutional reform therefore sometimes requires public recognition of (and sometimes public apologies for) these failures.

1. Kant's Conception of a Minimally Just State ("Rechtsstaat")

This section opens with a general exploration of Kant's conception of domestic right and focuses on what the public authority is such that it is the means through which both ideal and non-ideal problems characterizing interaction in the state of nature can be solved. Two ideas are central here: First, the state must posit, apply, and enforce laws that transform the principles of innate and private right into laws that reciprocally regulate citizens' interactions as private persons. Understanding this idea helps us capture two ways in which states fail by denying citizens their basic right to freedom. One way is by subjecting them to rules according to which either some citizens are deprived of certain basic rights of freedom, as, for example, most so-called sodomy or obscenity laws do, or some citizens are denied (full) access to civil society, as, for example, the denial of a right to marry for same-sex or symmetrical polyamorous relationships does. Although I defend Kant's general claim that we do not have a right to revolution—"to burn it all down" to use a contemporary colloquialism—because rightful relations are, in principle, impossible in the state of nature, neither do I defend the view that citizens are politically obligated to obey barbarous rules nor that there is no place for coercive resistance.

A second way in which states often fail to secure conditions of justice for their citizens concerns the way in which states must assume control over all systems on which their citizens' exercise of freedom are made dependent. A core idea here is that the state must establish a rightful public law-governed monopoly on coercion, which it does by ensuring that the legal-political institutional whole is reconcilable with each citizen's right to freedom. It must do this by regulating those systems (upon which its citizens' exercises of freedom are dependent) by means of public right (public law). This idea of public right explains why just states have a series of distinctly systemic responsibilities and entitlements that no private individuals can be thought to have in relation to one another as private persons. Because it is through these systems that citizens secure legal access to acquire and possess means (homes, goods, services, incomes, and savings), states must ensure that such system-dependence does not subject some citizens' exercise of freedom to other citizens' arbitrary, private choices, and that all citizens' exercises of freedom are only subjected to and dependent upon public laws, laws that treat all as free and equal. This idea helps us understand why, for example, public spaces are regulated by law in ways private spaces are not, why we have laws that secure equal access to the economy and the financial system, and why behaviors such as stalking, blackmailing, and harassing—behaviors that often have sexualized or gendered patterns—are outlawed in just states. This idea of public right also enables us to appreciate why the state (but not any private individual) has an enforceable right and duty to deal with systemic problems concerning poverty and oppression, including problems associated with the fact that around the globe many sex workers are women and/or come from poor, oppressed socioeconomic situations. Throughout these analyses, I emphasize how explanations that are internally connected to our innate right to interact in rightful ways give us the general legal framework within which we can then accommodate concerns arising from our specifically *human* nature. Overall, we will see that Kant has a well-rounded view of to whom legislation according to principles of freedom matters, and, contrary to what many think, right and human flourishing are not at war with one another on this view.

1.1 The Form of the Public Authority I: Republican Principles of Innate and Private Right

Let us begin exploring Kant's conception of the public authority. To start, it is useful to note that Kant explicitly rejects an assumption that was common in much legal-political philosophy of his time and that is still common today—the assumption that private individuals can realize justice on their own by interacting virtuously or in ways consistent with respecting each other's basic rights. The details of this argument in the literature and the ways in which this argument relates to Kant-interpretation are beyond our interests here. Instead, it suffices to repeat that my approach is located in the liberal, republican interpretive tradition, and to give a brief outline of the main relevant interpretive and philosophical ideas constitutive of it.[2] In short, on my reading (2008, 2010b, 2016), Kant agrees that non-ideal problems of realizing justice for beings with natures as crooked as ours make justice very *difficult* to realize in the state of nature. Nevertheless, it is *ideal* problems of assurance (secure enforcement) and of indeterminacy regarding the specification and application of the (*a priori*) principles of right to actual interactions that lead him to conclude that rightful interaction is *in principle* (ideally) *impossible* in the state of nature. Kant argues that only a distinctly *public* authority can solve these ideal problems of interaction in a way that is reconcilable with each person's innate right to freedom, which is why he rejects any liberal position (e.g., libertarian positions such as Locke's) according to which individuals have a natural right to enforce their basic rights (a so-called "natural executive right").[3]

Because Kant views himself as having refuted the idea of a natural executive right using only ideal arguments about freedom (rather than, say, non-ideal, prudential, or epistemological arguments), he opens his discussion of the rights of the state (domestic public right) with this claim:

> however well disposed and [right-loving] [hu]man [beings] might be, it still lies *a priori* in the rational idea of such a condition (one that is not rightful) that before a public lawful condition is established individual human beings…can never be secure against violence from one another, since each has [their] own right to do *what seems right and good to [themself]* and not be dependent upon another's opinion about this.   (MM 6: 312)[4]

There are no rightful relations in the state of nature, because there is no assurance (security) against violence and all disagreements (indeterminacies) regarding the specification of right (of the general principles and of the application of these general principles to particular interactions) must be solved through each person's private "opinion" ("what seems right and good" to each, or each person's private arbitrary judgments). Thus, in the state of nature, *might* (violence) rather than *right* (law-governed force) ultimately governs all uses of coercion, which is why *only* the establishment of a public authority can enable interaction in ways that are reconcilable with each person's innate right to freedom. Only a public authority can ensure and enable interaction that is consistent with the rights constitutive of exercising our innate right to freedom, namely the rights analytically connected with the innate right to freedom (our rights to rightful honor, bodily integrity, and free speech) and the rights synthetically connected with this right (our acquired, private rights to private property, contract, and status relations). Only a public authority can solve the problems of assurance and indeterminacy without violating anyone's innate right to freedom in the process. The public authority can solve these problems of assurance and indeterminacy because it represents the will of each and yet the will of no one in

---

[2] An overview of the interpretive traditions in the scholarship on Kant's Doctrine of Right are found in the introduction to Part II.

[3] Central to the argument is that there is no objective valuing of material, including natural, resources. For my engagement with Locke and contemporary Lockeans on this point, see Varden (2012b).

[4] To stay faithful to Kant's own text, I have replaced Gregor's translation of "rechtliebend" ("law-abiding") with "right-loving." As I have consistently throughout the book, I have also rendered the text truer to Kant's original by replacing Gregor's "man" with "human beings."

particular, embodying the idea of an inherently shared authority (the representation of a general will). Because the public authority is representative in this way, by being "united *a priori*" or by being an "*omnilateral*" will (MM 6: 263), it can regulate on behalf of everyone when we interact. For these reasons, the public authority is the only means through which our interactions can become subject to coercive external laws that restrict everyone's external uses of freedom reciprocally (rather than being subject to someone's arbitrary, private choices).

As mentioned, a second, related difference between Kant and much contemporary legal-political thought is that he explicitly challenges the (typically implicit) assumption that the reasoning and actions of the public authority should be thought of as fundamentally like the reasoning and actions of virtuous private individuals.[5] On such readings, public reason is thought to refer to that which *virtuous* individuals would or could hypothetically consent to. In contrast, Kant maintains that the perspective of the public authority is not an idealized perspective of personal virtue but rather a public perspective constitutive of a rightful condition. In ways more familiar to us today through John Rawls's writings on public reason, Kant argues that the reasoning and actions of the public authority should be *public* in the sense that any decision it makes or action it undertakes should be such that *all citizens* could hypothetically consent to it *as citizens* (MM 6: 314). And, as citizens, they try to bring about a condition in which rightful interaction is possible, which is only the case in civil society. The realization of such a distinctly public way of reasoning by means of which we regulate our interactions as citizens is constitutive of rightful interaction. To represent the citizens properly, then, the representatives of the public authority must reason within a framework set by the citizens' rights against one another as private persons (private law) and as against their public institutions (public law). And because public reasoning is a distinct way of reasoning, it takes time to learn how to do it well, and to develop good laws and related legal-political institutions and practices, which is one reason the process of learning how to govern ourselves wisely through public institutions grounded on principles of freedom is such a slow endeavor.

---

[5] Similarly, Kant's refutation of a natural executive right explains why he maintains that public right covers any action that amounts to a private crime, such as a serious contractual lie. An act of aggression, or coercion against another person is also an attempt to undermine the state's rightful monopoly on coercion. Thus, all violent aggressions, including serious contractual lies, are crimes covered by public law—what we call "private crime laws." They are not regulated by private law (MM 6: 331). Public law also governs the public authority's administrative offices (MM 6: 328). Only so can it subject its citizens to the authority of these offices without thereby subjecting them to other citizens' (the public officers') arbitrary choices. Public law regulation of public administrative offices creates the distinction between reasoning as a public officer and as a private citizen. Right, therefore, requires more than properly functioning public reason. It also requires that public officers respect what Kant calls, somewhat misleadingly, the "private" reasoning constitutive of their office (WE 8: 37f.). The distinction between "scholarly" or public reasoning qua citizen and "private" reasoning qua public officer is necessary for reconciling the public authority's power with each citizen's right to freedom. Thus, public offices can represent citizens and ensure interaction that is subject to universal laws of freedom rather than to anyone's particular choices. For more on Kant's distinction between private and public reason, see Ripstein (2006), Jonathan Peterson (2008); for comparisons of public reason in Rawls and Kant, see Deligiorgi (2012a), and Niesen (2018).

When a state comes into being, Kant explains in The Doctrine of Right, "[t]he general will of the people has united itself into a society which is to maintain itself perpetually" (MM 6: 326). When exploring what Kant means by the general will here, we find a third way in which Kant diverges from much contemporary legal-political thought, namely by claiming that the minimally just state ("republic/"Rechtsstaat") need not be a democracy. For Kant thinks that there are three possible forms the state can take: the public authority can be held by one person (autocracy: one active citizen), by a few persons (aristocracy: a few active citizens), or by many persons (democracy: many active citizens) (MM 6: 338f.). In *Anthropology*, Kant advances a similar line of reasoning. There, he makes this point in connection with his argument that the main ingredients of external freedom—force, freedom, and law—can be combined in four different ways, yielding "anarchy," "barbarism," "despotism," and the "republic":

Freedom and *law* (by which freedom is limited) are the main pivots around which civil legislation turns.—But in order for law to be effective and not an empty recommendation, a middle term must be added; namely, *force*, which, when connected with freedom, secures success for these principles. Now we can conceive of four combinations of force with freedom and law:

A. Law and freedom without force (anarchy).
B. Law and force without freedom (despotism).
C. Force without freedom and law (barbarism).
D. Force with freedom and law (republic).

One sees that only the last combination deserves to be called a true civil constitution; by which, however, one does not have in view one of the three forms of state (democracy), but understands by *republic* only a state as such.   (A 7: 330f.)

The state of nature, as previously noted, need not be a condition of injustice. Rather, it is a condition that is, at its best, devoid of justice. It is clearly the non-violent version of the state of nature to which Kant is appealing by employing his concept of "anarchy" here: We can imagine a situation in which everyone happens to agree on the general and particular specifications (positing and application) of the principles of right, and consequently no one ever experiences any (reasonable or unreasonable) disagreement regarding how their exercises of external freedom should be restricted in interpersonal interactions. Such a situation would also naturally lack any wrongful uses of coercion; indeed, it would lack any instances of coercion at all. This would be the best possible anarchical situation since although it is one in which we have not enabled justice (because there are no rightful uses of coercion in this condition), it is also one in which there is no injustice. Such an anarchical situation would be possible, but it would be, at best, a condition "*devoid of justice*," because if a dispute concerning right were to arise in this situation, "there would be no judge competent to render a verdict having rightful force" (MM 6: 312). A condition that is worse than the anarchic state of nature is one in which there is pervasive use of force but no freedom and no law enabling rights for all citizens (barbarism). In such a barbaric condition, the use of force is not restricted by considerations of freedom or law; there is only brute force (violence), which is why Kant considers it barbaric. Although neither condition is a condition of justice, "anarchy" is only devoid of justice, whereas "barbarism" is simply unjust.

The two other possible conditions Kant identifies are "despotism" and the "republic" (civil condition). Both combine force with law, but despotism does not combine force with freedom and so cannot succeed in realizing both freedom and law, which are the "main pivots around which civil legislation turns." There is no freedom in a despotic condition because there is no representation even in the most basic sense of the word, arising from the fact that there are neither any active citizens in this condition nor any basic rights to freedom necessarily secured. One major problem with despotism is that the individual or individuals wielding power take themselves to hold this power as private persons rather than as public officials who represent the people and who are entrusted to act *on behalf of* the people to enable rightful, lawful interactions between them as free, equal, and independent persons. There is, in other words, no public authority in a despotic condition; there is only private authority. In despotic legal-political systems, some person(s) holds power in a way that is fundamentally not representative; within such a system there is no way, even in principle, for conclusively rightful relations to be secured. More specifically, the various despotic bodies (in a despotic autocracy, only one person; in a despotic aristocracy, a few persons; and, in a despotic democracy, a subset of the citizens) subject and see themselves as subjecting all the others in their state to their private or personal authority (an authority they may, for example, view as being grounded in their own personal virtue, their family lineage, their deep religious insights, God having chosen them, etc.) rather than subjecting them only to laws that foster rightful interactions between them as free, equal, and independent. Hence, despotic societies lack freedom and are characterized by force and law only, or law-governed, private power. In such a society, then, there is a law-governed legal-political institutional framework, but there is no public law-based system grounded in the protection of all citizens' innate right to freedom (and its analytically and synthetically connected rights). Despotism is therefore not a true civil condition: only provisional justice is possible, and it *necessarily* cannot secure protection of the citizens through laws of freedom.[6] Therefore, provisional justice manifests whenever there is agreement and the use of coercion is made unnecessary *or* when particular (but not all or the sum of) laws in effect can reasonably be regarded as instantiations of the general principles of innate, private, and public right. Such a despotic condition cannot issue conclusive political obligations but only provisional and/or prudential obligations.

The republic (the minimally just state or *Rechtsstaat*), in contrast, is a condition in which force is combined with freedom and law in a way that "secures success for these principles" (of freedom and law). That is, the republic requires the establishment of a public authority that can take any of the three forms of state (autocracy, aristocracy, or democracy). In addition, however, a key feature of the republic is, as we have seen, that the persons wielding sovereign power in this condition are not authorized (by the law) to act as anything but delegates of the people by fulfilling their role as representatives of the public authority. The highest public authority in

---

[6] See, for example, how Kant argues that "All laws of the *summus imperans* {supreme sovereign} must arise *quasi ex consensus communi* {as if by common consent}, namely not **necessarily** contradict them. . . . If some laws are possible only *ex arbitrio private* (*unus adversum omnes*) {from private choice (one against all)}, then they are thuggish [*gewaltthätig*], hence despotic." (LDPP 19: 346; cf. 490).

the republic is also functionally and institutionally tripartite, and, relatedly, the one or ones who are legally entitled to vote on the laws are the active citizen(s). To establish a republican institution that represents the "general united will of the people" (MM 6: 314), we must therefore establish three artificial *public* authorities, or "thought entities" constitutive of a public will (MM 6: 338):

the *sovereign authority* ... in the person of the legislator; the *executive authority* in the person of the ruler (in conformity with the law); and the *judicial authority* (to award to each what is his in accordance with the law) in the person of the judge.   (MM 6: 313; cf. PP 8: 350ff.)

That the *tripartite* public authority has public legislative, judicial, and executive branches are part of why the public authority represents the general, united will of the people.

As we have seen, requiring the legal-political institutions to instantiate the rule of *public law* means that the legal-political authority must treat each of its subjects as free and equal (by legally securing each citizen's basic rights to freedom) and that the legislative authority must be regarded as having primacy with regard to the other two sovereign authorities (MM 6: 314; TP 8: 294f.). The legislative authority is prior to the others in that it posits the laws applied and enforced by the two others, and in that posited law must delineate the powers of the other two authorities. Only in this way can the tripartite public authority enable interaction that is reciprocally restricted by universal laws of freedom rather than interaction that is subjected to someone's arbitrary, private choices. This is why Kant says that in an important sense the legislative authority *is* the sovereign. The sovereign authority is primarily vested in the legislator by their authority to posit laws of freedom, whereas the executive authority enforces the law posited by the legislator and the judicial authority adjudicates actual conflicts between citizens by applying the relevant posited laws.[7] Kant illustrates this by explaining that the legislative authority can be thought of as the major premise in a practical syllogism ("the law of the [sovereign's] will"), the executive authority's resulting command as the minor premise ("the command to behave in accordance with the law"), and the judiciary authority's verdict as the conclusion ("the *verdict* ... what is laid down as right in the case at hand") (MM 6: 313). Despite the primacy of the legislative authority, however, the three constituents of the public authority complement one another and are simultaneously subordinated to each other in such a way that they do not usurp one another's functions. They must therefore be regarded as composed of three different but complementary principles, which secure and enable the rule of universal laws of freedom and, consequently, the establishment of an authoritative rather than merely powerful state power (MM 6: 316–18).

Notice that in a republican state, those who have voting power in the domain of legislation primarily should take themselves to be specifying the innate, private, and public laws of freedom by positing laws that can regulate rightful interaction. In addition, all public officials should strive to analyze public matters and wield public authority in an inherently public way, namely in a way that is aligned with the public

---

[7] Matters of guilt and innocence are determined by the people (as members of a jury). Because of this, if the jury is mistaken, the people have wrongly judged themselves (MM 6: 317f.).

laws and policies constitutive of their public offices. In a republic, public officials are obligated to take themselves only to be acting and are only legally authorized to act on behalf of each and all citizens in line with the relevant laws and policies regarding what doing so involves, and they do not view and are not legally entitled to view their public offices of authority as their own, private spheres of power and choice. When the public offices are treated as private spheres of dominance, they are corrupted. That those entrusted with public authority must act within the framework set by public law and policy does not mean that they are not entrusted with exercising their own judgment; surely, they are. There is space in all well-functioning legal-political systems for adapting its laws and policies to the particular situations for which they are designed. It is also not the case that those who hold public office do not have a role to play in the ongoing criticism of these institutions when they are not functioning sufficiently well. Indeed, as we will see below, Kant thinks that everyone also has a right to critically engage the actual functioning of the legal-political institutional system in public writings and debates. Rather, public officials do and must act within a legal framework set by the public laws and policies of their office when they act in their official capacities; they are and take themselves to be parts of a legal-political system that promotes conditions of rightful freedom for everyone.

The public authority comprises a system of law the objective of which is to enable rightful interaction in perpetuity, and the public officers of which are entrusted to serve as the citizens' delegates or deputies. Rather than identifying democracy as a minimal condition of state legitimacy, then, the minimum condition is that the public authority is exercised within the parameters set by a firm commitment to act on behalf of the citizens to enable and secure for them conditions of rightful freedom. The point is therefore not to construct an ideally virtuous, artificial *private* person but rather an artificial *public* person that, by reasoning in an inherently public way, represents each of its citizens and no one of them in particular. Therefore, the just state does something that private individuals cannot, in principle, do, namely to act *solely* as a representative of the people by establishing itself as a freedom-based rule of public law. Because the public authority represents itself as the solution to the ideal and the non-ideal problems characteristic of the state of nature in this way, it is the morally required (from both the points of view of right and virtue) as well as the prudent means through which rightful interactions are made possible.

An authority that is to be *public* (as opposed to private) also cannot have any private interests. For example, the public authority cannot own land or private property (MM 6: 323f.). Were the state to have these private interests, it would simply be a powerful private person and would thereby reproduce the problems of the state of nature in a ghastly form. Hence, all public land and property are, exactly, *public* and belong to the people and are regulated by public laws and policies. In addition, the public authority's monopoly on coercion must be reconcilable with each citizen's innate right to freedom, the rights analytically linked with it (the rights to honor, bodily integrity, and speech), and the rights synthetically linked with it (private rights: acquired rights to private property, contract, and status relations). Because the ideal objective of the public authority is to overcome the problems of assurance and indeterminacy in the state of nature and to establish reciprocal freedom under law, Kant maintains that its authority must be thoroughly delineated by posited law that is also consistent with the "*a priori necessary*...laws...[that] follow of themselves from concepts of external right as such" (MM 6: 313; cf. 315). And, as we have seen, this entails that the posited law must be consistent with the *a priori* principles of innate and private right; otherwise, our interactions cannot be described as exercises of freedom subject only to laws that restrict reciprocally and in ways consistent with each person's innate right to freedom. Making the principles of innate and private right determinate by positing related laws, which are then applied by the courts and enforced by the executive power, is therefore constitutive of establishing a public authority. The public authority's very legitimacy rests on its role in enabling reciprocal freedom under public law in this way.

In sum, then, constitutive of (necessary, but not sufficient for) the establishment of a minimally just state is a set of legal principles that secures each citizen's innate right to freedom, which include the (analytically or synthetically related) rights to rightful honor, free speech, bodily integrity, private property, contract right, and status right. If these principles are not legally secured and properly enabled, we do not yet have a minimally rightful state—a *minimal* realization of the idea of a judicial republic in a "Rechtsstaat"—and therefore we do not yet have a public legal-political institution that can issue conclusive political obligations for those subject to its power. On the contrary, in a *Rechtsstaat*

law itself rules and depends on no particular person.... Any true republic is and can only be a *system representing* the people, in order to protect its rights in its name, by all the citizens united and acting through their delegates (deputies). (MM 6: 341)

Moreover, the republic is the only legal-political condition in which citizens enjoy basic rights of freedom, so it is the only condition compatible with reform of existing legal-political principles that actually can lead to a future in which the people actively govern themselves through their public legal-political institutions. Once reform has succeeded, then *all* morally responsible citizens in the republic enjoy conditions in which they can work themselves into active participants in the public institutional framework, including by partaking in informed ways in public discussions and by being entrusted with holding various public offices. In contrast to a minimally just state, in a robustly just, flourishing republic, the people rule themselves through public self-governance, and the possibility of active participation in public discussions and public institutions is secured by the legal-political system as a whole. I return to these issues in section 2.2.

When it comes to issues of sex, love, and, gender, a first implication of this account of the public authority, contrary to a commonly held view, is that it is not the case that only democracies are minimally just, and so it is not the case that securing basic rights for women and sexual or gendered minorities is impossible without first establishing democracy. Indeed, one can have a democracy in place without thereby having a minimally just state (a republic or *Rechtsstaat*) in place. That is to say, as we seek to improve our legal-political institutions, it is important to distinguish the question of how to secure minimally just legal-political institutional frameworks (a *Rechtsstaat*) from the question of which form of government the state should have.

Notice, too, that this analysis is not a complete delineation of the conditions of a minimally just state on Kant's view, because there are additional public right principles that are also *a priori* and constitutive of a legal-political system that is based on each citizen's right to freedom. I return to these other principles in section 1.2. Before doing so, however, I want to engage Kant's defense of free speech and show how this account is consistent with legal regulation of public displays of erotica (section 1.1.1), as well as explore some ways in which the above discussion of the public authority helps us answer some general questions concerning forceful resistance in conditions under which the basic principles of innate and private right related to sex, love, and gender are not secured for all citizens (section 1.1.2).

1.1.1 FREE SPEECH AND PUBLIC DISPLAYS OF EROTICA

In Chapter 5, we saw that private citizens do not have legal claims concerning wrongdoing against one another regarding speech except insofar as their communications of thought are defamatory or are lies and as part of contractual relations, in which cases they deprive others of their rightful possessions by using speech. It is tempting, but mistaken, to conclude from those earlier discussions that a full liberal critique of free speech rights found in just states can be established using an account that is derived from private persons' rights against one another. If this were the case, Kant would be regarded as arguing that constitutional protections of free speech, for example, are merely concerned with ensuring that people are not punished when the speech does not constitute private wrongdoing. However, a Kant-based defense of free speech is both stronger and more interesting than this. In addition, as we will see shortly, Kant's strong defense of free speech is compatible with the outlawing of certain displays of erotica in public spaces, though the fact that we are making such laws for distinctly *human* beings is important for capturing central features of such laws.

The right to free political speech enables and protects engagement with, including criticism of, the public authority. Indeed, the right to speak out against the state is necessary for the public authority to be representative at all; in the absence of the right to political speech, the public authority cannot, in principle, act on behalf of the people. The right to free political speech is therefore constitutive of the legitimacy of the political authority (the public political relation). Because of this, the right to free political speech is neither derived from nor dependent on the justification provided by the private right argument that words cannot coerce. Instead, the political element of the right to free speech follows from the way in which the public authority must protect and facilitate its citizens' direct, critical engagement with the public, normative standards and practices as they pertain to right. The public authority is, after all, the means through which rightful relations between citizens are made possible; to deny the right to free political speech is to deny that the state is a *public* authority at all. Moreover, on this position, although we can identify the *a priori* principles of rightful freedom, there are no *a priori* prescriptions for how to actually formulate the wisest laws and policies for enabling rightful interaction in a particular state. The public authority can become enlightened about how and whether the current laws and institutions really do enable reciprocal external freedom for all citizens only by enabling public discussion about them that is protected by free speech. Only by protecting the citizens' right to freely express their often controversial and critical responses to the public authority's operations can the public authority regard its decisions as representing the common, unified perspective of all its citizens. If it does not know how its decisions affect its citizens, the public authority simply cannot function as a representative, public authority. Therefore, the state has the right and duty to legally recognize and protect its citizens' right to free speech; the right to free speech is constitutive of the rightful relation between citizens and their state.

There is clear textual support for the view that Kant provides the kind of twofold defense of free speech argued for here, a defense that combines arguments that communication of thought does not, as such, constitute private wrongdoing with arguments that the state must protect free speech so as to function as a representative authority. To outlaw free speech, Kant argues in the essay "What is Enlightenment?," is to "renounce enlightenment . . . [and] to violate the sacred right of humanity and trample it underfoot" (WE 8: 39). Outlawing free speech is not only imprudent, because it makes enlightenment or governance through reason impossible, but it is also wrong in that it goes along with denying people their innate right to freedom. Textual support for the claim that a government that outlaws free speech is a government "which misunderstands itself," which fails to recognize that its authority is *public* in nature, not private (WE 8: 41) is found in "Theory and Practice." There, Kant argues that legislation that outlaws free speech expresses irrational, unjustifiable behavior on the part of a government:

freedom of the pen . . . is the sole palladium of the people's rights. For to want to deny them this freedom is not only tantamount to taking from them any claim to a right with respect to the supreme commander (according to Hobbes), but is also to withhold from the latter—whose will gives order to the subjects as citizens only by representing the general will of the people— all knowledge of matters that [they themself][8] would change if [they] knew about them and to put [them] in contradiction with [themself].   (TP 8: 304; cf. WE 8: 39f.)

Free speech is the ultimate safeguard of the people's rights. A public authority cannot outlaw political free speech, because a ban on free speech would make "they them- self"—a functioning public authority—impossible. Such a decree would bring the sovereign "in contradiction with themself," because it would deny the sovereign the information without which the sovereign cannot act as the representative of the people or be a *public* authority at all. Additionally in "What is Enlightenment?," Kant expands on this point by claiming

[t]he *public* use of one's reason must always be free . . . . [B]y the public use of one's own reason I understand that use which someone makes of it *as a scholar* before the entire public of the *world of readers*.   (WE: 37)

---

[8] As throughout, I have changed Gregor's original translation which uses the male noun here ("he," "him," "himself") to the gender neutral "they," "them," and "themself" to stay truer to the original German. (In German, the word that generates Kant's use of the male pronouns is "der Befehlshaber," which is a male noun. A supreme commander is, however, a public position that can be held by people regardless of their gender identification, which entails that the better English translation would use gender neutral pronouns since nouns are not gendered in English.)

Every citizen must have the right to engage truthfully but critically in public affairs—to be a scholar—and so to raise their voice and explain why they believe the current public system of laws to be unjust or unfair. If such voices are not raised, the public authority cannot possibly serve as a means through which rightful relations and governance through public law are made possible. Without providing for public expression of the consequences of particular laws for right, the public authority lacks the information required to secure rights to freedom for all citizens and so to represent its citizens wisely. Indeed, not to protect freedom of speech makes it more difficult for the head of state to act and be wise, Kant argues in "Theory and Practice," as it is

to instill in the head of state concern that unrest in the state might be aroused by [the subjects'] thinking independently and aloud is tantamount to awakening in [them][9] mistrust of [their] own power and even hatred of [their] people.   (TP 8: 304)

This is why outlawing free political speech is something citizens cannot be thought as consenting to, and those entrusted with public office will (insofar as one is acting rationally) want citizens to have a right to free speech as this is necessary and makes it subjectively or emotionally easier for them to act wisely and be wise.

Notice that Kant's distinction between innate, private, and public right, combined with the fact that our laws of freedom apply to *human* beings, can be used to make sense of controversial issues regarding speech and sexuality, such as the legal regulation of displays of erotica in public spaces. To begin, erotic speech and images can be displayed in public spaces just as they can be published. There is no legal wrong, as such, in publicly displaying erotic images. The state can and should regulate where these public displays are made available, however, because it rightfully regulates ways in which private citizens can use public spaces. Because these spaces are intended for all to use, regulations circumscribe where and how private persons and businesses can make public statements, advertise their products, and perform other such activities within these spaces. Accordingly, the state should regulate the public presentations of erotica just as it should regulate all other material and products. What is more, once we incorporate the fact that the laws regulating public spaces are designed for beings that are not only rational, embodied, and social but also distinctly human, we can make sense of why public displays of erotica tend to be among the most restricted of public displays. On balance, human beings need time to emotionally and morally mature before being able to engage the complexity of erotica in morally (ethically and legally) responsible ways. Consequently, children as well as adults who have certain cognitive disabilities have a right not to be subjected to explicit sexualized or erotic writings and images—privately *or* publicly—until they are capable of being morally (legally and ethically) responsible for their own sexuality. For this reason, just states will not legally permit public displays of erotica that are unsuitable for audiences currently incapable of moral responsibility for their sexuality, just as it will not permit public displays of other human activities the viewing of which requires capability for moral responsibility.

---

[9] I have altered Gregor's translation here too to make it gender neutral.

1.1.2 SEXUALITY AND SEDITIOUS SPEECH, RESISTANCE, AND THE RIGHT TO HAVE RIGHTS

Like many philosophers before him, Kant argues that seditious speech should be outlawed. To understand why, remember that Kant takes himself to have shown that right is in principle (ideally) impossible in the state of nature and that, consequently, a natural executive right does not exist. Because Kant believes he has successfully refuted any notion of a natural executive right, he takes himself to have shown that no one has a *right* to stay in the state of nature. This, in turn, explains why Kant can and does consider seditious speech a public crime. The intention behind seditious speech is not just to criticize the government or, say, to critically discuss theories of government. To qualify as seditious, the speaker's intention must be to encourage and support efforts to subvert the government or to instigate its violent overthrow— or to foment a revolution. To have this right would be to have the right to destroy the state and return to the state of nature. Because the state is the only means through which rightful interaction is possible, to have a supposed right to overthrow it would be to have the right to annihilate right, which is impossible (a contradiction in terms) (MM 6: 320). That is to say, because right is impossible in the state of nature, the right to subversion would be the right to replace *right* (rightful use of force or rightful coercion) with *might* (pure force or violence). Because the state is the only means through which right can replace might, just states outlaw seditious speech. And, because it is a crime that "endanger[s] the commonwealth" as such (rather than citizens qua private persons), it is a public crime (MM 6: 331).

That one does not have a right to revolution does not entail that anyone is politically obligated to obey barbarous laws, but it does mean that it is never justifiable simply "to burn it all down."[10] To see why, notice that the account just described entails that constitutive of the minimally just state is a legal-political framework based on each citizen's right to freedom, which is matched by a series of rights analytically connected with this right for embodied beings (namely, to rightful honor, bodily integrity, and free speech) and a set of private rights synthetically connected with it (namely, to private property, contract, and status relations). To grasp the importance of this point, first consider a couple of paradigmatic

---

[10] In one of the fragments from his *Lectures and Drafts on Political Philosophy*, Kant expresses this point regarding resistance in this way: "The *summus imperans* {supreme sovereign} does something wrong and could be coerced with power [*Gewalt*]. The subjects* are right but do not have any authorized power and avail themselves of what they have, in this case they do not wrong the *imperans* but it is *formaliter* wrong. They act against the form of both the commonwealth and its contract. The resistance of the subjects contradicts itself as well as the constant call of their happiness, the former decides . . . * they can never oppose but only resist, i.e. refuse to do what is in itself morally impossible and endure the consequences. The reason for this is because a human being is an animal that is good only under coercion, and he who is to coerce him is himself a human being. No wrong is done in this way to the one who wants to sever the bonds of right" (LDPP 19: 487; cf. 591, 593f.). So, again, the people do not have a right to engage in revolution, but they can refuse to go along with what is wrong from the point of view of right (what would amount to being denied their basic rights), in which case they will do a formal wrong, but not a material wrong (against the human being who holds the supreme sovereign office and who is trying to wrong them through this office).

historical examples that do not concern sex, love, and gender. First, it follows from this account that until slavery was abolished in the US, it was not a minimally just state (a *Rechtsstaat*); after all, the innate right to freedom just is the right not to be enslaved. Second, once Jews were denied the right to own private property, Nazi Germany ceased to be a minimally just state (a *Rechtsstaat*), because once (some) citizens are denied a property right, they cannot rightfully acquire material objects with which to exercise external freedom. In addition, without private property rights they are denied the possibility of access to a place where they can exist and to which they can deny other private persons access.

Let us now move to cases where the basic legal-political legal framework (such as the constitution) meet the general conditions of being minimally just, but where pockets of law regarding sex, love, or gender are not. As noted several times, it is constitutive of minimally just states that they posit, apply, and enforce the *a priori* principles of right outlined in Chapters 5 and 6 in such a way that all persons have—to borrow Hannah Arendt's phrase—the right to have rights. Arendt's idea of having a right to have rights is similar to what Kant seems to mean when he says that a "rightful condition is that relation of human beings among one another that contains the conditions under which alone everyone is able to *enjoy* [their] rights" (MM 6: 305f.). Arendt develops her idea of the right to have rights in relation to refugees and their right to become members of states. Here, however, my main point is that Kant's philosophy can help us develop Arendt's thought by enabling us to see that there are two ways in which we can be denied a right to have rights even though we live in states whose general, fundamental legal-political framework (the constitution) is minimally just: (1) We can find ourselves in states where some aspects of our lives are subjected to inherently unjust laws and thereby find some aspects of our lives subjected to threats of violence and injustice characteristic of a barbaric state of nature; and (2) we can be denied use of our rights by being denied access to and protection by some of the laws constitutive of civil society, yielding the result that some of our relations are forced to remain in the anarchic state of nature (where anarchic relations devoid of justice are the best that we can do). In both cases, it will be that one does not need to change the basic, general legal principles by means of which laws are justified in the state to show that these particular laws (such as laws making sodomy or abortion illegal or same-sex marriage legally impossible) are unjustifiable, even if *de facto* upheld. Let us begin with the case in which some interactions—pockets or compartments of the legal-political reality—are subject to barbaric (inherently unjust, violent, or brutalizing) laws. Then we will move to cases where one is denied access to law and therefore finds oneself forced to effectively live in an anarchic state of nature where these rights are concerned.

First, consider cases in which some group of citizens is subjected to inherently unjust laws, laws that deprive them of their most basic innate or private rights. Remember that if my Kantian theory of justice is correct, then people have the right to have secured the rights internally linked with their innate right to freedom, either analytically (i.e., the rights to rightful honor, free speech, and bodily integrity) or synthetically (i.e., the rights to private property, contract, and status relations). It follows that if, for example, the constitution is grounded on rights all citizens have, but the legal system (property law further downstream from the constitution) upholds that women cannot own private property, then the related use of coercion is not justifiable because the state fails to recognize and secure for roughly half their population the right to have this basic right (to private property). Instead, the state makes women's right to legally exist somewhere and their legal access to private spaces of their own dependent on somebody else's (men's) private choices about the matter. Again, there is a *possible* path by means of which solid legal-political argumentation that demonstrates the injustice of this—the one that is consistent with and expressive of a firm commitment to each citizen's right to freedom—is available, but at the moment the legal-political forces make this course of reform *de facto* unavailable. Similarly, if a state (again, not as a constitutional matter) criminalizes abortion or fulfillments and expressions of one's LGBTQIA identity (by criminalizing sodomy or gender-affirming surgeries, for example), it again denies some citizens (women and members of the LGBTQIA community) their right to have rights to bodily integrity protected. The enforcement of such laws is simply an exercise of violence, a mere use of unjustifiable force in the coercive denial of this sphere of rights: it is barbarism. Such laws even require the state's own institutions to participate in the wrongdoing. Women and sexual or gendered minorities therefore do not wrong materially anyone in particular when they resist such violence, while those who participate do participate in the wrongdoing: women and sexual or gendered minorities undertake only formal (and not material) wrongdoing, whereas those who partake in such violence against the women and sexual or gendered minorities engage in both formal and material wrongdoing.

Another example is states that use legal-political coercive means to deny women the right to wear the clothes they want to wear in public—whether these laws require them to remove religious clothing in public (currently, in some countries, burkas and niqabs must be removed when entering public spaces) or to wear specific religious clothing (in other countries, burkas and niqabs must be worn when entering public spaces). These states cease to be minimally just in these regards. Although any solid legal-political argument based on the innate right to freedom can show that such uses of violence against women are inherently unjust, again, at the moment such legal-political paths are blocked by destructive and damaging political forces. Accordingly, when women find themselves in such situations, they do not materially wrong anyone in particular, including the public officers when they defend themselves from such violence—such as by lying about what they have done or by using force to stop someone from reporting them to the police—but nevertheless they do formal wrong, in the highest degree, when they so resist. As argued in Chapter 3, they are being forced into situations from which there are no morally good—let alone emotionally healthy—ways out. Similarly, if erotica as such is criminalized or if people who choose to sell sexual services or goods are criminalized for so doing, the state fails to be minimally just in this regard. All these kinds of rules are necessarily inconsistent with basic principles of freedom (innate and private right) and therefore cannot be laws for free persons. Obviously, people may choose not to break such rules for prudential reasons, but they are under no rightful obligations to comply with them. If they use force to protect themselves in this regard, they do not commit material wrongdoing against anyone, but they do engage in formal wrongdoing. In contrast, those who participate in such uses of violence against sex workers, women, or people who enjoy erotica, engage in both formal and material wrongdoing in so doing.

Second, unlike in the types of cases just discussed, sometimes the problem facing people is that states refuse to legally recognize the many ways in which we can live together as an "us." This refusal of legal recognition does not thereby transform relevant spheres of force into barbarism, however; rather, it forces those affected by these legal restrictions to live together in the state of nature, where they can, at most, live together peacefully but not rightfully (live in ways "devoid" of justice). This is a different sense in which one can be denied the right to have rights, namely by being denied full entrance into civil society. So, if states refuse to recognize legal marriage for interracial, same-sex, or symmetrical polyamorous relationships, they do not thereby institute barbarism, but they do fail to perform their basic function of establishing rightful conditions for their citizens. By denying them access to a shared life governed by family law, these states force those people to live together in the anarchic version of the state of nature, where the best they can do is live together in ways that are devoid of justice. (It would be the institution of barbarism if it were made a legal wrong or crime to live together in these ways.) Similarly, if states prohibit artificial insemination for lesbian couples or refuse the right to adopt for singles, non-straight couples, or members of non-monogamous loving relationships, they wrong members of these groups by denying them entrance into civil society. By being denied such access to civil society, members of these groups are denied the legal protection and facilitation of their shared lives and homes to which they have a right, which would be recognized were they being treated as free and equal subjects of family law. Again, such refusals of legal recognition are serious failures on the part of states, because they deny people access to civil society, but they do not institute barbarism (violence) as they are merely despotic (efforts by means of which some use the legal-political system to force others to live in accordance with their private choices on important personal issues). I return to some of these issues towards the end of the chapter, where the topic is the reform of our inherited legal-political institutions. But first, given our interests here, let us move from the consequences of the denial of protections of innate and private right (private law) to examine a different set of legal, systemic protections in Kant's account of public right (public law).

1.2 The Form of the Public Authority II: Republican Systemic Principles of Public Right

We have seen some of the principles constitutive of the public authority. I now turn to other, distinctly systemic principles that Kant proposes as necessary legal-political effects of the establishment of civil society. Throughout this analysis, I argue that the main principle constitutive of ensuring systemic justice is that the state cannot allow its citizens to become dependent on its monopoly on coercion unless it also ensures that the legal-political institutional system as a whole is consistent with their innate right to freedom, namely their right not to have their freedom subjected to anyone's arbitrary, private choices but only to public law. All principles of public, systemic right therefore follow from one of two normative facts: (a) from the fact that the state must institutionally reconcile its monopoly on coercion with each citizen's innate right to freedom and secure its own rightful existence in perpetuity; or (b) from the fact that any systems on which the citizens' exercise of freedom is made dependent must treat the citizens as being free and independent in relation to one another and subject only to a set of laws that reciprocally restricts them (as equals). Public right (public law) is the main tool the state uses to ensure that the law-governed monopoly on coercion as a whole operates in this way and, so, to deal with both systemic facts characteristic of civil society. As we will see, this approach becomes very useful as we try to understand and address the many problems of harassment and oppression that characterize the lives of women and sexual or gendered minorities.

1.2.1 SEX, LOVE, AND GENDER AND EQUAL ACCESS: PUBLIC IDENTIFICATIONS, PUBLIC FORMS, PUBLIC MARKETPLACES

"*Public right*," Kant explains, refers to the rule of law necessary to enable and secure individuals' rights as well as to "[t]he sum of the laws which needs to be promulgated generally in order to bring about a rightful condition" (MM 6: 311). Kant positions his public right discussion of systemic justice in a "general remark" section entitled "On the Effects with Regard to Rights that Follow from the Nature of the Civil Union" (MM 6: 318) in The Doctrine of Right. This section of The Doctrine of Right critiques public right principles as they pertain to systemic issues concerning the structure of the public authority, as previously outlined (MM 6: 318–23), and the systemic issues concerning land ownership, the economy, the financial system (MM 6: 323–5), poverty and religious institutions (MM 6: 326–8), public offices (MM 6: 328–30), and punishment (MM 6: 331–7). Each of these principles of public right is, as emphasized above, grounded on how the state must ensure a systemic legal-political institutional whole under which citizens can interact as individuals who are free, equal, and independent in relation to one another, and as subject only to public law. The main focus in this section is on how Kant's argument for the legal regulation of the economy and the financial system relates to issues concerning equal access.

Before proceeding, however, allow me to note one more general equal access issue that applies to all of the systems mentioned above: the question of equal access to public spaces, which is a question of particular importance to some members of the LGBTQIA community. All interaction in public spheres—from interaction with the legal system to interaction with the economy, financial system, and public administration—requires that we be able publicly to identify ourselves. Access to public identification papers is a precondition for traveling, for engaging in economic exchanges (including by buying homes or acquiring jobs), for accessing the public administrative system, and so on. Because the state is necessarily in charge of their availability, it cannot make access to these public identification papers dependent on interacting and presenting oneself as someone one is not. Citizens must be able to acquire identification papers that identify them as themselves and not as those who others may want them to be. Making it possible for each citizen to specify (insofar as gender or sexual specification is necessary for public identification purposes at all) or change their gender (if the gender one was assigned at birth is mistaken) is consti-tutive of the state's fulfillment of its function in this area.

With respect to the regulation and administration of the economy, Kant defends a public systemic solution to what he considers a systemic problem. The public authority is, Kant argues, a legal-political guarantor of the economy: It must act as "supreme commander" of the economic system. Regardless of the type of economic system the state allows to develop, the state must assume a special authoritative role in relation to the way in which means (goods and services) are exchanged by ensuring that it secures what we might call a public marketplace (the economy). The state fulfills this role by positing and enforcing laws that secure each person's right to access and participate in the public marketplace on equal terms. Specifically, it posits laws that regulate the ways in which people participate as buyers and sellers in the public marketplace. The right to access the public marketplace to exchange one's means preserves the right to freedom in a market-based system, where people must engage in trade to legally access means with which they can set and pursue ends of their own. Accordingly, the state must ensure that the economic system does not deny access to citizens who have the relevant means or deny citizens access to trade on equal terms. Insofar as citizens' exercise of external freedom is made dependent on the economic system, in other words, the state must regulate actual economic practices to ensure equal systemic freedom. Distinctions between permissible and impermissible ways of engaging in economic activity (trade) will be drawn precisely at the limit at which equal systemic freedom is denied.

To illustrate the general principle, let me first offer a couple of examples not related to sex, love, or gender. To begin, the principle entails the state can prohibit the emergence of monopolies in a capitalist system. The power enjoyed by a monopoly enables it to control the supply of goods and services in a market, which makes it impossible for others to compete with it. Such a dynamic is inconsistent with a public capitalist marketplace—where competition and prices enable supply to meet demand—and instead consists of subjecting some citizens' exercise of freedom to the private choices of others (those in charge of the monopoly, the supply). Thus, such an asymmetrical, systemic dependency relation is impermissible in a free society that has adopted the capitalist system. Another example is the public requirement that businesses enable everyone, including physically incapacitated persons, to enter their stores. If the public marketplace is inaccessible to those who have physical incapacitations and the state has made the citizens' exercise of external freedom dependent on trade (the economy) to access goods and services, the state must institute regulations that ensure access for all (again, conditions of equal systemic freedom).

Turning to examples involving sex, love, and gender, first note that once citizens' exercise of freedom is made dependent on markets, the state must require businesses to recognize all citizens as equal customers. Private people (and their businesses) cannot demand to participate in the public market solution to the provision of land, goods, and services and simultaneously insist on treating the public market as if it is simply their private sphere. That is to say, if one wants to be part of the public market solution to the provision of goods and services for all citizens, one must also be willing to do so in a way that involves treating all citizens as free and equal. Accordingly, in just states private businesses participating in the economy will be legally required to treat all citizens as equals. In just states, private businesses cannot deny access to certain customers based on these customers' sexual identity or gender or sexual orientation, for the same reason they cannot deny them access because of their religion, ethnicity, disability, etc. If it is difficult for someone to interact with others in rightful ways because doing so is perceived as inconsistent with one's deep religious or first-person ethical convictions, then one must assume responsibility for this, such as by hiring someone who can serve all customers in ways that are consistent with these customers' rights to be treated as free and equal. Similarly, insofar as the transactions require publicly recognized or official forms listing one's family members, such as when people apply for loans or purchase homes, these forms will use gender-neutral concepts as much as possible. It must also accommodate same-sex and symmetrical polyamorous marriages. Only when citizens' equal access to markets and financial institutions is secured can citizens' market dependence be reconciled with their right to freedom, that is, their right to be subject only to general laws that restrict reciprocally (symmetrically and non-contingently). In these ways, public institutional regulations on the economy secure citizens' innate right to have their external freedom subject only to public law and not to the arbitrary, private choices of other citizens.

The same assumption of protection must guide the public authority's establishment of a financial system. For example, the state guarantees conditions of equal systemic freedom in relation to the way it permits the introduction of money by assuming responsibility for regulating the financial system. External freedom is the ability to set and pursue ends of one's own, so people's means are constitutive of their external freedom. If the value of a person's means is determined by a monetary system, the value of money must be subject to public regulation. The state must ensure that the value of a person's means is not arbitrarily determined by some other private person but only by public law. Only in this way can it ensure that permitting a financial system is consistent with everyone's innate right to freedom. The complexity of the financial system will affect the details of regulations required to ensure that the system does its job, but the legal-political test will be whether the state provides its subjects with conditions under which they can enjoy equal systemic freedom. Presumably, the following conditions must be met with regard to money: the state must determine what counts as legal tender; ensure that legal tender is recognized as having the same value for all participants in the public marketplace; and assume sole control over the supply of legal tender. If it does not meet these conditions, it clearly has not passed the test. A system of law that allows what counts as legal tender to be arbitrarily determined, that allows private persons to determine whether legal tender is recognized and what value it is given in the marketplace, or that allows private persons to print as much money as they wish clearly does not ensure that (the value of) one private person's means (as money) is protected from the arbitrary choices of other private persons.

Similarly, insofar as the people's savings are made dependent on a financial system, all legally responsible persons must be treated as equals under this financial system. For example, being a woman cannot disqualify one from opening a bank account or taking out a loan (under the same conditions as men). Again, because external freedom is characterized by being able to use one's means to set and pursue ends, if these systemic requirements are not met, one private person's external freedom is subjected to another private person's arbitrary choice rather than to public law, and the person is thereby denied access to conditions of interaction that are reconcilable with one's innate right to freedom. If the state fails to regulate the financial system but still makes its people depend on it to exercise their freedom, the citizens cannot be seen as politically obligated to obey its authority, just as they cannot be obligated to obey laws that deny them equal systemic freedom as participants in the economy. Once we also accommodate the reality that these systems are made for and by human beings, with the particular emotional makeup and histories that human beings have, we will regard failures to interact in these ways as particularly serious failings, because they enable and foster humiliating and shaming behaviors towards women and sexual or gendered minorities.

1.2.2 REFUSING TO INTERACT AS FREE, EQUAL, AND INDEPENDENT: STALKING, BLACKMAIL, AND SEXUAL HARASSMENT

This Kantian account of equal freedom also helps us understand why just states outlaw other kinds of behavior that undermine public spaces by making them into spaces of interaction characterized by private, asymmetrical dependency relations. In addition, as usual, once we account for the typical emotional effects of such behaviors on human beings, especially on those whose social identities have histories characterized by oppression and violence, we can understand why such laws identify those unjust behaviors as being not only serious but also heinous. To illustrate this general idea, I discuss three kinds of unjust behaviors—stalking, blackmail, and harassment—that often target women or that target people because of their sexuality or gender.

Let me begin with stalking. The reason just states prohibit stalking is relatively straightforward: Public spaces of interaction are such that each and all can use them to set and pursue ends of their own (including consensually with others) subject to laws that restrict them reciprocally. To engage in stalking behavior is to refuse to interact in this way. Stalking is to follow another person around, making this person's end-setting correspond to or determining for one's own ends. It encompasses trying to create a private (secret) relationship between oneself and another without the other's consent. The stalker assumes, in self-deceived ways, that they have a right to set ends together with the person they are stalking or to participate in their end-setting. Once we also account for the fact that stalking is done by and to human beings, additional challenges arise: being stalked can be deeply scary for the one being followed around; there is a pattern of men being the stalkers and women being the stalked; stalking often follows relationships that have ended; there is a real danger that the stalker escalates the bad behavior and uses force to realize the imagined relationship with the victim; and there is a positive correlation between stalking and physical violence against women and intimate partner murder.[11] In light of these factors, it is not surprising that laws for *human* beings should treat stalking as particularly serious and heinous.

Next, consider blackmail, which often involves the threat of unauthorized use of private sexual or erotic images. Why is blackmail outlawed by a just state? After all,

---

[11] For statistics on stalking in the US, see, for example, http://victimsofcrime.org/our-programs/stalking-resource-center/stalking-information

one might puzzle, private rights protect people's use of their own means to pursue their own ends. In addition, we have seen that no one has a right to anyone else's silence as such. If this is correct, why can I not offer to be silent about my knowledge (not share it publicly) of another's history in exchange for that person's payment? The reason I do not have a right to blackmail is that this kind of silence concerns the public sphere, and in this sphere, as we have seen, all citizens must be provided conditions in which they can interact as free, equal, and independent individuals. Instances of blackmail subvert these conditions of rightful interaction by having one person subject another person's exercise of freedom to their private choices. Accordingly, though I am legally permitted to make whatever truthful information I *rightfully* have about someone available to the public—such as by publishing it online or selling it to a newspaper or a magazine—I am not legally permitted to approach the person in question with an offer to exchange my silence for some of their means. Doing so is to attempt to force the other into a private dependency relation with me (in contrast to interacting as free, equal, and independent) by coercing them to set their ends in accordance with my choices about the matter. For these reasons, just states criminalize blackmail.

In addition, for *human* beings, handling others' intrusion into our lives in these ways is particularly difficult; there is a sense in which such invasion can make us feel like we no longer control our own lives. Because of the effects of blackmail on human beings, good laws consider blackmail particularly odious. Moreover, as explained in Chapter 5, if I have obtained someone's private (oftentimes erotic or sexual) images or writings illegally or through having shared an intimate private moment with the other person (as is often the case in instances of so-called "revenge porn"), I can be punished both for blackmail and for particularly serious breaches of privacy. Finally, because we are not only rational, embodied, and social beings but also *human* versions of such beings, and because such wrongdoings can inflict serious psychological damage on embodied, social beings such as we are, these transgressions are heinous and should be subject to particularly harsh punishment.

This account can furthermore explain why we have harassment laws, including sexual harassment laws. Public spaces of interaction and private workplaces are important targets of these public laws because, as previously discussed, in market-based economies, the state has permitted its citizens to become dependent on private employment to secure legal access to means (and to thereby exercise external freedom). Just as the state must ensure that all public spaces are spheres within which its citizens can interact as free, equal, and independent bearers of rights, the state must ensure that an economy on which its citizens are dependent for legal access to means (an income) functions in the same way. That is, insofar as the state permits the market-based system to become part of the public solution to enabling access to and securing rightful private property for each and all, it must also govern that economic system through public law. The state cannot permit such systemic dependence without also ensuring that the systems are not means through which some private persons harass others. To permit this would be to permit some private citizens to form unjustifiable dependency relations with their fellow citizens. Some private persons, such as those who are relatively well-off (materially and/or socially), would be able to give other private persons, such as those who are relatively less well-off (materially and/or socially), offers and advances they cannot refuse because they do not have the socioeconomic resources to prevent such refusals from yielding devastating effects.[12] Permitting such private dependency relations necessarily conflicts with the state's function, which is to reconcile its monopoly on coercion with each citizen's innate right to freedom. The right to freedom, as we have seen, is the right to *independence from* rather than dependence on any private person's arbitrary choices, which is realized only by subjecting interacting persons' freedom reciprocally to universal laws of freedom as enabled by the public authority. By issuing and upholding harassment laws that govern all systems on which citizens' exercise of their rights depends, including private businesses, the state secures rightful conditions for all.

Even if we accept this account, however, it is not immediately clear why we have not only general laws that forbid harassment but also *sexual* harassment laws,[13] where the "sexual" component adds a level of serious heinousness to the harassing behavior. According to my Kant-based position, the answer to this question requires us to once again pay attention to how laws of freedom accommodate specifically *human* concerns, because these concerns are crucial to understanding the ways in which some of the kinds of speech and behaviors that amount to harassment track severe and pervasive historical oppression. One can be harassed and stalked without such historical patterns doing explanatory work, but a lot of harassment as we (human beings) know it consists of personal insults and invasion of personal spaces motivated by factors such as gender or sexual identity, sexual orientation, race, ethnicity, disability, and socioeconomic class. Also, explaining the nature of insults often requires us to appeal both to the fact that the relevant interacting beings are rational, embodied, and social as well as to the fact that they share a distinctly *human* nature and a history that is characterized by significant oppression of groups with which the insulted person shares an identity. For example, though blonde jokes can annoy me, they do not insult me, whereas sexist comments about my gender *are* insults—and being constantly subjected to them typically interferes with people's ability to stay focused on the job and tasks at hand.[14]

Harassment generally contains a refusal to interact with others in professional and public spaces in ways consistent with respecting them as free, equal, and independent individuals. It involves a threat to or an invasion of the personal space of another. These problems are intensified insofar as they track the state's historic and current inability to provide some group(s) of citizens with rightful conditions of interaction, because this inability makes harassment more threatening, invasive, and likely to occur without consequence for the wrongdoer. Harassment laws are public laws that attempt to remedy the fact that some citizens have been and still are considered "more equal than others." Consequently, if the state finds that it is still unable to

---

[12] I think this argument applies to any private system on which the state allows its citizens to depend for the exercise of their rights.

[13] Note that libertarian theories of justice struggle to make sense of any of these kinds of regulation. Because they are committed to the view that the rights of the state are reducible to those of individuals, any restrictions must be understood in terms of private harms.

[14] See Cudd (2006) and Hay (2013) for excellent discussions of these features of oppression.

successfully provide conditions under which the protection and empowerment of its historically oppressed and therefore vulnerable groups are secured, it is within its rightful powers not only to impose general harassment laws to improve its ability to provide rightful conditions but also to clarify that certain groups are given special protection under these laws because these groups are more likely to be subjected to it and are more prone to psychological harm from such behavior. By putting its weight behind historically oppressed and vulnerable citizens, the state seeks to overcome the problems caused by its lack of proper protection in the past (as revealed in the patterns of oppressive behaviors). Note that this argument does not, nor must it, determine *which* uses of speech and behavior amount to (sexual) harassment and so should be outlawed. It only explains *why* certain instances of speech and behavior can and should be outlawed in the name of harassment. The former assessment is a matter for public debate and reflection and then translation into public regulation on behalf of all citizens.

1.2.3 POVERTY AS SYSTEMIC INJUSTICE

Having discussed some effects of the establishment of states on public regulation directed at securing citizens' interaction as free, equal, and independent individuals within the economy, the financial systems, and public spheres, I finish this section by turning to the issue of poverty relief. As mentioned in the general introduction to Part II, for a long time, most Kantians found Kant's position deficient because of his alleged failure to address issues of economic justice in general as well as the problem of poverty in particular.[15] Because of this problem, some Kantians, such as Onora O'Neill and John Rawls, found it necessary to move away from Kant's own theory to develop more egalitarian Kantian theories of justice.[16] In contrast to these interpretations, I defend a liberal republican kind of interpretation of Kant according to which considerations of economic justice lie at the very heart of Kant's conception of right, not only because of the requirements to ensure equal systemic freedom previously outlined but also because unconditional poverty relief is a minimal condition of the rightful state.[17] Besides, although the conditions on a minimally just state are not very demanding in terms of economic justice, I will argue, this does not mean that the Kantian position cannot also defend more robust forms of economic justice in materially and institutionally more resourceful conditions.

Kant discusses the state's duties to the poor in section "C" of public right (MM 6: 325-8), where he is concerned in part with how the public authority reconciles its monopoly on coercion with each subject's right to freedom by arguing that a systemic solution is necessary to rectify the systemic problem of poverty. Only through an institutional guarantee of unconditional poverty relief can the state make rightful the

[15] For examples in the earlier secondary literature, see Gregor (1963: 36f.); Williams (1986: 196-8); Kersting (1992a: 153, 164 n.7), though contrast the later with his modified view in Kersting (1992b: 356f.); Höffe (1994: 184f.); Rosen (1996: 197); and O'Neill (2000: 65).

[16] For example, see O'Neill (1990: 219-34, 1996: 122-212); Rosen (1996: 173-208); Rawls (1999: 221-7); and Guyer (2000: 262-86).

[17] My view that economic justice lies at the very heart of Kant's conception of political legitimacy stands in contrast to the interpretations of Kant given by, for example, Williams (1983); Kersting (1992a); Höffe (1994); Murphy (1970); and Guyer (2000).

dependency relation between itself and those who have no means. As I argue elsewhere,[18] to reconcile its rightful monopoly on coercion with the rights of the poor, the state must ensure that no private persons find themselves without any legal access to means because external freedom is impossible without material means. Therefore, the state must guarantee unconditional poverty relief to fulfill its role of providing conditions under which persons can exercise their innate right to freedom. In the absence of unconditional poverty relief, the poor cannot exercise their innate right to freedom, because insofar as they do not have means, any legal access to means goes through some other private person's consent, such as richer private persons' arbitrary choices to provide employment or charity to them. Therefore, unless unconditional poverty relief is guaranteed by the state, the possibility of poor persons exercising external freedom is subject to the arbitrary choices of the richer ones (those who have means). To put the point differently, insofar as we are citizens who have private property under our control, our exclusion of others from our private property is not conclusively rightful unless there exists a public solution for those who, for whatever reason, currently do not have any. Our relations to one another as citizens are made minimally rightful only if each citizen is publicly guaranteed legal access to means, in part so that no citizens find themselves in a condition in which they cannot access means unless they commit a crime or another private person happens to choose to share some of their means with them. Consequently, as the state upholds its monopoly on coercion, it must also institutionally ensure that the poor do not find themselves so subject to the private choices of the richer. Therefore, Kant maintains, insofar as the state upholds its monopoly on coercion, the state has a right and a duty to tax the rich to provide unconditional relief for the poor, even though no individual private person has the right to coerce another to provide charity (beneficence). A state that takes this measure provides the kind of condition that is constitutive of making the current private property holdings conclusively (rather than merely provisionally) rightful.

A reason many read Kant's argument differently is that he makes claims such as the following: Because the wealthy owe their existence to the state and the state has an indirect right to preserve the people, the state will use taxation to provide for the poor people's "most necessary natural needs" (MM 6: 326). Kant's formulation might tempt us to conclude that he is simply confused, because a claim that "natural needs" can give rise to demands of justice would undermine much of Kant's account of justice as rightful freedom. So, even if Kant is expressing a desire to incorporate into his theory of justice some notion of poverty relief, he clearly fails to do so. In my view, however, the stronger interpretation of Kant's position on poverty relief pays careful attention to how this argument is made within public right and how public right is principally concerned with how the sovereign must set up their institutional framework to reconcile their monopoly on coercion with the rights of each citizen. When Kant speaks of how the wealthy owe their existence to the state, I suggest, he is referring to the fact that the conclusive rightfulness of their private property is enabled and secured by the state.[19] As well, his reference to the state's indirect

---

[18] See Varden (2006, 2010b, 2012a).   [19] See also Kant's (2001) lecture notes (LDPP 27: 540).

right (corresponding to the citizens' duty) to preserve society suggests that the primary objective for the public authority is to maintain and preserve for its people a rightful condition in perpetuity. It does this by institutionally guaranteeing each person's innate right to freedom, which includes providing unconditional poverty relief so that none of its subjects ends up in a situation in which they have committed no legal wrongdoing and yet they find their legal access to means dependent on another private person's arbitrary choices about the matter.[20] The state cannot force its subjects into such private dependency relations because if it does it thereby fails to represent those citizens. In the absence of an institutional guarantee of unconditional poverty relief, the state is not minimally just and political obligations do not exist. Unquestionably, our *human* embodiment entails that we have natural needs, but on the more plausible reading of this point, in my view, this is another instance of Kant making space for our distinctly *human* nature within the framework set only by *a priori* principles constitutive of rightful freedom. Human beings have certain natural needs because of our particular kind of embodied, social nature, which entails that the amount and kinds of means that need to be legally guaranteed is determined by these features of our particular kind of embodied, social being. That is to say, our distinctly *human* needs must figure into a deliberative determination of what kind of and how much relief is necessary and reasonable; this is yet another place where an *a posteriori* aspect to our legal-political realities is accommodated within the *a priori* framework set by the principles of freedom.

Note that the claim in the previous paragraphs is not that the state, to be minimally just, must have an extensive welfare system. The claim is only that it must take institutional steps to guarantee the availability of means for those who, for whatever reason, have none. Notice, too, that these arguments concerning the state's role as guarantor of equal systemic freedom and unconditional poverty relief entail that the state's rights exceed the rights of private individuals. More specifically, the state's rights to ensure equal systemic freedom and unconditional poverty relief are rights that private individuals cannot have, because were we to understand them as private rights, they would be tantamount to the right to enslave or steal from others. Furthermore, together with the arguments in the earlier sections of this chapter that the state must provide these institutional protections is another reason why Kant's position is not absolutist. By requiring the state to provide public systemic solutions to what he considers public systemic problems, Kant tries to show that there are institutional requirements of the public authority that cannot be set aside without its legitimacy being thereby undermined. For example, to make sure that women have safe places to be and independently of anyone else's private choices about the matter—so that they can, for example, flee from abusive husbands, not have to marry, or not to be forced into trade in sexual services or goods—is not a matter of charity or benevolence; it is plainly a matter of justice on this approach. Notice too that the focus thus far has been only on the minimal conditions of equal systemic freedom and poverty relief that must be met for the state's monopoly on

---

[20] Those who find other textual interpretations of Kant more compelling can, of course, still view this account as capturing the stronger Kantian philosophical position.

coercion to be justified and for the state to be minimally just. As said above, however, this is not the end of the story, and, in the next section, I will address the question of how we make our inherited legal-political framework not only *minimally* just but also *robustly* just—one that is conducive to human beings' being able to flourish and govern themselves through public reason, namely through active engagement in public discussions and public offices. As we will see, this matters greatly as we are trying to make our states safer and better for historically oppressed groups like women and sexual or gendered minorities.

2. Reforming Our Imperfect, Inherited Legal-Political Frameworks into Well-Functioning, Robustly Just States

This section addresses the question of how we can reform our inherited, imperfect public institutions as we find them in our actual political societies so that they can better enable and protect rightful, sexual, loving, and/or gendered relations for each and all. I start by exploring these reform processes in general terms, following Kant's lead by considering how right should accommodate politics and not the other way around. I then turn to more specific issues regarding sex, love, and gender. First, I argue that states should seek to develop legal-political means—such as constitutions, judicial review, and participation in supranational and international conventions on human rights—to secure their citizens' ability to defend and exercise their basic rights. This is important, I argue, for securing rights for members of oppressed and vulnerable social groups domestically as well as for advancing our shared global fight against wrongdoing that takes advantage of the vulnerability of members of oppressed groups, such as child pornography and sex trafficking.

Second, I explain how states that (correctly) understand their own authority in terms of their citizens' right to freedom can, and sometimes do, deal with their current failure to protect all their citizens by taking legal measures such as abstaining from enforcing certain laws, permitting certain kinds of legal defenses, and abstaining from legislating over some areas of interaction. This argument is important for appreciating some ways in which states seek to address their inability to secure safe abortions for women, to protect women from domestic abuse, or to protect sex workers from assault and abuse. Third, just states can and should use systemic means to fight economic and social oppression that tracks historic or current state failures to secure rightful conditions for citizens. Such means include robustly just states' efforts to provide safe shelters for women and children who are fleeing domestic violence, legislation that secures access to gender-affirming surgeries for those needing them, legislation that secures access to safe housing for members of the LGBTQIA community, and so on. Fourth, I briefly explain why states should continuously make efforts to secure their citizens' right to privacy. Finally, I argue that states should seek to reform their public institutions so that they increasingly serve as public legal-political institutional means through which citizens can actively govern themselves. A central measure employed to achieve this goal should be expanding access to (higher) education for all citizens. As states reform themselves, I argue throughout, they are also increasingly able to build public institutions that are sensitive to our distinctly human needs.

2.1 From Right to Politics

As I have noted several times, in *The Metaphysics of Morals*, Kant argues that the necessary counterpart to a metaphysics of morals—or a system of *a priori* moral principles—in a complete practical philosophy is a moral anthropology. Turning our attention explicitly to a right and duty to reform our inherited, legal-political institutions, we find in "On the Supposed Right to Lie from Philanthropy" a complementary idea concerning how to realize *a priori* principles of right in our particular political circumstances. Kant says,

> in order to progress from a *metaphysics* of right (which abstracts from all conditions of experience) to a principle of *politics* (which applies these concepts to cases of experience) and, by means of this, to the solution of a problem of politics in keeping with the universal principle of right, a philosopher will give 1) an *axiom* that is an apodictically certain proposition that issues immediately from the definition of external right (consistency of the *freedom* of each with the freedom of everyone in accordance with a universal law); 2) a *postulate* (of external public *law*, as the united will of all in accordance with the principle of *equality*, without which there would be no freedom of everyone); 3) a *problem* of how it is to be arranged that in a society, however large, harmony in accordance with the principles of freedom and equality is maintained (namely by means of a representative system); this will then be a principle of *politics*, the arrangement and organization of which will contain decrees, drawn from experiential cognition of human beings, that have in view only the mechanism for administering right and how this can be managed appropriately. Right must never be accommodated to politics, but politics must always be accommodated to right.
>
> (SRL 8: 429; cf. TP 8: 277ff.)

When we explore Kant's conception of enforceable rights in relation to particular legal-political issues, in other words, the analysis will distinguish between the juridical *idea* of various issues (understood as the exposition of the relevant principles of right that abstracts from empirical conditions of experience) and the legal-political *ideal* of these same issues (understood as the exposition of a fuller legal-political conception of these issues in which empirical cognition of experience is given its due space). The main difference between the juridical *idea* (the minimally just state, or *Rechtsstaat*, previously explored) and the legal-political *ideal* (the most robustly just state), then, is that the fuller legal-political ideal incorporates not only the general moral psychological and anthropological reality that we are embodied, social human beings (the relevant concerns of animality and humanity, as found in Kant's account of human nature[21]) but also the fact that we live in particular societies with distinct geographical circumstances, histories, and cultures. In the remaining sections, I employ these distinctions to suggest some ways of reforming existing legal-political institutions to more effectively combat historical oppression and violence based on sex, love, and gender.

---

[21] As always, for more on Kant's account of human nature, see Part I.

2.1.1 BUILDING LEGAL SAFEGUARDS: CONSTITUTIONS, JUDICIAL REVIEW, AND INTERNATIONAL CONVENTIONS

Considering Kant's accounts of human nature (including the human propensity to evil) and right, it is unsurprising that many modern states (many states that understand their own authority in terms of their citizens' rights to freedom) develop various legal-political means for securing and promoting the progress of their development and for safeguarding against regress. Indeed, given these accounts, it is not surprising that in some of his personal notes on legal-political philosophy, Kant comments,

> Protect citizens from one another not only through laws but also through human-made institutions where everyone is safe from everyone else through laws. Be subordinated in no other way but according to the law. No advantage except when one has right on one's side. Easy access to administration of justice. Insight into legislation and wisdom in directing the administration.   (LDPP 15: 628)

An important legal-political means that has served these roles is founding legal documents (such as constitutions) that specify the basic principles of freedom (on the account we have discussed, the citizens' innate, private, and public rights) and that provide citizens a legal pathway for challenging particular laws' reconcilability with their basic rights to freedom. Constitutions empower citizens by securing for them a legal pathway for arguing in the highest court of the country—for example, the Supreme Court in the US or the Federal Constitutional Court in Germany—that a particular law is inconsistent with the legal-political foundation of civil society, that is, it is unconstitutional. Some states have also instituted judicial review, which allows the judiciary to critically engage (review) the legislation and policies passed by the other two branches of government. The right to legal representation—access to legal defense through trained and licensed legal professionals—is another way in which many states seek to secure each citizen subjection to laws only. A further means modern states have used to promote progress and hinder regress is by signing on to supranational and international conventions on human rights. Again, this is a legal means through which states defend against state-organized wrongdoing and failures to protect citizens' basic rights—however self-deceived those in charge of the state powers are in so perpetuating these wrongdoing and failures—by providing the citizens with a legal route by which they can challenge the justifiability of the laws to which they are subjected in a court founded on basic legal-political principles of freedom. Signing on to these legal institutions also gives states a starting point for building cooperative international legal-political institutions to fight crime that crosses state borders, including sex crimes, such as child pornography and sex trafficking, and crimes against women who work as servants in foreign countries.

In my view, according to Kant's legal-political philosophy, the fact that we seek to establish legal-political instruments of these kinds is not accidental. These measures enable us both to correct current and inherited mistakes by recognizing what our commitment to freedom requires of us, and to safeguard against similar mistakes in the future. We are, after all, prone to want to replace objective principles of freedom with contingent principles—to subject right to politics rather than politics to right.

As Kant emphasizes in *Anthropology,* our propensity to evil remains a constant threat to civil society:

In a civil constitution, which is the highest degree of artificial improvement of the human species' good predisposition to the final end of its destiny, animality still manifests itself earlier and, at bottom, more powerfully than pure humanity . . . . The human being's self-will is always ready to break out in aversion toward his neighbor, and he always presses his claim to unconditional freedom; freedom not merely to be independent of others, but even to be master over other beings who by nature are equal to him . . . . This is because nature within the human being strives to lead him from culture to morality, and not (as reason prescribes) beginning with morality and its law, to lead him to a culture designed to be appropriate to morality. This inevitably establishes a perverted, inappropriate tendency: for example, when religious instruction, which necessarily should be a moral culture, begins with historical culture, which is merely the culture of memory, and tries in vain to deduce morality from it.   (A 7: 327–8)

Kant's example here concerns the way in which the combination of the early development of our existentially powerful capacities to animality and the social (not pure) aspects of humanity with the vices trailing them (our desire to feel absolutely unrestricted or powerful) is internally linked to the fact that religious instruction so often understands itself as beginning with "historical culture" rather than with "moral culture," or what can be justified to morally responsible beings (persons).[22] Religious instruction (as an actual practice) often understands and presents itself as being justified by the culture of memory (its own historical culture) rather than by the participation of (social) beings who are *also* capable of moral responsibility (true freedom). This mistaken approach towards religion is terribly tempting to us because of the way in which it feeds our propensity to evil, namely by fostering a sense of importance (being part of some grand, historical enterprise that surpasses all the rest) or a sense of superiority over others that impairs our ability to interact with everyone as equals (in ways respectful of our inherited, cultural differences).

The same mistaken approach also manifests in the case of nations. One problem with certain forms of bad nationalism is that they purport to justify the claim that one nation is better than others and that the inherited culture (whatever it is taken to be) of that nation sets the framework for freedom rather than the other way around. Political leaders who participate in such bad nationalism try in vain to argue that there are special Norwegian, French, British, Chinese, Korean, Japanese, South African, American, Russian, etc. (or, as is similarly common, "African," "Western," or "Eastern," etc.), values that somehow set the framework for permissible exercises

---

[22] It is somewhat difficult to follow Kant in this passage because of how he discusses animality and "pure" humanity. To make his point easier to understand, he could have written that the capacities to animality and humanity are existentially very important and that the capacity to humanity necessarily presents the possibility of choices (because this capacity requires reason, albeit not practical reason). It is therefore tempting for us not to engage others in the ways that "pure" humanity would require of us, namely by regarding each other as having "*equal worth,*" and to instead regard others as having unequal worth (R 6: 27). In addition, morality as such—what is justifiable to all morally responsible persons— cannot possibly be deduced from these two predispositions, because, as we have seen in previous chapters, morality is necessarily enabled by the third predisposition, the predisposition to personality. Hence, these forms of religious instruction are terribly tempting to beings such as us but are also profoundly confused.

of freedom in their own nations rather than maintaining that our shared capacity for freedom (moral responsibility) is what must always set the framework within which any claims to accommodation of cultural, national, and religious differences are justifiably made.[23] Cultural and religious beliefs are inherently contingent and cannot set the framework for rightful coercion. Again, the objective (*a priori*) principles of right that enable rightful freedom must set the coercive legal-political framework within which we can then accommodate and develop our cultures and religions. Legal paths for challenging current norms and practices can, in other words, enable citizens of just states to constructively address and challenge normative claims that seek justification by appeal to our animality and social aspects of our humanity and that currently wrongly override or are inconsistent with respect for us as the particular beings we are. Only then can the legal-political framework as a whole be owned as "ours," that is, as a legal-political framework that makes it possible for each and all of us to bring into union our pursuits of happiness and commitments to morality (ethics and right). In addition, it assists us in our efforts to gradually sharpen our ability to analyze legal-political disputes in terms of principles that are grounded in each citizen's right to freedom.

2.1.2 REFUSING TO LEGISLATE OR ENFORCE: ABORTION AND SEX WORK IN TRANSITIONARY STAGES

In early stages of a state's development, when it is not yet able to protect its most vulnerable citizens, another important legal tool is permitting behavior that under more ideal conditions would be outlawed. Consider, for instance, the following case, which continues our discussion of concerns related to sexuality: no citizens have a right, as such, to privatize public spaces by, for example, using them as their private space for conducting business or as their personal space. Accordingly, under conditions in which the state can secure safe shelter for all and people have the means necessary for engaging in economic activity, the state can outlaw sleeping in public spaces or selling sexual services on the streets. Most states in the world today, however, are incapable of providing their citizens and others living within their territory safe shelter or conditions under which those who sell sexual services can do so in safe, private establishments. Because our actual circumstances are non-ideal in this way, states may reasonably abstain from positing or enforcing laws that make it illegal to sleep in public spaces and to sell sexual services on the streets. When there is an insufficient number of safe shelters for those without homes, enforcing laws that make it illegal to sleep in public spaces makes little sense. Focusing only on sex work, simply not to posit or enforce such laws can be the best option under some historical circumstances. Whether in a given circumstance this is the best way to protect sex workers who have no real options except selling sex on the street is a question to which there cannot be an *a priori* answer. The answer must be found by empirical studies, including ones that dialogue closely with sex workers. Such empirical investigations must involve asking questions that can guide solutions, such as the

---

[23] Nationalism can be bad in much more horrifying ways than this, of course. For my current take on this, see Varden (2014a).

following: what legal steps can the state take now to improve the situation of these workers? What steps should the state take in the near future and in the long run to enable and better secure rightful conditions for these workers? The answers to these questions are not found *a priori*, and they are not among those that philosophers are particularly good at answering. However, if the arguments we have discussed are compelling, philosophy can explain why the good answers can be found only by doing empirical research that places the sex workers themselves at the center of the process of developing laws and policies that can facilitate a transition to better future conditions. Not only do the sex workers know a lot about the challenges they face that most others do not, but these laws are about their persons, bodies, and lives.

Similarly—and as anticipated in Chapter 5—under conditions in which a state cannot guarantee access to safe abortions for all women, it seems that assuming responsibility for this failure in transitionary stages of state reform should require that the state, at minimum, enforce no legal time limit on abortions, though it may also follow Canada's lead and simply not legislate this issue at all. A reasonable condition for enforcing time limits on abortions is that a state be able to provide conditions under which women can safely access abortions. Until a state can do so, it seems best to give only the pregnant women the right to decide when in the pregnancy to abort. In addition, if states do enforce abortion laws but do not provide safe access to abortions, in cases where a woman has a later abortion (but not because of any medical emergencies), it seems she can permissibly appeal to the legal defense that it was impossible for her to access a safe abortion earlier. Allowing this kind of legal defense can also serve as a plausible legal strategy as we struggle to build better safeguards for women and children who are subjected to domestic abuse. For example, it seems reasonable that when states are unable to provide safe exit routes for women who live subject to serious domestic abuse, they should permit these women to plead self-defense also in cases where they have planned the killing of their violent, abusive husbands.[24]

2.1.3 SECURING SOCIOECONOMIC CONDITIONS CONDUCIVE TO ACTIVE CITIZENSHIP

So, what ideal of socioeconomic justice should we seek to realize as we reform our imperfect states? While commenting on the importance of ensuring that the legal-political framework can also be seen as acceptable from the point of view of the poor, Kant emphasizes that it must always be possible for them to be

> aware that, if [they do] not reach the same level as others, the fault lies only in [themselves] ([their lack of] ability or earnest will) or in circumstances for which [they] cannot blame any other, but not in the irresistible will of others who, as [their] fellows subjects in this condition, have no advantage over [them] as far as right is concerned.   (TP 8: 293)

That is, as we strive to make our states not only minimally but more robustly just and we build increasingly complex systems that determine how successfully we exercise our rights—such as educational systems, economic systems, political systems, etc.—

---

[24] For a Kantian developing a legal defense of this kind, albeit not one developed using Kant's texts and arguments, see Byrd (1991).

we must try to do two things to improve the socioeconomic conditions of justice: (1) institutionally guarantee that each citizen's legal access to means as such does not depend on another private person's choice about the matter (by legally guaranteeing unconditional poverty relief); and (2) ensure that the freedom-determining systems are themselves accessible to all as free, equal, and independent individuals, in part so that if we work resiliently within these systems we can, within a reasonable amount of time, obtain any kind of public position (insofar as our mental and physical abilities allow). Securing this kind of social mobility, in other words, is inherent to building complex societies in which the exercise of rights increasingly depends on access to systems.

To illustrate, in my view these two principles are reflected in what may be seen as a two-stage, historical development of Scandinavian welfare systems. I will discuss the systems of the Scandinavian country I know best: Norway. Roughly until oil was discovered in Norway, there was little to no welfare system in place beyond unconditional poverty relief (in Kant's first minimal sense). Real change took place after oil was discovered, as a significant percentage of the oil revenue was used to fuel the build-up of a welfare system, from the late 1960s onwards. Today, Norway no longer only secures unconditional poverty relief, but it has a rather extensive welfare system, the purpose of which may be described as providing conditions of freedom, equality, and independence in Kant's second, more robust sense. Currently, at age 18, all Norwegian citizens deemed capable of full legal responsibility are independent (including economically independent, and so independent from their parents). At this age, all citizens acquire a right to emergency shelter, to a home of their own, health care, student loans, etc., namely conditions required to work oneself into any type of position in society, including any education required to hold any kind of public office. What any citizen will actually be able to obtain will depend, as Kant also emphasizes, on factors such as luck and talent, and there are many imperfections in the system. But there are no legal restrictions on what anyone can do (as compared to anyone else), and the set of public rights that protects each citizen actually provides such equal systemic opportunities. Additionally, even if certain citizens fail in their endeavors, such as by personal bankruptcy, systemic protections ensure that they will not end up on the street (they may, at worst, end up back where the 18-year-olds are, starting from scratch with just the basic welfare protections in place). In this way, public law as a whole should ensure that everyone is free and equal and that their exercise of freedom depends only on law. Each citizen is independent of other private persons and has the opportunity (through education and sufficient means) to actively participate in the public authority by engaging in informed public debates, including scholarly debates, and by holding public positions. This, I believe, is the direction in which Kant is pointing by claiming that the purpose of liberal societies is to create conditions under which each citizen is free, equal, *and* independent, because this ideal is achievable only in tandem with citizens' freedom being subjected only to law (and not to each other's private choices) and as governing themselves through public institutions grounded on each person's innate right to freedom.

To further illustrate the logic of redistributive economic justice on this approach, let me engage a recent line of criticism against Kantians such as myself on the topic of unconditional poverty relief. In "Property and Homelessness," Christopher Essert

(2016) argues that eliminating homelessness is a necessary condition of a minimally just state, and he also believes his position to be different from that of Kantians.[25] I think Essert is right that Kant's position is not that strong, but I think Kant is right not to make it that strong. In contrast to Essert, I have argued in this chapter that the public guarantee of the provision of safe shelters (in Kant's time, "poor houses") that minimally satisfy the "most necessary natural needs" of human beings can be regarded as satisfying the condition of a minimally just state (cf. MM 6: 326). The reason they meet this condition is not that shelters satisfy these needs particularly well but that the minimal condition is that the state *unconditionally guarantees* that there is always somewhere to go and exist legally and safely, and basic existence must be understood in ways that make appropriate space for the fact that we are *human* beings who have particular human needs.

Kant's account of human nature, as explored through the predisposition to good in human nature and the accompanying propensity to evil, furthermore gives us good reasons to think that privacy[26] is constitutive of emotionally healthy, morally good *human* being and that ensuring that people can quickly work themselves into a condition in which they have a home is generally the best way (according to what we can surmise empirically) to make proper space for this kind of living. Surely, we can imagine finite beings who exercise external freedom perfectly and who do not (subjectively) feel the need for privacy (although they have a right to it), but *human* beings do need privacy. Privacy is constitutive of human beings' efforts at realizing their animality (self-preservation, sex drive, and basic community) and the self-recognitional aspects of our humanity in emotionally healthy, morally responsible ways. Such a minimal guarantee of privacy may therefore reasonably include requiring a shelter to provide conditions of privacy for those staying there.

Nevertheless, though this legal guarantee satisfies the minimum condition, as I have argued just now, Essert would be right to criticize if Kant's story ended here. However, as we have seen above, aiming merely for this guarantee would be an unwise strategy for a people (a group of human beings) "who has united itself into a society which is to maintain itself perpetually" (MM 6: 326). Kant argues that it must be possible to work oneself out of this (passive) condition into an active one and given human beings' particular phenomenology, we have good reason to think that just states must do more by eliminating homelessness as soon as possible; they must ensure that people can transition from living in shelters to having homes of their own rather speedily, especially if they have children.[27] Hence, even though Kant did not explore this issue further, he did leave us the philosophical resources to explore it on our own. And if we do, we see quite quickly that public initiatives directed at the elimination of homelessness are a developmentally early undertaking for states that are striving to secure more robust conditions of justice (just as they were in the

---

[25] Essert argues specifically against Weinrib (2003), but his argument can be seen as applying to much of the work in the liberal republican tradition over the last couple of decades. For more on this discussion in the Kant literature, see the introduction to Part II.

[26] I explore more fully this question of privacy in "Kant and the Right to Privacy" (2020c).

[27] I have set aside the issue of children in this chapter. See Varden (2012a, 2020b) for an account of how children are consistently incorporated into this approach.

Scandinavian welfare projects). As Kant maintains, all citizens must be seen as having the right to work themselves into an active condition (MM 6: 314f.), and enabling people to establish homes of their own is an early stage in this attempt at promoting the emotional health and moral improvement of human beings.

In addition, as I will emphasize shortly, because the current distribution of wealth is the product of histories characterized by tremendous injustice and violence and because some people's identities make them and their loved ones subject to great dangers, securing access to homes (and not just temporary shelters) for all should be a first priority for minimally just states trying to reform themselves into more robustly just states. On the one hand, as embodied social beings interacting in the world, as we saw in Part I, we are aware of how others see us. In response to this recognition, we present ourselves socially or privately. For example, gender presentation is fundamentally about how I present myself in the social world, and I present myself in a way that is meant to be readable to others. This is quite different than the way I present myself privately or intimately, such as when I invite someone to a sexual interaction or when I explore how I want to best realize my own sense of embodiment (whether on my own or together with others). When I present myself in such private ways, I am personally open and vulnerable—to being engaged, affirmed, or rejected as the person I am—in a way that I am not when I present myself to the social world. Thus, though the combination of the right to bodily integrity and the right to freedom of thought gives us what we need to explain the corresponding right to privacy, spelling out the account of human nature allows us to see why taking special care to safeguard privacy should be a priority for states. Surely, to realize our sexual, loving, gendered selves well, for example, we typically need to explore it together with other responsible beings for whom we feel sexual attraction. Importantly, however, though we can assume *moral* responsibility for these aspects of ourselves by using our self-reflective capacities and capacity for reason (we have personality), these emotions (of affectionate love and sexual love) are importantly unreflective, and being responsible for them intimately involves relating to them as such. The point here is not that what goes on in these spaces could not be seen by others; of course it could, and, in an important sense, there is nothing to hide or to be ashamed of. Rather, the point is that what we seek to do in these private spaces insofar as they are part of ongoing relationships that are constitutive of who we are is not something we want strangers to be part of, just as (emotionally healthy) strangers would not want to be uninvited parts of it either. Having access to such private, intimate spaces helps to ground the lives of human beings in their relationships to themselves and others. Lack of access to a permanent home makes such grounding relationships infinitely more difficult, especially for those who have historically oppressed identities and for whom presenting socially typically carries greater risk.

On the other hand, because of the increasingly system-dependent lives we live (e.g., there is virtually no livable unowned land still available for appropriation on the planet) and the rather horrible history of private property appropriation worldwide, having only emergency poorhouses and shelters that provide unconditional poverty relief seems an unwise and unjustifiable idea for most existing states. Many of the consequences of sexism, racism, xenophobia, and so on can be effectively combatted by securing for members of these identities a situation in which their access to a home for themselves is no longer subject to other private persons' determining choices, and this consideration yields further support for the view that public initiatives targeting homelessness should be an early priority for states. That is to say, my Kantian account of human nature and evil previously outlined shows us that the personal spaces not protected by privacy are morally dangerous. Our identities as embodied, social beings and our liability to do bad things make us vulnerable to losing our way and to being violated in specific ways. For example, in the sexist, homophobic, racist, xenophobic worlds we currently find ourselves, the real danger of violence in temporary shelters make them particularly unsuited for this complex task and, so, is part of why it is especially important that we build legal-political institutions through which everyone can secure a home as soon as possible. In addition, because of various kinds of immaturity, bad character (pathologies), and the sheer temptation to seek power over others, one can be terribly tempted to publicly share (publish in the wider social world) information about, communications with, or images of another with which one has been entrusted in an intimate, private sphere.[28] Because of the way in which we are embodied, social beings, such information can, when leaked non-consensually by those with whom we have entrusted it, humiliate us and make it difficult for us to hold onto ourselves exactly because it reveals aspects of ourselves that we share only with selected, trusted people. Indeed, because we are inclined to seek power over others, domination may take the form of violation or lack of respect for the embodied and social aspects of others. All of this speaks to the urgency of securing legal rights to homes for each and all, as states stabilize and material resources make this possible.

On the third hand (yet again, appealing to an imaginary being seems necessary in this book), securing access to homes for each and all seems a particularly apt way to fight problems of domestic abuse. When one chooses to share a private home with another (by marrying, having children, or taking on jobs that consist of assisting another person in that person's home or personal life), one thereby acquires a legal responsibility to be committed to that person's well-being. Accordingly, one can never appeal to privacy to legitimize domestic violence, whether physical or emotional in nature. Indeed, doing so is legally punishable as such as well as a particularly heinous way to act (since the effects of such behavior are so radical for human beings).[29] Nevertheless, it is also the case that serious personal abuse is more likely in the domestic sphere than it is in other spheres of life—because they are characterized

[28] To return to the revenge porn example, notice that regardless of whether one thinks that privacy is necessary for or constitutive of healthy personal lives, the argument is consistent with, for example, Danielle Keats Citron and Mary Ann Franks's recent work (2014), which argues that revenge porn should be understood as a sex crime, although I do not agree that the reason why it should be considered a sex crime is because it is a kind of assault. On my position, revenge porn is not a sexual assault because it is not a physical but a social attack. Nonetheless, it is a particularly serious legal wrong and should be considered a crime because it deprives a person of privacy in its most intimate form; namely it attacks their feeling of being safe in the world, including when they are being intimate with others. Indeed, because of the psychological makeup of human beings, the psychological effects of such attacks on *human* beings can resemble those caused by physical assault.

[29] Though Marilea Bramer (2011) does not use Kant's account of status right and human nature to develop her account, I believe my reading is consistent with the main thrust of her approach and her conclusion about the terrorizing nature of domestic abuse.

by opportunities to exercise power over others—and men, for example, have inherited unjustifiable socially privileged identities that make it relatively easy and tempting for them to abuse their wives and children, especially when things are challenging. In addition, because of the devastating effects of living under abusive domestic conditions and the difficulty of finding safe, private spaces for relocation, it is even more imperative that the state should offer solutions that go beyond the minimal judicial idea. Making paths for transitioning from emergency houses to safe homes available to escaped violated spouses (and their children) should be a primary legal-political concern of any minimally just state.[30] Human beings need homes— safe spaces in which they can be and become increasingly emotionally healthy, morally good humans—and no state seeking to reform itself can justify not making it a major public objective to provide conditions under which people whose histories track violent oppression can acquire safe homes of their own within a reasonable amount of time.

On the fourth hand, the way in which our embodied, social natures are constitutive of who we are (the sense we have of ourselves) makes us vulnerable in specific ways. As embodied social beings, we can be violently attacked (whether through assault and battery, rape, shaming, or harassing behavior, etc.), which can leave us feeling invaded, violated, and threatened at the core of our being. Grappling with rape, for example, is so stressful for many not only because it is physically painful but also because it can unground survivors emotionally. Rape can make survivors feel unsafe in their own bodies and in the world, and can make them feel deprived of their value as human beings. Of course, upon reflection, *ceteris paribus*, they know that they are just as safe as they were before—the danger of rape remains the same—and they may know just as they did before that their value as human beings is infinite. Nevertheless, they can find themselves unable to help feeling invaded, violated, threatened, or worthless— emotions related to the predisposition to animality and this part of humanity—or unable to control those feelings using reflective means, because these emotions are not inherently reflective, moralizable emotions. Their unruly character is what makes them so difficult to assume moral responsibility for and why it is so difficult to move on for many when such bad things have happened. The way to heal is not by undergoing a process of *thinking about* what happened but rather by learning to *live with* what happened. Securing access to safe homes for everyone is a prudent way to protect survivors of violations such as assault, battery, rape, shaming, or harassment as they heal, precisely because a safe place to be also operates at the grounding, unreflective level. The fact that such violence is more likely to be perpetrated against members of vulnerable groups—sometimes the same groups that are more likely to be homeless in our oppressive societies, such as members of the LGBTQIA community—makes it even more important to make the fight against homelessness a public task early in the process of reforming our states into more robustly just states.

The above list of reasons why a state that seeks to reform itself and improve its ability to secure a rightful condition for its citizens will fight homelessness is obviously neither exhaustive nor necessarily applicable to every actual state. It could

---

[30] See also Varden (2016a).

not be. After all, the list is based on contingent concerns that are based on empirical cognition, that is, on observations of empirical challenges that face many today. For reasons of space, let me now switch focus by turning to some reasons why the state's reform project will include an effort to facilitate conditions in which all citizens can become capable of active self-governance through public institutions.

2.2 Active Self-Governance through Public Institutions

Let me explore the distinction between a minimally just and a more robustly just state further by engaging Kant's distinction between active and passive citizenship, because one implication of this account is that it is possible in a minimally just state (*Rechtsstaat*) for all but one person to be what Kant calls "passive" citizens. That is, a minimally just state can be one in which only one person (the monarch, say) can vote on legislation. And, because voting on legislation is how one exercises the power to determine exactly how to limit freedom in the name of freedom, everyone but this one person would be passive subjects rather than active members of the state. Let me explain this by approaching it from a different angle: Kant defines a citizen in terms of freedom, equality, and independence, and he distinguishes between active and passive citizens on the basis of whether they are given full freedom, which means having the right to vote on the actual laws governing their interactions with one another. The reason for this twofold distinction is that being an active citizen requires that one is "fit to vote" (MM 6: 314). At the same time, Kant explains, sovereign authority may simply not be accessible to anyone other than those who already have it, or, for that matter, to those who have the public power to attain it. That is, sovereign (legislative) or other public power may be restricted to only one person and this person's descendants (as in a hereditary monarchy), to a few families (hereditary aristocracy), or to some group of citizens (e.g., only sufficiently wealthy cis male citizens), while all others are obligated to obey as mere subjects. In the latter case, a minimally just state may be a democratic state where almost all citizens are "passive" citizens because they lack the means to be independent (to be "active" citizens). Because they lack sufficient means (lack the necessary ability) to live independently of others, the reasoning goes, they depend on others' means (including powers) to access a satisfactory livelihood.[31] And, as we saw previously, this means that until they rid themselves of this dependence through work, they may not, on Kant's theory, have the right to vote. Again, the only legal condition that must be fulfilled in a society where most people are poor, according to Kant, is that "anyone can work [one's] way up from this passive condition to an active one" (MM 6: 315).[32] So, where the socioeconomic conditions are such that many people can earn a livelihood only

---

[31] As is clear by now, my view of a guarantee of unconditional poverty relief is a minimal condition of a just state. Accordingly, in the absence of such a provision, the state is not even minimally just. This is why I write "satisfactory livelihood" here rather than, say, "survival."

[32] This is emphasized by Kant in many places. For example, in "Theory and Practice," he says that "From this idea of the equality of human beings as subjects within a commonwealth there also issues the following formula: Every member of a commonwealth must be allowed to attain any level of rank within it (that can belong to a subject) to which his talent, his industry and his luck can take him; and his fellow subjects may not stand in his way by means of a *hereditary* prerogative (privileged [reserved] for a certain rank), so as to keep him and his descendants forever beneath the rank" (TP 8: 292; cf. 293f.).

by making themselves dependent on others (become servants), it must still be possible for them to work themselves out of such a condition.

Kant's judgment, then, is that though a lack of material independence affecting large portions of the population is a real worry for the minimally just state (a core issue it must address as it reforms itself), as long as social climbing is not illegal and as long as any factors restricting such climbing are not based on contingent considerations of human nature (that can be disproven through real-life exception cases), the result does not deprive anyone of their basic rights. As noted in previous chapters, Kant suggests that there can be two plausible sources of such lack of ability: (1) "nature," which he suggests in several places explains why minors or children and women can never have the status of active citizens; and (2) lack of means to be one's own master, a factor that excludes "a domestic servant," "an apprentice in the service of a merchant or artisan," "the private tutor," and "the tenant farmer" from active citizenship (MM 6: 314f.; cf. TP 8: 294ff.). Thus, in this legal framework (of freedom), considerations of prudence (in response to considerations of our unruly human nature, here the complicated material circumstances of a group of people which makes it possible for their "masters" to put pressure on their vote and to give very rich people in effect more votes than others) can play their stabilizing role. Because a state exists in particular historical circumstances, and because what is being stabilized is not inherently unjust, such considerations of prudence are permissible or acceptable. Similarly, in The Doctrine of Right, Kant states that an *inherited*

nobility of a country that is not under an aristocratic but a monarchical constitution is an institution... [that] may be permitted for a certain period of time and may even be necessary by circumstances. But it cannot be asserted that this state can be established in perpetuity... a state has the right to alter its form (e.g. to reform itself into a republic).[33]   (MM 6: 370)

In other words, for reasons of prudence and history (e.g., a state has evolved from a feudal society), a state may give certain historically powerful families inherited public privileges, for example, exclusive access to becoming monarchs, marrying monarchs, or sitting in the monarch's council or government. Because the monarch's exercise of power is still subject to laws of freedom (that recognize each citizen's basic innate, private, and public rights) and because the monarch (from a legal point of view) is a thoroughly public person (i.e., not a private person owning the nation's wealth as private property), such discretionary political use of power (in response to actual circumstances) is permissible for a limited period (although it is "despotic" in this regard since the state has no "active" citizens). This type of arrangement may be necessary, for example, to stabilize a society emerging from war. Nevertheless, this legal-political practice is not strictly consistent with right, because it contains notions of hereditary public power, so it must be treated as a "temporary" rather than

---

[33] This last sentence is slightly confusing, because it seems that Kant is saying that the republic is to be contrasted with aristocracies and monarchies—and, as we have seen in earlier discussions, this is not his view. I believe one can read this sentence in one of two ways: (1) The use of "republic" refers to how the highest executive authority would be a president or prime minister; *or* (2) it concerns the ways in which various non-republican (i.e., inherited) elements of the actual operation of the state can be reformed. Considering all the other textual evidence, including that which we have previously encountered, I believe the latter reading is the one intended here (though it would be philosophically consistent to read it either way).

permanent feature or as an "accident" of the legal-political system (MM 6: 370). As we will see more clearly shortly, *hereditary* public privileges are one impactful feature the elimination of which will be required by the reform of minimally just states into more robust, flourishing versions of themselves. After all, the notion of hereditary public privileges contradicts the concept of a state that is reconcilable with each person's right to freedom.

It is important to keep in mind, then, that the main purpose of reform is to make the actual operations of the public power adhere more closely to the idea of the true state (republic)—by bringing it from a minimally just to a more robustly just state— so that the public authority is the means through which we act and which enables rightful interactions between us as free, equal, and independent individuals. The public authority is, as we have said many times, not yet another private person, but, ideally, a representation of an "us" through which rightful interaction is possible. And so, the main point of reform is to ensure that the public authority—or the legal-political institutional force—is not linked to any particular person or family (inherited power) or social identity (e.g., cis men, members of a particular family or religion, etc.) but is an authority with which any one of us can be entrusted. What is more, being entrusted with this authority means being entrusted to do our very best to ensure that the legal-political institutional system functions as it should and thereby becomes increasingly trustworthy for each and all. In addition, it may be prudent and therefore actually stabilizing to give certain social identities or families privileges that do not track these people's actual ability (merit) to hold public offices if we find ourselves in certain extreme, unstable circumstances. However, if a state allows such practices for determining whom is entrusted with public offices to continue indefinitely, Kant warns, the state will "fall into the hands of sheer incompetence" (MM 6: 328). As conditions improve, there are no good reasons not to let election or appointment to these offices track merit (actual proven ability). Also, as we continue reforming our system, we will want to develop rather than eliminate public officials' abilities to reason as our representatives, namely by analyzing legal-political issues in terms of each citizen's basic rights (innate, private, and public rights) and then making space for appropriate concerns of human nature. To do this, we must also strive towards a legal-political culture in which such reasoning is expected and encouraged in public discourse.

If not the first, Kant was among the first to give a genuinely freedom-based, complex account of public reason that accommodates appeals to our distinctly human needs and desires. Public reason includes, as we have seen, the kinds of ideals to which we, as citizens of states grounded on principles of rightful freedom, must hold those entrusted with public authority accountable, which are the ideals those vested with public power must maintain as they reason and uphold the rule of law (as they posit law, as they apply law in particular cases, and as they enforce it). However, public reason also concerns those who hold lower public offices and the ways they are required to reason (in that capacity), namely as determined by the public policies constitutive of their public office.[34] In section "D" of public right, Kant addresses the

---

[34] We find the main arguments that yield Kant's account of public reason in The Doctrine of Right (MM 6: 238), the "What is Enlightenment?" essay (WE 8: 36–42), and the "Theory and Practice" paper (TP 8:

question of how to reform the minimally just state into a civil condition (a true republic) with respect to lower-level public offices and dignities (MM 6: 238–30). According to Kant, the sovereign authority has the right to distribute both public offices (or "salaried administrative positions") and "*dignities*, which are eminent estates without pay, based on honor alone" (MM 6: 328). As in the case of his discussion of the tripartite sovereign authority, central to Kant's analysis of how to reform a minimally just state's system of public officials is the idea that the system must be purged of hereditary positions and honors. On the one hand, one reason for which some were given such positions and honors to begin with (historical and social advantage) when the state established its minimally just monopoly on coercion[35] is the same reason for which the practice should end. This reason is prudence (stability); we need these offices to be filled on the basis of merit such that they do not devolve into "sheer incompetence" (MM 6: 328). On the other hand, we want to rid the system of such elements because they are inconsistent with right; no one is born an official or as "more equal" than others, so, we correct this mistake by

letting [hereditary privileges] ... lapse and not filling vacancies in these positions.... So it has a provisional right to let these titled positions of dignity continue until even in public opinion the division into sovereign, nobility, and commoners has been replaced by the only natural division into sovereign and people. (MM 6: 329)

I do not believe that this entails that we cannot or should not maintain notions of public dignities. Rather, we want to rid the system of its notions of *inherited* public dignity, which are inconsistent with the basic idea that all have innate dignity as human beings, as expressed by the idea of the innate right to freedom. The only conception of public offices that is consistent with the idea of each citizen having a right to freedom is one according to which *everyone* can work their way into any public position, even if whether any particular person will successfully do so will depend, to some extent, on factors such as talents and luck. As Kant explains in The Doctrine of Right, "the intention of the state ... requires that everyone be able to rise from lower to higher offices" (MM 6: 328). As we have seen, the speed of this process of social reform and exactly how we go about changing it are open for debate and require sound political judgment about how we can achieve stability for the right reasons—now and in the future.

In the United Kingdom, for example, the institution of the Crown officially recognizes a number of British persons each year (usually on the recommendation of Parliament) for their outstanding public contributions to the nation—as artists, scholars, soldiers and military leaders, industrialists, social workers, politicians, teachers, and so on—by conferring on them various titles, such as titles of damehood or knighthood (Baroness (Onora) O'Neill of Bengarve is a notable Kantian example; Sir Elton John a similarly notable member of the LGBTQIA community). Again,

---

289–307). See also Peterson (2008), Deligiorgi (2012a), and Niesen (2018) on Kant's conception of public reason.

[35] Kant says, "The anomaly of subjects who want to be more than citizens of the state, namely born officials (a born professor, perhaps) may have crept into the machinery of government from older times (feudalism, which was organized almost entirely for war)" (MM 6: 328).

Kant's practical philosophy sees nothing wrong with this—quite the contrary—but it does maintain that even though one might find oneself in a historical condition in which such honors are inherited, as one's state becomes a more well-functioning state, these honors will only track citizens' outstanding merit, bravery, or service to the country. And, indeed, this seems to be the ideal that currently informs how the UK bestows such honors onto selected citizens. Without delving into details about how to understand the British processes of reform,[36] it suffices to say that one plausible argument for why it has been so slow—why reform of the political power of the Crown, House of Lords, House of Commons, judiciary, etc., has at times stagnated—is for permissible reasons of political stability. The Crown (the monarchical institution) and the House of Lords are considered stabilizing and non-partisan though increasingly representative elements of the public legal-political structure—and, at least so far, are not regarded as being easily replaceable, whereas the government is chosen through a representative, democratic process. And I take it that another good reason for doing these things slowly, pursuing a mix of popular and merit-based selections, and allowing for some inheritance arises from concerns about our human nature, including concerns to promote healthy political emotions and to tame unhealthy ones. We seek to build legal-political institutional structures that secure freedom and law for all but that have built into them safeguards and measures that will increase the likelihood that they are stable too, to address the reality that we are not only social creatures but also beings who can so easily act very badly and destructively. Indeed, as Kant says in *Anthropology*,

> If one now asks whether the human species . . . is to be regarded as a good or bad race, then I must confess that there is not much to boast about in it. Nevertheless, anyone who takes a look at human behaviour not only in ancient history but also in recent history will often be tempted to take the part of *Timon* the misanthropist in his judgment; but far more often, and more to the point, that of *Momus*, and find foolishness rather than malice the most characteristic mark of our species. But . . . foolishness combined with a lineament of malice (which is then called folly) is not to be underestimated in the moral physiognomy of our species.
>
> (A 7: 332f.)

Our efforts to change institutions somewhat slowly and by combining actions addressing concerns about our histories with actions addressing concerns about proven merit (including by popular choices) might, in other words, be viewed as attempts to increase the chances that the operations of our public legal-political institutions are wiser than any one of us is able to be on our own, including when we are entrusted with a public office. Also, because of the crucial stabilizing roles many monarchs have played, including during the historically recent World War II, it is not far-fetched, I believe, to suggest that among the important reasons many countries are not simply ridding themselves of this institution (the monarchy) is that it would be unwise to do so before they have found a good replacement, some other way of institutionally securing stability and continuity over time. To be sure, it is not as if those countries that have democratically elected presidents have more

---

[36] For my Kantian interpretation of the transformation of the UK legal-political institutional whole, composed of its monarchic, aristocratic, and democratic elements, see Varden (2016a).

impressive histories. These countries, too, seek to secure various stabilizing features, as exemplified by how US presidents remain presidents for life (and thereby remain possible partners in dialogue for the sitting president) and have lifelong stipends (salaries). There is, in other words, no simple *a priori* solution for how states should realize the idea of a rightful state (*Rechtstaat*) into more flourishing ideals thereof in actual states with their complex and complicated histories and compositions. Building solid conditions of right in various actual legal-political conditions is a difficult, slow endeavor. This, I believe, is true both generally and in the case of issues concerning sex, love, and gender. Insofar as progress towards establishing conditions of rightful freedom for women and sexual or gendered minorities has been achieved, the constructive forces have used different legal-political means of reform. Sometimes the legal system, sometimes politics, sometimes monarchs and presidents have been friends, but sometimes they have been foes; none of these public institutions nor any of the particular persons entrusted with these offices have always been constructive forces that women and sexual or gendered minorities can rely on—in combination with resilient resistance against injustice insofar as possible or as needed. The aim, as Kant argues, is simply to keep working on making the law itself what people can depend on—not the particular people entrusted with upholding and developing these institutions at any given time—and strive never to be naïve in thinking that this task is ever completed once and for all.

3. Concluding Remarks

In this chapter, we first focused on Kant's analysis of the need for and the difficulties involved in establishing minimally just states. Part of the difficulty, we saw, is that it takes human societies a long time to develop from being focused on basic survival and a sense of safety ("animality"/"a technical or mechanistic condition") to being able to cultivate a flourishing sociality or culture ("humanity"/"pragmatic condition") and, finally, to being able to enable and secure moral conditions of freedom for all, including by establishing minimally just legal-political institutions ("personality"/ "moral condition") (A 7: 322–5). We then saw that there are also distinctive difficulties contained in transforming our minimally just states into more robust, flourishing versions of themselves by promoting the development of our abilities to govern ourselves actively through public reason and public institutions, where some of the challenge is to do this in a way that is appropriately responsive to human nature in general and to the particular legal-political, historical situations into which we happen to be born. We have a natural tendency to want to try to derive what is right from culture, and we also want to describe ourselves as whole and good, which leads to its own challenges because we tend to be self-deceptive in our descriptions of our current interactions and of our histories.

Notice that if this is true, constitutive of our reform efforts should also be a state's public recognition of its own current and historical failures to protect vulnerable groups, namely failures that have resulted in putting citizens in situations where they have been either subjected to terrible wrongdoing or forced to protect themselves to the best of their abilities against barbaric violence by doing wrong in the highest degree. Because legal-political institutions are made for and by human beings whose historical progress as a moral species requires truthful histories, it is important that this process sometimes also includes public apologies. It is constitutive of rightful interaction to publicly recognize people for the lives they have lived—to record our shared public histories in ways that acknowledge our failures to interact in accordance with our right to freedom and corresponding duty of rightful honor. And in light of our distinctive kind of phenomenological structure, doing so is important to secure our current accomplishments and to move towards the future in ways consistent with a reasonable hope that it will be a better, more just one. After all, histories of injustice do not simply happen, people make them happen and even if one does or did not actively take part, when it is done by the state, it is done in everybody's or our shared name. Being entrusted with public offices is to be entrusted also with the responsibility of keeping us committed to truthfulness in how history is recorded, and in acknowledging and sometimes apologizing for our shared, public failures. It is therefore not an accident, but a good sign that some public leaders in recent years have apologized for their states' failures in relation to sexual or gendered minorities.

Concluding Part II
Justice as Rightful, Human Freedom

In his marginalia in his copy of Achenwall, Kant says,

The great difficulty in the problem of establishing a civil constitution is: that the human being is an animal that demands rights and yet does not willingly concede his right to anyone else, who thus has a need of a master who in turn can always only be a human being. From such crooked timber no Mercury can be cut.   (LDPP 15: 644)

It is unclear why Kant uses "Mercury" to refer to perfection here (cf. IUH 8: 23). He could use Mercury to denote the Roman god of merchants who was, among other things, the fleet-footed messenger of the gods. Or, perhaps he wants to pick out the planet Mercury, which he elsewhere describes as more balanced than other planets because of its proximity to the sun (UNHTH 1: 280). Being so balanced could be why Kant also claims that inhabitants of Mercury would be less developed (as they would have less impetus towards development) (UNHTH 1: 359). Regardless, he is clearly concerned with the general problem that individuals demand rights but resist granting them to others. And anyone we entrust to be the master to check us (to ensure rights for everyone) is just as fallible as we are. Our limitations affect any human being entrusted with holding sovereign (public) office(s), thus no particular legal-political system will ever overcome the problem once and for all. Rather, as we have seen in Chapter 7, Kant proposes that handling well these non-ideal problems of human justice requires that we not only continue making the public rule of law function in conformity with the ideal, universal principles of right. In addition, we must build legal-political institutions designed for human beings, institutions that wisely deal with the challenges stemming from our ever-so-human nature and particular histories and cultural circumstances as we strive to better engage in the distinctive public reasoning constitutive of civil society. We saw how this effort involves building an increasingly robust legal-political framework based on the ideal principles of right and that also protects us from one another by making our exercises of freedom dependent only on public laws. In such a system, all advantages always track only those who are acting within their rights, and it is actually possible for people living there to actively secure their rights by exercising their legal-political rights. Besides, in such societies, we seek to reform our legal-political institutions so that we can get rid of the bad effects of historical oppression and make the institutions better means through which human (and not only spatio-temporal rational) beings can realize their rights.

Sex, Love, and Gender: A Kantian Theory. Helga Varden, Oxford University Press (2020). © Helga Varden.
DOI: 10.1093/oso/9780198812838.001.0001

If we return to the puzzles posed in the general Introduction to this book, we can now see them in light of the reconciliation of ideal (universal) and non-ideal (contingent) concerns. The Kantian conception of rightful human sexual, loving, and gendered relations presented in Part II offers one way to overcome many of these current splits in legal-political philosophy. First, the accommodation of (non-ideal) concerns of moral psychology and moral anthropology within the (ideal) account of innate, private, and public right shows one way to combine concerns of both ideal and non-ideal theory. Second, and relatedly, the account can capture communitarian theories' characteristic emphasis on the particularity of societies and historical contexts when critiquing actual legal-political societies. Third, the way in which ideal and non-ideal concerns are combined shows one way to overcome the analytic-continental split with regard to issues of human sexual, loving, gendered nature, and justice. For the position does not hold that the reflective, rational (analytic) point of view of freedom is the entire human perspective. Rather, our unreflective aspects as well as our ineliminable tendency to evil and to self- and other-deception, have their own important and distinctive roles to play, which allows the account to capture what continental philosophy has been particularly good at accounting for, namely heinous violence and unruly embodiment and sociality.

Fourth, the analysis of rightful human relations (in terms of innate, private, and public right) can be seen as combining core libertarian and other liberal ideas as well as accommodating central ideas found in the legal positivist tradition. Although this position agrees with legal positivists' typical emphasis on the need for posited law— indeed my account even provides ideal (and not only prudential) reasons for this need—it challenges legal positivists' claim that almost any kind of positive law or legal system can engender legal and political obligations in particular societies. Instead, my position is able to capture and acknowledge what legal positivism typically cannot: namely, people's historical struggles for freedom. For example, in spite of centuries of posited law, men have never been right in denying women the right to participate in public life or to own private property; and sodomy laws that criminalize non-binary or homosexual interactions have always been wrong. Furthermore, although all arguments in this second part should be persuasive also to libertarian theorists, my account avoids serious problems characteristic of these positions. For example, my account avoids Lockeans' notoriously problematic view that it is possible to give one universal, legal specification of the universal laws of freedom (or nature) such that virtuous individuals can realize justice on their own in the state of nature, or that the rights of the state are co-extensive with the rights of individuals—both of which arguments are necessary for any defense of philosophical anarchism or Locke's natural executive right. At the same time, the Kantian position presented here can accommodate a theme central also to much libertarian thought, which is the idea that all rightful uses of coercion must be reconcilable with each person's right to freedom. A major difference (and a virtue) of my account is that it can show why the state not only enables rightful private interactions, but also rightful systemic interactions through public law, the latter being necessary for understanding and solving basic problems concerning, for example, sexual oppression and the exploitative nature of much current trade in sexual services and goods.

Fifth, my account's employment of ideas concerning embodiment and asymmetrical dependency relations—again, through its analysis of innate, private, and public right and the space created for concerns of moral psychology and anthropology—engages and develops ideas found in much feminist thought, including the care tradition. The human self is no longer a detached, rational subject that is prior to all it attaches to, and relations of care are no longer understood on the model of autonomous agents. Rather, as we have seen, care relations require their own legal analysis (as status relations) and the robustly just state seeks to build institutions that enable caregivers, among others, to have not just safe places (shelters) to go with their families, but homes.

Kant's legal-political political philosophy is therefore not one according to which right and human flourishing are inherently in conflict. Indeed, even in only a minimally just state, structures are in place to secure the possibility of a robustly just state, which is achieved insofar as the legal-political institutional whole functions in the following way: first, people's flourishing is made independent of other private persons and dependent only on public law; and, second, the people actively govern themselves through their public institutions. This is furthermore not a vision of human beings as perfect (Mercury) or as disembodied (rational aliens). The theory of justice offered here is, through and through, a theory that takes seriously the fact that human beings are rational *yet also* embodied, social beings of a specific kind. Our human embodied sociality is neither viewed as something we should always abstract away when we think about where we should be heading. Nor is it something that we should try to rid ourselves of to the extent that we can. Finally, as emphasized in the general Introduction, the claim in this book is not that my Kantian account is the *only* way to bridge these gaps between the traditions or to transcend them by merging their many insights. Rather, the suggestion throughout has been that it is *one* fruitful way to do so by offering a more complete philosophical theory of sex, love, and gender with the room needed to address at least most of the philosophical concerns such a theory needs to address.

Bibliography

Abramson, Kate and Leite, Adam (2011). "Love as a Reactive Emotion", *The Philosophical Quarterly*, 61(245): 673–99.

Albrecht, Ingrid (2015/17). "How We Hurt the Ones We Love", *Pacific Philosophical Quarterly*, 98(2): 295–317 (electronic publication Oct. 24).

Alcoff, Linda Martín (2018). *Rape and Resistance*. Cambridge: Polity Press.

Allais, Lucy (2008a). "Forgiveness and Mercy", *The South African Journal of Philosophy*, 27(1): 1–9.

Allais, Lucy (2008b). "Wiping the Slate Clean: The Heart of Forgiveness", *Philosophy and Public Affairs*, 36(1): 33–68.

Allais, Lucy (2008c). "Dissolving Reactive Attitudes: Forgiving and Understanding", *The South African Journal of Philosophy*, 27: 1–23.

Allais, Lucy (2013). "Elective Forgiveness", *The International Journal of Philosophical Studies*, 21(5): 1–17.

Allais, Lucy (2015). *Manifest Reality*. Oxford: Oxford University Press.

Allais, Lucy (2016). "Kant's Racism", *Philosophical Papers*, 45(1–2): 1–36.

Allais, Lucy (unpublished manuscript). "Kantian Determinism and Contemporary Determinism."

Allison, Henry (1983). *Kant's Transcendental Idealism*. New Haven: Yale University Press.

Allison, Henry (1990). *Kant's Theory of Freedom*. Cambridge: Cambridge University Press.

Allison, Henry (1996). *Idealism and Freedom: Essays on Kant's Theoretical and Practical Philosophy*. Cambridge: Cambridge University Press.

Altman, Matthew C. (2010). "Kant on Sex and Marriage: The Implications for the Same-Sex Marriage Debate", *Kant-Studien*, 101(3): 309–30.

Altman, Matthew C. (2011). *Kant and Applied Ethics: The Uses and Limits of Kant's Practical Philosophy*. Malden, MA: Wiley-Blackwell.

Ameriks, Karl (2000). *Kant and the Fate of Autonomy*. Cambridge: Cambridge University Press.

Arendt, Hannah (1973). *The Origins of Totalitarianism*. Chicago: Harcourt, Brace, Jovanovich.

Baehr, Amy R. (2004). *Varieties in Feminist Liberalisms*. New York: Rowman & Littlefield.

Baier, Annette C. (1993). "Moralism and Cruelty: Reflections on Kant and Hume", *Ethics*, 103: 436–57.

Baier, Annette C. (1996). "The Need for More than Justice", in *Moral Prejudices: Essays on Ethics*, pp. 18–32. Cambridge, MA: Harvard University Press.

Baron, Marcia W. (1985). "Servility, Critical Deference and the Deferential Wife," *Philosophical Studies*, 48(3): 393–400.

Baron, Marcia W. (1995). *Kantian Ethics Almost Without Apology*. Ithaca, NY: Cornell University Press.

Baron, Marcia W. (1997a). "Kantian Ethics and Claims of Detachment", in Robin M. Schott (ed.), *Feminist Interpretations of Kant*, pp. 145–70. University Park: Pennsylvania University Press.

Baron, Marcia W. (1997b). "Kantian Ethics", in Marcia W. Baron, Philip Pettit, and Michael Slote (eds.), *Three Method of Ethics*, pp. 3–91. Oxford: Blackwell.

Baron, Marcia W. (2002). "Love and Respect in the *Doctrine of Virtue*", in Mark Timmons (ed.), *Kant's Metaphysics of Morals: Interpretive Essays*, pp. 391–407. New York: Oxford University Press.

Baxley, Anne Margaret (2010). *Kant's Theory of Virtue: The Value of Autocracy*. Cambridge: Cambridge University Press.

Beauvoir, Simone de (1949/2011). *The Second Sex*, trans. C. Borde and S. Malovany-Chevallier. New York: Vintage Books.

Beever, Allan (2003). "Kant and the Law of Marriage", *Kantian Review*, 18: 339–62.

Brake, Elizabeth (2005). "Justice and Virtue in Kant's Account of Marriage," *Kantian Review*, 9: 58–94.

Brake, Elizabeth (2012). *Minimizing Marriage: Marriage, Morality, and the Law*. New York: Oxford University Press.

Bramer, Marilea (2010). "The Importance of Personal Relationships in Kantian Moral Theory: A Reply to Care Ethics", *Hypatia*, 25(1): 121–39.

Bramer, Marilea (2011). "Domestic Violence as a Violation of Autonomy: The Required Response of the Kantian State", *Social Philosophy Today*, 27: 97–109.

Butler, Judith (2006). *Gender Trouble: Feminism and the Subversion of Identity*. New York: Routledge.

Byrd, Sharon B. (1991). "Till Death Do Us Part: A Comparative Approach To Justifying Lethal Self-Defense by Battered Women", *Duke Journal of Comparative & International Law*, 1: 169–211.

Byrd, Sharon B. and Joachim Hruschka (2010). *Kant's Doctrine of Right: A Commentary*. New York: Cambridge University Press.

Cahill, Ann J. (2001). *Rethinking Rape*. Ithaca, NY: Cornell University Press.

Calhoun, Cheshire (2000). *Feminism, the Family, and the Politics of the Closet: Lesbian and Gay Displacement*. Oxford: Oxford University Press.

Card, Claudia (2002). *The Atrocity Problem—A Theory of Evil*. New York: Oxford University Press.

Card, Claudia (2010). "Kant's Excluded Middle," in Sharon Anderson-Gold and Pablo Muchnik (eds.), *Kant's Anatomy of Evil*, pp. 74–92. Cambridge: Cambridge University Press.

Citron, Danielle Keats and Franks, Mary Anne (2014). "Criminalizing Revenge Porn", *Wake Forest Law Review*, 49: 345; and *University of Maryland Legal Studies Research Paper*, 1: 1–38.

Cohen, Alix (2008). "The Ultimate Kantian Experience: Kant on Dinner Parties", *History of Philosophy Quarterly*, 25(4): 315–36.

Cohen, Alix (2009). *Kant and the Human Sciences: Biology, Anthropology and History*. London: Palgrave Macmillan.

Cohen, Alix (2016). "The Role of Feelings in Kant's Account of Moral Education", *Journal of Philosophy of Education*, 50(4): 511–23.

Cohen, Alix (2017a). "Rational Feelings", in Diane Williamson and Kelly Sorensen (eds.), *Kant and the Faculty of Feeling*, pp. 9–24. Cambridge: Cambridge University Press.

Cohen, Alix (2017b). "Kant on Beauty and Cognition: The Aesthetic Dimension of Cognition", in Steven French and Otavio Bueno (eds.), *Thinking about Science and Reflecting on Art: Bringing Aesthetics and the Philosophy of Science Together*, pp. 140–54. London: Routledge.

Cohen, Alix (2017c). "Kant on Emotions, Feelings and Affectivity", in Matthew Altman (ed.), *The Palgrave Kant Handbook*, pp. 665–81. London: Palgrave Macmillan.

Cohen, Alix (2017d). "Kant on the Moral Cultivation of Feelings", in Alix Cohen and Bob Stern (eds.), *Thinking about the Emotions: A Philosophical History*, pp. 172–83. Oxford: Oxford University Press.

Cohen, Alix (2017e). "The Natural and the Pragmatic in Kant's Anthropology: The Case of Temperaments", *Early Science and Medicine*, 22: 1–18.

Cohen, Alix (2018). "Kant on Moral Feelings, Moral Desires and the Cultivation of Virtue", in Dina Emundts and Sally Sedgwick (eds.), *International Yearbook of German Idealism*, pp. 3–18. Begehren: Desire.

Clement, Grace (1996). *Care, Autonomy, and Justice.* Boulder, CO: Westview Press.

Cudd, Ann (2006). *Analyzing Oppression.* New York: Oxford University Press.

Darwall, Stephen (2006). *The Second-Person Standpoint: Morality, Respect, and Accountability.* Cambridge, MA: Harvard University Press.

De Laurentiis, Allegra (2000). "Kant's Shameful Proposition: A Hegel-Inspired Criticism of Kant's Theory of Domestic Right", *International Philosophical Quarterly*, 40: 297–312.

Deligiorgi, Katerina (2012a). *Kant and the Culture of Enlightenment.* Albany: SUNY Press.

Deligiorgi, Katerina (2012b). *The Scope of Autonomy: Kant and the Morality of Freedom.* Oxford: Oxford University Press.

Deligiorgi, Katerina (2017). "Interest and Agency", in Markus Gabriel and Anders Moe Rasmussen (eds.), *German Idealism Today.* Berlin: De Guyter Verlag.

Deligiorgi, Katerina (2018). "The 'Ought' and the 'Can'", *Con-Textos Kantianos: International Journal of Philosophy*, S.l(8): 323–47.

Denis, Lara (2001). "From Friendship to Marriage: Revising Kant", *Philosophy and Phenomenological Research*, 63(1): 1–28.

Denis, Lara (2015). *Moral Self-Regard: Duties to Oneself in Kant's Moral Theory.* London: Routledge.

Deering, K. N., Amin, A. Shoveller, J., Nesbitt, A., Garcia-Moreno, C., Duff, P., Argento, E., and Shannon, K. (2014). "A Systematic Review of the Correlates of Violence Against Sex Workers", *American Journal of Public Health*, 104: e42-54.

Dewitt, Janelle (2014). "Respect for the Moral Law: The Emotional Side of Reason", *Philosophy*, 89(1): 31–62.

Digby, Tom (2014). *Love and War: How Militarism Shapes Sexuality and Masculinity.* New York: Columbia University Press.

Dillon, Robin S. (1992a). "Care and Respect", in Eve Browning Cole and Susan Coultrap–McQuin (eds.), *Explorations in Feminist Ethics: Theory and Practice*, pp. 69–81. Bloomington, IN: Indiana University Press.

Dillon, Robin S. (1992b). "Respect and Care: Toward Moral Integration", *Canadian Journal of Philosophy*, 22: 105–32.

Dillon, Robin S. (1992c). "Toward a Feminist Conception of Self-Respect", *Hypatia*, 7: 52–6.

Dillon, Robin S. (1992d). "How to Lose Your Self-Respect", *American Philosophical Quarterly*, 29: 125–39.

Dillon, Robin S. (1997). "Self-Respect: Moral, Emotional, Political", *Ethics*, 107: 226–49.

Dillon, Robin S. (2001). "Self-Forgiveness and Self-Respect", *Ethics*, 112: 53–83.

Dillon, Robin S. (2003). "Kant on Arrogance and Self-Respect", in Cheshire Calhoun (ed.), *Setting the Moral Compass: Essays by Women Philosophers*, pp. 191–216. Oxford: Oxford University Press.

Dworkin, Andrea (1981). *Pornography: Men Possessing Women.* London: Women's Press.

Dworkin, Andrea and MacKinnon, Catharine A. (1988). *Pornography & Civil Rights: A New Day for Women's Equality.* Minneapolis, MN: Organizing Against Pornography: A Resource Center for Education and Action.

Dworkin, Andrea and MacKinnon, Catharine (1997). *In Harm's Way: The Pornography Civil Rights Hearings.* Cambridge, MA: Harvard University Press.

Eaton, Anne W. (2007). "A Sensible Antiporn Feminism", *Ethics*, 117(4): 674–715.

Ebbinghaus, Julius (1953). "The Law of Humanity and the Limits of State Power," *The Philosophical Quarterly*, 3(10): 14–22.

Ebels-Duggan, Kyla (2012). "Kant's Political Philosophy", *Philosophy Compass*, 7(12): 896–909.

Engelhardt, H. Tristram, Jr. (1974). "The Ontology of Abortion", *Ethics*, 84(3): 217–34.

Engstrom, Stephen (1996). "Happiness and the Highest Good in Aristotle and Kant", in Stephen Engstrom and Jennifer Whitting (eds.), pp. 102–39. Cambridge: Cambridge University Press.

Engstrom, Stephen (2002). "The Inner Freedom of Virtue", in Mark Timmons (ed.), *Kant's Metaphysics of Morals: Interpretive Essays*, pp. 289–316. New York: Oxford University Press.

Essert, Christopher (2016). "Property and Homelessness", *Philosophy & Public Affairs*, 44(4): 266–95.

Fahmy, Melissa Seymour (2009). "Active Sympathetic Participation: Reconsidering Kant's Duty of Sympathy", *Kantian Review*, 14: 31–52.

Fahmy, Melissa Seymour (2010). "Kantian Practical Love", *Pacific Philosophy Quarterly*, 91: 313–31.

Feldman, Susan (1998). "From Occupied Bodies to Pregnant Persons: How Kantian Ethics Should Treat Pregnancy and Abortion", in Jane Kneller and Sidney Axinn (eds.), *Autonomy and Community*, pp. 265–82. Albany, NY: State University of New York Press.

Finnis, John (1994). "Law, Morality, and 'Sexual Orientation'", *Notre Dame Law Review*, 69: 1049–76.

Fischer, Molly. 2016. "Think Gender Is Performance? You Have Judith Butler to Thank for That", *New York Magazine: The Cut*. (https://www.thecut.com/2016/06/judith-butler-c-v-r.html?mid=fb-share-thecut).

Flikschuh, Katrin (2008). "Reason, Right, and Revolution: Kant and Locke", *Philosophy and Public Affairs*, 36(1): 375–404.

Flikschuh, Katrin (2017). "A Regime of Equal Freedom: Individual Rights and Public Law in Ripstein's *Force and Freedom*", in Sari Kisilevsky and Martin J. Stone (eds.), *Freedom and Force: Essays on Kant's Legal Philosophy*, pp. 55–74. Portland, OR: Hart Publishing.

Friedman, Marilyn A. (1985). "Moral Integrity and the Deferential Wife", *Philosophical Studies*, 47(1): 141–50.

Friedman, Marilyn (2008). "Care Ethics and Moral Theory", *Philosophy and Phenomenological Research*, 77(2): 539–55.

Frierson, Patrick (2003). *Freedom and Anthropology in Kant's Moral Philosophy*. Cambridge: Cambridge University Press.

Frierson, Patrick (2013). *Kant's Questions: What Is the Human Being?* London: Routledge.

Frierson, Patrick (2014). *Kant's Empirical Psychology*. Cambridge: Cambridge University Press.

Frye, Marilyn (1983). *The Politics of Reality: Essays in Feminist Theory*. Trumansburg, NY: Crossing Press.

Gaus, Günter (1964). "Zur Person." Interview with Hannah Arendt (https://www.youtube.com/watch?v=dsoImQfVsO4&t=19s).

Gensichen, Hans-Peter (2004). "Wie Schwul war Kant?" *Geschichte*, March: 43–7.

George, Robert P. (1997). "Public Reason and Political Conflict: Abortion and Homosexuality", *The Yale Law Journal*, 106(8): 2475–504.

Gillespie, Norman C. (1977). "Abortion and Human Rights", *Ethics*, 87(3): 237–43.

Gillian, Carol (1993). *In a Different Voice: Psychological Theory and Women's Development*. Cambridge, MA: Harvard University Press.

Greasley, Kate (2017). *Arguments about Abortion: Personhood, Morality, and Law*. Oxford: Oxford University Press.

Gregor, Mary J. (1963). *Laws of Freedom*. Oxford: Oxford University Press.

Grenberg, Jeanine M. (2005). *Kant and the Ethics of Humility: A Story of Dependence, Corruption, and Virtue*. New York: Cambridge University Press.

Grenberg, Jeanine M. (2013). *Kant's Defense of Common Moral Experience: A Phenomenological Account*. New York: Cambridge University Press.

Guyer, Paul (1993). "Kant's Morality of Law and Morality of Freedom", in R. M. Dancy (ed.), *Kant and Critique*, pp, 43–89. Dordrecht: Kluwer Academic.

Guyer, Paul (1995). "Moral Anthropology in Kant's Aesthetics and Ethics: A Reply to Ameriks and Sherman", *Philosophy and Phenomenological Research*, 55(2): 379–91.

Guyer, Paul (1996). *Kant and the Experience of Freedom*. Cambridge: Cambridge University Press.

Guyer, Paul (2000). *Kant on Freedom, Law, and Happiness*. Cambridge: Cambridge University Press.

Guyer, Paul (2007). "Naturalistic and Transcendental Moments in Kant's Moral Philosophy", *Inquiry*, 50(5): 440–64.

Haas, Ann P., Rogers, Philip L., and Jody L. Herman (2014). *Suicide Attempts among Transgender and Gender Non-Conforming Adults: Findings of the National Transgender Discrimination Survey*. New York and Los Angeles: American Foundation for Suicide Prevention and the Williams Institute (williamsinstitute.law.ucla.edu/wp-content/uploads/AFSP-Williams-Suicide-Report-Final.pdf).

Hampton, Jean (2004). "Feminist Contractarianism", in Amy R. Baehr (ed.), *Varieties in Feminist Liberalisms*. New York: Rowman & Littlefield.

Hay, Carol (2013). *Kantianism, Liberalism, and Feminism: Resisting Oppression*. New York: Palgrave Macmillan.

Held, Virginia (2006). *The Ethics of Care: Personal, Political, and Global*. New York: Oxford University Press.

Herman, Barbara (1993a). *The Practice of Moral Judgment*. Cambridge, MA: Harvard University Press.

Herman, Barbara (1993b). "Could It Be Worth Thinking about Kant on Marriage?", in Louise M. Antony and Charlotte E. Witt (eds.), *A Mind of One's Own: Feminist Essays on Reason and Objectivity*, pp. 53–72. Cambridge: Westview Press.

Herman, Barbara (2008). *Moral Literacy*. Cambridge, MA: Harvard University Press.

Herman, Barbara (2011). "Embracing Kant's Formalism", *Kantian Review* 16(1): 49–66.

Hill, Thomas E., Jr. (1973). "Servility and Self-Respect", *The Monist*, 57(1): 87–104; reprinted in (1993). *Autonomy and Self-Respect*, pp. 4–19. New York: Cambridge University Press.

Hill, Thomas E., Jr. (1991). *Autonomy and Self-Respect*. Cambridge: Cambridge University Press.

Hill, Thomas E., Jr. (1992). "A Kantian Perspective on Moral Rules", *Ethics*, 6: 285–304.

Hill, Thomas E., Jr. (2002). *Human Welfare and Moral Worth. Kantian Perspectives*. Oxford: Clarendon Press.

Hobbes, Thomas (1996). *Leviathan*, ed. Richard Tuck. Cambridge: Cambridge University Press.

Hoffman, A., Borowski, L. E., Jachmann, R. B., and Wasianski, C. A. (1902). *Immanuel Kant, ein Lebensbild nach Darstellungen der Zeitgenossen Jachmann, Borowski, Wasianski*. Halle a. S.: Hugo Peter (https://archive.org/stream/immanuelkanteinloohoff#page/n3/mode/2up/).

Holtman, Sarah Williams (2004). "Kantian Justice and Poverty Relief", *Kant-Studien*, 95(1): 86–106.

Huseyinzadegan, Dilek (2018). "For What Can the Kantian Feminist Hope? Constructive Complicity in Appropriations of the Canon", *Feminist Philosophy Quarterly*, 4(1).

Höffe, Otfried (1992). "'Even a Nation of Devils Needs the State': The Dilemma of Natural Justice', in H. L. Williams (ed.), *Essays on Kant's Political Philosophy*, pp. 120–42. Chicago: The University of Chicago Press.

Höffe, Otfried (1994). *Immanuel Kant*, trans. Marshall Farrier. Albany, NY: State University of New York Press.

Jauch, Ursula Pia (1988). *Immanuel Kant zur Geschlechterdifferenz. Aufklärerische Vorurteilskritik und bürgerliche Geschlechtsvormundschaft.* Wien: Passagen Verlag.

Jauch, Ursula Pia (2014). *Friedrichs Tafelrund & Kants Tischgesellschaft—Ein Versuch über Preussen zwischen Eros, Philosophie und Propaganda.* Berlin: MSB Matthes & Seitz Berlin Verlagsgesellschaft mbH.

Johnson, Robert (2011). *Self-Improvement: An Essay in Kantian Ethics.* Oxford: Oxford University Press.

Kant, Immanuel (1974). *Anthropology from a Pragmatic Point of View,* trans. M. J. Gregor. The Hague: Martinus Nijhoff.

Kant, Immanuel (1996). *Practical Philosophy,* trans. and ed. Mary J. Gregor. New York: Cambridge University Press.

Kant, Immanuel (1996). *Religion and Rational Theology,* trans. and ed. Allen W. Wood and George di Giovanni. New York: Cambridge University Press.

Kant, Immanuel (1999). *Critique of Pure Reason,* trans. and ed. by Paul Guyer and Allen W. Wood. Cambridge: Cambridge University Press.

Kant, Immanuel (1999). *Correspondence.* New York: Cambridge University Press.

Kant, Immanuel (2001). *Lectures on Ethics,* ed. P. Heath and J. B. Schneewind. Cambridge: Cambridge University Press.

Kant, Immanuel (2007). *Anthropology from a Pragmatic Point of View* in *Anthropology, History, and Education,* ed. Robert B. Louden and Günter Zöller, trans. Mary Gregor, Paul Guyer, Robert B. Louden, Holly Wilson, Allen W. Wood, Günter Zöller, and Arnulf Zweig. New York: Cambridge University Press.

Kant, Immanuel (2012). *Universal Natural History and Theory of the Heavens, or Essay on the Constitution and Mechanical Origin of the Entire Universe, treated in accordance with Newtonian Principles,* trans. Ian Johnston. Arlington, VA: Richer Resources Publication.

Kant, Immanuel (2016). *Lectures and Drafts on Political Philosophy,* ed. Frederick Rauscher, trans. Frederick Rauscher and Kenneth R. Westphal. Cambridge: Cambridge University Press.

Kelsen, Hans (1992). *An Introduction to the Problems of Legal Theory,* trans. Bonnie Litschewski Paulson and Stanley L. Paulson. Oxford: Clarendon Press.

Kersting, Wolfgang (1984/1993). *Wohlgeordnete Freiheit. Immanuel Kants Rechts- und Staatsphilosophie.* Berlin: de Gruyter/Frankfurt: Suhrkamp.

Kersting, Wolfgang (1992a). "Kant's Concept of the State", in Howard L. Williams (ed.), *Essays on Kant's Political Philosophy,* pp. 143–66. Chicago: Chicago University Press.

Kersting, Wolfgang (1992b). "Politics, Freedom, and Order: Kant's Political Philosophy", in Paul Guyer (ed.), *The Cambridge Companion to Kant,* pp. 342–66. New York: Cambridge University Press.

Kittay, Eva F. (1999). *Love's Labor: Essays on Women, Equality, and Dependency.* New York: Routledge.

Kleingeld, Pauline (1993). "The Problematic Status of Gender-Neutral Language in the History of Philosophy: The Case of Kant", *The Philosophical Forum,* XXV(2): 134–50.

Kleingeld, Pauline (2007). "Kant's Second thoughts on Race", *The Philosophical Quarterly,* 57(229): 573–92.

Kleingeld, Pauline (2010). *Kant and Cosmopolitanism: The Philosophical Ideal of World Citizenship.* New York: Cambridge University Press.

Kleingeld, Pauline (2014). "Patriotism, Peace and Poverty: Reply to Bernstein and Varden", *Kantian* Review, 19(2): 267–84.

Kneller, Jane (1993a). "Kant's Immature Imagination", in Bat-Ami Bar On (ed.), *Modern Engendering: Critical Feminist Readings in Modern Western Philosophy.* Albany, NY: State University of New York Press.

Kneller, Jane (1993b). "Women and Imagination in Kant's Theory of Taste", in C. Korsmeyer and H. Hein (eds.), *Feminist Aesthetics*. Bloomington, IN: Indiana University Press.

Kneller, Jane (1997). "The Aesthetic Dimension of Kantian Autonomy", in Robin M. Schott (ed.), *Feminist Interpretations of Kant*, pp. 173–90. University Park: Pennsylvania University Press.

Kneller, Jane (2006). "Kant on Sex and Marriage Right", in Paul Guyer (ed.), *The Cambridge Companion to Kant and Modern Philosophy*, pp. 447–76. Cambridge: Cambridge University Press.

Kneller, Jane and Axinn, Sidney (1998). *Autonomy and Community: Readings in Contemporary Kantian Social Philosophy*. Albany, NY: State University of New York Press.

Korsgaard, Christine M. (1986). "Kant's Formula of Humanity", *Kant-Studien*, 77(4): 183–202.

Korsgaard, Christine M. (1992). "Creating the Kingdom of Ends: Reciprocity and Responsibility in Personal Relations", in J. Tomberlin (ed.), *Philosophical Perspectives, 6, Ethics*, pp. 305–32. Atascadero, CA: Ridgeview Publishing Company.

Korsgaard, Christine M. (1996a). *Creating the Kingdom of Ends*. Cambridge: Cambridge University Press.

Korsgaard, Christine M. (1996b). *Sources of Normativity*. Cambridge: Cambridge University Press.

Korsgaard, Christine M. (1996c). "From Duty and for the Sake of the Noble: Kant and Aristotle on Morally Good Action", in Stephen Engstrom and Jennifer Whiting (eds.), *Aristotle, Kant, and the Stoics: Rethinking Happiness and Duty*. Cambridge: Cambridge University Press.

Korsgaard, Christine M. (1997). "The Normativity of Instrumental Reason", in G. Cullity and B. Gaut (eds.), *Ethics and Practical Reason*. Oxford: Oxford University Press.

Korsgaard, Christine M. (1998). "Motivation, Metaphysics, and the Value of the Self: A Reply to Ginsborg, Guyer, and Schneewind", *Ethics* 109: 49–66.

Korsgaard, Christine M. (2002). "Internalism and the Sources of Normativity", in Herlinde Pauer-Studer (ed.), *Constructions of Practical Reason: Interviews on Moral and Political Philosophy*, pp. 50–69. Stanford: Stanford University Press.

Korsgaard, Christine M. (2003). "Normativity, Necessity, and the Synthetic A Priori: A Response to Derek Parfit" (http://www.people.fas.harvard.edu/%7Ekorsgaa/Korsgaard. on.Parfit.pdf).

Korsgaard, Christine M. (2009). *Self-Constitution*. Oxford: Oxford University Press.

Kuehn, Manfred (2001). *Kant—A Biography*. New York: Cambridge University Press.

Langton, Rae. 1992. "Duty and Desolation", *Philosophy*, 67: 481–505.

Langton, Rae (2009). *Sexual Solipsism: Philosophical Essays on Pornography and Objectification*. Oxford: Oxford University Press.

LaVaque-Manty, Mika (2006). "Kant's Children", *Social Theory and Practice*, 32(3): 365–88.

LaVaque-Manty, Mika (2012). "Kant on Education", in Elizabeth Ellis (ed.), *Kant's Political Theory: Interpretations and Applications*, pp. 208–24. University Park: The Pennsylvania State University Press.

Lloyd, Genevieve (1993). *Man of Reason: "Male" and "Female", Western Philosophy*. London: Routledge.

Locke, John (1988). *Two Treatises of Government*, ed. Peter Laslett. Cambridge: Cambridge University Press.

Louden, Robert B. (1986). "Kant's Virtue Ethics", *Philosophy*, 61: 473–88.

Louden, Robert B. (2000). *Kant's Impure Ethics: From Rational Beings to Human Beings*. Oxford: Oxford University Press.

Louden, Robert B. (2011). *Kant's Human Being*. New York: Oxford University Press.

MacKinnon, Catharine A. (1979). *Sexual Harassment of Working Women: A Case of Sex Discrimination*. New Haven: Yale University Press.

MacKinnon, Catharine A. (1987). *Feminism Unmodified: Discourses on Life and Law.* Cambridge, MA: Harvard University Press.

MacKinnon, Catharine A. (1989). *Toward a Feminist Theory of the State.* Cambridge, MA: Harvard University Press.

MacKinnon, Catharine A. (1994). *Only Words.* Cambridge, MA: Harvard University Press.

MacKinnon, Catharine A. (2003). *A Dialogue with MacKinnon: On Pornography and Prostitution.* Tokyo: Fuma-shobo.

Marquis, Don (1989). "Why Abortion is Immoral", *Journal of Philosophy*, 86(4): 183–202.

Marwah, Inder S. (2013). "What Nature Makes of Her: Kant's Gendered Metaphysics", *Hypatia*, 28(3): 551–67.

Maus, Ingeborg (1992). *Zur Aufklärung der Demokratietheorie. Rechts- und demokratietheoretische Überlegungen im Anschluss an Kant.* Frankfurt: Suhrkamp.

Mendus, Susan (1987). "Kant: An Honest but Narrow-Minded Bourgeois?", in Ellen Kennedy and Susan Mendus (eds.), *Women in Western Political Philosophy*, pp. 21–43. Brighton: Wheatsheaf Books.

Merritt, Melissa (2018). *Kant on Reflection and Virtue.* Cambridge: Cambridge University Press.

Mikkola, Mari (2011). "Kant on Moral Agency and Women's Nature", *Kantian Review*, 16(1): 89–111.

Miller, Sarah Clark (2012). *The Ethics of Need: Agency, Dignity, and Obligation.* New York: Routledge.

Moen, Marcia (1997). "Feminist Themes in Unlikely Places: Re-Reading Kant's *Critique of Judgment*", in Robin M. Schott (ed.), *Feminist Interpretations of Kant*, pp. 213–56. University Park: Pennsylvania University Press.

Mohr, Richard D. (1988). *Gays/Justice: A Study of Ethics, Society, and Law.* New York: Columbia University Press.

Mohr, Richard D. (1992). *Gay Ideas: Outing and Other Controversies.* Beacon Press.

Mohr, Richard D. (2007). *The Long Arc of Justice: Lesbian and Gay Marriage, Equality, and Rights.* New York: Columbia University Press.

Moran, Kate A. (2012). *Community and Progress in Kant's Moral Philosophy.* Washington, DC: The Catholic University of America Press.

Murphy, Jeffrie G. (1970). *Kant: The Philosophy of Right.* New York: St. Martin's Press.

Nagel, Thomas (1969). "Sexual Perversion", *The Journal of Philosophy*, 66(1): 5–17.

Naragon, Steve (2017). "Kant's Life", in M. C. Altman (ed.), *The Palgrave Handbook*, pp. 29–47. London: Palgrave Macmillan.

Niesen, Peter (2008). *Kants Theorie der Redefreiheit.* Baden-Baden: Nomos.

Niesen, Peter (2018). "Kant and Rawls on Free Speech in Autocracies", *Kantian Review*, 23(4): 615–40.

Nozick, Robert (1974). *Anarchy, State and Utopia.* New York: Basic Books.

Nussbaum, Martha C (1999). *Sex and Social Justice.* New York: Oxford University Press.

Nussbaum, Martha C. (2000). *Women and Human Development: The Capabilities Approach.* New York: Cambridge University Press.

Nussbaum, Martha C. (2010). *From Disgust to Humanity: Sexual Orientation & Constitutional Law.* New York: Oxford University Press.

Okin, Susan M. (1989). *Justice, Gender, and the Family.* New York: Basic Books.

O'Neill, Onora (1990). *Constructions of Reason: Explorations of Kant's Practical Philosophy.* Cambridge: Cambridge University Press.

O'Neill, Onora (1996). *Towards Justice and Virtue: A Constructive Account of Practical Reasoning.* Cambridge: Cambridge University Press.

O'Neill, Onora (2000). *Bounds of Justice.* Cambridge: Cambridge University Press.

Palliakkathayil, Japa (2017). "Persons and Bodies", in Sari Kisilevsky and Martin J. Stone (eds.), *Freedom and Force: Essays on Kant's Legal Philosophy*, pp. 35–54. Portland, OR: Hart Publishing.

Papadaki, Linda (2010). "Kantian Marriage and Beyond: Why It's Worth Thinking about Kant and Marriage", *Hypatia*, 25(2): 276–94.

Pascoe, Jordan (2011). "Personhood, Protection, and Promiscuity: Some Thoughts on Kant, Mothers, and Infanticide", *APA Newsletter on Feminist Philosophy*, 10(2): 4–7.

Pascoe, Jordan (2012). "Hunger for You: Kant and Kinky Sex", in Sharon M. Kaye (ed.), *What Philosophy Can Tell You About Your Lover*, pp. 25–36. Chicago: Open Court Press.

Pascoe, Jordan (2013). "Engagement, Domesticity, and Market-Based Metaphors in Kant's Rechtslehre", *Women's Studies Quarterly*, Fall: 195–209.

Pascoe, Jordan (2015). "Domestic Labor, Citizenship, and Exceptionalism: Rethinking Kant's 'Woman Problem'", *Journal of Social Philosophy*, 46(3): 340–56.

Pascoe, Jordan (2018). "A Universal Estate? Why Kant's Account of Marriage Speaks to the 21st Century Debate", in Larry Krasnoff and Nuria Sanchez Madrid (eds.), *Kant's Doctrine of Right in the Twenty First Century*, pp. 220–40. Cardiff: University of Wales Press.

Pauer-Studer, Herlinde (1994). "Kant and Social Sentiments", *Vienna Circle Institute Yearbook*, 2: 279–88.

Peterson, Jonathan (2008). "Enlightenment and Freedom", *Journal of the History of Philosophy*, 46(2): 223–44.

Pogge, Thomas (1988). "Kant's Theory of Justice", *Kant-Studien*, 79: 407–33.

Rawls, John (1996). *Political Liberalism*. New York: Columbia University Press.

Rawls, John (1999). *A Theory of Justice*, rev. edn. Cambridge, MA: Harvard University Press.

Rawls, John (2001a). "The Idea of Public Reason Revisited", in *Collected Papers*, ed. Samuel Freeman, pp. 573–615. Cambridge, MA: Harvard University Press.

Rawls, John (2001b). *Justice as Fairness: A Restatement*. Cambridge, MA: Harvard University Press.

Reath, Andrews (2006). *Agency and Autonomy in Kant's Moral Thought*. Oxford: Oxford University Press.

Rinne, Pärttyli (2018). *Kant on Love*. Berlin: Walter de Gruyter (Kant-Studien, Kantstudien-Ergänzungshefte).

Ripstein, Arthur (2004). "Authority and Coercion", *Philosophy and Public Affairs*, 32: 2–35.

Ripstein, Arthur (2006). "Private Order and Public Justice: Kant and Rawls", *Virginia Law Review*, 92: 1391–438.

Ripstein, Arthur (2009). *Force and Freedom—Kant's Legal and Political Philosophy*. Cambridge, MA: Harvard University Press.

Robinson, Elizabeth (2017). "Kant and Hume on Marriage", in Elizabeth Robinson and Chris W. Surprenant (eds.), *Kant and the Scottish Enlightenment*, pp. 181–96. London: Routledge.

Rousseau, Jean-Jacques (1997). *The Social Contract and Other Later Political Writings*, ed. Victor Gourevitch. New York: Cambridge University Press.

Rosen, Allen (1996). *Kant's Theory of Justice*. Ithaca, NY: Cornell University Press.

Schaff, Kory (2001). "Kant, Political Liberalism, and the Ethics of Same-Sex Relations", *Journal of Social Philosophy*, 32(3): 446–62.

Scholz, Sally (2010). "That All Children Should be Free: Beauvoir, Rousseau, and Childhood", *Hypatia*, 25(2): 394–411.

Schott, Robin M. (1997). *Feminist Interpretations of Kant*. University Park: Pennsylvania University Press.

Sedgwick, Sally (1997). "Can Kant's Ethics Survive the Feminist Critique?", in Robin M. Schott (ed.), *Feminist Interpretations of Kant*, pp. 77–100. Pennsylvania: Pennsylvania University Press.

Sedgwick, Sally (2011). "'Letting the Phenomena In': On How Herman's Kantianism Does and Does Not Answer the Empty Formalism Critique", *Kantian Review*, 16(1): 33–47.

Sensen, Oliver (2016). *Kant on Human Dignity*. Berlin: de Gruyter.

Shell, Susan Meld (2009). *Kant and the Limits of Autonomy*. Cambridge, MA: Harvard University Press.

Sherman, Nancy (1997). *Making a Necessity of Virtue: Aristotle and Kant on Virtue*. Cambridge: Cambridge University Press.

Simmons, A. John (2000). *Justification and Legitimacy: Essays on Rights and Obligations*. New York: Cambridge University Press.

Singer, Irving (2000). "The Morality of Sex: Contra Kant", *Critical Horizons*, 1(2): 175–91.

Soble, Alan (2002). "Sexual Use and What to Do about It: Internalist and Externalist Sexual Ethics", in Alan Soble (ed.), *The Philosophy of Sex*. New York: Rowman & Littlefield.

Sumner, Wayne L. (1974). "Toward a Credible View of Abortion", *Canadian Journal of Philosophy*, 4(1): 163–81.

Sumner, Wayne L. (1983). *The Morality of Abortion*. Princeton: Princeton University Press.

Stark, Cynthia (1997). "Decision Procedures, Standards of Rightness, and Impartiality", *Nous*, 31(4): 478–95.

Strawson, P. F. (1962). "Freedom and Resentment", *Proceedings of the British Academy*, 48: 1–25.

Sussman, David G. (1996). "Kantian Forgiveness", *Kant-Studien*, 1: 85–107.

Sussman, David G. (2001). *The Idea of Humanity: Anthropology and Anthroponomy in Kant's Ethics*. New York: Routledge.

Sussman, David G. (2008). "Shame and Punishment in Kant's 'Doctrine of Right'", *The Philosophical Quarterly*, 58(231): 299–317.

Sussman, David G. (2009). "On the Supposed Duty of Truthfulness: Kant on Lying in Self-Defense", in Clancy Martin (ed.), *The Philosophy of Deception*, pp. 225–43. Oxford: Oxford University Press.

Thomason, Krista K. (2018). *Naked: The Dark Side of Shame and Moral Life*. New York: Oxford University Press.

Thomson, Judith Jarvis (1971). "A Defense of Abortion", *Philosophy and Public Affairs*, 1(1): 47–66.

Timmermann, Jens (2007). *Kant's Groundwork of the Metaphysics of Morals: A Commentary*. Cambridge: Cambridge University Press.

Tooley, Michael (1972). "Abortion and Infanticide", *Philosophy and Public Affairs*, 2(1): 37–65.

Tooley, Michael (1983). *Abortion and Infanticide*. Oxford: Clarendon Press.

Tronto, Joan (2004). "An Ethic of Care", in Ann E. Cudd and Robin O. Andreasen (eds.), *Feminist Theory: A Philosophical Anthology*, pp. 251–63. Malden, MA: Blackwell Publishing.

Uleman, Jennifer K. (2000). "On Kant, Infanticide, and Finding Oneself in a State of Nature", *Zeitschrift für philosophische Forschung*, 54(2): 173–95.

Uleman, Jennifer K. (2010). *An Introduction to Kant's Moral Philosophy*. New York: Cambridge University Press.

Varden, Helga (2006). "Kant and Dependency Relations: Kant on the State's Right to Redistribute Resources to Protect the Rights of Dependents", *Dialogue—Canadian Philosophical Review*, XLV: 257–84.

Varden, Helga (2007). "A Kantian Conception of Rightful Sexual Relations: Sex, (Gay) Marriage and Prostitution", *Social Philosophy Today*, 22: 199–218.

Varden, Helga (2008). "Kant's Non-Voluntarist Conception of Political Obligations: Why Justice is Impossible in the State of Nature", *Kantian Review*, 13(2): 1–45.

Varden, Helga (2009). "Review of Ann Cudd's *Analyzing Oppression*", *Symposia on Gender, Race, and Philosophy (SGRP)*, 5(1).

Varden, Helga (2010a). "Kant and Lying to the Murderer at the Door...One More Time: Kant's Legal Philosophy and Lies to Murderers and Nazis", *Journal of Social Philosophy*, 41(4): 403–21.

Varden, Helga (2010b). "Kant's Non-Absolutist Conception of Political Legitimacy: How Public Right 'Concludes' Private Right in 'The Doctrine of Right'", *Kant-Studien*, 3: 331–51.

Varden, Helga (2010c). "A Kantian Conception of Free Speech," in Deirdre Golash (ed.), *Free Speech in a Diverse World*, pp. 39–55. New York: Springer Publishing.

Varden, Helga (2012a). "A Kantian Critique of the Care Tradition: Family Law and Systemic Justice", *Kantian Review*, 17(2): 327–56.

Varden, Helga (2012b). "The Lockean 'Enough-and-as-Good' Proviso: An Internal Critique", *Journal of Moral Philosophy*, 9: 410–22.

Varden, Helga (2012c). "A Feminist, Kantian Conception of the Right to Bodily Integrity: The Cases of Abortion and Homosexuality", in Sharon L. Crasnow and Anita M. Superson (eds.), *Out of the Shadows*, pp. 33–57. New York: Oxford University Press.

Varden, Helga (2013). "Review of Carol Hay's *Kantianism, Liberalism, Feminism: Resisting Oppression*", *Notre Dame Philosophical Reviews*, 11(5): 10–11.

Varden, Helga (2014a). "The Terrorist Attacks in Norway, July 22nd 2011— Some Kantian Reflections", *Norsk Filosofisk Tidsskrift/Norwegian Journal of Philosophy*, 49(3–4): 236–59.

Varden, Helga (2014b). "Patriotism, Poverty, and Global Justice—A Kantian Engagement with Pauline Kleingeld's *Kant and Cosmopolitanism*", *Kantian Review*, 10(2): 251–66.

Varden, Helga (2015a). "John Locke: Libertarian Anarchism", in Guttorm Fløistad (ed.), *Philosophie de la justice/Philosophy of Justice, Contemporary Philosophy*, 12: 157–76. Dordrecht: Springer.

Varden, Helga (2015b). "Immanuel Kant: Justice as Freedom", in Guttorm Fløistad (ed.), *Philosophie de la justice/Philosophy of Justice, Contemporary Philosophy*, 12: 213–37. Dordrecht: Springer.

Varden, Helga (2015c/2017). "Kant and Women", *Pacific Philosophical Quarterly*, 98: 653–94. doi: 10.1111/papq.12103

Varden, Helga (2016a). "Self-Governance and Reform in Kant's Liberal Republicanism: Ideal and Non-Ideal Theory in Kant's Doctrine of Right", *dois pontos*, 13(2): 39–70.

Varden, Helga (2016b). "Rawls vs. Nozick vs. Kant on Domestic Economic Justice", in Andrea Luisa Bucchile Faggion, Nuria Sánchez Madrid, and Alessandro Pinzani (eds.), *Kant and Social Policies*, pp. 93–123. London: Palgrave Macmillan.

Varden, Helga (2018a). "Kant's Moral Theory and Feminist Ethics: Women, Embodiment, Care Relations, and Systemic Injustice", in Pieranna Garavaso (ed.), *The Bloomsbury Companion to Analytic Feminism*, pp. 459–82. London: Bloomsbury Academic.

Varden, Helga (2018b). "Kant on Sex. Reconsidered: A Kantian Account of Sexuality. Sexual Love, Sexual Identity, and Sexual Orientation", *Feminist Philosohy Quarterly*, 4(1): 1–33.

Varden, Helga (2020a). "Kant and Moral Responsibility for Animals", in Lucy Allais and John Callanan (eds.), *Kant on Animals*, pp. 157–75. Oxford: Oxford University Press.

Varden, Helga (2020b). "Kantian Care", in Asha L. Bhandary and Amy R. Baehr (eds.), *Caring for Liberalism: Dependency and Political Theory*, pp. 50–74. New York: Routledge.

Varden, Helga (2020c). "Kant and Privacy", in Ansgar Lyssy and Christopher L. Yeomans (eds.), *Kant on Morality, Humanity, and Legality: Practical Dimensions of Normativity*, pp. 229–52. London: Palgrave.

Varden, Helga (2021). "On a Supposed Right to Lie from Philanthropy", in Julian Wuerth (ed.), *The Cambridge Kant Lexicon*, pp. 691–95. Cambridge: Cambridge University Press.

Varden, Helga (forthcoming). "Universality and Accommodating Differences: Religious, Racial, Sexual, Gendered", in Sorin Baiasu and Mark Timmons (eds.), *The Kantian Mind*. London: Routledge.

Waldron, Jeremy (2006). "Kant's Theory of the State," in Pauline Kleingeld (ed.), *Toward Perpetual Peace and Other Writings on Politics, Peace, and History*, pp. 179–200. New Haven: Yale University Press.

Walla, Alice Pinheiro (2013). "Virtue and Prudence in a Footnote of the Metaphysics of Morals (MS VI: 433n)", *Jahrbuch für Recht und Ethik/Annual Review of Law and Ethics*, 21: 307–22.

Watson, Lori (2007). "Pornography and Public Reason", *Social Theory and Practice*, 33(3): 467–88.

Watson, Lori (2010). "Pornography", *Philosophy Compass*, 5(7): 535–50.

Watson, Lori (2013). "Pornography and Obscenity", *International Encyclopedia of Ethics*, Hugh Lafollette (ed.). Oxford: Wiley Blackwell.

Watson, Lori (2014). "Why Sex Work Isn't Work", *Logos—A Journal of Modern Society and Culture*, 13(3–4).

Watson, Lori and Flannigan, Jessica (2019). *Debating Sex Work*. New York: Oxford University Press.

Weinrib, Ernest (1995). *The Idea of Private Law*. Cambridge, MA: Harvard University Press.

Weinrib, Ernest J. (2003). "Property and Poverty in Kant's System of Rights," *Notre Dame Law Review*, 78: 795–828.

Weinrib, Jacob (2008). "The Juridical Significance of Kant's 'Supposed Right to Lie'", *Kantian Review*, 13(1): 141–70.

Wiestad, Else (1989). *Kjønn og ideologi. En studie av kvinnesynet hos Locke, Hume, Rousseau og Kant*. Solum Forlag.

Wilde, Oscar (1990). "The Case of Warder Martin: Some Cruelties of Prison Life", in *The Complete Works of Oscar Wilde*. Leicester: Blitz Editions.

Williams, Bernard (1976). "Character and Morality", in Amélie O. Rorty (ed.), *The Identities of Persons*, pp. 197–216. Berkeley, CA: University of California Press.

Williams, Howard L (1983). *Kant's Political Philosophy*. New York: Palgrave Macmillan.

Wilson, Donald (2004). "Kant and the Marriage Right", *Pacific Philosophical Quarterly*, 85: 103–23.

Wilson, Holly L. (1997). "Rethinking Kant from the Perspective of Ecofeminism", in Robin M. Schott (ed.), *Feminist Interpretations of Kant*, pp. 145–70. University Park: Pennsylvania University Press.

Wilson, Holly L. (1998). "Kant's Evolutionary Theory of Marriage", in Jane Kneller and Sidney Axinn (eds.), *Autonomy and Community*, pp. 283–306. Albany, NY: State University of New York Press.

Wood, Allen W. (1999). *Kant's Ethical Thought*. Cambridge: Cambridge University Press.

Wood, Allen W. (2007). *Kantian Ethics*. New York: Cambridge University Press.

Wuerth, Julian (2014). *Kant on Mind, Action, and Ethics*. Oxford: Oxford University Press.

Zammito, John H. (2002). *Kant, Herder, and the Birth of Anthropology*. Chicago: University of Chicago Press.

Zuckert, Rachel (2007). *Kant on Beauty and Biology*. New York: Cambridge University Press.

Index

For the benefit of digital users, indexed terms that span two pages (e.g., 52–53) may, on occasion, appear on only one of those pages.

Printed and bound by CPI Group (UK) Ltd, Croydon, CR0 4YY